Atlas
Architectures of the 21st Century
America

Luis Fernández-Galiano (Ed.)

Atlas
Architectures of the 21st Century
America

Fundación **BBVA**

The BBVA Foundation's decision to publish this book does not imply any responsibility for its content, or for the inclusion therein of any supplementary documents or information facilitated by the authors.

No part of this publication, including the cover design, may be reproduced, stored in a retrieval system or transmitted in any form or by any means, electronic, mechanical, photocopying, recording or otherwise, without the prior written permission of the copyright holder.

First edition: December 2010

© Of the texts: their authors, 2010
© Of the photographs: their authors, 2010

Published by:
© Fundación BBVA, 2010
Plaza de San Nicolás, 4. 48005 Bilbao

Edition and Production:
Arquitectura Viva S.L.
Gina Cariño, Beatriz G. Casares, María Cifuentes, Raquel Congosto, Luis Fernández-Galiano, Laura Fernández, Cuca Flores, Laura González, Luis Játiva, Beatriz Lazo, Covadonga Lorenzo, Laura Mulas, Leticia Olalquiaga, Jesús Pascual, José S. Yuste

Translations:
Gina Cariño, Laura Mulas

Printed by: Artes Gráficas Palermo, S.L.
Bound by: De la Fuente
ISBN: 978-84-92937-06-6
Legal Deposit: M-51906-2010

Printed in Spain

This book is printed on totally chlorine-free paper in conformity with the environmental standards required by current legislation.

Atlas
Architectures of the 21st Century
America

9 Luis Fernández-Galiano
   So Many Americas. An Architectural Trip from the Arctic to Patagonia

1. Canada
14 Trevor Boddy
    Mega and Micro. Canada, Invention at the Extremes
24 Patkau, **Gleneagles Community Center,** Vancouver, British Columbia
28 MacKay-Lyons & Sweetapple, **Architectural Laboratory,** Nova Scotia
30 Teeple Architects, **Apartment Building at 60 Richmond,** Toronto, Ontario
32 Frank Gehry, **Art Gallery of Ontario,** Toronto, Ontario

2. United States
36 Thomas Fisher
    America, America. United States, a Crucible of Cultures
44 David Chipperfield, **Anchorage Museum Expansion,** Anchorage, Alaska
48 Renzo Piano, **Academy of Sciences,** San Francisco, California
54 Norman Foster, **Winspear Opera House,** Dallas, Texas
60 Joshua Prince-Ramus/Rem Koolhaas, **Wyly Theater,** Dallas, Texas
66 Carlos Jiménez, **Data and Library Service Center,** Houston, Texas
70 Miró & Rivera, **Pedestrian Bridge,** Austin, Texas
72 Steven Holl, **Nelson-Atkins Museum of Art Expansion,** Kansas City, Missouri
78 James Corner/Diller Scofidio+Renfro, **High Line Promenade,** New York
82 Frank Gehry, **InterActiveCorp Headquarters,** New York
86 Jean Nouvel, **Nouvel Chelsea Apartment Building,** New York
90 Morphosis, **Academic Building for the Cooper Union,** New York
94 SANAA, **New Museum of Contemporary Art,** New York
98 Herzog & de Meuron, **Miami Art Museum,** Miami, Florida

3. Mexico
104 Louise Noelle
     Persistences and Challenges. Mexico, the Weight of History
112 Teodoro González de León, **Contemporary Art Museum,** Mexico City
116 LAR/Fernando Romero, **Soumaya Museum,** Mexico City
118 Nicholas Grimshaw, **Museum of Steel,** Monterrey, Nuevo León
122 Mauricio Rocha, **School of Plastic Arts,** Oaxaca
126 BIG/Michel Rojkind, **Tamayo Museum Extension,** Atizapán, Mexico State

4. Central America, Caribbean
130 Roberto Segre
     A Splintered Mirror. Central America and the Caribbean, the Shadows of Politics
138 Toro & Ferrer, **Aula Verde,** Río Piedras (Puerto Rico)
140 Victor Cañas, **Portas Novas House,** Guanacaste (Costa Rica)

5. Venezuela
144 Maciá Pintó
     Urban Contrasts. Venezuela, Administered Informality
152 Urban Think Tank, **Metrocable,** Caracas
156 Matías & Mateo Pintó, **Communal House,** Caracas
158 Productora/Lucio Muniaín, **CAF Headquarters,** Caracas

6. Colombia

162 Silvia Arango
The Public Realm. Colombia, One Country and Three Geographies
170 Giancarlo Mazzanti, **España Library,** Medellín, Antioquia
176 Juan Manuel Peláez, **Las Mercedes School,** Medellín, Antioquia
180 Planb & Jprcr, **Orquideorama,** Medellín, Antioquia
184 Torres, Piñol, Ramírez & Meza, **Public Library,** Villanueva, Casanare
188 Husos, **Garden-House for Taller Croquis,** Cali, Valle del Cauca

7. Peru, Ecuador, Bolivia

194 Frederick Cooper
The Aesthetics of Scarcity. Peru, Ecuador and Bolivia, Rigor as Identity
202 JSa, **Apartment Building,** Lima (Peru)
204 Sáez & Barragán, **Pentimento House,** Quito (Ecuador)
208 Carlos Villagómez, **Archaeological Museum in Tiwanaku,** La Paz (Bolivia)

8. Brazil

212 Hugo Segawa
Paradoxes of Modernity. Brazil, the Fascination of an Emerging Power
220 Mendes da Rocha, **Chapel of Our Lady of the Conception,** Recife, Pernambuco
222 Forte, Gimenes & Marcondes Ferraz, **FDE Public School,** São Paulo
226 Triptyque, **Office Building,** São Paulo
230 Marcio Kogan, **Paraty House,** Rio de Janeiro
234 Procter & Rihl, **Slice House,** Porto Alegre, Rio Grande do Sul

9. Argentina, Uruguay, Paraguay

240 Jorge Francisco Liernur
Panorama after the Crisis. Argentina, Uruguay and Paraguay, Green Shoots
248 Rafael Iglesia, **Quincha I and II,** Rosario, Santa Fe (Argentina)
252 AFRA-LGR-Fernández Prieto, **Mausoleum,** San Vicente (Argentina)
254 Diéguez-Fridman Arquitectos, **Apartment Building,** Buenos Aires (Argentina)
258 Gualano & Gualano, **Shelter at the Salto del Penitente,** Lavalleja (Uruguay)
262 Solano Benítez, **Father's Tomb,** Piribebuy, La Cordillera (Paraguay)
264 José Ignacio Linazasoro, **Spanish Embassy,** Asunción (Paraguay)

10. Chile

270 Fernando Pérez Oyarzun
Excellence at the Limit. Chile, a Critical Fortune Put to the Test
280 Alejandro Aravena, **Quinta Monroy Social Housing,** Iquique
282 Coz, Polidura & Volante, **Museum of the Atacama Desert,** Antofagasta
286 Cristián Undurraga, **Retiro Chapel,** Auco, Los Andes
290 José Cruz Ovalle, **Graduate Center,** Peñalolén, Santiago
294 Alberto Mozó, **Office Building,** Providencia, Santiago
298 FAR, Frohn & Rojas, **Wall House,** Santiago
302 Pezo & Von Ellrichshausen, **Parr House,** Chiguayante, Concepción
306 Smiljan Radic, **Copper House 2,** Talca
310 Grupo Talca, **Tourist Shelter and Observation Decks,** Panguilemo, Talca
314 Germán del Sol, **Hotel Remota,** Puerto Natales, Patagonia

319 Photographic credits
320 Contributors

Atlas
Architectures of the 21st Century
America

THIS ATLAS is the second volume of a series of four which update and substantially develop the work published in 2007 by the BBVA Foundation, *Atlas. Global Architecture circa 2000.* The initial project dealt in a single volume with the architecture of the planet at the threshold of the millennium, and aimed to take stock of the most important works completed after the Fall of the Berlin Wall in 1989, an event that marked the end of the Cold War and also the end of the 'short 20th century' that began in 1914 with World War I. With the perhaps too ambitious purpose of reflecting at the same time the 'state of the world' and the 'state of the art', the book combined what Franco Moretti calls 'distant reading', through ten long essays by experts on the different regions of the globe, with the 'close reading' provided by the detailed documentation on the most noteworthy buildings of the period, grouped into the same geographical areas. Inspired by the conceptual history of Reinhart Koselleck, this collective project tried to offer a broad panoramic account of the recent past through something like a convergence of stories, tightly interwoven to create a tapestry where all the main currents that shape our time are combined with the distinctive features of the regions and the singularity of events, so that the smooth continuity of patterns becomes the weft that ties together the changes, innovations and events that alter the course of history.

The positive reception of the first project encouraged the BBVA Foundation to take on an even more ambitious endeavor: documenting with four volumes, published in consecutive years, the latest architecture of the different continents. With the same intellectual coordinates and publishing characteristics as the previous edition, this project has several new features, beyond the very obvious one of multiplying the extension by four and the less evident one of increasing the works published per volume to almost double the initial number. In the first place, it only covers works completed very recently, transforming the broad historical balance of the first book into an attempt to register the realities of the present; with a similar purpose, it includes unbuilt projects, extending its reach to an immediate future; lastly, it eliminates the restrictions of the first *Atlas,* which only featured three works per region and one building per office (compelled by the synthetic nature of the account), so allowing the most significant countries and the architects with greater international presence to assert their dimension and influence. The result, as can be seen in this volume, are publications less stringently modulated than the initial *Atlas:* while maintaining the division of each book into ten geographical chapters, the extension of the essays and the number of featured works and projects are commensurate with the relevance of the region in question.

Dividing the planet into four areas necessarily called for a continental criterion, though somehow modified to make the volumes even in extension. The insufficient demographic size of Oceania was solved by adding the Pacific to the Asian continent; the smaller economic scale of Africa was made up for with the inclusion of the Middle East; the Americas are dealt with in a single volume; and Europe includes the Russian territories in Asia. Hence, the first volume, *Asia and Pacific,* took off in the territory of 'The Great Game' and traveled through the continent all the way to the ocean; the second of the series, *America,* explores it from the Arctic to the Southern Cone; the third, *Africa and Middle East,* will go from South Africa to the Bosphorous; and the fourth, *Europe,* will start the itinerary in Russia to conclude it at the *finis terrae* of the Iberian Peninsula. This volume covers the second stage of the journey, with an architectural tour through a continent shaped by the European impact on the native populations and cultures, and where the route goes through the great world power of our days – the country that marked the past century – but also through new emerging actors that are showing their resilience in the current crisis, and areas where prosperity and freedom are still elusive: architecture takes stock of this itinerary of lights and shadows, witness and symbol of the hopes and achievements of a time in which the only constant is change.

Luis Fernández-Galiano
So Many Americas
An Architectural Trip from the Arctic to Patagonia

The prosperous northern countries and the emerging southern ones shape in America a stimulating and varied sequence of urban and architectural stages.

THE ECONOMIC earthquake that stirs the planet had its epicenter in an American island. At the threshold of the second decade of the century, Manhattan suffered a financial catastrophe whose aftershocks soon spread to the production economy, and later – after massive rescue and stimulus plans – also to sovereign debt, creating a new political and ideological landscape. Just like a volcanic eruption transforms the territory, changing the coastline and spoiling fertile landscapes with slag and ashes, the collapse of Lehman Brothers on 15 September marked in 2008 the beginning of a historical period that is altering the world's geopolitical profiles, with devastated areas and emerging agents that define a new topography of prosperity and power. This systemic earthquake shook our financial, economic and tax structures, but also many political certainties and social hopes. While the dust is still setting, we try to chart the landscapes of the continent where the tremor began, and we do so with articles, works and projects that span this transit – reflecting both the immediate past, the changing present and the uncertain future –, and also span the extreme diversity of an America that we have often felt tempted to name in plural, because beyond its physical shape, few places have the cultural and socioeconomic contrasts of the Rio Grande, or the variety of institutional reactions seen after the recent catastrophes of New Orleans, Haiti or Chile.

The trip through these motley Americas necessarily begins in the vast territory of Canada, a nation proud that the urban caution shown by its cities – well-organized, rich and conservative – has allowed its banks, equally cautious, to weather the crisis better than any other country of the G8. As Trevor Boddy explains, the vitality of Vancouver, Toronto or Montreal is supported by the combination of qualified immigration and financial firms willing to grant long-term capital for real estate investments in the urban centers. Architectural experimentation, which in other countries preferably occupies the intermediate scale of cultural facilities, is located here at either end of the dimensional range, in the high-density hybrid mega-developments and in the small pavilions in nature, befitting the coexistence of an extreme degree of urbanization and vast extensions of virgin land. The mega-developments, fascinating because they strive to integrate rich and poor, immigrants and natives, provide a metaphor of the Canadian social inclusivism, in contrast with the romantic individualism of the pavilions, exquisite in their traditional craftsmanship and aesthetic refinement, reflecting the dream of the frontier and the love of nature in a country that is at once consistently urban and seductively wild, still under physical and human construction.

Also its southern neighbor is a work in the making, formed by the contributions of immigrants and 'itinerants', as argued by Thomas Fisher, who agrees with Walter Lippman when he stresses that if the great social adventure of the United States in the 19th century was the conquest of the wilderness, in the 20th the challenge was the absorption of many different peoples and cultures. His text reflects the opportunities open to talent and the richness of this diversity through the commentary of a selection of works conceived by native and immigrant American architects, and also by Europeans and Asians, whom together compose a kaleidoscopic portrait of this unique country, which left its mark on the past century, and whose decline before Asia's rise is perhaps heralded prematurely. There, a Canadian of Polish descent, Frank Gehry, may be the most prominent architect, and the best European or Asian professionals – British like Foster or Chipperfield, French like Nouvel, Italians like Piano, Dutch like Koolhaas, Swiss like Herzog & de Meuron or Japanese like Sejima & Nishizawa – may obtain coveted commissions. From Alaska to California, and from Texas to Florida, but

Atlas: America 9

The dramatic contrast between the uniform layout of the planned city and the chaotic growth of spontaneous construction characterize the urban landscapes of America, from the endless grid of Mexico City (below) to the crowded favelas in the hillsides of Rio de Janeiro (next page, top), passing through the intimate coexistence of formal and informal building that can be seen in the view of Caracas (next page, below).

with an inevitable concentration in New York, still the capital of the world, imported or 'itinerant' talent builds the symbolic face of the first world power.

On the other side of Rio Grande the view is very different, because the weight of the native population, the deeply rooted local cultures and the close mixture between the vernacular and the colonial have given Mexico a strong personality that does not easily accept exterior influences, causing – as Louise Noelle highlights – the historical alternance of times of self-withdrawal and others of openness to the world. Today we are experiencing one of the latter, because the advance of economic globalization and the key role of the mass media have fostered the popularity of international trends, which however do not usually express themselves through works of star architects, but rather through their imitation by the country's younger generation. These new architects coexist with the veteran representatives of the traditional Mexican scene, and though all of them have endeavored to address social demands in the fields of housing, health or education, it is probably in culture where the most outstanding results have been achieved, and this field is also perhaps the one that best reflects the current crossroads of a country divided between its bold singularity and the homogenizing impulses of an interconnected and interdependent world.

In contrast with the solid identity of the 'New Spain', the fragmentation of Central America and the Caribbean – the isthmus and the islands sum almost twenty countries – has made it difficult to define a personality other than that encapsulated in the touristic myth of the Tropic: a nature so friendly (though cyclically ravaged by hurricanes and earthquakes) that it can be easily tamed with the elemental cabin of the hotel bungalow. In his text, Roberto Segre narrates the creation of the so-called 'Caribbean environmental syncretism', documents the seduction of the Tropic that led so many architects from the first modernity to the Antilles, and laments the poverty and violence – as well as the dictatorships of all colors – that have forced many to flee to the United States, sinking the region into a political darkness that contrasts with its past cultural splendor, and that has frozen in time spectacular cities like Havana. Today, the architecture of the region moves between the real estate dynamism of Panama, the protection of the colonial legacy and touristic construction with vernacular flavor, finding its best expressions in the small Costa Rica, which has created a school of builders that shows both environmental responsibility and aesthetic refinement,

within the context of a luxuriant nature, also protected in an exemplary manner.

If the portrait of the Caribbean conveys a bittersweet frustration, the chronicle of 21st century Venezuela by Maciá Pintó describes a landscape of striking contrasts. After ten years of socialist experiment, the country that competed in modern achievements with Mexico and Brazil during the second half of the past century is today an architectural scenario characterized by the contradiction between change-oriented projects and the stubborn persistence of everyday life. In spite of the construction of transportation infrastructures like the remarkable and popular Metrocable – a cable car that gives access to the tightly-knit neighborhoods of informal housing around Caracas – or of the improvement of sports and service facilities which has been made possible by the considerable oil income of the country, social polarization has created an atmosphere of insecurity that makes both difficult and uncertain the necessary transformation of Venezuelan cities. Territorial expression of the dramatic inequalities of the country, the contrast between the modern planned metropolis and the hillsides covered with the spontaneous construction of favelas has sometimes been used to praise an 'informality' that often slides into disorder or chaos, and that is very distant from the interventionism which has historically characterized socialism.

Belonging to the same Bolivarian mythical realm as Venezuela, but in constant political and ideological clash with it during recent years, the cultivated and sophisticated Colombia has suffered the stigma of drug trafficking and violence as an undeserved disease, but it has managed to overcome this social tragedy with the firm leadership of the government, and with a series of imaginative initiatives in the cities that have brought about some of the most admired urbanistic and architectural episodes in the continent during the past decade. Silvia Arango orchestrates the narration of this blooming describing the achievements of the different generations of architects – from the orthodox and contextual modernity of Salmona's contemporaries to the more experimental approach of the younger generations, two professional groups that have polarized the internal debate – in the three most significant regions: the Atlantic Coast, centered in the exceptional Cartagena, a colonial city where the impact of tourism has served as stimulus for the preservation of heritage, but has also promoted the Miami-Panama urban model; the Antioquia region, where a sequence of visionary mayors has turned Medellín into

the best urban laboratory of Latin America, and a breeding ground for experiences that have had a powerful media icon in the España Library of Giancarlo Mazzanti; and the Bogotá Savannah, where for fifteen years the municipal government has been able to combine large-scale projects related to the river basin, interventions in urban public space and the construction of social facilities.

The central Andes region shares a culture that, as Frederick Cooper notes, was forged first in the Inca Empire, and then in the Viceroyalty of Perú during colonial times. Between the Pacific and the Amazonian plateau, Peru, Ecuador and Bolivia form a geographic space that is subjected today to the impact of globalization, which operates over a still weak economic base. This limitation determines the reduced scale of the most ambitious culturally-oriented architecture, as well as the formal austerity its works show, two features that detach it from the spectacularity of mediatic stardom. Hence, the houses or small interventions in archaeological environments try to turn scarcity into an aesthetic virtue, practicing a rigorous laconicism that is a reflection of its time, no matter how these may be located in the margins of the great currents that shape cities: the spontaneous construction of the peripheries, that so many countries of Latin America try to regenerate; and the merely commercial or speculative architecture of urban centers, that practically nobody knows how to tame and place at the service of the public domain.

Leader today of the ten countries of South America, Brazil is living an extraordinary moment that goes beyond the adjective 'emergent', because under Lula's leadership – now followed by that of Dilma Rousseff – it has achieved historic goals, internationally endorsed by its routinary inclusion in the BRIC (Brazil, Russia, India, China) group of new world economic powers and for its election as venue for the celebration of sports events like the World Cup of 2014 and the Olympic Games of 2016, to be held in Rio de Janeiro. This boom, as Hugo Segawa points out, finds its reflection in architecture and urbanism, with the renewed popularity of masters like Oscar Niemeyer and Paulo Mendes da Rocha, and the responsibilities taken on by figures like Luiz Paulo Conde, whom as mayor of Rio promoted the urbanization of favelas led by Jorge Mario Jáuregui, and Jaime Lerner, whom as mayor of Curitiba turned his city into an imitated reference in the field of sustainable mobility. But these are only the most important names within a large group of architects who are

following their own path along the trail of the modern Brazilian tradition, and who have their main hub and place of encounter in the vibrant São Paulo.

Argentina is undoubtedly a different case, because after the dramatic crisis it suffered at the turn of the century, its economy has recovered enough so as to trigger a vigorous real estate activity, with the largest project under way at the Puerto Madero of Buenos Aires. Unfortunately, as stressed by Jorge Francisco Liernur – who also briefly covers Paraguay, with Solano Benítez as its main figure, and Uruguay, with a stimulating young scene shared by local and Argentinian architects –, this dynamism has not sparked creative ambition in everyday construction. The most noteworthy episodes are often far from the capital, in the region of Mendoza or in the research on materials carried out by Rafael Iglesia in Rosario, and the Buenos Aires that was once a flourishing center of architectural culture is today faded, even though it continues to export talent to the United States and Europe, where countries like Spain have profited from successive waves of Argentinian immigration, moved by political or economic reasons as those that once spurred our own exodus.

It is only appropriate to end this itinerary in Chile, because this country of unusual geography, which in a thin strip between the Andes and the Pacific contains all the climates of the planet, is the one which has produced the continent's best architecture in the last decades. With a solid economy and an efficient government, from Europe it is perceived as a remote place, and yet both its long coast along the ocean shared with the emerging Asia, and the competitive advantage of its austral agriculture, give it a paradoxically central position. Fernando Pérez Oyarzun avoids explaining the quality of recent Chilean architecture from the point of view of its international success, and prefers stressing the quality of education, the theoretical ambitions of groups like the School of Valparaíso, and the crossbreeding with European experiences. From the radical oeuvre of Smiljan Radic to the lucid activism of Alejandro Aravena, passing through the landscape works of José Cruz or Germán del Sol, the material poetics of Cristián Undurraga or the lyrical houses of Pezo & Von Ellrichshausen, Chile is a stage filled with talent, where architecture as discipline finds its *raison d'être* in reconciling artistic purpose with social awareness, within the commendable frame of a public sector that has managed to react with exemplary efficiency to catastrophes like the recent earthquake or the trapping of the miners.

Canada

Firmly established in its affluence, Canada owes its current urban vitality to the enviable stability of its financial institutions and their readiness to invest huge amounts of capital in real estate markets. This, in combination with federal government programs aimed at revitalizing social housing policies, has given rise to the construction of colossal high-density multi-use buildings in several cities, such as 60 Richmond by Teeple Architects in Toronto, and to ambitious interventions in heritage restoration, like the expansion of the Art Gallery of Ontario by Frank Gehry. Complementing these big projects in the urban centers are small-scale constructions located in natural environments that resort to wooden structures and sustainable technologies, represented in this chapter by the Architectural Laboratory that the firm of MacKay-Lyons & Sweetappple has built in Nova Scotia or by the Gleneagles Community Center that the office of Patkau has raised in Vancouver.

Trevor Boddy
Mega and Micro
Canada, Invention at the Extremes

James Cheng, Shangri-La Hotel, Toronto, Ontario (2008)

Colossal and high-density hybrid megaprojects rising in the urban centers contrast with modest pavilions situated in natural environments.

The idea of a high-density multipurpose building is a radical concept that endeavors to foster the integration of social classes, the juxtaposition of functions, and the combination of construction strategies.

THERE MAY BE no more Canadian a proposition than to suggest that the state of our architecture is linked to the state of our banks. A large and conservative country, Canadians are proud of their large and conservative banks, which weathered the financial crises of 2008-2010 better than financial institutions in any other G8 country. Canadian banks are more regulated than those in the United States, Britain or many European countries, and less prone to risky investments. Canadian banks are particularly fond of investment in real estate, and the relative vitality and diversity of Canada's largest cities – like Vancouver, Calgary, Toronto and Montreal – is due, in part, to the availability of large pools of patient capital for investment in commercial and residential buildings in our central cores. This real estate investment is sustained by high levels of immigration of well-educated new citizens from around the world, assuring a continuing market for bold city-building. This is all very good news for Canadian architects and other city-builders.

There is a flip side to the conservative nature of our banks, and the wealthy but conservative culture they serve. While the United States has thousands of banks, Canadian federal regulations keep our total to about a dozen, and they are not nearly as aggressive in supporting new or innovative businesses (or new and innovative forms of real estate development). They prefer established businesses to new enterprises, tired business formulas to novel ones, the packaged franchise to the new commercial concept, the reliably analogue to the quixotically digital, the established typology to experiment in form, predictably modest results to potential windfalls (or disasters). Risk management is something of a national obsession. The same is true of our architecture, and I am convinced that the same national ethos edits out design flare and technical brilliance in our buildings in favour of bland competency.

It is in the nature of global surveys like this series of architectural books to avoid bland competency and make room for each nation's most innovative and creative buildings. In compiling a sampling of Canadian architecture from the past decade that will be of interest to an international audience, my list tends to the very big and the very small: developer-driven behemoths of urban momentum, and tiny wooden pavilions. These small works are aesthetically conservative – essays in self-conscious Neo-Modernism, where art historical allusions are plain to see –, but they are invigorating and beautifully crafted. Ironically, the big projects are the radical ones, proposing new kinds of urban living, conjunctions of rich with poor residents, unprecedented hybrids of building uses within the same walls, all the while pushing structures and living densities to their limits. This essay is thus split between 'mega' and 'micro' sections, presenting the two spectrum ends of excellence in Canada's design culture. Except for a few words at the conclusion, I will pass by the 'muddled middle', the usual range of architecture for architects (cultural buildings, showpieces for corporations and universities, local implementations of the global marketing strategies of 'starchitects'; massive private residences brimming with quirky innovation) and provide a little historical background on why Canadian architectural culture has evolved towards these twin poles of excellence, along with a run-through of the projects and personalities that have inspired this unusual pattern of accomplishment.

Mega, Hybrid Buildings
The first of the macro designs I will discuss is not the largest in size, but it has grand ambitions and is a considerable accomplishment. 60 Richmond by Teeple Architects is a housing co-operative co-sponsored by a trade union for hotel and restaurant workers, located just east of

Commissioned by a syndicate of individuals who are employed in the hotel and restaurant sector, the new building at 60 Richmond Street in downtown Toronto is the first housing co-operative to go up in the Canadian city in over a decade, forming part of the implementation of a long-term strategy of the federal government towards revitalizing social housing policies and programs, which were suppressed in the 1990s.

Toronto's downtown core. As in much of Europe, downtown housing in Canadian cities has become very expensive, meaning that service workers like these must endure long commutes to more affordable lodging in the suburbs. Some new creative development and financial policies now make 60 Richmond the first housing co-operative built in Canada's largest city in over a decade; following the elimination of social housing programs in Thatcher's Britain and Reagan's United States, in the 1990s Canada had eliminated funding for co-operatives and other modes of publicly-sponsored affordable housing. It was decided, in re-developing the site of the 1960s vintage Regent Park social housing complex further east, that it would be good to develop some of their social housing allotment off-site, funding it by selling some of Regent Park lands for private-market housing on what was once an American-style large 'housing project'. This notion of a satellite construction funded the creation of 60 Richmond in an otherwise gentrifying part of the city.

Central to the Canadian megaprojects is the notion of the hybrid, understood in the sense of an intentional mixture of social classes, an unusual grouping of building programs, and the use of un-typical combinations of tectonic or environmental strategies. 60 Richmond demonstrates all of these characteristics. Residents are now a few blocks walk away from the hotels and restaurants where they work, and the city is richer for having a more diverse range of residents both here and at Regent Park, with its new private condos where once there was only social housing. Most of the residents are recent immigrants to Canada, mainly from Asia, and the building program adapted to their needs, notably with a training kitchen and restaurant at ground level, where they learn and improve their skills. In raised beds on decks cut into the black mass of the floors, they produce herbs and vegetables for the restaurant. These decks, along with a large white-painted light well at the centre of the block, are part of an ambitious green strategy which also includes a green roof with rainwater retention, a verdant 'grow wall' on the interior court, heat recovery devices, and a palette of environmentally friendly materials and finishes.

Stephen Teeple's design demonstrates an adeptness at turning medium- and high-density housing into architecturally bold living environments. His strategy was to build residential floors out to the maximum building envelope permissible, then carve into it horizontally (the skydecks with the gardens) and vertically (the central circulation and daylight court.) His colour and material palette broadcasts these strategies, with black metal panels on the elevations touching the limits of the site, with a turn to white for the multiple-storey balconies and inner courts. Some smaller balconies have their inside walls painted bright colours, while apartment windows are set at a variety of depths in from the outer envelope, for a more plastic elevation.

The assertive use of colour and the maximization of residential density on a difficult site are themes shared with the next example of Canadian 'mega', the Spectrum project of James K.M. Cheng Architects for Vancouver's Concord Pacific Developments. Framed by two sports stadia, some freeway ramps and a 15 metre escarpment, this site near downtown Vancouver had long been passed up as unbuildable. Lower floors – below the datum of the stadia, ramps and hill – were not suitable for housing, yet higher perches yielded unblocked views of False Creek and Burrard Inlet. Vistas equal value in Vancouver's real estate 'cult of the view'. A hybrid of building programs was the strategy here, in this case by covering the entire site with the first Costco (a big-box store similar to a Carrefour hypermarket) ever to be built in any downtown, and above

Teeple Architects, Apartment building at 60 Richmond, Toronto, Ontario (2010)

Considered worthy examples of the current called Vancouverism, which arose in Canada at the close of the 1980s, are a colossal residential highrise accommodating a luxury hotel on its top floors, a project of the Canadian architect James Cheng, a precursor of the movement, and the complex designed by Henriquez, with high-density hybrid towers that bring together university premises and social housing units.

that went a multi-levelled parking garage, and on the roof, at a level to match flanking downtown streets, new lanes lined by townhouses. Sprouting up and out of all this are four apartment towers of 35 to 45 storeys, with Lego-like coloured highlights on their outward surfaces, but more modest hues on those facing the other towers and new streets. More than any other architect, James Cheng is considered the inventor, in the late 1980s, of the initial architectural typology of Vancouverism, the thin high-rise apartment tower set on a continuous townhouse base. Spectrum takes what has been named the tower-podium typology to new heights, somewhat literally, through its raised deck at downtown street elevations, resulting in new streets in the air lined with townhouses and framed with high-rise towers; an utterly new streetscape for one of the world's youngest major cities.

Henriquez Partners, Woodwards Building, Vancouver, British Columbia (2010)

Elsewhere in Vancouver are hybrid combinations of uses within the same building not found elsewhere, not even in Asia: an entire university and office tower built over a once-failing suburban shopping mall that never stopped operating through construction; other big-box stores laminated onto supermarkets, their roofs home to entire villages of townhouses. High land prices and enlightened urban planning have pushed Vancouver further to intensifying urban spaces this way, and architects like Cheng are doing so with architecture of verve and elegance. Consider the suburban equivalent to Spectrum: a large big-box store, a huge ground-level parking lot, hundreds of suburban bungalows and the roadways needed to connect them. Vancouverist projects like Spectrum are more conserving of land, energy and natural resources, and the single most effective green strategy available is to build dense and diverse cities reliant on public transport.

James Cheng's latest hybrid, high-density project is also the largest single building ever built in Vancouver. The Fairmont Pacific Rim features a luxury hotel on its lower 21 floors and condo apartments above; in total 76,090 square meters, more floor space than the LMN Architects-designed new convention centre across the street, on Vancouver's waterfront. Urban design and 'view corridor' restrictions shaped the tower, and Cheng's plan provides 70% of apartments with guaranteed harbor views forever, an increasingly rare commodity. Each typical highrise floor is 1672 square meters, triple the size of Vancouver's more typical apartment towers, so the architect uses compositional and material changes on the elevations to bring down the perceived scale. Wrapping the base of the hotel where kitchens and ballrooms are located is a stainless steel exo-elevation on outriggers, where laser-cut holes and stamped dimples of differing diameters combine, pixel-like, to form an image of a coastal rain forest; a detail adapted from Herzog & de Meuron's treatment at the De Young Museum in San Francisco. In any case, Cheng's major feat at Fairmont Pacific Rim is using proportion and detail to temper the often overpowering scale of 'mega' construction.

The most dramatic and socially ambitious paradigm of Vancouverism is Woodwards. Designed by Henriquez Partners, the location is Vancouver's Downtown Eastside, the notorious 'favela' adjacent to downtown that is home to Canada's poorest residents and to an out-of-control drug problem. Here, a late 19th- and early 20th-century department store called Woodwards had sat empty for nearly 20 years. Henriquez's design restores a portion of this store to serve as offices for community and arts organizations serving local residents. Mid-block are an interior atrium and several outdoor 'piazzetas', but the most dramatic elements are the high-density towers around, Vancouver's most extreme hybrid of building programs yet. One wing features studios, theatres, classrooms and offices for the 2,000 students of Simon Fraser University's School for the Contemporary Arts. Using profits derived from the extra density granted for adjacent private condos, the developer has built social housing on the university's roof for several hundreds of the city's poorest residents, many of them both addicted and suffering from mental illness. In one of the more radical conjunctions of use and social class that is Vancouverism, they gaze across at expensive private condos in the W-43 Tower, which features an exterior trellis in red-painted metal that will be home to a wall of ivy.

Less visually spectacular but just as socially amenable is the adjacent Abbott Tower, with private residences on top, affordable rental housing (increasingly scarce in ever more resort-like Vancouver) for families at the middle, and on the lower floors, offices for city and federal government cultural agencies. This mix

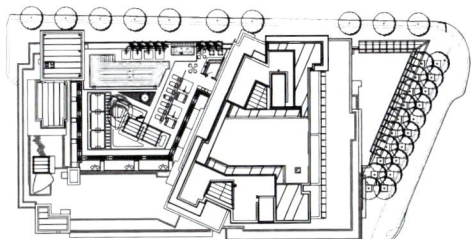

James Cheng, Fairmont Pacific Rim, Vancouver, British Columbia (2010)

required complex legal pacts between the developer and all levels of government, making it take nearly 20 years to forge an agreement and complete construction. There is a Utopian streak at the heart of Vancouverism, with its notion that public amenities can compensate for extraordinarily high living densities, that rich residents can live happily beside poor ones, that conservation of old buildings in a slum will not get in the way of marketing flashy condos in a slick tower. The marketing slogan for the project was 'Be Bold or Move to Suburbia', a sentiment that might just as well be inscribed at all of the bridges leading to island-like, peninsular downtown Vancouver, one of the first cities of the 21st century.

The multi-use, high-density, city-in-one-building idea in Canadian architecture began not in Vancouver, but in Montreal, during its Expo 67 era of architectural innovation. In the sci-fi inspired architectural argot of the day, Place Bonaventure was labeled a 'megastructure' for its multiblock scale and its collection of uses: metro and mainline rail stations; a large shopping centre; a convention hall; five floors of a merchandise mart and offices; all capped by a 395-room rooftop hotel set around garden courts. Designed by Ray Affleck and his team at ARCOP Architects, Place Bonaventure has matured as a hub of Montreal's underground city and an engine of its metropolitan vitality. While the large and hybrid mode of Canadian city-building began with ARCOP's Place Bonaventure, that tendency is now most associated with Vancouver, and to a lesser extent Toronto, Calgary and Edmonton.

The Canadian megaprojects are sponsored by private developers and financed by our banks, but in terms of urbanism and architecture, they are truly radical creations. They are socially radical in attempting to mend the striation of class, often combining social housing with luxury condominium apartments in the same complex or even the same building. This same tendency extends to building programs, with hybrids of functions seldom found in the same buildings elsewhere in the world: Place Bonaventure, to start, and more recently Surrey Central City by Bing Thom Architects, an office tower and university for 4,000 students built on top of a continuously operating shopping mall constructed 30 years earlier. Technical innovation is crucial to megabuilding as well, demonstrated in Surrey Central City's experiments in the use of wood as structural element, or in the innovative engineering that allows Spectrum's towers to rise up over a large open-span store. Canadian civic and political culture means that developers are nearly always required to construct a significant public amenity to get approval for their ever-higher-density projects: a public plaza, an arts facility, a daycare centre, a conservation of heritage, a health center or housing for the homeless. All of the large Vancouver projects have significant ranges of public benefits, not to mention the even more pronounced benefit of building in the most sustainable manner possible: a high-density, diverse and equitable city.

In concluding the 'mega' section of this essay, a few words are necessary regarding the designer whose work most furthered the notion of large, integrated city-building in Canada. Arthur Erickson died in 2009, but his half-century of domination of his homeland's architectural culture continues. Some of his best domestic designs of the 1960s, such as West Vancouver's Smith II and the Graham houses, are barely over 100 square meters, but have an unexpected presence and authority generated by their confident form-making and visual extension out into the landscape. Their craft and repertoire of details inspire such lauded current practices as Shim-Sutcliffe in Toronto, Pierre Thibault in Quebec City, or Battersby Howat and others in Vancouver.

Despite having built nothing larger than several small wooden houses, Erickson and then-partner Geoff Massey won the 1963 design competition for the mountaintop-covering campus of Simon Fraser University, east of Vancouver. Erickson and Massey reconsidered the idea of a university, breaking down notions of faculties and barriers between students and faculty within a unified architectonic frame that aspired to the condition of landscape. While Erickson's wooden houses engage a courtly dialogue with landscape, SFU and the other large commissions that followed, such as the University of Lethbridge, are raised up in scale and ambition to function as entire landscapes of buildings. Inspired by a nearby railway bridge, the University of Alberta integrates student housing and teaching space in a unified structure that spans across a deep valley in the prairie.

James Cheng, Fairmont Pacific Rim, Vancouver, British Columbia (2010)

Atlas: America 17

A mix of new sustainable technologies with wooden structures that respect the natural environment characterizes the various constructions that have gone up beside the LaHave River estuary for the workshops and classrooms of a center for architectural education run by its founder, MacKay-Lyons, as well as the nature interpretation museum by the veteran studio Baird Sampson Neuert along the banks of the French River.

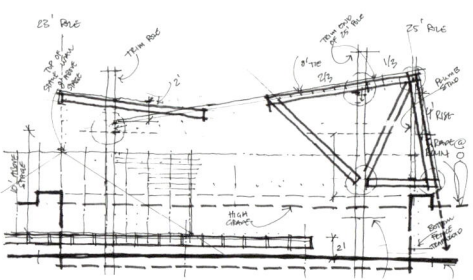

Architecture workshop, Upper Kingsburg, Nova Scotia (2007)

This same sensibility takes an urban turn with the three-block complex that functions as the heart of downtown Vancouver, Robson Square. Erickson devised a progressive brief for a courthouse complex: the corridors and solar-heated public spaces are visually open to the street, rendering the legal process literally transparent. The two other downtown city blocks of Robson Square feature the renovation of a former courthouse into an art gallery, and a sublime range of gardens, walkways and watercourses set on top of a provincial government office building. After Robson Square, Toronto's Roy Thomson Hall, Ottawa's Bank of Canada, Los Angeles's Bunker Hill development and countless other projects in the Middle East (nearly all of them unbuilt, save for the Kuwait Ministry of Petroleum tower) furthered Erickson's notions of large-scale city-building tempered by handsome detail and a dialogue of built form with landscape form. Right to the end of his career, Erickson continued to design houses (admittedly, grander ones) while crafting further ground-breaking essays in large-scale city-building.

West Vancouver's Gleneagles Community Centre by Patkau can be seen as an extension of this Ericksonian trajectory. While John Patkau worked briefly for Erickson, what is most true to this pattern of building is the use of a very generously-sized roof to provide an organizing framework for the building, almost an element of landscape, analogous to the entire block-sized glass roof on the Robson Square Law Courts building, the space frame over the key plaza of Simon Fraser University, or the internal streets of the one-building University of Lethbridge. Nestled under Gleneagles's spectacular wooden roof are the complete range of aerobics studios, gymnasia, classrooms and other spaces for this suburban recreation hub. The opposite of the programmatic expressionism common to high modernism (the notion that every building function should have a different spatial and/or material expression), the large roof and other strategies of large-scale integration become representations of society and community. As with hybrid building programs and technologies, 'mega' devices are tropes for Canadian society generally, architectural symbols for a nation that often attempts to replace American-style romantic individualism with more statist attempts to bind rich to poor, immigrant to native-born, city to hinterland, and so on. The architectural ambitions of the 'mega' projects can appear artificial and over-reaching at times (as can the laws and funding needed to accomplish these goals), but in the warm inclusivity of a building like Gleneagles Community Centre, the possibility of a stable and integrated society seems very real indeed.

Micro, Pavilions in Nature
Different in size (sometimes) and sensibility (always), much of Canada's architectural avant-garde is adept at crafting artful pavilions which are completed in nature, not only buildings for the intensification of cities. Canada is one of the most highly urbanized countries in the world, but it is also home to immense stretches of wilderness. It is perhaps understandable why Canada's most innovative architects would be attracted to the two extremes of scale and built purpose. If the ethos of the megaprojects is Utopian – the creation of equitable, energy-conserving, diverse and lively contemporary downtown areas –, the ethos of the microprojects is romantic and spiritual – provisional pavilions in the lap of nature, the constructed dwelling set artfully amidst the splendor of wilderness or farmland.

Many of the leading designers specialize in microprojects because they avoid the complications, perilous finances, complex approval-obtaining and political

Brian MacKay-Lyons, Architecture workshop, Upper Kingsburg, Nova Scotia (2007)

French River Visitor Center, Alban, Ontario (2006)

Baird Sampson Neuert Architects, River Visitor Center, Alban, Ontario (2006)

interventions needed for 'mega' city-building. Some of the Canadian microprojects are even hand-built by their designers, or their regular collaborators, often students. This type of project has proven attractive to professors of architecture, the investment of time and attention for megaprojects being way beyond the capabilities of full-time teachers of design. Canadian architecture schools differ from those in Europe and the United States in that they grant professorships to those who excel in teaching, rather than building, so very few of our most lauded designers have full teaching appointments. In turn, whereas the Canadian megaprojects largely lack a critical or interpretive literature, these microworks may be the world's most over-explicated sheds, with a monograph or exhibition to match every wood-framed experiment. (Further to the ellipsis in the previous sentence, the importance of these documents in advancing the academic careers of both architecture students and professors cannot be under-emphasized.)

The School of Architecture of Dalhousie University in Halifax has been one of the leaders of the 'micro' movement in contemporary Canadian design. Brian MacKay-Lyons has deep family roots in Atlantic Canada and has taught there for 25 years, while producing a highly regarded string of rural vacation houses throughout the continent and some larger public buildings in the Halifax area. Using a portion of his own rural estate on the seashore south of Halifax, MacKay-Lyons has organized an influential string of 'Ghost Camps' that investigate the art of building, interrogating the nature of place through design. What sets his creation apart from architecture school 'design camps' and the cult of the woodshop-crafted details popular in the 1990s are the meticulousness and intellectual ambitions of these workshops. The first camps of 1994 and 1995 consisted almost entirely of Dalhousie students and faculty, but over the past years prominent architectural writers including Kenneth Frampton, Juhani Pallasma and Robert Ivy and such practitioners as Rick Joy and David Miller have joined in. In the 2007 Ghost Camp, participants included faculty and students from 20 different universities, plus a number of design firms.

The collaborative designs resulting from this iterative workshop sequence have grown in scale and ambition, from simple-performance platforms and observation towers early on, to fully finished dwellings (completed by MacKay-Lyons Sweetapple) and residences for future campers. The built results are more interesting in their collectivity – an ensemble arrayed on a magnificent landscape – than they are viewed as individual pieces. The camp is better than the cabins from which it is composed. As is the case for most other design camp creations across North America,

The scale of important cultural buildings like the National Library of Quebec in Montreal, a work of the experienced partnership of John and Patricia Patkau, strikes a contrast with the modest dimensions of the wooden pavilions that have been constructed in almost artisan manner by the firm Kohn Schnier or the exquisite single-family residences designed and executed by the office of Brigitte Shim and Howard Sutcliffe.

Kohn Shnier, Pavilion for two families, Toronto, Ontario (2010)

the default aesthetic here is a structurally expressionist take on a vernacular wood frame construction, helped along by the fact that mainly summertime use means little need for the full building enclosure that would hide the artful wood framing and self-conscious connections.

With MacKay-Lyons's deep local roots, participants get to meet and converse with local builders, fishermen, musicians and farmers of the place. 'Ghosts' of the local building vernacular of barns, houses and lighthouses appear in the camp's annual constructions, but a key difference is that they are almost entirely unpainted, in a region where house paint colours and highlights announce each owner's pride and ethnic identity. These naked and graying wood pavilions – empty most of the year – baffle some of the local residents. Ghost Camp is sometimes compared to the works produced by Auburn University's Rural Studio. But the formal invention and community engagement of the Alabama collaborative constructions made under Sambo Mockbee's direction make the Canadian experiments seem conservative, and, well, intra-faculty. Speaking of faculty, some of the micropavilions produced by MacKay-Lyons's Dalhousie colleagues are more inventive and visually interesting. Such constructions by Richard Kroeker as the 2003 Eskasoni Studio and the 2004 Cheticamp Theatre Petit Cercle have a more gestural quality, his unfinished or organically closed-in use of wood frame drawing attention to building conventions by corrupting them.

It is a peculiar quirk of Canada's contemporary architectural culture that the micropavilions have come to predominate in its architectural exhibitions, publications and, especially, design awards. The Governor General's Awards for Architecture are the nation's highest design prizes, administered by the Canada Council, the federal arts agency. The dozen GG medals awarded for 2010 certify the predominance of microworks – especially houses or pavilions in natural settings – at the centre of the nation's architectural culture. Five of these prizes went to small houses in natural settings, and another four went to park pavilions and interior renovations. The two significant megaworks of Canadian city-building that were granted medals in 2010 – John and Patricia Patkau's National Library of Quebec in Montreal and Marianne McKenna/KPMB's Toronto Telus Centre for Performance and Learning – were both actually designed in the 1990s, but took long periods for approvals and funding, and, it seems, even longer to be recognized by a national awards jury. For the first time in the history of the Canadian design awards, three of the dozen medals went to but one firm, the wife-husband team of Brigitte Shim and Howard Sutcliffe of Toronto. All three were for exceptionally small designs, little more than a room: a workspace addition to one of their previous medal-winners, from 1997; the conversion of a heritage building's interior for an art dealer; and a guesthouse in a Toronto ravine. This trio cements the 'micro' sensibility of the times in Canada, a preference for exquisite string trios over grand orchestral works.

The ravine house is a serene pavilion situated in a wooded park, and it is a useful summary of the magical creations of this talented firm. Most of the architecture is devoted to a single-room porch set in front of a simple sleeping room, top-lit by an almost absurdly oversized ring of clerestory windows, a large cap defining the activity

John & Patricia Patkau, National Library of Quebec, Montreal, Quebec (2004)

Shim-Sutcliffe Architects, Craven Road Studio, Toronto, Ontario (2010)

space of the porch below through light and shadow. The roof is suspended on a brace frame of steel I-beams, with a secondary frame of wooden beams permitting exterior walls to be spared structural duties. Wide wooden doors open up onto vistas of the rocks and maple trees of this hardwood forest not far from downtown Toronto, views chanelled by the structure above and the wooden decks, bridge and reflecting pond in the foreground field of vision. A double-sided cast concrete fireplace is virtually the only 'furniture' in the room, its planimetric power balanced by a thick concrete wall that serves as an entrance screen. The site works recall Frank Lloyd Wright and Wright via Scarpa, while the pavilion form and details are indebted to Alvar Aalto as well as to the west-coast Canadian modernism of the early houses of Arthur Erickson and Ron Thom. The house is an unusually balanced essay in nature-worshipping romanticism, laminated to architectural ideas reduced to intellectual essences, their roots and intentions showing.

At the core of Canada's architectural culture is the 19th-century British notion of the Picturesque, the composition of built form with raw natural features into pictorial spatial sequences. The Picturesque informs many of the works in this section, and before them countless houses and public buildings, even Canada's Houses of Parliament, with their Gothic Revival forms perched on top of a forest-covered bluff on the Ottawa River. An attraction to the 'sublime and terrible' found in raw nature, in dialogue with the artful composition of sympathetic built forms, is a common strategy for 'mega' works, especially Erickson's. Just as with Parliament Hill's Gothic buttresses framed by raw granite outcroppings and a maple forest, Canadians are drawn to this interplay of cosmopolitan aesthetics and wilderness in its most unprocessed state.

Sensibilities of this kind are given an invigorating update in the French River Visitor Centre by the Toronto firm of Baird Sampson Neuert. This small museum interprets the geology, biology and cultural history of the river that courses from Lake Nippissing to Georgian Bay. In a steeply-sloping site above the river, the museum is one large room cantilevered over a single cast concrete branching pillar shaped into an abstracted tree-like form. Inside and uphill are support spaces, with trays of teaching and public events spaces outside nestled within concrete terraces and under generous roof overhangs. Inside, glu-lam beams and a wooden ceiling warm the space, while open wood lattices serve as vertical display services for museum artifacts and interpretive information.

The spatial effects here are as powerful as its visual details. The vertigo of the down-slope glass end-wall that terminates the main museum rood wall is amplified by having its vertical surfaces tapered in and its floor dropping slightly down. Visitors are drawn through the natural and cultural history of the displays, then towards this viewing perch in the trees. This spatial sequence has a bit of narrative irony, the end-wall window doing a kind of 'so what?' to the rest of the pavilion, as if to say "What you have seen in here is nothing, just look outside!"

Neuert's partner George Baird is founder of their firm and has had a longtime interest in phenomenology as a means to both understanding and making architecture, as presented in the essay 'La Dimension Amoreuse in Architecture', which appeared in the *Meaning in Architecture* collection

Shim-Sutcliffe Architects, Ravine Guest House, Toronto, Ontario (2010)

Atlas: America **21**

Frank Gehry, Art Gallery of Ontario, Toronto, Ontario (2009)

that he himself co-edited with Charles Jencks. Published in 1969, it was one of the first analyses of what came to be called 'postmodern cultural theory' in architecture. Shortly afterwards Baird disassociated himself from Jencks and from the ProTo-PoMo of his former Toronto architecture dean Peter Prangnell to explore the continuities of modernism, a direction that has been deeply influential on an entire generation of Canadian architects, especially in Toronto. Whatever its intentions, the self-consciousness of their quotations from the modern canon indicate to me that many of this generation adhere, instead, to that camouflaged but ongoing subspecies of postmodernism called Neo-Modern. Of course its practitioners deeply resent any allusion to this, but a version of Neo-Modernism definitely dominates the design scene in Canada's largest city.

The irony here is that while much of the early professional career of Baird was tied up in urban design studies, he is at last getting a reputation as a collaborating architect of buildings through a string of interpretive centres and small museums where nature, much more than cities, is the generative factor. Conversely, it is an unreconstituted modernist like James Cheng who is having the most profound impact on city-building, pushing densities and hybrid building programs to places never before seen, while seldom quoting a precedent in his design details; there is no time for Neo-Modernism in the rapidly-building cities of the West.

As a new city without a metropolitan history but bounded on all sides by resplendent nature, it is Vancouver that is blazing new trails into formats and assemblies of urban architecture in Canada. Toronto, at the polluted geographic heart of one of the world's greatest industrial agglomerations around the Great Lakes, is drawn to a romantic engagement with fading nature, combined with a kind of credentialism which semi-guarantees second-hand beauty via quotations from the certified masterpieces of modernism, mainly villas. Vancouver, in its Asian-fired newness, goes Mega, while Toronto, in its moment of self-doubt and decline of smokestack industries, goes Micro. Toronto, in its intellectuality, quotes chapter and verse from the built history of modernism, while Vancouver, in its eager naivety, renews the social and technical ethos that powered modernism when it was new. There are arguments for both sensibilities, and maybe some way can be found towards their reconciliation.

Conclusion: The Muddled Middle
If I have made any kind of case for the strength of contemporary Canadian design at the large- and small-scale ends of the built spectrum, what accounts for the weakness in the middle, the usual range of cultural institutions, corporate and university showpieces or large houses occupying much of architectural publishing? As is the case with its banks, Canada has a mid-range of safe corporate architectural practices producing these buildings in a competent but risk-averse manner that usually stymies invention. For those outside our borders there is little of interest for these conservatively middling designs.

Because of a cultural inferiority complex, coupled with a reluctance to allow its most talented designers to break into larger commissions, Canadians continually grant the B-teams of international 'starchitects' commissions for their largest and most important cultural institutions. This began in the 1980s, with Philip Johnson gaining the design commission for the Toronto headquarters of our most important cultural institution, the Canadian Broadcasting Corporation, the result being a forgettable embarrassment. After the city endured a difficult economic period in the 1990s, civic

Frank Gehry, Art Gallery of Ontario, Toronto, Ontario (2009)

Two ambitious expansion and restoration operations stand out in Toronto: the enlargement of the Art Gallery of Ontario by Frank Gehry, with its unique spiral staircase connecting the existing building to the new construction; and the renovation of the Royal Ontario Museum by Daniel Libeskind, with new exhibition halls provided within a group of angular prisms inspired by the institution's collection of minerals.

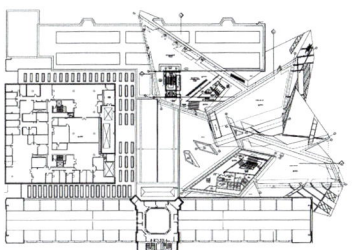

Royal Ontario Museum, Toronto, Ontario (2007)

leaders and provincial funders started an ambitious cultural building program.

In my view, the most successful architectural creations of this multi-billion dollar sequence were two theatres for music designed by local architects: Diamond & Schmitt's Four Seasons Opera House and Marianne McKenna/KPMB's Telus Performance and Learning Centre. The results from the imported 'starchitects' are decidedly more mixed. The best of this lot is Frank Gehry's re-planning and additions to the Art Gallery of Ontario. The strength here was the rationalization of spaces and the flow of patrons after a confused sequence of previous additions. I am less enamoured of AGO's two flashy architectural set pieces. First is a sculptural stair derived from the one Gehry designed 25 years previously for Loyola University's Law School in Los Angeles; the original was better. The second is the linear gallery in curving sections of Douglas fir laminate beams and glass, looking out over the downtown neighbourhood where the Canadian-born architect spent his first eleven years.

Daniel Libeskind's fractured and impractical addition to the Royal Ontario Museum verges on self-satire. Will Alsop's colourful floating box addition to the Ontario College of Art and Design is a dumbing-down, spatially and materially, of his own Peckham Library in southeast London. The 'starchitect' turn has been imitated by provincial cities in Toronto's orbit, notably for Winnipeg's Museum of Human Rights (Antoine Predock doing a variation on his Gateway Center for the University of Minnesota) and the Art Gallery of Alberta in Edmonton (Randall Stout, project architect for one of Gehry's worst buildings, EMP in Seattle, now out producing low-rent imitations of his ex-employer's signature style.)

Quebec has fostered a climate where architects successfully evolve into artful and ambitious middle-range buildings. This is

Daniel Libeskind, Royal Ontario Museum, Toronto, Ontario (2007)

largely because – due to provincial government encouragement – this is the only area in North America where design competitions are routinely held for public and cultural sector buildings. This gives an opportunity – largely unavailable to designers elsewhere – to break through from promising 'micro' designs to confident constructions in the middle range. From his Pointe à Callières Museum in Old Montreal to a string of ambitious university buildings, Dan Hanganu is a designer of the first rank. Saucier & Perrotte have evolved an eloquent idiom, both in their Quebec work and in such creations as the Perimeter Institute at Ontario's University of Waterloo. Pierre Thibault of Quebec is as interested in a dialogue with nature as the Toronto 'micro' designers, but has evolved a more personal and original take, shaping cultural buildings of increasing scale and import.

To depart with a question, is there any hope of reconciling the extremes, the 'mega' city-builders of Vancouver with the 'micro' pavilion-shapers of Toronto? The example set by Canada's acclaimed architect Arthur Erickson is useful in answering this. While a Vancouverite through and through, he maintained a Toronto office for much of his career, and through it produced such excellent examples of city-building as the Roy Thomson Hall in Toronto and the Bank of Canada in Ottawa. With Simon Fraser University, Robson Square and the University of Lethbridge, Erickson set the standard for Canadian megabuilding. But his reputation had first been set with a string of small wooden houses in dramatic natural sites, notably the second house he designed for Gordon and Marion Smith in West Vancouver. Erickson – city-builder, small house deviser, social engineer, poet of post and beam – is an example, for all Canadian architects, of the idea that architectural brilliance knows no boundaries of scale, place, or source of ideas.

Patkau
Gleneagles Community Center
Vancouver, British Columbia (Canada)

Client
Corporation of the District of West Vancouver
Architects
Patkau Architects
Collaborators
Omer Arbel, Greg Boothroyd, Joanne Gates, Samantha Hayes, Patrick O'Sullivan, John Patkau, Patricia Patkau, David Shone, Craig Simm
Consultants
Vaughan (landscaping); Fast & Epp (structure), Earth Tech Canada (installations); Webster (engineering); Gage-Babcock, Susan Morris Specifications (consultants); Mc Squared System Design Group (audiovisuals); Gallop/Varley (signage); Maurice J. Ouellette (project manager)
Contractor
Country West Construction
Photos
James Dow

A GENTLE SLOPE next to the Gleneagles Golf Course is the site of this community center. To minimize the area of the building footprint, the program is organized on three levels. Through a subtle reshaping of the site's cross-sectional topography, the lower and intermediate levels can both be located at grade, opening directly to complementary outdoor activities. The design of the building's section energizes and animates the center. That is, the gymnasium volume rises through all three levels, and the walls that separate it from the adjacent spaces are glazed, creating a visual connection between the major program components (gymnasium, childcare, classrooms and a multipurpose hall) and offering a complex variety of simultaneous views of multiple activities.

The structural system is composed of cast-in-place concrete slabs, insulated concrete-finished double wythe wall panels, and a timber roof. This massive structure is an important part of the building's interior climate control system, acting as a huge thermal storage mass that absorbs and emits energy. Hot and cold water flows through piping embedded in the concrete structure, so the floors and walls act as radiant surfaces for air temperature regulation. The energy required to heat and cool water is obtained by means of heat pumps in combination with a ground-source heat exchanger situated beneath the parking lot.

Ventilation is achieved through a displacement system. Fresh air is tempered and supplied at low velocity in the low levels. This air rises, pushing contaminant particles to the higher levels, where reheated air is captured. As air is not used for the heating and cooling of the building, doors and windows can be opened without affecting the performance of the system. The energy needed for the community center's performance is 40% less than that consumed in conventional buildings.

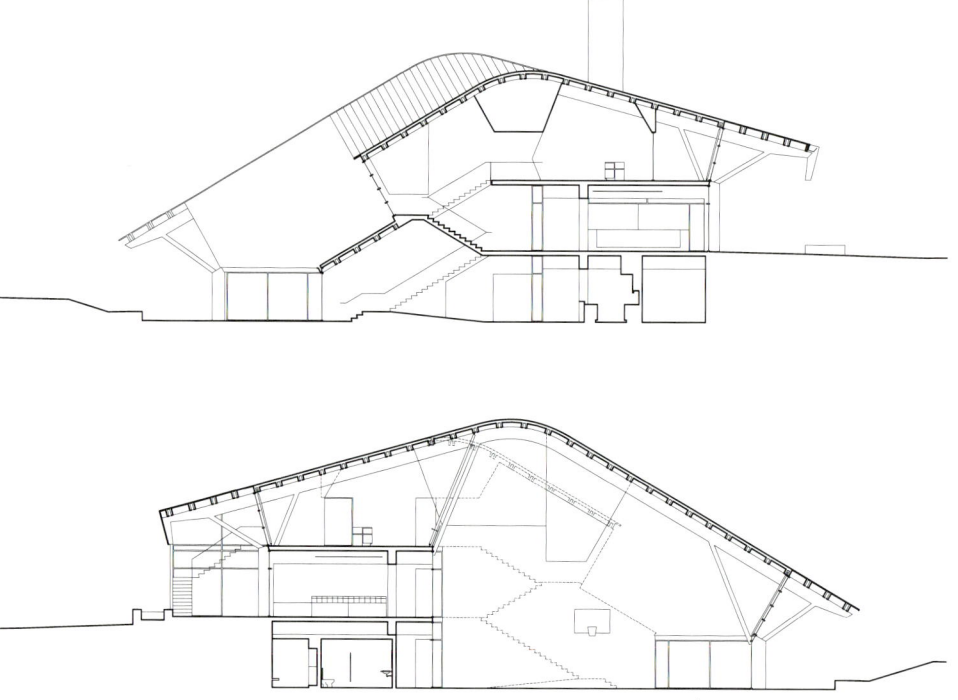

Taking from a palette of materials that are connected to Canadian building tradition, this innovative building was raised with a structure and a set of installations conceived to minimize consumption of energy.

The new civic center has a total floor area of 7,315 square meters distributed on three different levels. The two lower stories open on completely to the surrounding landscape, taking advantage of the natural slope of the plot. The large wooden roof acts as a huge thermal storage mass and its generous overhangs serve to protect the building's interior spaces from excessive solar radiation while shielding them from the rain.

The building combines wood – the most widely used construction material in the country – with concrete, chosen for its capacity as a massive material to absorb and emit heat. The way the main uses are arranged on section contributes to the center's animated and dynamic character; hence the gymnasium rises all three levels and the adjacent spaces look onto it through glazed walls that create a play of visual connections.

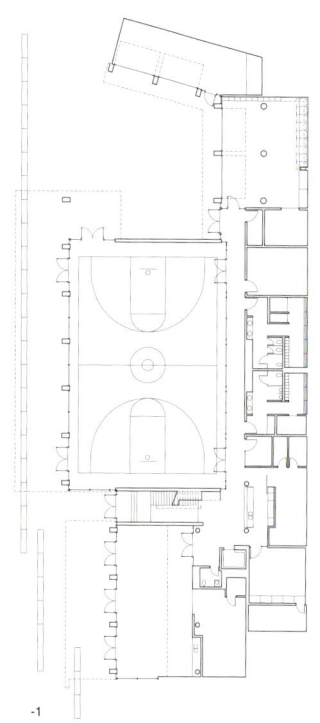

-1

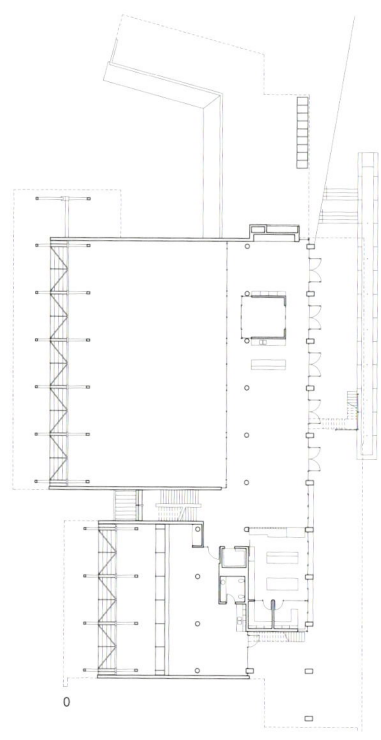

0

Systems of thermal conditioning by means of air are avoided, in favor of the installation of radiant surfaces in the floors and walls, through pipes inside where cold and hot water circulate. For a correct ventilation of the interiors, fresh air is tempered and supplied at low velocity in the lower levels of the rooms, to subsequently rise and push containment particles to the higher levels, where, finally, part of the reheated air is captured.

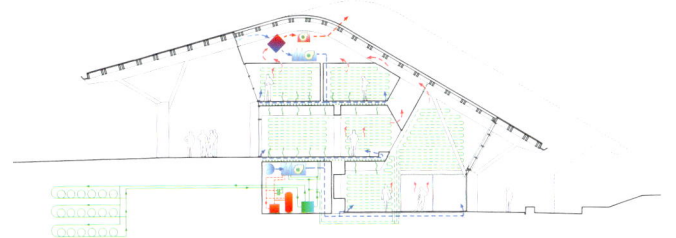

MacKay-Lyons & Sweetapple
Architectural Laboratory
Upper Kingsburg, Nova Scotia (Canada)

Architect
Brian MacKay-Lyons,
Talbot Sweetapple
Collaborators
Ted Flato, Bob Benz
Consultant
Michel Comeau (engineering)
Photos
MacKay-Lyons & Sweetapple

SITUATED ALONG the LaHave River estuary on Nova Scotia's Atlantic coast, the Ghost Laboratory is an architectural education center in the tradition of Frank Lloyd Wright's Taliesin and Samuel Mockbee's Rural Studio. The compound has several constructions – a tower, a studio, cabins and a barn – that provide accommodation for the program and a venue for community events. Each component is the result of a self-build project carried out by students of the center in the course of a two-week workshop held every summer. The tower and the barn – which contains a tool shed and stalls for horses besides sometimes being used as an additional classroom-atelier – are the only structures that are sited outside the actual fenced grounds of this small campus, and they are built with a frame of simple wooden posts that have no cladding whatsoever. As for the studio and the four cabins, each of which contains two bedrooms for use by students, they were constructed over reinforced concrete foundations and are supported by a wooden structure clad with eastern cedar shingles. All the buildings are executed using local building systems, sustainable technologies, and recycled materials coming mostly from nearby sawmills.

Using recycled materials, sustainable technologies and local building systems and techniques, all the facilities of this architectural education center have been designed and constructed by its own students.

Within the fenced grounds of the campus are the study center and the four cabins that contain accommodations for students, raised over a foundation of reinforced concrete with a wooden structure coated with cedar shingles. In turn the tower and the stable, which is used as a classroom-workshop, are found outside the premises and are built with a structure of wooden posts that have no cladding whatsoever.

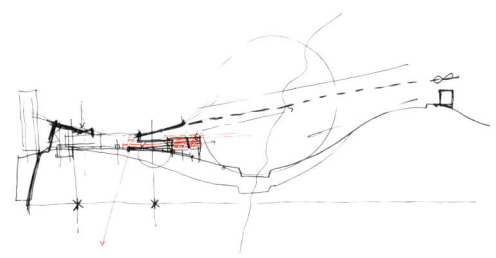

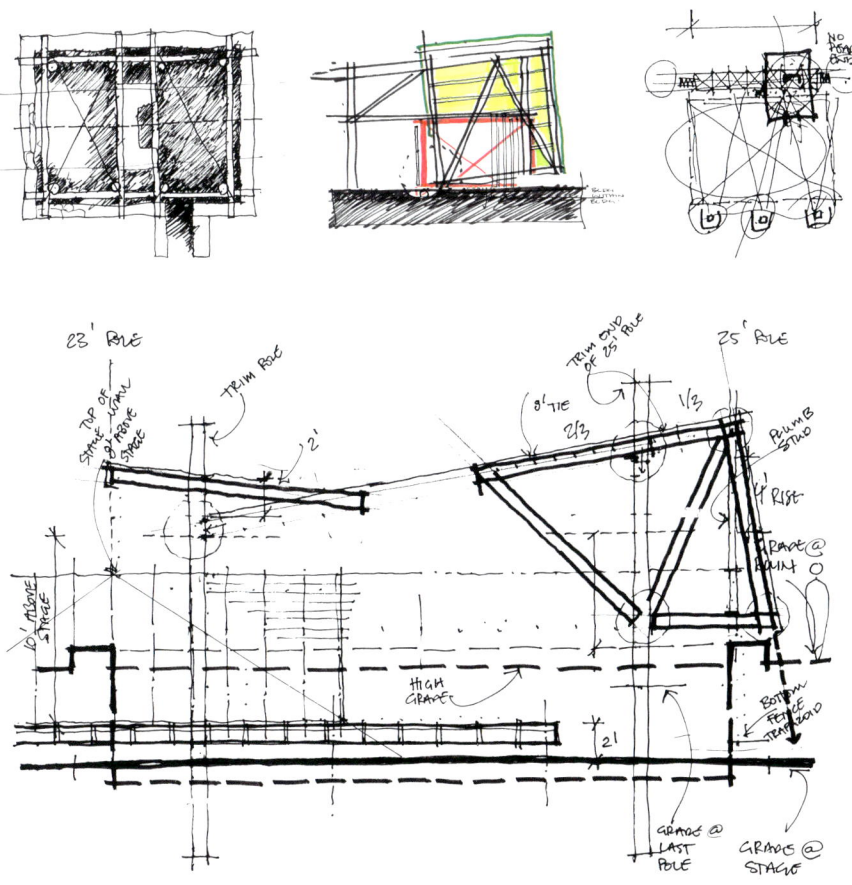

Teeple Architects
Apartment Building at 60 Richmond
Toronto, Ontario (Canada)

Client
Toronto Community Housing Corporation
Architects
Stephen Teeple, Chris Radigan, Richard Lai, William Elsworthy
Consultants
CPE Structural Consultants (structures), Jain & Associates (installations and electricity), Aercoustics Engineering (acoustics), IKO (roof)
Photos
Shai Gill Photography

Conceived in the manner of a large perforated mass, the building has communal open-air areas within it that allow the natural lighting, airing and thermal conditioning of the living units and give good views of the urban context.

IN THE URBAN CORE of Toronto rises a solid, 11-story volume containing 85 living units and multipurpose communal spaces. The client, a housing co-op for employees of the hotel and restaurant industry, was concerned with economic sustainability. This was key to defining the project, which goes by 'permaculture', a new concept having to do with designing sustainable human habitats that are a small-scale imitation of the full-cycle ecosystems found in nature. Premises of this kind led to the creation of a variety of spaces accommodating an integrated system for the production and generation of food products. A restaurant situated at street level, collectively owned and operated by the residents, is supplied with vegetables, fruit and herbs grown in a kitchen garden on the sixth-floor deck, irrigated by storm water coming down pipes from the roof. Organic waste generated by culinary activity serves as compost for the ecological garden.

The building on 60 Richmond is an iconic design that showcases an innovative approach to urban infill. Unlike the glass condominium towers that abound in the downtown landscape, it was conceived as a solid mass carved-into to form openings and skydecks at various levels. The result is a dynamic solution that visually connects the interior to the urban surroundings while being instrumental in the creation of open-air kitchen gardens and other green and amenity spaces. The perforations in the volume of the building contribute to the natural lighting, airing and thermal conditioning of the apartments. The client's demand for low maintenance costs also inspired the use of a broad range of sustainability technologies. Durable materials were combined with energy-saving strategies such as thermal bridging and heat recovery systems. Carbon footprint reduction is further achieved with the green roof and through rainwater collection for the terrace gardens.

In downtown Toronto, at 60 Richmond, stands an 11-floor mixed-use construction that contains 85 cooperative housing units for employees of the hotel and restaurant industry, a resident-owned and -operated restaurant at street level, communal multipurpose spaces, and open-air areas including ecological kitchen gardens that foster a way of life based on precepts having to do with sustainability and respect for the environment.

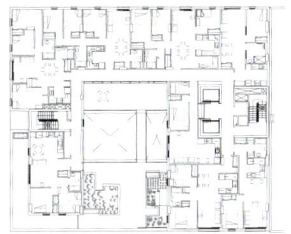

Atlas: America 31

Frank Gehry
Art Gallery of Ontario
Toronto, Ontario (Canada)

Architect
Frank Gehry
Consultants
Halcrow Yolles Engineering (structures), H.H. Angus & Associates (installations), Mulvey & Banani (electricity), L'Observatoire (lighting), Trow Associates (geotechnics), Anderson Associates (civil engineering), Hough Group/Planning Partnership (landscaping), Adamson Associates (local achitects), Royal Danish Consulate, Teknion Furniture Systems (furniture)
Photos
Iwan Baan, Sean Weaver/AGO Photo Resources (p. 33)

A new sculptural spiral staircase connects the existing gallery building to its latest expansion, a prismatic volumen rising five stories that provides additional space for the permanent collection of the Canadian museum.

Since its opening in the year 1918, the Beaux Arts-style stone building of the Art Gallery of Ontario has undergone several transformations, including a first expansion in the 1920s, the addition of a modern sculpture center and a museum store in the 1970s, and the construction of a 2-story brick building over what was the main facade, an operation which moved the institution's main entrance to the side. This new intervention brings the main entry back to its original position and facilitates direct access into Walker Court, the historic heart of the AGO.

The most distinctive feature of the expansion is the new glazed facade, stretching to a length of 180 meters and rising 20 meters above ground level, that has been built with a skeleton of wooden ribs recalling the structure of a ship's hull. Because it is completely open towards the street, the visitor can enjoy views of the city from inside the gallery. The same kind of transparency that characterizes the new hall for displaying sculptures on the north side of the building allows passers-by outside to appreciate the works of art from the street. The whole building enjoys natural light, thanks, too, to a new glass roof built over Walker Court.

The project also incorporates a new south wing providing additional space for the museum's permanent collection. A 5-floor volume with a tinted titanium and glass facade overlooking Grange Park, this addition will house a center for contemporary art and an event space, Baillie Court, with capacity for up to 450 guests. Finally, a unique space that is conceived as a public place, open to all, includes a 2-level gift and book shop, a restaurant serving contemporary comfort cuisine, a casual café, the Jackman Hall lecture theater, and the Young Gallery, a free space for exhibiting the works and projects of new and upcoming artists.

The new expansion of the building incorporates a titanium and glass facade that stretches to a length of 180 meters and rises 20 above street level. It is built with a skeleton of wooden ribs that recalls the structure of a ship's hull. Completely open towards the street, it offers views of the city of Toronto from all points of the visitor's route inside the gallery. The same transparency enables passers-by outside to appreciate the exhibits.

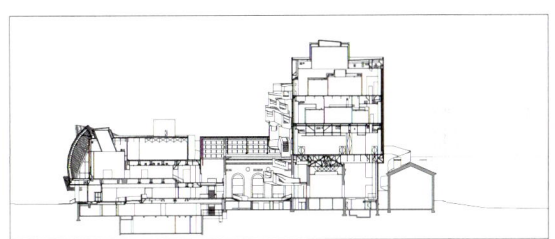

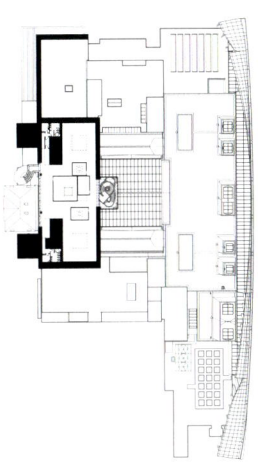

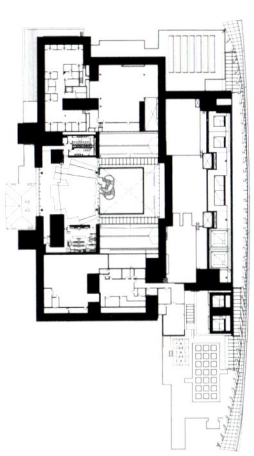

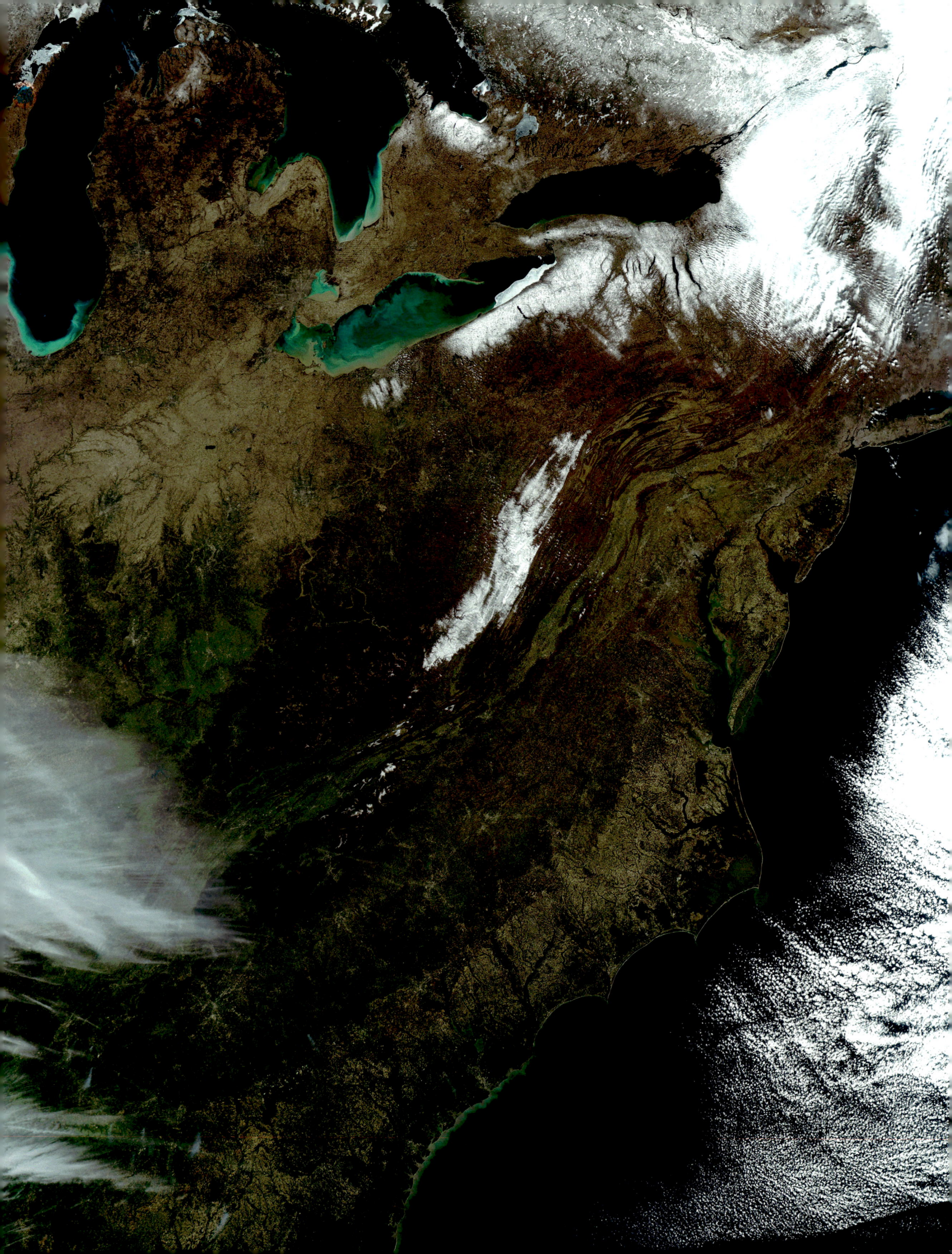

United States

The convergence of myriad ethnic groups has made the United States a multicultural nation, and this manifests itself in architecture, with works built by natives and immigrants alike reflecting the values that embody American culture. The fascination with nature is present in the High Line promenade by Diller & Scofidio with Renfro and James Corner, the California Academy of Sciences by Piano, the Nelson-Atkins Museum by Holl and the bridge by Miró & Rivera. The upholding of an open society is expressed in the free forms of the New Museum by SANAA, the Wyly Theater by REX and OMA, the Data and Library Center by Jiménez and the Anchorage Museum expansion by Chipperfield. The civic spirit is patent in public spaces like the Winspear Opera House by Foster and the MAM by Herzog & de Meuron. Finally, deference to the digital era is evident in the IAC by Gehry, the apartment tower by Nouvel, and the Cooper Union building by Morphosis.

Thomas Fisher
America, America
United States, a Crucible of Cultures

Marked by the enormous cultural diversity of its new generations, the country's architectural production reflects a wide range of contrasts.

The industrial revolution of the United States, which began with the 'machine in the garden', has given rise to a 'green' revolution that upholds sustainability and the integration of architecture with the landscape.

THE UNITED STATES, despite its financial influence and military might, remains a work in progress, shaped by the contributions of immigrants and itinerants. As Walter Lippmann wrote in the early 20th century, "the great social adventure of America is no longer the conquest of the wilderness but the absorption of fifty different peoples". That infusion of talent has made America what it is, evident in the work of American-born citizens whose ancestors arrived as immigrants generations ago, and of foreign-born residents who come because of the opportunities an open society offers. American architecture has benefited from this talent pool, allowing architects to imagine projects that could not occur elsewhere. As J. Hector St. John De Crevecoeur wrote in 1782, "an immigrant when he first arrives… no sooner breathes our air than he forms new schemes, and embarks in designs he never would have thought of in his own country". The following projects reinforce that point, reflecting the quality of the internationally respected talent, American and foreign-born, working in the USA in the 21st century.

Return to the Land
Let's start with the few American-born architects whose work appears in the following pages. Most of them – Steven Holl, Weiss/Manfredi and Diller Scofidio – have projects connected in some fundamental way to the land. Americans have long had a paradoxical relationship with nature: on one hand "draining swamps, turning the course of rivers, peopling solitudes, and subduing nature", as Alexis de Tocqueville observed in 1835, and on the other hand finding "in wilderness… the preservation of the world", as Henry David Thoreau wrote sixteen years later. That tension emerges here in different ways.

Steven Holl's addition to the Nelson-Atkins Museum of Art in Kansas City takes a Thoreauvian stance toward nature. Rather than build on the land, as the other competition entrants did, Holl built most of the museum below ground, with five translucent-glass 'lenses' projecting above grade to let light into the galleries below. "The addition is not an object," says Holl. "We envisioned a new paradigm fusing landscape and architecture." Yet the contrast in Holl's addition between the undulating land and the crystalline structures recalls the metaphor of the 'machine in the garden' that the historian Leo Marx saw as central to America's development: the love of technology at odds with the love of nature. Holl suggests at Nelson-Atkins that technology, rather than dominate nature, can enhance it, with the machine not subduing but supporting the garden.

Another tension in American culture evident in Holl's design involves the frontier. While the American cowboy and Wild West remains a powerful myth in the minds of Americans and non-Americans alike, the frontier ended, officially, in 1890, according to the U.S. census. Americans had to accept becoming a largely urban (and suburban) nation, even as many longed for the frontier mentality and the rugged individualism that went with it. In Holl's addition, you see his sensitivity and sophistication, but he also epitomizes the rugged individualist, receiving this commission by ignoring what the competition brief requested and putting the addition below ground and in a spot no one thought could serve as a site. Rewriting the rules remains a classic American characteristic, suggesting that the frontier exists not physically, but in the imagination of our artists and thinkers.

Diller Scofidio and Renfro's work on New York City's High Line, in conjunction with James Corner, reveals another facet of American culture's fascination with nature. The High Line – a raised rail line in Manhattan converted to a promenade – shows how the industrial revolution in the United States, which began with

The big cities undergo major urban renewal operations including the construction of new promenades flanked by greenery and the creation of large urban parks featuring terraced gardens and open-air spaces for displaying large-scale sculptural installations. In turn the new buildings seek to bond with the natural environment through sustainable technologies and organic forms evoking the surrounding landscapes.

Weiss/Manfredi, Olympic Sculpture Park, Seattle, Washington (2008)

machines in the garden, has ended with a green revolution, as the garden takes back the space once occupied by machines. The designers describe the High Line as "a postindustrial instrument of leisure reflection about the very categories of 'nature' and 'culture' in our time". They do not separate planted areas from paved ones, but interweave them. Nor do they hide the rusted elements of the former rail line. Instead, they use the rails to support wood-plank benches and lounge chairs, some mounted on wheels.

Such elements reflect not only the shifting view of nature and culture in America, but also the changing nature of our economy. In a country built on the manual effort of farmers and laborers, America now depends on knowledge workers and creative innovators, giving American architecture a new role: not just to accommodate our physical and social needs, but to stimulate the imagination of what Richard Florida calls the 'creative class'. That makes the leisure reflection prompted by the High Line not an idyll activity, but an essential part of America's postindustrial economy.

The other landscape-based project here, the Olympic Sculpture Park in Seattle by the American firm Weiss/Manfredi, also provides a place for contemplation and the stimulation of ideas, and in a similar way. Instead of appropriating a rail trestle, Weiss/Manfredi built over train tracks and a highway to link downtown to the waterfront, with space for large sculptures.

As such, it reflects another change in American architecture: the rise of infrastructure as a realm ripe for rethinking by designers. While the park has an elegant glass-enclosed pavilion on its upper end for exhibitions, lectures and special events in Seattle's rainy climate, the bridges and the gravel and grass terraces function as the real 'building' here. And Weiss/Manfredi has handled this infrastructure with great verve as it zigzags down the slope and over transportation cuts like a giant sculpture, showing the tremendous potential that exists in the integration of imaginative architectural and engineering design. Likewise, the Olympic Park mirrors the trend toward the integration of architecture and landscape architecture in the USA. That integration stems from a common interest in sustainability and from the realization that landscape architects often know more about ecosystems than their most committed architect colleagues. In that context, Weiss/Manfredi's park has become iconic, a symbol of American architecture and the landscape, the built and natural environment enfolding back into each other.

This merging with nature becomes explicit in Miro Rivera Architects' pedestrian bridge, which spans 80 feet over a lake between a house and guesthouse in Austin, Texas. The architects bent the steel-reinforcing rods that form the bridge deck

M.H. de Young Museum (Herzog & de Meuron) and California Academy of Sciences (Renzo Piano) in Golden Gate Park, San Francisco, California

Atlas: America **37**

Herzog & de Meuron, Miami Art Museum, Florida

over the structure's 5-inch-diameter pipes to create a railing and skirt that echo the reeds along the shore. Its rope railing and spiky profile also recall the bamboo bridges of tropical cultures, reminding us that we have much to learn from such 'primitive' people, whose ability to live in balance with nature greatly exceeds our own.

Seeking a Big Tent
In American politics, the idea of a 'big tent' – a movement large enough to encompass the diverse opinions and interests of Americans – remains an elusive goal. That idea has nevertheless influenced American architecture, evident in some of the projects here, where a big roof reaches out to cover passers-by who may have thought they had no interest in the activities going on within. That foreign-born architects have designed these buildings suggests that the appeal of the 'big tent' extends beyond Americans to all who find the idea of an inclusive community appealing.

Renzo Piano's California Academy of Sciences in San Francisco offers an environmental version of that idea. It has a 2.5 acre green roof that extends out to the edge of the podium on which the museum stands, welcoming people to come inside. Envisioned by Piano as a piece of the park lifted in the air, with the museum slipped in underneath, the building echoes a long-running tension in American culture between a scientifically grounded pragmatism and a naturally inspired romanticism. Americans' love of science and technology comes through in the building's mechanistic-like museum spaces, with automated features that regulate cooling and photovoltaic panels generating power. At the same time, our love of the land emerges in the building's undulating planted roof, reflecting the domed volumes below and echoing the rolling hills of San Francisco around it.

Herzog & de Meuron, Parking Garage, Miami, Florida (2010)

38 Atlas: America

Conceived with a strong civic spirit, the new cultural and recreational centers tend to reach out to the public by means of huge metallic canopies or imposing slabs of reinforced concrete that extend beyond the enclosing walls of the buildings, creating large outdoor premises for the citizenry that are protected from weather inclemencies and offer greenery, commercial premises and spaces for exhibiting sculptures.

Norman Foster, Winspear Opera House, Dallas, Texas (2009)

The representation of that tension in the building's big roof also suggests a resolution of the reason/romanticism conflict. Americans remain, as the historian Michael Kammen wrote, a "people of paradox, in which one extreme simultaneously begets its opposite". As novelist James T. Farrell put it, "America is so vast that almost everything said about it is likely to be true, and the opposite is probably equally true". That paradoxical character has led, recently, to political polarization in America, but Piano's museum expresses a both/and alternative. It accommodates supposedly irreconcilable differences – science and nature, people and plants, museum and park – on different planes, allowing them to exist simultaneously and invisibly with each other on or under one roof.

Foster & Partners' Winspear Opera House in Dallas evokes other forms of reconciliation in America. One of the bonds among Americans lies in the regional diversity of its geography and climate, creating extreme conditions that have brought people of very different backgrounds together. Foster's building has a broad canopy that shades the public space around the enclosed opera house from the intense sun and heat of Texas. Whether opera-goers or not, passers-by can find relief under that louvered roof and participate vicariously in opera activities.

While Foster's building responds well to its climate, it also expresses another characteristic of the United States: its place as a nation of laws, a classical idea that had its origins in the Enlightenment. The country's classical roots find expression in the neoclassical design of everything from its currency to its iconic buildings in Washington, D.C., and you can see that influence even in modern buildings like the Winspear, with its broad roof, columned porticos, and curved opera house rising up through the center like a dome. The building echoes the American paradox of a modern nation still in love with classicism, since without the rule of law inherited from the Enlightenment, the United States would hardly be a country at all.

The third big-roof project here, Herzog & de Meuron's Miami Art Museum, suggests another interpretation of America as a nation defined by its system of laws rather than by a population of common ethnic origin. As in the Piano and Foster projects, this museum has an expansive roof that shades outdoor public space, but unlike the vaguely classical porticos around the other two buildings, the columns in the Miami Art Museum serve as a structural system within which the museum's various volumes float. This three-dimensional matrix evokes the functional flexibility and physical freedom that has long characterized American culture. The commentator Marilyn vos Savant aptly asked: "What is the essence of America? Finding and maintaining that perfect, delicate balance between freedom 'to' and freedom 'from'".

You see that delicate balance inside the Miami Art Museum as well. The architects have designed the galleries to allow visitors a wide range of routes through the building, and curatorial staff an equal degree of freedom to arrange exhibitions. This also occurs in Herzog & de Meuron's retail and parking structure at 1111 Lincoln Road in Miami Beach. Comprising a series of thin, cantilevered concrete slabs, located at various heights and alignments and supported by a number of angled and trapezoidal concrete columns, the garage turns the often-forgettable activity of parking and storing cars into a dynamic, three-dimensional experience that echoes the act of driving along the similarly detailed, elevated highways of American cities. At once functional and freeing, the building interweaves the retail stores not only along the pedestrian-oriented Lincoln Road and its adjacent side streets, but also on an upper

The availability of new materials as well as the latest construction systems and techniques makes it possible to deck buildings with aluminum mesh enclosures that alter slightly with the day's changing light, perforated envelopes of intense colors, neutral claddings executed with reflecting curtain walls, and unique skins erected with slender cylindrical aluminum bars, in the manner of semi-transparent screens.

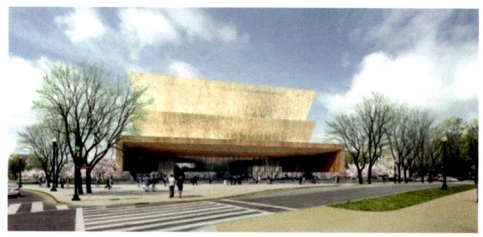

David Adjaye, Museum of African American History, Washington, D.C.

floor. So it recalls Americans' paradoxical love of both cities and suburbs, wanting to walk to stores and also drive up to them. The urbanist Jane Jacobs wrote that "there is a widespread belief that Americans hate cities. I think it is probable that Americans hate city failure, but, from the evidence, we certainly do not hate successful and vital city areas". 1111 Lincoln Road proves Jacobs's point: its vitality has turned a parking garage into a tourist destination.

Embracing Diversity
Many on the political left think that finding an overall order or 'big tent' broad enough to encompass the diversity of America is a futile effort. Better, they argue, to accept and express the contentiousness that comes with such a large and varied population. Some of the buildings that follow do just that.

SANAA's New Museum in New York City, for example, seeks no overarching system or overhanging roof to handle the range of spaces in the building. Instead, the architects stack up a series of metal-mesh-clad boxes, each slightly shifted off the other, aptly expressing not only the energy and vibration of the contemporary art inside, but also the jostling and competitive nature of American society itself. As Supreme Court Justice Louis Brandeis observed, Americans believe "in differentiation, not in uniformity".

With that belief comes an emphasis on the autonomous individual, a belief captured in the work of artists and expressed in SANAA's museum, with its autonomous, windowless boxes stacked in a seemingly random, individualistic way. Individualism, of course, can also create tensions in society. The tension in the SANAA museum lies not in the building itself, but in its contrast with the buildings around it. As the sociologist Georg Simmel said, "the deepest problems of modern life derive from the claim of the individual to preserve the autonomy and individuality of his existence in the face of overwhelming social forces".

David Chipperfield's Anchorage Museum Expansion takes a related approach to that problem. As in SANAA's museum, Chipperfield envisions the Anchorage building as a series of anonymous forms sliding past each other. But Chipperfield has clad his addition in a minimally detailed glass curtain wall, evoking not the autonomy of artists so much as the anonymous corporate sponsors whose funding often keeps museums alive. This corporate veneer enclosing work that often challenges corporate culture seems particularly appropriate in a state like Alaska, whose residents remain famously individualistic despite the dominance of oil and mining companies in their economy.

Such paradoxes pervade American society, leading to a growing divide in the country between facts and ideology, between how people live and how they believe they should live. Chipperfield's museum reflects that divide. Unlike SANAA's museum, whose central elevator and stair core follows the circulation pattern of a typical highrise building, Chipperfield's museum expansion overturns the conventions of corporate offices. He has pulled the core – the stairs and elevators – to the perimeter of the building and opened up the center the entire height of the structure. This reversal of expectations captures something important about Americans, whose conventional exterior appearance often disguise unconventional interior lives.

OMA and REX take that paradoxical aspect of American culture to its logical conclusion in the Wyly Theater in Dallas. Its anonymous exterior has the quality of a literal curtain wall, with a tubular-metal undulating surface recalling the folds of a theater curtain, even as the theater space itself has a glass wall backed by an actual curtain. Behind that uniform and almost ugly exterior stands a wide array of front- and

SANAA, New Museum of Contemporary Art, New York, New York (2007)

40 Atlas: America

David Chipperfield, Anchorage Museum Expansion, Alaska (2009)

back-of-house functions and a large, flexible performance space, stacked vertically like a three-dimensional jigsaw puzzle. The pragmatic directness of the design, with its combination of an unexceptional exterior and an unexpected interior, captures those same qualities of so many Americans. "This is the story of America," wrote Jack Kerouac. "Everybody's doing what they think they're supposed to do".

As OMA's Rem Koolhaas understood, beginning in *Delirious New York,* America is a social experiment of accommodating diversity in an infrastructure of equality, leading to irrational combinations of activities in apparently rational systems. In elevation the Wyly appears rational – a glass-walled recessed entry, a glass-enclosed performance space, and a metal-wrapped 'super fly' space that seems uniform, despite the random combination of metal tubes in the curtain wall. In section the seemingly irrational mix of performance and rehearsal space, audience and administrative functions, storage and staging areas, is evident. The Wyly, like many OMA projects, embodies the conflict between equality and diversity and reflects the extremes that the idea can take in America.

The Problem of Skin
You can often spot a group of American students abroad not by their clothing or the technology they carry, which have become ubiquitous in a world united by global trade, but by their ethnic diversity, most apparent in the variation in the color of their skin. Skin has been a divisive issue in the United States not only in the past, with the subjugation of African Americans as slaves, but still to this day, with the controversial law in Arizona allowing the state to interrogate, prosecute and deport anyone looking like they may be an illegal immigrant. Perhaps because of the sheer size and ethnic diversity of the country, some Americans still judge others by the color of skin, however illegal it is to act on such prejudices. Recent American architecture has reflected this struggle over skin.

David Adjaye's National Museum of African American History and Culture, planned for a key site on the National Mall in Washington, D.C. celebrates the skin of the building in a fitting rejoinder to the dark underbelly of American racial prejudice. A few blocks from the White House, where the first African American president now resides, Adjaye's museum will feature a stone-clad, glass-walled base opening up to the Mall and a perforated bronze screen that wraps around the building's upper stories. The splayed form of those upper stories recalls the shape of African headdresses, but the punctured metal cladding also brings to mind the pain that African Americans have suffered because of their 'bronze' complexion and the riches that await those who overcome racial prejudice and get to know the person behind the skin.

Adjaye himself makes that point. A black British architect, born in Tanzania, Adjaye's background shows how much America, like most of the world, now provides a degree of mobility that lets people achieve their potential like never before. America might not have the benefit of talent like Adjaye's were the anti-immigration biases in places like Arizona widespread. And as his museum will no doubt demonstrate through its exhibits, racial prejudice runs counter to economic vitality and opportunity, which makes ethnic profiling not only illegal, but also stupidly self-defeating. As Prime Minister Winston Churchill once said, "you can always count on Americans to do the right thing – after they've tried everything else".

With the waning of racial bias in America has come the rise of an equally pernicious prejudice: ethnic intolerance, most recently against people from the Middle East and predominantly from Muslim countries. This

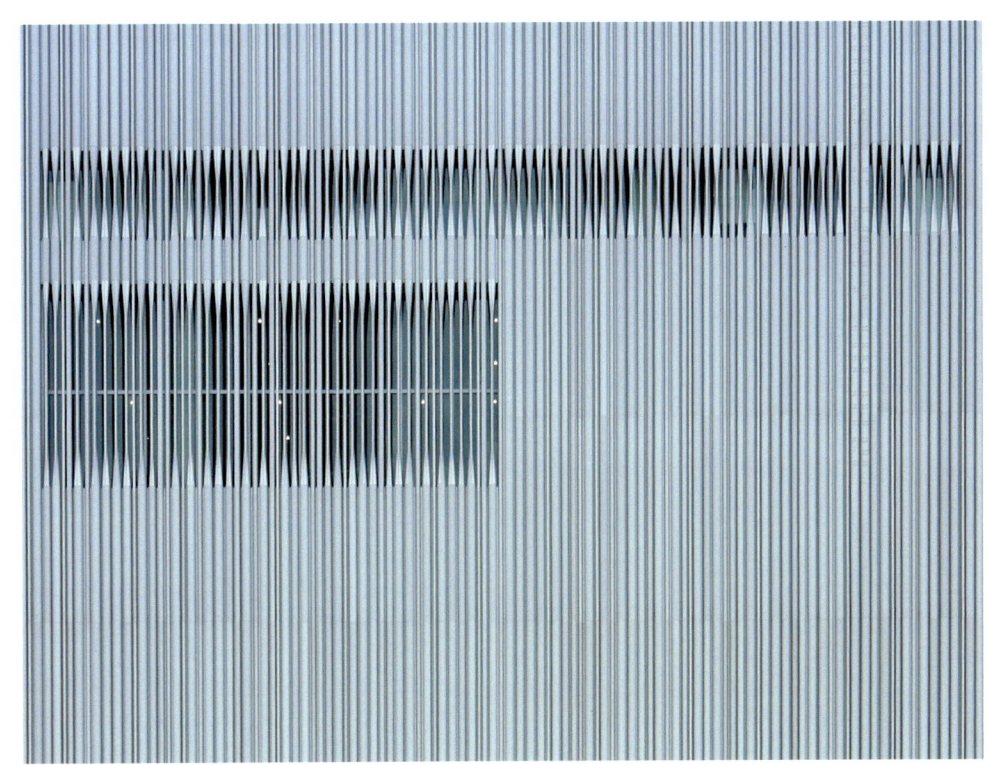

Joshua Prince-Ramus & Rem Koolhaas, Wyly Theater, Dallas, Texas (2009)

Atlas: America 41

In clear simulation of the digital virtual models that are generated by the sophisticated computer programs for parametric design, the materialized buildings take on sinuous forms that are executed by means of complex structural frames, unique steel sheet enclosures ripped here and there to show the interior, peculiar skins folding up like origami paper, and crooked, twisted, undulating curtain walls speaking of movement.

Morphosis, Cooper Union Building, New York, New York (2009)

has stemmed in part from the fear-mongering of the Bush administration for political reasons, but also from the rise of religious fundamentalism worldwide, replacing rational discourse with irrational dogma. In that context, Zaha Hadid's selection as the architect of the Eli and Edythe Broad Art Museum at Michigan State University has symbolic as well as architectural importance. An Iraqi-born London-based architect, Hadid's success in building in the American Midwest – the contemporary art center in Cincinnati, Ohio and now this museum in Lansing, Michigan – shows how art and the academy serve as counter forces, in the United States, to the political and religious prejudices of some people threatened by America's diversity.

Hadid's design has a white pleated skin, recalling not only the folded paper of origami, but also the stacks of books and papers that populate nearby professors' offices and the serrated rows of field crops across the midwestern landscape. Inside, the public circulation space crosses the center of the building, with galleries in the corners – an organization much like that of towns across America – formed around the crossing of two roads that seem to extend, like Hadid's museum, to the horizon. Hadid's design, like the art inside, asks us to contemplate the overlapping layers that bind us as human beings and to question the rough-edged bigotry that has beset a nation built upon the idea of equality.

Among American architects, Frank Gehry has done more to explore the possibilities and implications of skin than almost anyone else. The exteriors of his buildings refer not to the prejudices of people who judge others by their ethnicity or color of their skin, but to the yearning of people who come to places like America for the freedom and mobility it offers. In buildings like his Beekman Tower in New York City, Gehry wraps the 76-story apartment building in a folded, creased and waving stainless-steel curtain wall that makes the structure look like it flaps and billows in the breeze, recalling the classic image of the American driving down the highway. As the writer Laurence Peter observed, "America is a country that doesn't know where it is going but is determined to set a speed record getting there".

Gehry evokes not only the American love of motion, even in something as heavy and fixed as a building, but also the American fascination with the idiosyncratic artist who defies conventions or expectations. The American poet e.e..cummings knew this when he said that "America has colossal faults, but one thing cannot be denied: America is always on the move. She may be going to Hell, of course, but at least she isn't standing still". Gehry never stands still, nor do his buildings. Though carefully programmed and pragmatically laid out, like the Beekman Tower apartments, his architecture is always on the move, with skins like swelling sails, filleted fish or crumpled cars, all propped up like scenery in Hollywood studios near Gehry's office. That this Toronto-born son of Polish Jews could come to America and become one of the world's most famous and sought after architects says a lot about what this country, for all its faults, still has to offer.

Virtual Worlds, Return to Reality
To achieve his kinetic buildings, Gehry's office has developed computer tools that have transformed American architectural practice as much as architecture itself. That digital revolution has enabled architects, engineers and contractors to work together in a more integrated way and create buildings of much greater complexity than ever before. You see that new complexity in Jean Nouvel's Tower Verre next to the Museum of Modern Art of New York City. Comprising museum galleries, a hotel and apartments, the tower has a spiderweb-like structure designed to resist the various forces affecting a building that

Jean Nouvel, Tower Verre, New York, New York (2009)

Zaha Hadid, Eli and Edythe Broad Art Museum, Lansing, Michigan

tall. The tapered profile of the tower also reflects an ability to make adjustments in the dimensions of buildings that are almost impossible drawn by hand.

Like Tower Verre, Morphosis's Cooper Union building, also in New York City, shows how real buildings in the United States have started to simulate the digital models of them. Now that BIM software lets designers construct a structure virtually and resolve most problems before it gets erected, architects have the ability to build almost anything they can model in the computer. This has resulted in buildings of complex curves and sinuous shapes that seem almost uncanny in their contexts. The Morphosis building exemplifies that phenomenon. Having seemingly descended on its tight urban site like some phantom, the building's undulating metal-mesh cladding, which shields the glass curtain wall behind it from the sun and weather, has a gash in it that echoes the twisting atrium and central staircase inside the building. That atrium and stair, serving as a gathering place and seeming to extend to infinity, recall the effects one can get in computer-generated environments. With students spending a great deal of time in such environments, it makes sense to simulate that experience in physical space, as Morphosis has done here. As in so many other aspects of American life, the building also blurs the boundary between fantasy and reality, which serves as a source of much of our creative energy. "Americans," says the comedian Bill Maher, "live in an infantile fantasy land, where reality is whatever we say it is."

Yet the opposite is also true. A growing number of people react to the virtuality and fantasy of American life by again seeking authentic experience in the physical world. That takes a couple of forms. In the St. Edwards University dormitory in Austin, Texas, the Chilean Alejandro Aravena has highlighted the materiality of the building with an exterior whose irregularly laid bricks emphasize the single masonry unit and provide a rich texture to the wall, in contrast to the colorful glass curtain wall lining the inside courtyards. Aravena's treatment of the overall form of the building, with narrow deep-set windows and a chamfered roof edge, give it an almost geological presence on the landscape, like some sedimentary mesa eroded by the wind.

That sense of expansive space and time has helped define the American character. As Gertrude Stein said, "In the United States there is more space where nobody is than where anybody is. That is what makes America what it is." And it is what makes Aravena's dormitory so provocative and powerful, with its rough-hewn exterior referring to the vastness of the western landscape and its tight internal courtyards providing physical and psychological protection from that emptiness.

If Aravena's building evokes the land, Carlos Jiménez's projects return to where we began, with the machine in the garden. But unlike the work of Holl, Diller Scofidio and Weiss/Manfredi, the Costa Rican Jiménez treats the metal-clad Library Service Center and Data Center for Rice University in Texas like rational objects set off from the land. Yet Jiménez draws attention to the sheer artifice of these buildings by painting them a bright green and corrugating, paneling or louvering their outer walls to stress their mass-produced nature.

These structures also reveal the reality that most American architecture has become, reduced to the efficient enclosure of the maximum amount of space. That Jiménez can make compelling architecture out of such a constrained condition reinforces the talent and tenacity of the best architects working in the United States. The poet Carrie Latet observed that "America is not just a country but a way", and the architects whose work follows shows the truth of this. Each has found a way to express something profound about America and the way it is.

Frank Gehry, Beekman Tower, New York, New York (2010)

Atlas: America 43

David Chipperfield
Anchorage Museum Expansion
Anchorage, Alaska (United States)

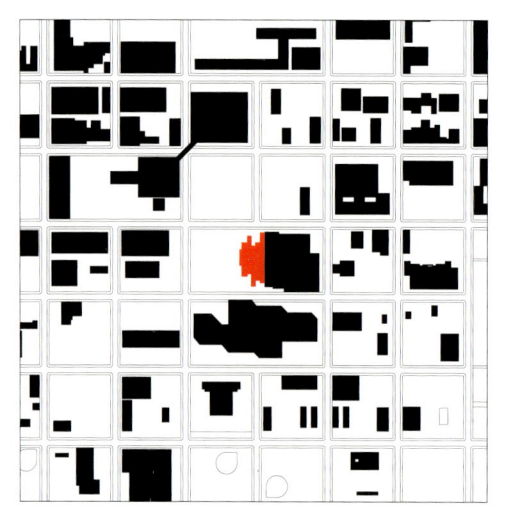

Client
Anchorage Museum at Rasmuson Center
Architects
David Chipperfield Architects;
Kumin Associates (architects of record)
Collaborators
F. Borho, P. Castelo, M. Ebert, I. Heide, M. Johnston, V. Jessen-Pike, C. Junge, P. Kleine, M. Kunz, M. Mitchell-Heggs, A. Philips, B. Prendergast, J. Sattler, R. Wolter, D. Schwarzer;
Kumin Associates: C. Banister, D. Brown, M. Griffith, M. Komkov, J. Kumin, D. Nunn, E. White, R. Timm, P. Wilm
Consultants
Magnusson Klemencic Associates, BBFM Engineers (structures); Affiliated Engineers NW, RSA Engineering (services); Davis Langdon: M. Gordon, J. Young (quantity surveyors); W.J.Higgins and Associates (facades); George Sexton Associates (lighting); Ralph Appelbaum Associates (exhibition designers); Charles Anderson Landscape Architects, Earthscape (landscaping)
Contractor
Alcan General
Model photos
David Chipperfield Architects, Richard Davis (p. 47)
Photos
David Chipperfield Architects, Christian Richters/View/Album (pp. 44, 45)

LOCATED IN the heart of Alaska's largest city, the Anchorage Museum at Rasmuson Center began as a public-private partnership to celebrate the 100th anniversary of the purchase of Alaska from Russia. The museum opened its doors in 1968 with an exhibition of 60 borrowed paintings and a collection of 2,500 historic and ethnographic objects loaned from the local Historical Society.

In the 1980s, with the flood of revenues from oil development, the state funded community-wide building projects. 'Project 80s' led to a major, 13,000 square meter expansion of the Anchorage Museum in 1986. Funds were raised to complete the Alaska Gallery, a showcase of the museum's permanent historic and ethnographic collection, which now numbers 17,500 objects plus an education collection of 2,000 artifacts and 350,000 photographs.

This new 8,000 square meter expansion has also created a new entrance to the museum. The organization of the new building is based on five linear volumes of varying length and height arranged along the western face of the existing building. It is this arrangement that forms a new facade and entrance facing downtown Anchorage. The Common, created at the front of the museum, provides a new public space for the city. Openings on the facade allow the outside onlooker a view of goings-on within, while reorienting the visitor inside to the urban context and the natural setting beyond. The glass facade of the four-story building is fritted with a striped mirror pattern, providing views out of and into the museum and reflecting the sky and surrounding mountain landscape. The interior design concept exposes the concrete structure as part of the character of the new exhibition spaces, which are defined by dividing walls built between columns.

The expansion also accommodates the Arctic Studies Center, with its collection of 600 Alaska Native ethnographic artifacts from the Smithsonian Institution's National Museum of Natural History and National Museum of the American Indian.

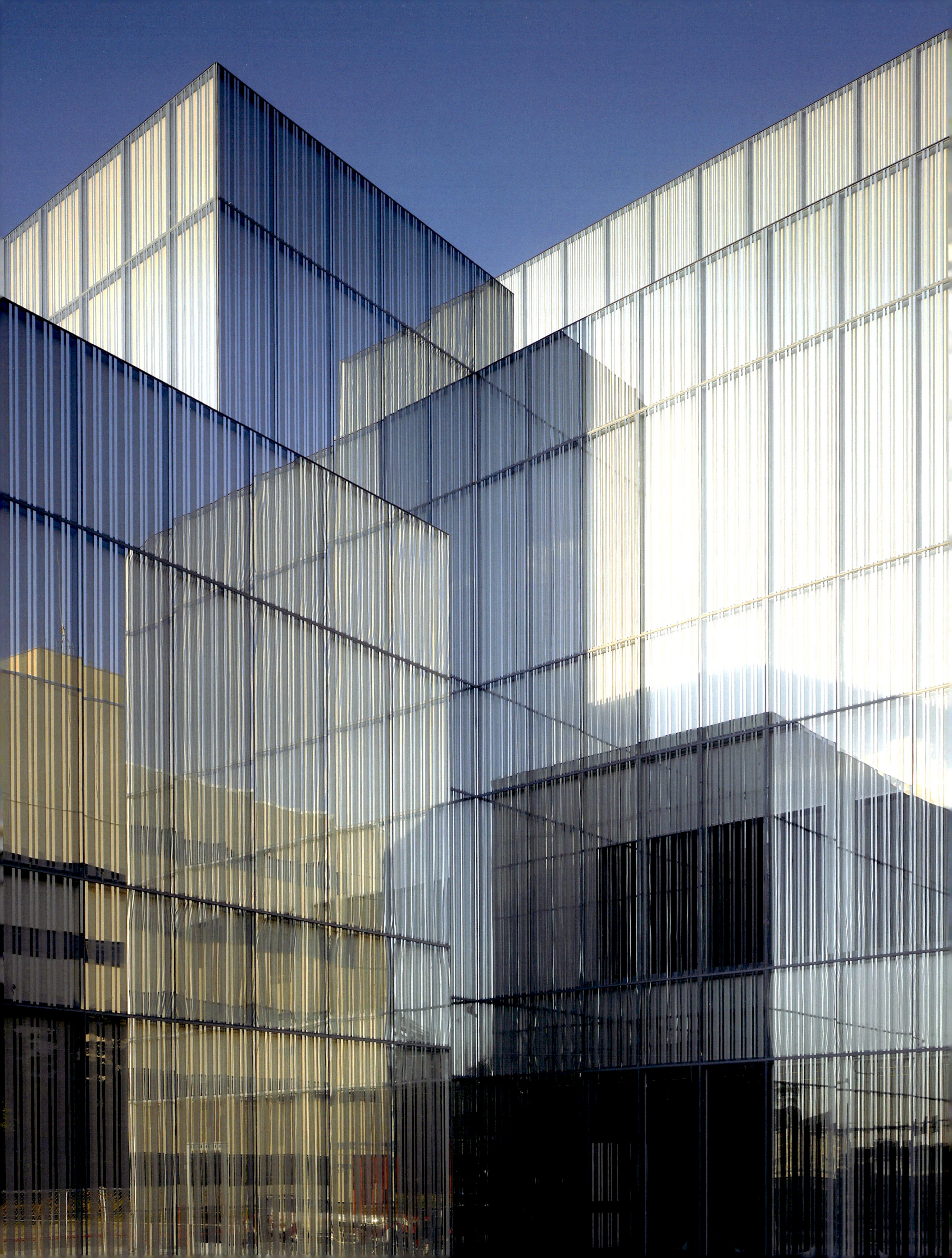

The new expansion of the Anchorage Museum is compactly attached to the preexisting building, freeing up a vast surface for public use along the western face, where the new entrance into the institution is located.

A vertical striped mirror pattern on the glass facades of the complex's five volumes gives visitors inside a view of the landscape beyond, while allowing onlookers outside a look at activities taking place within.

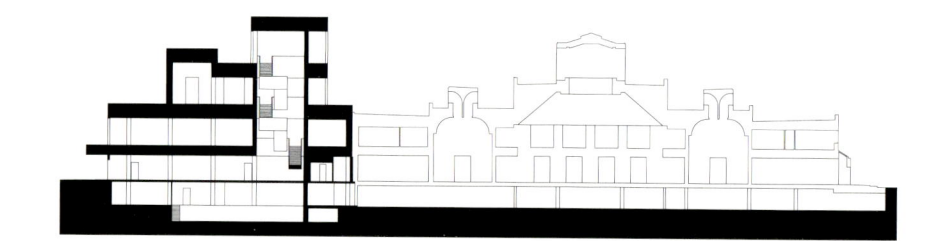

46 Atlas: America

First floor

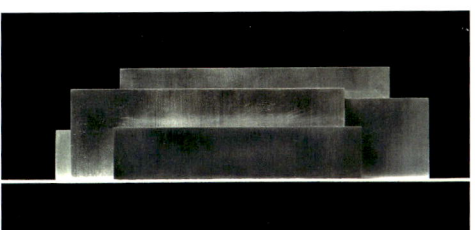

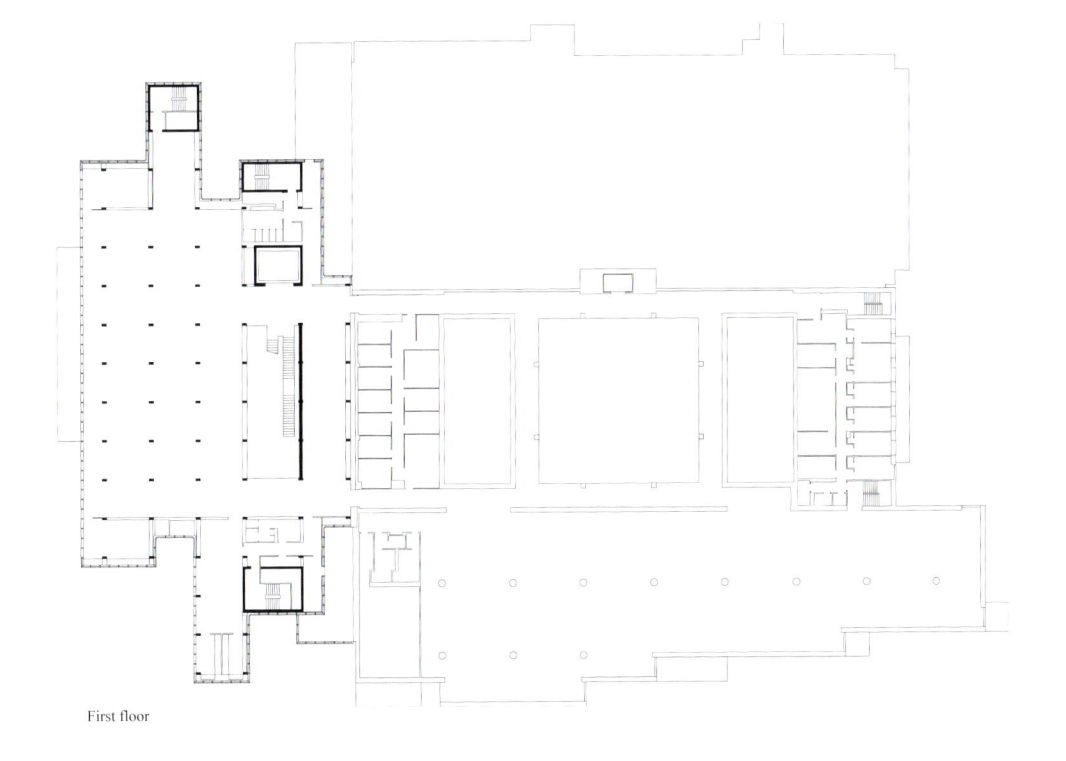

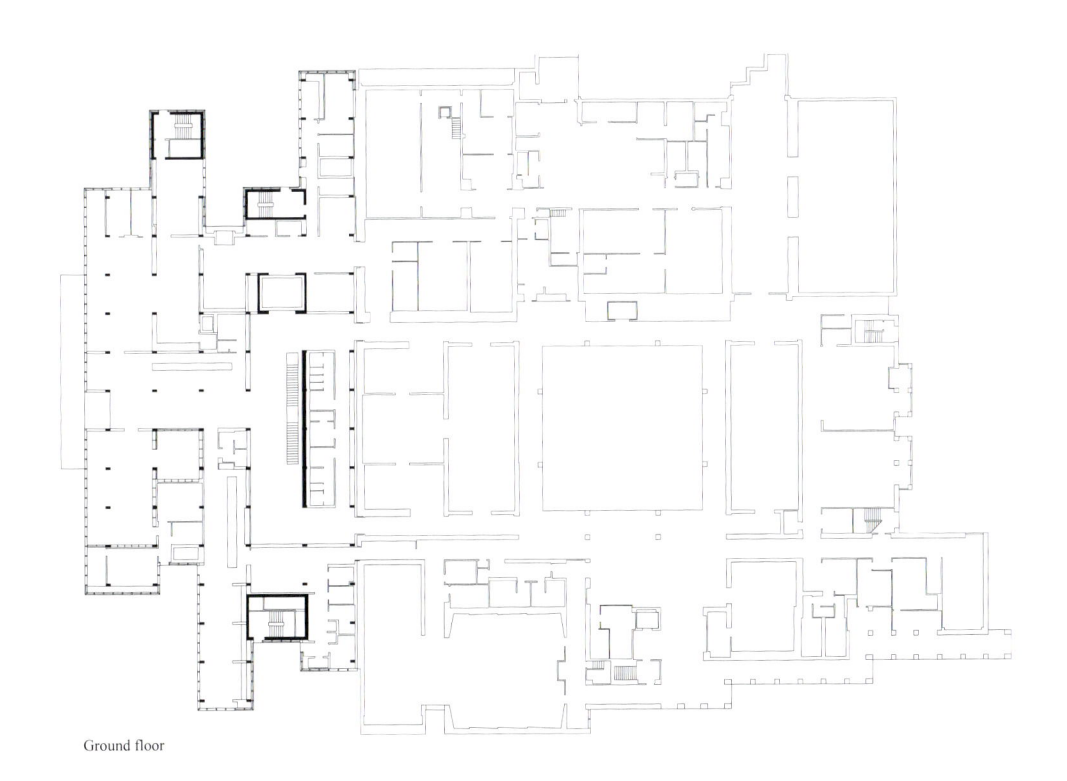

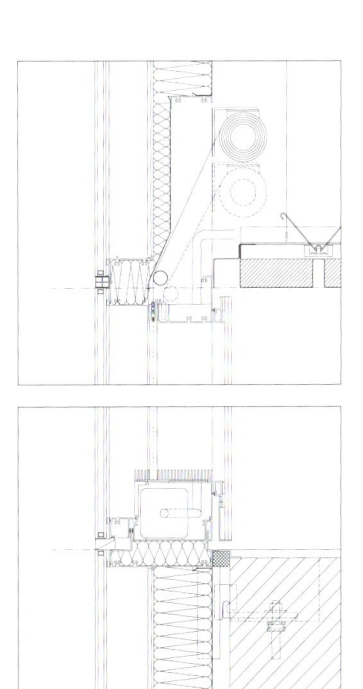

Ground floor

Atlas: America 47

Renzo Piano
Academy of Sciences
San Francisco, California (United States)

Client
California Academy of Sciences
Architects
Renzo Piano Building Workshop, Stantec Architecture
Collaborators
M. Carroll, O. De Nooyer, S. Ishida, B. Terpeluk, J. McNeal, A. De Flora, F. Elmalipinar, A. Guernier, D. Hart, T. Kjaer, J. Lee, A. Meine-Jansen, A. Ng, D. Piano, W. Piotraschke, J. Sylvester; C. Bruce, L. Burow, C. Cooper, A. Knapp, Y. Pages, Z. Rockett, V. Tolu, A. Walsh (design team); I. Corte, S. D'Atri, G. Langasco, M. Ottonello (CAD Operators); F. Cappellini, S. Rossi, A. Malgeri, A. Marazzi (models)
Consultants
Ove Arup (engineering); Rutherford & Chekene (civil engineering); SWA Group (landscaping); Rana Creek (living roof); PBS&J (aquariums); Thinc Design, Cinnabar, Visual-Acuity (exhibits)
Contractor
Webcor Builders
Photos
Tim Griffith (pp. 48, 51 bottom);
Tom Fox (pp. 49, 50, 51 top);
Nic Lehoux (p. 53)

THE MISSION STATEMENT of the almost centenary California Academy of Sciences – "to explore, explain and protect the natural world" – supplied the inspiration for the design of its new home on the same site of the old complex of buildings in San Francisco's Golden Gate Park. Facing Herzog & de Meuron's M.H. de Young Museum, the new Academy houses beneath its undulating green 'living roof' a program combining exhibition uses with modern facilities for scientific research and the storage of specimens.

As before, all the functions of the institution have been organized around a central covered court, the *piazza*. Three other elements of the previous Academy have been maintained: African Hall with its original dioramas, California Hall, and the entrance to the Steinhart Aquarium. The *piazza* is flanked by two spheres – one opaque and the other transparent – containing a planetarium and a rainforest ecosystem, respectively. The research activities, the storage of specific specimens, and administrative functions are concentrated in two volumes flanking the rear access, where the colonnade leading to the aquarium has been reconstructed, giving to the *piazza* and investing it with a respectable civic character.

The institution sought to be a model of sustainability by adopting a holistic approach. This is patent in everything from the recycling of materials salvaged from the old Academy to the emphasis on natural light and ventilation, efficient use of water and in situ energy generation. The roof is the main ecological feat. Coated with native succulent plants requiring no irrigation, it returns greenery to the park, produces a large amount of thermal inertia and gathers rainwater. The protruding perimeter incorporates 55,000 photovoltaic cells that generate 5% of the energy the building consumes. To guarantee natural ventilation in the central space, hindered by its position in a cross as well as by the spheres and the *piazza,* simulations and calculations were made through computational fluid dynamics. Consuming 30% less energy than required by standard building codes in California, the Academy has received the highest award there is in the environmental field: the Platinum-level LEED certification.

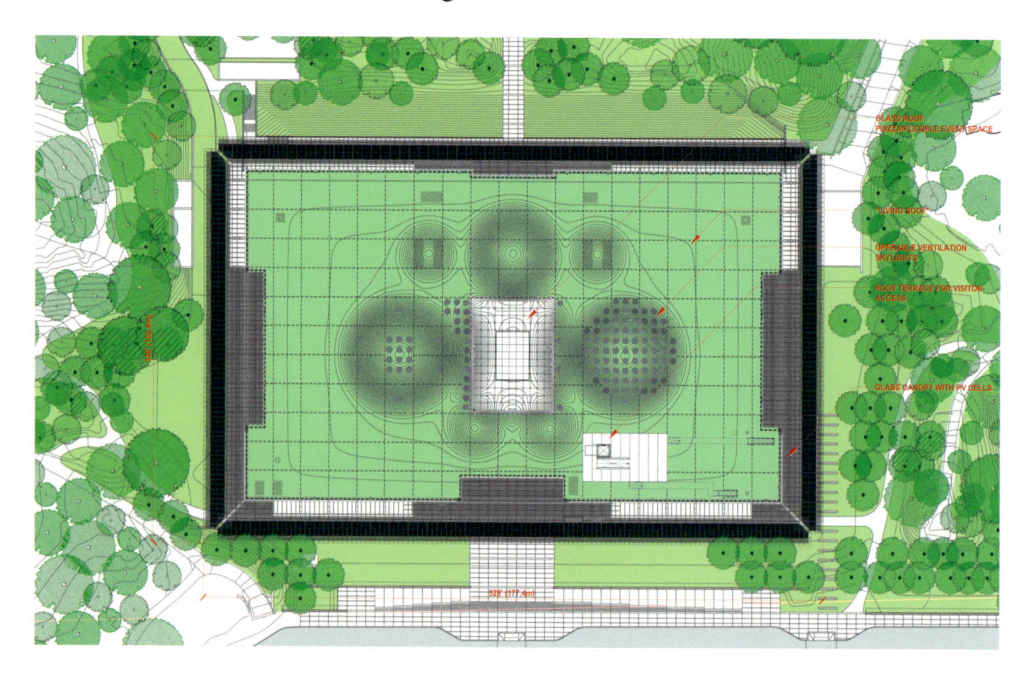

The Music Concourse of the Golden Gate Park in San Francisco is flanked by the M.H. de Young Museum, by Herzog & de Meuron, and the new California Academy of Sciences, whose green waving roof, which was present since the earliest sketches, reveals the forms found within: two spheres containing the planetarium and the visitable recreation of a rainforest ecosystem, and a central covered court that acts as a *piazza*.

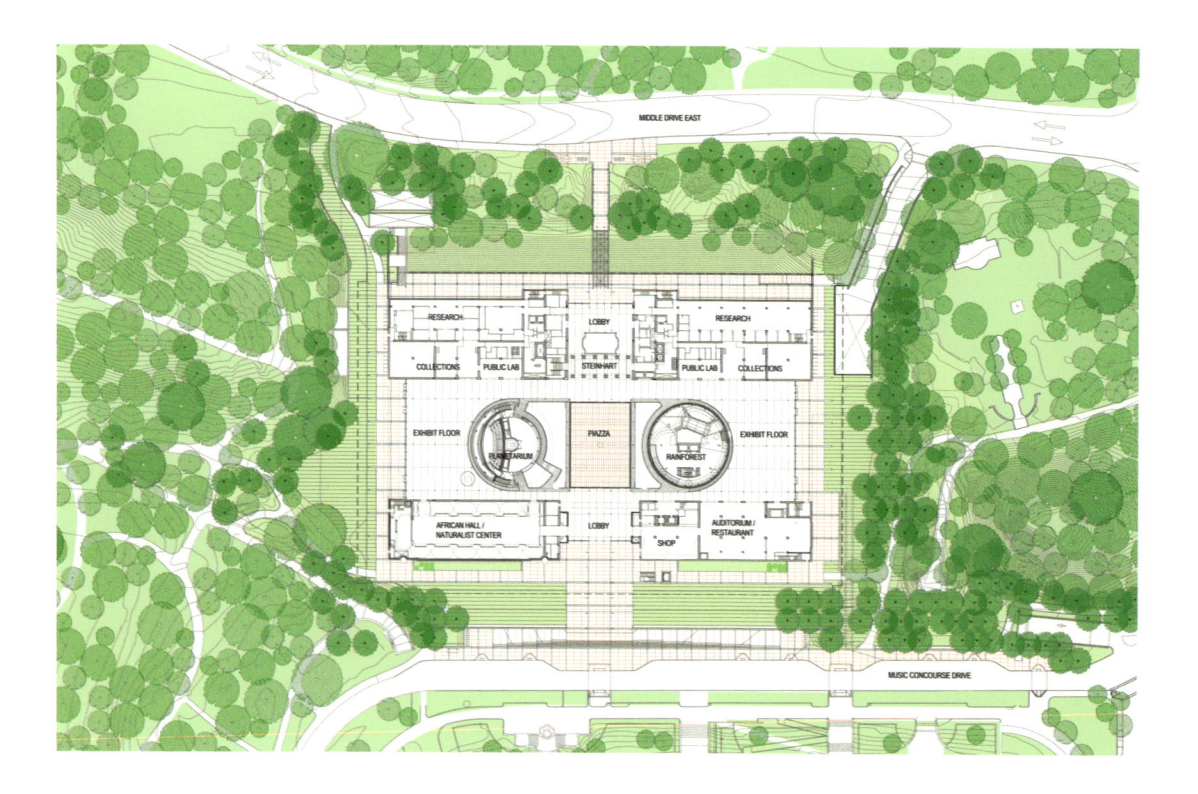

The landscaped roof of the Academy acts as an efficient ecological mechanism: the vegetation that coats it includes a wide diversity of native species that need no irrigation, and a cistern layer that serves to gather rainwater for subsequent use. All this together gives the building a high degree of thermal inertia. The large skylights open to ventilate the interior spaces and the glazed perimeter incorporates photovoltaic cells.

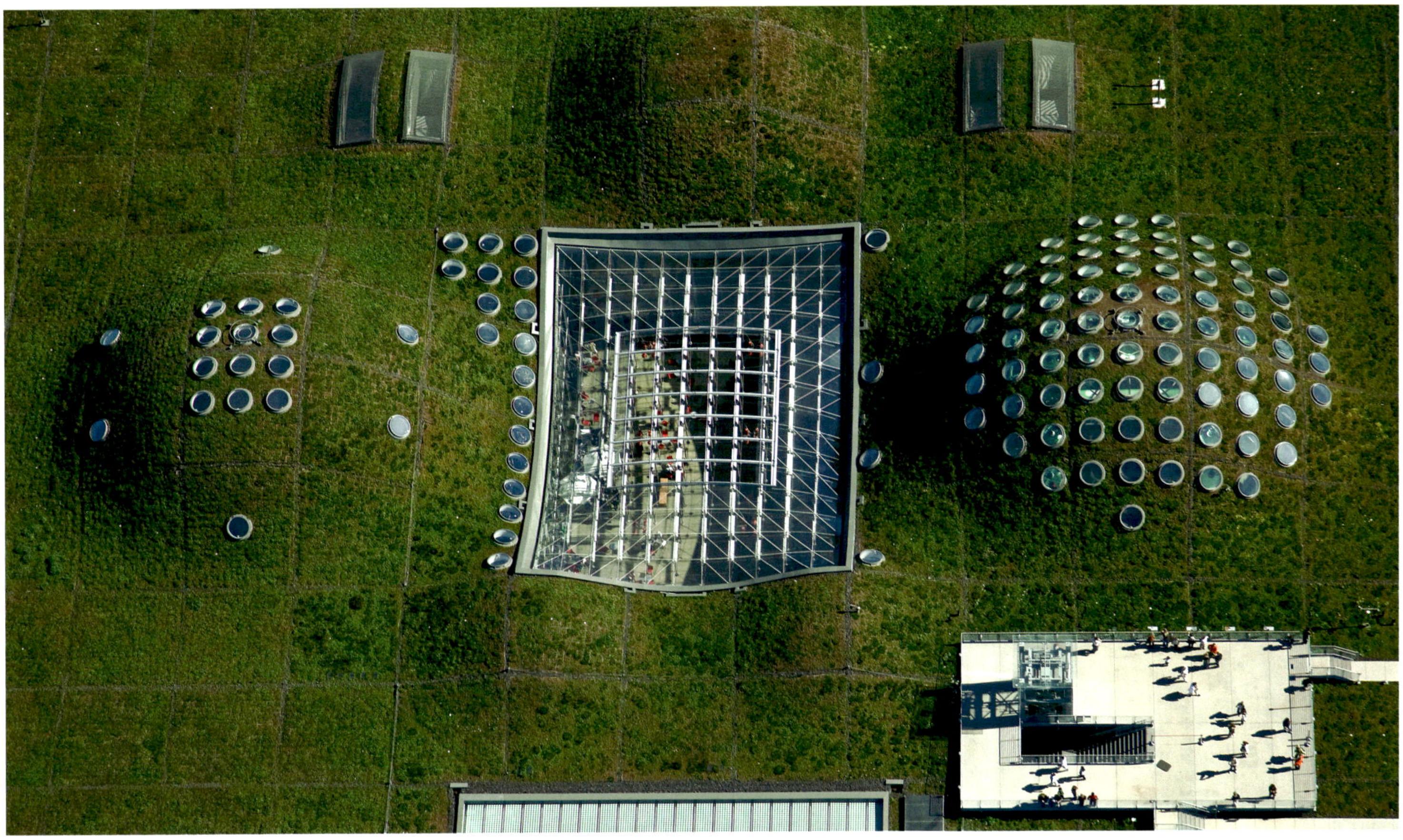

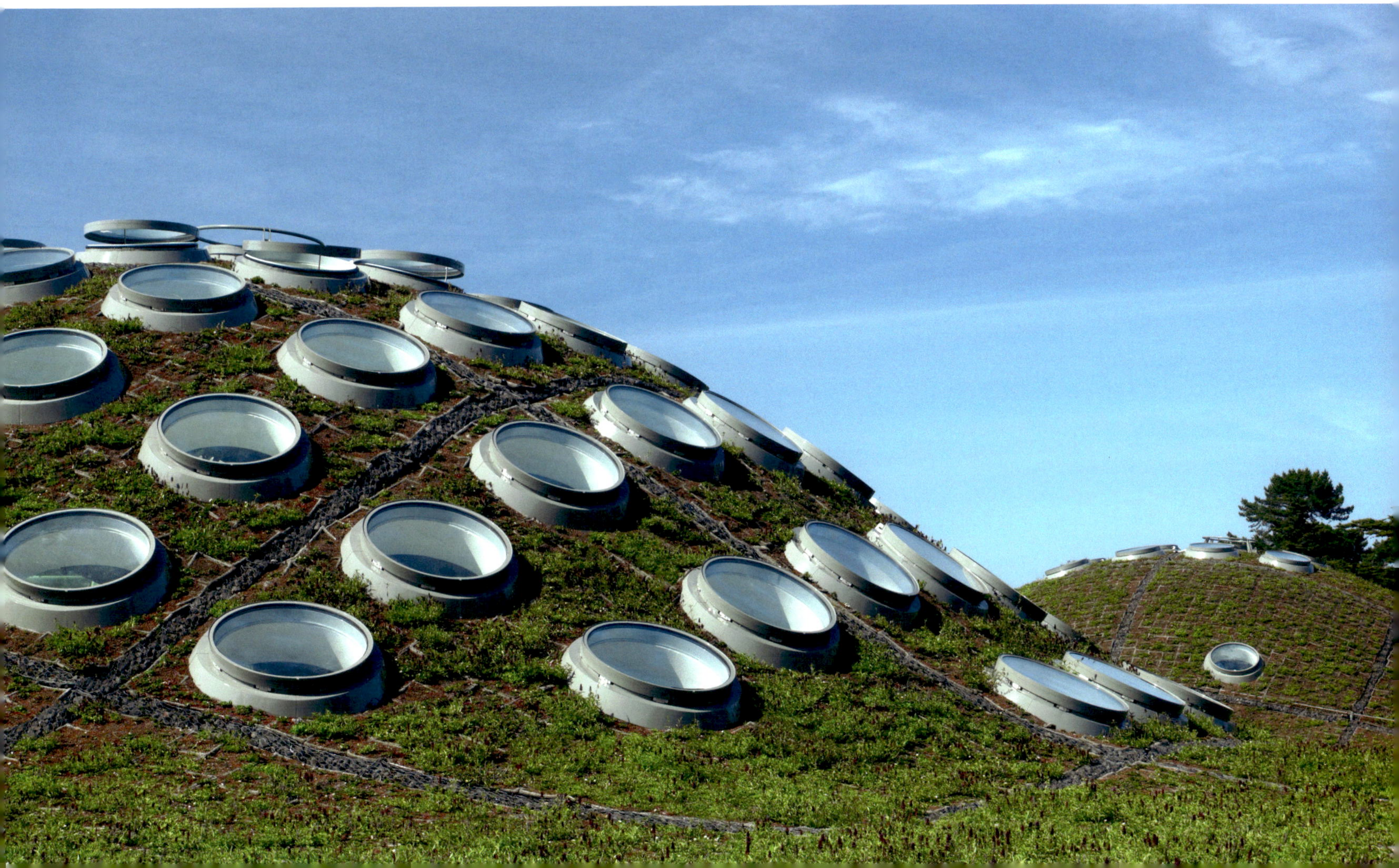

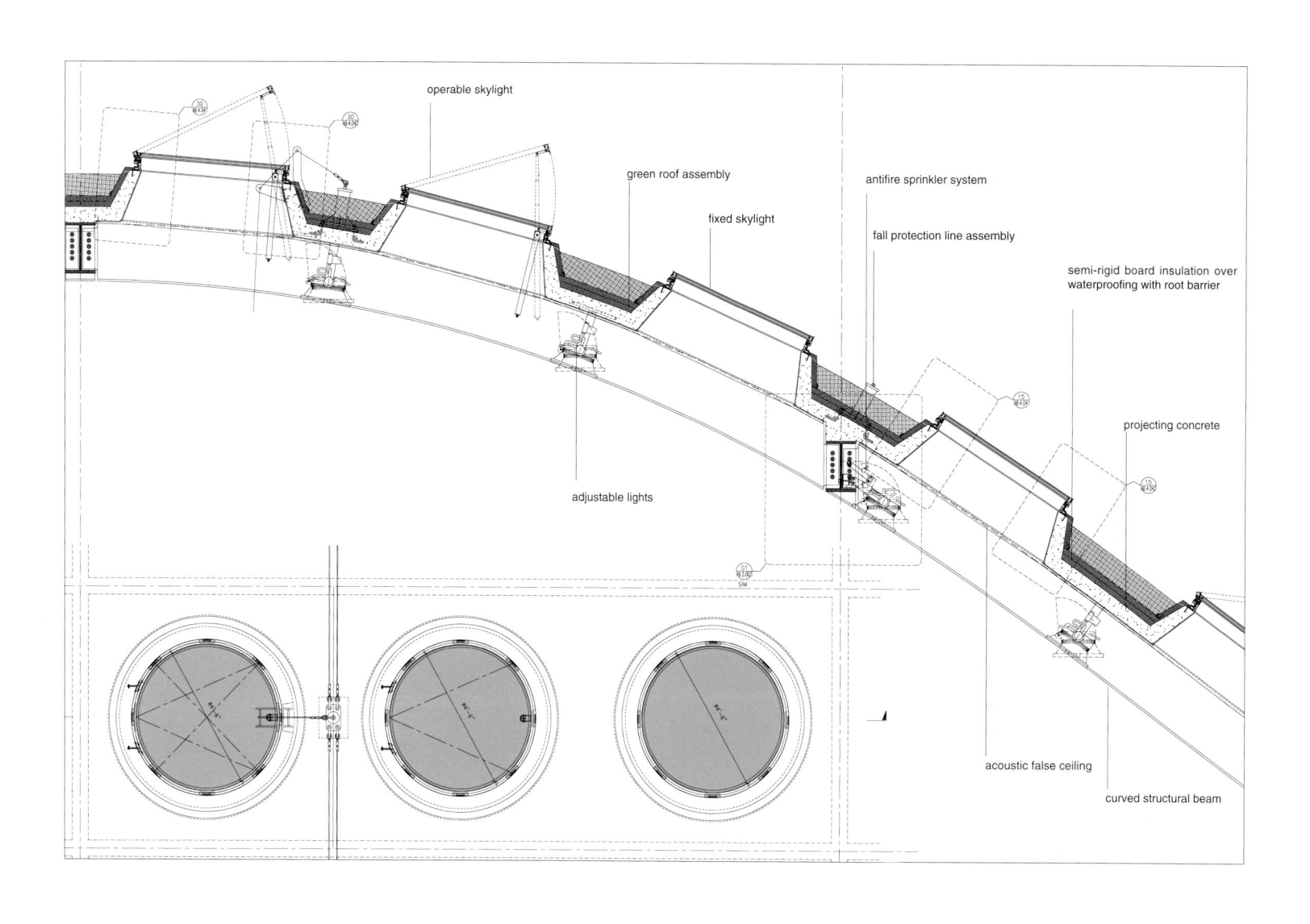

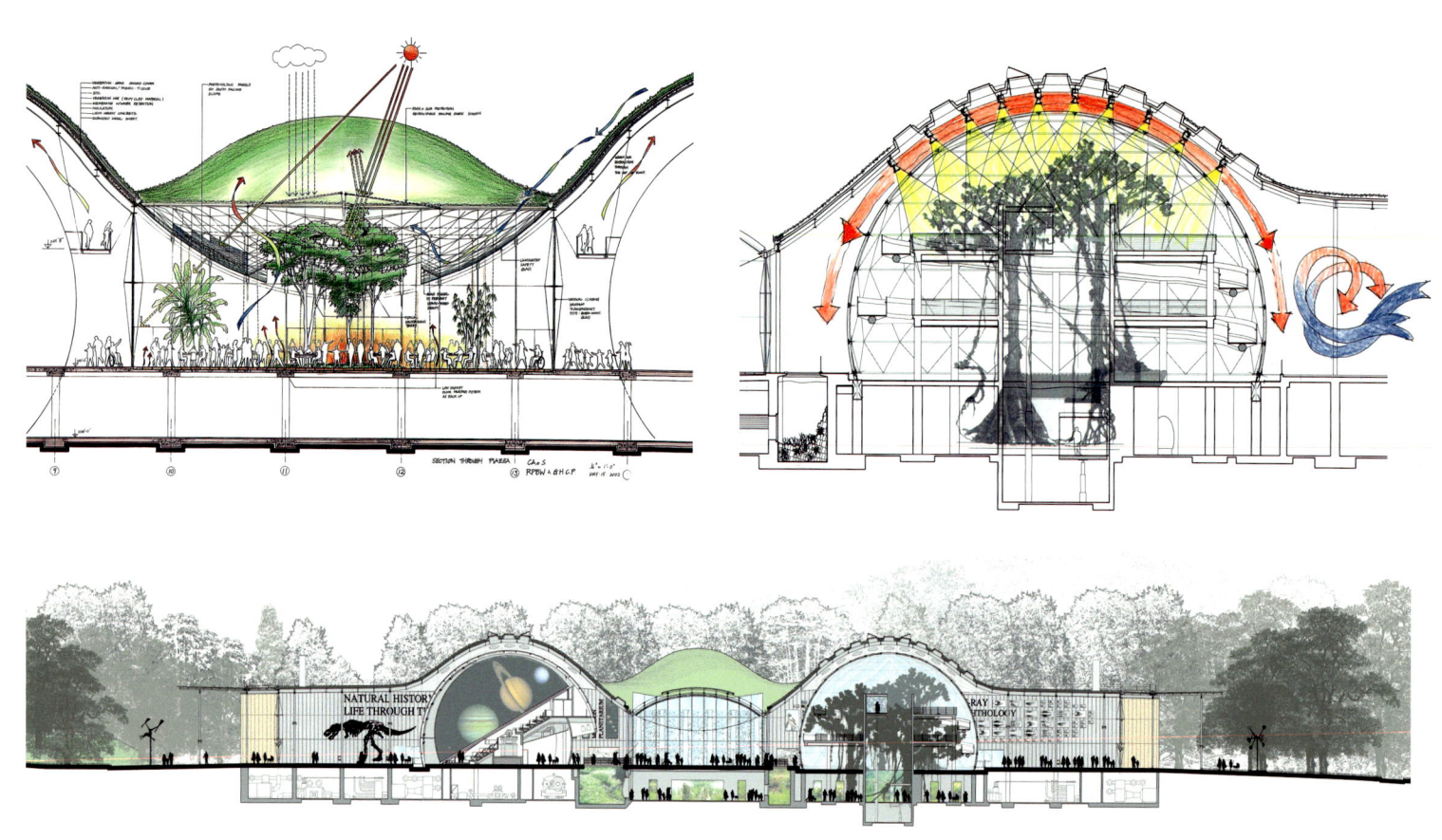

- operable skylight
- green roof assembly
- antifire sprinkler system
- fixed skylight
- fall protection line assembly
- semi-rigid board insulation over waterproofing with root barrier
- adjustable lights
- projecting concrete
- acoustic false ceiling
- curved structural beam

52 Atlas: America

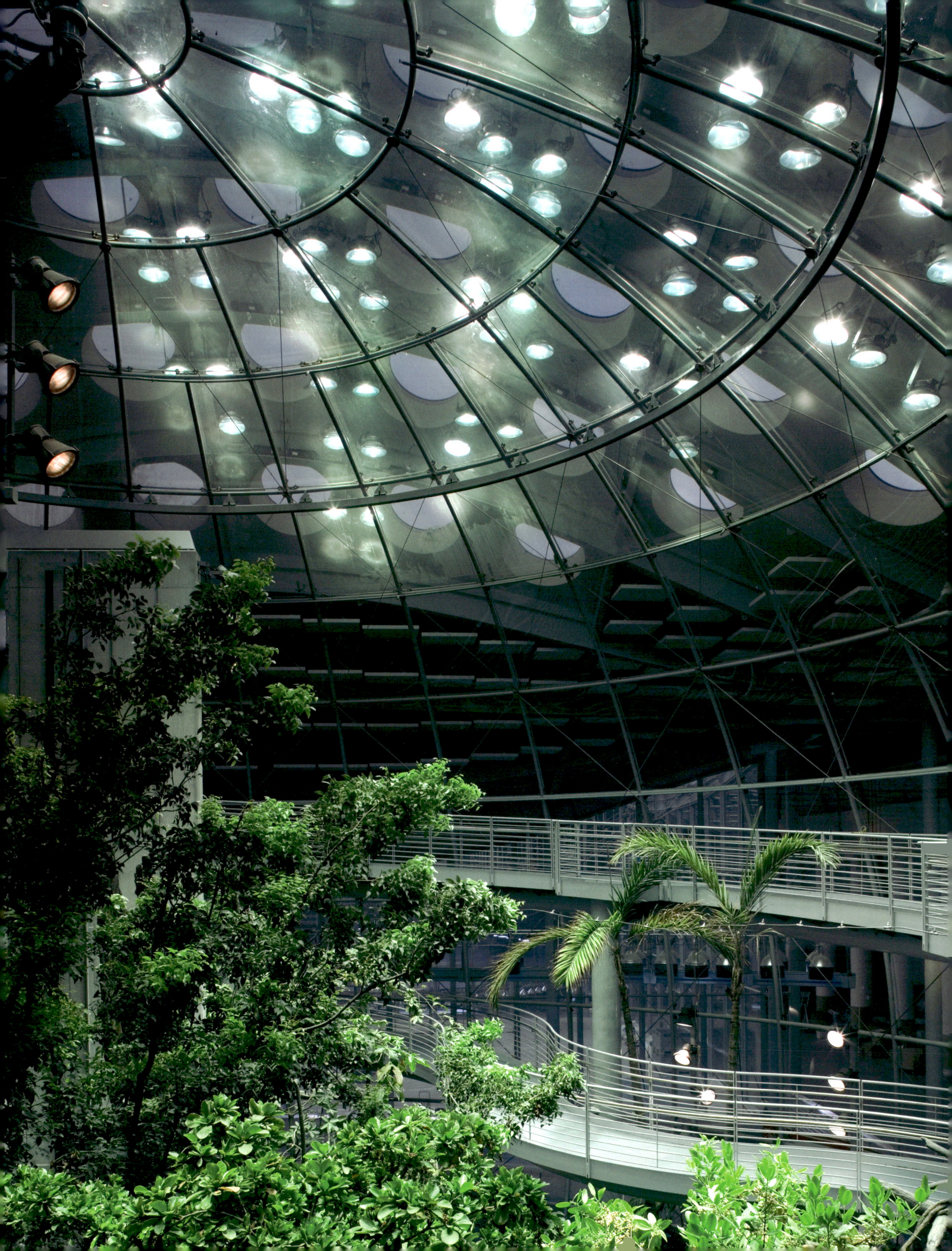

Norman Foster
Winspear Opera House
Dallas, Texas (United States)

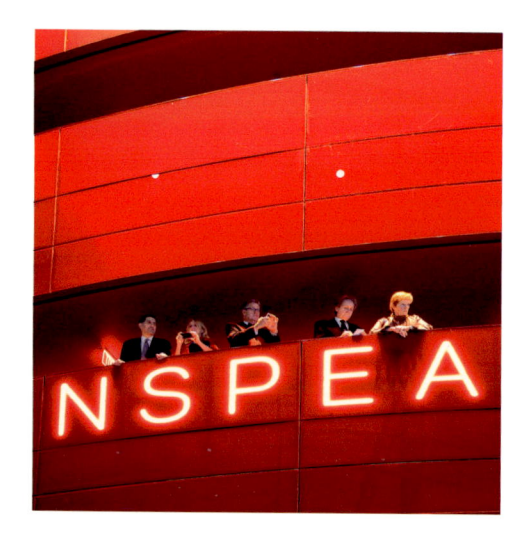

Client
AT+T Performing Arts Center
Architect
Norman Foster
Collaborators
Spencer de Grey, Stefan Behling, Michael Jones, James McGrath, Bjørn Polzin, Laszlo Pallagi, Morgan Fleming, Leonhard Weil, John Small, Ingrid Sölken, Hugh Whitehead, Francis Aish (team); Kendall Heaton (collaborating architects)
Consultants
Sound Space Design (acoustics); Theatre Projects (theater consultant); Buro Happold, Thornton-Tomasetti (structures); Battle McCarthy (services); Claude R. Engle (lighting); Pielow Fair (codes); Donnell (costs)
Contractor
Linbeck Construction
Photos
Iwan Baan; Nigel Young (pp.54 top, 57 bottom y 58 top)

A classic auditorium with a horseshoe plan and several levels of balcony seating is clad with panels of a bright red color; a high foyer marks the transition between the interior and the large shaded public plaza.

THE NEW WINSPEAR Opera House in Dallas redefines the essence of an opera house for the 21st century. Responding to the torrid Texan climate, a generous canopy surrounds the building, revealing a glazed 18 meter high lobby. This establishes a direct relationship between inside and outside. Beneath the canopy, a shaded plaza gives the city a new public space. Because of its position in the Dallas Arts District, the Winspear is its focal point. Among the outdoor spaces it connects with is the Annette Strauss Artists' Square, with its open-air performance venue for 5,000 spectators, a café terrace and the main entrance to the opera house, with access to the parking garage.

Organizationally, the Winspear creates a series of publicly welcoming transparent spaces that wrap around the rich red drum of the 2,200-seat auditorium. Its long opening hours and the presence of a café and restaurant make it a popular destination in its own right, independently of shows inside. The transition from the canopy area into the auditorium has its climax in the foyer, whose multi-height design turns opera-goers into 'see and be seen' actors.

The grand staircase, skirting the drum and linking all the lobby spaces, also provides a high place from which to admire the building. As for the actual auditorium, a classic horseshoe plan and the stacking of seating balconies together bring the audience as close as possible to the stage while guaranteeing excellent acoustics. The balcony fronts have a white gold irregular finish and their interiors are clad in dark red velvet, details improving the resonance of sound. To heighten the drama of the spectacle, a huge chandelier made of hundreds of transparent rods and creating an inverted cone of light ascends into the ceiling before the performance begins. The curtain was designed by the Argentinean artist Guillermo Quintero.

Punctuated with indigenous trees, the public spaces beneath the canopy benefit from a cool microclimate. The Grand Plaza responds to the grid of the canopy with a scored pattern set into the pavement, referencing the wider urban scheme of Dallas. In the Donor Pool of black granite, a film of water glistens over the names of the project's benefactors, which are written on the stone in stainless steel letters.

To bring the spectacle of the opera to as wide an audience as possible, the Winspear premises are made transparent. The actual performance auditorium at the core – which can be described as a rich red drum – hooks up with a gridded canopy that serves to delimit and shade the plaza constituting a new public zone for the city. All this, along with Annette Strauss Artists' Square, is part of the Dallas Art District.

0   +1   +2

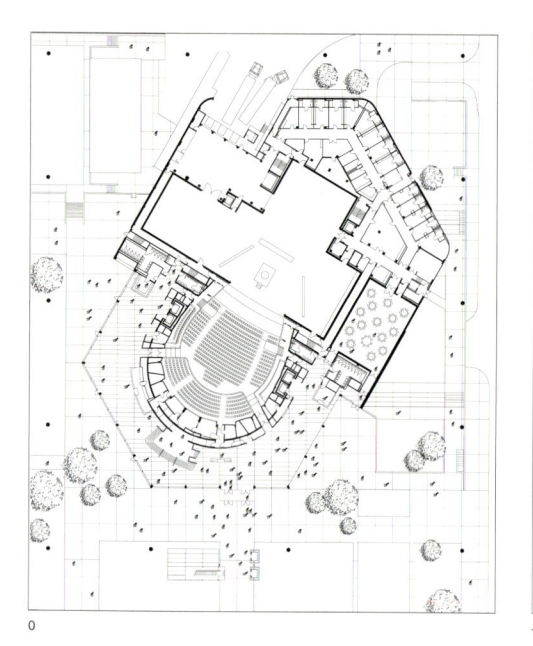

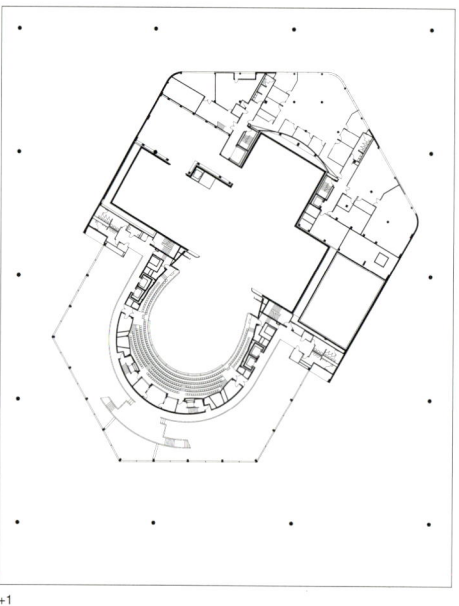

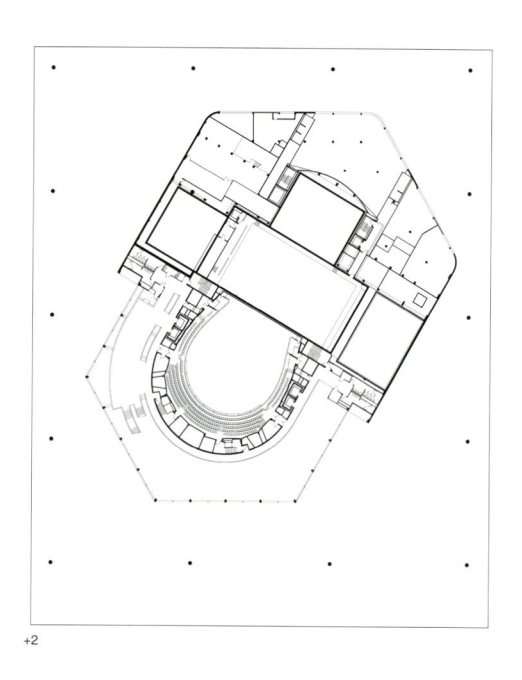

56 Atlas: America

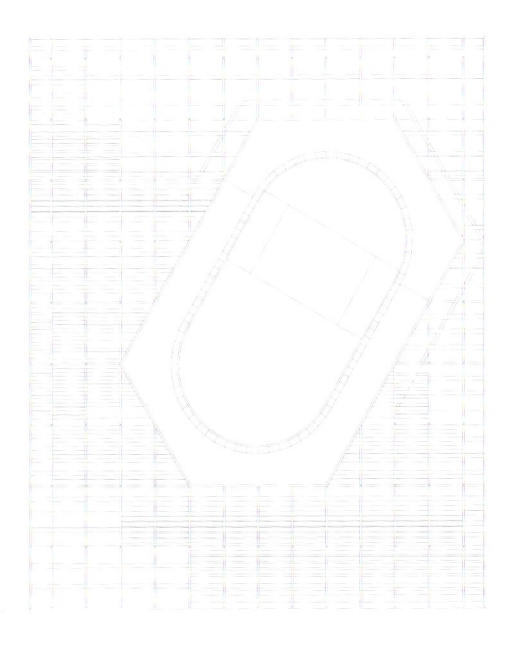

The closed premises of the Winspear Opera House are preceded by a metal canopy that surrounds it and gives rise to a shaded outdoor space decked with vegetation and pools of water. Skirting around the drum of the auditorium, the grand staircase that can be seen from the 18 meter high glazed foyer turns audiences into performers of the social act of going to the opera. The classic horseshoe shape of the auditorium and the stacking of several levels of balcony seats bring the audience as close as possible to the stage while guaranteeing excellent acoustics.

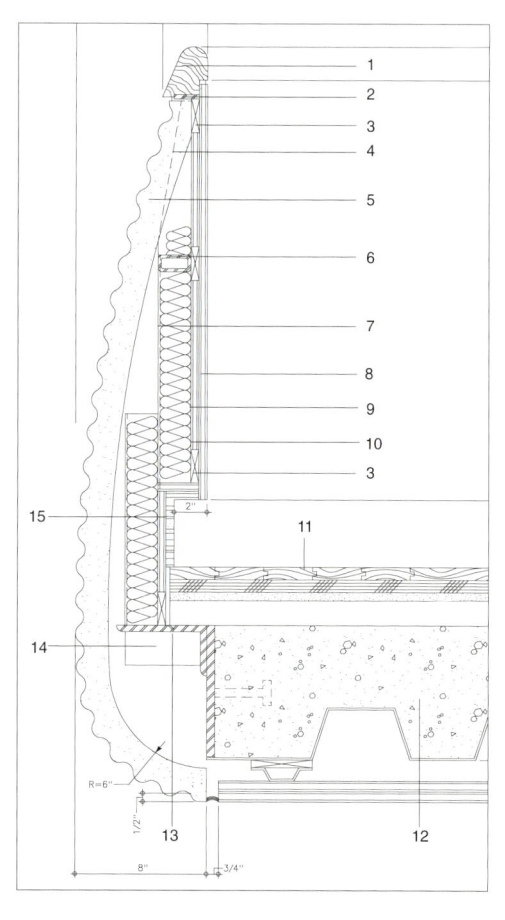

1. solid walnut cap attached to steel plate
2. steel bar welded to vertical bar
3. wood blocking attached to steel bars
4. tapered steel bar welded at top and bottom
5. 50mm thick fluted fiberglass-reinforced GFRG panel
6. continuous HSS 25x50x3mm welded to top of steel tubes
7. wire mesh attached to steel tube
8. 2 layers gypsum board
9. sound attenuation batt attached to wire mesh
10. 50x50x30mm light rail support tube welded to adjacent tube
11. floor assembly
12. reinforced concrete slab
13. steel angle welded to embed plate at each vertical tube
14. 50x50x8mm stub at each vertical tube
15. 13mm hardwood trim stained to match flooring

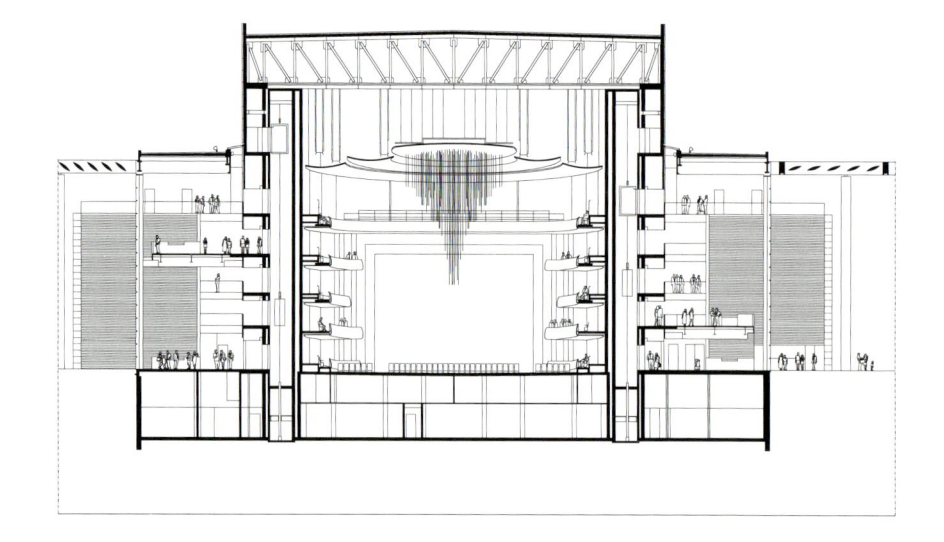

Atlas: America 59

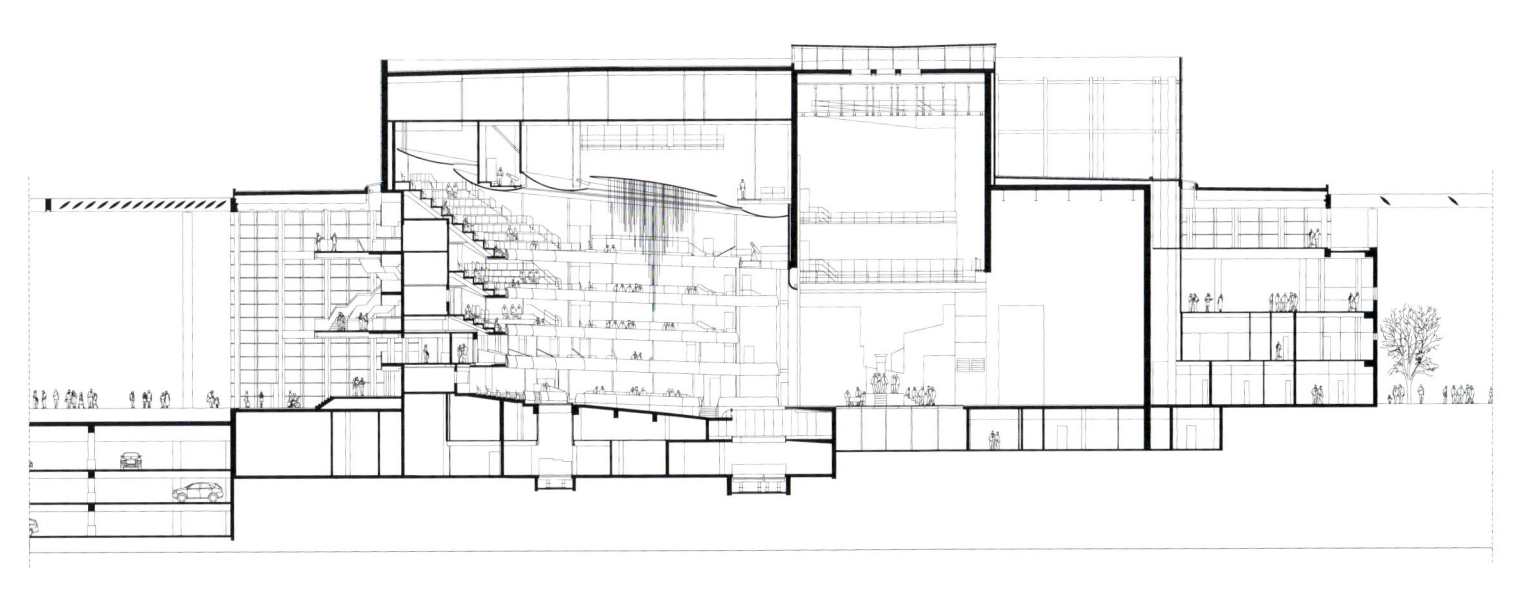

Prince-Ramus/Koolhaas
Wyly Theater
Dallas, Texas (United States)

Client
AT+T Performing Arts Center
Architects
REX / OMA (project): Joshua Prince-Ramus (partner in charge) / Rem Koolhaas
Collaborators
E. Ella, V. Bandy, V. Kassabian, T. Archambault; Kendall/Heaton
Consultants
Cosentini (MEP/FP), Donnell (costs), Dorsserblesgraaf (acoustics), Front (facades), HKA (vertical transport), Magnusson Klemencic (structures), McCarthy (construction management), Quinze& Milan (furniture), Theatre Projects (theater design), Tillotson (lighting), Transsolar (MEP/FP design), 2x4 (graphics/wayfinding)
Photos
Iwan Baan;
Tim Hursley (p.65 bottom)

A flexible stage is the protagonist in this prism of striated aluminum, the interior of which presents a series of stacked boxes of varying height that contain the different elements of the program.

THE DALLAS THEATER Center (DTC) is known for its innovative repertoire, the result of the provisional nature of what was long its home, the Arts District Theater, an old industrial shed in which companies were freed from the limitations imposed by fixed-stage setups. The directors who worked there constantly defied theater conventions, reconfiguring the stage and performers' engagement with the audience as they pleased. The ADT was renowned as the most flexible theater in America. In later years, however, for financial reasons, DTC had been forced to fix its stage into a three-sided 'thrust-cenium'.

Imagining a replacement for DTC's old home raised several challenges. First, the new theater would have to reproduce the makeshift character of its predecessor. Second, it needed to be flexible and able to take on many forms while reducing operational costs to a minimum. The Dee and Charles Wyly Theater rose to these challenges by turning around conventional theater design. Instead of circling front-of-house and back-of-house functions around the auditorium and fly tower, the Dee and Charles Wyly Theater stacks these facilities below-house and above-house. This strategy turns the building into one big 'theater machine'. At the push of a button, the theater can be transformed into a wide array of configurations, including the proscenium, the thrust and the flat floor, giving directors the freedom to choose the stage-audience arrangement that best suits their artistic purposes. The stage and auditorium surfaces are made of easily replaceable materials and can be cut, drilled, painted, nailed and stitched at limited cost.

Stacking ancillary facilities above- and below-house also liberates the performance chamber's perimeter, allowing the mix of reality (the exterior) and fantasy (the interior). Directors can choose to incorporate the Dallas skyline and streetscape into their plays. Panels of the facade can also be opened to let patrons or performers bypass the lobby and enter the auditorium directly from outside, through a ramp that descends and forms part of the plaza.

By investing in infrastructure that allows ready transformation of the chamber and liberation of its perimeter, the Wyly Theater gives artistic directors the freedom to determine the entire theater experience, from audience arrival to performance configuration and finally to departure. In this way, the Wyly can consecutively program a Shakespeare work on an Elizabethan stage and a Beckett play with actors and audience on the same level.

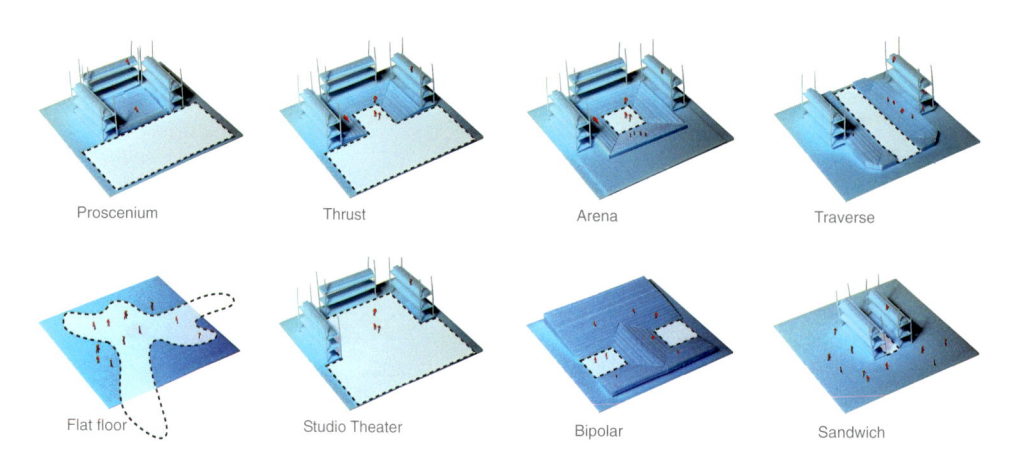

Proscenium | Thrust | Arena | Traverse
Flat floor | Studio Theater | Bipolar | Sandwich

60 Atlas: America

The Dee and Charles Wyly Theater rises opposite the Winspear Opera House on the same plane, which descends in the form of a landscaped ramp; the function of a foyer preceding the auditorium is transferred to a lower level, liberating the perimeter of the performance hall. The theater machinery makes it possible to configure the floor-level stage in many ways, depending on the particular artistic purposes of each director.

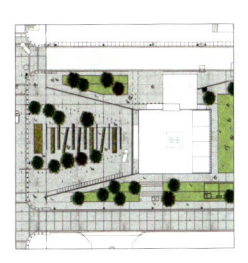

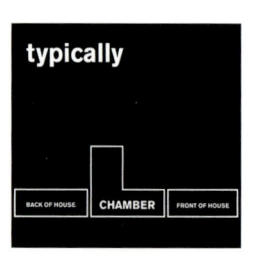

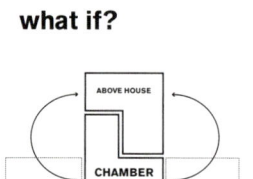

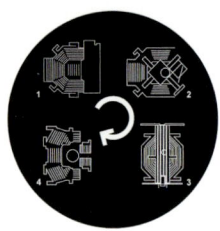

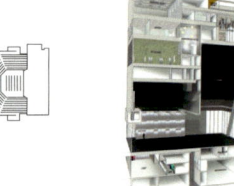

The project's early schemes sum up the Wyly's basic strategy, which rather than placing all the facilities on either side of the performance chamber, puts them at the service of the hall vertically, in the process freeing up the level where the audience and the stage are situated. The tall fly tower is inserted into a cubic volume whose industrial appearance reinforces the aluminum facade that envelopes the building.

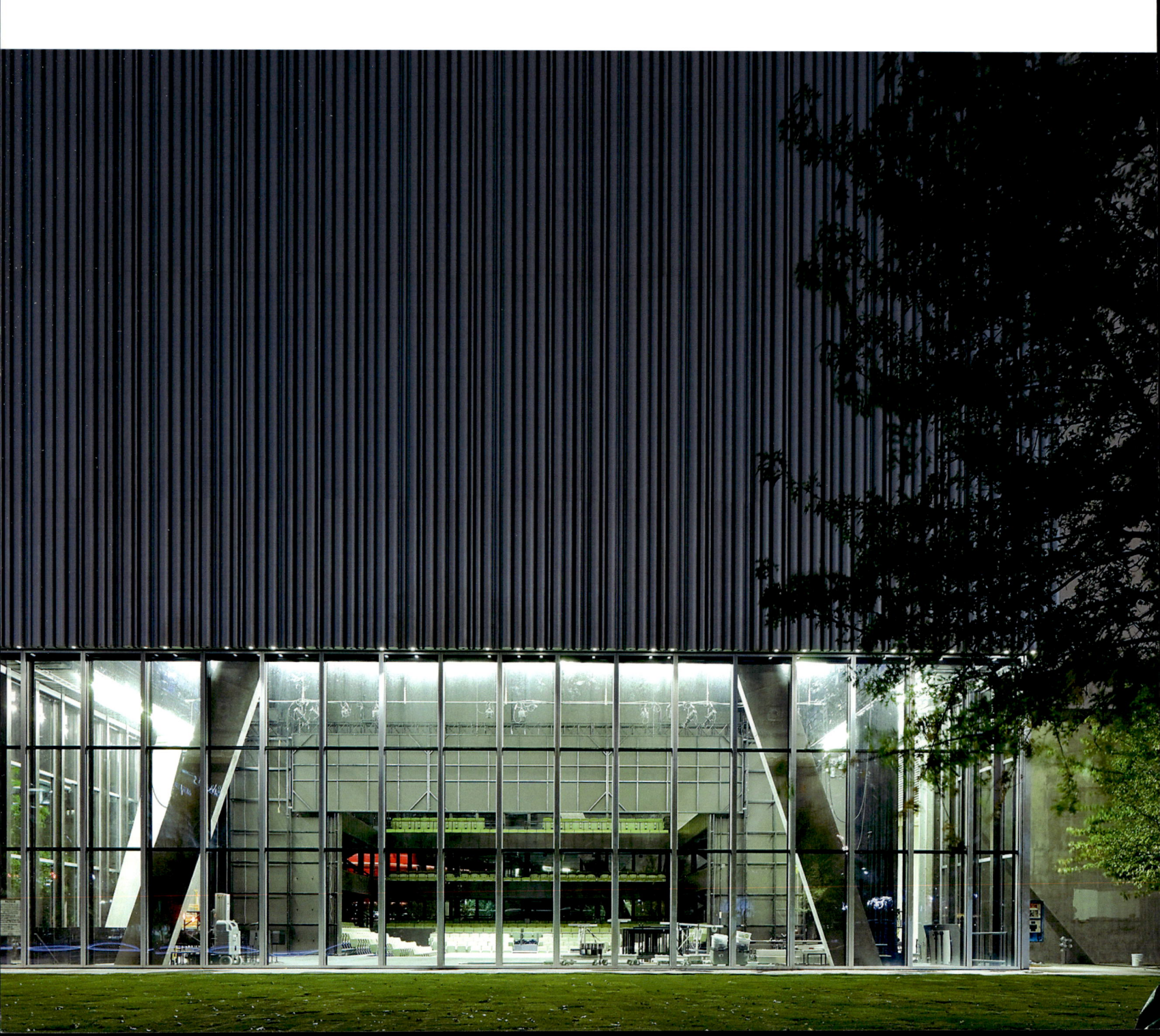

+4

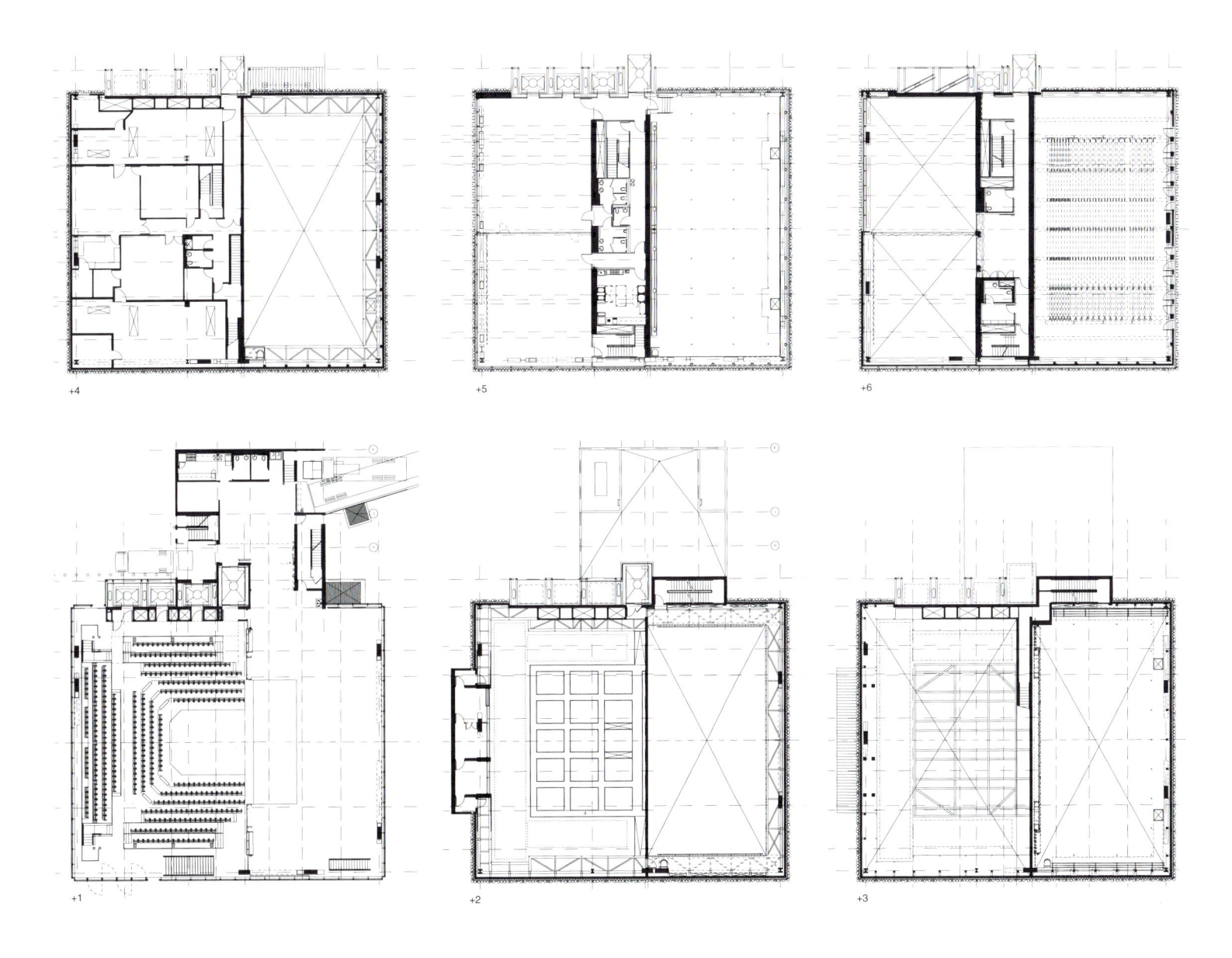

+5

+6

+1

+2

+3

Atlas: America 63

1 waterproofing system
2 aluminum extrusion support angle
3 insulation type
4 bird barrier
5 Taj light fixture
6 pivot door
7 acoustic glass
8 black out shade
9 color concrete
10 150x150x5mm tube steel
11 polyboard and plywood flooring
12 50x50mm tube steel
13 door operator
14 pivot door closing sensor
15 25mm steel plate welded to tube steel
16 250x150x6mm tube steel
17 175x100mm continuous aluminum angle
18 200x600mm steel section
19 thermally broken deglazing aluminum extrusion
20 250x200mm catwalk

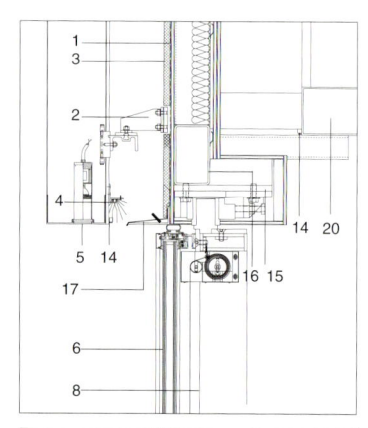

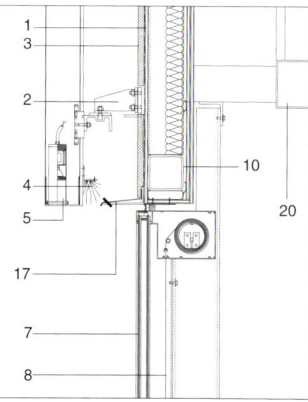

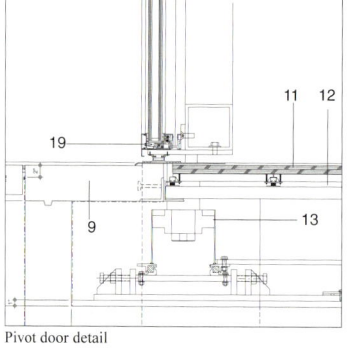

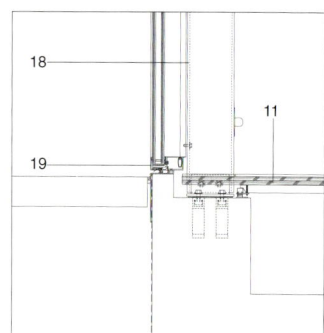

Pivot door detail

Fixed glass detail

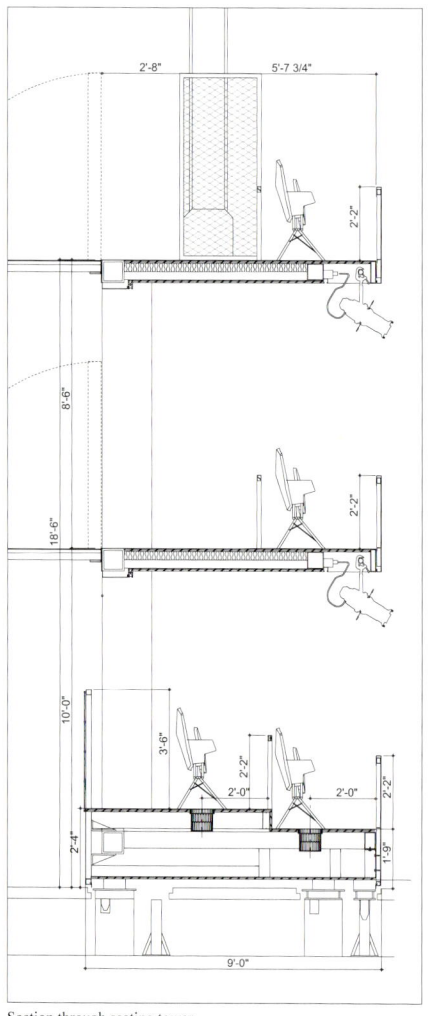

Section through seating tower

64 Atlas: America

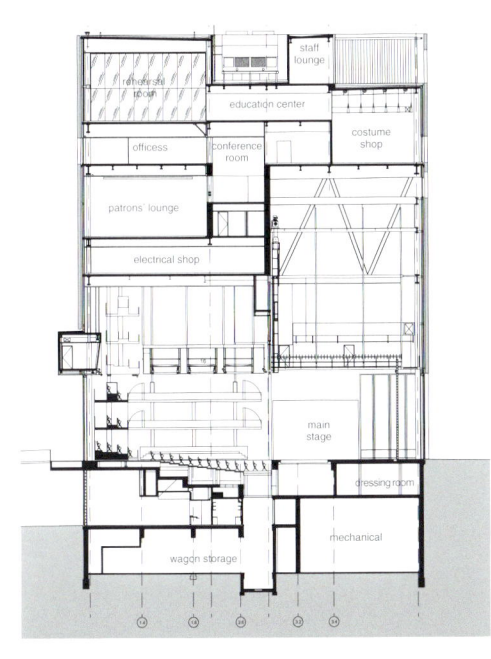

A highly sophisticated theater machinery system makes multiple configurations possible, both for the stage and the audience, which can be situated on the same level; the materials used in the performance hall are readily 'replaceable' and therefore easy for directors to manipulate in accordance with their artistic purposes. On the top floor, a unique terrace lined with artificial grass frames magnificent views of the city skyline.

Carlos Jiménez
Data and Library Service Center
Houston, Texas (United States)

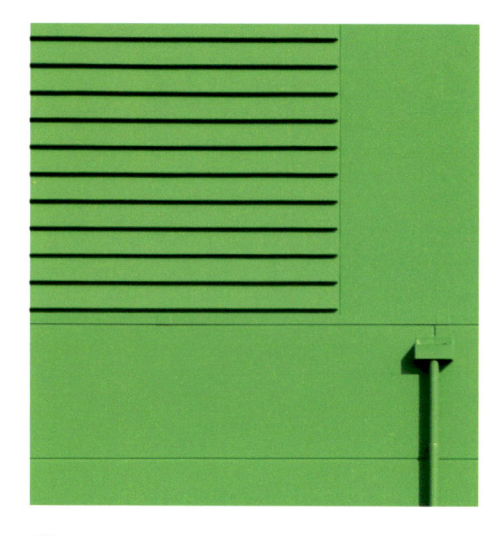

Client
Rice University
Architect
Carlos Jiménez
Collaborators
David Vargo AIA (project leader);
B. Zamore, M. Braisted, V. Murillo;
Kendall Heaton Associates: B. Kendall,
J. O'Connel, P. Akney, J. Ahn
(associate studio)
Consultants
Haynes Whaley (structure);
CHP (installations); Carter & Burgess
(engineering); Dill & Company
(book storage); Office of James
Burnett (landscaping)
Contractor
Spaw Maxwell
Photos
Paul Hester/Hester+Hardaway

Built with prefabricated materials, the volumes of the two new facilities, each painted a tone of bright fluorescent green, rise on the lawn of the university campus like a pair of long and perfectly trimmed hedges.

RICE UNIVERSITY expands its facilities with a new 13-hectare complex situated eight kilometers south of the original, 120 hectare campus. It is meant to provide the institution with storage space besides accommodating other uses, not necessarily exclusively of an academic nature.

The masterplan defines an elongated central ring with different buildings planted along its perimeter. Close to the south end of the premises rise the first two constructions of the new complex. The one situated more to the north is the Data Center, a hermetic-looking volume containing a total floor area of 7,700 square meters. The storage of academic data is to be concentrated here. This high-security building must also guarantee that the university's information networks function uninterruptedly.

Just a few meters away stands the Library Service Center, a book deposit facility that can take in somewhere between 1.75 and 2 million titles, surpassing the Fronden, Rice's main library, by offering vast spaces and innovative and efficient systems. The 5,600 square meter building has two parts: a volume containing an office and a two-level processing area, and a three-story construction for the actual storage of publications in modular bookstacks 10 meters tall. It incorporates an environmental control system that keeps the temperature at 10°C and humidity at 30%, ideal conditions for the preservation of paper products as well as microfilms, videos, tapes and slides. Since this building has been the first to go up on the new grounds, it sets a palette of materials that should serve as a reference for future constructions.

Inspired by industrial structures, the two volumes rise over a concrete slab foundation, on which stands a frame of slender metal profiles that have been concealed with prefabricated panels of concrete. The uniqueness of the solution lies in the attention and care that have gone to the execution of all the details and finishes.

The concrete panels have a texture that has the effect of investing the facings with scale, even in the absence of windows. The volumes are painted in two tones of a bright fluorescent green, thereby taking on the image of geometric hedges on an immense green field that have just been trimmed.

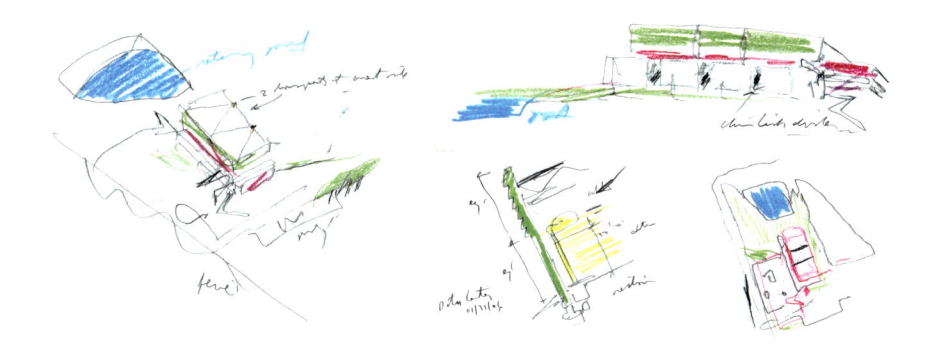

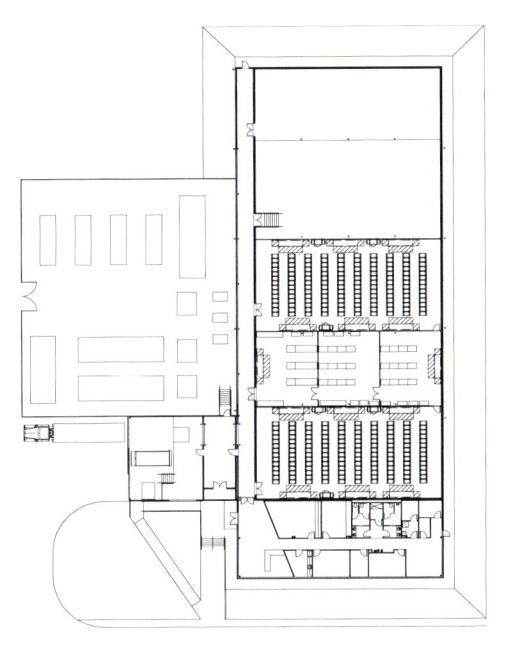

The expanded campus of Rice University is now equipped with a Data Center (1): a hermetic-looking building covered with concrete panels that have been prefabricated in a single piece stretching from ground to roof, with sawtooth profiles in the high parts. Beside it is the first volume of the complex to have gone up, the Library Service Center (2): a 5,600 square meter building containing administrative offices and storage for books.

68 Atlas: America

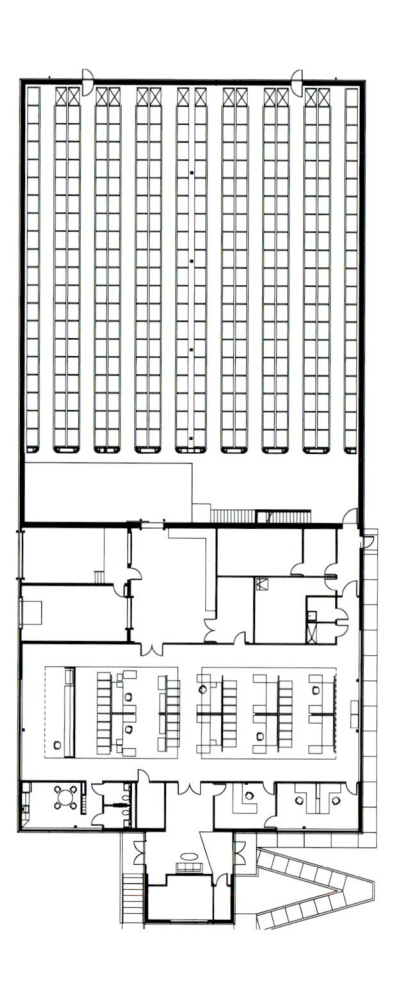

The Service Center is conceived as a support for the main library located on the original grounds, providing innovative storage space with capacity for 1.75 and even up to 2 million volumes, and incorporating an environmental control system that keeps thermal and humidity conditions ideal for preserving books, microfilms, tapes, videos and slides. Like the Data Center, it follows the building system of a conventional industrial construction, with a metal structure, composite flooring and facades of prefabricated concrete panels, but is unique in the exquisite care that has gone to the design and execution of the details and the different finishes.

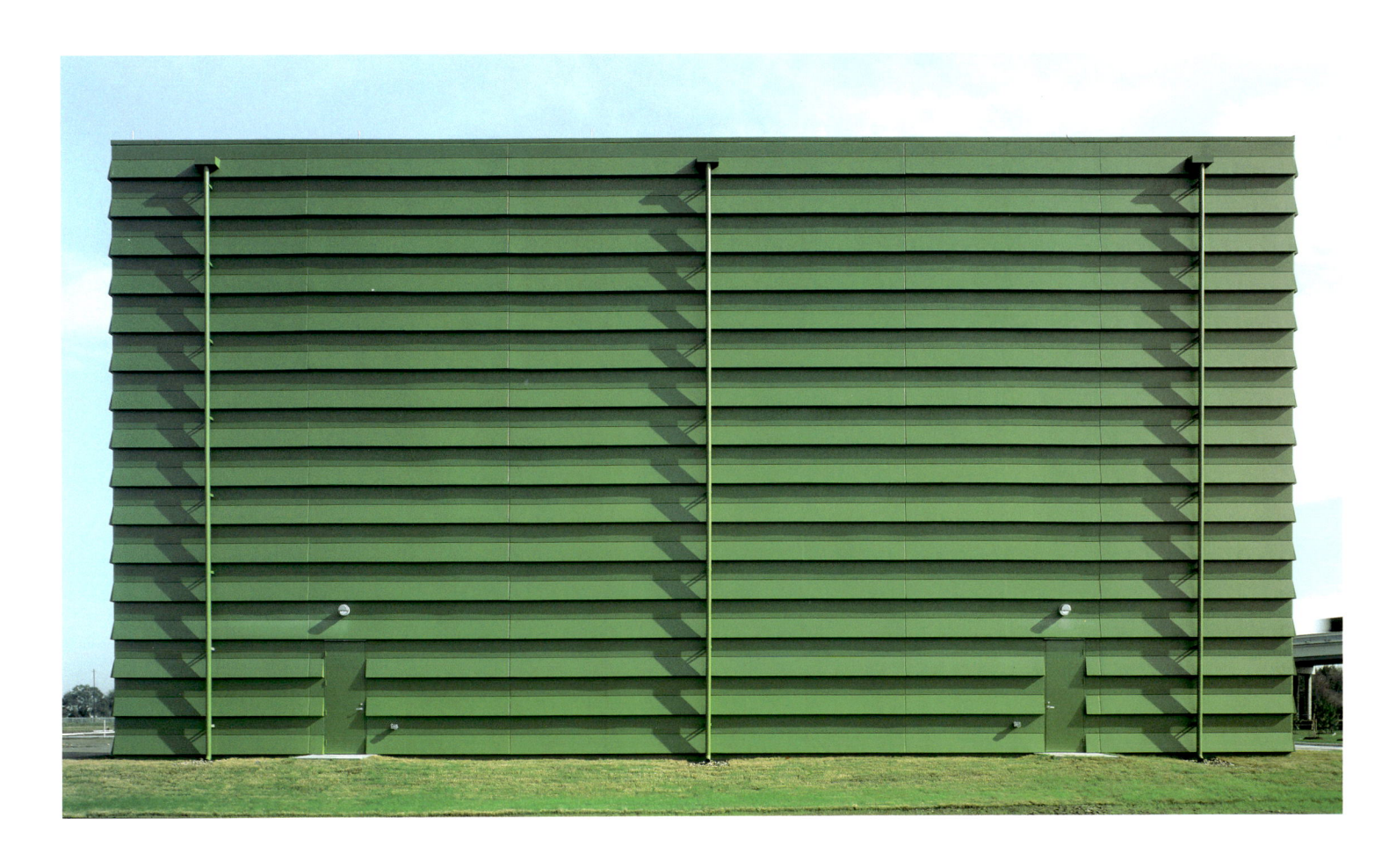

Miró & Rivera
Pedestrian Bridge
Austin, Texas (United States)

LOCATED IN a densely vegetated site at Lake Austin, in a reserve of the Colorado River that is home to a delicate ecosystem, this pedestrian bridge was built to span a body of water on private property and thus connect the main house to the newly constructed guest house on the opposite bank. Surrounded by wetlands that serve as a migratory stop for egrets, cranes and swans, the project forms part of a comprehensive ten-year plan for the preservation of the landscape in the area.

The design of the 24 meter long bridge takes inspiration from the native flora that covers the shores of the lake. Comprising five steel pipes with circular sections, the main arch supports slender vertical steel bars whose varying lengths and close spacing simulate the reeds that grow around the site. Thanks to them, the bridge merges with the mangroves colonizing the riverbank. The handrail is a simple rope secured with small steel wire rings to a tube welded to the structure, which stretches the entire length of the bridge. At the abutments, raised stone ramps give access to the bridge's main platform, and the intertwining here of bars and reeds camouflages the reinforced concrete pieces to which the loadbearing structure is anchored.

Architect
Juan Miró
Consultants
Architectural Engineers Collaborative (structures), Environmental Survey Consulting (landscaping)
Contractor
DCI
Photos
Paul Finkel, Piston Design

Surrounded by densely vegetated wetlands, a pedestrian bridge 24 meters long has been constructed over the lake to connect a private one-family residence to its guest house located on the opposite bank.

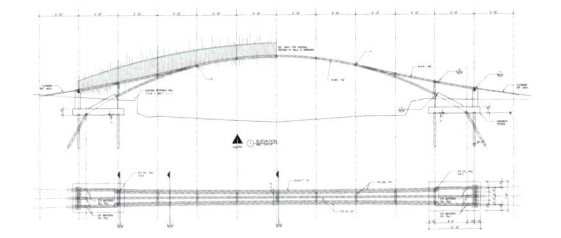

Simulating the reeds that grow in abundance on the shores of the lake, slender bars of varying length are vertically and with irregular spacing fixed to a structure consisting of five steel pipes with circular sections. These pipes in turn are anchored to two pieces of reinforced concrete situated at the bridge's abutments. The handrail is a simple rope secured with small steel wire rings to a horizontal metal tube that is welded to the vertical bars.

Steven Holl
Nelson-Atkins Museum of Art Expansion
Kansas City, Missouri (United States)

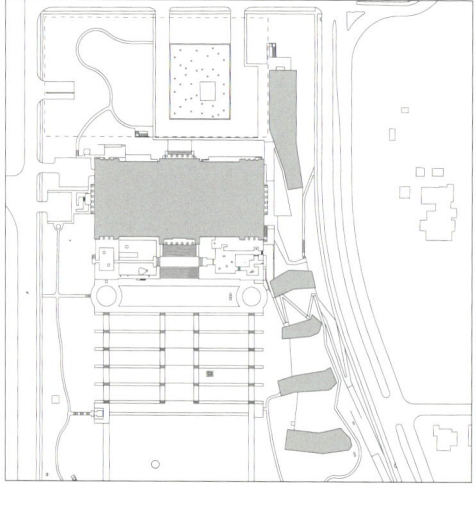

ON A HILL overlooking a vast plain, the Nelson-Atkins collection was housed in a building erected in 1933. Austere and introverted, its distinguishing mark is an imposing colonnade of Ionic columns marking the main entrance. In 1999, the institution held a competition for a renovation that would involve refurbishing the original building, reorganizing the museum's vast multidisciplinary treasures, and raising the Bloch Building, this new expansion containing galleries for modern and contemporary artworks, photography, African art and temporary exhibitions besides documentation and administration areas, ancillary facilities and parking. Of the six projects submitted, only Holl's did not tuck away the expansion behind the original building. Instead it altogether transformed the museum's image through a play of complementary contrasts between old and new. Against the massive, hermetic opacity of the classical 'Temple of Art', the Bloch has light transparent facades, communicative spaces opening up to the surroundings, and free circulation routes set between the de-structured volumes of its halls.

The Block stretches underground along the campus's east boundary and manifests itself through five crystalline volumes rising

Client
Nelson-Atkins Museum of Art
Architects
Steven Holl, Chris McVoy
Collaborators
Berkebile Nelson Immenschuh McDowell Architects (local architects); M. Cox, R. Tobias, M. Blass, G. Barman-Kramer, M. Blieden, E. Chryssochoides, R. Edmonds, S. Giostra, A. Goderbauer, M. Hoang, M. El Kadi, E. Lalonde, L. Hu, J. Korhammer, L. Lee, F. Llonch, S. O'Dell, S. Sanchez, I. Vogt, U. Vogt, C. Wassmann
Consultants
Nordenson; Structural Engineering (structures); Ove Arup (mechanical engineers); R.A. Heintges (facades); Renfro Design Group (lighting); Gould Evans and Olin (landscaping)
Photos
Roland Halbe; Andy Ryan (p. 73 top)

In contrast to the massive and hermetic opacity of the original building, the new expansion of the Nelson-Atkins Museum has been conceived as a landscaping work, with five pristine glass volumes rising on the hill.

The underground route through the various subterranean exhibition halls is lit by means of five crystalline volumes that rise from the ground (referred to as 'lenses'), offering an interplay of new angles of vision, from the original building towards the horizon, through a sculpture garden. Spread out on the hill's south slope, this park forms a continuous green roof providing a good degree of thermal insulation.

from the ground. By day these 'lenses', as they are called, illuminate the galleries buried underneath, whereas at night they light up the sculpture park sprawled around. While visiting the museum, one is drawn into the interplay of light, art, architecture and landscape that is patent throughout, with views crossing between the different levels and the interior and exterior spaces.

The first lens marks the new entrance to the museum and contains the the cafeteria, the library, the bookstore and the main lobby, which connects with the large spaces of the original building through a transversal axis. From this lobby the public is invited to slowly go down the ramps leading to the different halls. The halls are lit from above by the successive lenses, whose layers of translucent glass concentrate, diffuse and refract light, coming across under certain conditions as blocks of ice and throwing light, by night, on the outdoor sculpture park. Laid out over the galleries, the park forms a continuous green roof providing good thermal insulation and allowing the regulation of rainwater. The principles of sustainability underlying the construction also govern the structure and installations. In this way, the cavities between sheets of structural glass on the facades retain hot air in winter and release it in summer, and the systems for regulating daylight make it possible to adapt the interior atmosphere, through simple means, to the needs of the art installations. Under the exhibition galleries, the lower level of the building contains the areas for loading and unloading material, storage facilities and service spaces.

The union of art, architecture and land art resulted from collaboration with the museum trustees and artists like Walter de Maria, author of *One Sun/34 Moons*. Situated at the entrance plaza, this work is a sculpture on a star-shaped pool of water through which the underground parking garage is lit.

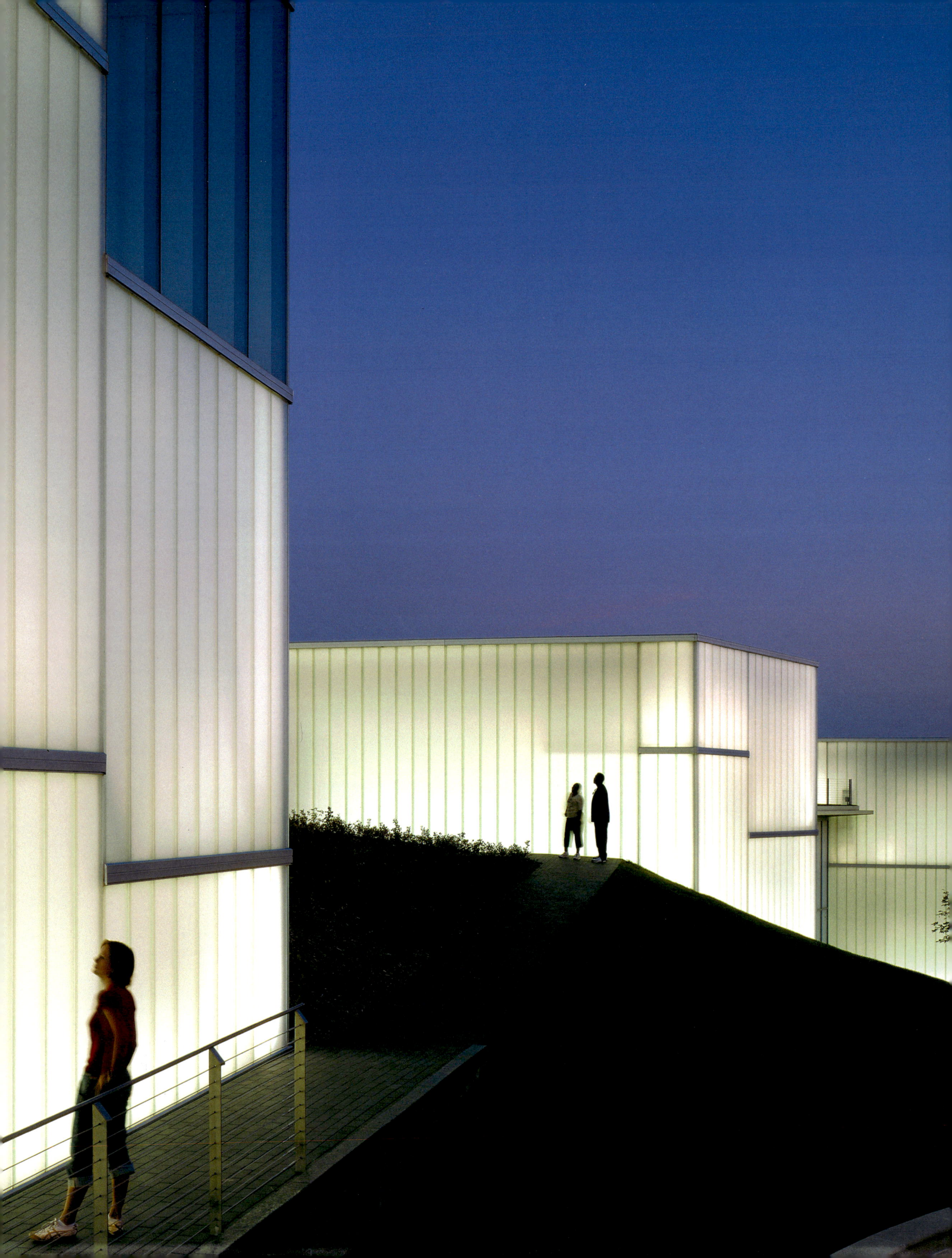

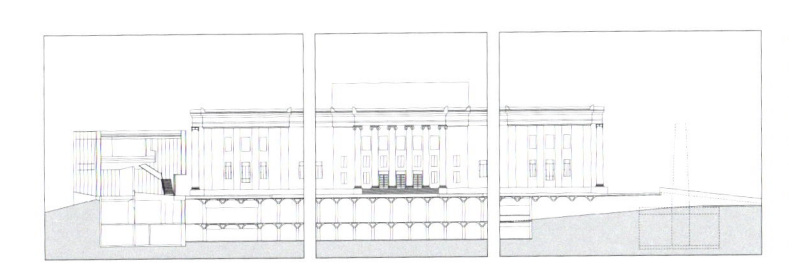

On the assumption that most visitors would be arriving at the museum by car, they were given direct access into the foyer from the parking garage on the basement level, which was conceived as a large public space.

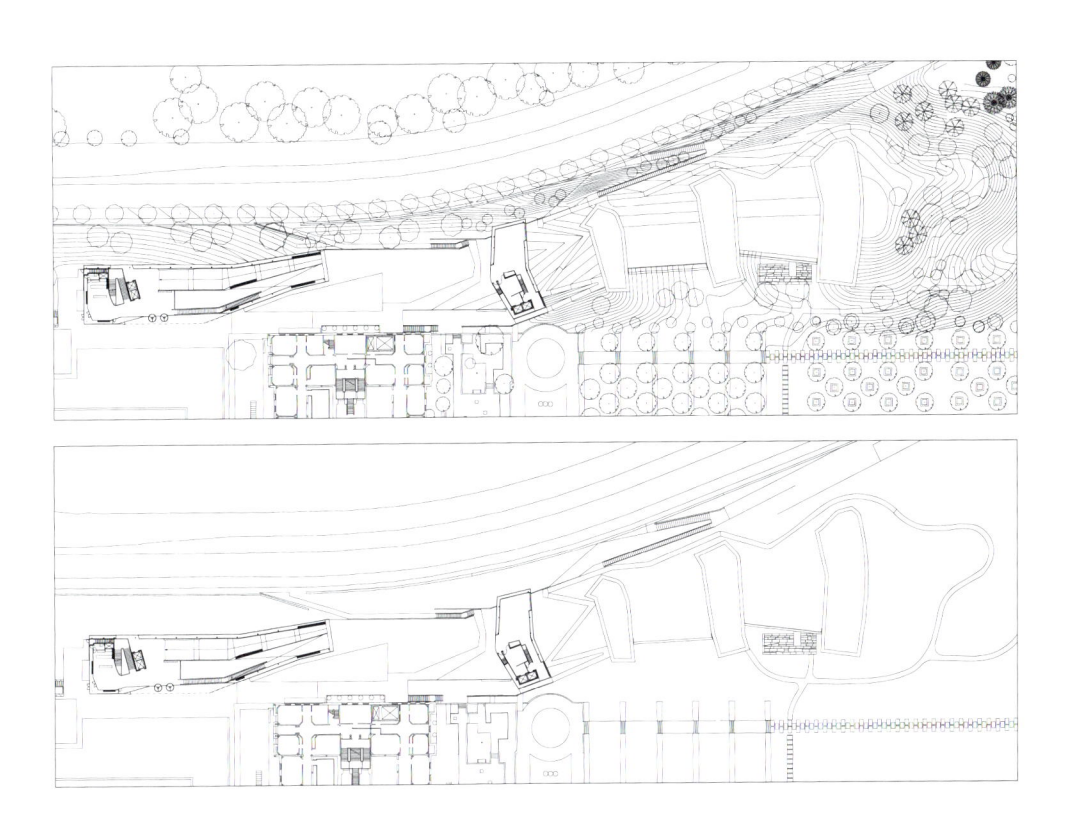

Atlas: America

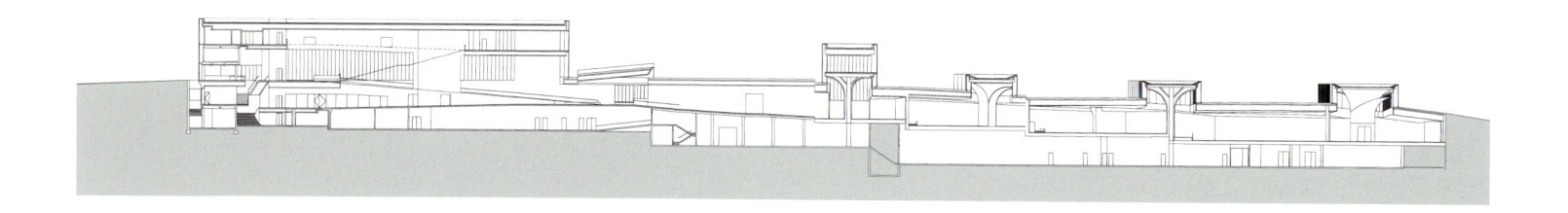

The unique T structure that characterizes the museum's exhibition halls bears the weight of the 'lenses' and their glass envelopes while serving to accommodate the air handling units. In turn, the air chambers situated between the sheets of structural glass of the facade work to accumulate warm air in winter and expel it in summer, making it possible to regulate the temperature of the building's interior spaces.

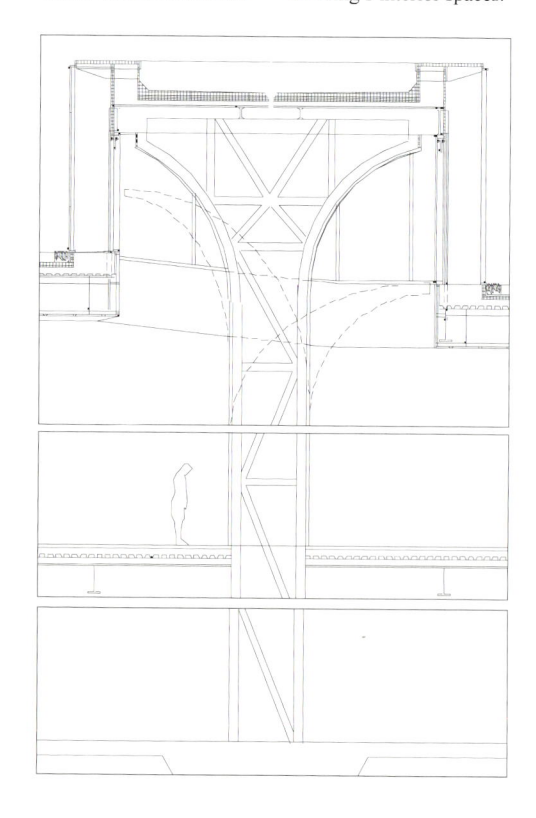

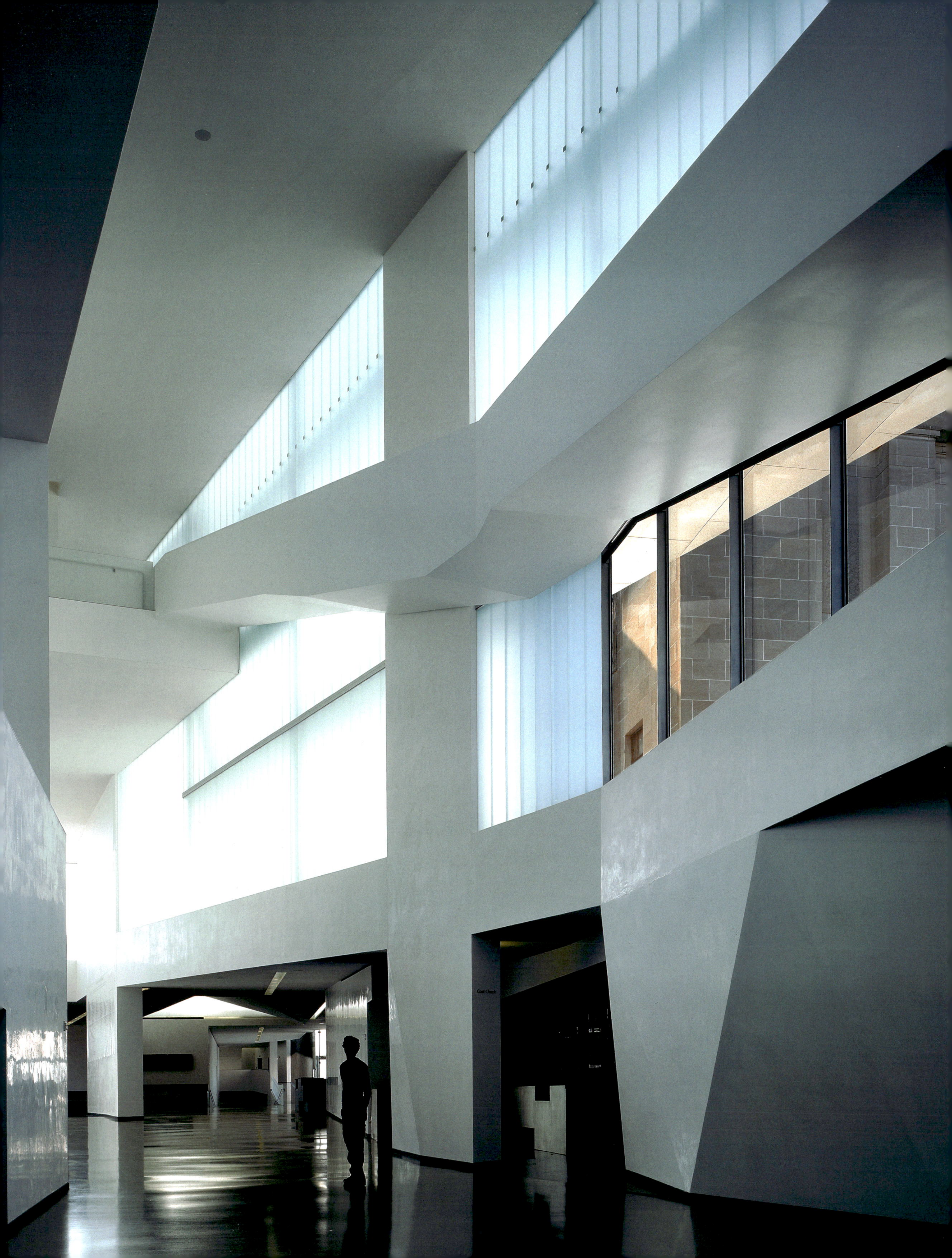
Coat Check

Corner/Diller Scofidio+Renfro
High Line Urban Promenade
New York (United States)

Client
New York City Department
of Parks; Friends of the High Line
Architects
Field Operations: James Corner; Diller
Scofidio+Renfro: Elizabeth Diller,
Ricardo Scofidio, Charles Renfro
Collaborators
L. Tziona Switkin,
N. Hwang; S. Bainbridge, T. Jost,
D. Martic, T. von Preussen, M.
Rockcastle, T. Ryan, L. Shihab-Eldin,
H. Yoon, H. Zhou (field operations);
M. Johnson; R. Condon, T. Hegemann,
G. Libedinsky, J. Linzee, M. Nelligan,
D. Sakai (Diller Scofidio+Renfro)
Consultants
Buro Happold (structures and
installations); Robert Silman
(structures and heritage preservation);
Piet Oudolf (planting design);
L'Observatoire International (lighting)
Contractors
KiSKA; SiteWorks Landscape
(construction management)
Photos:
Iwan Baan

In a unique operation involving urban recycling, a railway infrastructure that dates back to the year 1930 has been transformed into a public park raised above ground level and planted with wild flora.

In June 2009 the first stretch of a unique urban park opened in the old industrial zone known as the Meatpacking District, a neighborhood located on the banks of the Hudson River that in the past was home to hundreds of slaughterhouses and other constructions accommodating the meat industry. The park is located on the elevated structure through which merchandise trains servicing the area passed. Demolition was considered when the structure fell into disuse, but an association called Friends of the High Line firmly opposed this. The raised railway tracks were spared the pickaxe when it was established that the positive impact of transforming the obsolete infrastructure into a park, particularly on the value of the surrounding buildings, exceeded the price of the land on which it sat.

The part now open to the public is the first of three phases comprising the operation, and is 2.3 kilometers long. The leitmotiv of the park is the survival of the High Line. The pavement is a mosaic of elongated wedge-tipped pieces of concrete, in between which grass grows. Several stretches of the original train tracks were put back in place, with their corresponding wooden sleepers, and carefully selected seeds were sown here and there, in a way that would make the arrangement of the plants look like coincidence, thereby evoking the wilderness of the old railway tracks. Despite the absolutely artificial and controlled process behind it, the effect is that of a slice of nature that does not evade the city but actually merges with it, albeit on a platform set 9 meters above real ground level.

Prior to building the new landscape, in order to appraise the platform's resistance and ensure that it was in good state, everything that was on it had to be removed: steel tracks, ballast gravel, soil, rubble. This done, the structure was waterproofed and a gardening drainage system was installed. The steel elements of the structure were cleaned through sandblasting in order to eliminate the original coating of paint, which contained lead. Park furniture includes a series of benches that seem to unfold from the pavement and deck chairs made of thick wooden boards. Lighting is provided by LEDs inserted in the tracks and beneath our angle of vision, creating a cozy and safe promenade that also helps strollers adjust to the glare of the city's skyline.

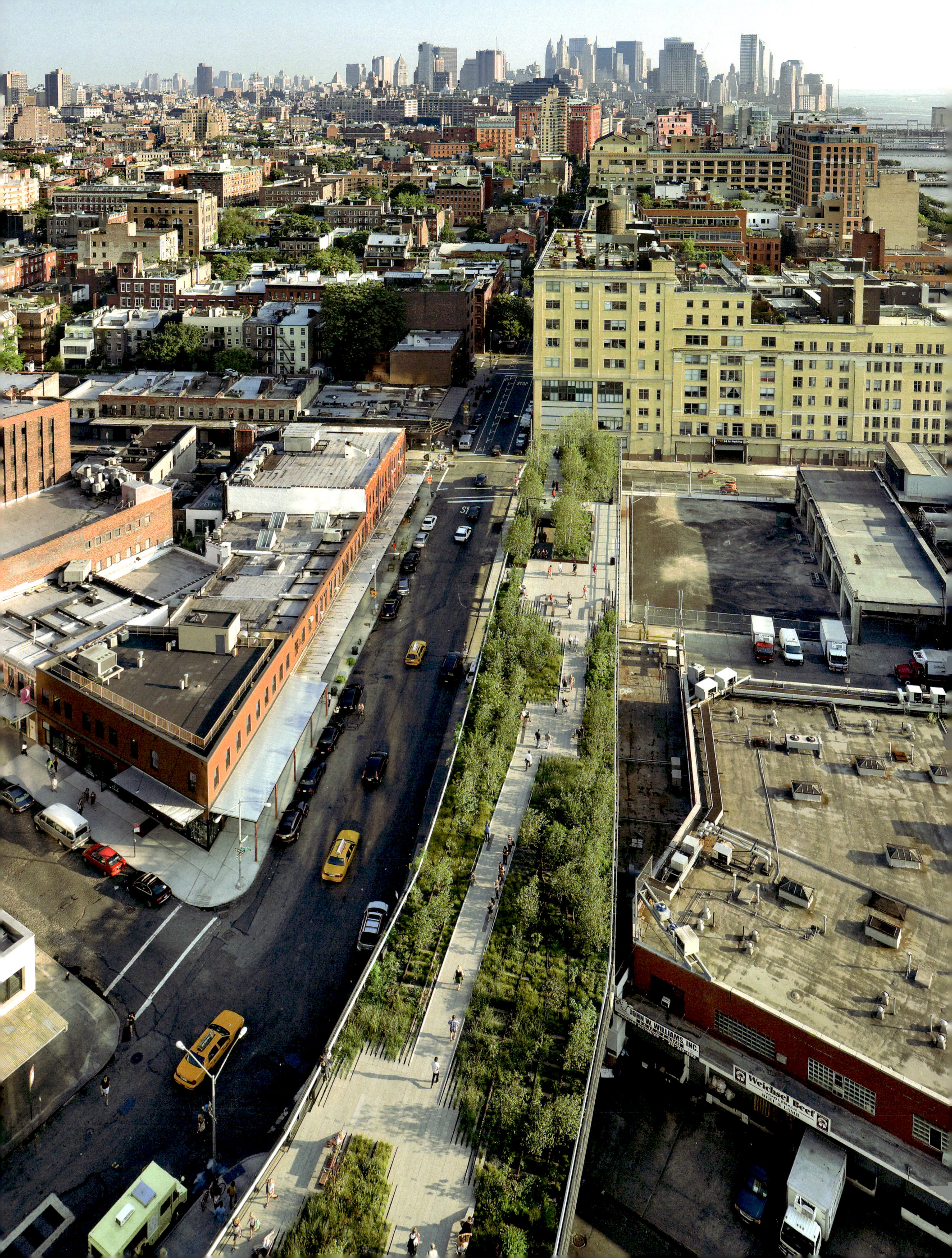

The first part of the High Line promenade stretches nine city blocks, passing close to Jean Nouvel's Nouvel Chelsea and Frank Gehry's InterActiveGroup offices (above), its landscapes evoking anything from a pasture to a small wood besides serving as a mirador and a solarium.

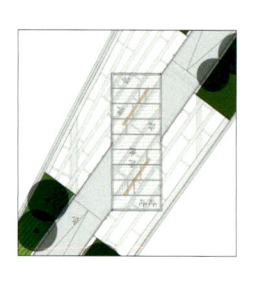

80 Atlas: America

Atlas: America 81

Frank Gehry
InterActiveCorp Headquarters
New York (United States)

Client
InterActiveCorp
Architect
Gehry Partners, LLC
Collaborators
Adamson Associates (associate architects); Studios Architecture (interiors)
Consultores
DeSimone Consulting (structural engineering); Cosentini Associates (mechanical engineering); Brandston Partnership Inc. (lighting); Israel Berger & Associates, TM Technology (security); Turner Construction (construction management); Langan (geotecnical engineering); McCann Systems LLC (audiovisuals); Bruce Mau Design (graphic design); McCann Systems LLC, Warren Z Productions, Tröllback + Company (video walls)
Contractor
Joel M. Silverman Associates
Photos
thomasmayerarchive.com

The ten-story building moderates its massive presence by setting back its top floors and softens its compact appearance through transparent glass bands placed across each middle section over an opaque white enclosure.

SITED IN THE Far West Side of Manhattan, in the Chelsea neighborhood, the headquarters of the firm InterActiveCorp – a conglomerate of companies owned by the media magnate Barry Diller – rises in the vicinity of the Hudson River like an imposing ship at full sail. The unique treatment of the glass curtain wall is the building's most complex feature. Up close it presents a striated texture, and clear across each middle section, at a point where people inside might stand to look out to the street and city beyond, the glass shades gradually to an opaque white, thanks to miniscule ceramic frit dots arranged in irregular waves that collect at the top and bottom.

The curvatures in the glass surfaces were achieved through a cold-bending process that was carried out on site, although surprisingly it is not the flexibility of the glass that determines a maximum torque (up to 4 centimeters), but the tensile strength of the silicone adhesive anchoring the fourth corner of each sheet of glass to the frame. The best place to see the effect is on the back side, where the building rotates up to 150° as it rises unbroken from the ground up.

Studios Architecture designed the interiors on all the floors except the sixth, which Frank Gehry undertook himself. Gehry also took care of the ground-level lobby, where the building's flashiest interior design feature is located. This is a 36 meter long video wall, a screen powered by eighteen 12,000-lumen projectors and streaming a collage of images of flowers, client product endorsements and artistic projects, in the manner of an art installation. As for the sixth story, where the company's executive offices are situated, it is marked by a predilection for bright colors, multiple textures and patterns, and shiny surfaces.

Each floor has a constant 2.5 meter wall that serves as a datum line to counteract ceiling heights, which oscillate between 2.8 meters on lower floors and 3.1 on upper ones. A plenum below each floor slab is recessed from the angled facade, creating space for a constant 1.5 meter deep perimeter cove light, which accounts for the building's nighttime glow.

Inside the building, elements that are arranged with an *ad hoc* haphazardness, producing a sense of energy and dynamism, are made to alternate with features that are placed more rationally. For example, the columns that are planted along the perimeter of the building all rise parallel to the glass envelope, which means that they tilt, sometimes as much as 20°, whereas the inner pillars stand straight, as if to tame irregularities and impose a sense of order.

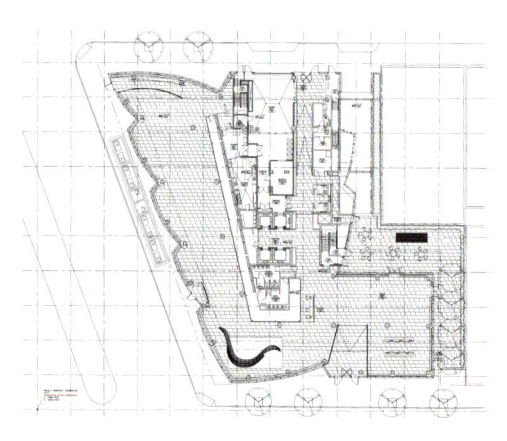

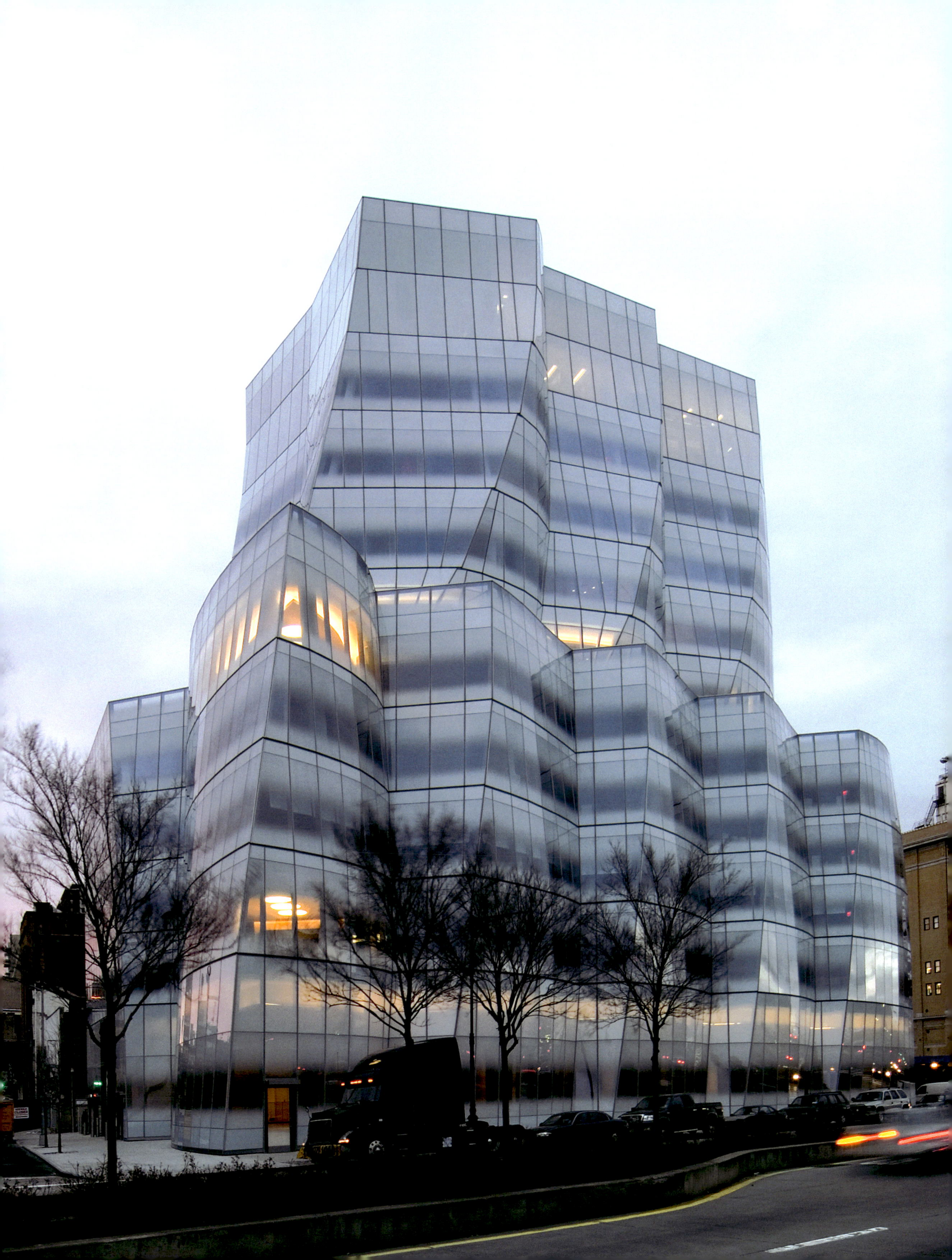

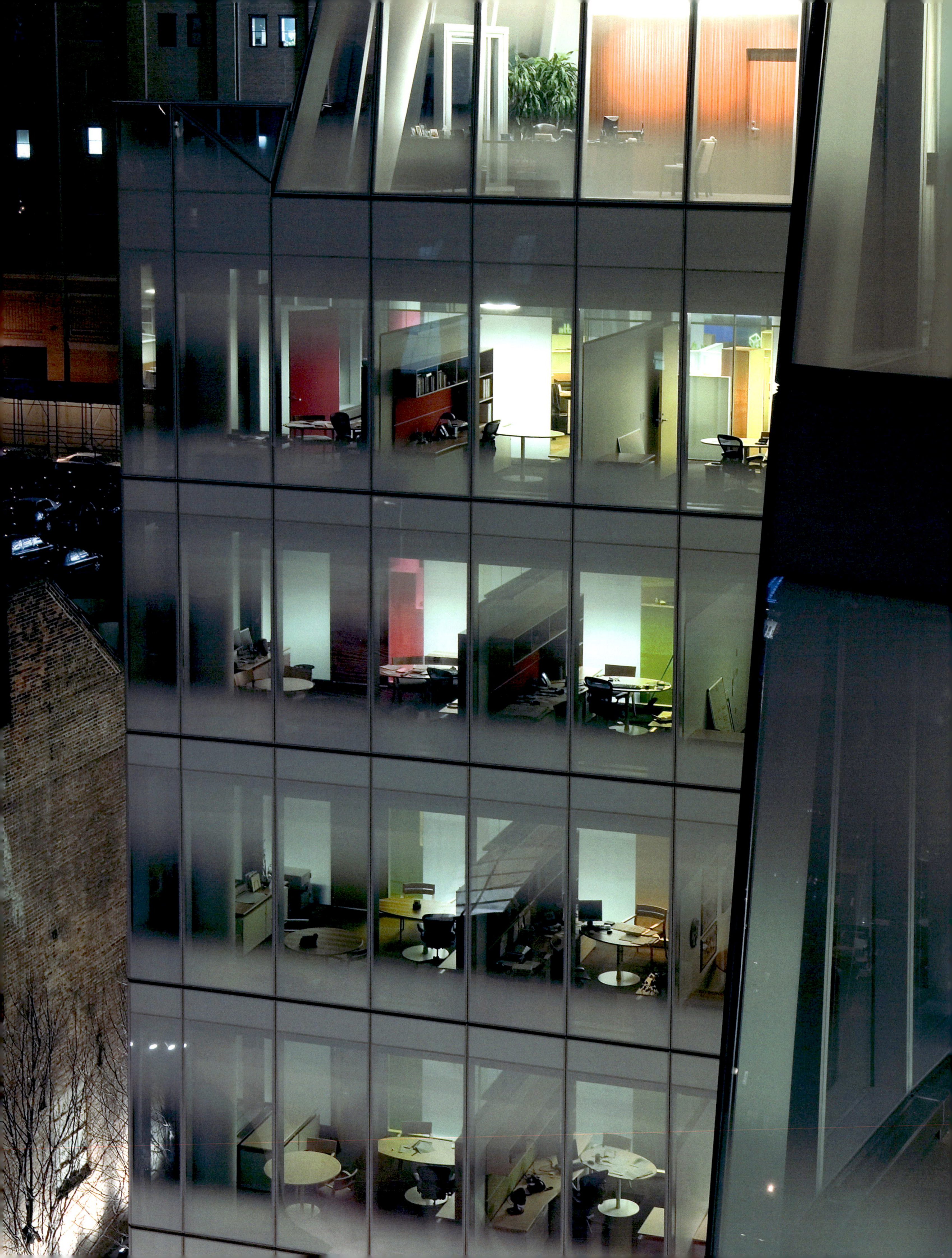

The facade's continuous surface was achieved by placing glass sheets curved on site through a cold-bending process, then anchored to the substructure by means of an adhesive silicone of high tensile strength.

In the ground-floor lobby, an enormous, 36 meter long video screen wall projects a collage of images of flowers, client product endorsements and artistic projects that are halfway between advertising and art.

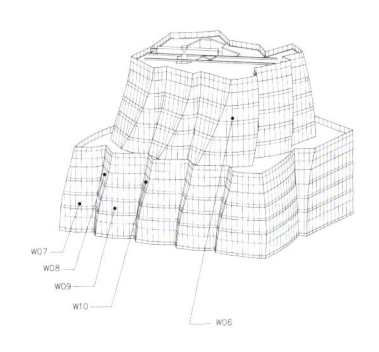

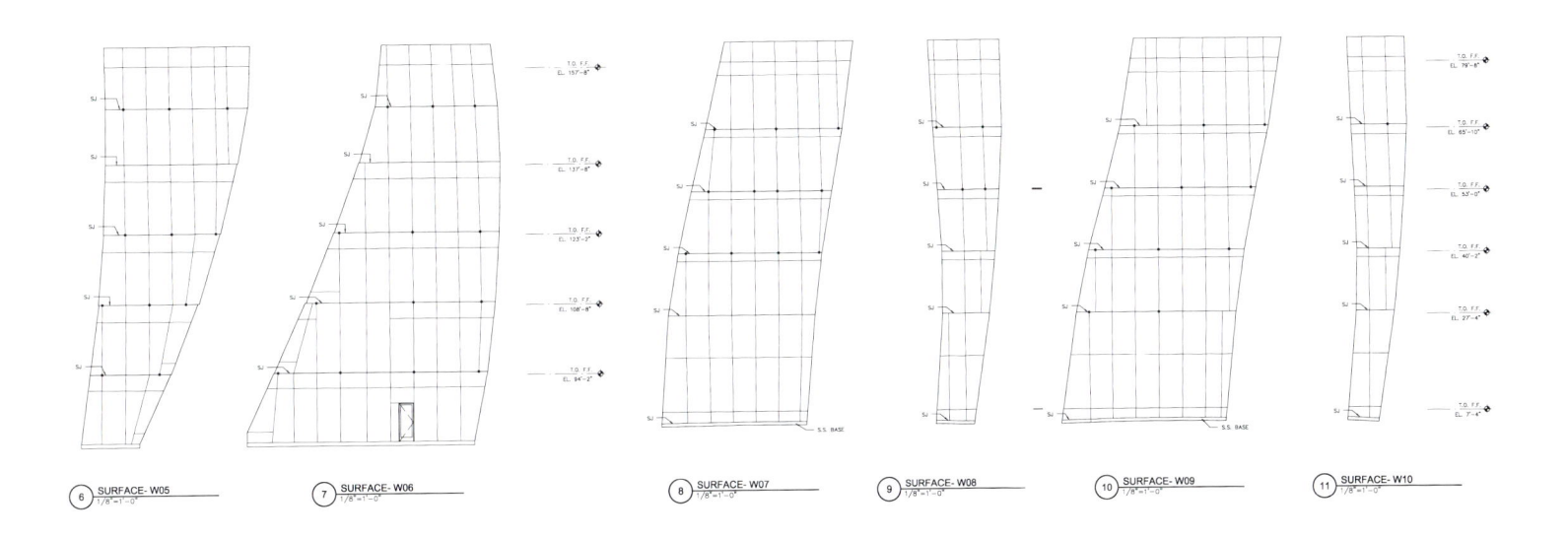

Atlas: America

Jean Nouvel
Nouvel Chelsea Apartment Building
New York (United States)

IN THE NEIGHBORHOOD of West Chelsea of southern Manhattan, close to High Line, a new public park, and next to Frank Gehry's IAC (InterActive Corp) office building, rises a new 23-floor deluxe apartment tower that combines a glazed and kaleidoscopic curved main facade with a severe, dark-brick rear envelope resembling the exteriors of the area's historical edifices. This is the condominium highrise originally known as 100 Eleventh Avenue, renamed Vision Machine, and finally called Nouvel Chelsea for marketing reasons.

The part in contact with the street – a 7-story plinth defined by a permeable metal framework distanced approximately 5 meters from the line of the building's facade – contains a half-open atrium where middle-sized trees are afloat, like in a hanging garden. This lower volume that engages in dialogue with the immediate surroundings also accommodates the terraces and the loggias – glazed spaces that are open and closed, respectively – of the first six floors of apartments and a semi-open court featuring the lobby-level restaurant and café. The building's communal facilities also include a 25 meter long swimming pool that is partly open-air and partly covered, a fitness center, a garden for use by residents, wine cellars,

Client
Alf Naman Real Estate, Cape Advisors
Architects
Jean Nouvel; Beyer Blinder Belle (local architects)
Colaboradores
G. Tolila (partner); F. Leiningr (project manager); S. Erard, Y. Rouby, A. Faraut, N. Zerrouki, T. Kubota, J. Romain Munvez, M. Kishi, JF. Winninger, R. Luna, N. Saccu de Franchi, R. Ishkinazi, S. Letourneur, L. Fontana, D. Thulstrup, E. Blanc, I. Djaorakitine, R. Turquin, M. Gabry, C. Cochard, N. Sasso, H. Aldogan, B. George, A. Zysman, S. Laromiguière, F. Imbert, E. Nespoulous, PE. Loiret
Consultants
Desimone (structure); Front (facade); Jam (zoning); AKF (installations); Bonny Whitehouse (lighting)
Photos
Philippe Ruault; Roland Halbe (p. 86 top, 88 bottom)

The deluxe apartment tower's better oriented facade is enveloped in a curtain wall that is discontinuous in appearance, pixelated by differently sized glass panes that reflect light at diverse angles.

The western light is reflected in the thousands of glass panes that make up the facade, and the built volume comes across as a glittering object facing the Hudson River. The curtain wall has been erected by means of steel-structured frameworks ranging in height from 3 to 5 meters, and is subdivided into rectangles onto which the window frames are fastened. On them go the sheets of glass of tones going from green to blue.

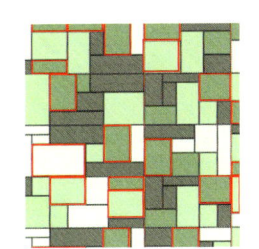

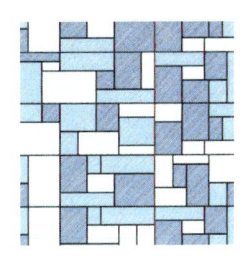

an Automatic Teller Machine (ATM) service and a 24-hour concierge.

The 72 luxury units offered by the building – one of them a 435 square meter duplex penthouse – have one, two or three bedrooms and floor areas ranging from 83 to 194 square meters. The typical story accommodates four apartments: the two at the far ends are the large units that open up on two opposite sites, while the two central ones are one-bedroom and face a single direction. Most of the apartments offer American-style kitchens equipped with terrazzo countertops designed by Jean Nouvel, Corian bathrooms with Jado plumbing fixtures also designed by the architect, and pivot doors.

The curved facade that characterizes the tower's dominant image takes up the entire width of the lot, maximizing both the amount of living area facing the street and the views that can be had from the building, with the result that all units receive direct sunlight and have views south and west. All have a street-side stretch of facade ranging in length from 10 to 53 meters, and floor-to-ceiling glazed facades divided into several panes of glass bordered by powerful frames. The curtain wall is made up of large steel-structure frames from 3 to 5 meters high and as much as 11 meters in span. Windows of different sizes are distributed along its surface, with the glass panes – in tones going from green to blue but turning gold or gray, depending on the light reflected – tipped vertically or horizontally, resulting in a discontinuous, almost pixelated surface. In effect, the building's shell comes across to the onlooker outside like a skin that changes as the day goes by, while offering residents mosaic-like views of the city. In contrast, the north- and east-facing rear facades are of black-painted exposed brick, although here, too, are openings of varying dimensions that are also turned vertically and horizontally.

Atlas: America **87**

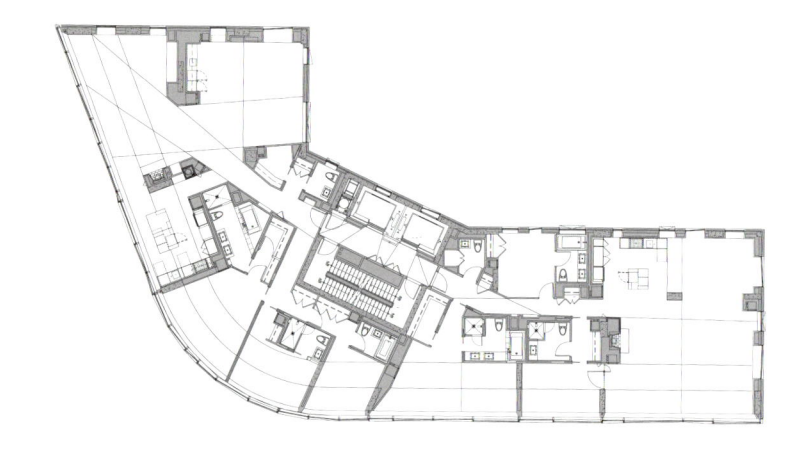

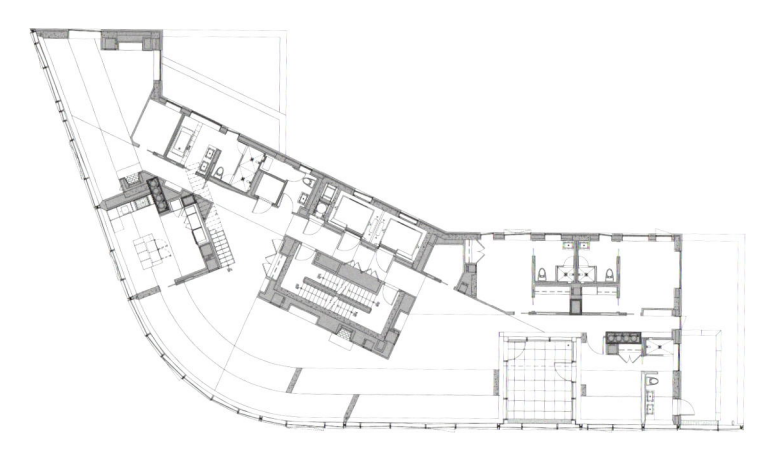

The highrise apartment building that has come to be called Nouvel Chelsea is located next to Frank Gehry's InterActiveCorp offices. The tower's different facades present a powerful contrast, depending on what they face: the front glitters towards the Hudson River whereas the elevations addressing the neighboring buildings are given a sober matt finish, mostly with sober brickwork. The 72 living units, varying in floor area between 83 and 435 square meters, are distributed in 23 floor levels. Every single apartment has a stretch of street-side facade, ranging in length from 10 to 53 meters, and huge floor-to-ceiling windows.

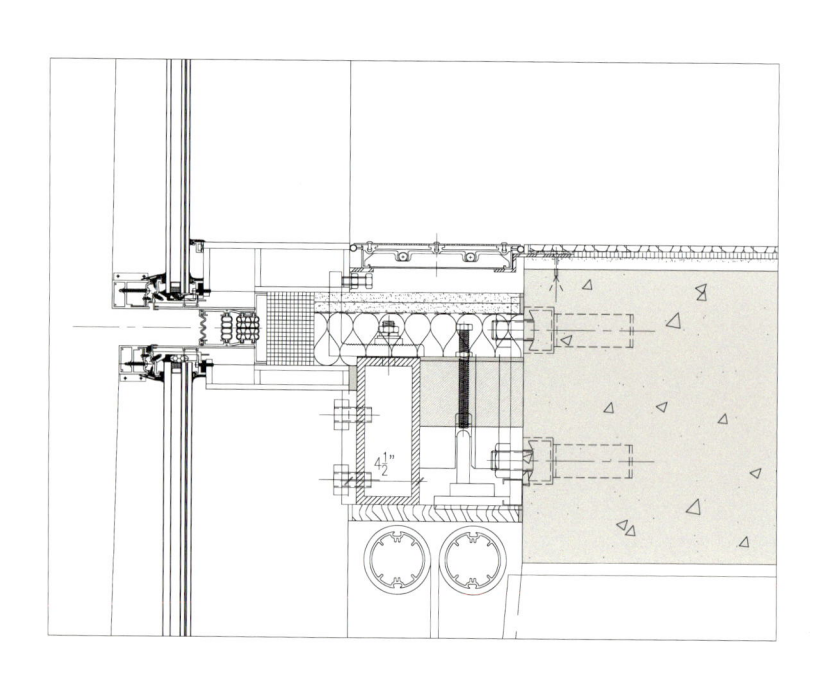

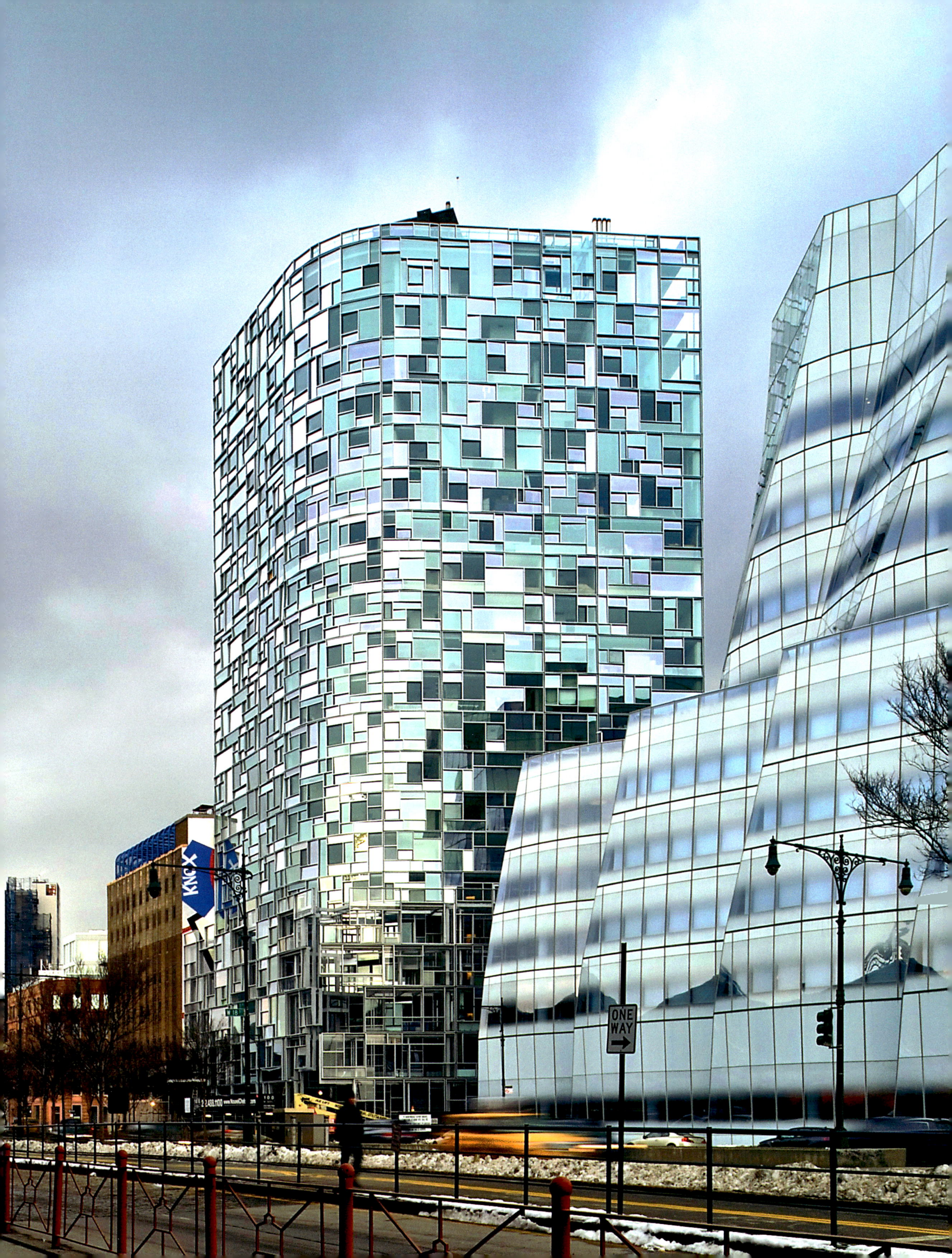
ONE
WAY

Morphosis
Academic Building for the Cooper Union
New York (United States)

Architects
Morphosis: Thom Mayne
Collaborators
Silvia Kuhle (project manager);
Pavel Getov (project architect);
Jean Oei (project designer), Chandler Ahrens, Natalia Traverso Caruana, Go-Woon Seo (design);
Irena Bedenikovic, Salvador Hidalgo, Marcin Kurdziel, Debbie Lin, Kristina Loock (team); Gruzen Samton (associate architect)
Consultants
Jonathan Rose (project management);
John A. Martin, Goldstein (structures);
IBE, Syska Hennessy (HVAC);
Gordon H. Smith (facade); Davis Langdon (sustainability)
Contractor
Sciame Construction
Photos
Iwan Baan; Wade Zimmerman (p. 92)

THE NEW BUILDING for The Cooper Union aspires to manifest the values and character of the school and the city it was founded in 150 years ago. The founder, the industrialist Peter Cooper, sought to provide education that was "as free as water and air". Among academic institutions in the United States, it is among the most advanced in the art, architecture and engineering fields.

Situated close to the original Foundation Building, the new facility – called the New Academic Building – occupies a rectangular lot facing Cooper Square, onto which its ground floor opens by means of a permeable perimeter. The eight floor levels contained within are not easily identifiable from without, where a deep crack on the square-side facade is its most recognizable feature. The interior is thought out to foster interdisciplinary dialogue among the three faculties it accommodates, which were previously housed in separate buildings.

The large central atrium – with its undulating and broken envelope and its 20 foot wide staircase for social, intellectual and creative exchange – is the heart of the new building. From the double-height entrance lobby, the grand stair rises four stories to a glazed lounge, also double-height, that offers views of the city. From the fifth floor to the ninth, a range of meeting opportunities, including seminar rooms, locker areas and seating zones overlooking the cityscape is organized around the central void. Bridges span this atrium void, connecting these venues for informal meetings. Reinforcing the dynamic mood of social and intellectual exchange is the 'skip-stop' circulation strategy, which increases both physical movement and chance encounters: the main elevators stop only at the first, fifth and eighth floors, encouraging the use of stairs and bridges. To comply with the Americans with Disabilities Act and facilitate the moving of materials, equipment and artwork, a secondary set of elevators stops floor by floor.

The atrium, central space of the interior, is echoed in the facade, where a large number of functions is concentrated in a double skin. The exterior is a semi-transparent layer of perforated stainless steel panels that protects the inner glazed envelope, providing a thermal control mechanism that also serves to give the onlooker a peep into goings-on indoors.

41 Cooper Square, built to the LEED Gold standards of the U.S. Green Building Council, is as much as 40% more energy efficient than a standard edifice of this type. It features a broad range of energy-saving devices: the skin of perforated stainless steel panels that reduces the impact of heat radiation in summer and insulates the interior spaces in winter; the radiant heating and cooling ceiling panels installed in the ceilings; the atrium that rises the entire height of the building, facilitating circulation for both users and air; the green roof, which diminishes the 'heat island' effect as well as rainwater runoff and pollutants; and the cogeneration plant that supplies electricity and recovers waste heat, thereby doing much to bring down the building's energy bills.

An opaque skin of steel sheets presents rips at the front, revealing the atrium around which classrooms and workshops of one of America's most prestigious and advanced institutions of higher education are arranged.

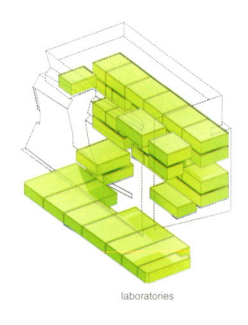

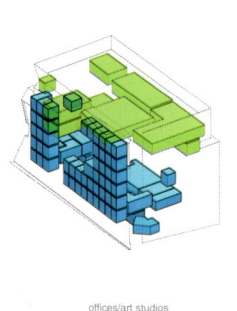

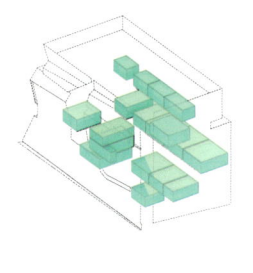

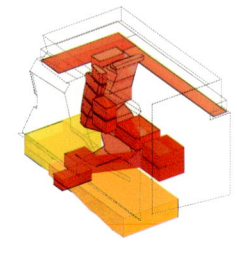

laboratories | offices/art studios | classrooms | public/social space

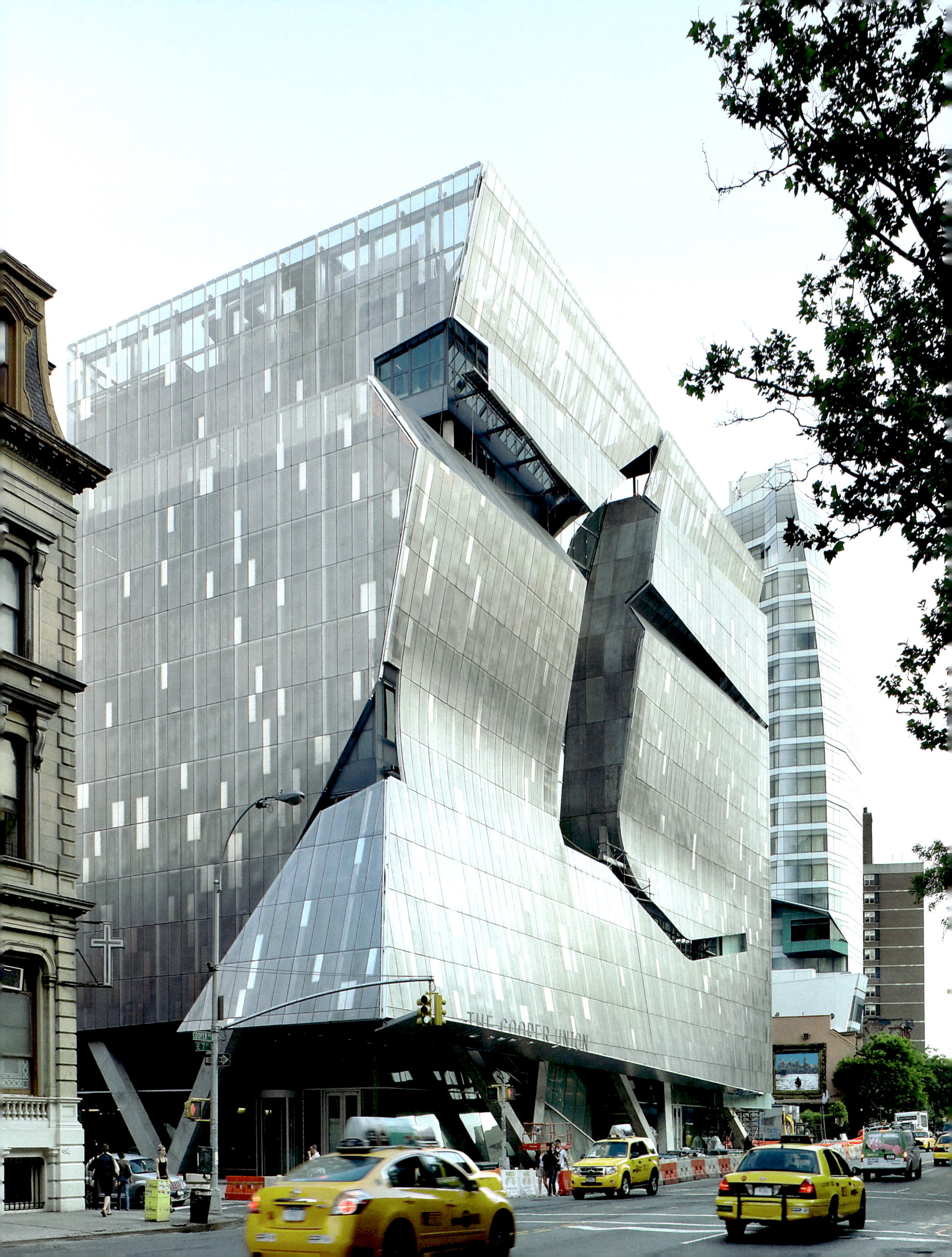
THE COOPER UNION

The width of the grand stair – which is wrapped in an undulating atrium that brings in natural light from above – and its central location at the heart of the school serve to add a lounge function to its circulation use. The 'skip-stop' system whereby the elevators stop on only some of the eight floors makes the students use the staircase as a meeting place. The atrium rises the entire height of the building and is discerned on the facade.

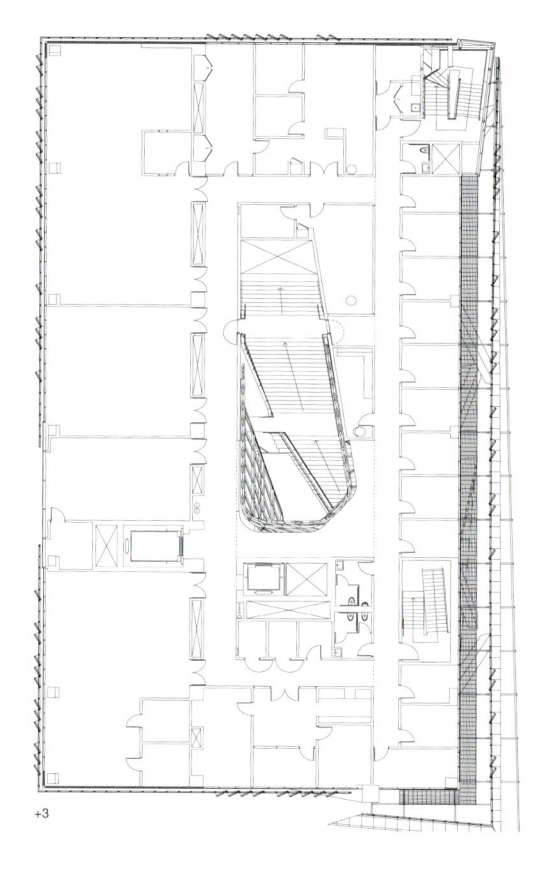

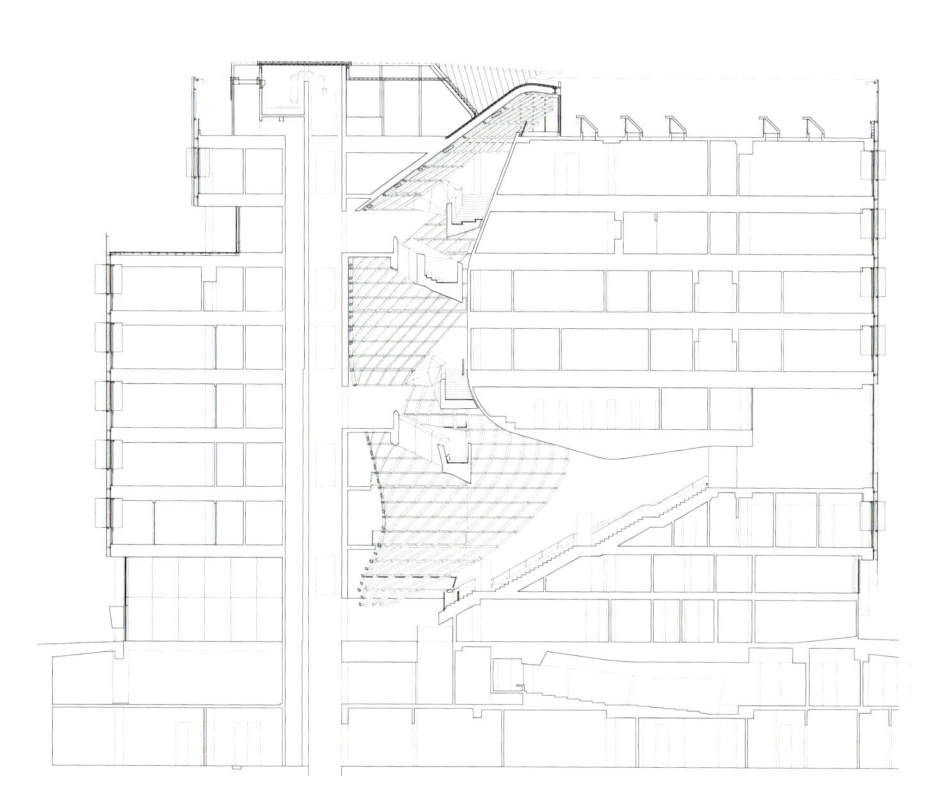

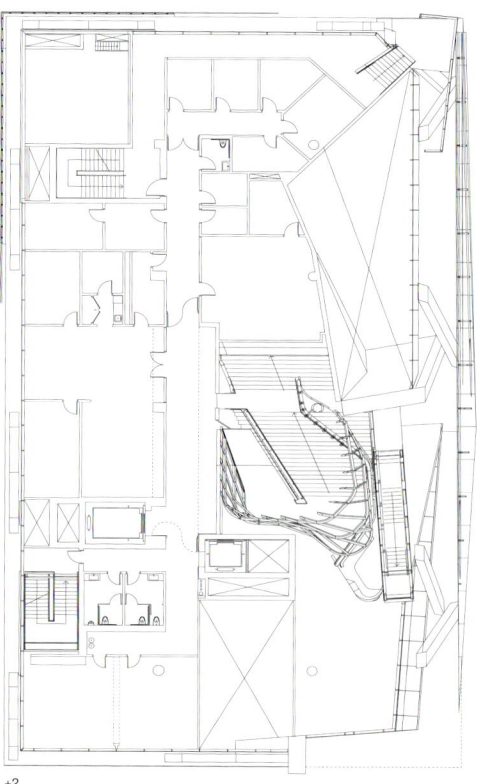

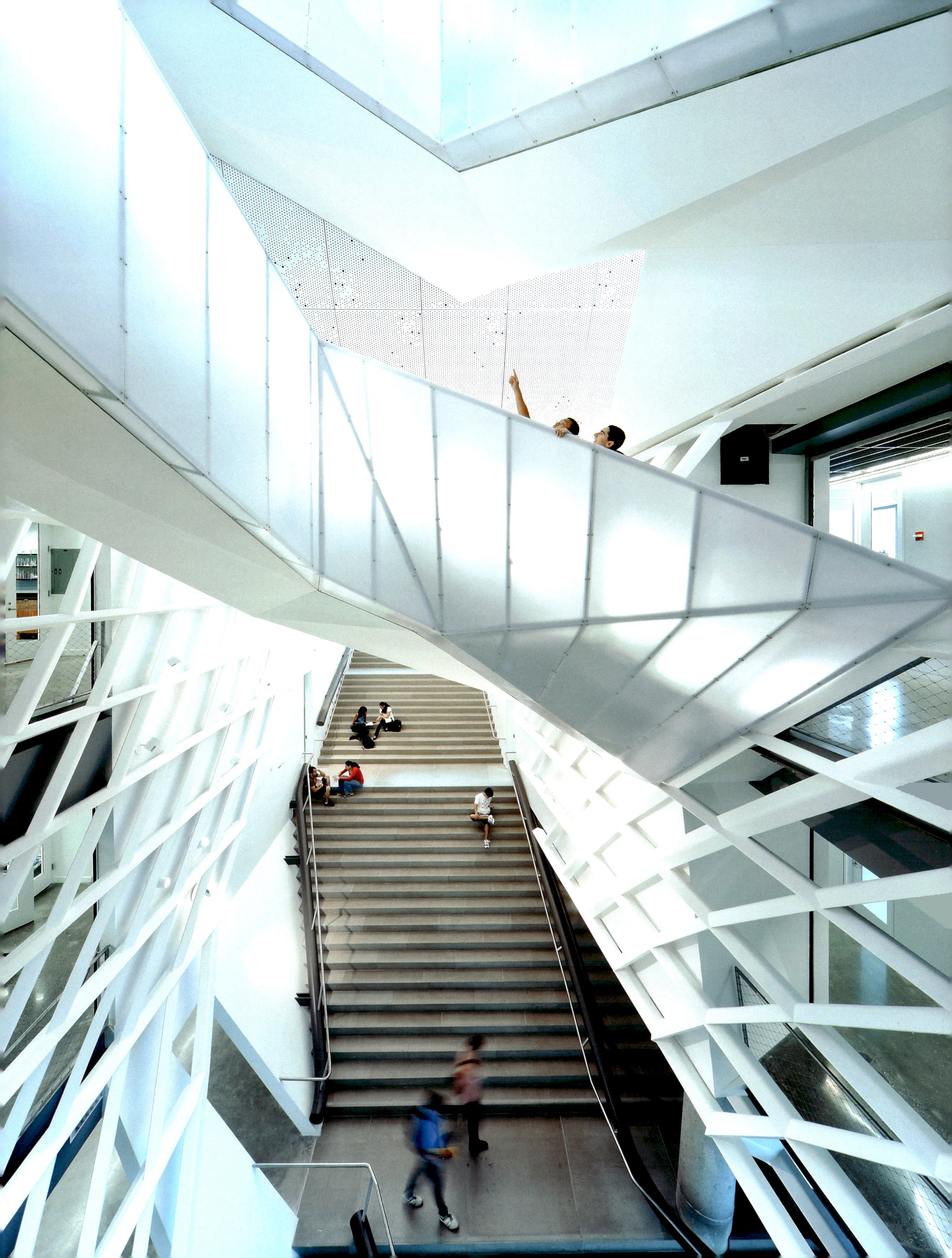

SANAA / Sejima & Nishizawa
New Museum of Contemporary Art
New York (United States)

Client
New Museum, Zubatkin
Architects
SANAA / Kazuyo Sejima,
Ryue Nishizawa
Collaborators
F. Idenburg, T. Oki,
J. Elding, K. Yoshida, H. Katagiri,
J. Haddad, E. Hidaka, T. Kondo,
F. Haakma-Wagenaar, T. Nakatsubo;
Gensler: M. Burke-Vigeland, W. Rice,
K. Pedrazzi, K. Gregerson, J. Chow,
W. Rohde, S. Moon, C. Duisberg,
E. Papazian (associate architects)
Construction Management
Sciame
Consultants
Plaza Construction Corporation
(project management); Guy Nordenson
(structural engineers); Arup
(mechanical/HVAC engineers); Simpson
Gumperts & Heger (facade); Jenkins &
Huntington (vertical transportation)
Photos
Christian Richters; Dean Kaufman
(p. 95); Wade Zimmerman (p. 94 top,
97); Iwan Baan (p. 96 left)

Thirty years after its founding, the art center has now opened in a degraded zone of New York City a spectacular building of its own, the second American work of the acclaimed Japanese duo of architects.

THE ONLY New York City museum dedicated to the latest in contemporary art now has its own freestanding premises in the Bowery, a longtime degraded zone of the Lower East Side that has been undergoing major redevelopment to become an animated hub of commercial activity and a new cultural center for the island of Manhattan. Conceived as a pile of boxes varying in dimensions and randomly shifted in relation to one another, with no apparent aligning axis or order, the building unfolds vertically to fit the institution's entire program within the confines of a small plot in a dense urban fabric. Each of the stacked volumes accommodates a distinct function, and they are all interconnected by a core containing the elevator shafts and staircases. Thanks to the shifting cantilevers of the boxes, the actual exhibition spaces can be naturally toplit through skylights.

The load-bearing steel structure has a white aluminum cladding that is protected by a second skin of perforated panels, also of aluminum. These panels are joined together in an almost imperceptible way, resulting in a continuous milky shine that strikes an stunning contrast with the facades of the surrounding buildings. At street level it gives way to a transparent glass enclosure that gives passers-by a glimpse of goings-on inside, as if in assertion of the public character of the institution.

The ground floor includes an area for the loading and unloading of artworks, visible from outside, and a main entrance hall that articulates the space between the information desk, a small café and the museum shop. The sense of fluidity and spatial continuity is repeated on the top floor, where a cafeteria opens on to a terrace that gives spectacular views of the skyscrapers inhabiting the downtown Wall Street area. Three intermediate levels house the exhibition galleries, while office and educational facilities including a library and reading room are distributed on the fifth and sixth stories. With its total floor area of approximately 5,500 square meters, the new building doubles the space previously available for exhibitions, and reinforces the museum's didactic program.

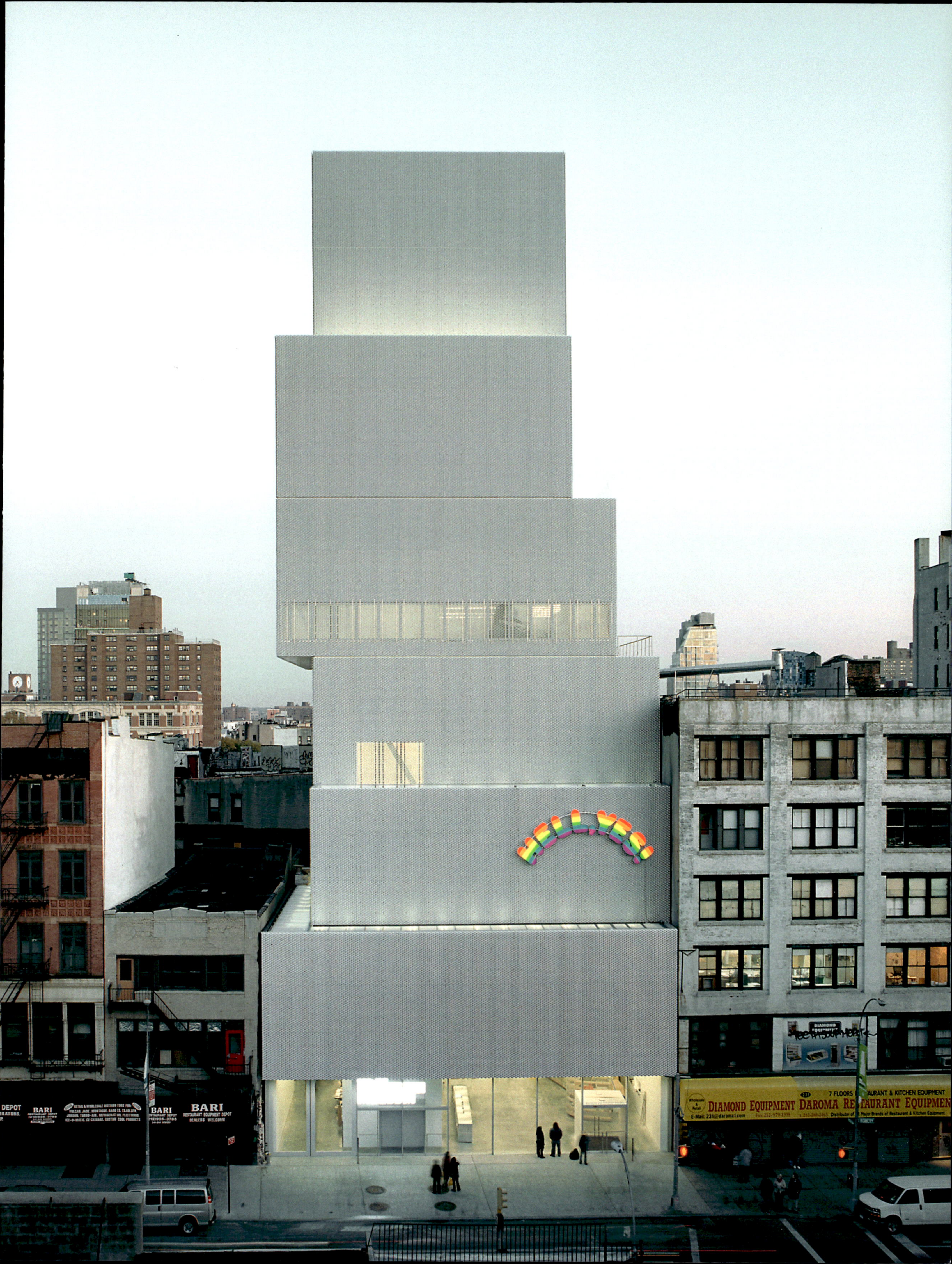

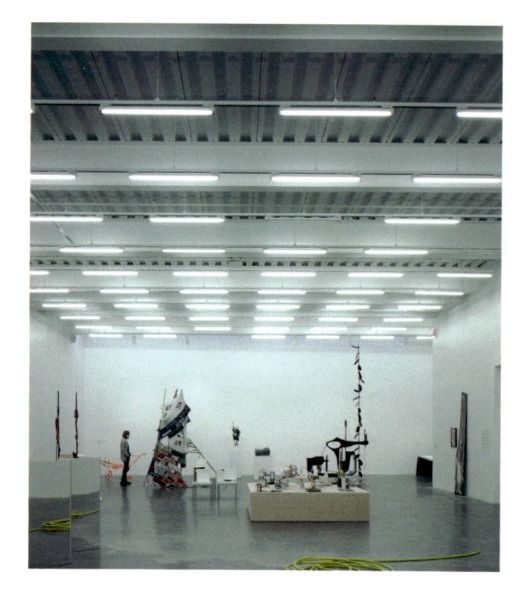

Clad with a sophisticated aluminum skin protected by a second envelope of perforated panels, a series of stacked volumes are threaded together and spatially connected by a vertical core containing the staircase and elevator shaft. Because they are not piled atop each other in a straight axis, but shifted in relation to one another, the boxes containing the exhibitions all have skylights that incorporate daylight into the interior spaces.

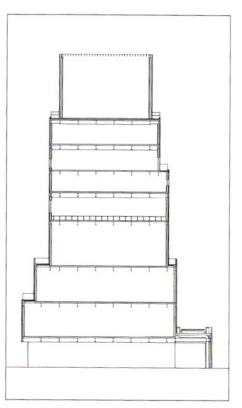

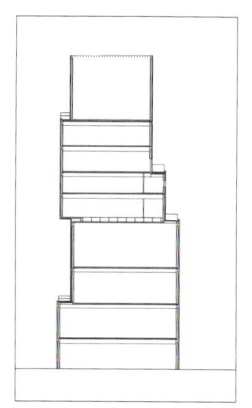

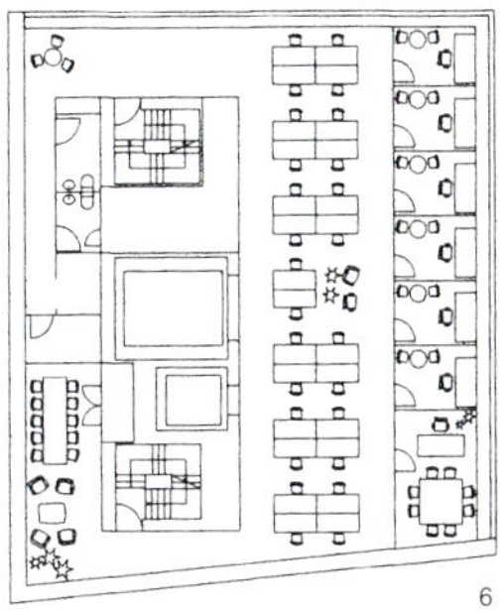
6

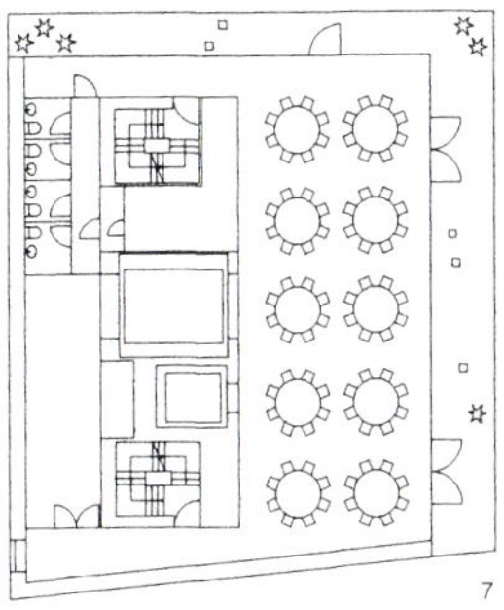
7

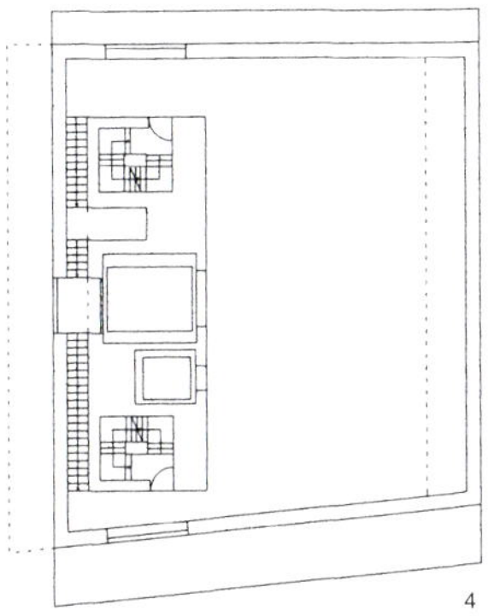
4

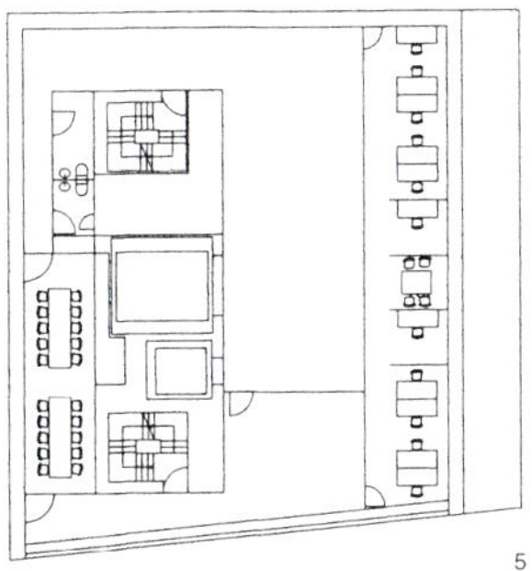
5

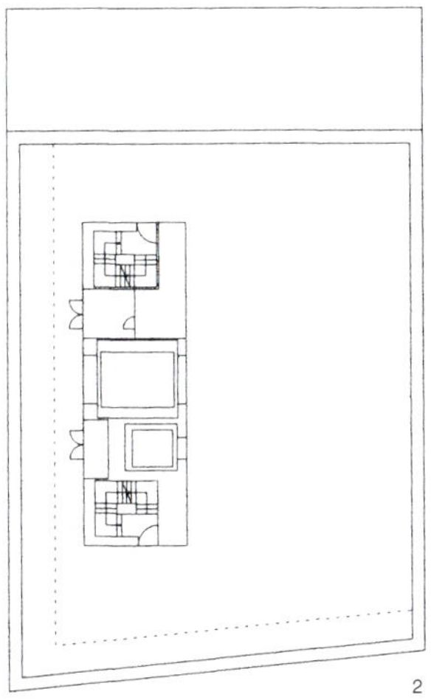
2

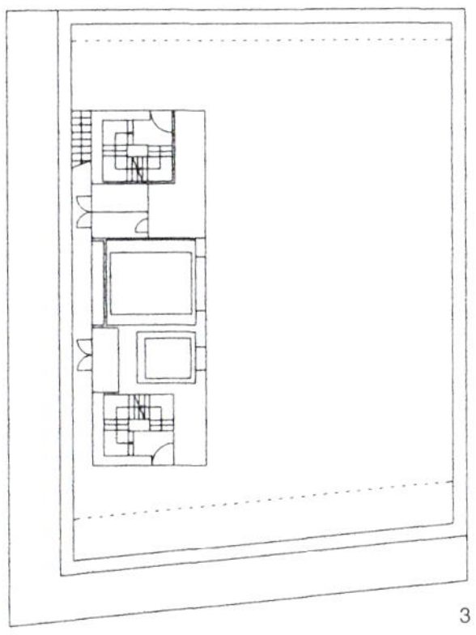
3

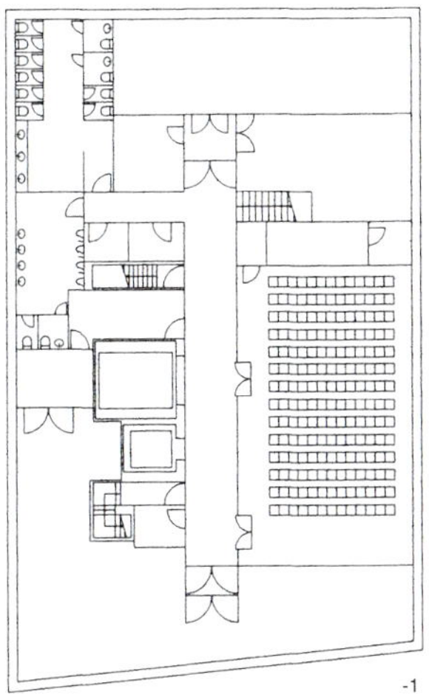
-1

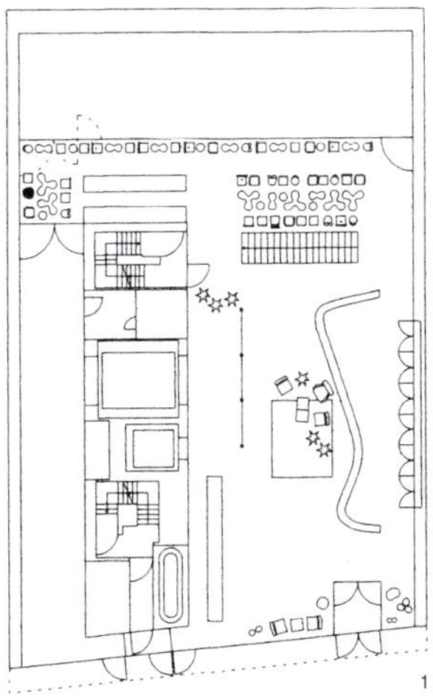
1

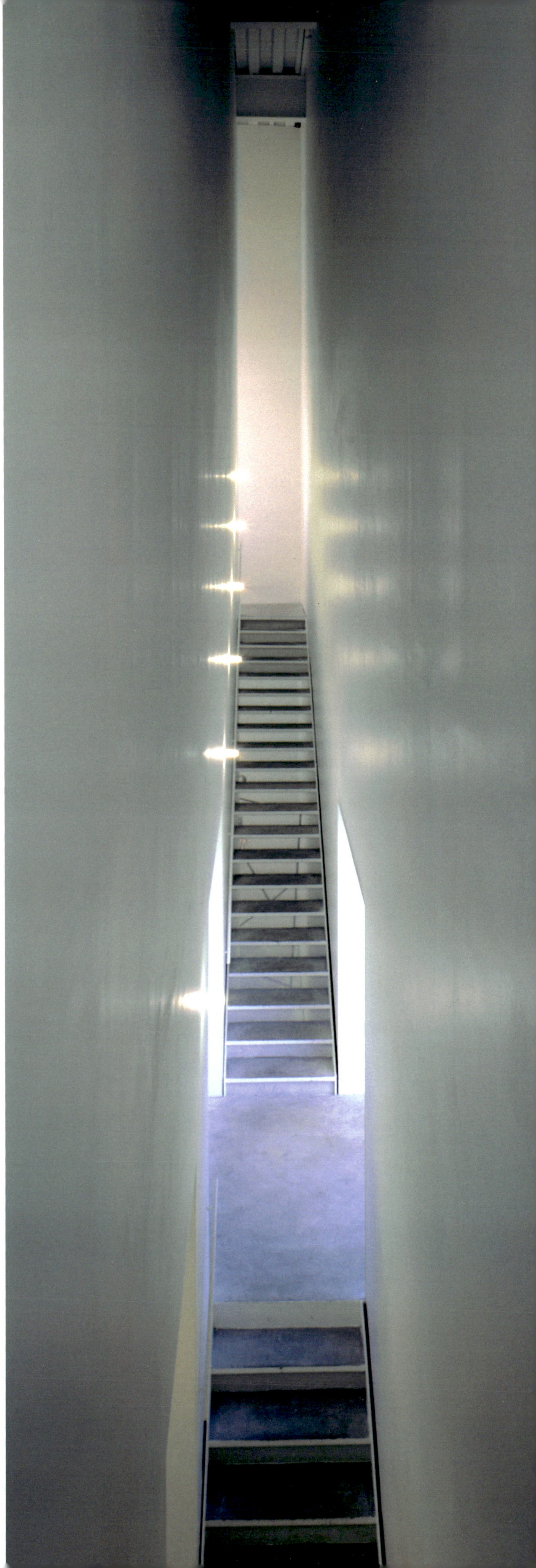

Herzog & de Meuron
Miami Art Museum
Miami, Florida (United States)

Client
Miami Art Museum, Paratus Group
Architects
Jacques Herzog, Pierre de Meuron, Christine Binswanger
Collaborators
Kentaro Ishida, Stefan Hörner, Joana Anes, Ida Richter Braendstrup, Margarida Castro, Yuko Himeno, Yuichi Kodai, Hugo Moura, Adriana Müller, Valentin Ott, Jeremy Purcell, Nils Sanderson, Masato Takahashi
Consultants
Arup (structural/mechanical engineering, lighting); Transsolar (climate engineering); Arquitectonica Geo (landscaping); Front (facade); Ada Engineering (civil engineering); Kaderabek Company (geotechnical); Maurice J. Ouellette (project manager)
Photos
Herzog & de Meuron

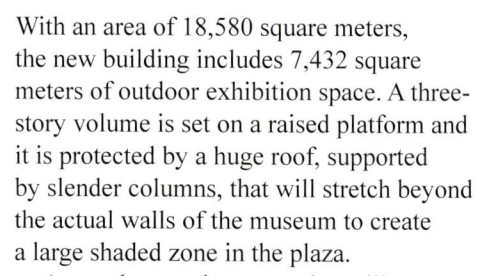

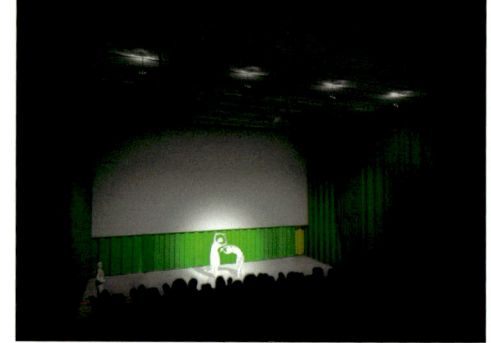

An enormous canopy supported by a sequence of slender columns protects the different volumes of the museum, amid which an outdoor sculpture garden that incorporates native plant species has been laid out.

IN AN ENDEAVOR to expand the scope of the institution and redefine its position in the world of the arts, the new premises of the Miami Art Museum will be thrice the size of the current facilities, located in the city center. The new building is going up in Bicentennial Park as part of a large-scale urban redevelopment operation that is being undertaken with the express mission of consolidating Miami as a major focus of attention in the international art scene, in accordance with a masterplan drawn up by Cooper, Robertson & Partners which knits together an entire collection of green spaces dotting the waterfront.

The MAM will stand along the north edge of the park and open on to a plaza that it will share with the Miami Science Museum, designed by the British architect Nicholas Grimshaw. The privileged location will allow it to simultaneously orient its front facade toward the bay, thereby becoming a highly visible landmark of the cityscape.

With an area of 18,580 square meters, the new building includes 7,432 square meters of outdoor exhibition space. A three-story volume is set on a raised platform and it is protected by a huge roof, supported by slender columns, that will stretch beyond the actual walls of the museum to create a large shaded zone in the plaza.

An outdoor sculpture garden will go beneath this enormous canopy, amid landscaped zones featuring native vegetation and tropical plants typical of Florida. The selection of botanical species will be based on their hardiness in terms of exposure to sun, wind and hurricanes, and the open structure of columns will use advanced horticultural techniques to make the tropical flora and the actual structure of the building blend together completely. A network of ramps and stairs will connect the different volumes of the museum to one another, creating a promenade that will stretch on to the new park by the waterfront.

The artist and botanist Patrick Blanc collaborated in the design of the garden areas underneath the perforated roof, and a series of advanced horticultural techniques were applied and adapted to integrate the tropical vegetation into the structural system of columns and platforms completely, ultimately making it possible to incorporate sustainable technologies in the air conditioning of the exhibition halls inside.

100 Atlas: America

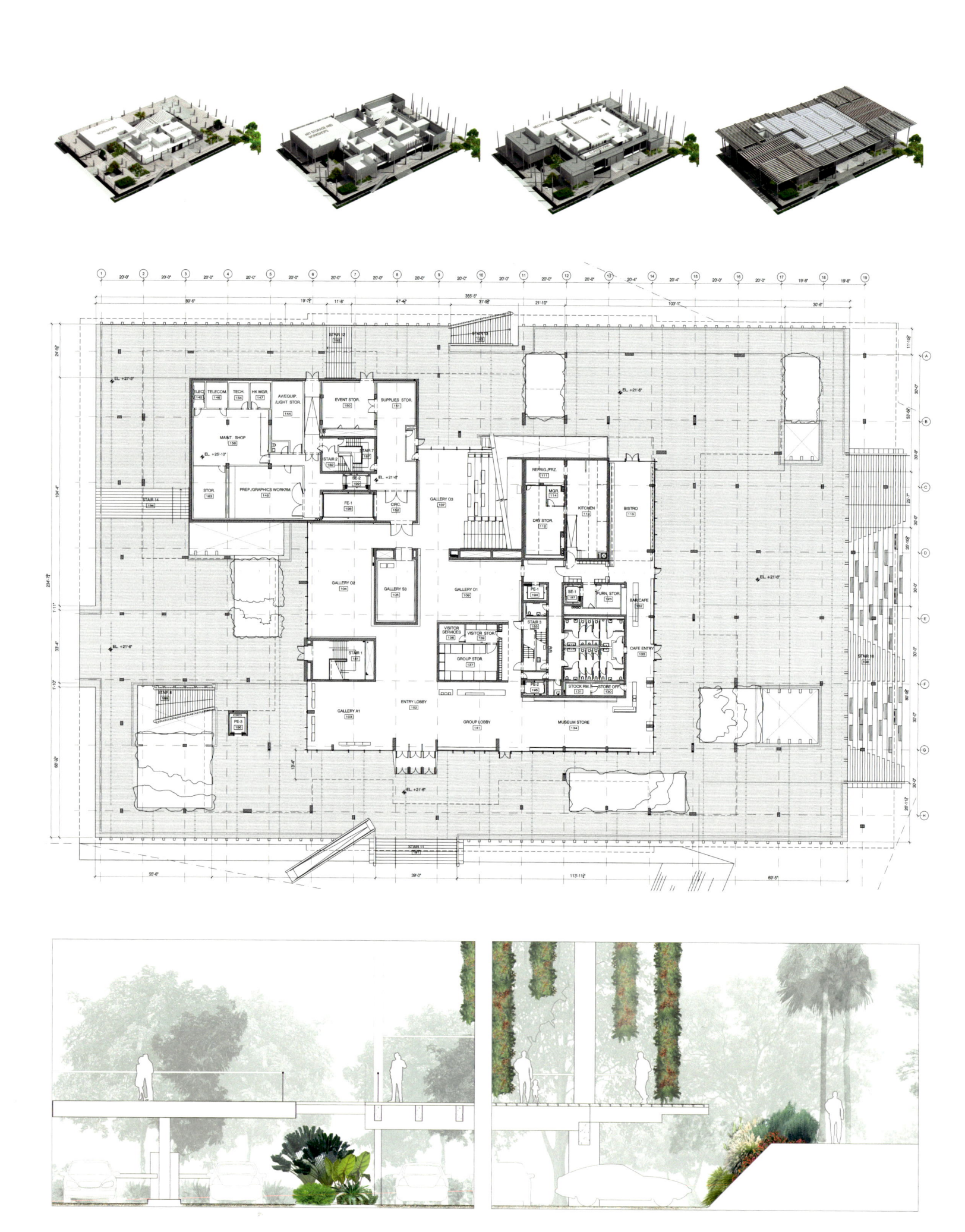

The new building has a total floor area of 18,580 square meters distributed on three levels containing the actual museum spaces and ancillary cultural facilities. The exhibition galleries, both for the permanent collection and for temporary shows, are situated on the first and second floors, while the top story contains the auditorium, the library, a range of classrooms and workshops, and administration offices and other staff rooms.

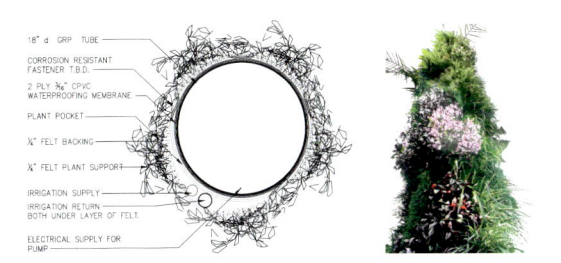

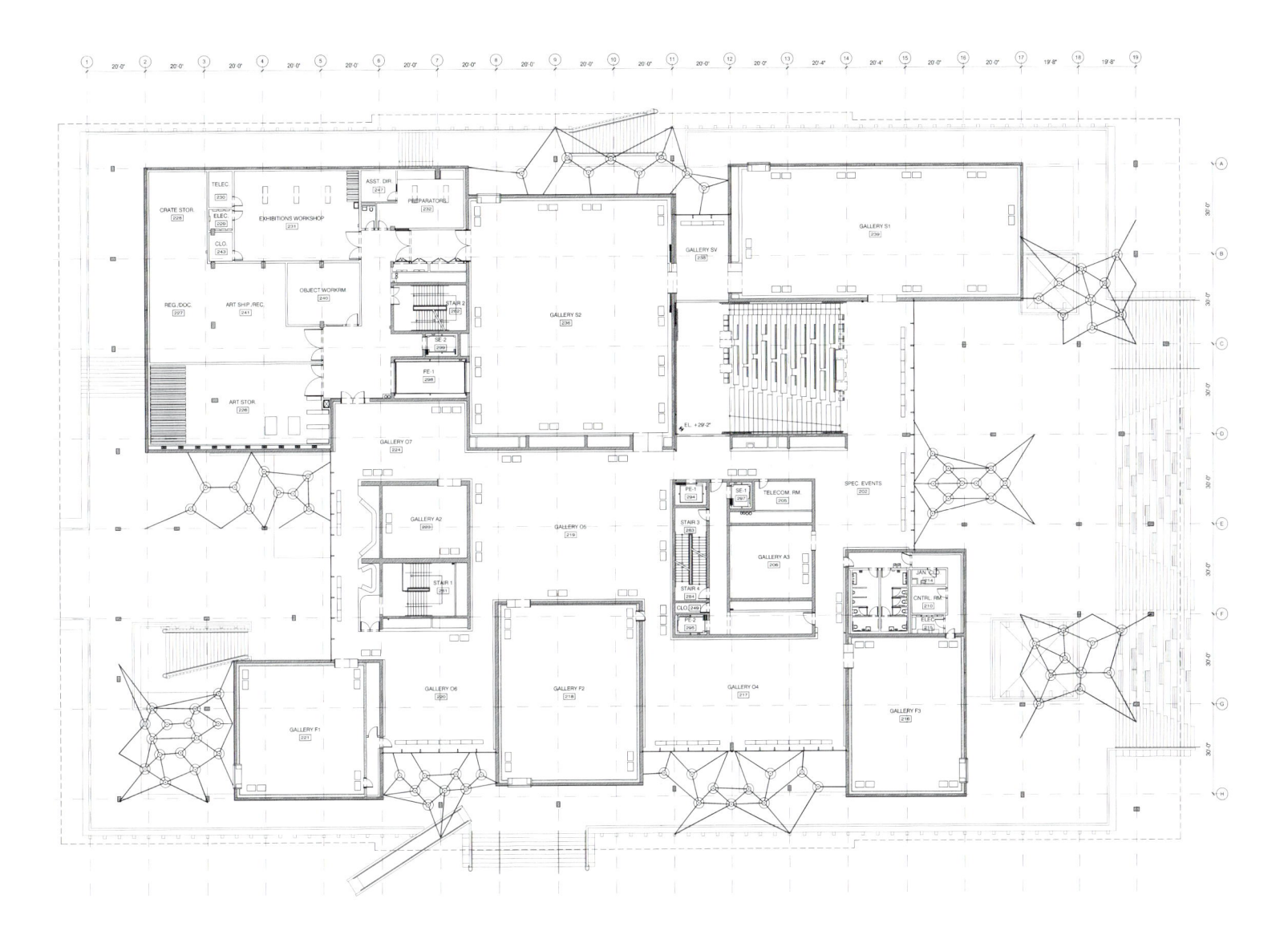

Atlas: America

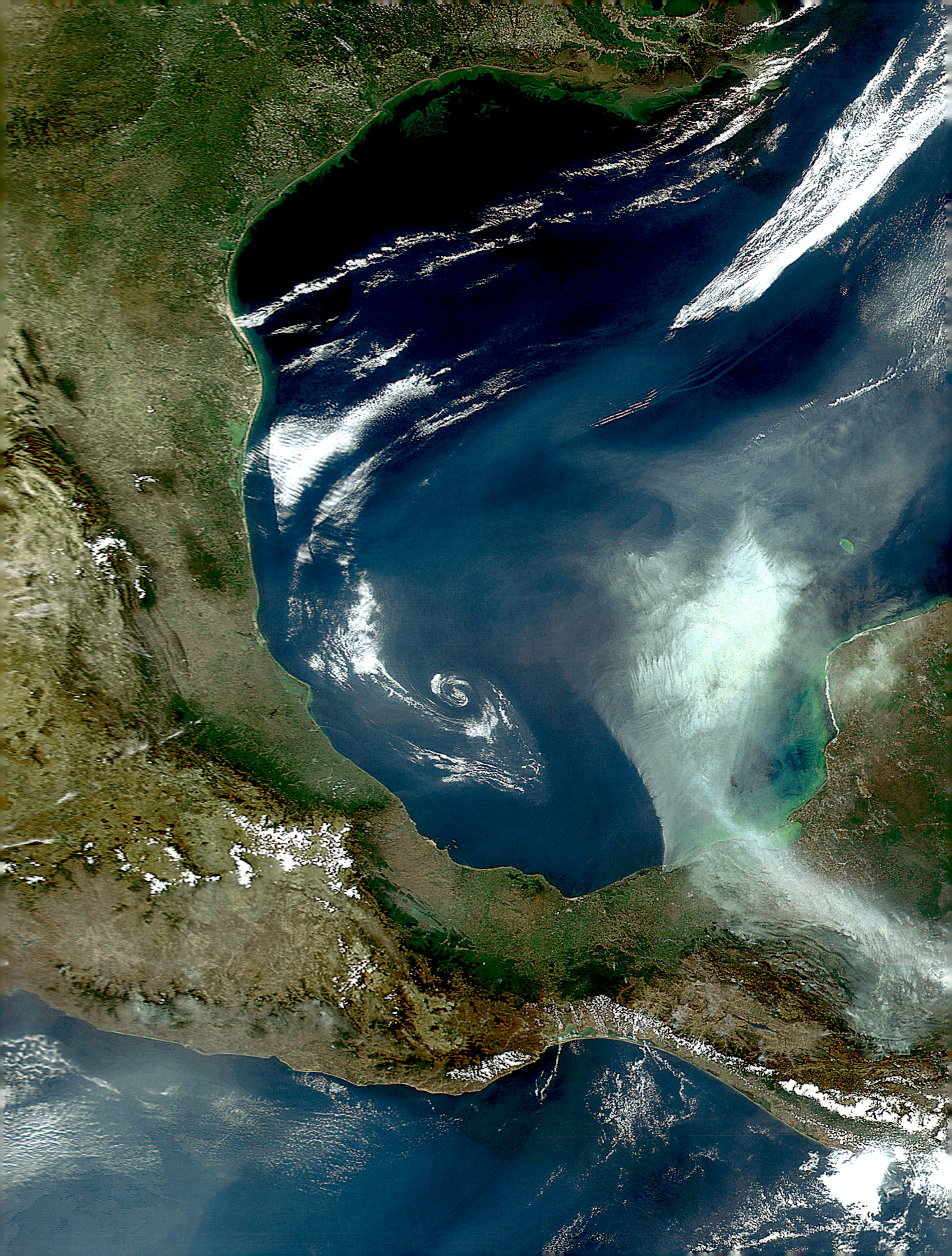

Mexico

Because of its geographical proximity to one of the world's great economic powers, Mexico is strongly influenced by the international tendencies that result from globalization. In the field of architecture, this comes through in works delivered by foreign architects, such as the Museum of Steel in Monterrey by Nicholas Grimshaw, as well as in projects carried out by members of the new generations of Mexican architects, including the Soumaya Museum in Mexico City by Fernando Romero and the new site of the Tamayo Museum in Atizapán by Michel Rojkind and the Danish office BIG. The latter two, however, share with the interventions of grand masters, represented here by the Contemporary Art Museum of Teodoro González de León, an adherence to a monumentality of the kind inherited from ancient Aztec culture, present as well in the School of Plastic Arts at Benito Juárez Autonomous University in Oaxaca, a work of Mauricio Rocha.

Louise Noelle
Persistences and Challenges
Mexico, the Weight of History

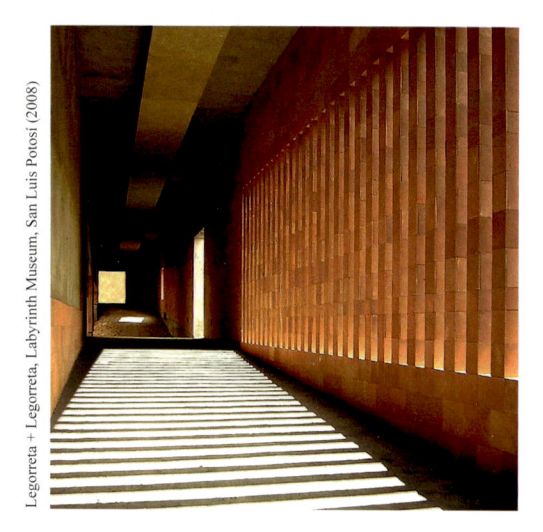

In the new interventions, the monumentality inherited from pre-Hispanic culture merges with the rationalism of the Modern Movement.

Legorreta + Legorreta, Labyrinth Museum, San Luis Potosí (2008)

To allow the natural lighting of the interior spaces as well as protect them from the harsh rays of the sun and the high temperatures, the buildings incorporate large canopies and lattices around the courtyards.

OVER THREE decades ago, the renowned art historian Jorge Alberto Manrique wrote this in a primordial article that was published in the book *El proceso de las artes:* "Mexican culture seems to be composed of successive moments, with periods of openness alternating with periods of closedness". He added, however, that none of these leanings ever gained absolute supremacy at any given time, tending instead to coexist with others. With this we have come to understand that the success of each inclination is not at all a matter of superiority, but of integration. At this particular moment in Mexico, there is a discernible preference for following and exalting international tendencies, a result of the various crises that followed one another at the end of the 20th century and the increased rate of globalization caused by economic forces and the media.

On the other hand it is important to note that the vast territory of Mexico has over the years produced a broad range of expressions, a result of both its geographic diversity and the variety of cultures that comprise it. And yet right now one could speak of a unity, a unity derived from the historic conditions behind its origins. At the close of the 15th century our territory was occupied by Mesoamerica, a region formed by ethnic groups boasting a high degree of cultural development. In the 16th century, native Americans suffered physical and moral conquest by the Spanish crown, which occupied the territory for three long centuries. The ultimate result was a nation that inevitably bore the mark of Europe and its amalgamation with local traditions: the spirit of a new world, as it were. Subsequently, at the dawn of the 19th century, New Spain gained its independence from the metropolis, not without undergoing a series of vicissitudes and problems of self-definition with regard to both its territory and its imagery. The rise of Mexico

Teodoro González de León, Contemporary Art Museum, Mexico City (2008)

The proposals that have been put forward by the new generations of Mexican architects share with the works of the great masters an adherence to the bold, monumental features of the artistic manifestations of Aztec culture, the use of color that is typical of the architecture built during the colonial period, the innovative spirit of the Modern Movement, and the functional refinement that is important in International Style.

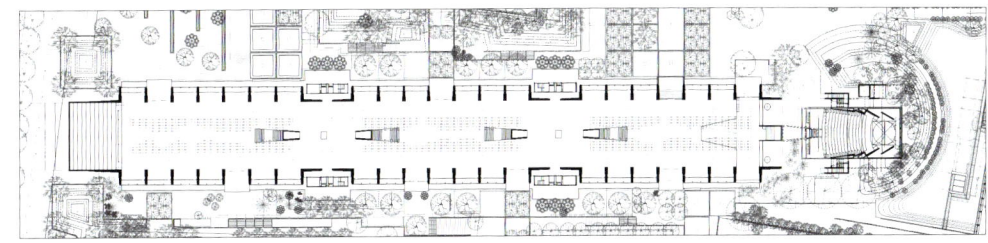

Alberto Kalach, Vasconcelos Library, Mexico City (2006)

as a country rich in artistic and cultural expressions was manifested in fields like literature, the fine arts, and in the last quarter-century, also architecture.

With these premises, the start of the 20th century forms the base upon which current contributions in architectural material rest. At the birth of the previous century, the appearance of new building systems and materials, accompanied by a series of theoretical proposals that were non-conformist, allowed the construction of important buildings, and with these, the changes that were just beginning to take shape. With the onset of the diverse movements that gave form to the modern movement – or functionalism, as it was then called –, the figure of Le Corbusier played a preponderant role in Mexico, as everywhere in Latin America. In a way, through the period's leading publications, the continued dependence of our young countries kept professionals abreast of the European and North American avant-gardes and advances. But various circumstances made the ideas of the Swiss master a greater presence. Architects like Mario Pani, a graduate of the School of Fine Arts in Paris, or Enrique del Moral and Luis Barragán, who traveled to the 'City of Lights' on finishing their studies, gained firsthand knowledge of his provocative precepts. To be sure, though they offer local variants, their interest in the theme of mass housing was inspired by Corbusian projects.

Another important theme in relation to architecture of the heroic years is the analytical and theoretical thinking that developed around the new tendencies. It was the presence of these architects in university classrooms, along with their writings, that formed the foundations of a school of thought that, while being inspired by texts of 19th-century theorists including Leonce Reynaud, Eugène-Emmanuel Viollet-le-Duc and Julien Guadet, would eventually find local expression. First of all we can mention José Villagrán García and his 'theory of architecture', the innovative principles of which, combined with his professional practice, have earned him the title of 'father of contemporary Mexican architecture'. But it is also important to remember the proposals of professionals like Jesús T. Acevedo, Federico Mariscal, Guillermo Zarraga, Juan O'Gorman, Enrique del Moral and Alberto T. Arai.

In the mid-20th century, Mexico saw an unlimited triumph of the so-called International Style, with advances in building materials and technologies giving rise to buildings inspired by the precepts put forward by Mies van der Rohe. Architects like Augusto H. Álvarez and Juan Sordo Madaleno set off on this road, one where technological concerns were as important as the purity of the results. During this same period, and parallel to this road, other tendencies appeared that presented alternative postures. This is the case of the collaborations between architects and muralists in search of arts integration. At the same time, as a consequence of the Spanish Civil War and World War II, Mexico saw the arrival of qualified European professionals who would open up further paths of creativity, among them Félix Candela, the precursor of innovative light concrete structures and author of lucid texts like *Toward a New Philosophy of Structures*. Another figure was Mathias Goeritz, who would have an important presence in university classrooms and write texts as determinant as *The Manifesto of Emotional Architecture*. Goeritz's importance was enhanced by his connection to the renowned master Luis Barragán, author of innovative architectural proposals.

This brings us to the subject of the University City of the UNAM (1950-1952), which was declared a UNESCO World Heritage site. With the planning carried out by Enrique del Moral and Mario Pani,

Alberto Kalach, Vasconcelos Library, Mexico City (2006)

Atlas: America 105

Using massive, heavy self-supporting walls of stone and enclosures executed with blocks of recycled rammed earth, the new cultural edifices that seek to preserve traditional construction methods and systems strike a marked contrast with those that choose to utilize novel technologies, characterized by light structures of steel wrapped with claddings of brightly colored corrugated metal sheets.

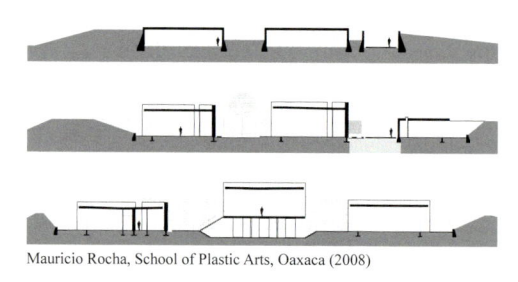

Mauricio Rocha, School of Plastic Arts, Oaxaca (2008)

in collaboration with over fifty architects, it found its place in the cusp of 20th-century Mexican architecture, as much for the quality of the design and construction as for its agglutination of the principal tendencies of the time. Also worthy of mention is Latin America's contribution to landscaping, exemplified by works like Roberto Burle Marx's works in Brazil and Luis Barragán's original urban development of El Pedregal, in Mexico.

Two decades later, with International Style in decline, a series of proposals materialized by a new generation of architects took shape. On one hand is the bold monumental gesture of Abraham Zabludovsky and Teodoro González de León, leaders of a large group of professionals. A smaller group is formed by the formalist architects, with Agustín Hernández and Manuel González Rul playing a dominant role. And perhaps the largest contingent is that which subscribed to the proposals of Luis Barragán and Enrique del Moral, as well as to the ones of those we have come to call regionalists, led by Ricardo Legorreta, Carlos Mijares and Antonio Attolini. Finally, a group of young architects has sought to emulate the novel approaches being put forward beyond our borders, managing to place themselves in the international scene.

The presence of these groups and their ventures in the architectural world persisted at the start of the new millennium, but new proposals sprung up, enriching the scene with novel postures that could be risky and unexpected. The diverse proposals sought to solve the enormous problems that still plagued Mexico in the areas of social architecture, housing, education and health, while trying to offer specific solutions for different public and private initiatives.

New Residential Alternatives

Perhaps one of the principal problems afflicting Latin America is the lack of proper housing for the majority. For this reason, since the early 20th century there has been sustained interest in providing dwellings to citizens belonging to the lowest economic rungs. In recent times the range of architectural proposals has broadened, and so has the financial rank of the users. If we study the latest operations, we can see that architects are attentive to urban insertion aspects and form, but without forgetting cultural and geographic context. Hence they are able to come up with buildings that address local demands.

We should mention proposals like those drawn up by the studio Taller de Arquitectura X, headed by Alberto Kalach, where spaces of the city are recomposed, or those of the firm Higuera & Sánchez, with a good number of apartment buildings carried out in the capital. In turn the studio Serrano & Monjarraz address the demands of new generations through residential developments like Puerta Alameda (2009), which offers lifestyle alternatives in the center of Mexico City by incorporating a wide range of commercial services situated at the ground level. Another young team that is working towards this novel approach in designing and developing residential buildings is the firm of Migdal Arquitectos, which is run by Jaime Varon, Alex Metta and Abraham Metta.

The past few decades have also seen a number of architects pursuing an interest in renovating existing buildings in different parts of the city, particularly in marginal neighborhoods. Operations of this kind have been much present in the capital since the earthquake of 1985, thanks to the Popular Housing Renovation program, in which numerous professionals have participated. To this we add the generous and innovative works of Carlos González Lobo and María Eugenia Hurtado in diverse communities throughout the country as well as beyond, in places as far away as Nuakchot, capital of Mauritania.

In this sense it is possible to address here a genre that has had a great capacity to combine concepts and been a champion of avant-garde ideas, particularly in Mexico but also on a global scale: domestic architecture. The production of dwellings for citizens of all social strata is immense, making it difficult to properly appraise in this study. Picking out a few recognized names is likely to be an act of injustice towards those not mentioned, but it is a risk to take. Richness of composition and freedom of design characterize most examples, with traditional materials perfectly combining with novel forms and occasionally arriving at a simplicity bordering on asceticism. In other projects, more importance is given to the matter of adapting to both the geographic environment and the climate, putting forward a congruence of conditions that ultimately aims for the well-being of the user. All these examples are clearly of a contemporary cut, of the kind occasionally influenced by lessons derived from popular wisdom, but always in line with the desire

Mauricio Rocha, School of Plastic Arts, Oaxaca (2008)

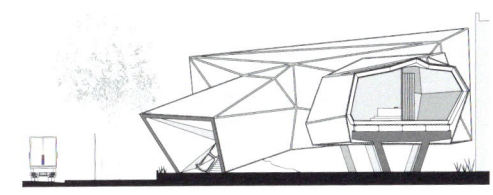

Michel Rojkind, Chocolate Museum, Toluca (2007)

to satisfy the user both aesthetically and functionally, in an emphatic gesture that seeks to draw the attention of the high-tech world to a theme that is fundamental in developing countries.

While architects of renown like Ricardo Legorreta, Antonio Attolini and José de Yturbe have continued to travel the path of 'emotional architecture', others like Carlos Mijares and Pablo Quintero have opted for a return to the rationality of brick constructions. As for Bernardo Gómez Pimienta, Gonzalo Gómez Palacio, Isaac Broid, Arcadio Artis, Gutiérrez Arquitectos, Lucio Muniain and Jorge Covarrubias with Benjamín González, they all present an architecture that is refined and functional. Then there are the place-specific approaches like those being put forward in cities like Guadalajara, where Ricardo Agraz and Juan Ignacio Castiello work; Mérida, where Augusto Quijano stands out; or Monterrey, featuring the likes of Ricardo Padilla, Jorge Estévez and Alejandro Penoir. In this latter category we can also mention Diego Villaseñor and the vacation houses he has built in different spots along the coast.

Cultural and Educational Facilities
A sector that has recently seen significant endowments is education, with libraries and institutions of higher learning going up in regular succession. Here we can observe a certain continuity with the paradigmatic university complexes that sprung up during the mid-20th century, and there are outstanding interventions in these same campuses. Worthy of mention because of their creativity are architects like Francisco Serrano, with the Ibero-American University, where he has been adding buildings for the past twenty years, and Agustín Hernández, with the Autonomous University of the State of Mexico in Toluca (2006), while Fernando González Gortázar has designed spaces of great visual quality and lure at the Los Altos University Center in Tepatitlán (2003).

The case of Legorreta & Legorreta is of special interest because the practice has intervened in institutional centers of higher learning in Mexico City and Monterrey, but also abroad. Prominent here are the Visual Arts Center in Santa Fe, New Mexico and the buildings for Stanford University in California and the University of Chicago, for the American University in Cairo, and for the Texas A&M Engineering College (2007) and the College of Business and Computer Science (2008), both located in the capital of Qatar. Conceived as institutions of higher learning that seek to preserve local culture, the buildings are rendered in architectural languages that are adapted to the particular parts of the world they are located in, using certain traditional elements, including patios, to stimulate and foster communications and exchange between students.

Two new art schools have gone up in the past years, one in Oaxaca and the other in León. The former, built by Mauricio Rocha in 2008, is outstanding for the careful way it is blended into the place and for its use of an innovative building technique using rammed earth taken from the actual site.

Michel Rojkind, Chocolate Museum, Toluca (2007)

Like the projects for single-family private houses, the large-scale public buildings that address complex programs endeavor to connect with the existing landscape through simple mechanisms, such as taking advantage of inclinations in the terrain to build platforms of stone extracted from the actual site, over which plain volumes of prismatic shape are then built with a wide variety of traditional materials.

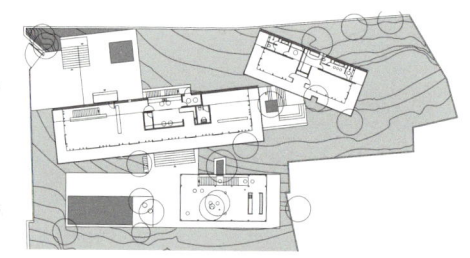

House in the Forest, Valle de Bravo (2010)

The latter, completed in the year 2005, is the result of the architects Augusto Quijano, Jorge Carlos Soreda and Javier Muñoz Menéndez working together to design a complex of great conceptual clarity and proven functionality. For his part, Gonzalo Gómez Palacio carried out the National School of Conservation, Restoration and Museography of the INAH (National Institute of Anthropology and History) in 2003, where the brick construction painstakingly addresses the specific requirements of educational centers of this kind. It would likewise be of interest to mention some complementary examples, such as the controversial, audacious Vasconcelos Library in Mexico City (2004-2006), a work of Alberto Kalach, as well as the project for the Public Library of Jalisco (2005), by the architects Sara Topelson, José Grinberg, Francisco López Guerra and Antonio Toca.

Parallel to this, in relation to culture and leisure, we can affirm that museums have been the protagonists in the last quarter-century, not only in Mexico but worldwide. At home, since the building in 1964 of the paradigmatic National Museum of Anthropology by Pedro Ramírez Vázquez, Carlos Campuzano and Rafael Mijares, the rate of creation of exhibition spaces has increased exponentially. The past years have seen the completion of a good number of specialized museums that not only address museographic requirements, but also provide facilities demanded by the public, from interactive spaces to bookstores and gift shops. The buildings are designed for all kinds of programs, from traditional museums that cover the arts and the sciences to those conceived for children or those planned around archaeological digs. Standing out are the impressive sculptural forms that Fernando González Gortázar designed for the Museum of the Mayan People in

Covarrubias & González, House in the Forest, Valle de Bravo (2010)

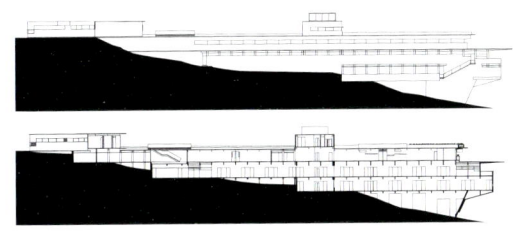

Faculty of Veterinary Medicine, Querétaro (2008)

Isaac Broid, Faculty of Veterinary Medicine, Querétaro (2008)

Yucatán, on the Dzibichaltun site, conceived as a tribute to prehistoric cultures.

As for spaces thought out for children, on one hand is the exuberance of forms proposed by Abraham Zabludovsky in the Papagayo Children's Museum (2005), located in Villahermosa. On the other hand is the singular language developed by Legorreta & Legorreta in the Labyrinth of Sciences and Arts Museum (2008), in San Luis Potosí. Both works are characterized by a large tower and rooms surrounding a large patio. Among proposals for art we must mention the project drawn up by the Mexican Michel Rojkind, in collaboration with the Danish studio BIG, for the enlargement of the Tamayo Museum in Atizapán, besides Teodoro González de León's Contemporary Art Museum, an unhesitating intervention in the cultural zone of the National Autonomous University of Mexico (UNAM).

Two museums related to the theme of science and technology opened in 2007. The Chocolate Museum, built by Michel Rojkind beside a Nestlé plant, is notable for its contrast between the sober interior and the provocative exterior, with stunning volumes designed as a welcome to the factory premises. The second, a work of Nicholas Grimshaw, sprung from the desire to preserve the preeminence of Blast Furnace #3 at the Museum of Steel in Monterrey: the museographic space is practically entirely buried underground. Indeed, most of these highly unique buildings implant themselves on the environment without assaulting it, offering instead the very best of the creativity of the architects and museographists involved. Some are inserted between preexisting constructions, forcing the architects to show their capacity to adapt, a quality that is increasingly important in reusing buildings that to a greater or lesser extent form part of a country's historic heritage.

A third area that has always been a concern of Mexican architects is the health care building. Here we come upon a series of recognized hospitals built by the office of Enrique Duarte Aznar in the Yucatán peninsula, including the State Center of Oncology in Campeche (2009), which shows a desire to create pleasant spaces for patients without impairing the primary functions of a specialized medical center.

We can analogously refer to other cases falling under the same theme. On one hand we find the National Laboratory of Genomics for Biodiversity (2009) by Enrique Norten's studio TEN Arquitectos, which is part of a group of facilities serving the field of agricultural research and is characterized by at once powerful and simple volumes that blend nicely with the surrounding nature. In a way this is what Isaac Broid achieves in the UNAM Faculty of Veterinary Medicine and Animal Husbandry (2008), in Rancho Tequisquiapan, whose deep red volume acting as a mirador towards views of the valley won the Gold Medal of the Biennial of Mexican Architecture. In turn Foster & Partners, in collaboration with Mario Schjetnan's Grupo de Diseño Urbano, has drawn up the masterplan for the City of Knowledge Biometropolis Campus, inserted in a 25-hectare protected area reserved for hospitals and study centers mixed with offices, homes and shops.

Government Buildings
Architecture has also been regularly asserting itself in other genres, such as government buildings, where official intentions have been teaming up with private proposals. We have to consider that these buildings have choice locations in the urban scheme, and that in appearance they express the dignity of the institutions that they house. Topping the list is the Senate building, currently under construction on the Paseo de la Reforma, the capital's main artery, in

A strong influence of modern functionalism rings in the public buildings, whose sober compositions of austere concise forms allow a rational distribution of different functions in straightforward prisms. Executed with exposed reinforced concrete or with metal enclosures, the interior spaces of these constructions are naturally illuminated by means of light shafts and a series of perforations made on the horizontal slabs.

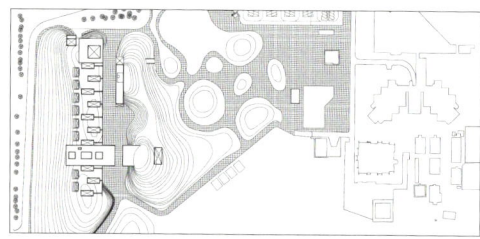

TEN Arquitectos, National Laboratory of Genomics, Monterrey (2009)

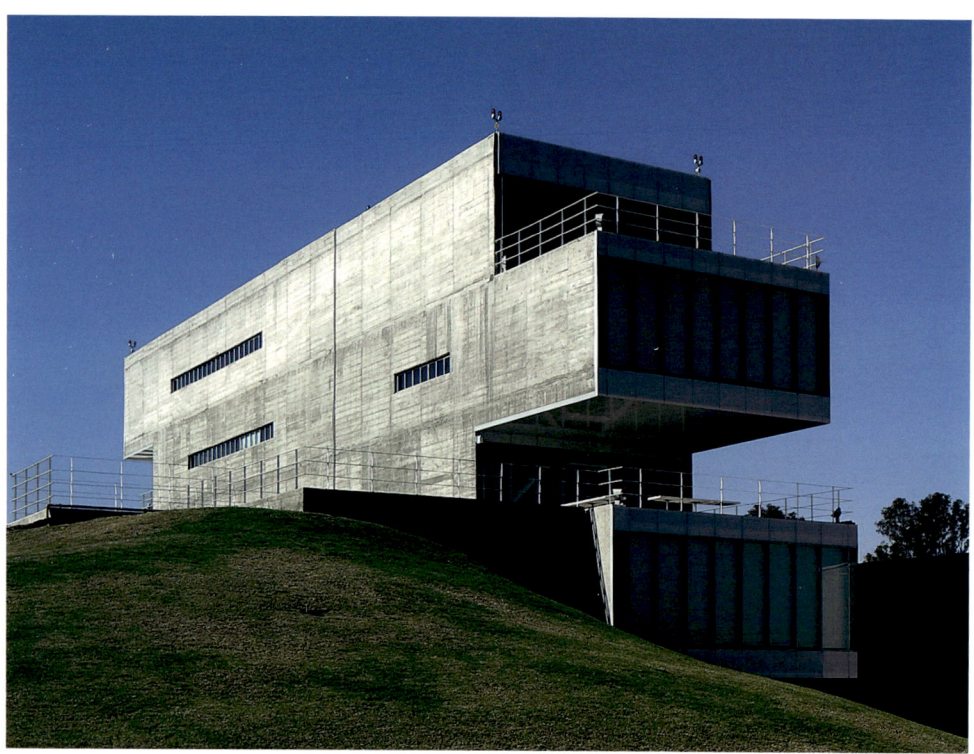

TEN Arquitectos, National Laboratory of Genomics, Monterrey (2009)

accordance with Javier Muñoz Menéndez's winning entry to the competition that was organized for the purpose. Another prominent work is Terminal 2 at the airport of Mexico City (2007), by Juan Francisco Serrano and his studio Serrano Arquitectos. Rendered with exposed white concrete and with circular perforations, its priority objective is to create the conditions for natural lighting and air conditioning. Known for its complexity is the Ciudad Azteca Multimodal Transit Station in the metropolitan area of Mexico City, a work carried out by CC Arquitectos under the leadership of Manuel Cervantes Céspedes. Here, besides the platforms and other elements that serve the different transport systems converging in the station, besides the complementary commercial, banking and other services, special attention went to the movement of passengers.

The building of three Mexican embassies in the past decade reflects the growing importance of the country's diplomatic presence abroad. Built by Teodoro González de León in conjunction with Francisco Serrano, the one in Berlin stands out with its facade of vertical elements that protects a foyer designed like a patio. The powerful language of both architects and the use of exposed white concrete are repeated in the embassies they built in Belmopan (Belize) and Guatemala City.

On a smaller scale but nevertheless of singular importance is the Ave Fénix Fire Station (2005), a work of Bernardo Gómez and AT.103 where functionality is on a par with the sober elegance of the design. Finally we can mention the Sailing School of La Paz (2007), by Sánchez Arquitectos, which was tackled as a repeatable prototype for future schools in Lower California. The multipurpose building's lightness and transparency reconciles its program with the federal government's desire to pep up the economy of the zone.

In the interest of benefiting the population at large, urban development has also had a place among the actions being carried out by various state organisms. A very significant action involved the state government of Nuevo León's efforts to turn the urban area previously occupied by the iron and steel company Fundidora Monterrey into Fundidora Park, which now features museums, movie houses and other cultural venues. Moreover, thanks to the state government's public works ministry and Abel Guerra Garza's coordination of architecture and landscape design, the Paseo Santa Lucía was created, connecting the park to the city center through a pedestrian street and a navigable canal.

As a corollary of public works we need to mention the national competition that has been held this year, 2010, in commemoration of the bicentenary of independence and the centenary of the Mexican Revolution. The competition to which 37 recognized professionals were invited called for blueprints for an arch that would be a monument to the start of the national independence movement. The winning project of 22 young Mexican architects led by César Pérez Becerril, named 'Trail of Light', is a slender vertical structure now under construction on the Paseo de la Reforma of the Mexican capital.

Private Initiatives
Most buildings resulting from private initiative address the demand for commercial spaces, offices and a whole range of mixed-use complexes. Every now and then a building of this kind seeks to flee from the everyday banality that favors pure consumerism, and it is often possible to save it from such a fate and integrate it into the life of the population. A case in point is the Arcos Bosques complex, by Teodoro González de León in conjunction with Francisco Serrano and Carlos Tejeda, and the Reforma 222 tower, also by González

Serrano Arquitectos, Terminal 2 at Mexico City Airport (2007)

de León, where apartments and offices combine with movie houses and a shopping center. Among recent examples it is important to mention office projects like the Cemex Building (2004) in Monterrey, by Landa García Landa Arquitectos, and the Tres Picos Building (2009), by Benjamín Romano, which offers an interesting technical solution to the problem of building on small lots. In turn, while the Explanada Studio (2008) of Tatiana Bilbao in collaboration with Francisco Pardo and Julio Amescua is a model for an art gallery located in a purely residential neighborhood, Felipe Leal's Puma store and Trophy Room in the Football Club of the UNAM (2004) is a compact intervention of clear minimalist character. Finally, a rather exceptional initiative is Technopark (2009), a high-tech corporate complex where Grupo de Diseño Urbano, under the leadership of Mario Schjetnan, took charge of landscaping and of the designing of squares, gardens, parking lots and a building serving to mark the entrance into the premises.

Hotels can be classified under buildings that depend on private investment. Tourist complexes are located in the nerve centers of the main economic capitals and are created to address a business demand for rooms to spend the night in and a variety of meeting venues, but they can also be seaside rest places. Surrounded by the reality of the large hotel chains that raise the same sort of buildings throughout the world, we find exceptions especially gratifying and memorable, such as the Four Seasons (2000) of Diego Villaseñor at Punta de Mita, Nayarit, or the recycled factory spaces of La Purificadora (2007) in Puebla, by Legorreta & Legorreta and Serrano Monjarraz Arquitectos. José Luis Ezquerra's nostalgic proposals have led him from Mexico's Pacific coasts to Morocco, where he finished the Shkirat Hotel-Club in 2005. And, as a final note, we should mention renovations, an area that seeks to safeguard built memory and which deserves mention for the quality of the proposals that have been drawn up by professionals dedicated to restoring and preserving our heritage.

References to the importance of Mexican architecture have been made in the past years, whether in connection to the work of certain architects or as a result of distinctions that their buildings and projects have reaped. It is evident that Mexico has been gaining international recognition, although a good number of the works awarded are by architects born during the first half of the 20th century, practicing in their years of lucid maturity.

But recent years have seen a group of young architects beginning their careers, confronting the difficult challenge of having to compete with consolidated veteran figures. This is a new generation, the seed that will bear fruit by facing the challenges of the new millennium. It is also safe to say that this country has in the past decade stood out for well-directed development which has yielded easily recognizable results in the field of architecture. Coexisting with these tendencies, which to a greater or lesser extent are linked to regional budgets, is a clear desire to find a differentiated expression through the inspiration of international avant-gardes.

We also have to appreciate how some Mexican professionals are more interested in finding solutions to specific problems than they are in coming up with plastic or aesthetic results, without this necessarily working against quality and beauty. Their primary interests are centered on fields like housing, health, culture and education, and they are always attentive to aspects of urban insertion in a certain socio-cultural context. Hence, at the dawn of the 21st century, it cannot be denied that Mexico is home to a well-nourished crop of architects who are committed to their profession as well as to the times it has been their lot to live.

Bernardo Gómez Pimienta & AT.103, Ave Fénix Fire Station, Mexico City (2005)

Teodoro González de León
Contemporary Art Museum
Mexico City (Mexico)

Client
National Autonomous University of Mexico
Architect
Teodoro González de Léon
Collaborator
Antonio Rodríguez
Consultants
Diseño y supervisión (structural design); Diseños Eléctricos Complejos (electrical installations); Garza Maldonado (plumbing installations); Ingeniería en Aire y Control (air conditioning); Lighteam (lighting); Saad acústica (acoustics); Entorno (landscaping)
Contractor
Ingenieros Civiles Asociados
Photos
Pedro Hiriart, Jorge del Olmo (p. 113), Fernanda Canales (p. 114)

Within the campus of the National Autonomous University, located in the Mexican capital, rise the prismatic concrete volumes that contain the exhibition galleries of the new museum of contemporary art.

LOCATED WITHIN the campus of the National Autonomous University of Mexico, in the capital, the new Contemporary Art Museum completes the cultural complex that constituted the second phase of the University City. Contained inside a circular enclosure are some white concrete volumes of prismatic shape that are arranged along a north-south axis. To the side of a new square, a facade that slants at a 45° angle presents a portico that welcomes one into the concert hall and the theaters of the cultural center. The entrance hall is conceived as a double-height space that traverses the building and connects the square to the National Library to the north of the complex.

The museum is organized in just two levels. The exhibition spaces take up the upper floor – situated at the same level as the square –, along with the reception area, a store and the educational area. Fourteen galleries are grouped in four sections that function as independent zones, connected to one another by three inner streets and lit by large skylights equipped with an ingenious system of inclined planes that can be regulated to control illumination. Three interior courtyards and two spatious terraces ventilate the rooms naturally. The design of the halls is based on a 12 meter module with dimensions that change with the height of the space, which varies between 6, 9 and 12 meters. The four halls placed along the main facade open out to the public plaza, which also serves as additional exhibition space.

The lower level, partly carved into the volcanic rock of the place, contains the media library, a conference room, an auditorium with seating capacity for an audience of about three hundred people, the cafetería, the restaurant, administration offices, storage for the collections of the museum, halls for temporary exhibitions, and the area for the restoration of art works.

112 Atlas: America

Situated to one side of a square set in the middle of the university campus, the principal facade of the building slants inward at a 45º angle to form a grand glazed portico welcoming the visitor into the concert hall and the various theaters included in the cultural center. The entrance hall is conceived as a double-height space that traverses the entire building and connects the plaza to the National Library towards the north of the complex.

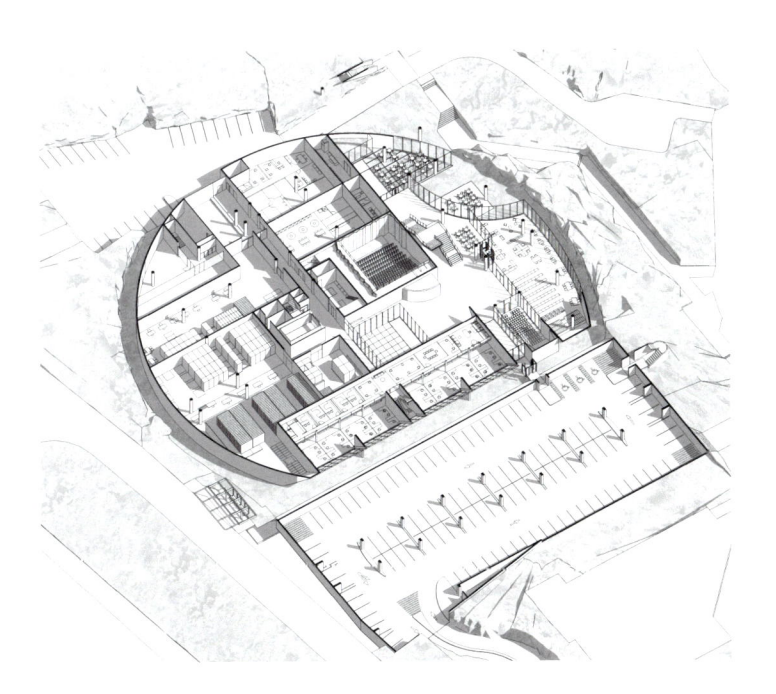

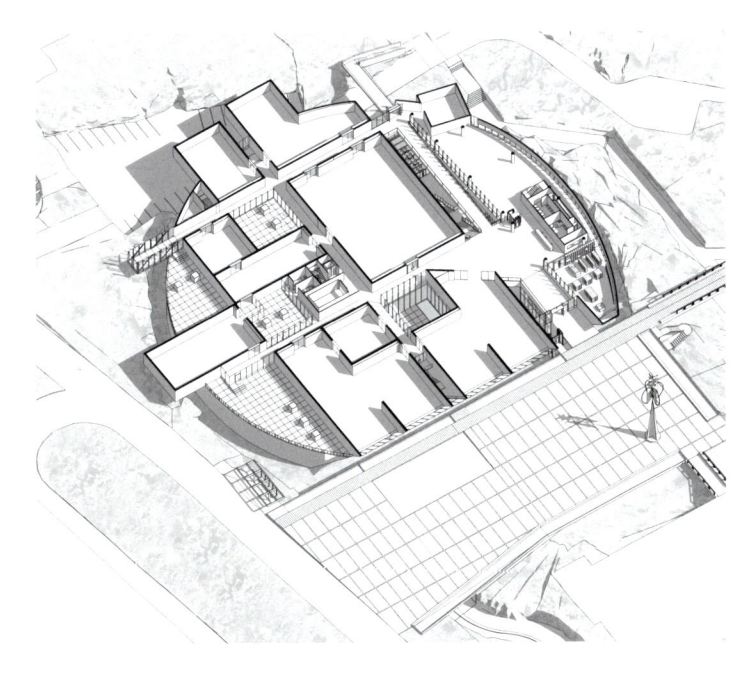

114 Atlas: America

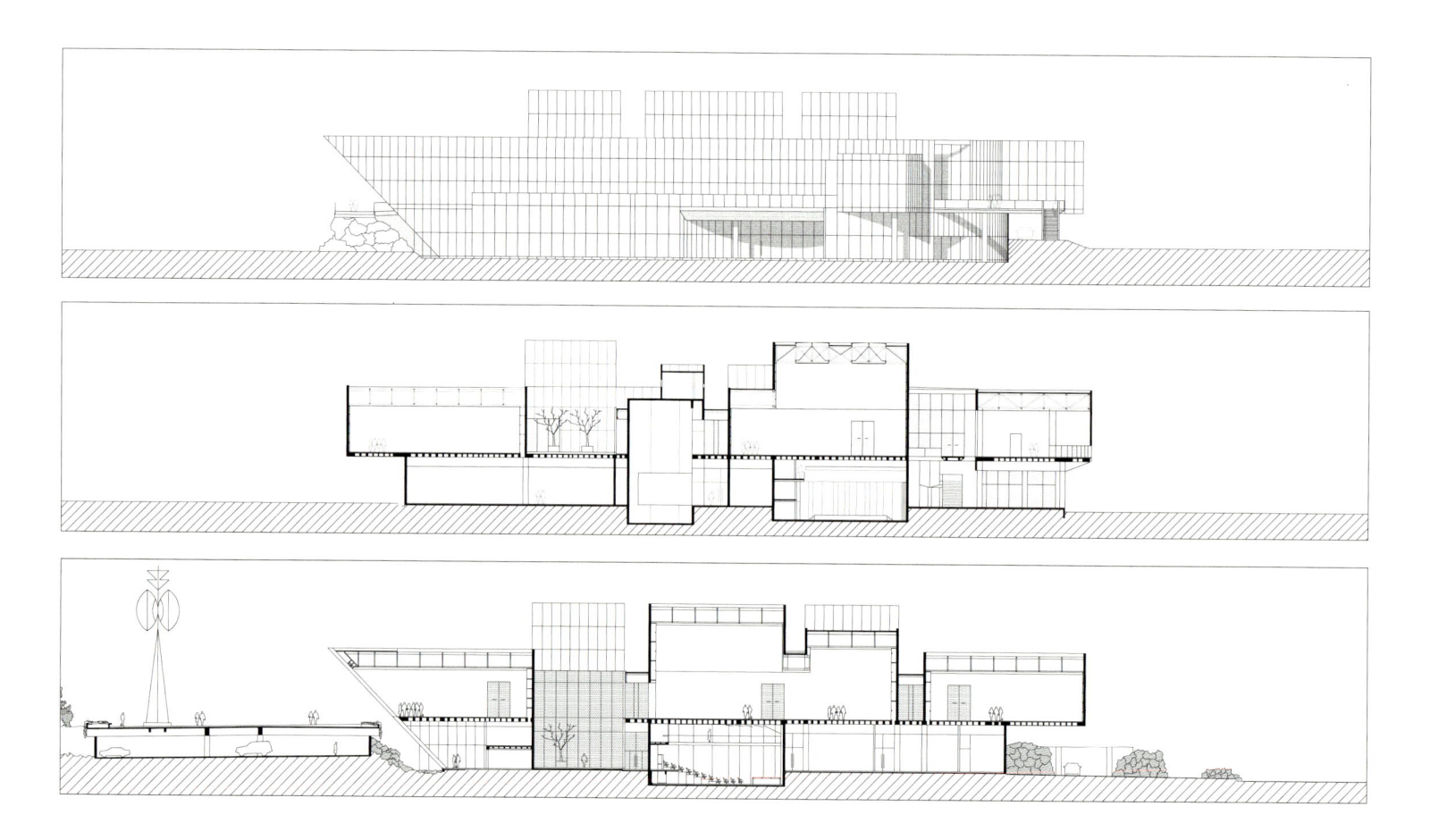

The museum has been organized in just two levels. The monumental grand staircase connects the fourteen permanent collection halls – all these located on the upper floor, along with the reception zone, the gift and book store and the educational area – to the facilities placed at ground level, namely a media library, a conference room, an auditorium, a cafeteria, offices, storage, temporary exhibition galleries and the restoration zone.

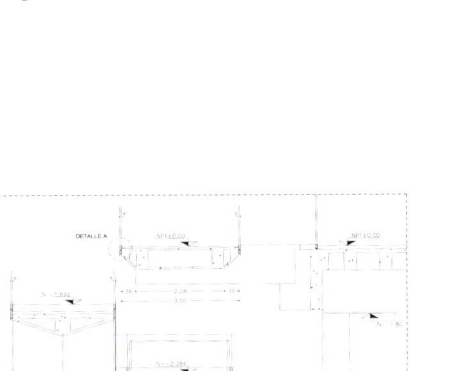

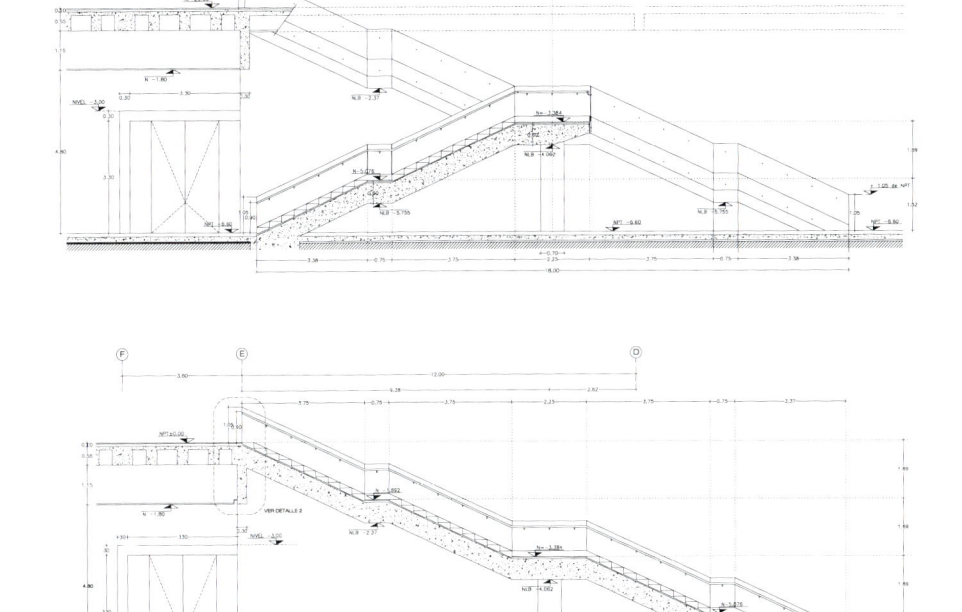

LAR/Fernando Romero
Soumaya Museum
Mexico City (Mexico)

IN MEXICO CITY'S Miguel Hidalgo delegation, in a new enclave of the northeastern part of the capital, the new Soumaya Museum will contain a floor area of 14,000 square meters in five levels, with 6,000 devoted exclusively to exhibitions. The rest of the program includes an auditorium seating 300 people, a library, staff offices, a cafeteria, all these preceded by a large main entrance hall. In addition, six underground stories are fitted out to accommodate a parking garage, storage space, and workshops where works of art are restored. A unique geometry that results from a series of rotation and torsion operations gives rise to floor plans of irregular forms with ring shapes of different sizes. On an enormous platform built with reinforced concrete, the structure is resolved by arranging 28 metallic pillars along the entire perimeter, and these support seven rings that go about adapting to the exterior curvature of the volume. Around this goes a slightly grooved metal enclosure, perforated with small openings, that has been constructed with hexagon-shaped pieces that themselves adapt to the curves at each point. The roof presents large skylights that make it possible for the gallery spaces inside to be naturally toplit.

Client
Carso Group, Soumaya Museum
Architects
Fernando Romero, Mauricio Ceballos
Collaborators
A. Medina, H. Gonzalez, O. Gerala Félix, S. Rebelo, A. Herrera, M. Mora, J. López, G. Mena, L. Castilla, R. García, M. Díaz, A. Aurioles, A. Gabriela Alcocer, L. Ricardo García, I. Ortiz, T. Pinto, L. Dominguez, J. Lopez, O. Gomez, H. Fernandez, J. Sidelko, E. Slim, N. Davolio, L. Warren
Consultants
Gehry Technologies (facade); Arup (engineering); Colinas de Buen (structures)
Contractor
PC Constructores
Photos
Adam Wiseman

The structure is solved through the arrangement of 28 metallic pillars along the perimeter of the building, on which rest seven rings of different sizes that go about adapting to the shape of the floor plans.

Over six underground stories containing a parking garage, storage space and restoration workshops rises a unique volume whose geometry is a result of a series of rotation and torsion operations, inside which are 6,000 square meters laid out for exhibition galleries apart from an auditorium for an audience of 350 people, a library, staff offices, a cafeteria and restaurant, all these preceded by a spatious entrance hall.

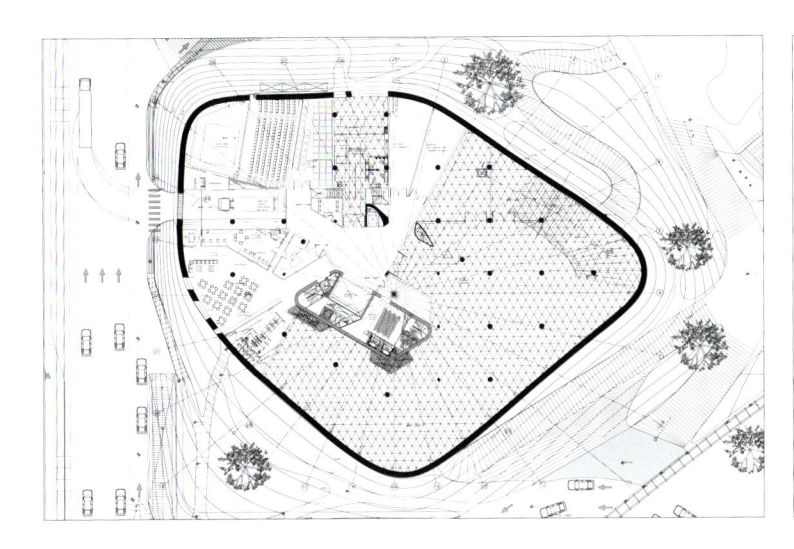

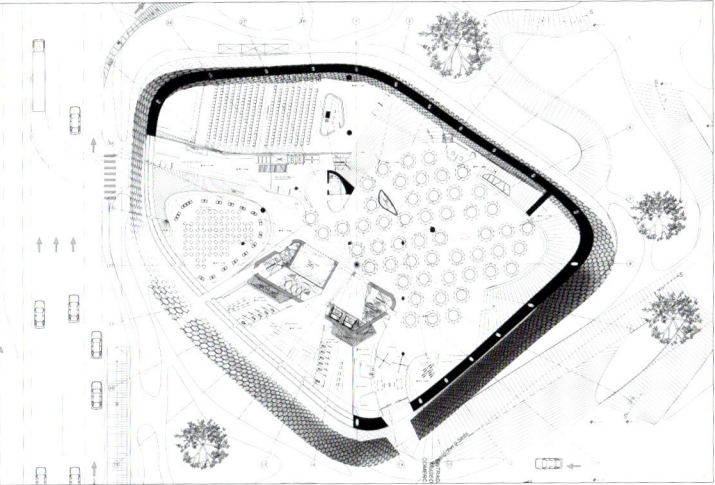

Nicholas Grimshaw
Museum of Steel
Monterrey, Nuevo León (Mexico)

Architects
Nicholas Grimshaw, Oficina de Arquitectura (associate architects)
Collaborators
Andrew Whalley, Vincent Chang, William Horgan, Christian Hoenigschmid-Grossich, Michael Blancato, Shane Burger, Paulo de Faria, Kenny Grossman, Nieves Monasterio, Robert Stuart-Smith, Chung Yeon Won, Richard Yoo, Casimir Zdanius
Consultants
Werner Sobek New York, Socsa (structures); Aldrich Pears (exhibit design); Claudia Harari (landscaping); Asesoria y Diseño (engineering); Arup (acoustics); Office for Visual Interaction (lighting)
Contractor
Aconsa
Photos
Paul Rivera/Archphoto, Christian Hoenigschmid/Grimshaw (p. 118)

The new museum is the result of restoring the metallic structure of Blast Furnace #3 of the former factory to accommodate some 15,000 square meters of exhibition areas showing the process behind steel production.

The Museum of Steel is located in a working-class neighborhood of the Mexican city of Monterrey and is one of the cultural facilities included within the public space known as Fundidora Park, which occupies the old grounds of the Monterrey Steel Foundry Company. After several years in disuse, in 2001 the National Institute of Anthropology and History set itself the task of restoring, maintaining and preserving the surviving factory constructions and turning them into a center of science and technology that would be a tribute to the old metallurgical industry.

The new building takes advantage of the structure of Blast Furnace #3 to create 15,000 square meters of exhibition spaces addressing the history and process of manufacturing steel. The program envisions four areas: the Gallery of History, fitted into the old entry; the Gallery of Steel, a new building over the former junk yard with an attractive roof of folded plates that form a geometrically unique circular plan; the Cast Hall, beside the mouth of the furnace, where the process of making steel is simulated for visitors; and finally the diagonally ascending elevator that once lifted materials to a height of 42 meters or more, and that now transports visitors to the top of the furnace for spectacular views of the city.

Wrapping up the program is a new pavilion that gives access to the complex, and the conversion of the control room into a cafeteria. In the exterior areas, the original platforms and other elements have been maintained. Steel is used in each and every detail of the intervention, from turnbuckles and profiles to railings and mullions, and especially in the sculptural, helical stair leading to the upper level. During the restoration, efforts were made to respect the existing building as much as possible. Even the rich patina of the original structure, accumulated through the years, was left as is.

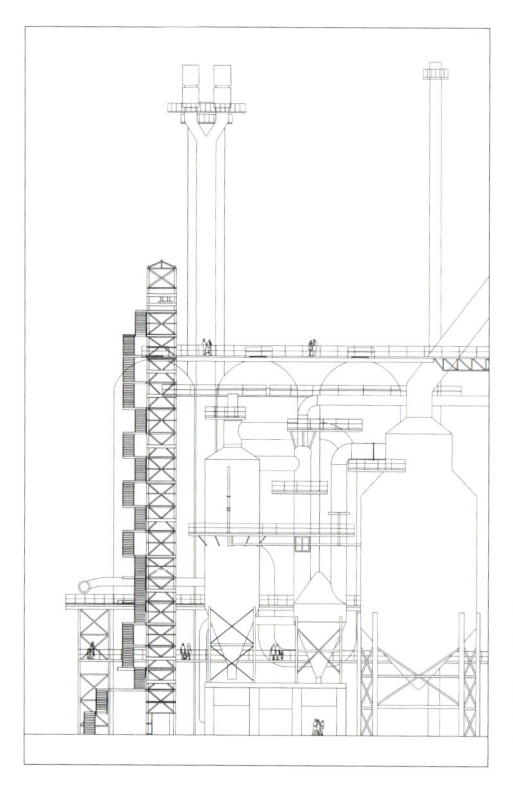

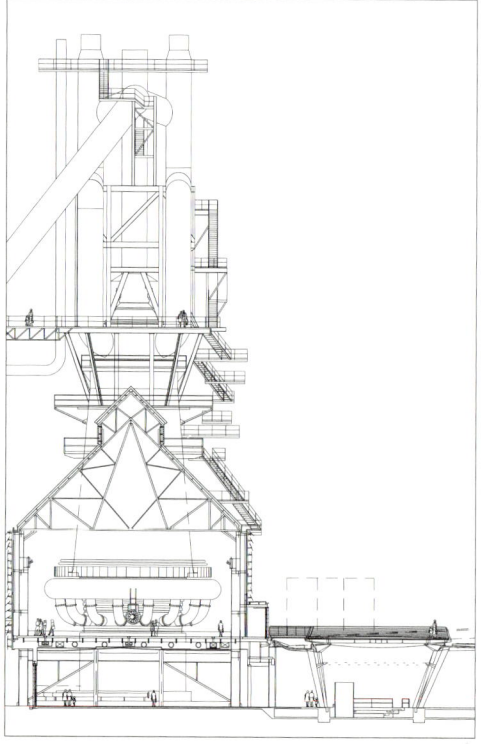

On the old grounds of the Monterrey Steel Foundry Company, the National Institute of Anthropology and History has set itself the task of transforming the existing factory buildings, long in disuse, into an avant-garde center designed with the aim of spreading scientific knowledge. The idea is to salvage and restore the surviving industrial structures and integrate them in a harmonious manner into the design of Fundidora Park.

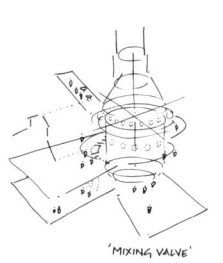

'MIXING VALVE'

The museum program envisions four principal areas for action: the Gallery of History, fitted into the old entrance space; the Gallery of Steel, a new building with a circular floor plan and a unique roof clad with folded metal sheets; the Cast Hall, located by the mouth of the furnace; and the diagonally ascending elevator that once lifted material to the top of the furnace and now takes visitors up for grand views of the city.

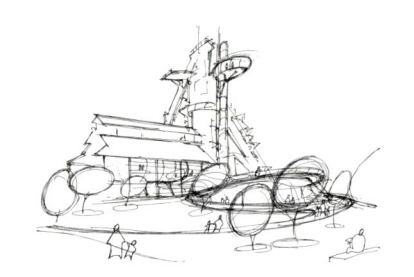

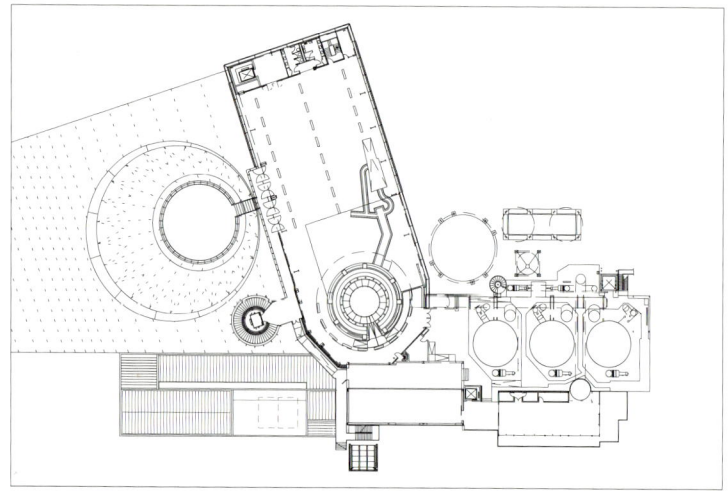

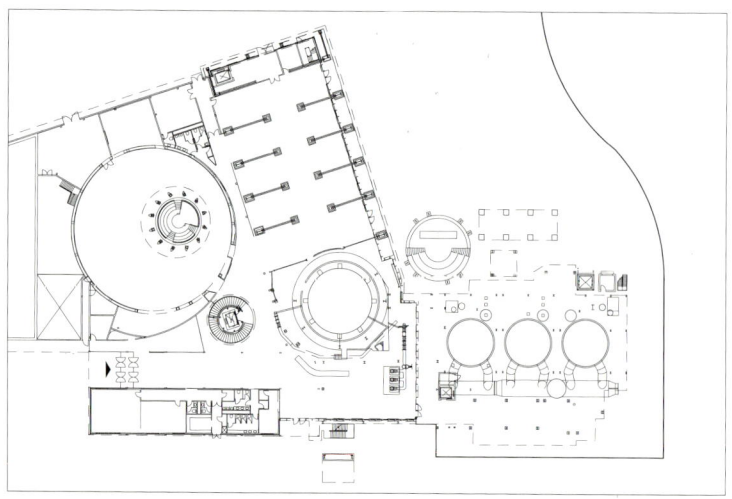

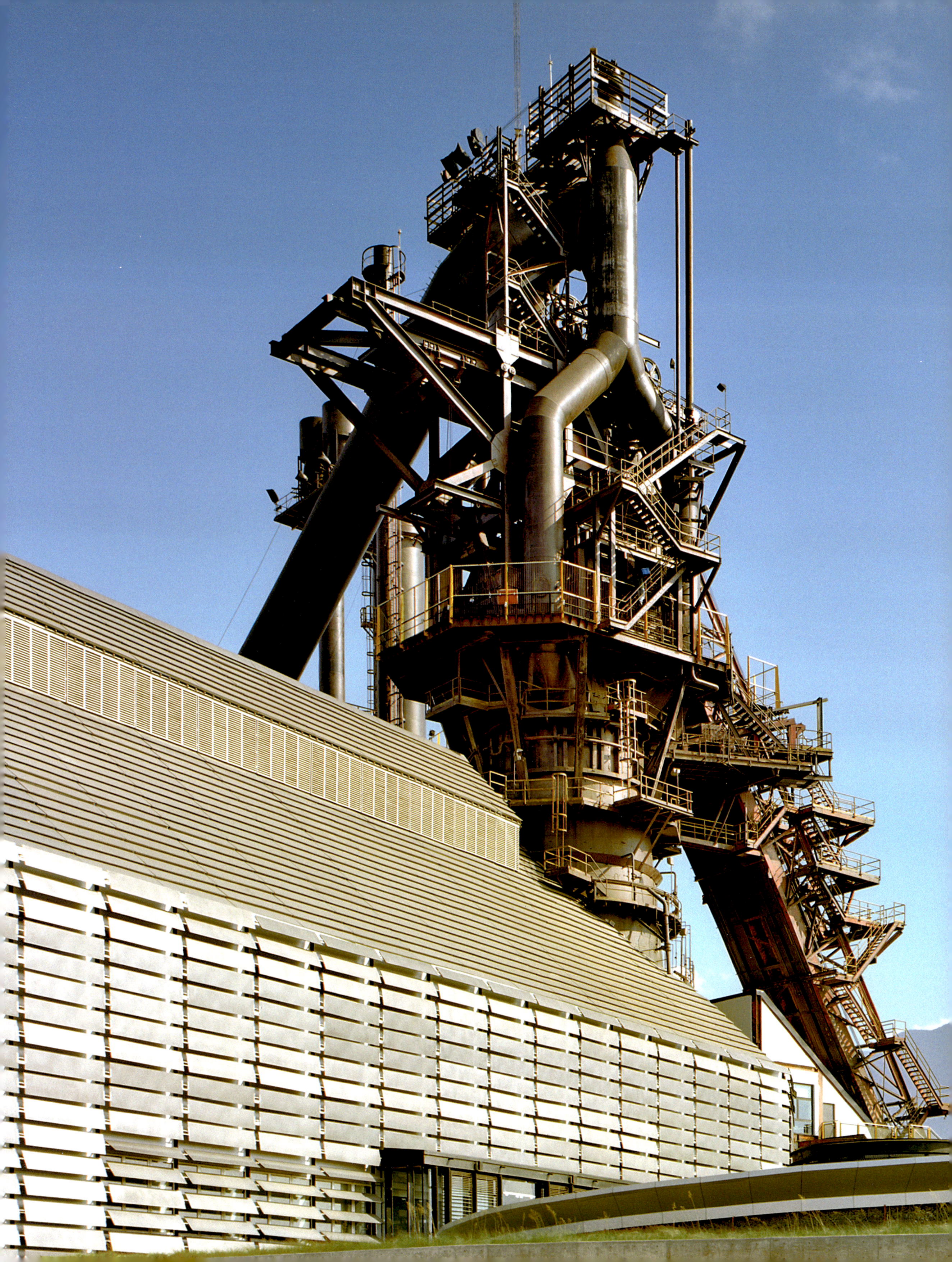

Mauricio Rocha
School of Plastic Arts
Oaxaca (Mexico)

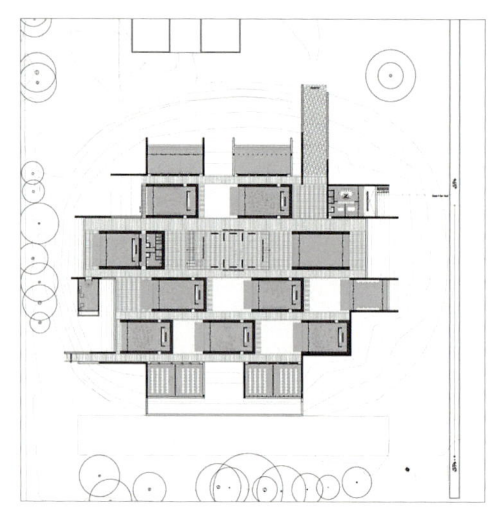

Architects
Mauricio Rocha, Gabriela Carrillo, Carlos Facio, Rafael Carrillo
Collaborators
Francisco López, Silvana Jourdan, Pablo Kobayashi, Francisco Ortiz, Juan Santillán
Consultants
Grupo Sai (structures); Tomás Rodríguez (installations); Yurik Kifuri (furniture); Prolur (lighting); Luis Zárate (landscaping)
Contractor
Cabrera y Asociados
Photos
Sandra Pereznieto, Luis Gordoa (p. 125)

Located in a university campus, the school blends into the environment thanks to the creation of a slope with moved soil and the construction of a series of small prismatic volumes with stone walls and rammed earth.

THE NEW BUILDING for the School of Plastic Arts of Benito Juárez Autonomous University, located in the city of Oaxaca, occupies an approximately 13,000 square meter lot close to the main entrance of the campus, between the space used at weekends for playing the ancient Mixtec-style ball game and an existing construction that has become the new cultural center of the university. Taking advantage of the large quantity of earth that was moved prior to the construction of a treatment plant on the site right next to the school, an artificial slope was created that has had the effect of blending the building into its environment.

The school incorporates heavy prism volumes raised with loadbearing stone walls three meters high that contain the above-mentioned slope, with free-standing buildings constructed with walls of rammed earth endowed with large openings. The first ones accommodate the theory classrooms, the media library and the administration areas, which look over courtyards and have small windows facing west towards the Mixtec ball games and a large tree-planted zone. The free-standing buildings, in turn, contain the main lecture hall, a multipurpose space and the workshops, which have some 80 square meters of floor area opening on to courtyards of identical dimensions that serve to enlarge the space available when needed. In all of them, cross ventilation regulates temperature and large windows facing north enhance the quality of light shining into the work areas.

Native plants and trees are planted in the courtyards, over a layer of gravel. The arrangement of *macuiles,* a deciduous species, creates outdoor work space shielded from the heat of the region. Moreover, the slopes are decked with touch-me-nots and other such low-maintenance native plants. The artist Francisco Toledo took part in the design of all the garden areas.

The heavy prismatic volumes built with stone walls, which contain the classrooms, media library and administration areas, strike a contrast with the free-standing buildings, raised with rammed earth, that contain the main lecture hall, a multi-use space and the drawing workshops. These have large windows facing north and overlooking open-air courtyards that make it possible to expand the available work space as required.

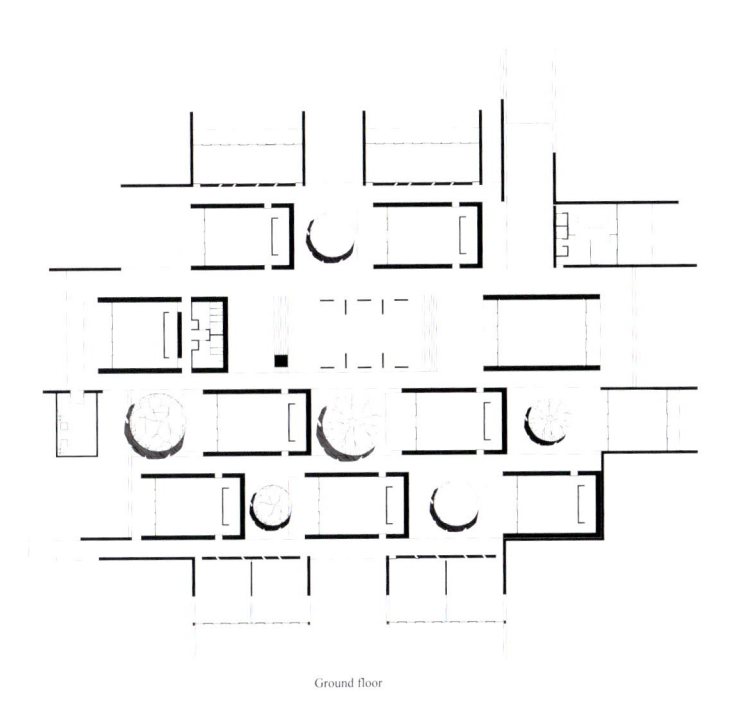

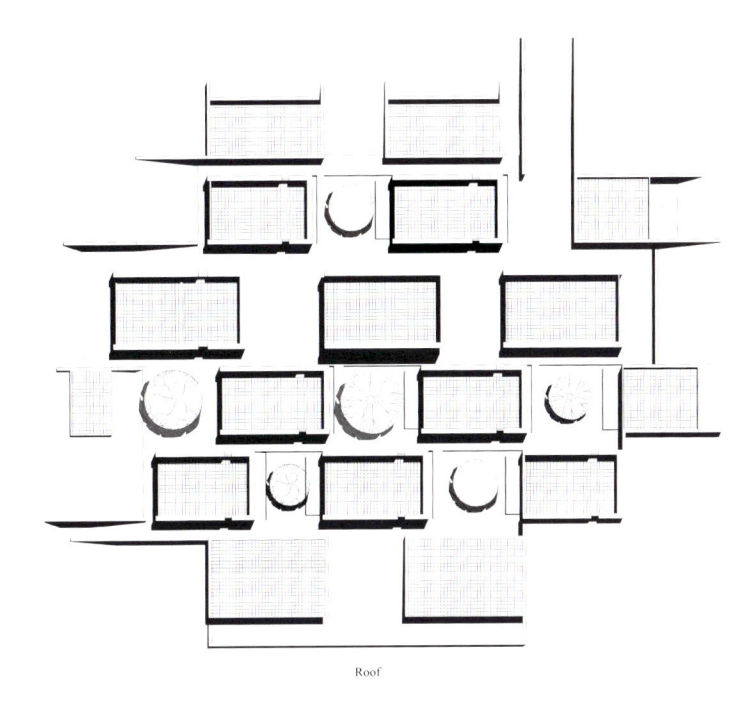

Ground floor

Roof

Atlas: America 123

1. 30x30 cm natural mud paving, 4 mm waterproof sheet membrane, 5 cm thick sloping reinforced concrete, nerved slab, polystyrene insulation, suspended ceiling
2. pvc drainpipe
3. 12 cm cement-sand block wall
4. 70 cm thick cement block wall
5. electrowelded metal rail
6. metal structure with painted finish
7. 8 cm hand-polished reinforced concrete slab fixed to wall with 20x12 cm beam
8. strip foundation
9. polished reinforced concrete floor
10. tie beam
11. concrete column
12. iron frame with 9 mm safety glass pane
13. steel profile
14. iron frame with 9mm transparent glass pane
15. strip light

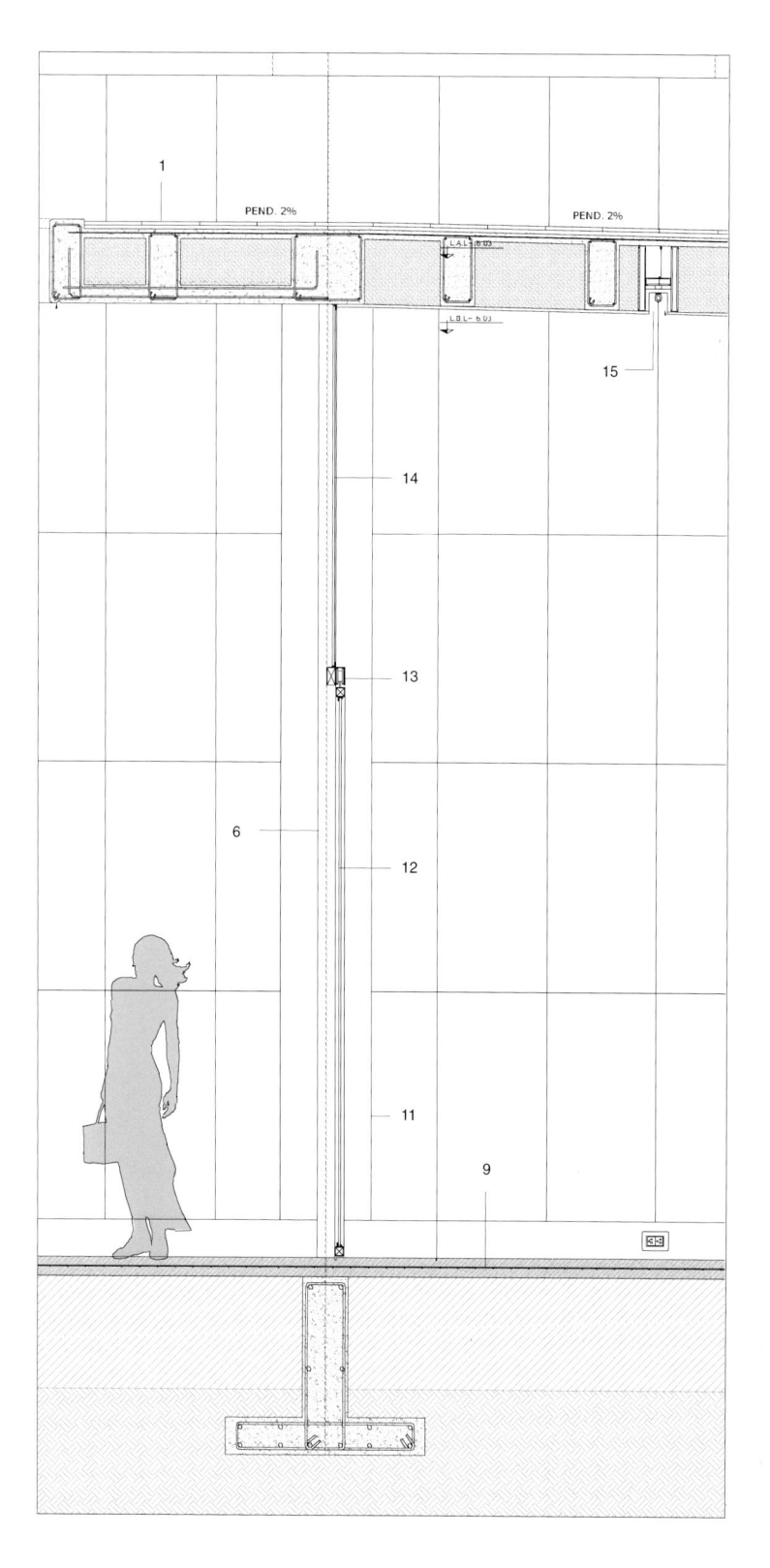

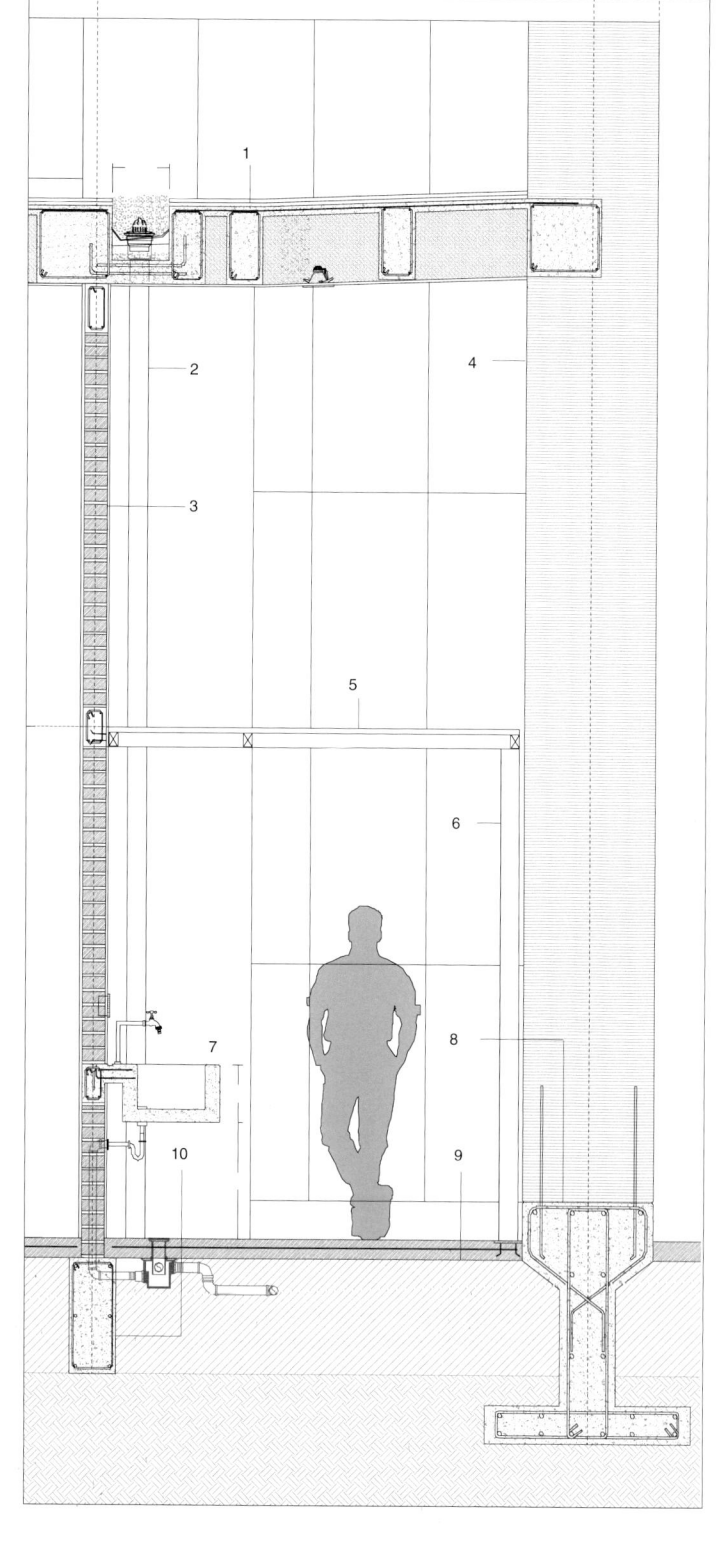

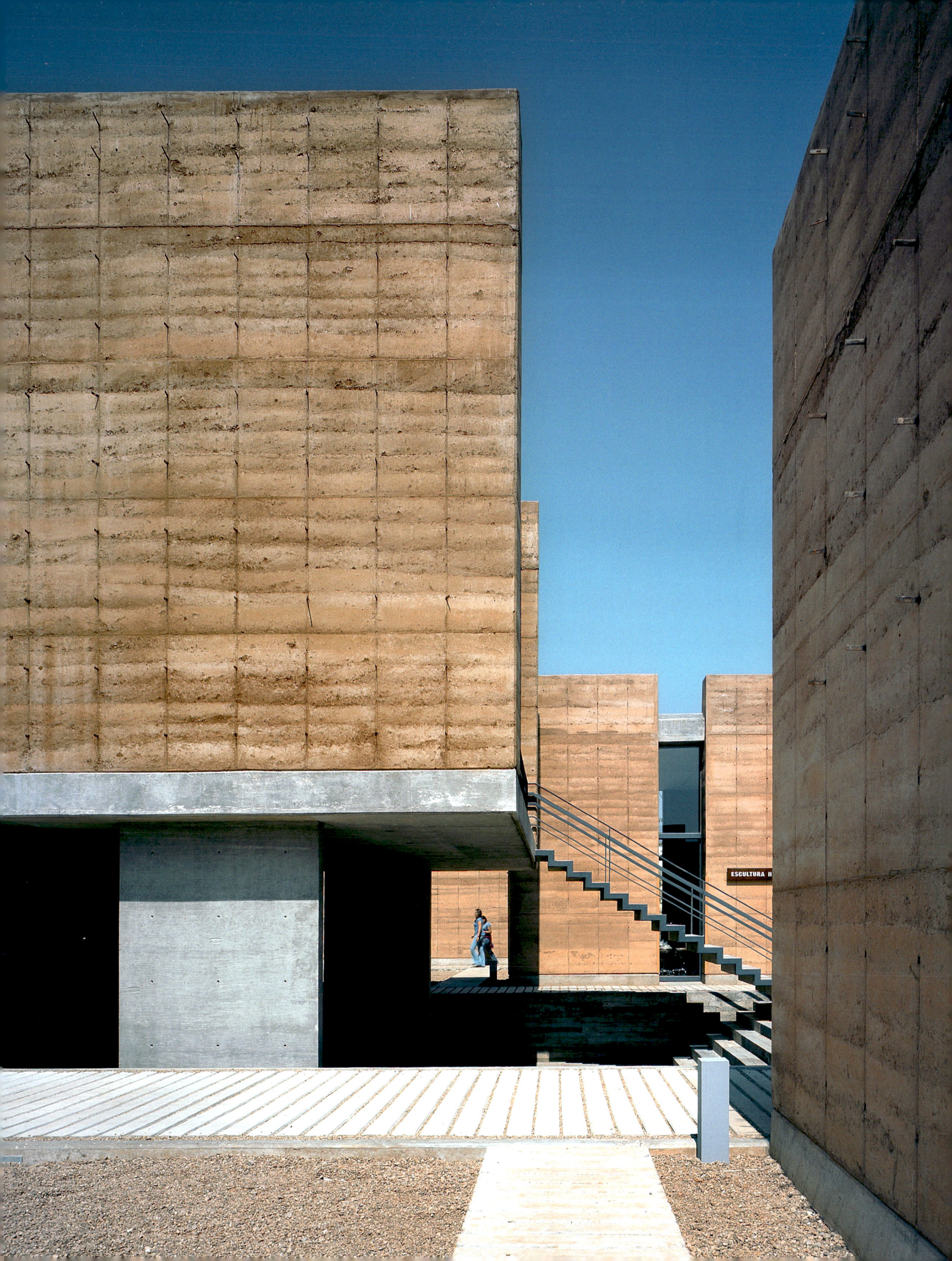
ESCULTURA II

BIG/Michel Rojkind
Tamayo Museum Extension
Atizapán, Mexico State (Mexico)

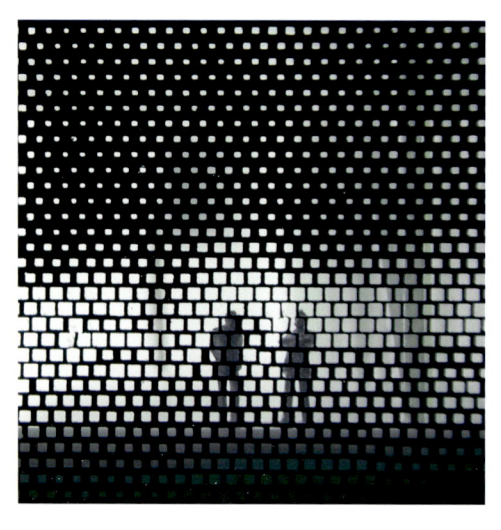

Client
Tamayo Trustees
Architects
Bjarke Ingels, Andreas Klok Pedersen, Michel Rojkind
Collaborators
Pauline Lavie, Maxime Enrico, Pål Arnulf Trodahl, Agustín Pereyra, Monica Orozco, María Fernanda Gómez, Tere Levy, Isaac Smeke, Juan José Barrios, Roberto Gil Will, Joe Tarr
Consultants
Romo y Asociados (engineering);
Romo y Asociados (landscaping);
SWA Group (landscaping);
Ernesto Moncada (graphic design)
Photos
Glessner Group

Iconic and recognizable thanks to its cruciform shape, the museum addresses the climate of the place by means of a perforated double enclosure that reduces the need for artificial cooling inside the building.

BUILT THIRTY YEARS ago by Teodoro González de León and Abraham Zabludovsky, the current Tamayo Contemporary Art Museum, situated in Mexico City's Chapultepec Forest, is a monumental concrete repository for the oeuvre of the Oaxaca-born artist Rufino Tamayo, credited to have brought modernity to Mexico. To make more space for the institution's permanent collection, plans for an expansion of the building were set in motion, and construction work on this annex is ongoing. In simultaneity with this on-site extension, the trustees of the Olga and Rufino Tamayo Foundation organized an international competition for ideas on an altogether new facility that would give the museum additional storage room and further increase its exhibition space by some 350 square meters.

Located in Atizapán, on a hillside on the outskirts of the metropolis, the new building follows a cross shape inspired by the concept of a box that unfolds and opens up to reveal its contents to visitors. The idea comes from a desire to show them the various stages that an art piece must go through, from the moment it arrives at the premises to the time it is put on display in the galleries. Visitor will have access to the workshops and be instructed on the logistics of art packaging, storage, restoration and montage.

The bulk of the program is organized in the main volume, taking up the cross's four arms: exhibition galleries, storage, restoration and conservation workshops, and a dock for the arrival of and loading and unloading of art works. A huge terrace has been laid out on the roof, overlooking the city, beside the cafeteria and restaurant. The sober interiors with white marble finishes constrast with the sophisticated outer skin, which acts as a shield against high temperatures while ventilating the rooms and filtering the natural light that comes into the exhibition halls.

The second site of the Tamayo Museum is located in Atizapán, on the slope of a hill on the outskirts of the Mexican metropolis, and gives the institution ample room for storing, restoring and preserving works of art apart from increasing its exhibition space by about 350 square meters. On the roof spreads a huge terrace, beside the cafeteria and restaurant, where one can enjoy magnificent views towards the capital.

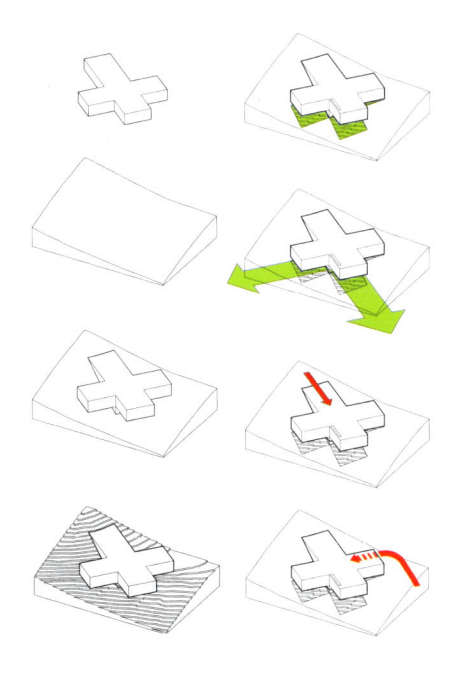

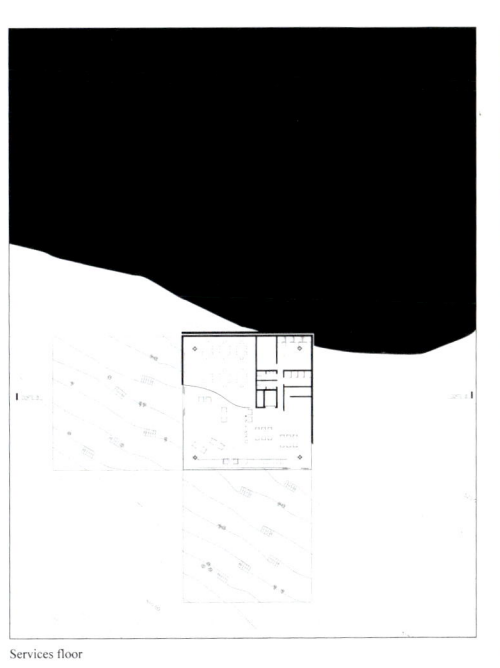

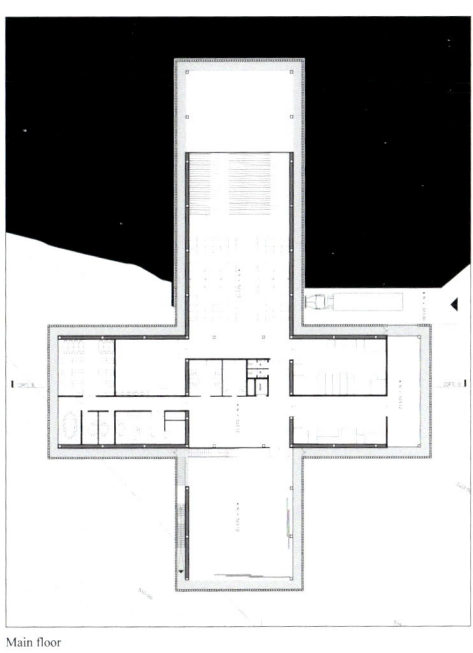

Services floor

Main floor

Atlas: America 127

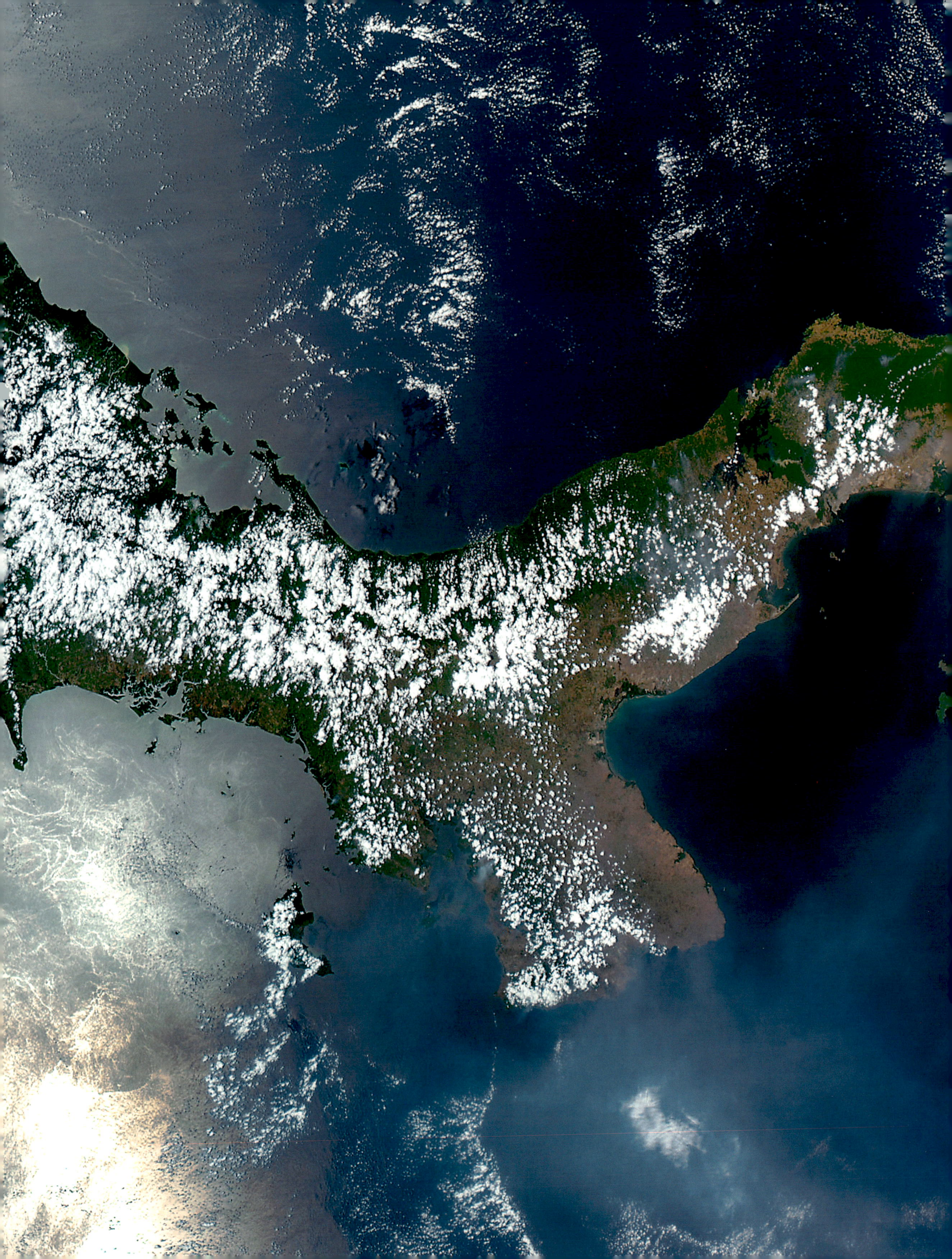

Central America, Caribbean

Nearly twenty countries make up this vast region situated between North and South America that is time and again shaken by natural catastrophes and social convulsions, and whose geographic fragmentation has been a hindrance to the formation of a united identity. Nowadays, architectural proposals in the area tend to fluctuate between the continuity of 'Caribbean environmental syncretism', the persistence of vernacular tradition, and an interest in preserving the urbanistic and architectural colonial legacy in the great historical urban centers. Standing out amid the commercial and speculative construction that the development of tourism generates are minimalist projects of sophisticated technology by Víctor Cañas, such as the Portas Novas House in Guanacaste (Costa Rica), and the environmentally sustainable architecture that Toro & Ferrer execute with soft technologies and materials, illustrated here by the Aula Verde in Río Piedras (Puerto Rico).

Roberto Segre
A Splintered Mirror
Central America and the Caribbean, the Shadows of Politics

Aerial view of Port-au-Prince, Haiti

The fragmentation of the territory of this vast region has hindered the appearance of common features in Caribbean architecture.

Successive hurricanes and seismic movements have devastated Antillean cities and towns throughout history, such as the recent earthquake in Haiti, which razed Port-au-Prince to the ground and left a death toll of 140,000.

THE CARIBBEAN BASIN covers 2.7 million square kilometers – the Mediterranean Basin, 2.6 million – and comprises nearly twenty countries with a total population of 50 million. Yet in global stocktakings of modern architecture that are published in Europe and the United States, the presence of this region of the Americas is practically null. Why the marginalization? Perhaps because of a stereotyped image that has reduced the area to either a place for tourist cruises and money laundering or a last redoubt of western socialism? First, the smallness, fragmentation and poverty of most of the countries in the basin prevented them from experiencing the same coherent development of architectural movements that took place in the continent's larger countries. Second, because Central America and the Antilles are a crossroads – a space for social systole and diastole –, external influences have had more weight than internal elaborations in architecture and urban planning. Nevertheless, from the colonial period onward, a natively Caribbean personality, popular and spontaneous, came to be. And in the 1930s, with the spread of the Modern Movement, this personality underwent a creative symbiosis that would characterize the region's architectural modernity. Thereafter, new generations of professionals have conceived novel solutions that are part of the international dialogue.

Since the Discovery, because of its exuberant nature, its docile, peaceful natives – excepting the ferocious Caribs –, and the millenary Maya culture in Central America, the Caribbean archipelago has been seen as Paradise on Earth and identified with the Hesperides and the island of Tropobana of Campanella's *City of the Sun*. Paradoxically, it has also been Hell on Earth, with hurricanes and earthquakes mercilessly devastating cities and populations: a tremor destroyed Antigua in 1773 and New Guatemala was founded; Old Panama was abandoned and Managua was razed in 1972; Port Royal in Jamaica was demolished in 1692 and up rose Kingston; and in Martinique, the eruption of Mount Pelée buried the city of Saint-Pierre and its 30,000 inhabitants. In the wake of the Haiti earthquake in January, little was left standing in Port-au-Prince, not to mention a death count of 140,000 and a million homes torn down. The annual hurricanes have also taken a toll on the Antillean capitals: the cyclones of 1926 and 1929 are still remembered in Havana and Santo Domingo, the latter also hard hit in 1999 by Georges. In 2008, four successive hurricanes left 800,000 homeless in Haiti and swept the province of Pinar del Río in Cuba. And on top of these natural catastrophes are the political and social convulsions that have characterized the history of the region for five centuries. With the conquest of America by Spain, the Caribbean and Central America became the nerve centers of European policies, marking what the Dominican Juan Bosch calls an 'imperial frontier'. Thanks to the presence of the fleet loaded with treasures from America, so coveted by the Netherlands, France and England, and thanks too to the narrowness of the Isthmus of Darien, which facilitated communication between the Atlantic and the Pacific, islands and continental areas were successively occupied by different European countries. This until the invasive presence of the United States brought on by President Theodore Roosevelt's Big Stick policy, which culminated with the occupation of Cuba and Puerto Rico in 1898. Since then and into the 21st century, even with the Cuban Revolution, the Caribbean was a North American lake, rendered evident by interventions and military bases established during the 20th century – Guantanamo in Cuba and San Juan in Puerto Rico (1898), Nicaragua and Panama (1909), Haiti (1915), the Dominican Republic (1916), Guatemala (1954) –, as well as by the more recent invasions of the Dominican Republic (1961), Granada (1983), Panama (1989) and Haiti

Presidential Palace after the earthquake, Port-au-Prince, Haiti

(1994), all executed to eliminate possible leftist governments. And yet we must remember that the first democratic republic of Latin America was instituted in Haiti in 1791, through a revolution headed by Toussaint-Louverture.

In *The Tempest,* Shakespeare foresaw the dependence and subjection link between colonizers and natives: the image of Prospero and Caliban is the image of the social reality that prevailed in the archipelago. In Central America, the Spaniards subdued the natives, whose population has been maintained to date, ensuring a certain degree of social uniformity altered only by the massive presence of Chinese and black Caribbeans used as manpower in the building of the Panama Canal. But in the Antilles, the rapid disappearance of natives led to the importing of Africans to work as slaves in the sugar plantations. And in the 19th century, with slavery abolished, labor came from China and India. What ensued was a racial and cultural interaction associated with the religious syncretism that dominated the region. The ups and downs of the island economies brought on high mobility rates in the population, in a continuous migration process that by the start of the 20th century, with poverty widespread in the region, became a diaspora towards the United States. Today, millions of Dominicians, Puerto Ricans, Cubans and Central Americans live in the main cities of the 'Colossus of the North'. A phenomenon not exclusively attributable to economic motivations, but to political ones as well: the persistence of dictatorships and authoritarian governments were also a cause of migratory flows – Somoza in Nicaragua, Trujillo in the Dominican Republic, Batista in Cuba, Duvalier in Haiti –, and in 1959, disagreement with Fidel Castro's socialist system gave rise to the exodus of over two million Cubans. In turn, the presence of guerrillas characterized the violence that was endemic in Central America during the second half of the 20th century.

If Caribbean architecture has recently become world-famous through Taschen 'coffee table books' publicizing examples of 'Caribbean Style', in fact the past two centuries have seen the gestation of a bona fide culture with an international presence: the Guatemalan writer Miguel Ángel Asturias won the Nobel Prize in Literature in 1967, the English Antillean Derek Walcott followed suit in 1992. And back in the 19th century, writers like José Martí in Cuba and Rubén Darío in Nicaragua paved the path of Latin American literary modernism. Dialogue between European surrealism and the Caribbean was intense: André Bretón marvelled at the nature and popular culture of Martinique under the aegis of Aimé Césaire, and the Cuban Alejo Carpentier discovered the 'marvellous real' when he climbed to King Henri-Christophe's citadel in Haiti. Surely music was key in giving the Caribbean a presence in the world: Ernesto Lecuona's habaneras, so well-known in Spain; Harry Belafonte's calypso and Bob Marley's rastafari reggae in Jamaica; the Dominican Juan Luis Guerra's salsa; the Puerto Rican presence in New York City through *West Side Story;* the universal success of the Cuban dancer Alicia Alonso and the Nueva Trova of the songwriters Silvio Rodríguez and Pablo Milanés.

Gestation of an Identity

What elements of architectural tradition did the modern architects adopt to elaborate a language for the dialogue between the universal and the local, and hence promote what would be called 'Caribbean environmental syncretism'? In Central America, the Maya ruins and adaptation of Spanish colonial constructions to the region's seismic conditions, with thick columns in courtyards and galleries, inspired the formal parameters of some contemporary

Refugee camp in Port-au-Prince, Haiti

Bruno Stagno, Holcim Offices, San Rafael, Costa Rica (2004)

works: the pyramid shape of Efraín Recinos's National Theater (1978) and Teodoro González de León and Francisco Serrano's volumetric Mexican Embassy (2007) in Guatemala City. But 19th-century constructions were the most important influence, as much for the new typologies formulated in 'tropical' dwelllings as for the functional solutions associated with banana plantations. On one hand, the use of the imported balloon frame structure in one-family homes and the replacement of the open patio with the shaded hallway, combined with the utilization, in warehouses and deposits, of prefabricated iron structures brought in from England to the United States, set the guidelines for solutions adapted to the climate; solutions so light and transparent as to allow the desired shade and movement of breezes inside the buildings. These are constants that appear in the recent works of the Costa Ricans Bruno Stagno, Víctor Cañas and Rolando Barahona, and the Panamanian Patrick Dillon.

In the Antillean world, the Spaniards found straw-roofed bamboo and wooden shacks comparable to the primitive Vitruvian hut. These were glorified by 18th-century European treatises and assimilated as contemporary models in resorts, clubs, and samples of fine architecture like the works of Óscar Imbert and Segundo Imbert in the Dominican Republic: we can mention the airport of Punta Cana (1985) and the Playa Caletón Club (2005). Developed by Philip II, the first work of regional scope was a system of fortifications with which to defend the territories against pirates. Huge masses of stone presiding over the cities – the Castillos del Morro of Havana and Santiago in Cuba and of San Juan in Puerto Rico – showed the talent of the engineers of the Antonelli family, to this day a reference for the architectural origins of the Great Caribbean. In the 20th century these fortifications had their modern version in the military bases that the United States set up in the area. The architectures imported from Spain were adapted to the tropical climate: openings were enlarged and surfaces providing protection against the white light appeared, as did arcades in the streets – Alejo Carpentier described Havana as the city of columns –, and tree-planted inner courtyards were made smaller and surrounded with shaded areas and wide galleries.

In the islands that were English, French and Dutch colonies, where sugar plantations reigned supreme, urban development was of little importance. Here, the simple shacks of the slaves contrasted with the industrial structures of iron and wood and the luxurious mansions of the landowners, the designs of which follow Palladian models and continue to be references in current projects. But the dominant tendency appeared in the 19th century with the generalized use of the balloon frame in dwellings and the metal constructions of markets and warehouses, which addressed climate conditions and possible earthquakes as well as the provisional character of production-related facilities. The lightness and transparency of these buildings defined the typology dominating Caribbean architecture, and also the Victorian decorative style of the gingerbread. But the academic interlude of the early decades of the 20th century disrupted the continuity of the vernacular legacy, which was taken up again with the assimilation, in the 1930s and onward, of the functional and aesthetic principles of the Modern Movement. So by the second half of the 20th century, the personality of modern Carribean architecture was well in the making.

The Seduction of the Tropics
While living on the islands could cause claustrophobia and desires to flee, the mysterious aura of the tropics, their exuberant nature and their multi-racial populations made them attractive to inhabitants of continental territories. The 20th century saw a stream of foreign professionals arriving in Central America and the Antilles. Influences from North America made themselves felt. With the Panama Canal opening in 1914, Frederick

Víctor Cañas, Holmes House, Guanacaste, Costa Rica (2004)

Rolando Barahona, Horizonte Emergente House, Cartago, Costa Rica (2002)

A reinterpretation of the balloon frame, imported from Great Britain and the United States and originally used in the construction of single-family dwellings and that of prefabricated steel structures for large industrial premises and warehouses, characterizes the current crop of architectural proposals, which are carried out with lightweight elements that, in addition, allow breezes to flow freely in the interior spaces.

Law Olmsted was invited as consultant in landscaping projects and Bertram G. Goodhue was tasked to design the Hotel Colón. After Miami, American tourists looked to the islands, generating the construction of grand hotels: Whitney Warren and Charles Wetmore built the Vanderbilt in San Juan (1923) and McKim Mead & White the National in Havana (1929). These kept within the academic vocabulary dominant from the 1920s to the 1940s, but others ventured into more original paths. Antonin Nechodoma, a Czech from Chicago, inserted Wrightian language into the Puerto Rican context. The Catalan Tomás Auñón developed a vernacular expressionism in the Dominican Republic, where, the French Dunoyer de Segozac combined Perretian structuralism with Corbusian brutalism in the Higüey basilica.

Richard Neutra was the great promoter of the Modern Movement in the Caribbean, what with his lectures and his projects and works in Cuba and Puerto Rico. Here he left his disciple Henry Klumb, whose huge architectural output established the bridge between modernity and tradition while adapting the modern language to the region's climatic and ecological particularities. The period from the 1950s on saw a succession of European masters visiting the Caribbean: Havana welcomed Walter Gropius, Mies van der Rohe, Josep Lluís Sert and Félix Candela; and Moshe Safdie designed Habitat Puerto Rico. The influence of the United States came through Welton Beckett, architect of the Havana Hilton (1958), and Edward Larrabee Barnes, who built the El Monte apartments in San Juan (1965). The questioning of International Style that began in Cuba with the National Art Schools, a project involving the Cuban Ricardo Porro and the Italians Roberto Gottardi and Vittorio Garatti (1961-2010), intensified in Costa Rica with Bruno Stagno and Jimena Ugarte, who had migrated there from Chile in 1973. Identification with Central

Patrick Dillon, Bird Observatory in Gamboa, Panama (2008)

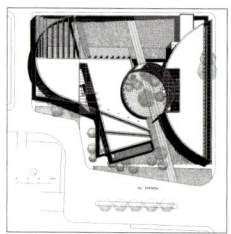

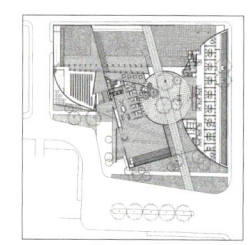

Mexican Embassy, Guatemala

Indicative of a desire to partake of the benefits of the so-called 'Bilbao effect', the presence of architects belonging to the international 'star system' finds material expression in the formal configurations of public buildings and in projects for cultural centers, which go from complex volumes seeking to be modern reinterpretations of the stone masses of pre-Hispanic ruins to fluctuating shapes with sinuous roofs.

American and Caribbean realities and awareness of the imminence of serious environmental problems made Stagno a champion of a 'tropical' architecture, not only in the Americas but on a planetary scale, in conjunction with Gustavo Luis Moré of the Dominican Republic, editor of *Archivos de Arquitectura Antillana* (AAA), the leading magazine on Caribbean architecture. Supported by the Prince Claus Foundation in the Netherlands and identified with the 'critical regionalism' thesis of Alexander Tzonis and Liane Lefaivre, in 1994 he founded the Institute of Tropical Architecture, which in successive seminars focussed on the creation of ecological and sustainable architecture has brought together key figures from five continents.

Two opposed situations drew international attention on the Caribbean. On one hand, enthusiasm over the economic bonanza that moved the globalized capitalist world from the 1990s up to the recent world crisis (2008), and brought about a building boom in the region that came hand in hand with the steady growth of tourism and real-estate speculation: Panama City, with little more than a million inhabitants, boasts 127 highrises. The phenomenon even gave rise to a sophisticated school of architecture and design (Isthmus) directed by the Colombian Carlos Morales – situated in the 'City of Knowledge' that occupies the old U.S. military bases of the Panama Canal –, whose international projection is aimed at training professionals practicing in the region. On the other hand, there is a concern for the profound social contradictions afflicting most of the countries, including the precarious living conditions of the most needy sectors of the population, which inhabit the edges of chaotic cities, removed from the reaches of urban planning. The presence of architects of the international star system is the result of an anxious desire to enjoy the benefits of the 'Bilbao effect' and give the region an urban visibility. Ricardo Legorreta designed the Metropolitan Cathedral of Managua (1991-1993) with a contradiction-filled language of dissimilar references; and Frank Gehry – married to a Panamanian – was invited to Panama to design the Museum of Biodiversity (2002) in Amador, at the gates of the canal, and conceived it as an encounter of the region's geological and social histories, with his usual typology of sinuous and fluctuating roofs. Closer to local history and tradition is the Mexican Embassy in Guatemala, by Teodoro González de León and Francisco Serrano (2007), a white complex of intricate volumes that endeavor to represent, on a modern note, the stony masses of Mayan pyramids. The schemes and transparencies that characterize Antillean tradition appear in the Ministry of Justice building in Fort de France, Martinique (2003), by Borja García Huidobro and Alexander Chementov. Finally, Rafael Moneo was called in by the Historian of the City of Havana to design a hotel in the historic center (2009). And in the utopian dimension of the developmentalist fantasy of neo-liberalism, two gigantic complexes serving tourism and finance were designed in the Dominican Republic. In 2004, in association with a Dominican team, Ricardo Bofill proposed the creation of an artificial island off the coast of Santo Domingo – Ciudamar, Novo Mundo XXI –, a million square meters of land for apartments, shopping centers, corporate offices and marinas. And Bernard Tschumi still hopes to build the largest financial center in the Caribbean, the Independent Financial Center of the Americas (2005), on virgin land situated 30 kilometers from Santo Domingo that would accommodate a stable population of 30 million. This is a reiteration in the Dominican Republic, since in 2001 the Catalan Tolo Cursach built the Barceló Bávaro Convention Center in Higüey, then considered the 'gateway into the Americas'. Interest in preserving

Teodoro González de León, Mexican Embassy, Guatemala City, Guatemala (2007)

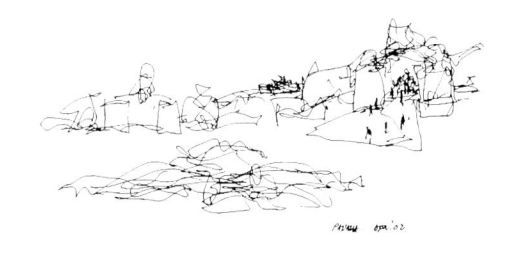

Caribbean architectural and urbanistic heritage, combined with efforts to safeguard traditional cities – threatened as they are, in most of the region's countries, by real-estate speculation – gave rise to an international movement in support of local initiatives to the effect. First, UNESCO added a large number of cities, works and natural contexts to its World Heritage List. Among them are the historic centers of Havana, Camagüey, Cienfuegos and Trinidad in Cuba; Santo Domingo in the Dominican Republic; Panama City; San Juan in Puerto Rico; and Antigua in Guatemala. In Spain, the Government of Andalusia published detailed guides of these cities. In Costa Rica, the Institute of Tropical Architecture and the publisher Líneas organized congresses and seminars attended by the likes of Josep Llinás, Josep Maria Montaner, Iñaki Ábalos, Glenn Murcutt and Ken Yeang. And several municipal organisms, architectural associations and university centers in Spain carried out projects and produced books having to do with interventions proposed in Cuba and the Dominican Republic. In 2000 Santiago de Compostela organized an international competition of projects for Latin American cities, in which Santo Domingo and Santiago in Cuba participated. To give continuity to this initiative, in 2002 the architect Antonio Vélez worked with the government of Santo Domingo in gathering urban planners to draw up solutions for the city. The group included Manuel de Solà-Morales, Manuel Gallego, Ramón López de Lucio, Bernardo Ynzenga, Felipe Peña and Ángela García de Paredes. Havana, in turn, brought several universities of the United States and Europe together in workshops on neighborhoods in precarious state; participants included the architecture schools of Harvard, La Villette, Seville, Granada and Barcelona. Under Andres Duany, the group New Urbanism put forward suggestions for the urban guidelines of the Vedado quarter and backed several publications, including the book featuring recent projects of Leon Krier. And the workshop held in Havana in 1996 with the participation of Coop Himmelb(l)au, Thom Mayne, Eric Owen Moss, Lebbeus Wood, Wolf Prix and Carme Pinós caused significant repercussions, with the results published in the book *The Havana Project*. Growing interest in the Caribbean culminated with seminars organized by Barry Bergdoll of the Department of Architecture of the MoMA in Jamaica (2008) and Santiago de los Caballeros (2010), and aimed at debating the specificity of Caribbean modernity.

A Vernacular Contemporaneity

Rare are the works, in the past decade, that are spared the anonymity of commercial and speculative architecture, the gratuitous formalism imposed by international fashions, or the influence wielded by Miami. These exceptions have managed to get materialized through the initiative of enlightened administrators who associate good architecture with the prestige of their companies, or thanks to cultured clients who like to personalize their homes in a way that distances them from the stereotypes of false vernaculars. As Miquel Adrià and Luis Diego Barahona demonstrated, Costa Rica is the Central American country that boasts the largest output of buildings with a high aesthetic level, carried out by Bruno Stagno, Víctor Cañas and Jaime Rouillón. In his extensive built work, Stagno looks for harmonious balance between formal Costa Rican typologies, traditional responses to climate and ecological conditions, economic sustainability, and the joint use of local materials and contemporary technology, all the while also aspiring to the 'divine proportion' between nature and architecture. Trained in the canonical tradition of the Modern Movement (having worked with Jullian in the project for Le Corbusier's church in Firminy), he has in his recent projects – the office buildings for Holcim (2004) and British American Tobacco (2008) – freed himself from rationalist shackles by using free sculptural forms for solar protection: in the former, light plastic canvases held up by metal tensors; in the latter, a system of undulating *brises soleils* that stretch along the facades. The interiors were also highly elaborated, with the architect achieving an atmosphere of shade and breezes to minimize the need for air conditioning.

Belonging to a younger generation, Víctor Cañas, Rolando Barahona and Jaime Rouillón feel less attached to environmentalist axioms and more attracted to deconstuctivist expressivity, minimalist modesty, and the spatial imagination associated with high-tech. Cañas's houses – Hovany (2003), Holmes (2004) and Portas Novas (2005) – are dominated by the alternation of opacities and transparencies in the ascetic interior spaces, imaginative use of solar panels, adaptation to the topography

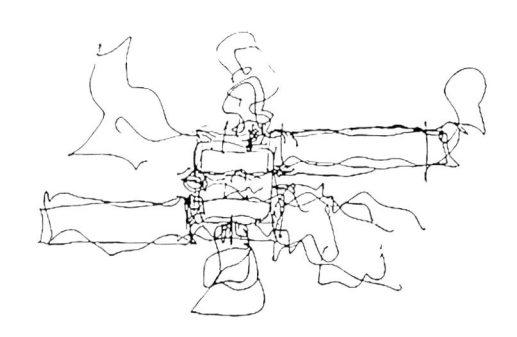

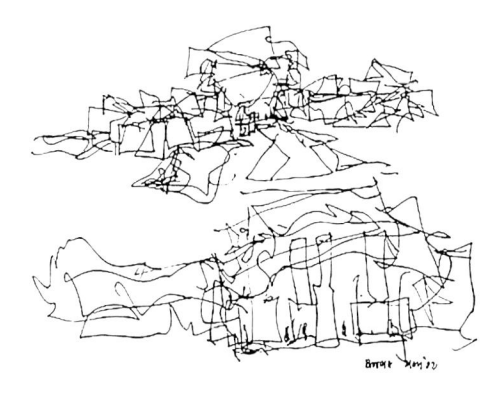

Frank Gehry, Biodiversity Museum project, Panama City

Gianni Botsford, Kiké House, Cahuita, Costa Rica (2009)

Taking the tropical climate into account, incorporating plant species that are native to the region, using vernacular construction traditions in combination with current technologies: all this is discernible in the projects being carried out today, whether small private one-family houses or medium-scale public buildings for cultural and recreational use, with materials recycled under the premise of producing an ecologically sustainable architecture.

of the place, and the creation of perspectives of the magnificent landscape, enhanced in mirror images created by the water of the ponds. In the Emerging Horizon and Habitable Sanctuary housing developments, Rolando Barahona establishes a dialogue between the geometric complexity of the floor plans and the exterior volumes adapted to the topography, with stone walls counterposed to the slender metal columns that frame the large glass surfaces giving views of the exterior space. And even though he lives in London, Gianni Botsford does not forget the ecological determinants of the tropics in the Kiké House (2009).

By combining vernacular traditions with contemporary expression, the Panamanian Patrick Dillon belongs to this tendency. In the Salo House in Veraguas he magnifies the virtual outer walls defined by wooden blinds, and invents a high-tech solution in the observation tower situated on the edge of a national park in Gamboa, the free, irregular form of which is the result of recycling materials taken from houses, offices, garages, sheds, and a demolished refinery in the area. We can also mention the efforts of Ángela Stassano in Honduras, who has managed to produce an economic and bioclimatic architecture without sacrificing aesthetic attributes. Her chromatic solution for the cottages of the Bed & Breakfast (2010) is highly original.

If residential architecture was more traditional in the Antilles, it was due to the greater pressure, there, of the vernacular traditions associated with international tourism and the search for a fleeting Lost Paradise. The Venezuelan Francisco Feaugas's luxurious houses in Casa de Campo (La Romana) – in the Dominican Republic, posh and exclusive domain of North American millionaires – try to strike a balance between contemporaneity and the use of traditional materials and forms.

Gianni Botsford, Kiké House, Cahuita, Costa Rica (2009)

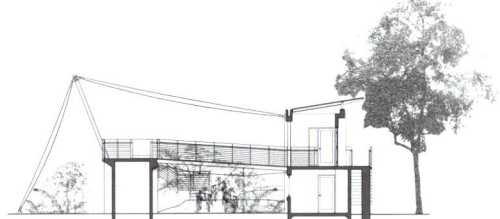

Toro & Ferrer, Aula Verde, Río Piedras, Puerto Rico (2002)

More innovative are the Martinique homes where Jerôme Nouvel experiments with inner courtyards and continuous external galleries, as is Carlos Weeber and Sofía Saavedra's chromatic residence in Willemstad (Curacao), which takes on the colorful heritage of Dutch architecture. The ecological experience of Abruña & Musgrave's small Absent House in Vega Alta, Puerto Rico is unique, its volumetric simplicity establishing a symbiosis between the elements and the covered space by capitalizing on rainwater, wind and solar energy. Concern for the poorest layers of the Puerto Rican population is patent in the dwellings built by Edwin and Iván Quiles for the inhabitants of a *villa miseria* (2009), and, in Río Piedras, the Aula Verde Center for Interactive Environmental Education (2002), a work of Toro & Ferrer in collaboration with Harvard University. Located on the edge of a forest and associated with a butterfly vivarium, the building is modest in its formal and constructional ascetism: the block for teaching activities is defined by a structure of exposed reinforced concrete and a rustic system of wooden window frames.

From Paradise to the Metropolis
We cannot end this panorama of Central America without mention of the urban theme and the operations underway in the historic centers. The dynamism of construction in Panama City and Santo Domingo contrasts with the immobilism of Havana. On one hand, the large architectural firms are carrying out monumental public works in the cities: Segundo Cardona, the Puerto Rico Coliseum (2004); Gustavo Luis Moré and Juan Cristóbal Caro, the Supreme Court of Justice (2001) and Andrés Sánchez and César Curiel, the Holiday Inn (2009), both in Santo Domingo; Seisarquitectos, the Industrial Bank in Guatemala City (2008); Mallol & Mallol, the government complex in Panama City (2002). On the other hand, there is a movement to preserve historic architecture: the buildings restored by Eduardo Tejeira Davis in the old quarter of Panama City, and the San Juan Museum (2000), located in the Old Market, by Bermúdez, Delgado & Díaz. At the same time, particularly in San Juan, there are efforts to socialize public spaces and their communal use. The landscaping work of Andrés Mignucci and the parks in different areas of the city are exceptional. Outstanding is the Window to the Sea (2006), situated by the beach amid the La Concha and Vanderbilt hotels, a space traditionally closed to the public. This operation has given rise to a movement advocating the everyday experience of urban space through social life, true to the Caribbean tradition of open-air activities – remember the traditional iron markets –, in opposition to the anti-urban, segregative dynamics of shopping centers and closed condominiums. Alas, the speculative interests that control tourism in the region are at odds with this desired blending of city and the tourist settlements of the resorts, by definition isolated and independent of the urbanistic infrastructures existing on the isles. So it is that Paradise is experienced by millions of visitors, oblivious to the realities of the Antillean universe.

Toro & Ferrer, Aula Verde, Río Piedras, Puerto Rico (2002)

Toro & Ferrer
Aula Verde
Río Piedras (Puerto Rico)

Client
Civil Action and Education Corporation
Architects
José Toro, Fernando de Jesús
Collaborators
Luis Rodríguez, Frank Bonilla
Consultants
Zapata & Zapata (structural engineers); Jorge Torres Scandali (mechanical engineer); Juan Requena (electrical engineer)
Contractor
Headma Construction
Photos
Marisol Roca

Conceived under the parameters of sustainable design, this environmental center includes a garden, a series of classrooms for school activities, a butterfly conservatory, and a pond for numerous species of tropical fish.

Aula Verde is part of a project to promote socio-economic development in a community suffering from high crime rates. It employs paroled members of the community to provide environmental workshops to nearly 10,000 schoolchildren from public and private schools in the area. Fostering human values and human rights as basic ingredients in the implementation of projects for sustainable development, the initative arose from the Civil Action and Education Corporation collective and receives support and funding from the Education Ministry.

The location is one of the most disadvantaged neighborhoods of the Río Piedras municipality's metropolitan area, on the edge of a small lush tropical wooded zone that provides the ideal setting for interactive learning of environmental topics. After a stroll through a gravel path in a part of the forest meant for the study of the trees and understory, the visitor reaches a small pond bordered by reinforced concrete slabs and wooden pavements mellowed by mosses and vines. From here one can proceed to the conservatory at the upper level, through a sloped wood and steel footbridge that also leads to a concrete platform offering a panoramic view of the butterfly conservatory below, an area covered by a fine net protecting the insects. Descending two other platforms, visitors enter an area surrounded by numerous butterfly species in a meandering gravel pathway that leads to a tropical fish pond.

The materials used for the building and adjacent spaces are suited to the limited budget. Steel for the columns and cables and reinforced concrete for the structure combine with more local, readily available materials, such as wood, for the interior finishes and joineries. Moreover, to reinforce its environmental nature, the project is oriented to take full advantage of prevailing tropical trade winds for cross ventilation.

A fine net fabric has been spread over the butterfly conservatory area which the visitor reaches by walking, from the upper level, down a sloped wooden ramp and a metal footbridge that offer a panoramic view of the tropical garden below. As a reinforcement of the environmental theme of the place, readily available materials like wood are used, and the project is oriented to take advantage of trade winds for cross ventilation.

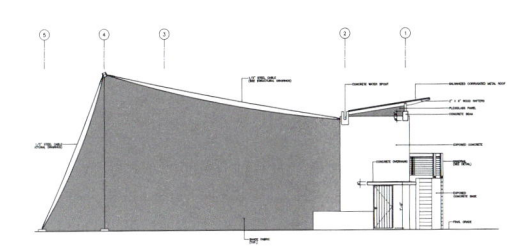

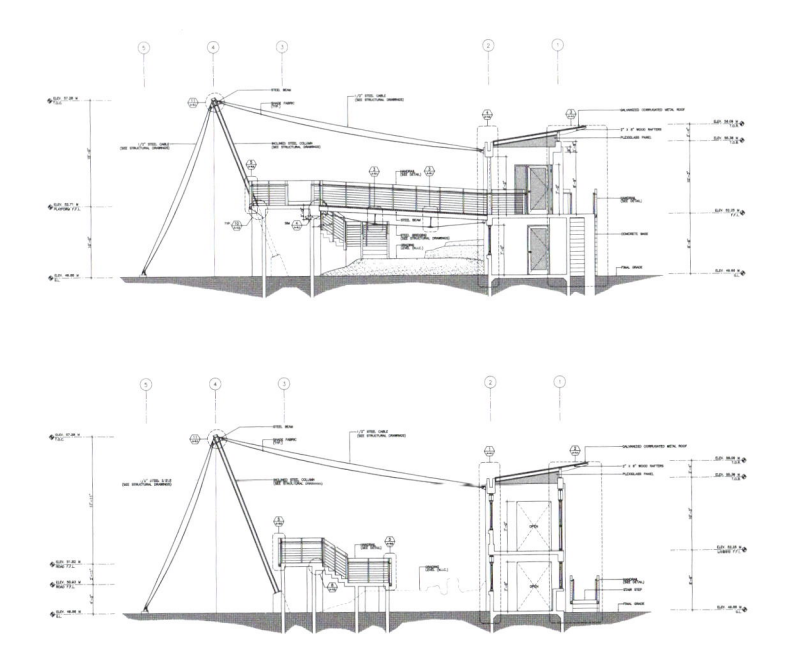

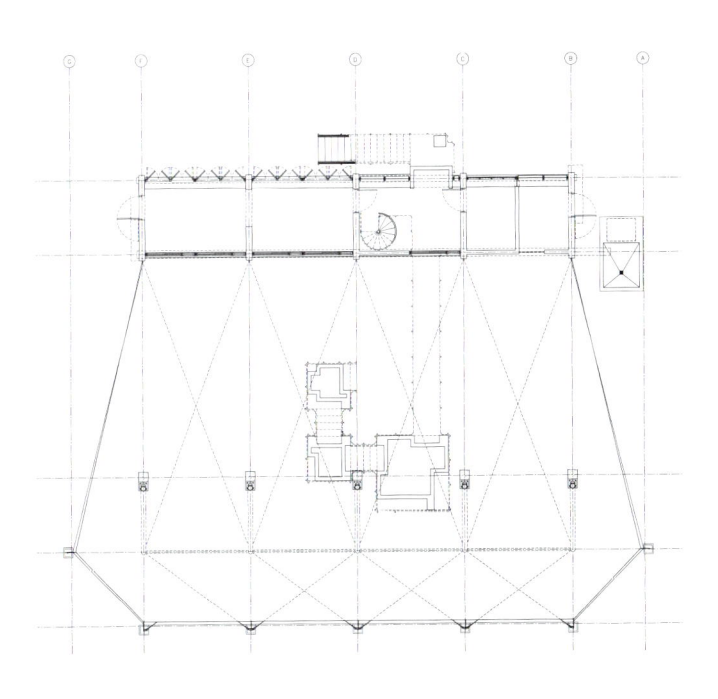

Atlas: America

Victor Cañas
Portas Novas House
Guanacaste (Costa Rica)

Architect
Victor Cañas
Collaborators
Andrés Cañas, Ricardo Chávez
Consultants
Ricardo Solano (structure), Elmer Arias (installations); Roberto Vargas Dengo (electricity); Juan Roca (swimming pool); Artiv Design (bathrooms); Arte en Luz, Artiv Design, Life Style (lighting), Nils Pinagel (electronics)
Photos
Jordi Miralles, Óscar Abarca (p. 141)

The different spaces of this private residence follow a longitudinal organization and are connected to one another by small gardens built with boulders and catwalks with wooden floors and glass walls.

SITUATED IN the northern part of Costa Rica, in an area with a dry tropical climate, the Portas Novas House stands on a hill that rises in the form of a peninsula endowed with magnificent views of the Pacific Ocean to the west; a cluster of islands, isles and peninsulas to the north; and a wooded valley with isolated private residential properties to the east. Access to this house is through two large aluminum doors, 3.5 meters tall, that protect a small courtyard. As one progresses through this space, views of the surrounding landscape gradually reveal themselves.

At one end of the courtyard, two small free-standing constructions accommodate the service areas. The principal volume of the complex unfolds from the entrance hall, following a longitudinal organization that is divided into three modules connected to one another by small gardens and platforms. The living room and lounge areas are located in the first module, a double-height structure with huge windows facing the sea. From here one proceeds to the other modules through catwalks that go about marking the transition and linking up the different spaces. One of the catwalks, protected by glass walls, stretches over the surface of the swimming pool to the main bedroom, while a sequence of small wooden platforms arranged in a Japanese garden leads to the guest rooms.

The house is designed to make the most of the characteristics of the privileged location. For instance, a sheet of water surrounds the main spaces of the house – the living room, the dining room and the master bedroom –, so that from inside, one can get to it through large sliding glass doors. In this way, a poolside space about 3 meters wide forms a 'sunken' terrace in which the users can bask in the sun. Finally, to ensure continuity with the outdoor premises, the floor of the living room is at the same level as the sheet of water.

Located in the northern part of Costa Rica, in an area with a dry tropical climate, the one-family house features a sheet of water around the main domestic spaces – the living room, the lounge and the master bedroom –, which is accessed through large glazed surfaces. In this manner a spatious 'sunken' terrace has been generated, from which one can contemplate magnificent views of the surrounding landscape.

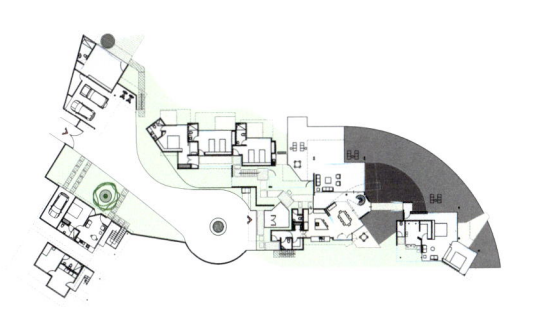

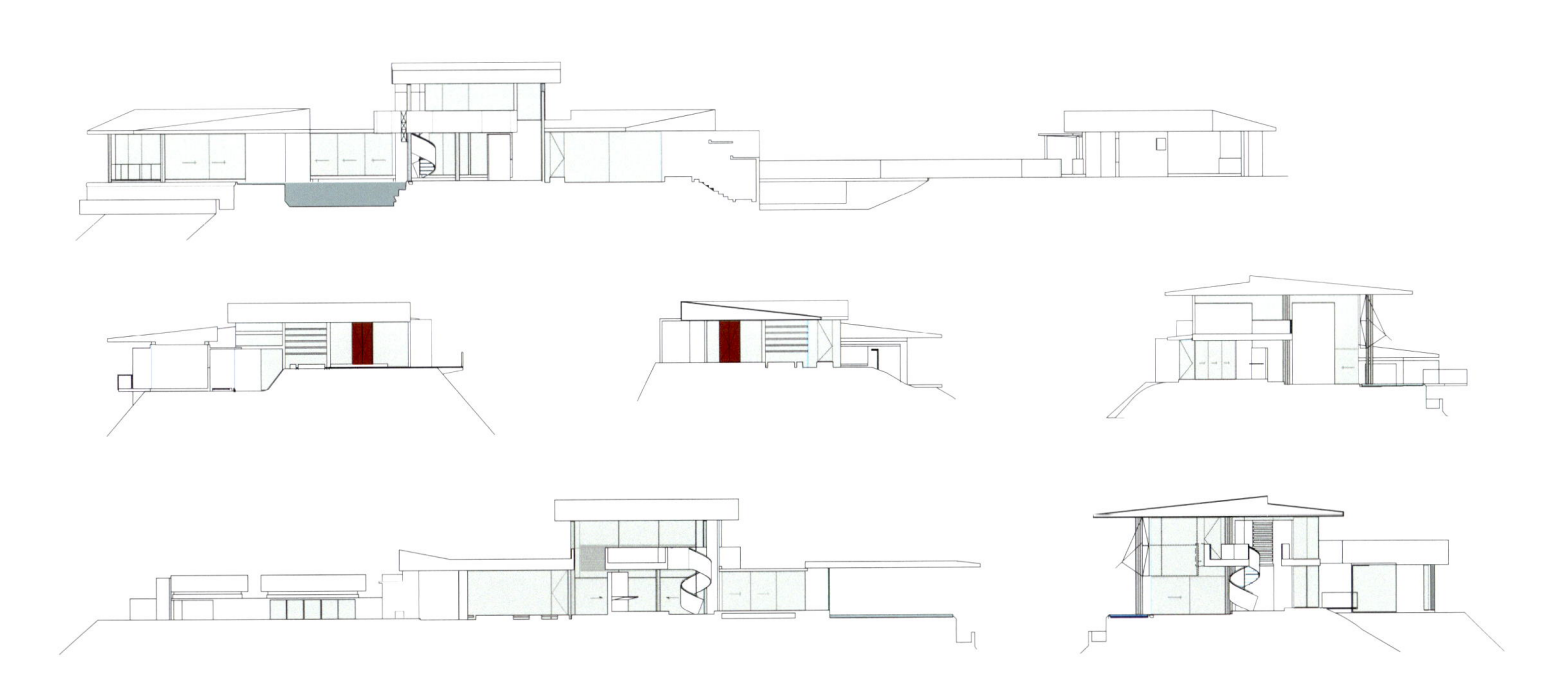

Atlas: America

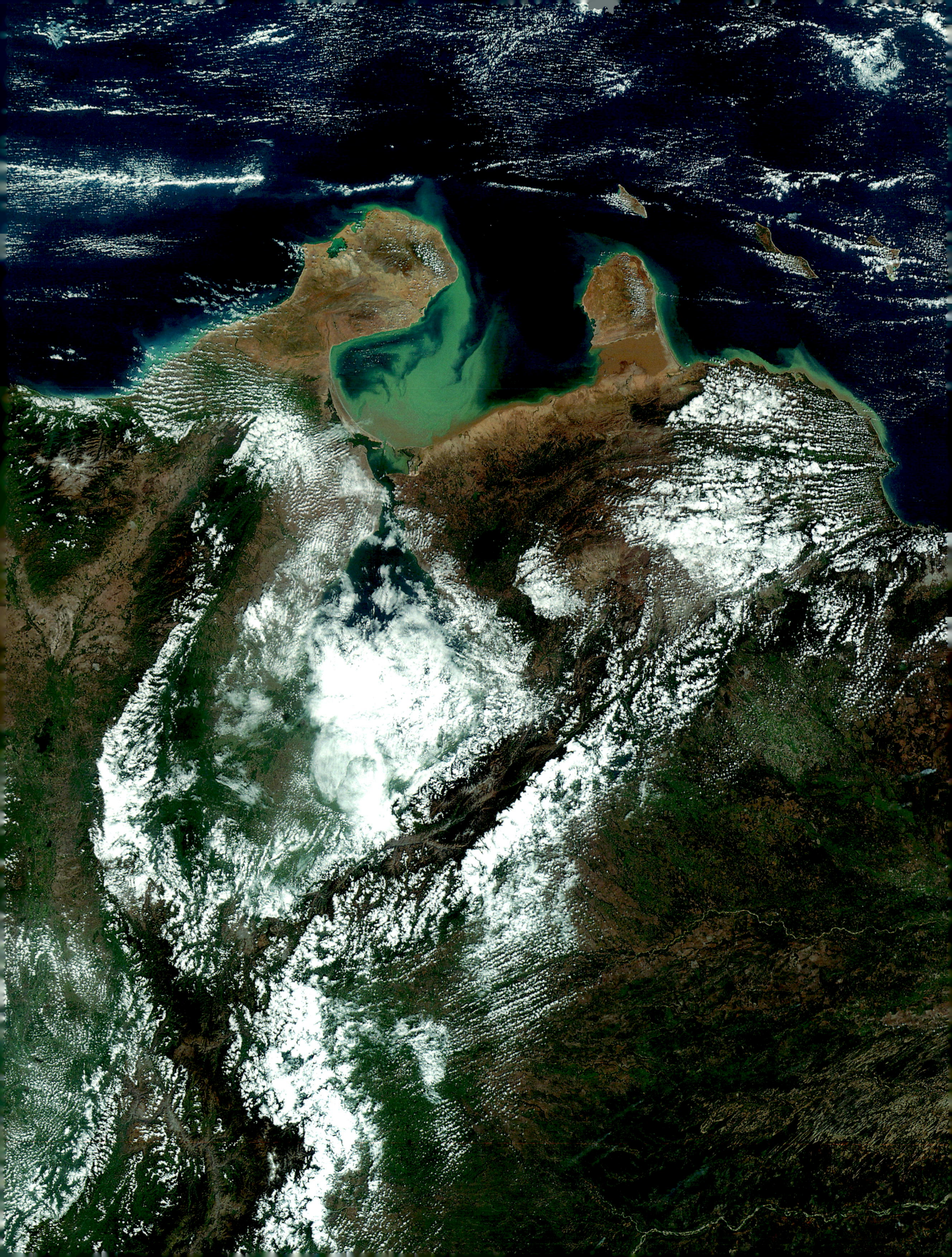

Venezuela

Faced with high levels of demographic concentration on the outskirts of the country's big cities, during the first decade of the current century Venezuela has not been able to address the tremendous growth of the urban centers, overwhelmed by marginal settlements that encroach on the territory without any kind of planning. In spite of this, thanks to public initiatives like the Program for New Facilities in 'Barrios', the past years have seen Caracas benefiting from urban renewal works and projects that provide citizens with unique transport infrastructures like the Metrocable connecting the San Agustín settlement to the town center, by Urban Think Tank, or new cultural facilities like the Communal House in San Miguel de la Vega, by Matías and Mateo Pintó, not to mention interesting proposals coming from the private sector, such as the highrise CAF Headquarters, won in international competition by the young Mexican studio Productora with Lucio Muniaín.

Maciá Pintó
Urban Contrasts
Venezuela, Administered Informality

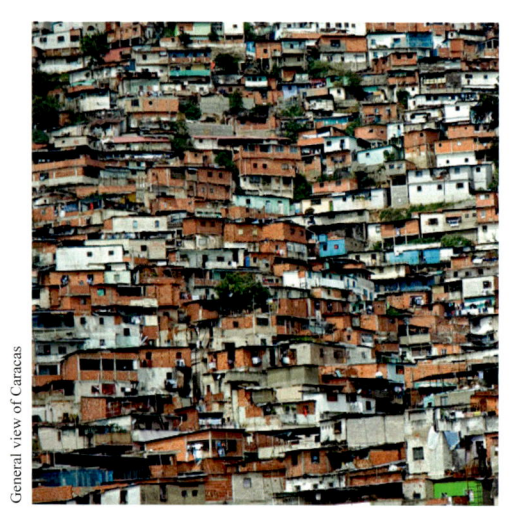

General view of Caracas

The country's acute social imbalances are reflected by the contrast between the formal planned city and the informal spontaneous one.

The 20th century saw Venezuelan architecture achieving an important niche in the international scene, boasting works and urban interventions conceived with the technical rationality of the Modern Movement.

Carlos Villanueva, El Silencio, Caracas (1944)

ONE IS HARD PUT to appraise the past Venezuelan decade, coinciding, as it does, with a political project that began in 1999 and is still ongoing, and that has a bearing not only in the political realm but also in institutional and professional spheres, particularly in the fields of architecture and urban planning. Political regimes come and go in Latin America, where we are accustomed to cyclic recurrences of the most varied denominations. Moreover, relations with the state and its instruments of power are not always the same, and neither are actions in the private sector and other areas necessary to democratic life.

Without meaning to justify or legitimize results, any discussion about our cities and the scarcity of architecture that is truly worth mentioning necessarily begins with a recreation of the context we are living. There have in fact been projects and building works in both the public and the private spheres, but considering the ten-year lapse and the quantity of resources that have entered the country, the final balance is not encouraging; much less if critical appraisals are guided by common sense.

It need not be so, but social housing policies and programs for infrastructures and facilities have proven insufficient, as have incentives or stimuli for investment. Nevertheless, things are really not all that bad. The network of metropolitan railway lines has expanded, incorporating more and more stations, and new institutional buildings, sport centers and public service facilities have gone up.

Order in Chaos
Formality and informality ought to interact in a desirable relative balance, if we refer to the city's structure as Francesco Milizia took it in *Principi Di Architettura Civile:* "it has to reign over order, but with some confusion; everything has to be straight and regulated, but without monotony; and from a multitude of regular parts must come a certain irregularity and chaos, which is something that suits large cities".

This balance, necessary to the dynamics of a city, is not reflected in the informality expressed as a transgression of the norm, nor in the insecurity and violence that eat away at the social fabric and destroy the physical environment. Néstor García Canclini, a scholar of the complex and contradictory American reality, points out two representations of the urban in the case of Mexico City, drawing a line between 'informality' and 'accident'. These representations correspond to the visions of two photographers: Paolo Gasparini, who captures the 'rituals of chaos' referred to by the writer Carlos Monsiváis, and Enrique Metinides, who makes it his task to illustrate the 'red chronicle' in Mexican newspapers.

Chaos and insecurity affect people, but also transform and degrade the physical environment of cities. Urban violence is felt in all areas: bars and other security systems create barriers by privatizing space, and architecture – armored, reinforced or surrounded by walls and wire fences – is secluded within gated domains. In 'Famous Writers', a story in one of his latest books, *Crimes,* the Venezuelan writer Alberto Barrera Tyszka constructs the parable of a country that awaits the promise of salvation without repentance, only to get a 'red balance': the balance of a country in moral breakdown, where life is worth nothing and death is the indeclinable literary, but real, end.

Like Brazil and Mexico, Venezuela reached a high level of modernity in the mid-20th century, independently of political systems. Perhaps owing to social and economic conditions of the time, its architecture achieved a level of importance internationally. And it was precisely art, architecture and urban planning that paved the way for modernity through imagination, technical rationality and the idea of progress.

The open spaces of a public character and the landscaped areas constructed around the residential buildings of large-scale developments during the 1950s, with the heyday of modernity in full swing, are now flooded with shantytowns and overcrowded with marginal dwellings that encroach on the territory with no kind of urban planning whatsoever, lacking the most basic services and infrastructures.

Carlos R. Villanueva, 23 de Enero Development, Caracas (1955)

One just has to glance at the past to see that Caracas in the 1950s and 1960s was in harmony with a vision framed by photographic modernity and shared by excellent professionals like Leo Matiz, the Colombian photographer who leaves us an invaluable testimony of that moment. We can see images of this testimony in a documentary put together by Alejandra Szeplaki, which shows a recently 'premiered', modern Caracas: a city full of space and prospects, with clear contrasted light entering the camara lens to give shape to a project or to the idea of a country that, with all its contradictions, had a sure future ahead. What a pity, then, that these vivid stories reflected by visual memory have given way to the disfigured city of today. Already in the introduction, Federico Vegas mentioned the sad paradox of a city like Caracas having "its best future in its most recent past".

This would seem to be the unavoidable destiny of our cities if we think that because of their very make-up, many Latin American countries are understood as expressions of a desire for the future, more than as realities. In *Alfredo Boulton and His Contemporaries: Critical Dialogues in Venezuelan Art, 1912-1974,* the philosopher and art critic Sandra Pinardi expresses this yearning for emancipation when she writes: "modernity and identity present themselves in Latin America as closely tied phenomena, not only because the very process of building identity is its process of implanting modernity, but also because Latin America is 'modernly' in constant re-inauguration, it is always re-founding itself". Our process has always been discontinuous, with advances and regressions determined "by a foundational will that installs itself each time as a beginning". We are made of a culture of substitutions "that do not bring about the establishment of permanences or

Carlos R. Villanueva, 23 de Enero Development, Caracas (2010)

Atlas: America 145

In contrast to the fragments of 'formal' city that define the urban fabric of the centers of the great metropolises, what rules on the outskirts is the form of growth that is most common nowadays: marginal urbanization, which spreads by adapting to the contour of the terrain and through the repetition of a single model for self-build housing that falls short of complying with the minimal standards of human habitability.

continuities, nor to any established thought, institutionality or culture".

In *Portable Country,* a novel by the Venezuelan writer and poet Adriano González León, the city is the main character and Caracas is an elusive reference marked by permanent barter and transformation, a mutable city where little is left or preserved and everything changes or is replaced or disposed of. Past and future are not only opposed, but inverted as places for temporal and spatial transit; they present themselves as spaces of mobility, and only ambiguous spaces are preserved, the new territories for the encounter of the public and private spheres. In this way, the certainty of permanently having a mortgaged or deferred project gets repeated.

An entire generation of excellent architects and urban planners prefigured a country and a city that was not only conceived as a utopia, but actually carried out. From the near-naïve fantasies of a visionary like Ramiro Nava to Maurice Rotival's masterplans for Caracas and other inland cities of Venezuela. From Oscar Niemeyer's unexecuted Museum of Modern Art project to the unfinished Roca Tarpeya Helicoid of Romero Gutiérrez, Pedro Neuberger and Dirk Bornhorst. From Tomás Sanabria's Hotel Humboldt on El Ávila Mountain to Cipriano Domínguez's Simón Bolívar Center towers on the Avenida Bolívar axis. From the houses built by Gio Ponti and Richard Neutra to the Caoma House of Carlos Raúl Villanueva in La Florida. From the latter's El Silencio Redevelopment – an urban renewal and public housing work in the central nucleus of Caracas – to the January 23 Superblocks and the vast popular developments built throughout the country by the Banco Obrero in the context of the National Housing Plan.

Carlos Raúl Villanueva is an indispensable reference because of the sheer volume and quality of his built work and his identification with Venezuela. Hand in hand with an important group of intellectuals, writers, poets, artists and architects, in the 1950s he achieved a certain degree of synchronization with contemporary works of the western world. The University City of Caracas stands out for the success of the 'Synthesis of the Major Arts' project, which brought together a good group of national and international intellectuals. But it was thanks to the unprecedented space of its most representative element, the Aula Magna lecture hall, a work of Villanueva in collaboration with the North American artist Alexander Calder, that the modern synthesis of the arts was made definitive and indissoluble. The big university complex, which unifies several works in one, represents the materialization of a city model where the best of modern urban planning finally comes true, and this is ratified by the UNESCO's decision, in 2000, to declare it a World Heritage Site.

Formal City and Marginal Urbanization
Formality and informality meet at the extremes, have a common denominator, and like political opponents are simultaneously contradictory and complementary. They are alike in their indefinition of limits and they exist side by side, superposing one another and interrelating in mutual interdependence. The two cities invade each other and intermix, expressing one same idiosyncrasy and becoming indistinguishable. Informality as a cultural phenomenon lies inside formality, and denies it from there.

Informality is present not only within the marginal or peripheral city, but in all

Aerial view of the University City, Caracas

Carlos R. Villanueva, Lecture Hall of the University City, Caracas (1954)

of the cracks of Latin American cities and metropolises. As a cultural phenomenon informality reflects the social, political, economic and especially educational situation of our countries, causing distorsions that work on the social body of a city understood as a whole. This is also physical, and although we must forget the false illusion of absolute control over urban form, we cannot deprive the city of its essential formal nature, which is directly linked to political and symbolic meanings. Informality and urban form are thus associated with the processes of generating and dissociating the fabric, with the make-up of the scheme, and with the loss of the city's physical and social framework.

In Caracas, the center and the periphery, the 'barrios' and margins, together form concentric circles of urban growth. In extent and presence, marginal urbanization has perhaps been the most significant growth pattern, creating an urban imagery that rests on a real or imagined base where we feel we are surrounded by 'ranches'. The marginal zones have sprung up on the hills surrounding the city, seamlessly adapting to the contour of the terrain and using the model of a house as a unit. That is, the 'barrio' has risen through the repetition of one same type, thereby establishing a certain formal unity in the fabric that visually gives a powerful effect of 'pregnancy' in the architectural unit, in the resulting cubic volume, and in the multiple windows through which to observe the formal city and from where the 'barrio' is perceived as a vigilant presence.

This 'city that sees us' – a concept referring to the title of a short film produced in 1996 by the poet Jesús Enrique Guédez, Venezuelan precursor of the socially-committed documentary –, thus maintains a certain 'proxemic' that defines the geographic distances between units, and incorporates, along with the topographic variable and the typology constructed, a certain order within the informality. In fact, several filmmakers have recorded the country's realities and their contradictions with the 'barrio' concept as starting point, in a dual gaze that puts two opposed visions in one and goes from informality to the formal city and then on to the 'informal', marginal condition of the 'barrios', left out of the urbanizing process and deprived of the most basic services and infrastructures.

General view of Caracas

Under the auspices of the official Program for New Facilities in 'Barrios', the country's new generations of architects have in the past years undertaken diverse urban renewal works and projects that set the pattern for exceptional public spaces, transport infrastructures, cultural and educational centers, dwellings and sport facilities seeking to renovate and restructure the deteriorated urban fabric of the peripheries.

Towards Urban Renewal

In the late 1990s and the start of the new century, studies and diagnoses carried out in university circles gave way to a Program for New Facilities in 'Barrios', an initiative of institutions and groups of outstanding professionals long working to organize communities and empower them for self-administration. We can mention the pioneer project: the urban intervention in Quebrada de Catuche. The first pilot projects for the urban design and physical refurbishment of the 'barrio' of San Miguel, in Caracas, were developed by the architect and urban planner Federico Villanueva and carried out with the support of AMHABITAT (Amigos del Hábitat), funding from the World Bank and the Inter-American Development Bank, and the management of the mayor of Libertador. With support from CONAVI (National Housing Commission) and under the direction of Josefina Baldó, several works and projects were undertaken in order to provide a great diversity of public spaces, different infrastructures, dwellings and sport facilities.

'Barrios' aside, public housing has been the big pending matter for years, and the deficit in this area has increased both quantitatively and qualitatively. In the relatively recent past, the inland cities of Venezuela maintained a degree of specificity and the distinctive features that gave them their identities, but these are fading, following the example set by Caracas. The city we have is not the one we wanted, nor is the city of the modern project, if in the face of a discontinuous series of partially undertaken operations, its ideas and dreams have remained mere theoretical references. Maybe we need other methods and categories by which to analyze the real city and appraise the architecture produced and consumed in it, which is generally exhibitionist and unconnected to the surrounding physical environment.

Upgrading the city, restoring some order within the multiplicity, can or should be the objective of urban renewal actions, which should be continuous, successive, and accompanied by architecture that is brave, sensible and commonsensical, that avoids the rhetoric of a different banner, the design gadgets picked up in our schools, and the paraphernalia of the most commercial brand of professional architecture.

Mentionable, for Caracas, are a novel above-ground metropolitan railway system, a funicular facilitating access to peripheral districts whose stations are designed by the studio Urban Think Tank, besides urban renewal works for improving the avenue Francisco de Miranda and other spaces in the municipality of Chacao, as well as buildings accommodating all kinds of community services, carried out by Town Hall in different periods. In 2001 Urban Think Tank/ Hubert Klumpner, Matías Pintó and Mateo Pintó, with the engineer Ignacio Carrillo,

Matías & Mateo Pintó, Communal House, Caracas (2000)

Urban Think Tank, Metrocable, Caracas (2010)

designed the Vertical Gymnasium: a sport center opened in 2004 and located in the barrio of La Cruz, in Bello Campo, on a site surrounded by buildings. In conception it relates to a previous project of theirs: the Communal House in La Vega, built with the engineer José Adolfo Peña and awarded in the 10th Biennial of Architecture held in Caracas in 2001. That same year, they drew up the Substitution Housing project for the El Petróleo sector, a construction that was left unfinished; a housing block and a social work center in La Ladera; and the Vertical Access Systems, all in La Vega. These experiences led to an important series of refurbishment projects, most of which have not been carried out.

For its part, the Juan de Dios Guanche School, a restrained building designed by Carlos Agell in Chacao, opened in September 2002, and for the same town, Manrique & Tamayo delivered a marketplace in 2008 and Alessandro Famigletti the Municipal Justice Court. Franco Micucci raised a city hall for Baruta, and in Los Teques, Harry Frontado built a metro station, a simple proposal dominated by a large diaphanous and luminous space. Despite these interventions, however, the exodus of young professionals choosing to work abroad, the dejected state of our architecture schools, and the lack of competitions and significant commissions for architects with solid professional track records together paint a picture that is not very bright.

The AM Group, led by Roberto Ameneiro, has carried out numerous projects throughout the country, including the Transport System Workshops and the stunning Footbridges of the Campo Elías Viaduct in Mérida, built in 2005 in collaboration with the engineer Rosendo Camargo. We can also mention the architects Carlos and Lucas Pou, whose many projects and built works include the Children's Cardiology Hospital in Montalbán and the ethereal La Villa del Cine building on the street Guarenas,

Urban Think Tank, Metrocable, Caracas (2010)

Enlace Arquitectura, Sabana Grande Boulevard, Caracas (2008)

Far from the sophisticated languages required by the public institutions for their infrastructural projects, characterized by a recourse to steel structures of huge dimensions, the simplicity of some of the proposals coming from private initiatives is laudable, centered as these works are on the quest for formal refinement and an efficient organization of the interior spaces through the use of sustainable technologies.

which was awarded in the 6th Biennial of Caribbean Architecture in 2007.

By way of contrast, we have what we can call the 'Sambil' phenomenon, in reference to the enormous and highly successful shopping centers built all over the country, by groups of private capital, in the worst of the most commercial kind of architecture of spectacle, closed and controlled to generate fictitious but safe 'public' spaces. This is a far cry from the typological precedent set in the 1970s and 1980s by the commercial complex that is open – like the Chacaito Shopping Center designed by Antonio Pinzani – and integrated into the public space of a city; or by the more recent San Ignacio Center of the architect Carlos Gómez de Llarena, a reference for a project he would later do in conjunction with Mendoza & Dávila, winner of a 2002 competition for ideas for the Shopping Center of the Rental Zone.

Perhaps today's finest example is the Millennium Shopping Center of the architects Francisco Pimentel and Óscar Capiello, which simultaneously opens up and goes underground to connect the metro to the parking lot, creating a space for intense public use: the Plaza Miranda. But even this building is not without a certain structural rhetoric that is disproportionate and superfluous. Winners of the 2009 competition for a hotel in the Rental Zone of Plaza Venezuela, the team has major works to its name, mostly centered on large condominium projects, and quality-wise is a reference for the finest and most serious architecture being produced in the country.

A phenomenon of a different nature are the so-called 'Chana Ranches' on Margarita Island: vacation houses in choice locations facing the sea, built with traditional materials and construction systems, that have become repeatable stereotypes. Independently of their spatial or environmental virtues, however, they constitute a contradiction by being expensive houses in exclusive areas. In a different context, but with certain similarities in the use of scarce elements at minimal cost besides environmental attributes, we have the Community Culture Spaces commissioned by the CONAC (National Culture Council) to a team headed by the architect Juan Pedro Posani. Built in several localities in the inland areas of Venezuela, the downside of these projects is that they do not last long.

Linked to the importance of the Youth Orchestra of Venezuela, we can mention the project for the Concert Hall in the Santa Rosa zone of Caracas – by Tomás Lugo, who built the Teresa Carreño Theater –, with its interior space that is good for acoustics, and the recent announcement of another ideas competition for several concert halls in the same area. But the most important

Grupo AM, Charallave North Station, Miranda (2006)

Productora/Lucio Muniaín, CAF Offices, Caracas (2008)

competition is perhaps the one for the new Caracas offices of the Andean Development Corporation (CAF). Out of 44 entries received, the jury formed by architects of renowned prestige gave first prize to the slender tower designed by the Mexican studio Productora in collaboration with the architect Lucio Muniaín, which stands out for its efficient functional layout and an on-target use of sustainability criteria.

Public and Private
For better or for worse, whether private or public, architecture generates effects on the city. What makes it deteriorate is total absence of planning and responsible, continued management. In Caracas, informality has paradoxically been the product of planning on the basis of guidelines and regulations that come from a static and two-dimensional view of the city. By 'administered' institutionalized informality we mean informality understood as a behavior and life system. But recognizing it as such should not lead us to justify and accept permanent disorder and chaos as something desirable. We must move from the city of anonymity back to the unique city; this is each one's responsibility, although it is collective and public. In cities, both the shifting and exchanging of roles between public and private and the marked obsolescence and abandonment of the public have left voids and gaps that are occupied by the informal commerce of street sellers, degrading communal space.

City and architecture, the 'public house' and the 'private city' point to the profound transformation of formalized urban roles, the dichotomy between public and private as a determinant of the cycles of urban life. In the current situation we should reconsider the architectural dimension of the urban and the urban signification of architecture in light of the phenomenon of informality, which essentially operates by exchanging permanence for mobility and material object for mediatic signals. The architectural form and the form of the city then cease to be mediums for representing society and culture.

Informality contains one distinct sign of life: the expression of a very particular urban culture where it is necessary to recognize oneself before finding others, and in this way carry out the difficult synthesis that will allow the essential features of the character of the informal to be fixed. After all, the city is an organism that can be recognized by means of an 'organizational pattern'; it is a system where disorder can be a source of order. Because of this, maybe a certain informality can be recognized as a new order; and maybe, too, understanding the process can bring good results. In any case, there is an enormous disproportion between the desire to solve the problems and the means with which to do so, and a tremendous ambiguity between analyses and proposals, between persuasion and the decision to take action.

Taking the project as an object of cultural agreement and as a body of knowledge calling for rationality requires formality. We design to change, and Caracas is a changing city, 'mutable' and in permanent mutation or transformation, not only in the sense of alteration, acquisition or loss of essential qualities, but also on account of its potential, which brings about another form of change. For better or for worse, this culture of informality – common to Venezuelan and Latin American cities – is a sign of vitality, variable and recurrent, which manifests itself in many elusive meanings that are hard to put a finger on through rational analysis, or in the objectivity or subjectivity of a subject reintegrating himself as an inhabitant. The Catalan philosopher Xavier Rubert de Ventós writes that we must step back the right distance with respect to the city, and adopt plural viewpoints, if we are to tackle it with a 'deference to difference'.

Productora/Lucio Muniaín, CAF Offices, Caracas (2008)

Urban Think Tank
Metrocable
Caracas (Venezuela)

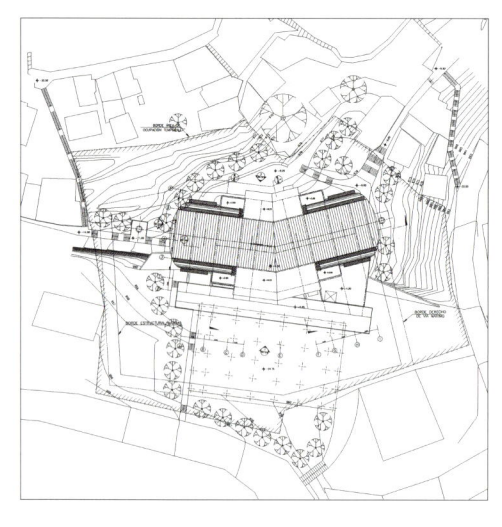

Client
Caracas Metro
Architects
Alfredo Brillembourg, Hubert Klumpner
Collaborators
José Antonio Nuñez, Carlos Bastidas, Patrick Edlinger, Elizabeth Florian, Cesar Gavidia, Dora Kelle, Rafael Machado, Claudia Ochoa, Regina Orvañanos, Juan Ponce, Matt Tarczynski, Michael Contento, Lindsey Sherman
Consultants
DAC (engineering); Topotek 1 (landscaping); Eduardo Lopez, Robert Silman (structures); Intégral Ruedi Baur (graphic design)
Contractor
Norberto Odebrecht
Photos
Iwan Baan

To link the marginal settlements on the edges of Caracas to the center, the building of a new aerial transport system using cable cars has been set in motion, connected to the metropolitan railway and bus networks.

LOCATED ON the peripheries of the city of Caracas, San Agustin has for years been a site for informal settlements of the kind inhabited by a constant agglomeration of immigrants arriving from the country's rural environments with few resources. It has been estimated that close to 60% of the 5 million people living in the Venezuelan capital reside in marginal communities of this type, situated on the hills surrounding the capital, totally cut off from any formal links to public transport and other civic services.

The official plans endeavored to slowly connect these areas to the center of the metropolis through new paved streets, but in 2003, a more radical strategy was proposed: the Metrocable. Numerous dwellings would be spared destruction thanks to this cable car system linked to other public transport networks and designed to allow quick and safe aerial linkage between the mountain zone settlements and downtown Caracas. The plan was approved by the relevant state organisms in 2006, and the first cable car line with its five stations, beginning at San Agustín and ending at Parque Central, has now been completed. Riding in cabins with a maximum capacity of 8 persons, as many as 40,000 citizens are said to benefit from this new infrastructure.

The result of studies, seminars and research conducted by architects, the plan centers mainly on the provision of a novel transport system and its stops, which also serve as transport interchange stations connecting the Metrocable to the existing metropolitan bus circuits. But it also speaks of the creation of 'plug-in' buildings that are attached to the stations and that offer a wide range of cultural and recreational programs for citizens, as well social services of a smaller scale, including gymnasiums, supermarkets and health centers.

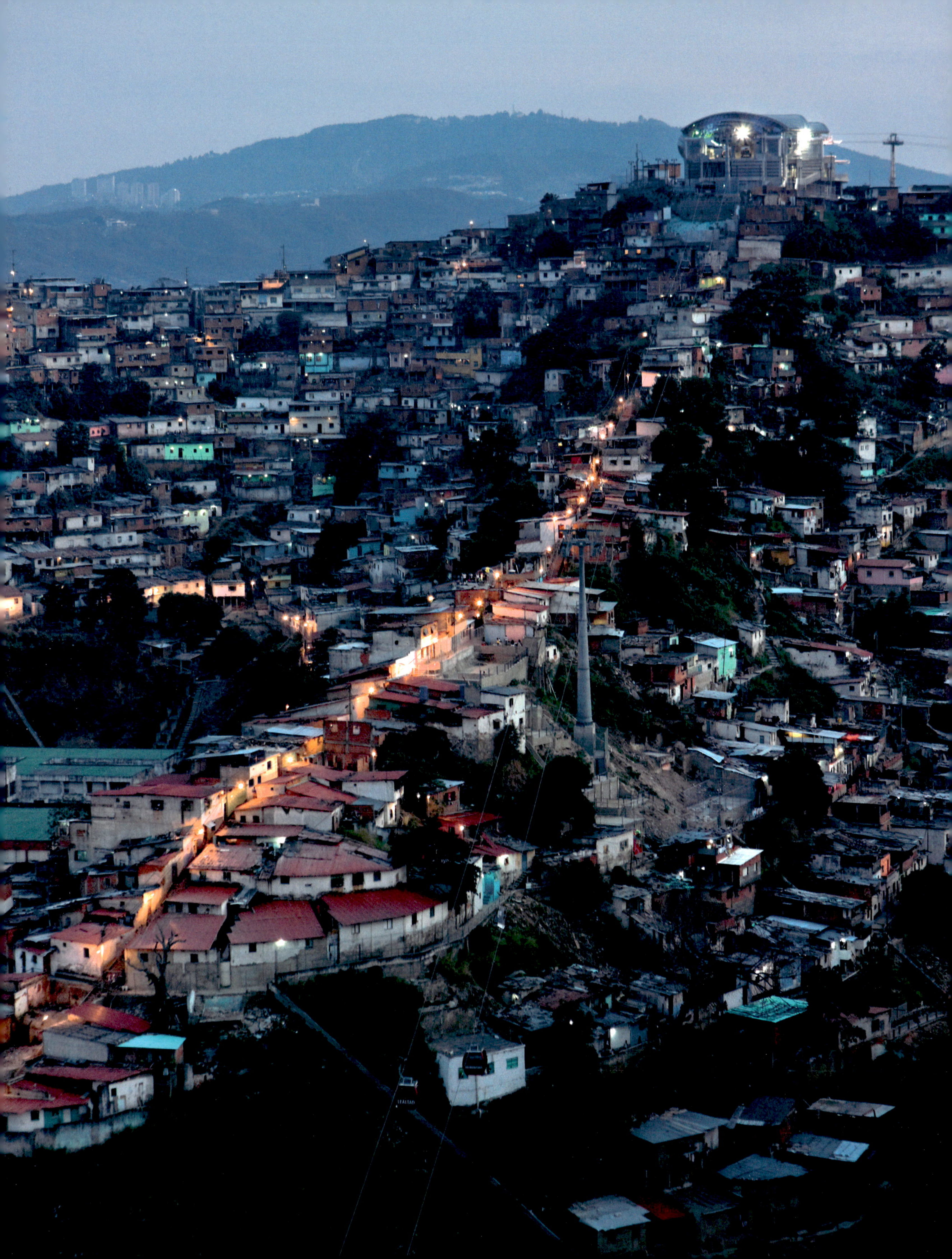

The Metrocable stops are conceived as transport interchanges connecting the cable car system to the existing public bus networks serving the capital. The overall plan also envisions the creation of 'plug-in' buildings that are attached to the stations and that offer a broad range of recreational and cultural programs for citizens, as well as civic services of a smaller scale, including groceries, gymnasiums and health centers.

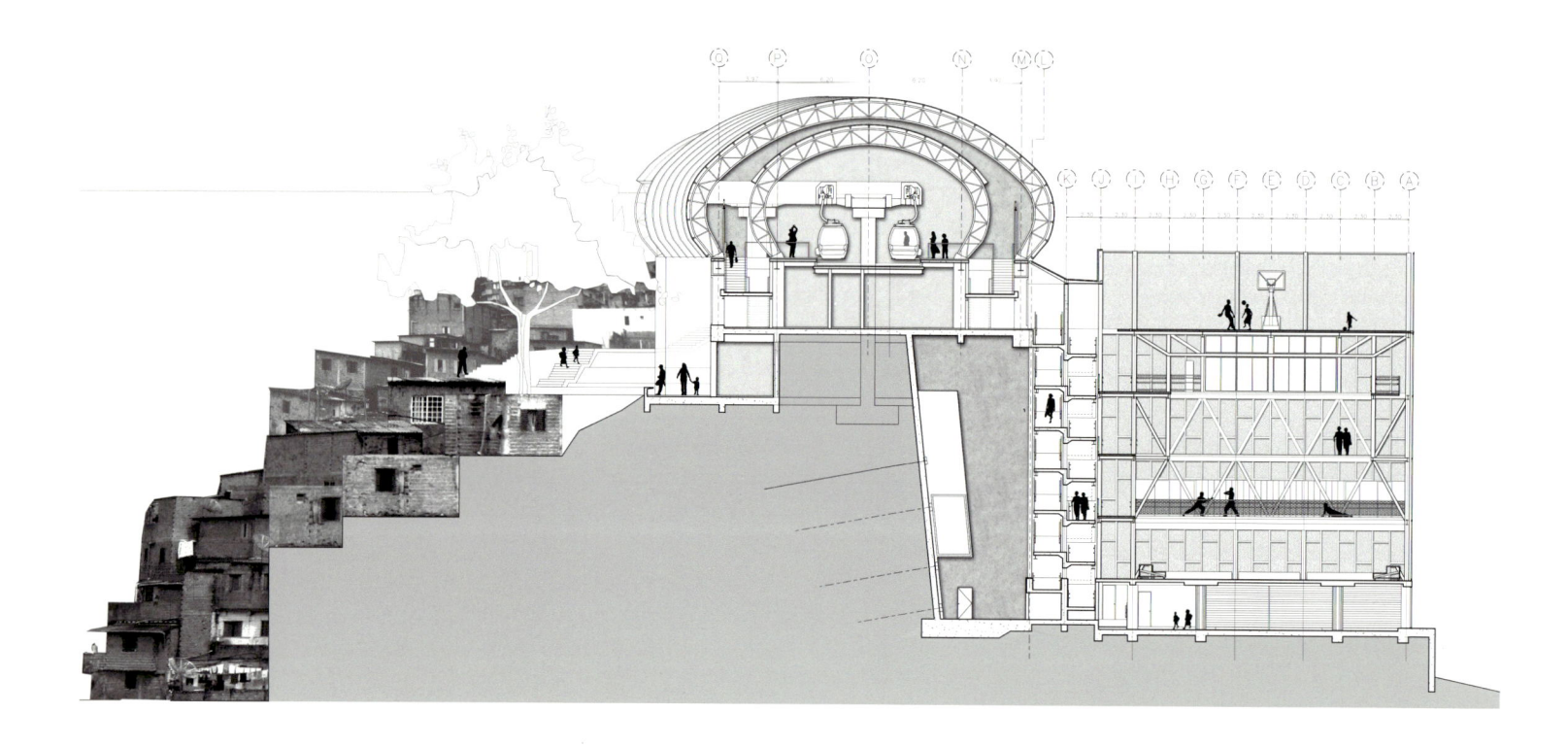

Atlas: America 155

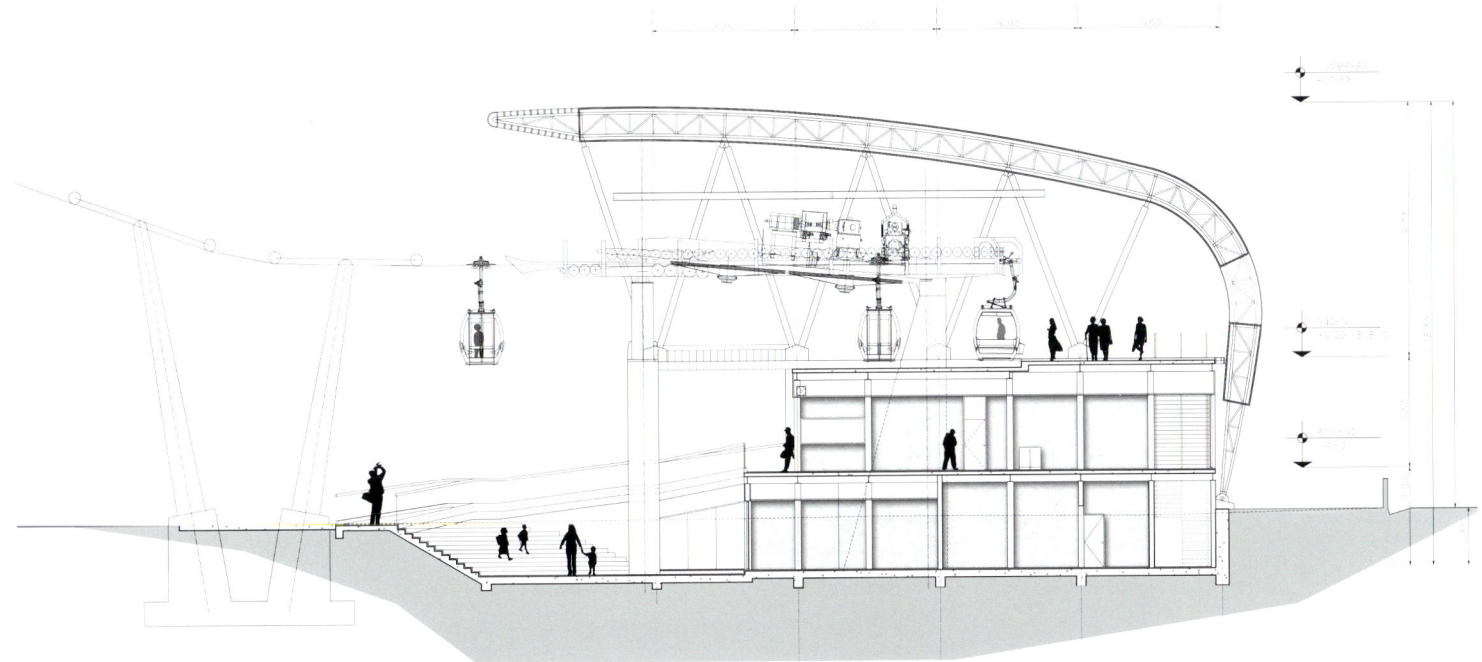

Matías & Mateo Pintó
Communal House
Caracas (Venezuela)

Client
Gran San Miguel Community Consortium
Architects
Matías Pinto, Mateo Pintó; Federico Villanueva (preliminary project)
Collaborator
Eduardo Kairúz
Consultants
José Adolfo Peña, Ignacio Carrillo (structures), Brewer Ingenieros (installations)
Contractor
Brewer Ingenieros
Photos
Matías & Mateo Pintó

CONCEIVED AS an enormous container, the building is equipped with the facilities necessary for basic social services to be provided in San Miguel de La Vega, among the most impoverished of the marginal neighborhoods surviving on the edges of Caracas. The idea for a Communal House started as one of several pilot projects comprising the Program for the Physical Refurbishment of Communities developed by the National Housing Council, along with a group of non-governmental associations formed by members of the community. This is just one of numerous isolated interventions that have been carried out as part of strategies for action directed at improving living conditions in the most degraded areas of the capital.

A simple volume, rectangular on plan, accommodates large spaces, thanks to a structure built with six towers of columns that allow huge spans. Organized in four levels, the building has an open space on the first floor, conceived as a multipurpose venue for social events. On the second floor are two interconnected rooms intended to serve as venues for cultural activities; one of them can be readily converted into a stage when needed. The third story accommodates service areas as well as small classrooms and study rooms that are organized along a perimeter corridor. From here, a bridge connects the center to the public spaces.

Finally, on the roof is a sport court, reachable through a catwalk and protected by a metal mesh enclosure, whose dimensions allow using it for a variety of sports. The structure has been raised with components of prefabricated concrete and steel, assembled right on the site, that simplify the montage process. The claddings are built with materials that are simple, economical, and easy to put together, making it possible for community members to take part in the building process.

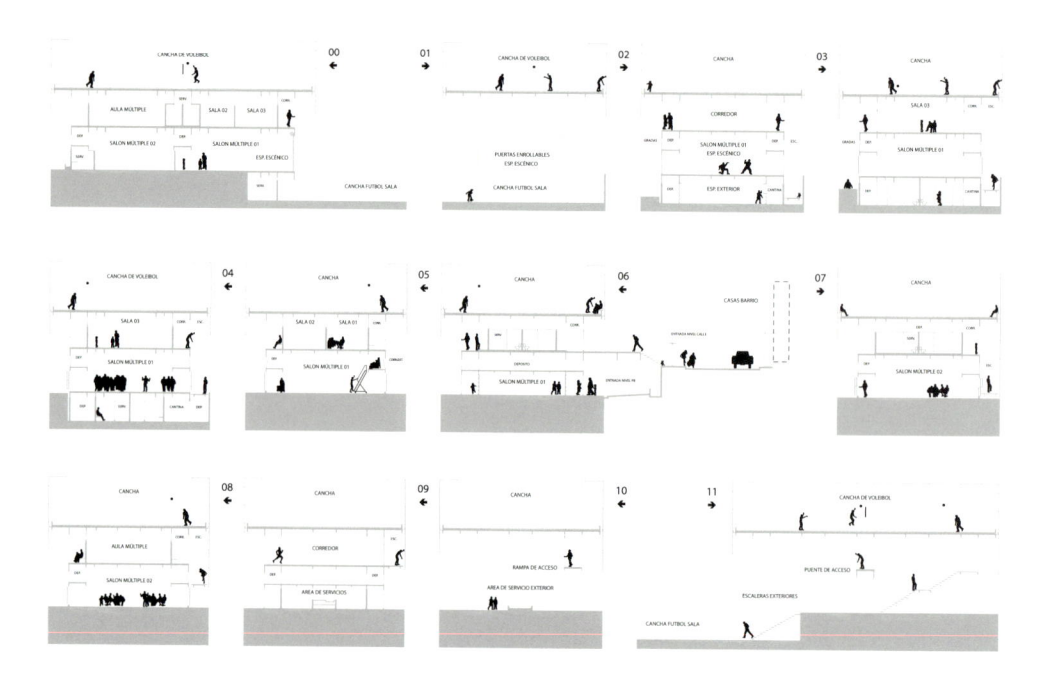

Organized in four floor levels, a straightforward prismatic volume contains a large multipurpose space, venues for various cultural events, rooms for recreational activities, and an open-air sport court on the rooftop.

Built with a structure of steel and prefabricated concrete components put together on site by means of joints with weldings, the Communal House was raised with the active participation, in the actual construction of the center, of members of the community. This was possible through the use of dry building systems that simplify the montage process, and through claddings made of simple, economical, easily assembled materials.

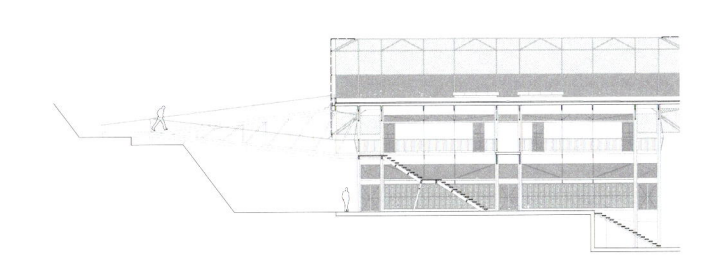

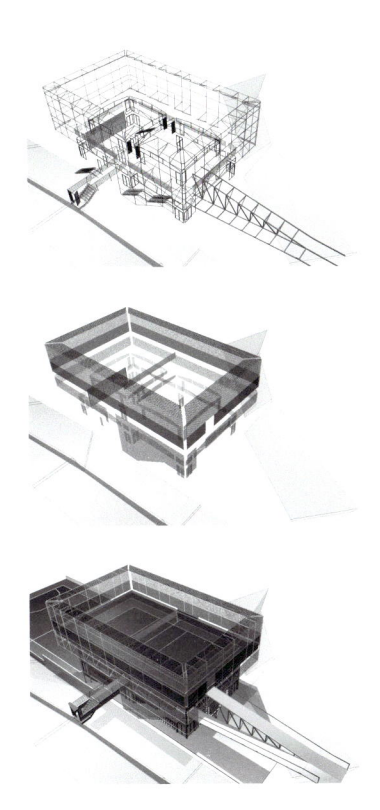

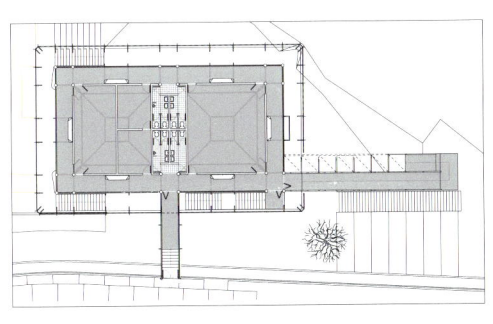

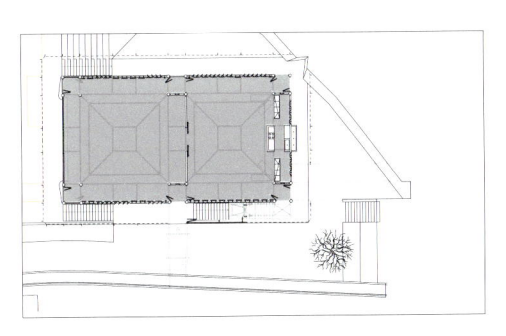

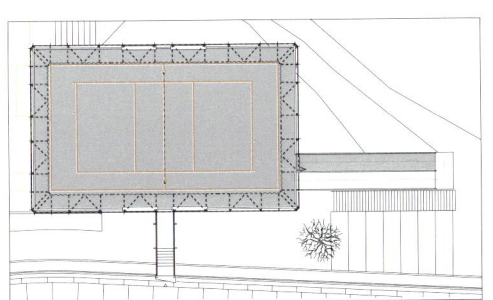

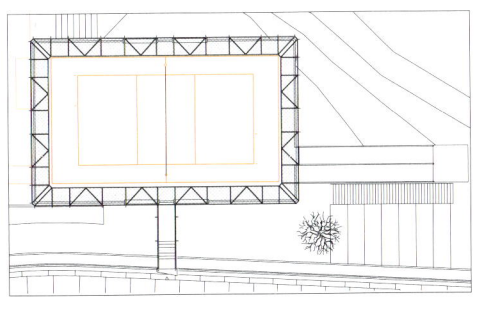

Atlas: America 157

Productora/Lucio Muniaín
CAF Headquarters
Caracas (Venezuela)

THE NEW HEADQUARTERS of the Andean Development Corporation (CAF) will rise in the urban locality of Chacao, the smallest of the five comprising the metropolitan area of the Venezuelan capital. Conceived to be a unique landmark within one of the city's most characteristic contexts, in an endeavor to contribute to urban fabric construction the tower engages in dialogue with the obelisk of Plaza Altamira. The result of an international competition held in the year 2008, the proposal stood out for its conception under criteria involving environmental sustainability, urban and architectural quality, and efficient functional layout. A slender tower rising 147 meters and 36 stories contains all the private functions and premises of the institution, to be complemented in the future with an adjacent building for those spaces and services that are open to the public. Distributing the program in two volumes with limited floor areas makes room for public spaces around. The two towers are connected underground, where the congress center and auditorium are placed above five parking levels. To make the tower meet standards of sustainability, the solutions adopted are those that can be maintained with locally available technology.

Client
Corporación Andina de Fomento (Andean Development Corporation)
Architects
Carlos Bedoya, Wonne Ickx, Victor Jaime, Abel Perles, Lucio Muniaín
Collaborators
David Ortega, Alfonso E. Gutiérrez, Jorge Arroyo, Christian Estavillo, Alejandro Zapata
Photos
Productora

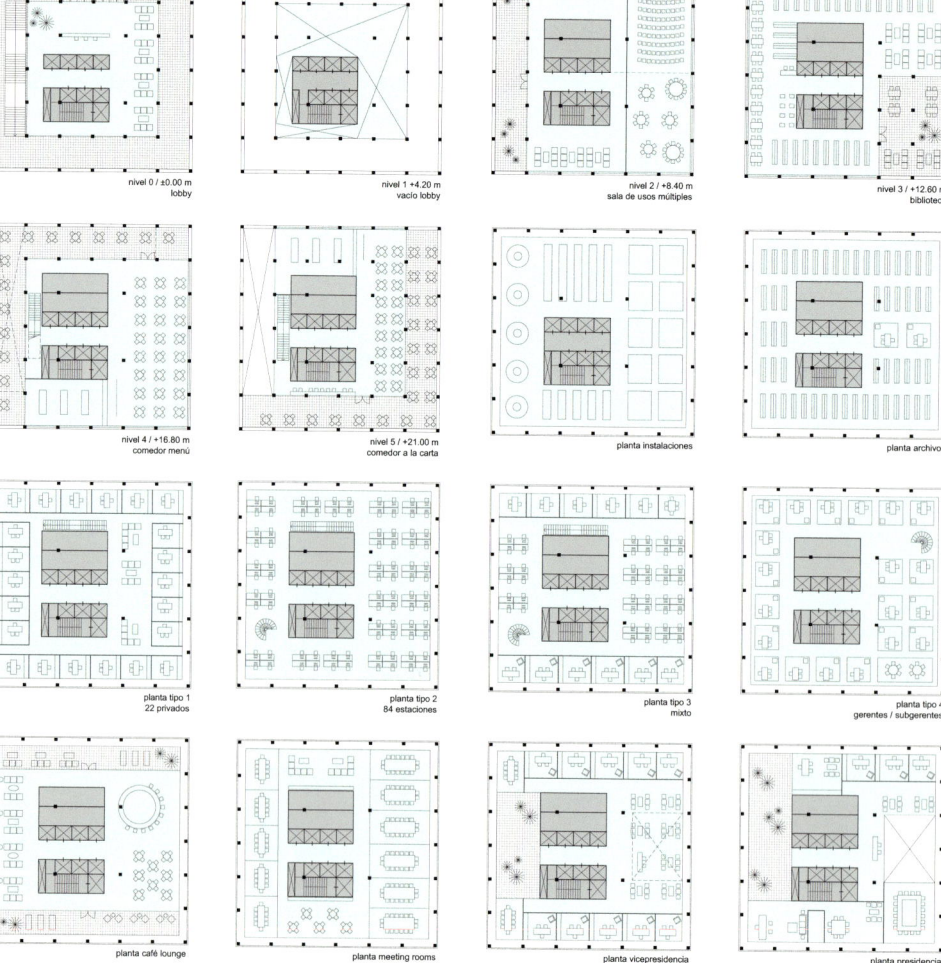

Designed under criteria involving environmental sustainability, the new CAF building excels in architectural quality, in how it interacts with the existing place, and in the efficient functional distribution of its spaces.

Rising a total of 147 meters and 36 stories, a slender tower contains all the private functions and premises of the major public works organism, to be complemented in the future by an adjacent building accommodating those services and spaces open to the public. Separated by a garden area, the two volumes will connect underground, with a congress center and an auditorium crowning the five levels of a parking garage.

Atlas: America 159

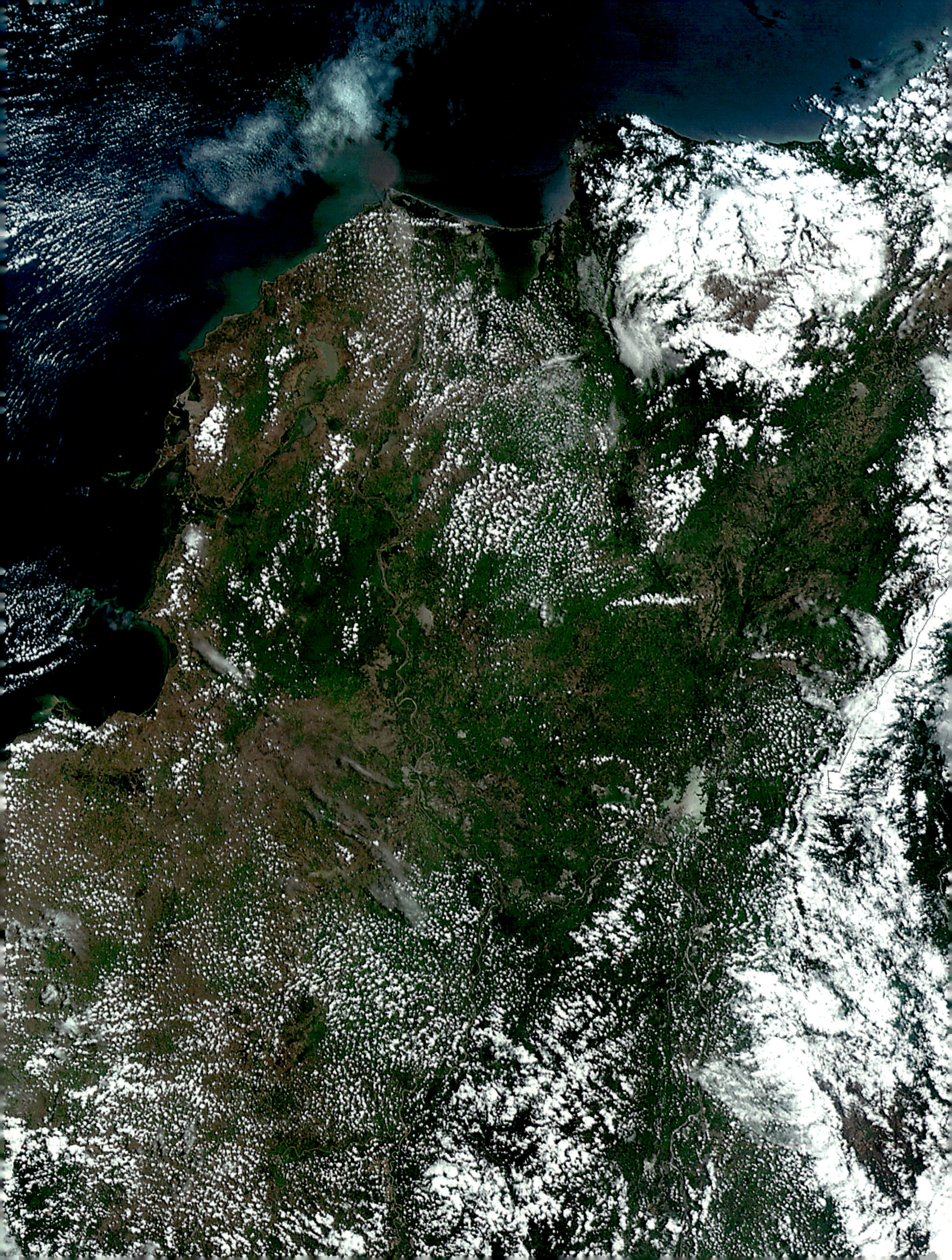

Colombia

Situated between the Caribbean, the Pacific Ocean, the Amazon region and the Andes mountain range, Colombia is rich in landscape and culturally diverse, embracing as it does three geographical areas: the Atlantic Coast, Antioquia – including the metropolitan area of Medellín –, and the Bogotá Savannah. Confronted with a population afflicted with serious social problems and high levels of violence, public institutions have set themselves the task of constructing innovative cultural buildings with the purpose of helping to transform the reality of the country. This is especially significant in the city of Medellín, the location of the España Library by Mazzanti, the Orquideorama by Planb and Jprcr, and the Las Mercedes School by Peláez. Alongside these works rises an architecture marked by elements of vernacular tradition, such as the Public Library in Villanueva, Casanare, by Torres, Piñol, Ramírez & Meza, and the Taller Croquis garden-house in Cali, by Husos.

Silvia Arango
The Public Realm
Colombia, One Country and Three Geographies

Simón Vélez, Cathedral of Pereira, Risaralda (2001)

The new architecture of Colombia bears features of its three geographical areas: the Atlantic Coast, the Antioquia zone, and the Bogotá Savannah.

Using a range of simple low-cost materials and traditional building systems, a large number of public buildings have been completed in small municipalities with the help of the respective communities.

COLOMBIA HAS stoically dealt with the mediatic avalanche that labels it as a dangerous country marked by drug trafficking. Contrary to this shallow image, Colombian architecture of recent years has been known to march in time with processes of social transformation, urban growth and intercultural integration. Although a short article cannot possibly touch on everything that is making Colombia an active and stimulating country where people strive to live a full and meaningful life, I will try to sketch the urban, political and social context in which the most important works of architecture of the first decade of the 21st century have arisen.

With its 48 million inhabitants, Colombia is Latin America's third most populated country, after Brazil and Mexico. This population is mostly distributed between the mountainous zone of the Andes and the Atlantic coast. As in other Latin American countries, urban growth in Colombia intensified in the course of the second half of the 20th century. At present, over 60% of the population is concentrated in sixty cities counting 100,000 inhabitants. Regions have consolidated by virtue of geography and history, with networks of cities that have a certain degree of autonomy and local cultural identity.

Before making a run-through of the three architecturally most significant regions – the Atlantic Coast, the Antioquia zone and the Bogotá Savannah –, it is worth mentioning some across-the-board works that are outstanding for their novel forms and structures and their utilization of simple, cheap and popular materials. In the Guanacas House, located in the municipality of Inzá, in an area of the Cauca Department where indigenous communities still thrive, the architect Simón Hosie – with the help of the community – designed a public library that doubles as a civic venue for gatherings. Known as the Casa del Pueblo, it stands out for how it blends with the landscape, for its interesting wooden structure, and for its intelligent interaction of use and form. Hosie subsequently designed a toll station at the exit of the city of Pereira, where he mixed industrial materials like steel with the traditional *guadua* (bamboo).

In the Public Library of Villanueva (2007), located in the town of Casanare and built by the architects Miguel Torres, Germán Ramírez, Alejandro Piñol and Carlos Meza, there is a contrast of walls: on one hand a heavy type of stone-filled gabions, and on the other a light wall of metal structures and wooden strips. Bamboo, abundant in the country's coffee-growing zones, is an important material in the projects that Simón Vélez has carried out in different parts of Colombia as well as far away abroad, including the Zeri Pavilion at Expo 2000 in Hannover, which later went up in a park of his home city, Manizales. For his persistence in building sustainable architecture, in 2009 Vélez earned a Prince Claus, a Dutch award that Rogelio Salmona had been honored with in 1997. As for building with earth and *bahareque*, several experiments have been undertaken by the HabiTierra group in Barichara, Santander and other places, forming a body of works that rarely get coverage in the media but are noteworthy for the natural, graceful way they are inserted in their locations.

The Atlantic Coast and Antioquia
In the Atlantic Coast region, which includes the coastal area and the inland savannahs, the three major cities are Barranquilla, Cartagena and Santa Marta. Mainly in Cartagena, a city of colonial origins whose historic center and ramparts remain intact, the impact of tourism growing at an alarming rate has had significant urban consequences. On one hand, in recent years the hotel sector has undergone a drastic process of verticalization through towers whose

The latest generations of Colombian architects have recourse to a range of bioclimatic solutions that are appropriate to the country's tropical climate, such as mixed structures in which traditional materials such as wood and bamboo are combined with prefabricated industrial components, or enclosures artisanly raised with frameworks made of wooden pieces and then supported on slender metal profiles forming light lattices.

Simón Vélez, Zeri Pavilion, Manizales, Caldas (2001)

volumetric gestures hardly conceal their commercial intentions. Though still short of the overdensification afflicting places like Panama City, this tendency augurs for the near future a disturbing coastal landscape resembling its model: Miami. On the other hand, tourism has served as a stimulus for the preservation and restoration of our architectural heritage.

In Cartagena, apart from the restoration of emblematic buildings – the Palace of the Inquisition (2003) by architect and restorer Alberto Samudio, for example –, numerous 17th- and 18th-century houses have been converted into homes and boutique hotels. Leaders in this trend are the works of Álvaro Barrera, in particular one of his very latest projects: fitting five apartments into the Casa de los Leoncitos (2009).

On a smaller scale, similar actions have been effected in Santa Marta, a seaside city that has demonstrated a keen interest in improving the public spaces of historic centers. Several promenades, squares and parks designed by Carlos Cabal were inaugurated late in 2009. Along these lines, a project of great importance on account of its ecological reach and the quality of its design is the Ronda del Sinú park along the Sinú River in the city of Montería, a work of Julio Parra, Carlos Montoya, Jorge Cortes and Alfredo Villamaría.

Most of the outstanding architectural works of the past years are located in the most populated and industrialized parts of the country: the Antioquia zone, with its epicenter in the Aburrá Valley, which includes the metropolitan area of Medellín with its population of 3.6 million; and the central part of the country, in the Savannah, which embraces the metropolitan area of Bogotá with its close to 8 million inhabitants. I prefer to talk here in terms of regional coordinates, because surely the disorderly and accelerated expansion phenomenon of urbanization makes us think in terms of the regions where these realities are happening, way exceeding the delimited notion of 'city'. So it is that the plans for re-ordering Medellín and Bogotá necessarily take on a regional and ecological scale, one where interventions of a more specific space can be inscribed.

During the mid-20th century, the Aburrá Valley – the 30 kilometer wide, 90 kilometer long valley of the Medellín River – was occupied by a few small towns with Medellín at the center. Today the territory is filled to the brim. Urbanization has chaotically gobbled up the municipalities that were once clearly discernible, separate units, pushing the two extreme sectors of the population – the richest and the poorest – up the mountain slopes. The urban picture therefore presents a compact and dense fabric in the lower valley against a mountain backdrop where an informal city of self-built dwellings resembling the favelas of Rio de Janeiro alternates with a serpentine city

Daniel Bonilla, Julio Mario Santo Domingo Building, University of the Andes, Bogotá, Colombia (2007)

Planb & Jprcr, Orquideorama, Medellín, Antioquia (2006)

In the Antioquia zone, with its epicenter in the Aburrá Valley – which embraces the metropolitan area of Medellín –, the new cultural centers and sport facilities are playing an important part in the regeneration of the urban fabric of the city. Connected to one another by an above-ground metropolitan railway system called the Metrocable, all of them have been made possible through the sponsorship of public organisms.

dotted with luxury houses and apartment buildings. The continuity of programs spearheaded by mayors like Sergio Fajardo since 2001 has given rise to urban and architectural interventions of enormous impact on the physical transformation of the cities, operations largely made possible by the launching, in 1995, of a surface metropolitan railway system that stretches parallel to the Medellín River.

Interventions undertaken within the consolidated city have served to connect two hubs of activity – one administrative-commercial, the other recreational-cultural, with a 3.5 kilometer distance in between – through the 'pedestrianization' of the street Carabobo. The first hub revolves around the Alpujarra Administrative Center (1980-1982), a work of Germán Samper and Fajardo Vélez in collaboration with Lago & Sáenz, a last holdover of the civic center proposed by Josep Lluís Sert and Paul Wiener in their masterplan of 1952. The idea of concentrating civic, administrative and cultural activities in a place other than the historic center has been on the minds of Medellín planners for fifty years now. In this sector, several buildings have been going up around refurbished town squares since 2000. That same year, to the west of the Alpujarra – across the 'intelligent' Public Companies of Medellín building (1996) of Carlos Julio Calle and beside the Metropolitan Theater of Medellín (1987) of Óscar Mesa –, the Park of the Bare Feet and the Public Companies Interactive Museum, both by Felipe Uribe de Bedout, Ana Elvira Vélez and Giovanni Spera, were inaugurated. The instant success of the park, of medium scale and including water play activities, led to the building of other public spaces in the area. In the vicinity Daniel Bonilla and Giancarlo Mazzanti built the Plaza Mayor complex (2002-2004): a compact block clad above with wooden

Felipe Mesa (Plan b) & Giancarlo Mazzanti, Coliseum of Medellín, Antioquía (2010)

Alejandro Echeverri, Explora Park Museum, Medellín, Antioquia (2007)

strips, containing a convention center, and a more elongated volume with a facade of superposed horizontal strips, accommodating an exhibitions center.

North of the Alpujarra was the traditional Plaza Cisneros and on one side stood the Carré and Vázquez buildings, raised at the start of the 20th century and last remnants of the edifices that surrounded the razed market square. Completed across them in the year 2005 is the Public Companies Library of Felipe Uribe de Bedout, with its inclined glazed facade recalling the work of Alfonso Eduardo Reidy, forming a space decorated with a forest of post-dimmers that is known as the Plaza de la Luz. Conceived by Juan Manuel Peláez, the square is ill-lit because the vertical light fixtures are turned on only occasionally. Finally, beside the Alpujarra, work on the Plaza de la Libertad began in 2007 and is still in progress. Designed by the studio Opus, a team formed by Manuel Jaén, Carlos Betancur and Carlos Montoya, it includes two interconnected office towers clad with strips of wood as a symbol of the freedom of Colombia's forest ecosystems. Overall, the interventions that have been carried out in the city center are reminiscent of CIAM urbanism, with open spaces surrounded by free-standing buildings of different forms and materials.

Prominent in the cultural-recreational area, at the other far end of Carabobo, is the Orquideorama (2006) of the architects Felipe Mesa, Jean Paul Restrepo and the latter's son Camilo Restrepo. Located in the city's Botanical Garden, more than a place for exhibiting varieties of the orchid – the national flower – the building is used as a venue for social events. The project consists of a series of hexagons formed by artificial trees – made of metal and clad in wood –, which in the manner of juxtaposed umbrellas cover an open area that connects with the rest of the park. Facing the Botanical Gardens is a train-like complex of red volumes that is the Explora Museum-Park (2007), by Alejandro Echeverri. Close by is the Park of Desires, a large space whose folded horizontal plane is bordered by the Planetarium and its support building, the latter and the park being works of Felipe Uribe de Bedout.

We also have to mention the sport facilities built for the 9th South American Games of 2010, situated some two kilometers west of this area. Standing out among them for its undulating roofs are Felipe Mesa (Planb) and Giancarlo Mazzanti's Coliseum of Medellín – containing basketball, volleyball, combat and gymnastics stadiums – and the Aquatic Complex of Paisajes Emergentes, a studio jointly run by Luis Callejas, Edgar Mazo and Sebastián Mejía.

Areas with low indexes of human development – poor mountain communes –, have since 2004 been seeing the materialization of the Integrated Urban Projects (PUIs) through a transport system known as the metrocable: booths fitting five people that hang from an endless wire and connect with the metropolitan railway system. The PUIs also envision the creation of public facilities – libraries, schools, daycare centers – whose designs adapt to the characteristics of their respective locations. The most advanced PUI so far is in the Northeastern Commune, with its twelve neighborhoods and 170,000 inhabitants already benefiting from three metrocable stations and various public spaces since 2006. Under the direction of Alejandro Echeverri, a municipal team endorsed by the participation of townsfolk carried out the painstaking task of scanning the area for places to act upon, and this led to specific designs: a chess balcony, a church atrium and a park count among the interesting new public spaces that act as architectural and social stitches.

In the same commune, Giancarlo Mazzanti's España Library in the Santo Domingo neighborhood (2007) – one of seven in Medellín – has received plenty of world attention. It developed from three conventional structures clad with sheets of black stone for an effect of sculptural faceted volumes that compromises the building's durability and its formal purity when seen up close. In the wake of the success of the Northeastern zone, projects based on similar precepts were launched in the Trece commune in 2009, and another five municipalities will be following suit in the near future. As for the metropolitan dimension, three thrusts are involved: creating linear parks around the gorges and passes that separate the various hills

Integrated Urban Projects, Metrocable, Medellín, Antioquia (2004)

The central part of the country, specifically the vast savannah where the city of Bogotá is situated, has been the scene of large-scale operations undertaken by the municipal government to provide the citizenry with more social facilities. These projects include park-libraries and public schools, as well as a new system of mass transit called Transmillennium, with articulated buses circulating along some lanes with priority.

Rogelio Salmona, Virgilio Barco Library, Bogotá (2002)

surrounding the city; fixing up and providing access to zones of ecological interest deep in the valley; and designing five 'centralities', conceived as corporate enclaves and urban developments, that serve to organize the boundaries between Medellín and the municipalities adjacent to it.

The Bogotá Savannah

The metropolitan area of Bogotá, the country's capital, is bordered to the east by mountains and surrounded in the other directions by a vast and fertile savannah where agriculture including livestock has been thriving for centuries. In an aerial view of the zone, the range of greens that make up the high plain has been disrupted in recent years by the plastic greenhouses used for the cultivation of flowers, now a leading export product. In any case, with mayors like Antanas Mockus, Bogotá has kept up a certain continuity in the creation of basic projects. Among those carried out in the past fifteen years or so are interventions on public spaces, newly created social facilities – park-libraries and schools – and designs for mega-projects in the watershed, of a metropolitan nature. Adapted from that implanted in the Brazilian city of Curitiba, the mass transport system known as Transmillennium was inaugurated in 2000, with articulated buses that stop at specific points and have priority on given lanes. Although it was an improvement over the chaos of the previous system, with its excessive number of private lines, the Transmillennium is by now saturated, so the prospect of building an underground metropolitan railway that can take in large crowds of commuters is high on the agenda of Bogotá's new mayor. Already backed by detailed studies, the initiative will hopefully come to fruition, a solid system of mass transport being vital to a city as huge and populous as Bogotá.

In simultaneity with the Transmillennium, an extensive network of bicycle lanes was created in various zones of the city to encourage people to bike and thereby curb the use of private vehicles. With the same intention of making citizens walk and bike, the outskirts were endowed with the so-called 'alamedas' (tree-lined avenues), which alternate with small plazas acting as meeting points. One of the most ambitious among these promenades is the Alameda del Porvenir – by MPG, the studio of Felipe González-Pacheco and Juan Ignacio Muñoz –, which stretches 17 kilometers and in the process connects several popular

Daniel Bermúdez, El Tintal Library, Bogotá (2001)

neighborhoods situated west of the capital. These promenades have two antecedents. First is the practice, begun in 1982, of restricting wheeled traffic on Sundays and holidays. On these days, the capital's main streets and avenues turn into spatious sport circuits for a varied citizenry – children, youngsters and grown-ups – equipped with an entire range of mini-means of locomotion: bicycles, skateboards, pedal cars and so on and so forth. The other antecedent dates further back in time: the tradition of alamedas and promenades that took root in Bogotá, as in many other Latin American cities, during the late 18th century and early 19th, and which has been reborn in the wake of Rogelio Salmona and Luis Kopec's pedestrianization of Avenida Jiménez (2000), the spinal column of the city center. Finally, public space projects included the creation of urban parks – the Third Millennium Park and Renaissance Park included – and the improvement of numerous green zones.

The Bogotá idea of library parks, later borrowed by Medellín, is of great interest because despite the pessimistic predictions that the book is doomed to disappear in the Internet era, Bogota's libraries have historically been among the most used in the world. In 2000, the Luis Ángel Arango Library of the Bank of the Republic, opened in 1958, recorded a daily visitor count of over 10,000, mostly secondary school and university students. With this for an antecedent, plans were made to build four mega-libraries surrounded by greenery and equipped with infrastructure for cultural events (auditoriums, functions rooms and exhibition halls). Three of them opened in the year 2001 as architectural landmarks. Southwest of the capital, the El Tintal Library was built by Daniel Bermúdez from an old garbage compactor facility, a solid concrete volume preceded by a wide ramp up which the garbage trucks used to be driven. Large skylights were opened to create a pleasant, uniformly lit interior. South of the city rises the El Tunal Library, which the architects Suely Vargas and Manuel Guerrero organized in such a way that an interior street connects the different rooms within a horizontal volume. In the northwestern sector is the El Salitre Library, also called the Virgilio Barco Library, a work of Rogelio Salmona, where an intimate symbiosis between architecture and park is emphasized by the access scheme, which ascends and descends while bordering a staggered fountain. The architectural composition, based on curved forms that emerge from a central space conceived as a newspaper library, can be appreciated from the terraces above, as can the mountains surrounding the city of Bogotá. Finally, the north of the capital is home to the recently completed Julio Mario Santo Domingo Library, a work of Daniel Bermúdez, which includes a theater for large-scale spectacles and an audience of 1,000 people.

Moving on to a more metropolitan scale, the most ambitious long-term project to be launched to date is the de-contamination and recuperation of the Bogotá River and its hydric system, which includes the brooks, streams and wetlands that flow down from the eastern mountains, cross the city and finally empty into the river. The masterplan, which includes a restructuring of a 380 kilometer sewage system, is due for completion by the year 2020. One of the most advanced projects within the ZMPA (Environmental Management and Preservation Zones) specified by the general plan involves the delta of the Juan Amarillo River and its adjoining wetlands, designed by a team spearheaded by Diana Wiesner and Eduardo Samper.

Besides the municipal projects, we should mention some private works undertaken with city-building intentions. Just a hundred meters from the foundational square, the Plaza de Bolívar, rise two cultural facilities of great importance. One is the Museum of Art of the Bank of the Republic by Enrique Triana, with its several interconnected courtyards arranged within a city block and a white facade preceded by a small sunken square. On the same street stand the offices

Daniel Motta, Carlos Pizarro School, Bogotá (2004)

With huge investments coming from public organisms, buildings for education constitute a particularly interesting laboratory for formal experimentation, giving rise to arrangements around large central squares open to the public to freely planned layouts with galleries that serve to link up interior spaces, passing through linear constructions containing classrooms and other spaces flanking corridors to circulate through.

Juan Manuel Peláez, Las Mercedes School, Medellín, Antioquia (2008)

of the Mexican Economic Culture Fund, known as the García Márquez Cultural Center, which was Rogelio Salmona's last project. Its transparency invites one to enter the circular plaza inside and go up the ramps to some terraces that offer views of the colonial architecture around.

The same concept of stitching up the city is behind two new interventions undertaken in the campus of the University of the Andes: the renovation of buildings B and W by Daniel Bermúdez. Both connect with preexisting buildings of different periods to create covered zones protecting pedestrians and the accesses to the different spaces, and are rendered with a sensitiveness that demonstrates a solid knowledge of the rituals and customs of university life. Meanwhile, in an area that is separated from the actual campus, Felipe González-Pacheco has built a sport center that fits a swimming pool and several covered courts inside a compact glazed volume protected by a cladding of horizontal aluminum strips.

It seems natural, though not in an obvious manner, for avant-garde architecture to go up in the country's two major metropolises, Bogotá and Medellín: natural because it is in these two cities that a great number of architecture schools and architects are based, making them the central hubs of debate, confrontation and interaction with the rest of the world; and not in an obvious way because the same conditions exist in other great cities of the continent, such as Cali and Barranquilla, and yet these have not in recent years demonstrated as vigorous an architectural dynamic. Perhaps the decisive factor behind the proliferation of projects in Medellín and Bogotá is the political clout and push of their mayors, who in breaking a long tradition of designing urban facilities on the sole basis of quantitative parameters, have succeeded in tying up social welfare objectives with architectural quality, upon the understanding that the construction of worthy buildings is an inexorable part of social regeneration.

Educational Buildings
In a general scheme of things, if I had to name a single typology as best representing the best of Colombian architecture of the past ten years, without any doubt it would be the architecture of education. Thanks to huge investments in public and private schools, along with the decision to avoid uniform

Adolfo Schleger Verano, Pies Descalzos Foundation, Barranquilla (2009)

models, which has allowed a great degree of freedom in design, this category has become a laboratory for formal and compositional experimentation. Without getting into labels of architectural language, simply in the spirit of spotting tendencies among the numerous examples, we can easily distinguish four compositional strategies. First, the centripetal organization is conceived as an orthogonal arrangement around a large courtyard or central plaza, as in the school of the Pies Descalzos Foundation (2009), a property of the popular Colombian singer Shakira, built in her hometown, Barranquilla, by the architect Adolfo Schleger Verano. A variation on this scheme is the Antonio Derka School – the enlargement of the Santo Domingo School –, the open spaces of which follow a sharp inclination of the land by unfolding in the form of a cascade. Located in Medellín, the project has been carried out by Obra Negra, the studio formed by the architects Carlos Pardo, Nicolás Vélez and Mauricio Zuluaga.

The second tendency, which is linear in character, is to arrange the classrooms and other school spaces on both sides of an internal circulation system that functions in the manner of a street. This is the case of the layout drawn up by Pedro Juan Jaramillo at the Gabriel Betancourt School in Bogotá, a work completed in 2005. The third compositional strategy consists of alternating filled spaces (classrooms and other rooms) with voids (patios) in a grid or mesh, as at the María Mercedes Carranza School in Bolívar City, a work of the architects Sergio Trujillo, Leonardo Álvarez and Diego Suárez, or at the Carlos Pizarro School in Bogotá, by Daniel Motta and Fernando Rodríguez. Finally, the fourth layout is like a necklace, with a free circulation scheme that snakes or zigzags in the process of connecting the different volumes, as at the Gerardo Molina School in Bogotá, by Giancarlo Mazzanti , or the Flor del Campo Shool in Cartagena, a project carried out by the same architect in collaboration with Felipe Mesa.

Four Generations
In the past years, a total of four generations of architects have coexisted in Colombia. The most veteran among them, headed by the figures of Rogelio Salmona and Enrique Triana, have an evident weakness for contextual architecture of the kind that interconnects immediate and intermediate circumstances within a profound sense of place, and breaks up masses into small fragments.

The generation that is now in maturity, represented by Daniel Bermúdez and Sergio Trujillo, presents features of continuity from the previous one, such as a similar preoccupation with context, but shows differences, such as a keen interest in technical and constructive questions and an inclination for bold, regular volumes built with durable materials like stone and concrete. The adult generation currently in power, as historically befits its age, counts the largest number of members working in the Colombian panorama. Architects like Felipe Uribe de Bedout, Giancarlo Mazzanti and Daniel Bonilla seem to be of a pragmatic cut, ignoring local traditions and preferring irregular volumes with skins that are porous and not very durable. Finally, the tradition of granting commissions through public competitions has given rise to the young crop of architects, represented here by Felipe Mesa, Juan Manuel Peláez and Simón Hosie. They have features of the generation before them, as is natural, but also present characteristics of their own, such as their interest in theories oriented towards the social and exact sciences, their systemic way of thinking, and their tendency to group into anonymous teams – such as Planb, OPUS, Ctgr or MGP – or tie up with other architects for project-specific commissions. This practice, which makes authorships difficult to ascribe, seems to be a reaction to the 'author architecture' of preceding generations. Over and above differences, however, all four generations are responsibly working to improve the living conditions of Colombians through a mix of social awareness and architectural quality.

Obra Negra, Antonio Derka School, Medellín, Antioquia (2009)

Giancarlo Mazzanti
España Library
Medellín, Antioquia (Colombia)

Client
Medellín Town Hall
Architect
Giancarlo Mazzanti
Collaborators
A. Sarmiento, J. Manuel Gil,
F. Pantoja, P. Saa, G. Vasquez,
I. Ucros, S. Tobon, A. Aschner
Photos
Iwan Baan, Carlos Tobón (p. 172),
Sergio Gómez (p. 173 bottom)

IN ONE OF THE most crime-ridden and poverty-stricken neighborhoods of the city of Medellín is a grand, imposing multipurpose complex whose three dark volumes include a library, learning centers, an exhibition gallery, administration areas and an auditorium. The España Library forms part of the so-called Integral Urban Projects, a series of works of architecture and urban planning that public institutions, academic sectors and social organizations have been carrying out in past years with the aim of addressing the serious problem of violence afflicting the district.

The project's location on the steep slopes of the Colombian city was determinant in the decision to construct a public platform that, by becoming a choice spot from which to view the valley below, has reinforced its function as a meeting point and gathering place and as a reference in the regenerated zone. This new plaza serves to connect the building to a sequence of lookouts positioned between the dense urban scheme and the metrocable station.

The three enormous bulks of the España Library complex rise over this platform. An articulated metal skeleton supports an enclosure built with slate panels and a system of reinforced concrete frames that frees the envelope from the need to take on any loadbearing function, allowing the zenithal illumination of all the interior spaces. This lighting from above would potentially bring the region's high temperatures into the building, but the use of stone, laminated glass and wood for the interior claddings, combined with an innovative thermal control mechanism that releases hot air by generating ascending air currents, keeps the spaces comfortably cool. All three slate-clad volumes are completely severed from the platform, which was constructed with a framework structure of metal pillars and a retaining wall built with reinforced concrete and stone gabions.

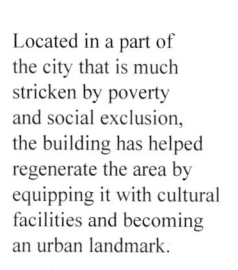

Located in a part of the city that is much stricken by poverty and social exclusion, the building has helped regenerate the area by equipping it with cultural facilities and becoming an urban landmark.

On a steep inclination in the Colombian city of Medellín stands this new cultural complex formed by three prismatic volumes hovering over a huge horizontal platform that takes on the added role of viewpoint over the valley. The whole program is fitted into this trio of dark-toned, slate-clad constructions containing, respectively, a library, a social center including classrooms and a gallery for exhibitions, and a large cultural center.

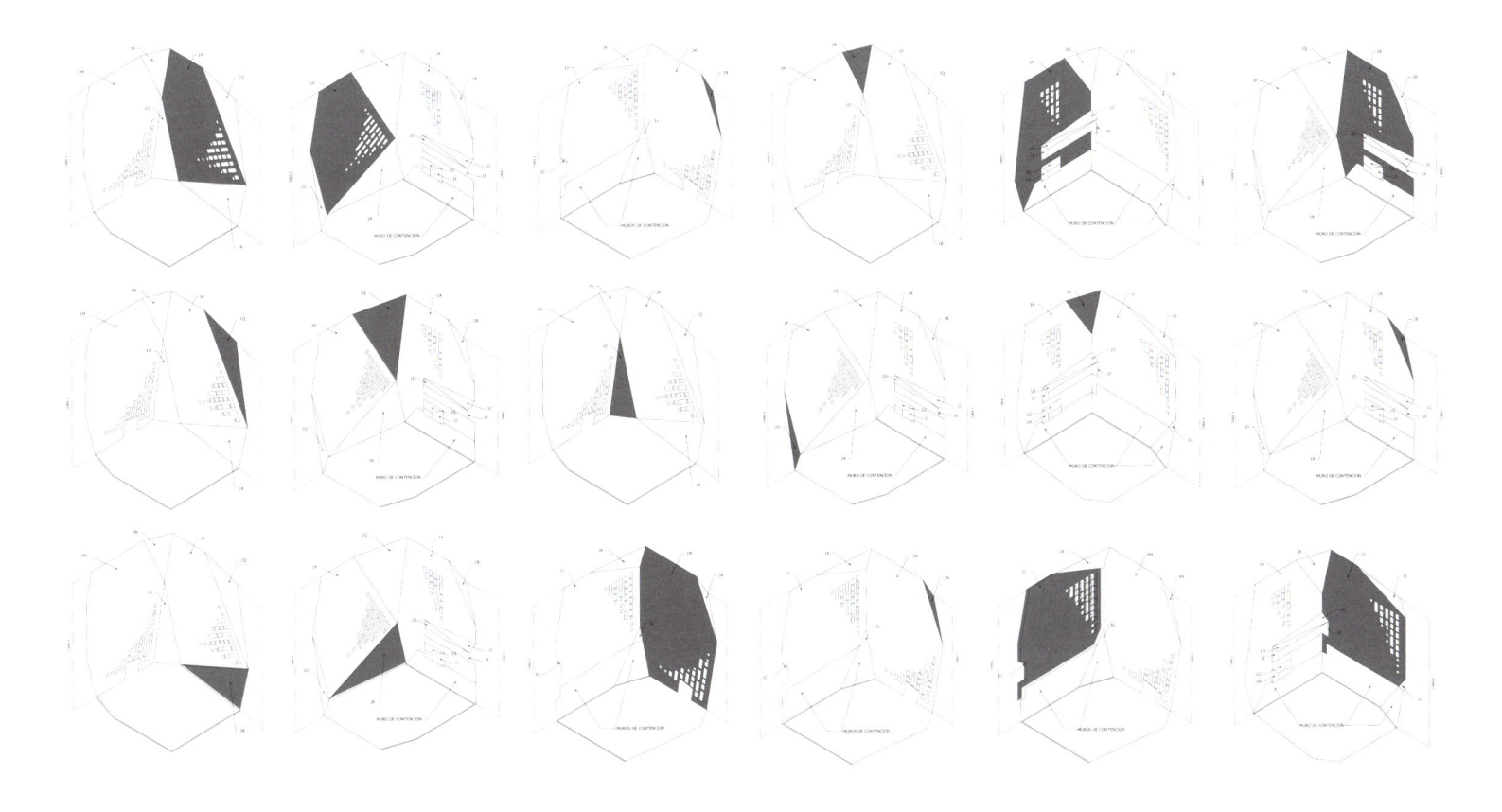

Atlas: America **171**

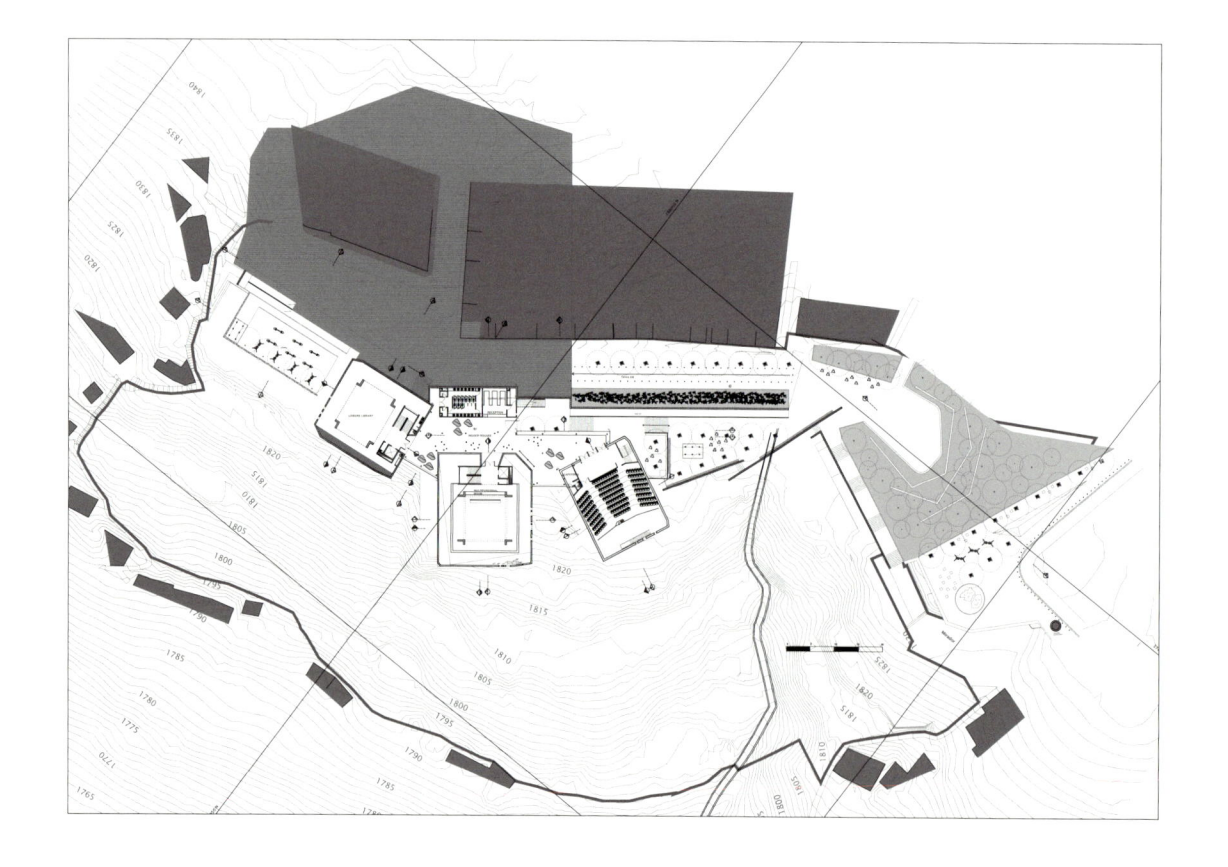

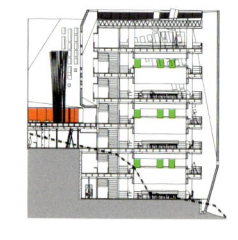

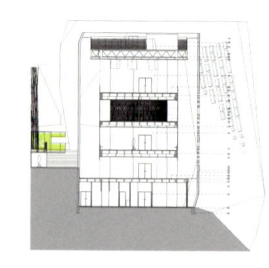

The building aims to provide this neighborhood, stricken by poverty and social exclusion, with new cultural facilities to spur the regeneration process of the area, becoming at the same time a new city landmark.

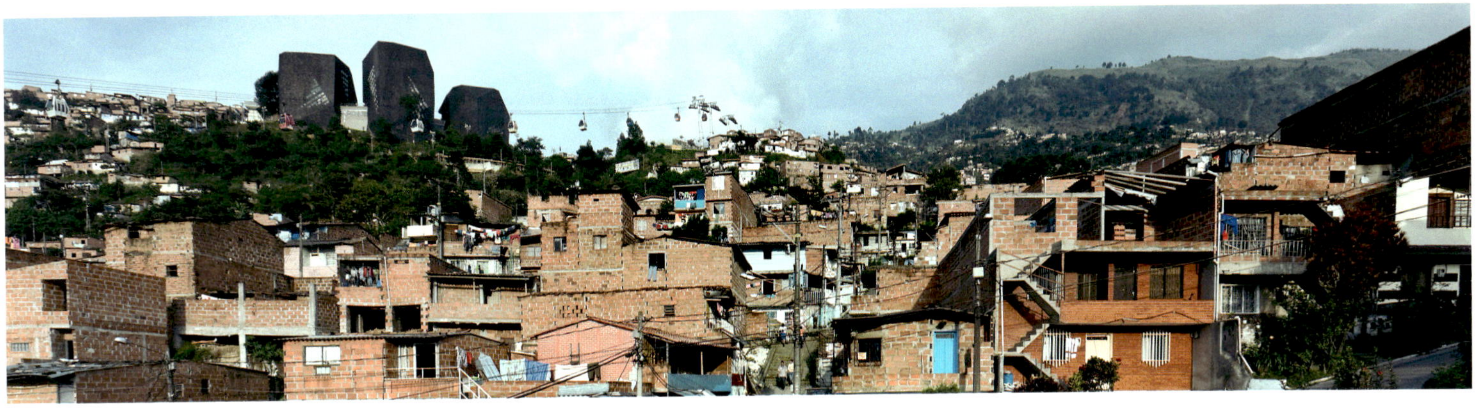

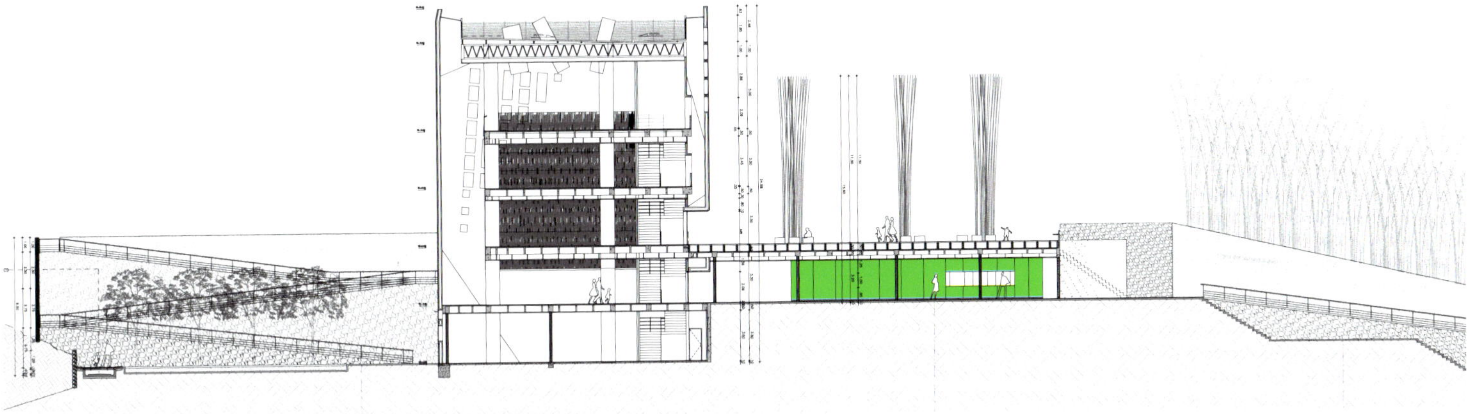

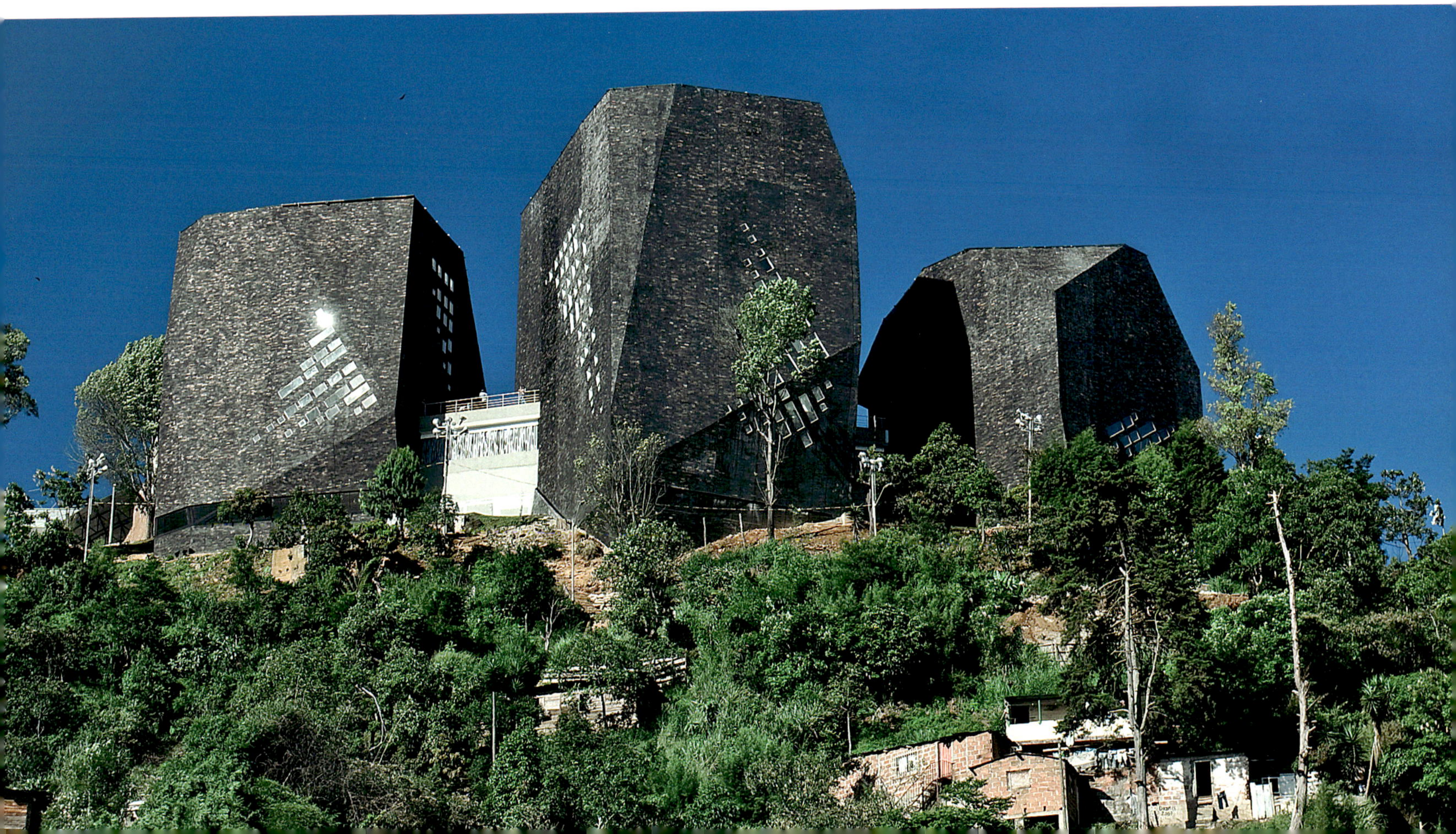

174 Atlas: America

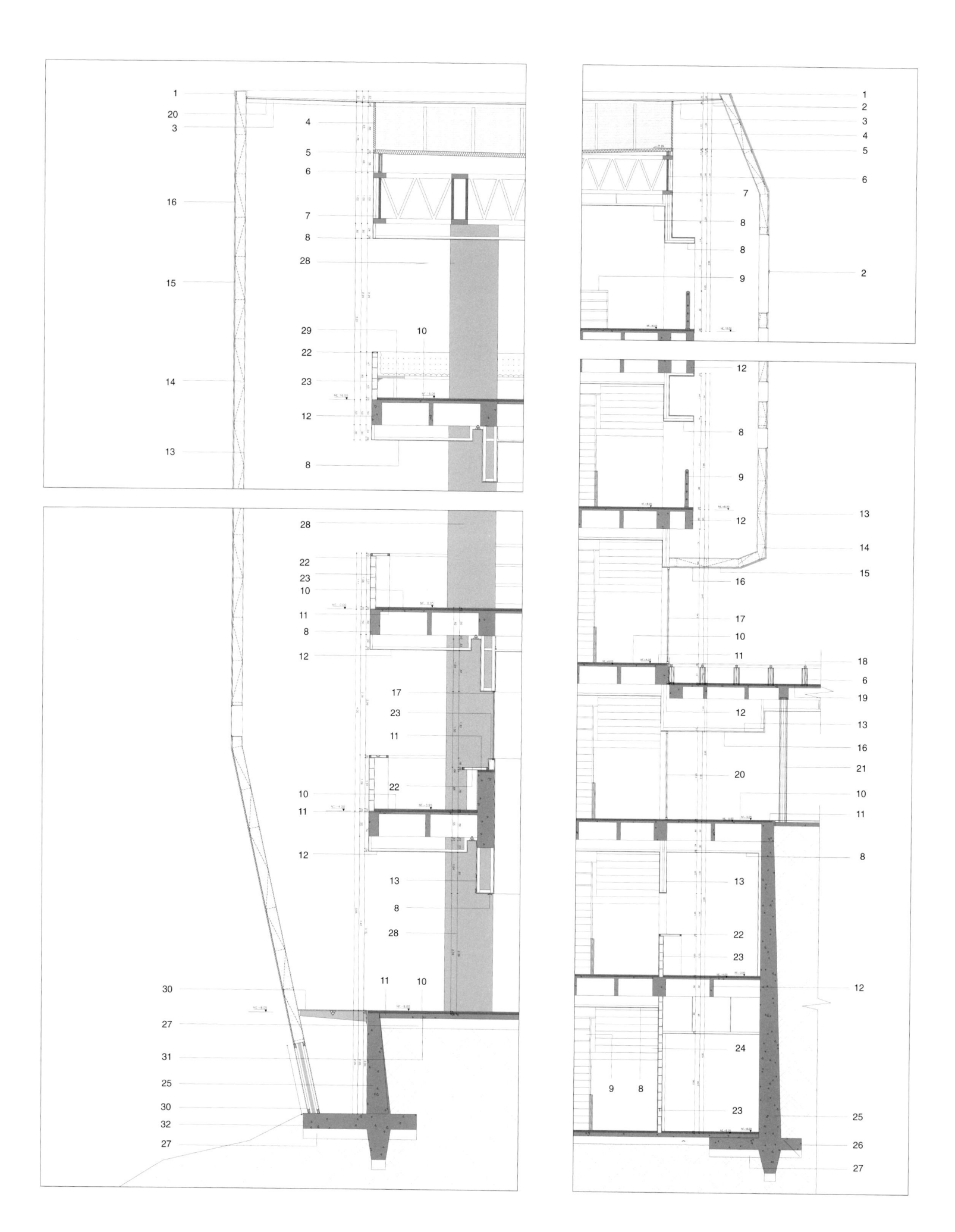

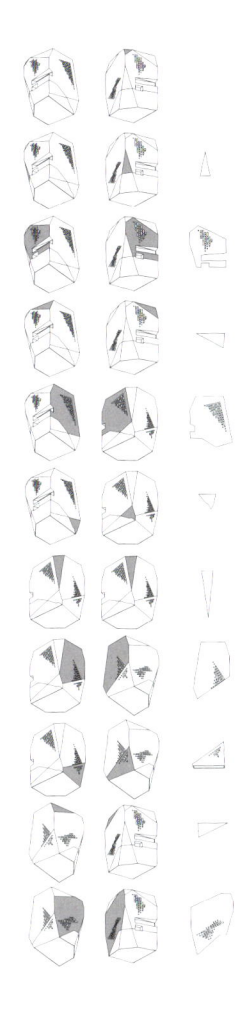

1   aluminum finish
2   10 mm laminated safety glass with anodized aluminum frame
3   1.8 mm tubular profile
4   blind metal profile
5   metal panel for covering, expanded polyurethane finished in aluminum on both sides
6   levelling die
7   metal roof truss
8   suspended ceiling painted in white
9   stainless steel banister
10 stone floor
11 levelling mortar
12 lightened concrete
13 plasterboard cladding
14 thermal glazing
15 fiber cement cladding
16 black stone slab
17 green laminated safety glass
18 metal frame
19 waterproof sheet
20 colorless laminated glass
21 circular metal tube
22 lacquered wood board
23 clay bricklaying
24 stone cladding
25 reinforced concrete retaining wall
26 concrete beam
27 ground compaction
28 reinforced concrete column
29 agglomerated sheet
30 steel grill
31 reinforced concrete slab
32 foundation

Juan Manuel Peláez
Las Mercedes School
Medellín, Antioquia (Colombia)

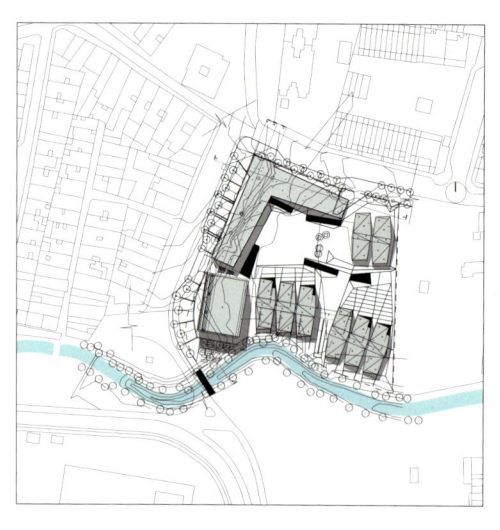

Client
Medellín Town Hall
Architect
Juan Manuel Peláez Freidel
Collaborators
Juan Esteban Ramírez, Edgar Mazo, Sebastián Mejía, Cesar Rodríguez, Jorge Gómez
Consultants
EDU: Empresa de Desarrollo Urbano (structural design)
Contractor
Coninsa
Photos
Sergio Gómez

The different volumes of an educational center, with its classrooms and laboratories for enrolled students combined with spaces for use by the community at large, stand out in a degraded sector of Medellín.

IN THE CONTEXT of the celebrations for the fiftieth anniversary of Empresas Públicas de Medellín (public companies of Medellín) – one of Colombia's most solvent firms, generating, distributing and commercializing telecommunications services, energy, gas and water –, the entity donated $80 million to Town Hall to finance the construction of 10 public schools and the refurbishment and improvement of 132 already existing ones. The new centers were to go up in a number of degraded areas of the city, neighborhoods characterized by high crime rates, conflictive social fabrics, and lack of basic infrastructures.

The Las Mercedes School is one of those centers. Aiming to address the scarcity of cultural facilities in its vicinity, the program was drawn up – in collaboration with associations and individual members of the community at large – in such a way that the place would be used by the student body and faculty in the course of the academic year, but made readily available to the rest of the community at weekends and during vacation periods.

The various functions of the school complex have been organized around a large central yard. A main construction offers multipurpose spaces intended to serve as venues for parents of enrolled students to hold activities in. Sport facilities are provided in a lower structure situated close to a densely tree-shaded garden ground, the administration areas, and the services and laboratories.

A broad rooftop terrace serves as a lookout to the city beyond, while benefiting the students with large open spaces. Finally, the classrooms are located at the heart of the premises, protected from the road by a gentle drop in the terrain. Placed in boxes with irregular shapes, they are built with a structure of reinforced concrete and enormous windows that allow natural lighting into all the interior spaces.

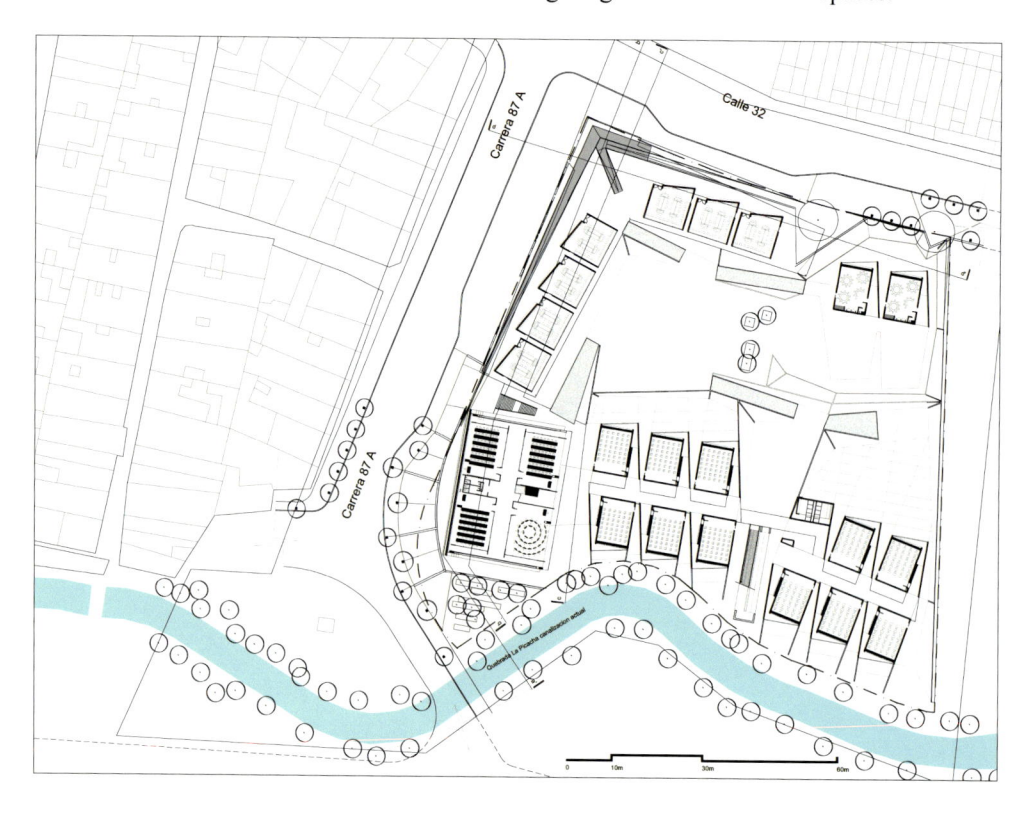

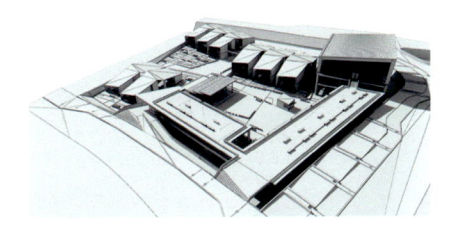

The different functions of the complex are arranged around a spatious central yard. Two large volumes contain the laboratories, the administration offices, some multipurpose spaces intended as venues for activities involving parents of enrolled students, and a broad rooftop terrace, while a series of smaller prisms with irregular shapes contain the classrooms, which are protected from the road by a gentle drop in the terrain of the site.

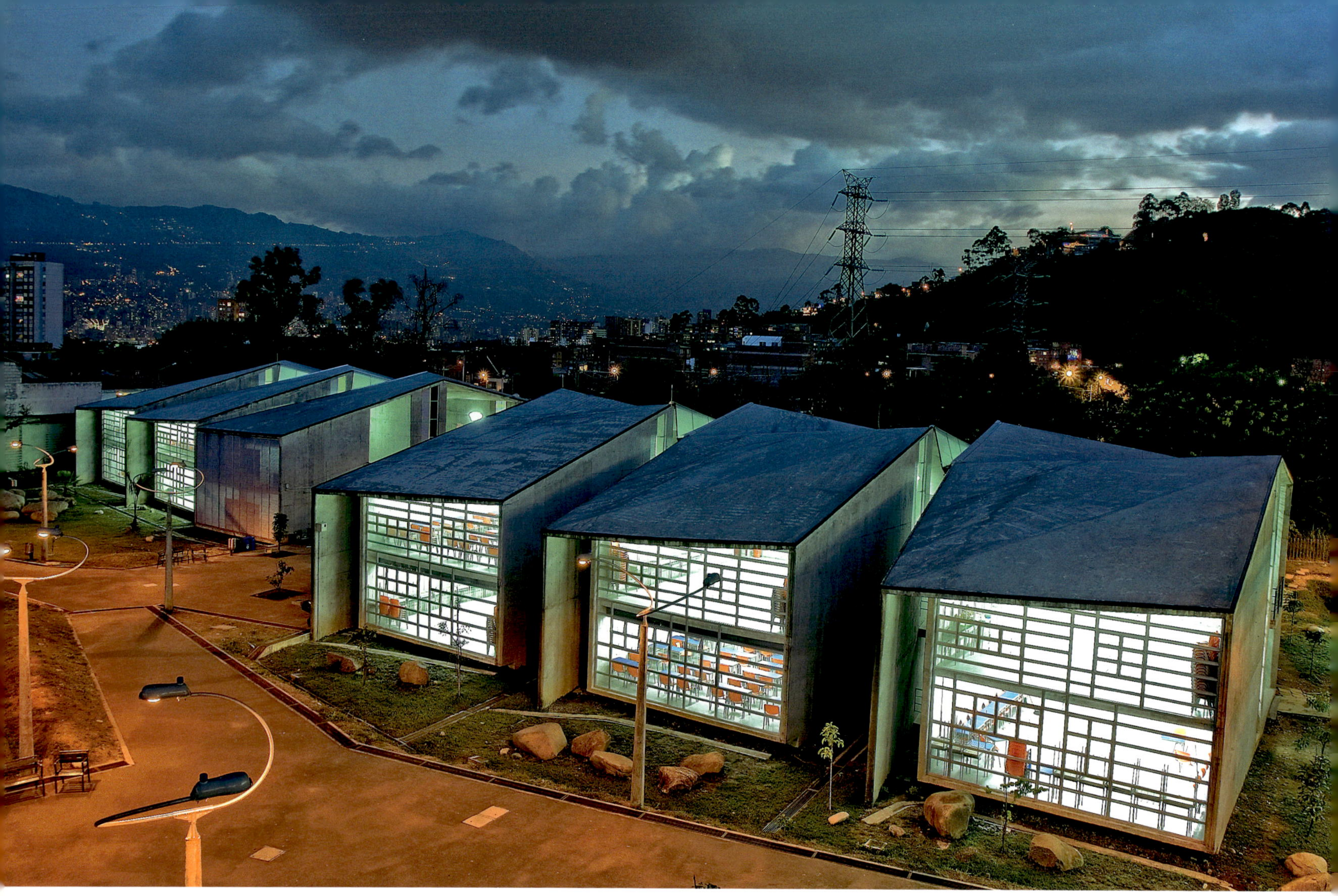

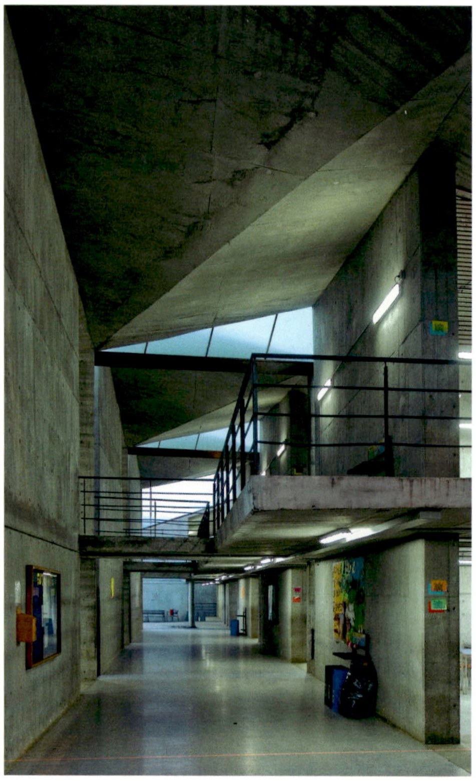

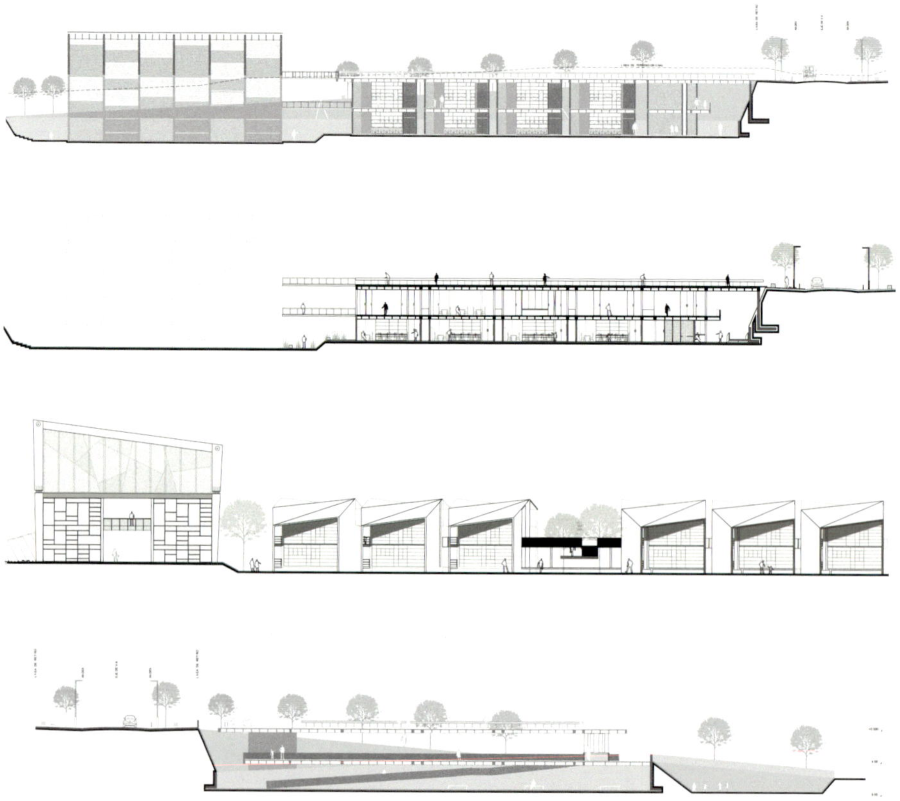

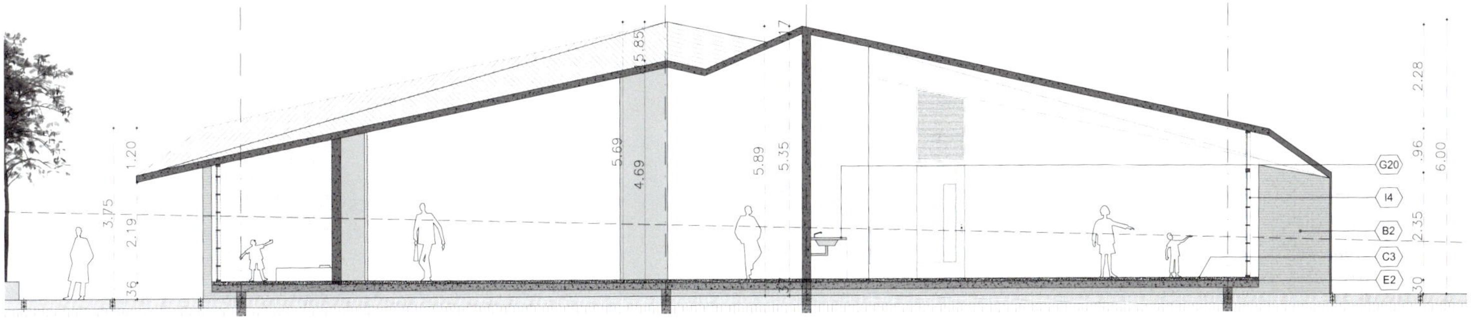
G20
I4
B2
C3
E2

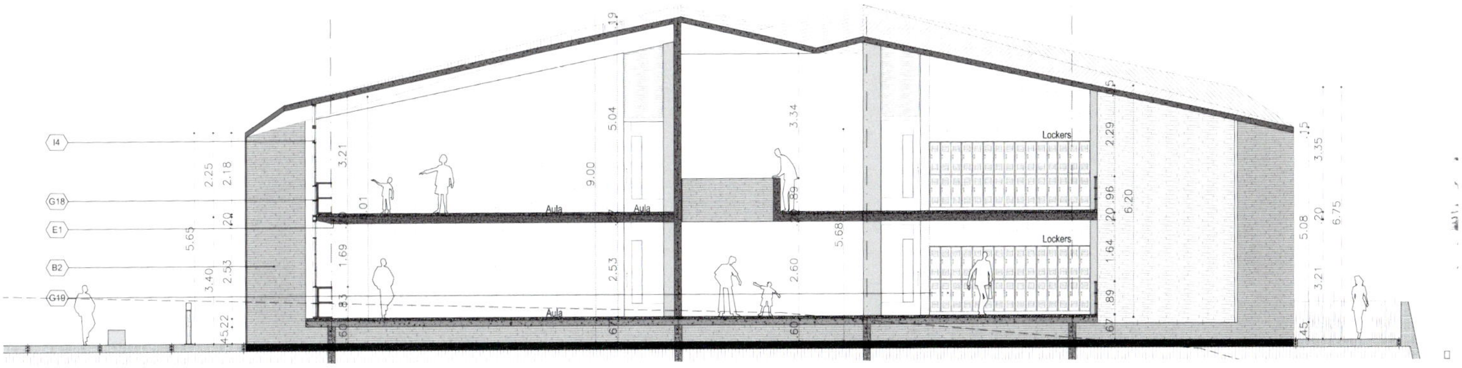
I4
G18
E1
B2
G19
Aula
Aula
Aula
Lockers
Lockers

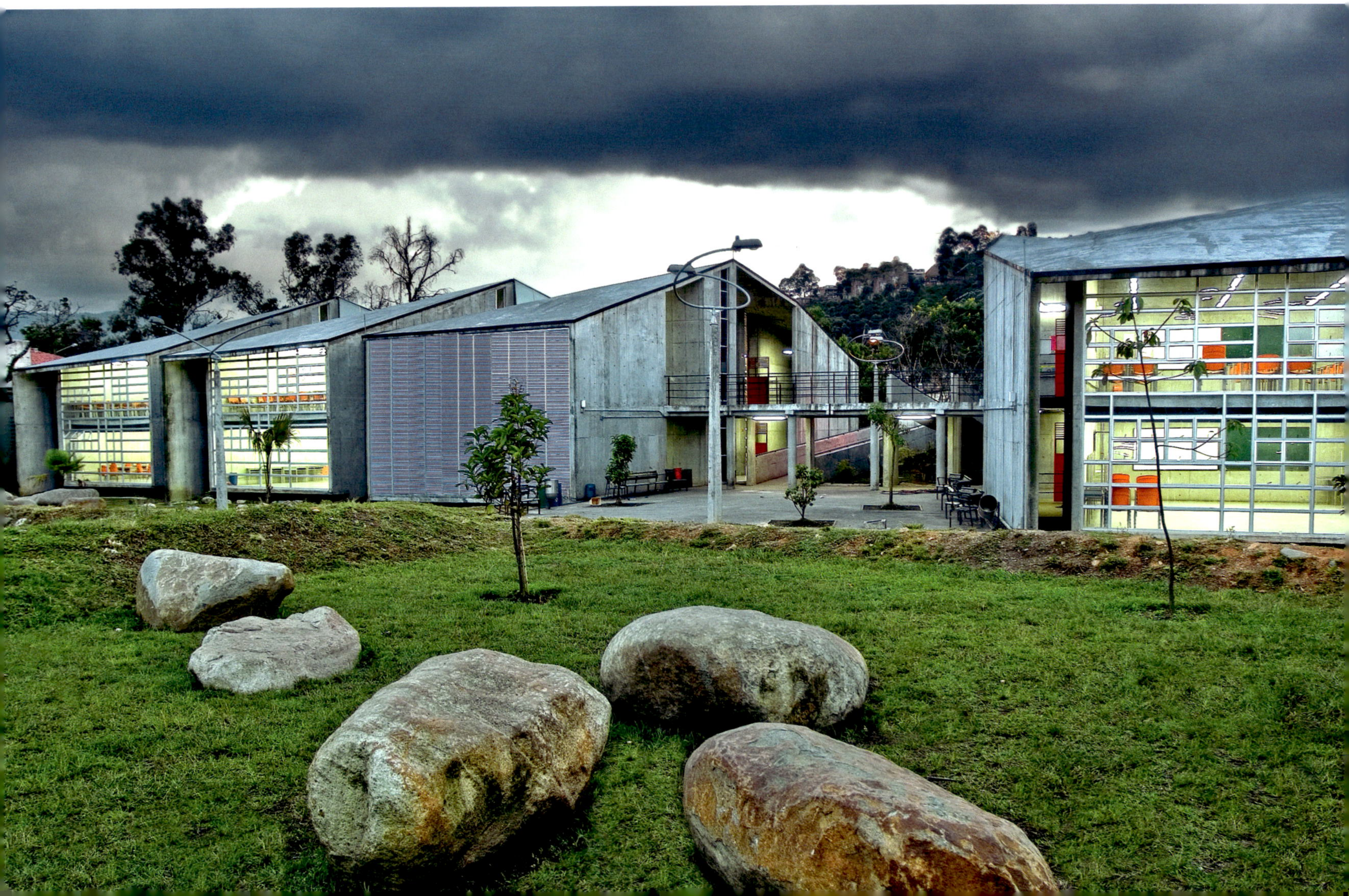

Planb & Jprcr
Orquideorama
Medellín, Antioquia (Colombia)

Client
Botanical Gardens of Medellín
Architects
Planb (Felipe Mesa, Alejandro Bernal) and Jprcr (Camilo Restrepo, J. Paul Restrepo)
Collaborators
Viviana Peña, Catalina Patiño, Carolina Gutiérrez, Lina Gil, Jorge Buitrago
Consultants
Ove Arup (engineering and sustainability); Rutherford & Chekene (civil works); SWA Group (landscaping); Rana Creek (roof); PBS&J (aquariums); Thinc Design, Cinnabar, Visual-Acuity (exhibitions)
Contractor
Ménsula
Photos
Iwan Baan; Carlos Mario Rodríguez (pp. 180 bottom); Sergio Gómez (p. 181 above); Felipe Mesa (p. 181 bottom)

Right within a tropical forest, amid native vegetation, rises a new mosaic of artificial trees with hexagonal geometries. It serves as a venue for events surrounding the national flower of Colombia.

THE FLOWER FESTIVAL, over fifty years old now, is a major event offered by the city in Antioquia. One of its features, the 'Orchids, Birds and Flowers' show, is held in the new Orquideorama, a canopy shelter for specimens of the largest family of flowering plants that is also a venue for weddings, fashion shows, festivals and concerts.

The commission called for a flexible program combining the artificial with a strong connection to the organic. The organic is reflected in two scales, each one defining different aspects of the project. On one hand, the micro scale establishes the principles of material organization, based on the structures of natural life. On the other hand, the visual-external scale of living forms allows us to relate to environmental phenomena and perceive the world. The micro scale of the organic, the way it is organized by exact laws into flexible geometrical patterns – a honeycomb, a cell tissue –, made it possible to create a module on plan, a 'flower-tree' formed by seven hexagons. The systematic repetition of this module then determined the rest of the project, defining its growth and expansion, its perimeter, the organization of the program, and the geometry of the floor. The larger scale of biomorphic structures, specifically flowers and trees, warranted perceiving a large forest or shaded garden, besides a structural system of hollow trunks or patios through which temperature, humidity and water collection are regulated.

The Orquideorama is built as flowers are sown. One 'flower-tree' grows and beside it sprouts another, until the system of flower-tree structures is defined. What arises is not a closed, clearly delimited form, but a modular system of groupings and flexible growth. The project bunches together ten 'flower-trees' but like a system on standby, one that can at any moment be modularly expanded or replicated elsewhere. Inserted in a clearing of the Botanical Gardens' native jungle, the roof of the Orquideorama restores the luminous and environmental qualities of the missing foliage. Rendered like petals with wooden slats and supported by metal pillars, the roof connects the biotic to the structural, and growth to geometry.

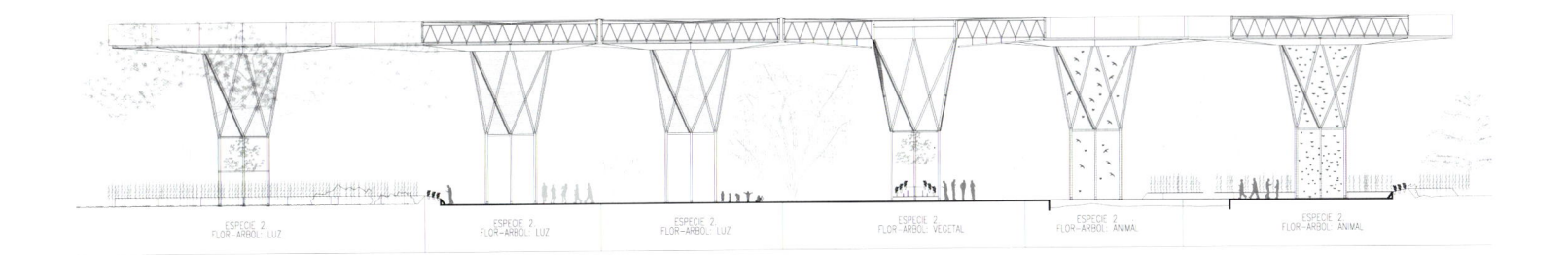

Replacing a building of an industrial nature, the Orquideorama inserts itself into a jungle of indigenous plants of Medellín's Botanical Gardens, and does so in the manner of a flower plantation multiplied in scale. The giant petals that form the roof of the construction stand in for the foliage that has been removed. More than a roof, it is a canopy of wooden slats supported by metal pillars, and it imitates the luminous environmental qualities of a tree's leafy parts.

Atlas: America **181**

182 Atlas: America

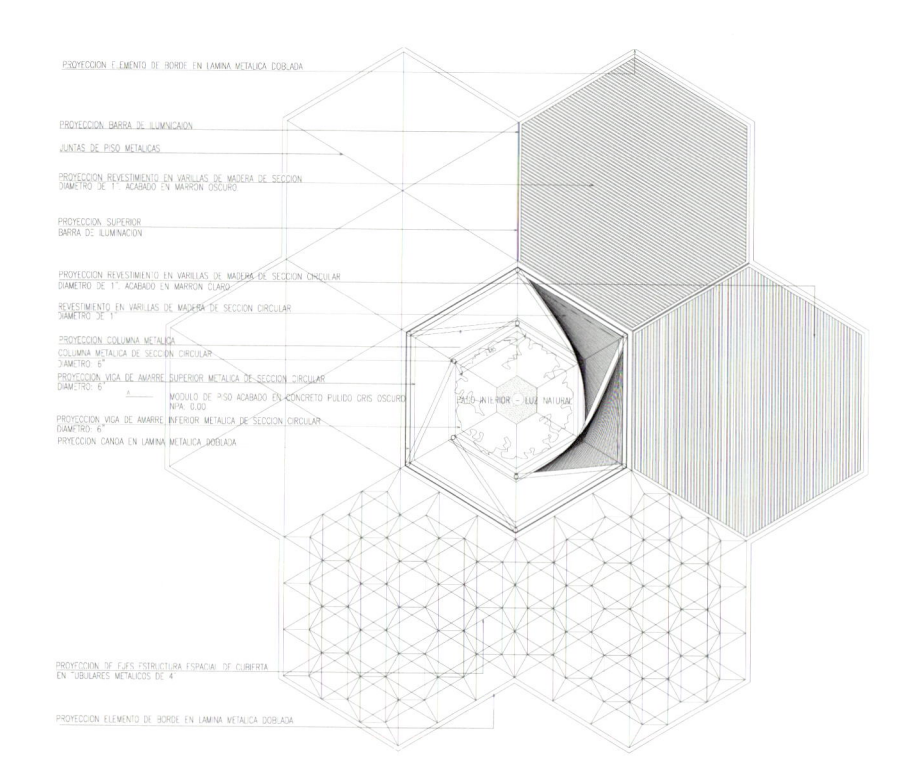

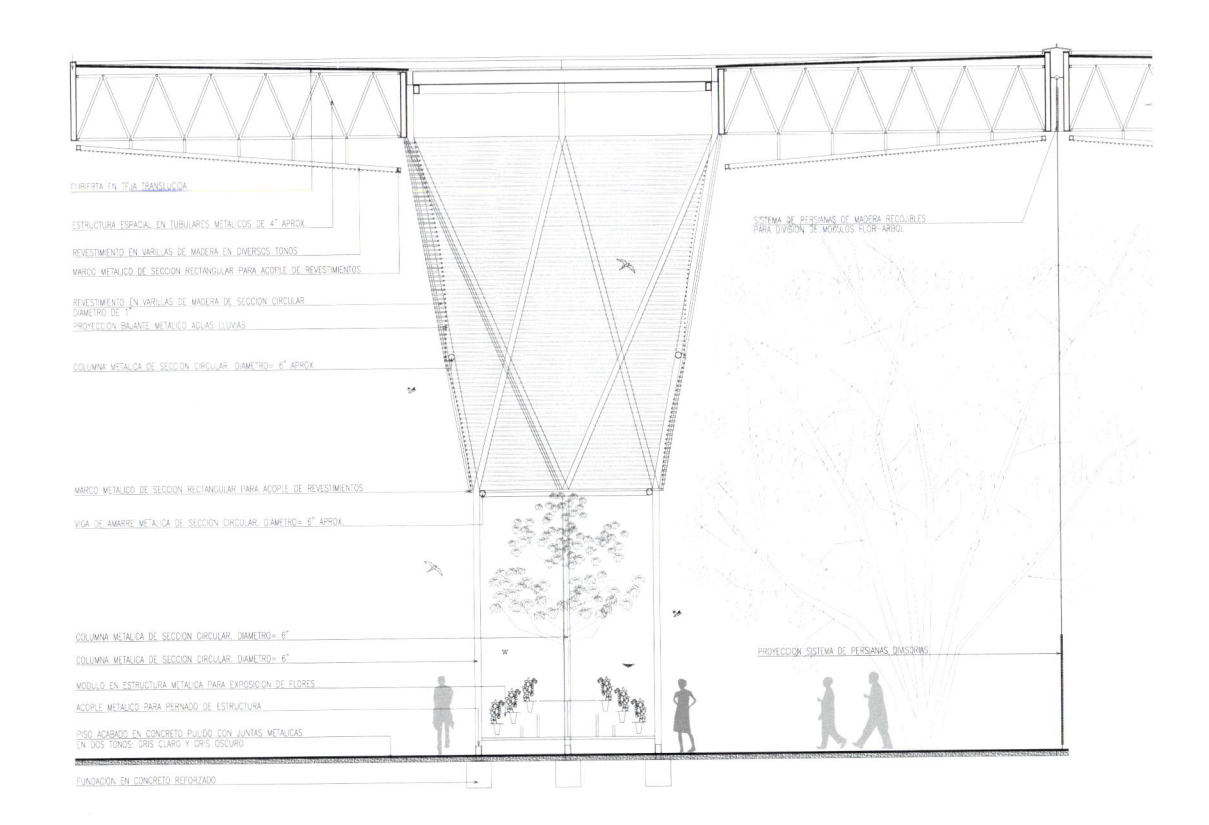

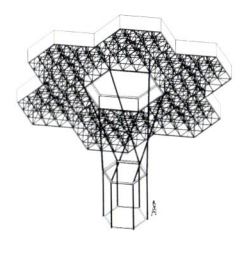

Each of the 'flower-trees' is held up by six metal pillars. The central hexagon of the module is covered with a synthetic fabric that serves to protect the plants against both rain and direct solar exposure. The 'petals' have been built with slats of patula pine wood. The flooring is formed by triangular paving stones of cement of a gray color, in a clear attempt to reproduce the module that is used in the roof.

Torres, Piñol, Ramírez & Meza
Public Library
Villanueva, Casanare (Colombia)

Architects
Miguel Torres, Alejandro Piñol,
Germán Ramírez, Carlos Meza
Collaborators
Humberto Correal, Lugi Neth
Gómez, Diana Pizarro, Andrés
Rodríguez, Humberto Amaya,
Humberto Valderrama, Jairo
Jaramillo, Nydia Linares
Consultants
Union Temporal Quimper (structure);
Geotecnia y Cimentación (foundations);
Steel Colombia (roof)
Photos
Nicolás Cabrera,
Alejandro Piñol (pp. 184, 186)

With its peculiar stone facade of walls of gabions raised in artisan manner, using boulders taken from the region, the new cultural facility cuts a striking figure in the landscape of the small Colombian city.

LOCATED IN the Colombian department of Casanare, Villanueva is a very young municipality that has become an important pocket of development, thanks to the efforts of public institutions in reinforcing agroindustrial, commercial and tourist infrastructure with new constructions and urbanistic operations. Conceived to function as a cultural center and a hub for social interaction, this public library includes a spatious covered gallery that serves as a public square and has the effect of unifying the destructured urban fabric surrounding it. The gallery is built with a series of white-painted circular-sectioned metal pillars that support a framework elaborated in artisan manner with wood from pine trees cultivated in the region.

The actual building was raised with gabion stone walls put together with boulders of the area. Constrained by a very tight budget, the construction of the center was possible through the use of modular containers attached to one another. These elements were built with stones of different sizes that were retained with a wire mesh of galvanized steel and reinforced along the edges. In forming the gabions, the stones were placed one at a time and by hand, resulting in an artisanal finish with gaps serving to let light and air seep in.

The enclosure was conceived as a piece of fabric that filters the air coming in to cool the interior spaces. There is no need for additional artificial ventilation systems. Extraction of hot air is carried out horizontally by means of cross ventilation through the circulation spaces, and vertically by convention through grilles placed on the roof that also provide natural lighting. The search for bioclimatic solutions appropriate to the tropical climate, the modularization of the loadbearing structure, the rationality of the distribution of spaces, and the use of recycled materials all point at a firm commitment to sustainabilty.

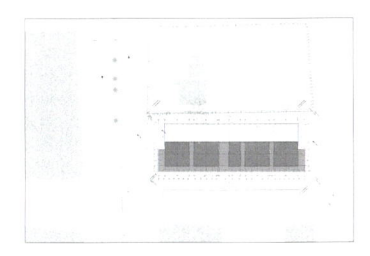

With very tight budget constraints, construction of the public library was made possible by the use of modular containers built by retaining stones of varying size with a wire mesh of galvanized steel. The gabions were raised with river boulders placed one at a time and manually, resulting in an artisanal finish with gaps in between the stones to bring light and air into the interior spaces for natural illumination and ventilation.

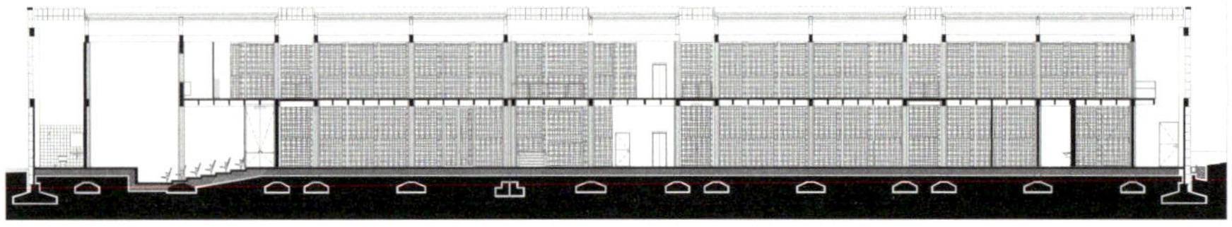

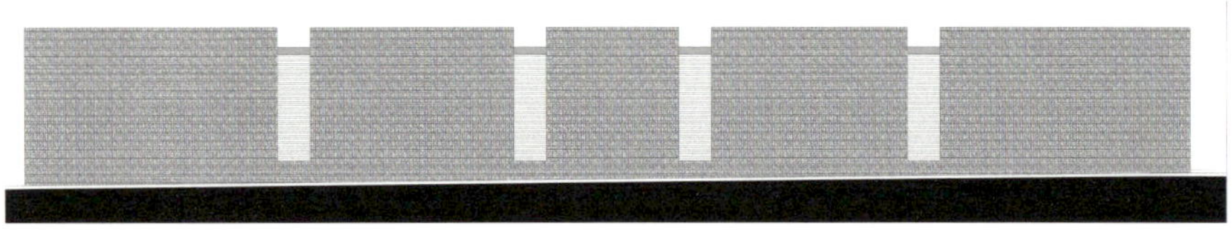

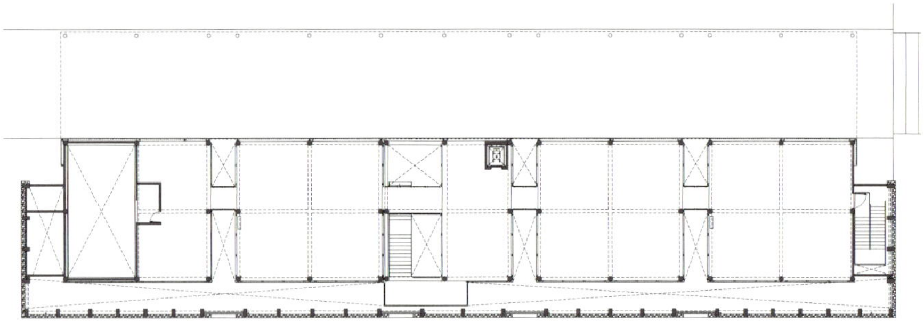

2

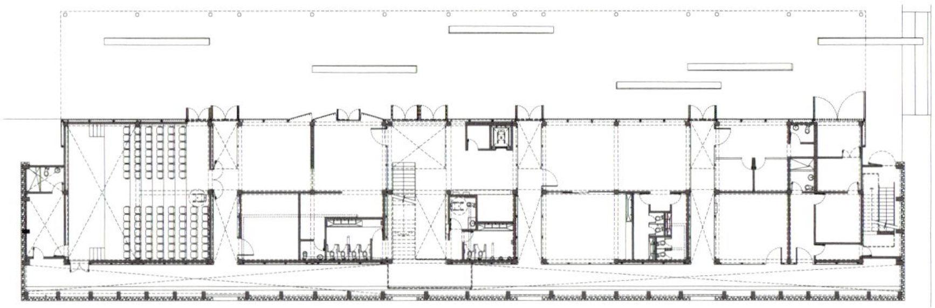

1

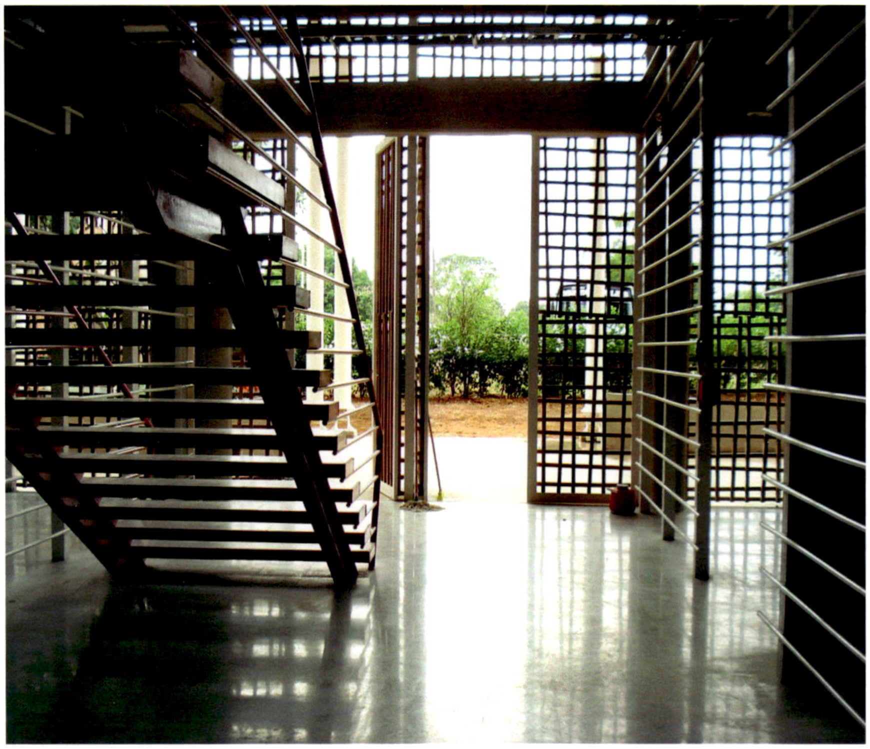

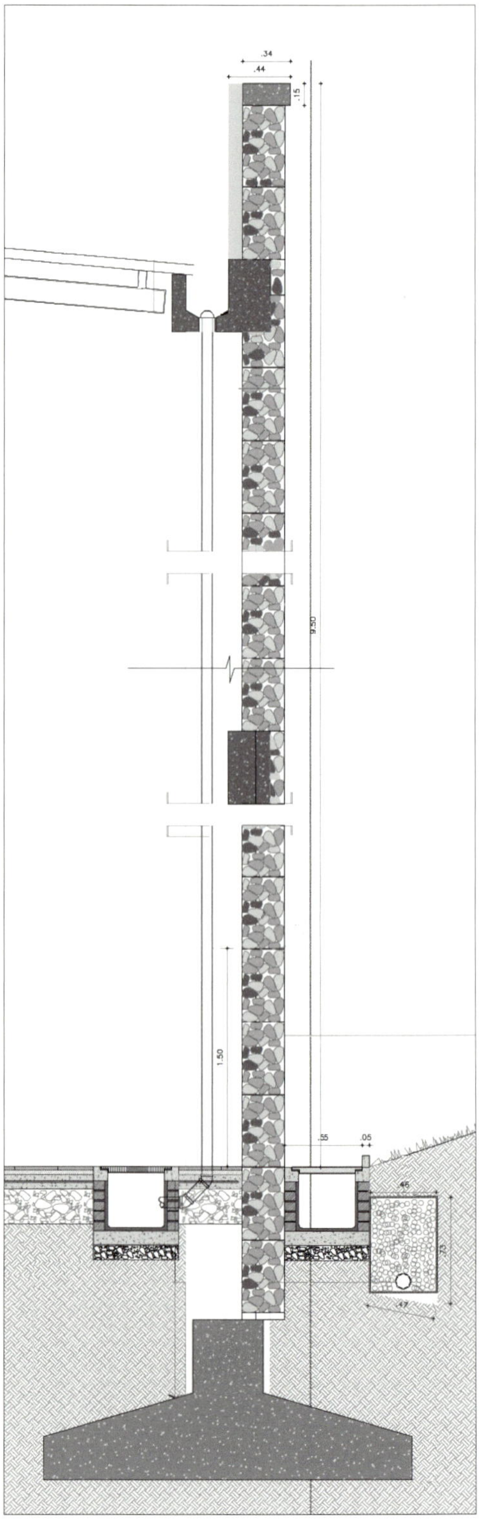

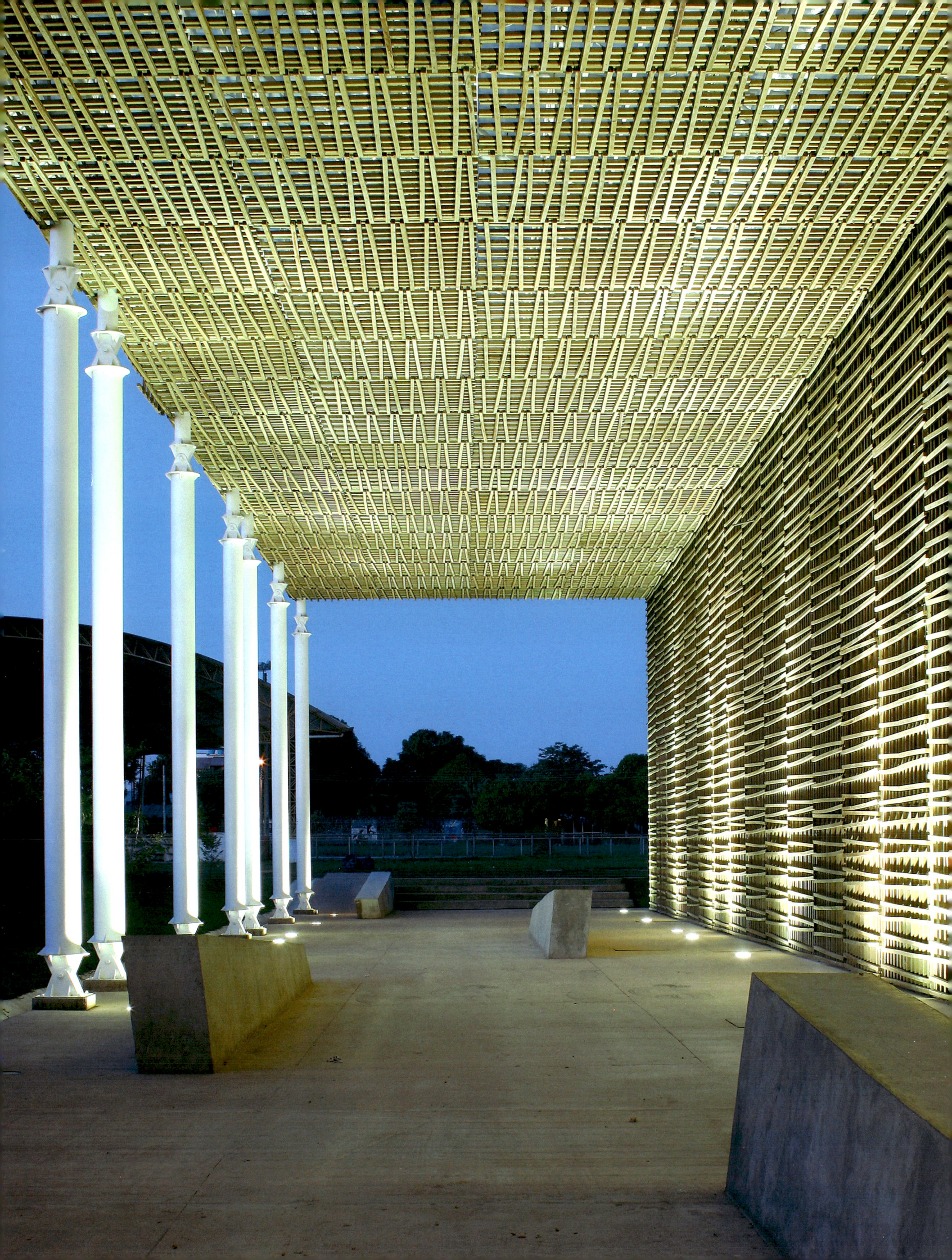

Husos
Garden-House for Taller Croquis
Cali, Valle del Cauca (Colombia)

Architects
Camilo García, Diego Barajas
Collaborators
Francisco Amaro (biologist),
Juan Pablo Arias, Antonio Cobo,
Junko Watanabe, Luis A. Ramírez
Consultants
Jorge Mejía (structure)
Photos
Javier García, Manuel Salinas,
Sylvia Patiño

Conceived as a garden of nectar and host plants for butterflies, the house-workshop of a small clothing and decoration design business has taken the lead in preserving the natural environment of the city of Cali.

THE PROJECT is the result of a private commission from a company called Taller Croquis (Croquis workshop), a small but growing clothing and decoration business run by five women. It is also the first implementation of an environment preservation plan for the city of Cali, a program launched by a network of civic associations concerned with sustainability issues. The building accommodates a one-family dwelling for the owner besides the spaces comprising the design workshop: a production area and a store where its products are sold. But the scheme also includes an intelligent garden, a kind of biometer or biological gauge that attracts butterflies of the region through the cultivation of plant species that nourish them and are their natural habitats. Butterflies are among the most effective bioindicators of an ecosystem's quality and diversity, and they are particularly abundant in this region that boasts the planet's greatest diversity of butterfly species. Apart from the benefits it generates in its immediate environment, the workshop organizes activities intended to inform and conscientize about the importance of preserving biodiversity in the city.

The plants are arranged over a steel structure that wraps the building. Besides improving atmospheric conditions, the plants attract butterflies, helping to establish natural circuits, through the city, for the movement of butterflies. For safety, a thick mesh has been installed at first-floor level. The mesh opens up at the higher levels so that the fruits of the various climbing plants can be easily picked. Inside, the party walls of the yard have been decked with differently sized bulbs of tropical shrubs, completing the system of host and nectar plants that butterflies need. The whole research project was designed, directed and coordinated by a team of biologists and entomologists, with technical support from the Cali Zoo.

A light steel structure that wraps the building is decked with a variety of climbing plants whose function it is to attract butterflies, helping to create the conditions for the establishment of a natural circuit, through the city, for the movement of butterflies. Twenty differently sized bulbs of tropical shrubs and bushes have been made to grow inside, on the party walls of the yard, completing the botanical system that the butterflies need.

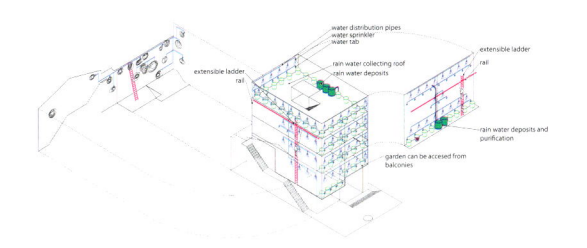

Atlas: America

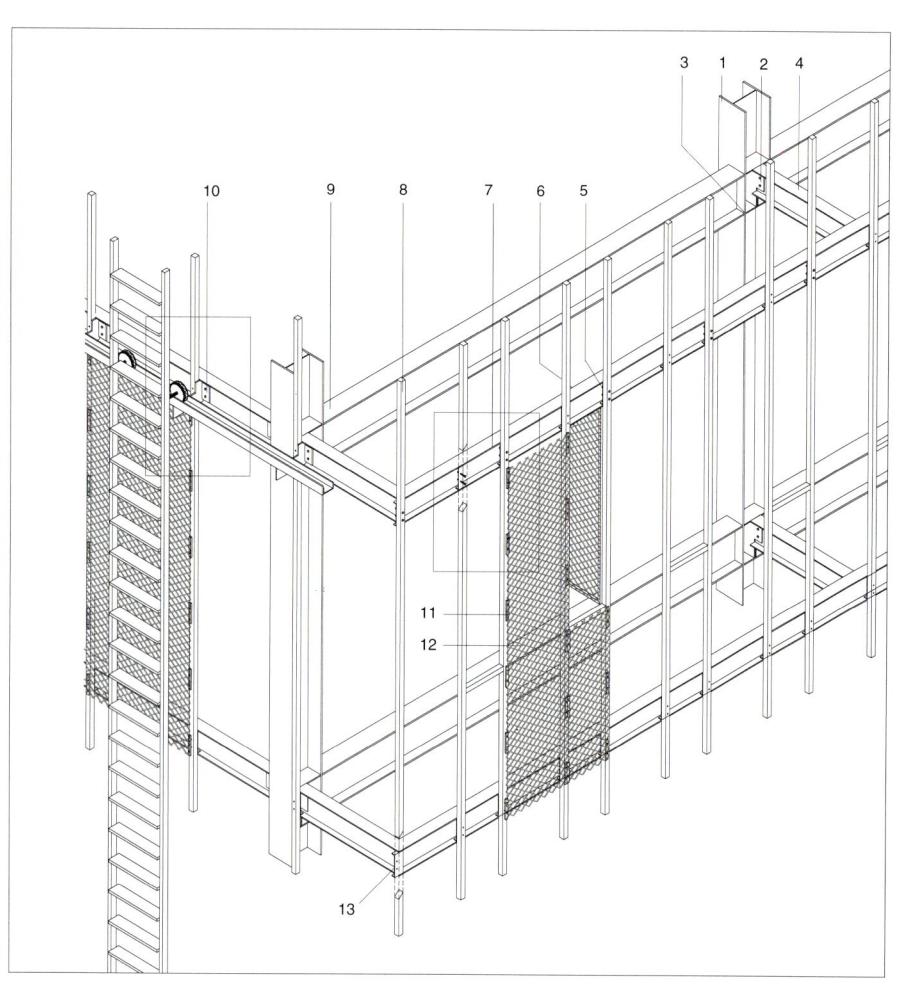

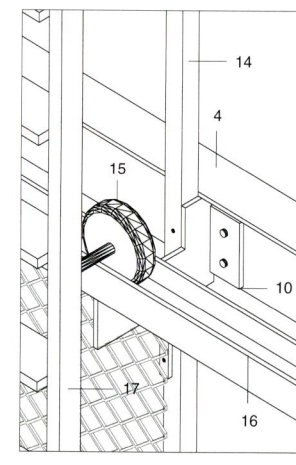

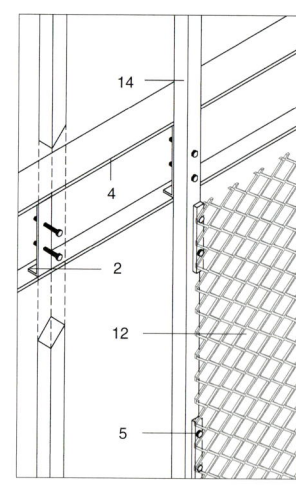

1. 260 mm HEA steel structural profile
2. 6 mm thick calibrated steel plate
3. 9 mm thick metal profile stiffener
4. IPE 200 steel profile
5. 7.5 mm diameter stainless steel screw for anchoring to steel structure
6. 5 mm calibrated metal plate anchor with U-shaped section
7. 20x20 mm structural metal tubing with square section
8. 40x40 mm steel profile, 2 mm thick
9. IPE 330 steel profile
10. metal plate anchor for supporting staircase rail, 8 mm thick
11. 165x20 mm calibrated plate welded to mesh, 10 mm thick
12. steel mesh with electrostatic paint finish
13. 5 mm metal plate anchor for supporting frame at corner
14. 40x40x2 mm steel profile, 2 mm thick
15. stainless steel wheel with rubber coating, 15 mm thick
16. UPN 100 steel profile
17. one-flight retractable aluminum staircase for maintenance of facade

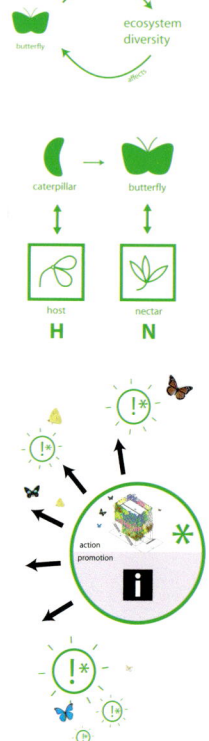

Atlas: America 191

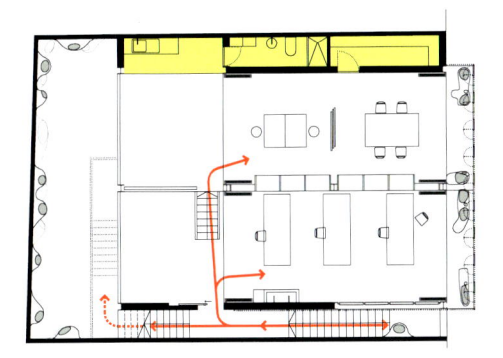

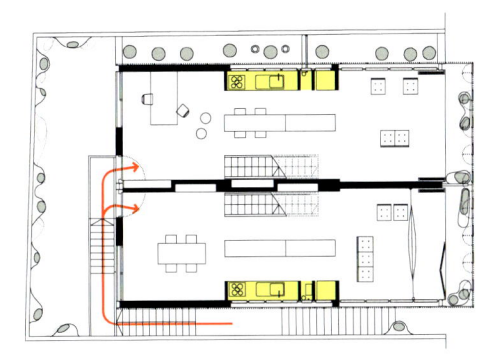

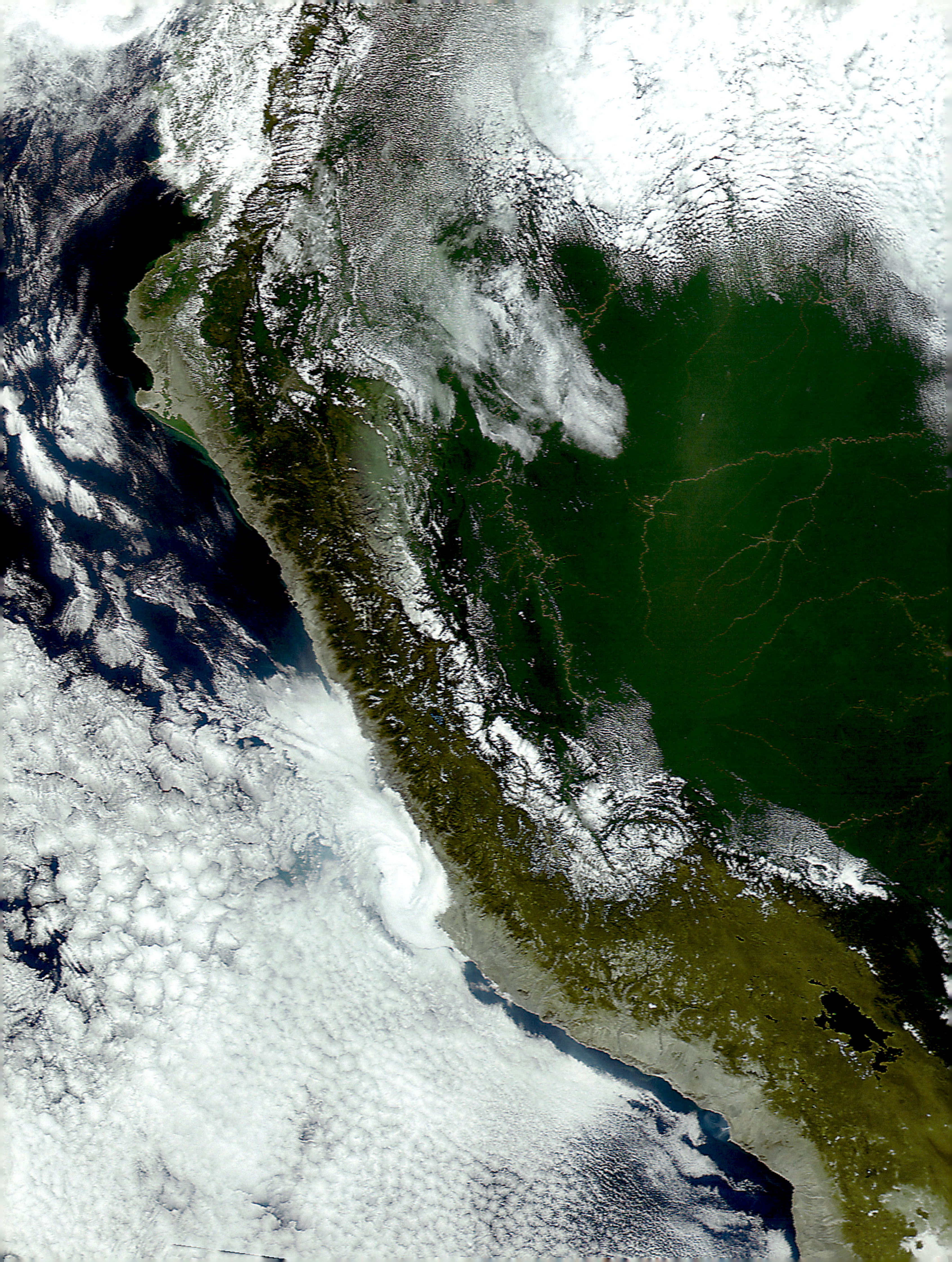

Peru, Ecuador, Bolivia

In the Central Andes – between the Amazon plain and the Pacific Coast –, the trio formed by Peru, Ecuador and Bolivia is the core of the Andean conglomerate. Sharing geographic and ethnic roots, the three countries have a cultural kinship that is reflected in an architecture of quality marked by a strict, formally austere rationalism, at odds with the stylistic excesses of real estate speculation. The Peruvian scene features the sobriety of domestic architecture of modest proportions, such as the apartment building raised by the studio JSa in a tourist area of the capital. The Ecuadorian panorama includes the structural rationality of proposals like the Pentimento House in Quito by Sáez & Barragán, which follows a construction system derived from vernacular tradition. In the Bolivian picture, finally, works like the Archaeological Museum in Tiwanaku by Villagómez draw inspiration from the bold, monumental forms of pre-Hispanic civilization.

Frederick Cooper
The Aesthetics of Scarcity
Peru, Ecuador and Bolivia, Rigor as Identity

Óscar Borasino, OIT Offices, Lima, Peru (2006)

Architecture in the Central Andean region is commendable for its modest scale and formal austerity, removed from mediatic frivolity.

In the three countries, joined by shared ethnic and geographic roots, some signature works of high quality stand out amid all the self-building and the stylistic deliriums that real estate speculation generates.

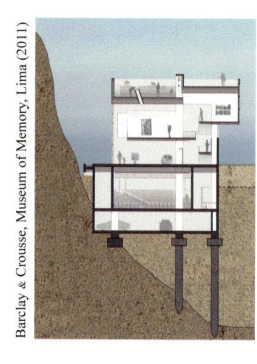

Barclay & Crousse, Museum of Memory, Lima (2011)

ONE HIDDEN EFFECT of globalization is that it has made us tend to see our cultural patterns as being imposed on us by the dominant countries or cultures. To a large extent, this is quite true. An overwhelming majority of the global population wears jeans, quenches its thirst for information through Google, drinks Coca-Cola, and increasingly frequents supermarkets. Of course Latin America does not escape this state of affairs, much less the central zone of the Andean region, a geographically heterogeneous territory that, with touches of a vernacularity not so much picturesque as pathetic, typifies the hapless universal panorama we know as underdevelopment. An impartial and rigorous scrutiny of the architecture that the new century has seen arising between the Amazonian plain and the Pacific coast – around the equatorial line and the high plain of the Andes – shows a society digesting the excesses of the global eclosion with surprising cultural wisdom. Maybe the narrowness can be the anteroom to a virtuous austerity instead of a reason for the immorality of poverty.

Ecuador, Peru and Bolivia – the central core of the Andean Latin American conglomerate – make up a geographic space, address a common culture and share socioeconomic difficulties, giving rise, as in the past, to a close affinity of features, at least in the large sense by which, for this article's purposes of making a superficial diagnosis, we can present a brief panorama of their recent architecture. United in a common crucible – first the empire of the Incas, later the viceregency of Peru –, and despite sporadic political differences, they empathize with one another culturally; an affinity sustained, no doubt, by their geographic concomitance, their shared ethnic roots, and a history that, *mutatis mutandis,* equally affects their citizens. And the homogeneity happily reveals itself in their architectural expression, an eloquent reality that in the past took on a Hispanic, Creole and Christian arrogance, but now professes a peculiarly evocative dichotomy.

If we have to put down common features, I would say that contemporary architectural production in the Andean region oscillates between three clearly differentiated strata. First: self-construction. Second, a very wide and conflict-laden range of stylistic deliriums that are a consequence of real estate speculation. Finally, a small crop of serious architecture that resists getting diluted in the banality of frivolous and inconsequential cultural environments. Self-construction – the genre that in the early 1960s was baptized by the London magazine *Architectural Design* as the architecture of democracy –, is the most dominant and problematic expression of the effects of massive urbanization in cities lacking political and social direction, an area where architecture in the real sense of the term (building as a deliberate act of social and aesthetic gestation) has practically disappeared. The mantles of shantytowns and slums that relentlessly expand the suburbs of the old colonial centers and their modern industrial enclaves are important for our purposes here not only because they accommodate the huge exodus of people from the rural zones to the cities, but also because they have actually usurped the place of the architect, and in doing so, pushed the limits of the rational and formal principles of modernity; a modernity rendered useless by its incapacity to meet demands for speed and expectations that are socially complex and culturally autochthonous. In contrast the mesocratic or speculatively commercial social segment – which mediatically claims architectural leadership for itself –, is culturally colonial, opportunistically bourgeois and formally eclectic. It includes the public and private works resulting from a real estate eclosion which feeds on both the irregular expansion of a middle class that is voracious and devoted to consumerist hedonism, and the improvised expansion

Barclay & Crousse, Equis House, Cañete, Peru (2003)

During the first decade of the current century, architectural production in Peru has been limited to modestly sized buildings designed under the premises of a strict rationalism that efficiently addresses the demands of complex programs, and to small one-family residences characterized by their aesthetic sobriety, their constructive rationality, and the extreme precision with which their details and finishes are handled.

of a residential and commercial market that lacks cultural references, and which is exposed to both the perversion of advertising and the boundless affluence surrounding foreign models, a product of the massive expansion of the modes of communication and information that are being disseminated without undergoing the elemental filters of critical mechanisms. It is here that we find the greater part of residential and commercial (malls and hypermarkets) architecture, whose drive for profit is based on the exploitation of a global rhetoric that is disseminated especially on television and the internet; an eclectic repertoire that is hungry for the unusual and ephemeral, or for decoratively sweetened conventional forms; a specter enclosing a cult to notoriety that oscillates between a strident avant-garde *soit disant* and an apocryphal arrivistic snobbery; an incidental fan much nourished by an architectural pedagogy that seeks to provide the mercantilistic and liberal market with a nonreflective, culturally submissive, socially frivolous professionality.

The other side of the coin, the architecture of resistance, is that lucid architecture of a handful of architects professing a more demanding and challenging sense of their craft. Being scarce, this architecture reaches notable levels of quality and congruence, but does not reap the material and mediatic benefits that the professional prestige dispensed by the real estate market brings in its train, nor the social gratification that can come when architects abdicate the profession's *raison d'être* in favor of peripheral alternatives, whether sociological, anthropological, political or urban. It subsists, stoked by its adherence to certain cultural values, which for these architects cannot be ignored, or perhaps because of a mature attention to global production; a culture of modernity that germinates in certain university circles or in small groups of like-minded professionals who remain true to the primordial principles of the craft.

Peru, Formal Austerity
In Peru, the architecture of resistance is represented by three commendable architects. Óscar Borasino stands out with the International Labour Organization (ILO) Regional Office in Lima, a building with a strict but formally amiable, accessible rationalism that intelligently reconciles complex programmatic demands with strict guidelines, executed with admirable attention to proportions and details.

Beach houses almost exclusively sustained the practice of architecture during the protracted economic crisis that afflicted Peru in the final five years of the 20th century, and the three making up Sandra Barclay and Jean Pierre Crousse's so-called X Houses superlatively represent a genre that is widespread and of mediocre quality. Designed and built one after the other, they embody the more valuable aspects of the kind of architecture which goes against the current of that coming from the predominant hedonist and frivolous consumerism of a voracious emerging bourgeosie, showing, as it does, a use of forms that is as rational as it is ingenious, and an austere sense of constructive materiality that is charged with a sensible expressivity deferring to the coast and the desert environments.

Barclay & Crousse, Equis House, Cañete, Peru (2003)

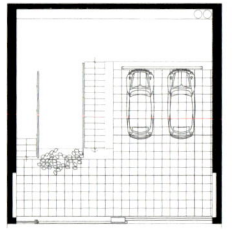

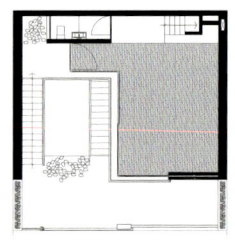

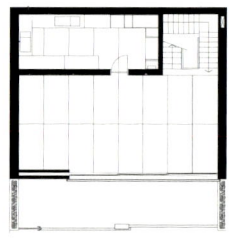

House in San Isidro, Lima

Peru's output of domestic architecture is governed by a formal austerity that goes about organizing the layout of rooms in accordance with balanced compositions charged with a sober dramatism, while Ecuador's modest one-family dwellings excel by virtue of a marked structural rationality that focusses on defining building systems inspired by the local materials and techniques of vernacular architecture.

Drawn up by the same architects, the project for the Museum of Memory is an especially vulnerable place in the scarce natural environment that subsists in Lima, a platform set on a cliff of the wide coastal arch that separates it from the Pacific. The building is set within a rural and symbolic landscaping treatment whose careful approach is read as a tribute to the victims of the terrorist violence that shook Peru during the last five years of the 20th century. Winner of a national competition that boasted an exceptional jury – foreigners Rafael Moneo, Kenneth Frampton and Francesco Dal Co, and locals José García Bryce and Wiley Ludeña –, its design has the qualities of a rationalism inspired by program and landscape, by professionality and the terrestrial sensitivity that has characterized the work of Barclay & Crousse since their return to Peru after twenty years in France. Adapting to a program rendered exceptionally complex by its deliberate imprecision (the competition was an ideas contest with no set script or museography), by the dubious resistance of the ground on the designated spot, by the difficult guidelines to comply with, and especially by the message the architecture was called upon to convey (the construction was to symbolize or actually embody the tragic terrorist experience and incriminating social arguments that brought on a mantle of death and destruction on Peru during the lapse of two recent decades), the chosen scheme absolved all that with an accurate balance, through a staid dramatism that comes from combining a correct rapport with a fragile coastal context and an architectural libretto marked by sobriety and aesthetic eloquence.

Finally, a house in Lima's San Isidro district by Alexia León reveals hidden but recurrent aspects of the Peruvian architectural lineage: a precise, disciplined experimental restlessness and a rigor forged through the project it embraces, from the original reading of the program and place to a perfectionist prolixity in the conception and execution of details. In the first decade of the new millennium, Peru's architectural production has been limited to a small range of typologies: one-family residences of modest proportions, largely anodyne apartment buildings, and shopping centers. With the state and town halls removed from the obligation to build the architectural infrastructure with which to provide the public services – schools, hospitals, universities, libraries, theaters, museums – that are inherent to an efficient and congruent democracy, the profession has not only lacked opportunities to update itself and compete, but has also seen the decline of its social and cultural hierarchy.

Alexia León, house in San Isidro, Lima, Peru (2005)

Ecuador, Regionalist Modernity
The Ecuadorian and Peruvian architectural scenes have similar features, the difference being that Ecuador's political hierarchy has proven quite more competent in planning urban development. With exemplary conciseness José María Sáez and David Barragán's Pentimento House reiterates the sense of austerity of an architectural rationality that, without making demagogic concessions to the dramatic geographical, socioeconomic and historical conditions that

196 Atlas: America

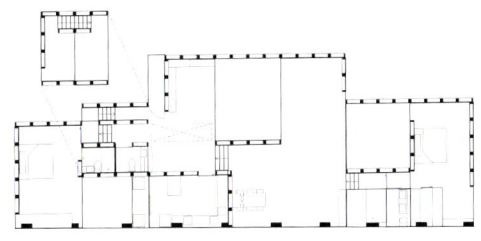

Sáez & Barragán, Pentimento House, Quito, Ecuador (2006)

tend to assert themselves as foundations of modernity in the region, exceptionally manages to translate these circumstances into proposals that are as consistent as they are innovative. Of small dimensions, confined to a narrow stretch of sloping land, the house rises over these limitations and reaches a category bordering on monumentality, an aesthetic rank whose impactful hierarchy is ostensibly rooted in the daring, challenging keystone of its structural and constructional option, the framework of a volumetric scaffolding that architects conceive as the virtual matrix for a sense of space that is as emotional as it is severely abstract. Open to multiple interpretations, its obstinate tectonic structure – a framework of modular pieces of reinforced concrete, conceived with a stereometric sense – becomes a rhetoric, which with expressive moderation takes on a rich variety of programmatic repercussions and a formal script wholly forged to orchestrate a materially austere and powerful aesthetic architectural content. In spite of its structural and abstract language, the house exudes a cordiality that borders on the vernacular and a sensitivity that comes from its mild settling in a conventional neighborhood. So close to the raised granaries of Galicia and the frames of rural constructions in the farming and fishing environments of the Andes, its architecture is of a universality that can only be understood as a consequence of its formal and tectonic coherence; a harmony resulting from the congruent way of stringing together the modularity of its constructive language and the walls and roofs, woven in accordance with one same pattern that is skillfully interpreted to achieve a soberly rhythmic and functionally expressive spatial and volumetric continuity. And so without being evocative, much less nostalgic, it appears to be so rooted on the site and so eloquent as an

Sáez & Barragán, Pentimento House, Quito, Ecuador (2006)

Industrial in execution and with an approach that is functional, economical and formally discreet – a moderation of spirit that is reflected in the way the interior spaces are arranged, – the quality architecture that currently most receives attention in Ecuador includes modest apartment buildings and diverse public facilities contained in compact volumes of prismatic shape that are raised with simple frame structures.

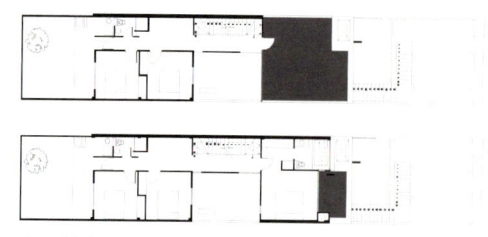

Kenny Espinoza Carvajal, row houses, Loja, Ecuador (2008)

expression of a local modernity that proclaims its contemporaneity, in clear allusion to an innovative sense that also comes from an architectural lineage encoded in subtle keys of ancestral proportions which remain in force in their village usage, and in the scale of spaces and volumes arising from a long building tradition.

Located in Loja, a small cluster of three row houses built by Kenny Espinoza Carvajal simultaneously deals with the narrowness of an elongated sloping lot and a demanding program with equal doses of sensitivity and maturity. Set on a moderate inclination facing the forest and flanked by party walls, the project addresses the contour of the parcel with notable good sense, putting the three dwellings in a single block, like a platform situated at half-height, with the evident purpose of obtaining a functionally efficient, economic, and formally austere arrangement. Audaciously discreet, the three segments comprising the single volume give rise to a homogeneous and classical rhythm, a modulation categorically marked by a porticoed pattern of four frontal walls that frame, under an uninterrupted roof and of the same thickness, a serene tripartite facade. Adding a sensible architectural corollary resolves the accesses through a syncopated interplay of stairs, terraces and sloping gardens, a combination whose modernity exudes a Serlian aroma, a rhetoric which in Ecuador has recourse to the sublime circular staircase that masterfully spans the grade difference between the plaza and the atrium of the Monastery of San Francisco in Quito. The formal austerity of the main facade also governs the internal organization, an arrangement of equidistances in the manner of the spatial economies of Mies and Le Corbusier, exempted from mimetic allusions to their well-known examples. Skillfully distributed on two levels between continuous slabs resting on rectilinear walls, each unit contains two symmetrical spaces partly separated by a staircase that splits them in the middle, relegating the humidity-exposed rooms – bathroom and kitchens – to the west side. With the ground floor slightly set back and continuous front balconies, these spaces give the facades a depth that not only separates them from the exterior visually, but also provides their compositions, along with the exterior development of the stairs and the staggered treatment of the portals of the garages and entrances, with a depth that is pleasant and consistent. The same formal austerity livens up the architecture of the interiors, spaces bathed in a luminosity that is subtle and calming, where sensible and exquisite details are dealt out in accordance with the distinction and quality of their external appearance.

Of a similar make is an apartment building in Cuenca by the architects Javier Durand and María Rosa Hermida. Again we have a block between party walls, with a simple porticoed structure whose structure looks over its two fronts, horizontally and vertically framing the exquisite proportions of the facades. Reiterating the austere aesthetic of an architectural option that evidently situates the aesthetic consistency of the composition in the careful calibration of the scaffolding of its slabs and loadbearing walls, the building adds to this format the studied design of the screens, lattices and railings taking up the wide open spaces; a formal strategy that effectively gives the design a subtle and restrained richness happily enhanced by the volume suspended over the accesses to the parking areas. This strategy gives the interiors a crystalline look and makes it possible to incorporate views and a moderate light into the resulting spaces. Without a doubt, the austerity is in accord with the elegance and sobriety of the architecture preexisting in Ecuador's cities and countryside. A fruit of those constants that Chueca Goitia spoke of, the design reconciles the conceptual conciseness of a rationalism that is still in force in the roots of an unextinguished modernity, to the austere formality of its colonial and pre-Hispanic lineage; a continuity that, far from being attributable to a tired, decadent spirit, is the result of a lucid, intelligent option.

Closer to a high-tech that is conceptually foreign to the Andean architectural tradition, Andrés Núñez's pavilion for the Passive Archive of the Metropolitan Hospital in Quito is proof of the good criteria with which this remote orientation can be used in circumstances so removed from those of its technological foundations. Conceived like an ingot of beautiful proportions and with a

Kenny Espinoza Carvajal, row houses, Loja, Ecuador (2008)

Andrés Núñez, Passive Archive of the Metropolitan Hospital, Quito, Ecuador (2004)

trapezoidal section, the building maintains the unneighborly austerity that impregnates the building with that formal and constructive severity accommodating the new materiality of its industrial make, the process that in pre-Hispanic times gave rise, for example, to the dilated structures of Racchi or Huaytará, and later, in colonial and republican times, to the long refectories or parrochial chapels. To this Andrés Núñez incorporates a transversal model of the building that adapts to its environmental conditions, virtually modifying the inclination of the roofs and the striation of its tiled roofs to insinuate a balanced continuity. The same reflection could be made with respect to the assembly of its structural framework and its enclosures, a new arrangement whose evident industrial rhetoric alludes equally to the rustic Inca and colonial frameworks.

Whereas the architectural experience in Ecuador has unfolded with neither the breadth nor the consistency of its small emblematic works, the theme of urban reform has been tackled with an earnestness not seen in Peru and Bolivia. The pioneer experience of radical change in Guayaquil was followed by others, all fruits of the political maturing that currently characterizes many of its municipal authorities. This may not translate into design stratagies comparable to those of Medellín, Bogotá or Curitiba, but it has curbed the deterioration that its main cities and towns have undergone on account of neglect or adulteration.

A case in point is the renovated Plazoleta La Merced in Cuenca, a work of the architect Boris Albornoz that brings to the public space a balance between an austere and intelligent modernity on one hand, and an innovative and sober handling of building preservation on the other. Albornoz tackles the renovation of a colonial square through three daring actions. First, by homogenizing the ground, making it a uniform plane that he then adds nuance to through a wide range of paving stones and granite surfaces, emphasizing the planters and paths with small plinths, bordering the pedestrian areas with stone spheres and equipping the spaces with subtly designed benches and light fixtures. Second, by harmonizing the eclectic facades that frame the space: colonial, republican and modern buildings whose contrasting styles are reconciled through an intelligent make-up job. And finally, by carefully handling color and the trees, the diversity of which is adjusted to the impecable sobriety of the complex. The case is exemplary, as the towns and cities of the central Andean region have generally been deformed in the past decades by the propagation of a corny and demagogical urbanistic rhetoric, by an opening towards a modernity that is uncontrolled and removed from the architectural roots of its streets and squares. So this operation is an exception to the voracious drive to impose a despicable, stridently sculptural and regionalist truculence in public spaces through materials, monuments and ornate architectural typologies that irreparably deform the serene roots of an urban morphology which originally had a quiet and anonymous public sense about it.

Durand & Hermida, Jacobo Building, Cuenca, Ecuador (2009)

Daniel Contreras, Sáenz García Building, La Paz, Bolivia (2006)

Bolivia, Modest Sobriety

The situation in Bolivia is similar, but its architecture is the result of a more intense, heterogeneous and localistic cultural idiosyncrasy. Equally advocating a regionalist modernity whose diversity covers the same areas described for Bolivia and Ecuador, there is at work a marked difference between Andean production and that of the tropical plain; an opposition that reflects a range not only of climate and ethnographic conditions, but also of radically opposed political and cultural behaviors. In the high regions – cities located on the Andean plateaus, between the mountain range and its deep valleys –, past decades have seen a heyday of self-construction and a mercantilistic, consumerist and formally superficial and demagogical architecture coexisting with a rationalist and regional modernity; a production that despite limited activity spearheads an avant-garde striving to correct the stylistic excesses of the aesthetic demagogy pervading the area.

An example is the enlargement of the Museum of Ethnography and Folklore in La Paz, built by architect Carlos Villagómez, a native of the city. The building elegantly and intelligently absorbs a diversity of foreign architectural models in a regional usage that is forceful and original. Around the multiple heights of an imposing covered atrium, its planning addresses the proximity of important heritage buildings of the 17th and 19th centuries, as well as the provision of new exhibition areas, in a block that discreetly marries its austere kind of contemporaneity to the adjacent monument. Villagómez correctly resolves this crossroads by resolutely interpreting the dominant role that modernity was to take on in the intervention, an audacious attitude that finds an accurate affirmative instinct in the handling of scale and materials, as well as in a deliberately protagonistic architectural repertoire. More rhetorical but no less powerful is Villagómez's project for the Tiwanaku Museum, which alludes to the Museum of Ethnography and Folklore in La Paz without diminishing the strong sense of drama and contemporaneity that characterizes his architecture.

The architecture of Daniel Contreras is another version, in La Paz, of the austere modernity that is predominant in the region, a modernity professed by the small number of architects who persistently try to give it an original and vigorous regional sense. The Sáenz García Building in La Paz clearly reflects this tendency, both in the boldness of its robust cubic geometry and in the choice of a thick and traditional materiality. Its softened, elegant brutalism has Kahnian roots inserted in the telluric rotundity of its Andean Altiplano context; a daring composition that Contreras proposes with haughtiness and conviction, and that gives its urban environment a landmark which is at once respectable and deferential.

In the Marina Núñez del Prado House-Museum, which involved considerably enlarging the picturesque residence of the celebrated Bolivian sculptress, Contreras generates a powerful expressivity based on the categorical volumetry that a new work of such imposing dramatism gives the complex. Allusive to the commemorative sense of its museological mission, a U-shaped structure looking and suspended over the old roof gives the new enlargement a desirable urban presence, but also serves to generate a large space, an open atrium that simulates a lap embracing the artist's memory. Inside, the spaces are strictly subjected to the structure and to a very accurate, skillful handling of light and circulation systems, an orchestration in accordance with the external format, particularly with the gesture of opening the section of the two upper bays toward the street, and of crowning the space with a discreet and pertinent floating ceiling.

Carlos Villagómez, Tiwanaku Museum, Tiwanaku, Bolivia (2001)

In simultaneity with the architecture going up in Bolivia's tropical plain, poor in quality because of its mercantile, consumerist nature, the Andean meseta is still the scene of works and projects conceived by profesionals who subscribe to a rationalist and regional modernity. Their bold and robust cubic geometries draw inspiration from pre-Hispanic and colonial traditions and are executed with a wide variety of traditional materials.

But it is his urban proposals that best illustrate the maturing of his architecture. In the refurbishing of Paseo Juan XXIII and Plaza Alonso de Mendoza, he imposes a decisive and elegant order on a typical Latin American neighborhood. In the plaza, he unfurls an exhaustive gamut of formal touches that, without being excessive, confer on the environment a powerful sense of neighborhood concealing the questionable quality of the surrounding architecture. On the boulevard, in contrast, Daniel Contreras proposes a more audacious industrial and popular rhetoric, a deployment of metallic structures containing commercial spaces, in what constitutes a daring attempt to bestow on a narrow, tortuous, anodyne street the rank of a modern public space.

Ricardo Aparicio's School of Our Lady of Mount Carmel, located in the tropical city of Riberalta, in the Beni region, translates the previously presented sense of formal austerity into a domestic format. A simple porticoed structure covered with a pitched roof generates a series of galleries and courtyards that alternate with prominent eaves and translucent lattices; a formal language clearly alluding to an architectural genre that is the product of a warm and rainy climate, with regional motifs that Contreras determinedly uses to come up with an architectural expressivity much in keeping with a modest use of economic resources. This commendable approach is seen especially in the sections and elevations, and is very close to the work of the Australian master Glenn Murcutt, as much in the rigor of the language as in the way it gives architectural technology a decisive role in forming spaces and volumes.

More sculptural and differentiated is Hans Kenning Moreno's project for the Private Technological University of Santa Cruz, a structure that, while invoking the functional nature of the installations – the gradients of the classrooms and stairs, the gravitation of the circulations in the generation of uncovered spaces –, uses those ingredients to work with a notable sense of affirmation, a formal identity that is both pleasant and pertinent.

Resistant Architecture
Despite the necessary brevity of this run-through of the architecture of a large and complex region where very diverse climates and societies coexist, we can find in all its buildings – whether self-built, speculative, or attached to colonially consumerist global styles, but above all, in architecture of the kind that is more resistant and rigorous – a common mode that finds, in the austerity imposed by a predominant economic deficit, a formal *raison d'être* that determines its aesthetic and technical foundations. Scarcity not being a plausible explanation for architectural sobriety, and in spite of the reduced scale of majority of the most ambitious and demanding works, recent productions all share a stoic sense of design, a formal inhibition that ultimately translates into an eagerness to give it a content clearly alluding to its economic limitations. In the fields of self-construction, speculation or consumerism, this scarcity tends to be compensated by decorative or stylistic impostations, by finishes, colors or plasterings creating the architectural identity – ethnic, social or typological – that is to be highlighted in each case. In contrast, in the work of the more mature protagonists – including the examples selected to formulate this diagnosis –, awareness of scarcity translates into options where the content of design attributes an important part of its aesthetic proposal to its austerity; a feature that has allowed it to maintain a degree of integrity which, in a way, keeps it at a distance from the hedonistic tendency afflicting the architectural avant-garde of the greater part of mediatic global stardom.

Rolando Aparicio, Our Lady of Carmen School, Riberalta, Bolivia (2004)

JSa
Apartment Building
Lima (Peru)

Located by a beach, approximately 50 kilometers from the city of Lima, the building contains four vacation apartments – each with an area of 185 square meters – for use by the members of one same family. With a jetty situated just two meters away, the building stands on a 389 square meter rectangular plot of land. The entire residential program revolves around a court, with the shared areas surrounding it at ground level: the swimming pool, a main living room, the kitchen and some service spaces. The rest is stacked over this communal floor in the form of three-, four- and five-bedroom units. With a full view of the seascape, each apartment has been conceived as an independent volume with a layout appropriate to its particular users. In all the units, the common spaces are put on the side toward the street, while the bedrooms and other private rooms face the inner court. An enclosure executed with operable wooden shutters installed over a plane of aluminum frames protects the interior spaces from the region's high temperatures and gives a nuance to the sunlight streaming in. On the main facade, huge windows opening on to large balconies offer vistas of the impressive scenery.

Architects
Javier Sánchez
Collaborators
Irvine Torres, Juan Reyes, Héctor Hernández, Francisco de la Concha
Consultants
JPR Proyectos (structure); Lumber (wood)
Contractor
Buckley, Konno
Photos
Eduardo Hirose

A rectangularly shaped beachside plot of land with an area of 389 square meters is the site of a residential building containing four separate vacation apartment units for use by the members of one same family.

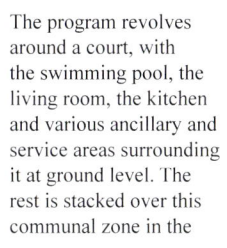

The program revolves around a court, with the swimming pool, the living room, the kitchen and various ancillary and service areas surrounding it at ground level. The rest is stacked over this communal zone in the form of three-, four- and five-bedroom units. With sweeping views of the seascape, each apartment is conceived as a completely autonomous volume with a functional layout appropriate to its particular occupants.

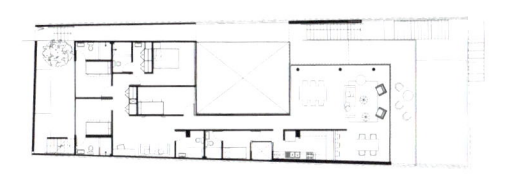

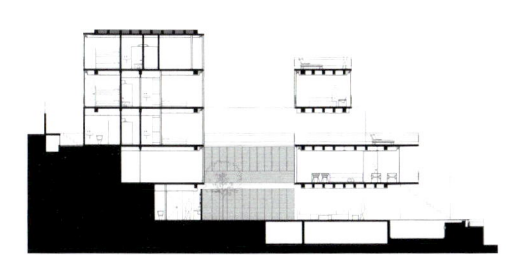

Atlas: America 203

Sáez & Barragán
Pentimento House
Quito (Ecuador)

Client
Desireé Marín
Architects
José María Sáez Vaquero,
David Patricio Barragán Andrade
Collaborator
Alejandra Andrade
Consultants
Héctor Sánchez (prefabricated elements); César Izurieta (structure)
Contractor
Jaime Quinga
Photos
Jose María Sáez, Raed Gindeya (p. 207 bottom)

Following a staggered configuration based on the prospects that the prefabricated concrete pieces present, the house unfolds in such a way that it blends into the landscape, incorporating the vegetation around.

IN THE HEART of a mountainous area east of Quito, a concrete platform adapts to the uneven terrain to both take on the role of superficial foundation and incorporate the existing cluster of trees into the project. The architecture blends into the natural landscape, with an enclosure that presents itself as an extension of the surrounding vegetation. The house unfurls on a single main level, crowned by a small lookout, as if to emphasize the project's aim of coming up with a simple, clear-cut, economical construction.

The composition unfolds on a staggered horizontal plane, and it is based upon a building system that shows the possibilities that arise when a single prefabricated piece of concrete, placed in four positions, configures the structure, the enclosure, the stairs and even the furniture.
The prefabricated units are attached to the concrete platforms with steel rods that are anchored to the spot with epoxy glue.

The rods and the elements joining the pieces together generate a tight structure of small columns and lintels that serves to help resist the seismic movements which are frequent in the region. The gaps that appear between the pieces are covered with acrylic, and they are thought of as filters for vegetation and sunlight, but here and there they are closed with wooden boards and transformed into a whole variety of domestic elements like shelves, seats and tables.

Responding to a reduced budget, the house has no finishes. The foundation slab is simply given a layer of pigment of a hardened black color. Both inside and out, the prefabricated concrete pieces are left as they are, their hardness mellowed only by the reddish tone of wood and the green of the oxidized copper flashings. The lookout has no ancillary components whatsoever, letting air and light pass and framing views of the distant mountains, connecting the residents to their environment.

This one-family house was raised with a single prefabricated piece of concrete that was placed in four different positions to resolve the structure, the enclosure, the stairs, the furniture, and even the garden facade that had been the original idea of the project. On the outside it is a neutral grid with the semblance of a hedge, while inside, each wall is different, adjusting to the particular function it is designed to serve.

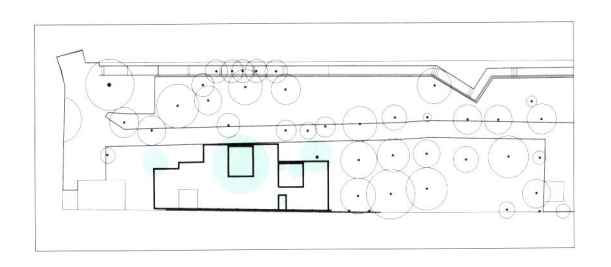

Constrained by a tight budget, the house makes do without finishes. The foundation slab is simply coated with a layer of hard black pigment and the concrete pieces are left as they are. Here and there, the gaps between prefabricated units are covered with acrylic elements that act as filters for vegetation and sunlight; in other areas they are closed up with wooden boards and transformed into domestic fixtures and furniture.

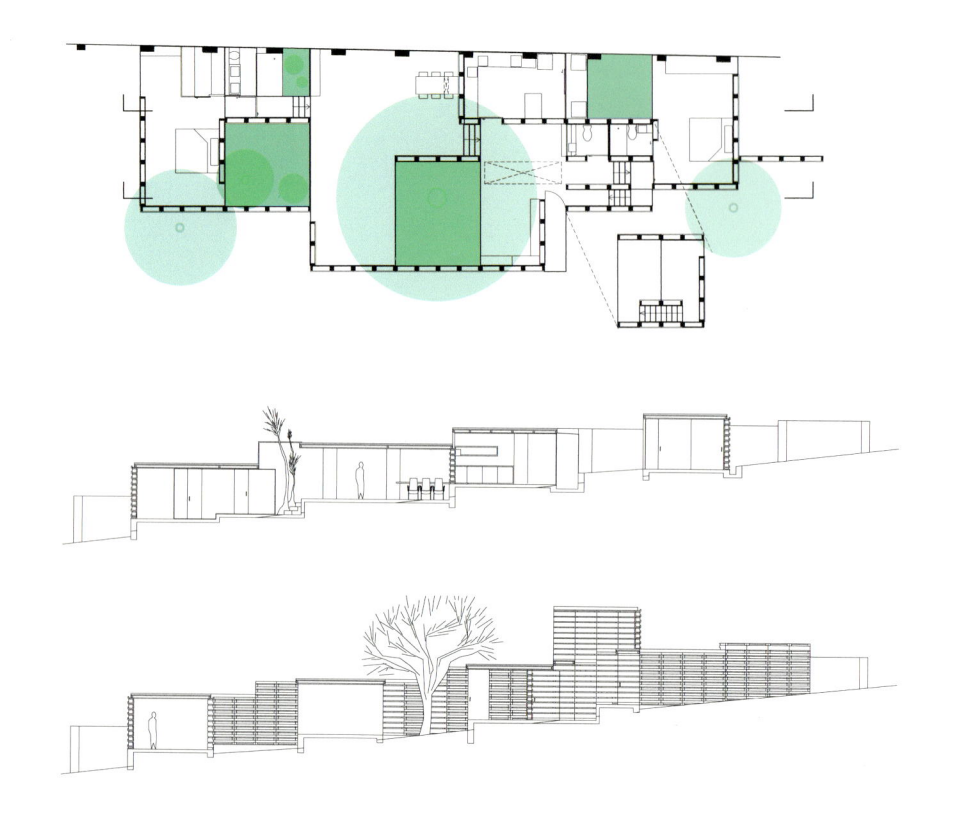

206 Atlas: America

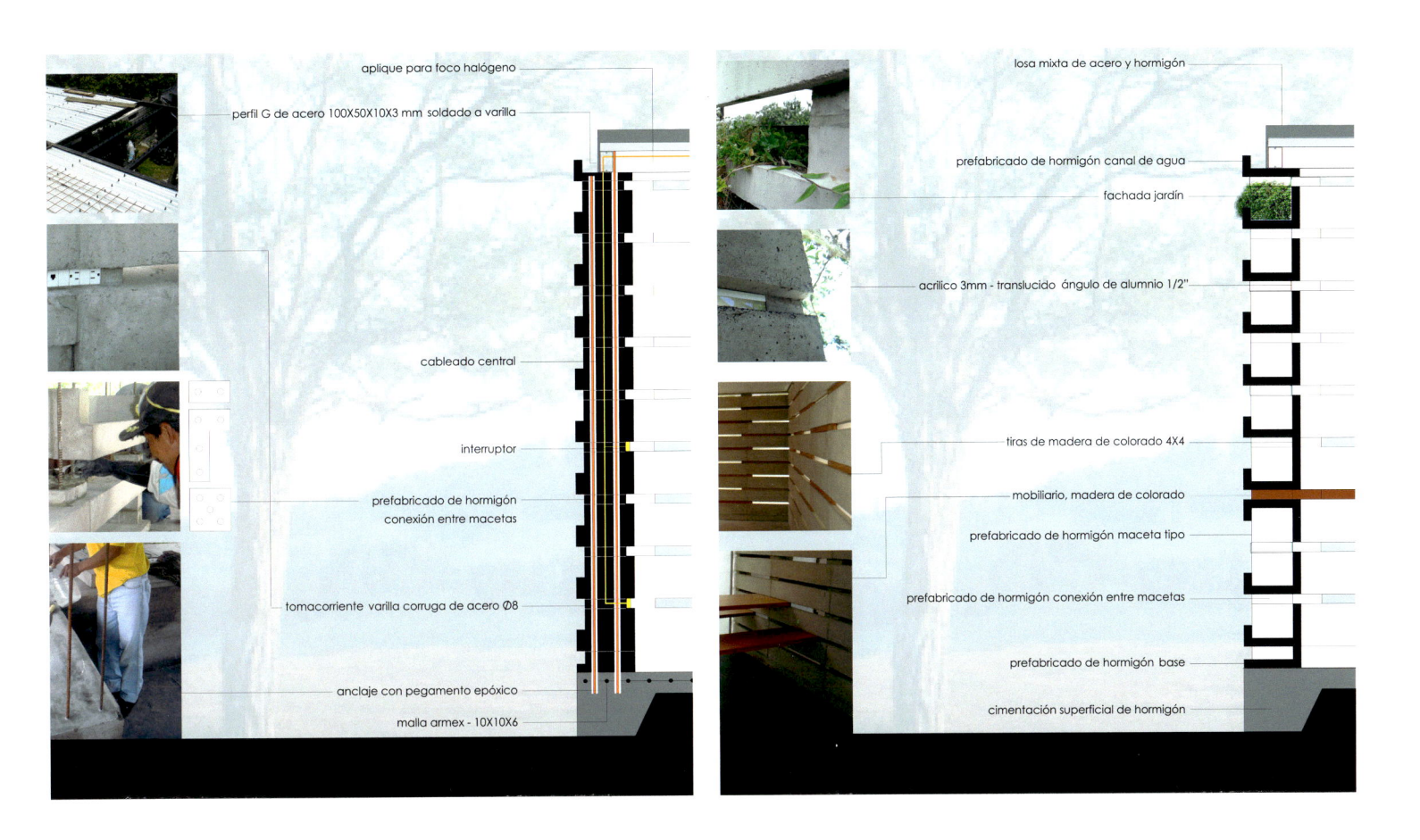

aplique para foco halógeno	losa mixta de acero y hormigón
perfil G de acero 100X50X10X3 mm soldado a varilla	prefabricado de hormigón canal de agua
	fachada jardín
	acrílico 3mm - translucido ángulo de alumnio 1/2"
cableado central	
interruptor	tiras de madera de colorado 4X4
prefabricado de hormigón conexión entre macetas	mobiliario, madera de colorado
	prefabricado de hormigón maceta tipo
	prefabricado de hormigón conexión entre macetas
tomacorriente varilla corruga de acero Ø8	prefabricado de hormigón base
anclaje con pegamento epóxico	cimentación superficial de hormigón
malla armex - 10X10X6	

Carlos Villagómez
Archaeological Museum in Tiwanaku
La Paz (Bolivia)

Client
Ministry of Tourism and Culture
Architect
Carlos Villagómez Paredes
Collaborators
Fernando Larrea, Ana María Steverlynck, Gabriela Urquiola
Consultants
Max Mollinedo (engineering)
Contractor
RAH Gómez
Photos
Daniel Contreras

On a floor plan shaped like the Andean square cross rise the different spaces of the museum, which contains the entrance hall and the exhibition galleries in eight modules arranged around a central space.

A TESTIMONY OF pre-Inca civilization, Tiwanaku is an ancient architectural complex and a current archaeological site in the central plateau of Bolivia, located 20 kilometers southeast of Lake Titicaca. Constructed in 1993, the Regional Museum of Tiwanaku Culture has now expanded its facilities to accommodate some 3,500 objects taken from archaeological digs carried out in the early 1990s by specialists working with the National Archaeology and Anthropology Directorship.

The new building salvages the most essential values of pre-Hispanic architecture and tries to give it an added value by drawing inspiration from Tiwanaku culture of the classical age. The floor plan is based on the square cross that is an icon of Andean culture and consists of nine modules. The entire premises take off from a central area, around which eight rooms are laid out. Both on plan and on elevation the geometry unfolds in modularized grids with units of 1.6 meter sides, the Andean measurement known as Jacha Luka. All geometric relationships are set by this measurement and its multiples and submultiples (Taipi Luka). The museum is entered on the east, and the main foyer, the information center and the staff offices are placed together, organized in two symmetrical volumes connected by a toplit central space. The other spaces contain the exhibition halls in a total approximate floor area of 400 square meters.

The building technology used is a local variant of an open prefabrication system that uses prefabricated concrete elements of different dimensions, colors, textures and finishes. All such elements here were produced with high-density vibrated concrete mixed with the reddish soil of the place, and utilized to raise the sepia-toned rock-like walls as well as the low-relief friezes inspired by the typical decorative motifs of the region.

With the explicit objective of integrating the museum into the archaeological site that it sits on, a local variation of an open prefabrication system was resorted to, using concrete blocks made with the characteristic reddish sand of the region. These elements were used to build the sepia-colored rock-like walls, and the friezes adorned with low reliefs inspired by the decorative motifs abounding in the objects found in the dig.

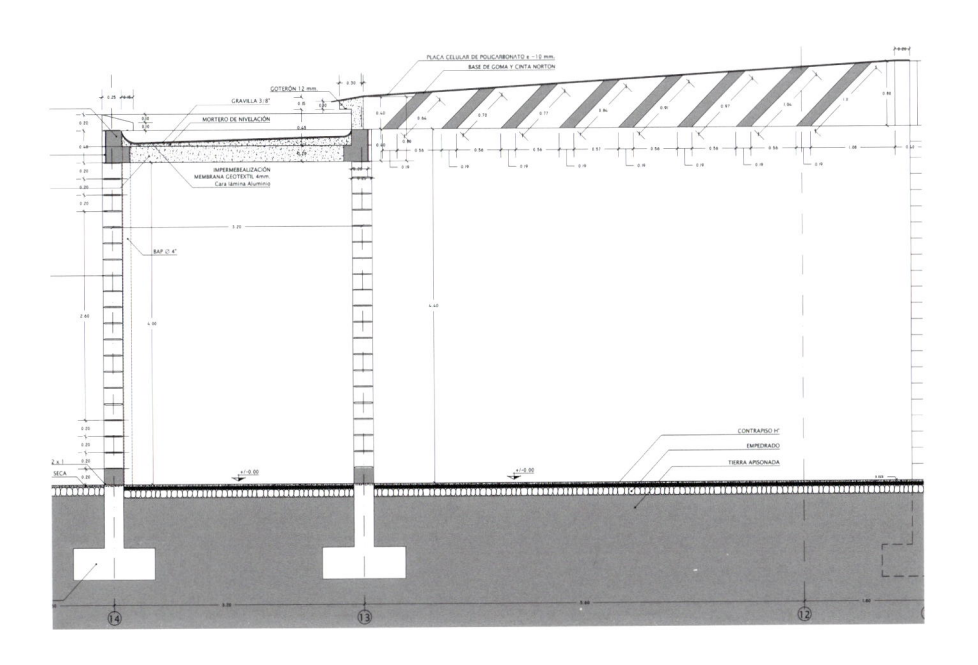

Atlas: America 209

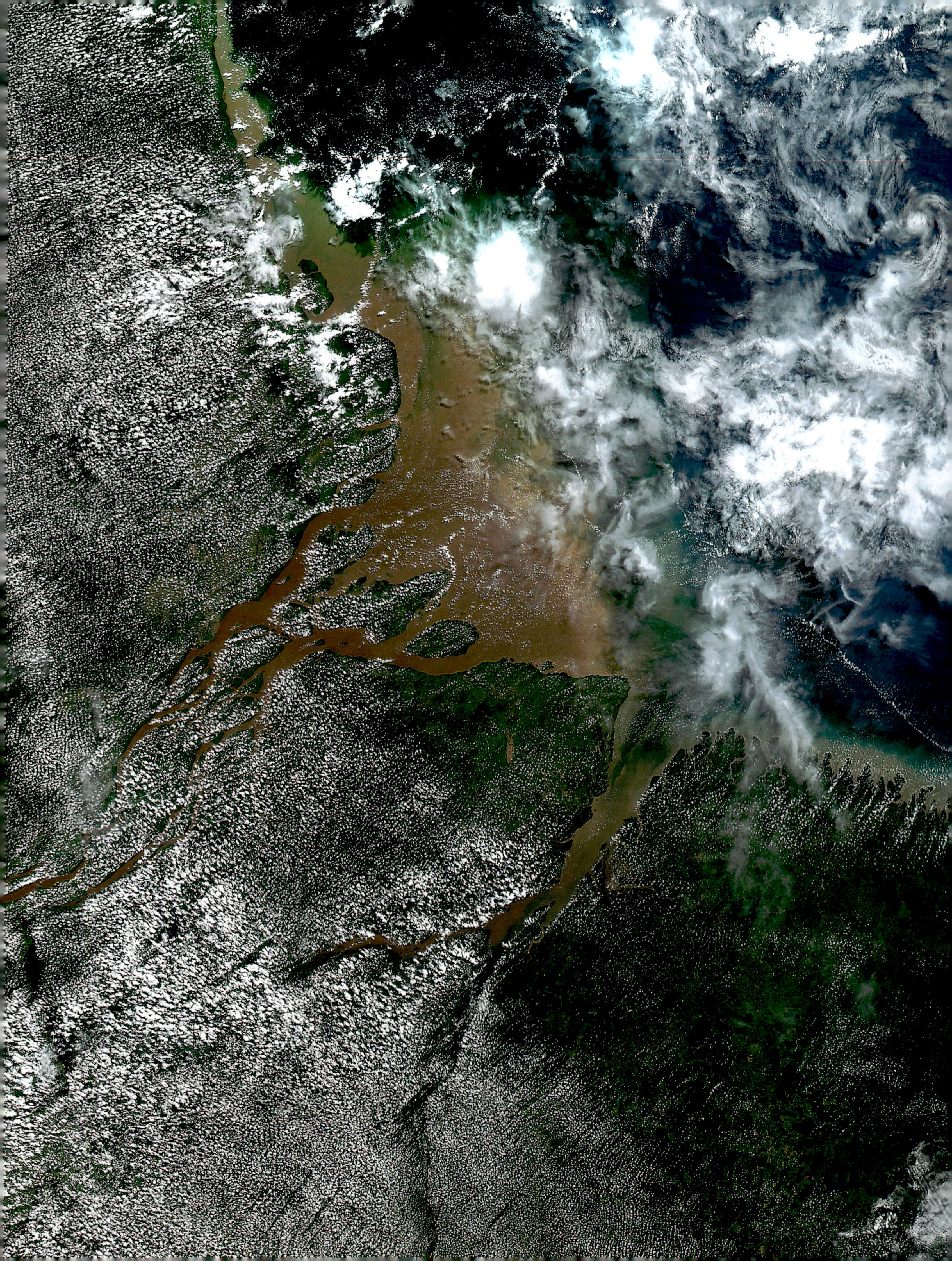

Brazil

With a total area exceeding 8.5 million square kilometers and a privileged geographical location in the tropics, Brazil is extremely rich in natural resources. In the past years, a rise in gross domestic product and increased participation in international trade have together made it one of the world's emerging economies. In the field of architecture, the continued hegemony of the grand masters – Oscar Niemeyer, João Filgueiras Lima and Paulo Mendes da Rocha, the latter represented in the following pages by the Chapel of Our Lady of the Conception in Recife – coexists with daring proposals coming from young Brazilian practices that are in the process of developing a new hybrid language, as is evident in the single-family residences built by Marcio Kogan in Paraty and Procter & Rihl in Porto Alegre, as well as in the office building raised by Triptyque and the FDE Public School constructed by Forte, Gimenes & Marcondes Ferraz, both of them in São Paulo.

Hugo Segawa
Paradoxes of Modernity
Brazil, the Fascination of an Emerging Power

Oscar Niemeyer, Honestino Guimarães Museum, Brasília (2006)

Besides the continuity of historic modernity, the country's economic development has spurred the appearance of new architectural languages.

New practices are on the rise and trying to make their way in the field with works that reinterpret modernity, faced as they are with the hegemony of the great masters whose prolific careers continue to evolve.

IN THE YEAR 2000, the last Mies van der Rohe Award for Latin American Architecture went to Paulo Mendes da Rocha for his remodeling of the State Pinacotheque, an unfinished early 20th-century building of academic physiognomy, to house a contemporary art museum. There was a subtle paradox in this recognition because it had Brazil, a country under the sign of modernity, presenting itself through an old building that, by certain parameters, was not that old. At the same time, an architect who was among the least predictable in interventions of this kind was receiving international applause, acclaim which he would follow up six years later with the Pritzker Prize. When Oscar Niemeyer capped the Pritzker in 1988 with Gordon Bunshaft, *Time* magazine called both him and Paulo Mendes da Rocha "unrepentant old Modernists" and *Progressive Architecture* printed an editorial titled 'Honors to the Old Guard'. Neither of the two was considered by professionals of the guild to be representative of architecture of the new millennium.

Latin American presence in the media in the last two decades of the 20th century, especially in the context of the fifth centenary of Christopher Columbus's arrival in America, threw the limelight on various Brazilian figures, including Éolo Maia, Carlos Bratke, Severiano Porto, Aflalo & Gasperini and Luiz Paulo Conde. The latter came to be urban planning councilor and subsequently mayor of Rio de Janeiro, from the positions of which he carried out initiatives like the Rio City Revitalization Plan, aside from operations in poor sectors like the Favela-Bairro Program. The development of his most publicized intervention was carried out by Jorge Mario Jáuregui, who is known for his involvement in the urbanization of favelas through projects that had positive repercussions at the close of the past millennium, including Harvard University's Veronica Rudge Green Prize in 2000. These successes are also the cause of the prestige of ex-mayor and ex-governor Jaime Lerner, an architect from Curitiba who *Time* included in a list of the world's twenty-five most influential thinkers. Some ideas of Lerner and his team, including the Rapid Transit Bus, preempted the current concern for urban sustainability by almost forty years.

The Turn of the Century
The final decade of the past millennium was a renaissance period for the veterans. Niemeyer, whom Gropius had called a 'bird of paradise' in the 1950s, became a real Phoenix. The Museum of Contemporary Art of Niterói opened in 1993 and was an immediate success in the non-specialized international press, which saw in it wild allusions to science fiction that were really nothing extraordinary in the career of the architect from Rio de Janeiro whose work had disturbed the most orthodox positions of the Modern Movement. Niemeyer more recently designed the Serpentine Gallery Pavilion of 2003, in London, and his, too, are the National Library and National Museum along the monumental axis of Brasília, which opened to the public in 2006. In January 2010, little over a month after the master turned 102, the Niemeyer Auditorium opened in the Italian city of Ravello. In March, the state of Minas Gerais inaugurated his Administrative Center, and in the coming months the Oscar Niemeyer International Cultural Center will open in the Asturian city of Áviles.

Also considered impactful is Paulo Mendes da Rocha's Brazilian Museum of Sculpture in São Paulo, which opened in 1995 and is regarded as the *tour de force* behind the career of its author, a native of that city. But Mendes da Rocha was no neophyte; although before this museum he had only built a few cult works, within an exclusive intellectual circle he was held to be the main representative of a current of

The active presence in the architectural scene of masters of the earliest generations of modern Brazilian architects – Oscar Niemeyer, greatest representative of the Rio de Janeiro school; Paulo Mendes da Rocha, leading exponent of the São Paulo school; and João Filgueiras Lima, better known as Lelé – is an unmistakable indicator of the continued vitality and solidity of the South American country's modern tradition.

João Filgueiras Lima, Sarah-Río Hospital, Rio de Janeiro (2009)

Brazilian architecture that was called the Paulista school, whose members gravitated around the Faculty of Architecture and Urban Planning of the University of São Paulo. Another prominent member was the architect João Batista Vilanova Artigas, whose name has in the past years begun to ring a bell beyond our borders.

The opening of the Sarah-Salvador Hospital in 1994, designed by João Filgueiras Lima (Lelé), was the first of a chain of hospitals specialized in the treatment of locomotor apparatus problems: Sarah-Lago Norte International Center for Neurorehabilitation and Neuroscience (1994-2003); Sarah-Fortaleza Hospital (1991-2001); Sarah-Macapá Pediatric Rehabilitation Center (2000-2005); Sarah-Rio de Janeiro Center for Neuroscience and Neurorehabilitation (2000-2002); Sarah-Belém Pediatric Outpatient Center (2003-2007); Sarah-Rio de Janeiro International Center for Neurorehabilitation and Neuroscience (2007-2009). For over half a century Lelé has pursued a professional path that stands out for his total mastery of the process of conceiving and materializing the architectural work – a variation of Walter Gropius's master builder concept –, for exploring the potentials of industrialization in construction – starting with a revision of Jean Prouvé's *homme d'usine* concept –, and for his work with the free form, with the refined sensibility inherited from Niemeyer. Lelé has even created a technology center with the capacity to design and produce anything from an orthopedic prosthesis to a building, such as the Housing Unit of Rio de Janeiro (2009).

Obviously Lelé's quest to rationalize building processes was born from the challenge and urgent need to build Brasilia, where Lelé worked as Oscar Niemeyer's assistant. Designing through in-depth analysis of needs and proposing rigorously elaborated programs – thought out in terms of rationalization, industrialization, labor considerations and economizing on means and resources – denote attitudes through which he has tried to address specific contexts. This is his conception of architecture: an empirical and pragmatic instrument for mediating between the social and economic environments, between technique and aesthetics.

Preserving the Modern
Revisiting the great masters also helps us find the references of the new crops of architects. As the Mexican critic Miquel Adrià observes, referring to Brazilian architecture, this is characterized by the maintenance of "continuity with respect to classic modernity for generations". Here the term 'classic modernity' refers to that which was established upon our own identity, reflected in two important publications: *Brazil Builds* (1943), the catalog of an exhibition held at the Museum of Modern Art in New York, and *Modern Brazilian Architecture* (1956), written by Henrique Mindlin. As for 'continuity', it expressed a concept generally used in Latin America to refer to the specific case of Brazil, which differs from the other countries of the region in that its successive periods of architectural production are bound together by many formal similarities. Whereas some Mexican architects, such as Alberto Kalach or Enrique Norten, reject any connection to previous Mexicanisms, Brazil's professionals of the same generation as Kalach and Norten acknowledge their admiration for masters like Oscar Niemeyer, Lucio Costa, Affonso Eduardo Reidy, Rino Levi, Oswaldo Bratke, Vilanova Artigas or Lina Bo Bardi. The longevity of the first batch of modern architects of Brazil – Lucio Costa died in 1998, Roberto Burle Marx in 1994, Oswaldo Bratke in 1997, Lina Bo Bardi in 1992 and Acácio Gil Borsoi in 2009 –, and the continued activity of some of them – Oscar Niemeyer, Paulo Mendes da Rocha and João

Paulo Mendes da Rocha, Parking Building, Recife, Pernambuco (2006)

Atlas: America 213

Núcleo Arquitectura, Jardim Angélica III School, Guarulhos, São Paulo (2004)

Filgueiras Lima – or their disciples – Marco Antônio Borsoi or Paulo Bruna – are a clear testimony of the vitality and solidity of the country's modern tradition.

Awareness of this modernity is also attributable to a level of academic activity that has broadened and intensified in the past two decades. Institutional strengthening of post-graduate programs in different parts of Brazil promoted the study of Brazilian architecture and urban planning as one of the more interesting themes of investigation. Tens of doctoral theses threw light on historical and critical aspects of this period and the high level, both quantity- and quality-wise, of the proposals presented. Moreover, discussion on the subject found solid support for its dissemination, in São Paulo, through the electronic magazine *Vitruvius* – edited by Abílio Guerra and with a substantial following abroad, it is the principal permanent forum for documenting history and criticism of Brazil's recent architecture –, and in the consolidation of the Brazilian chapter of DOCOMOMO (Documentation and Conservation of the Modern Movement) through national and regional biannual seminars held in different parts of the country, parallel to international gatherings.

Two important events reinforced the idea of continuity of the modern. The first was the exhibition 'Encore moderne: Architecture Brésilienne 1928-2005', held from October 2005 to January 2006 at the Cité de l'architecture et du patromoine in Paris. The curators Lauro Cavalcanti and André Corrêa do Lago, in resuming the canonical reading of the history of Brazilian architecture, identified a "clear influence and inspiration in the 'historic' Brazilian projects that followed the Modern Movement of the 1940s and 1950s". For this reason, they structured the different parts of the exhibition in accordance with Modern Movement references, crediting contemporary architects with an "interesting revisited modern style".

The other event that fortified the idea of a continued modern movement was the exhibition 'Coletivo: Arquitectura Paulista Contemporánea', inaugurated in São Paulo in 2006, at the ETH of Zürich in 2007, and at the IUL of Lisbon in 2008. This traveling exhibition brought together the production of six studios of the same generation, all run by graduates of the Faculty of Architecture and Urban Planning of the University of São Paulo: Andrade & Morettin, MMBB, Núcleo de Arquitetura, Projeto Paulista, Puntoni Arquitetos & SPBR and Una Arquitetos. Born in the 1960s, their affinities are rooted in their university training and in the invention of the tradition with Vilanova Artigas, as well as in references to Paulo Mendes da Rocha and Marcos Acayaba, with whom some of them have worked and even continue to. The professional career of each of them has been analyzed from a theoretical angle in the exhibition catalog and in writings by Ana Luiza Nobre of Rio de Janeiro, Ana Vaz Milheiro of Lisbon and Guilherme Wisnik of São Paulo. These three members of a new generation of recognized Brazilian and Portuguese critics represent something similar to what the critic Reyner Banham was for New Brutalism. Hence the celebratory spirit, not without polemic, that was felt in the arena of São Paulo's architectural culture. Evidently the six offices selected for the exhibition could not offer a global view of the architecture currently going up in São Paulo, highlighting the need for the organization of a systematic atlas of local production.

Some young professionals aligned with architectural practice in São Paulo stand out over the rest, with several quality works to their names that nevertheless are still short of establishing them as consolidated architects. Many of them, such as Héctor Vigliecca or those forming the team of Biselli & Katchborian, have also repeatedly stood out as winners or finalists in nationwide architectural competitions, but sadly some of the most notable projects have remained on paper. Vigliecca, in particular, boasts a brilliant track record with his forty

Yuri Vital, Box House, São Paulo (2009)

Marcelo Suzuki, Cuiabá Forum, Mato Grosso (2005)

Conventional systems using reinforced concrete are the rule in the formally expressive large buildings that have been undertaken in São Paulo, by public entities, to accommodate educational facilities, as well as in apartment buildings, whereas in the smaller cities the tendency has been to go for light metal structures in combination with traditional materials like earth for walls and wood for claddings.

awards received in national and international competitions, among which we ought to mention the shortlisted project for the José Vasconcelos National Library of Mexico and the honorable mention in the contest for the Grand Egyptian Museum. Parallel to all of this, Vigliecca has been carrying out urban and architectural interventions, prominent among which are the social housing projects he has built in São Paulo.

Metropolis, Megacity and Global City
In the first decade of the millennium, the mood of São Paulo has seemed to be the most 'vibrant' in all of Brazil. In the famous publication *Wallpaper City Guide*, the introduction to the city makes this comparison: "while Rio de Janeiro has always had beaches, samba schools and tourists, São Paulo has preserved an antiquated image, as if it were a vast urban sprawl in *Blade Runner* style. In fact, for those familiar with it, South America's largest city has always had the energy, sophistication and drive of the Modern Movement, thanks to which it has come to be a must destination for the most adventurous travelers". According to the United Nations, in the year 2007, with a population of 18.9 million São Paulo ranked fourth among the world's largest cities, after New York City, Mexico City and Tokyo. It is predicted to come in fifth in 2025, with 21.4 million people, after Dacca, New Delhi, Mumbai and Tokyo, which will continue in first place.

Will São Paulo be a 'global city', in accordance with the theorizing that has gained ground in past decades? Or just a megacity? Business, finance, consulting, academic and government sectors gamble on São Paulo's becoming part of the discourse on the new geographics of centrality, the internationalization of the finance industry – through a network of transactions on a world scale –, and the election of a small number of strategic places equipped with a network of services, resources and infrastructures adapted to the flows generation under the sign of globalization. The Study Group and Network of the think tank Globalization and World Cities (GaWC) classifies São Paulo as a 'Beta World City'. Some studies include it among the world's fifty global cities, with its capacity to attract resources, while others point to the fallacious character of the 'global city' as a vector of urban transformations. The world financial crisis of the last trimester of 2008 made it necessary to revise the concept, putting its redemptive character under suspicion.

Being South America's largest metropolis does not spare it from having the greatest social contrasts, with problems of a magnitude that is proportional to its size. Recent initiatives that have tried to face up to the challenge in concrete terms have had to do with educational infrastructures. Subordinated to the State of São Paulo's Education Ministry, the Foundation for Educational Development is carrying out a stimulus program to improve school facilities in small areas of the poor peripheries undergoing development, using conventional systems of prefabricated concrete that make execution quick and keep costs low. If these projects are better than the average, it is thanks to the participation of reputed São Paulo architects of different generations, such as Eduardo de Almeida, Paulo Bruna, Marcos Acayaba, the members of the Coletivo de Arquitetura Paulista Contemporánea, the Escritório Paulistano de Arquitetura, and the office of Forte, Giménez & Marcondes Ferraz, who despite being conditioned by prefabrication systems offered by the market and by scant budgets, have demonstrated that it is possible to build good architecture in extremely limited circumstances, with works spread all over the metropolitan region of São Paulo and some nearby cities.

On an urbanistic level, the most important operation in the educational field was developed by City Hall in the period 2002-2004. The Unified Educational Centers (CEU) were facilities that have sprung up as a result of a comprehensive administrative

Marco Antonio Borsoi, Hotel Tejú-Acu, Fernando de Noronha, Pernambuco (2006)

The large-scale urban interventions carried out in the marginal areas on the outskirts of the city of São Paulo, all linked to the construction of cultural, sport and educational buildings, as well as to the provision of new public zones and basic infrastructures, strike a contrast with the delicate operations that have been effected in protected landscape environments, where private residences merge with tropical vegetation.

Takiya, Delijaicov & Ariza, CEU Schools, São Paulo (2004)

action that is not common: eight municipal councils (education, culture, sports, environment, economy, juridical cabinet, planning, and infrastructures and public works), along with the parliaments and the communities, engaged in dialog to draw up a project for the city's poverty-stricken outskirts. More than just working out an iconic school building, the intention was to unify the fragmented make-up of the peripheries through the construction of an efficient urban space. The architects André Takiya, Alexandre Delijaicov and Wanderley Ariza of the Projects Division of the Building Department of the Ministry of Infrastructures and Works (EDIF) proposed an architectural structure originally meant to go up in 45 localities (only half of them were built in the end) with complex social, economic and geographic contexts. The program was conceived as a system made up of the actual school (kindergarten, primary and secondary school, unaccredited studies), a cultural area (theater, cinema, art and music workshops), sport facilities (gymnasiums, swimming pools, soccer field, skating rink), recreational spaces (plazas, gardens, parks, playgrounds, pools), and the infrastructures including basic plumbing, water pipes, the road system, light fixtures in the public spaces, public transport and sidewalks. Some of the peripheral communities were getting all this for the first time, thanks to the CEUs, and one cannot help seeing them as a new reading of the 'social condensers' of Soviet constructivists. The authors of the CEUs acknowledge the influence of Hélio Duarte's projects for the 'Educational Agreement' of the 1950s; the proposals of the Soviet constructivists; the masterworks of Le Corbusier and Richard Neutra; the Paulista architecture of Vilanova Artigas and Paulo Mendes da Rocha; the educational action proposed by Darcy Ribeiro in Rio de Janeiro; the Integrated Centers for Public Education (CIEP) built by Oscar Niemeyer in the 1980s; and the architecture of João Filgueiras Lima.
As the expert eye of the historian and critic Leonardo Benévolo observed in his book *L'Architettura del nuovo millenio,* "the naturalness with which the prototypes and models of the first modern revolution are again being put forward in the new century, as if time had not passed, is extraordinary. The seriousness of the matter of relating to the community of users acts as an intellectual brake to any digression".

The Renewal of Modernity
Despite the diversity of current Brazilian architecture and despite profound ideological differences, the architects of the new generations have been breaking into the scene with common references in their discourses. The first decade of the millennium has seen the appearance of large numbers of architects who were born in the 1950s to graduate in the 1970s, hinting at a stratigraphy of the generations quite a lot later than the heroic phase of Brazil's modern movement.
Lina Bo Bardi was a teacher for a while, in the 1950s, at the Faculty of Architecture and Urban Planing of the University of São Paulo. Although she stayed away from the classrooms in the final years of her life, the projects she carried out – such as the Pompéia Factory and the interventions in the historic center of Salvador – had the conditions necessary for young architects to get involved and have firsthand experience of her design practice. Marcelo Ferraz, André Vainer and Marcelo Suzuki collaborated with her in various works. Vainer later teamed up with Guilherme Paoliello, while Suzuki set up the studio Brasil Arquitetura with Fanucci & Ferraz. These architects form a front which differs from that represented by the followers of Artigas and Mendes da Rocha, but it is impregnated with the same values that are present in the University of São Paulo. The

Marcio Kogan, House in Bahía, Salvador de Bahía (2010)

office of Fanucci & Ferraz has in the last ten years or so produced a respectable body of works that includes recyclings, renovations and restorations, in coherence with the anthropological sensibility that we find in the oeuvre of Lina Bo Bardi. In 1997, over contestants like the Brazilian Éolo Maia and the Argentinian team formed by Justo Solsona and Clorindo Testa, Fanucci & Ferraz won the international competition for the intervention that was to be carried out in the Gelbes Viertel neighborhood of the center of Hellersdorf, in what was East Berlin. The brief stipulated a housing complex with 3,200 units for 12,000 people. More recent works of theirs include the KKKK Complex (1996-2001) in the city of Registro (São Paulo), the Bread Museum and Center (2005-2007) in Ilópolis (Rio Grande do Sul) and the Rodin Museum (2002-2006) in Salvador de Bahía, all of which seek a dialog between old and new through the refurbishing of old edifices to serve new functions. And counting among their very latest works are the Plaza de las Artes at the very heart of the city of São Paulo and a social housing development in the historic center of Salvador de Bahía, both of them currently under construction.

Isay Weinfeld and Marcio Kogan happen to share a past as graduates of the Mackenzie Architecture School in São Paulo, co-curators of exhibitions, colleagues in film productions – specifically writing and directing a feature film and several shorts –, and partners in some architectural projects, such as Hotel Fasano (2003) and the Minneapolis Building (2001-2004). But apart from this near-fraternal complicity between them, individually each has a long list of works to show for. They have separately been delivering sophisticated interventions in small spaces, interesting furniture and decorative objects, and numerous one-family residences, especially

Marcio Kogan, Paraty House, Rio de Janeiro (2009)

Arquitetos Associados, Environment Museum Expansion, Rio de Janeiro

The state of Minas Gerais is home to a new batch of young designers, such as Matoso Macedo or those at Arquitetos Associados, who studied in the 1990s under the influence of 'mineiro' postmoderns and currently work along the lines of geometric abstraction. Meanwhile, in Brasilia, the works of professionals including Gustavo Penna and studios like Projeto Paulista bear the unmistakable mark of their master, Niemeyer.

since the late 1990s. In the past years, the refined finishes and details of their small-scale constructions have been gaining ground in larger works. In 2009 the so-called 360º Building, an upscale residential block situated in São Paulo that Weinfeld designed, was honored for its innovativeness in the MIPIM Architectural Review Future Projects awards, a recognition given in connection with the huge event of the international real estate market that was held in Cannes, France. Kogan's architectural practice (Studio MK27) has also been internationally recognized. In 2008 it received an honorable mention, for the Primetime School, in the awards given by the United States magazine *Interior Design;* the Yellow Pencil Award granted by the British organization D&AD (Design & Art Direction), specifically in the Environmental Design and Public Space category; as well as one of the prizes in the Dedalo Minosse International Award, held in Italy. The Paraty House (2009) was the winner of the LEAF International Award and was hailed in 2010 as the best newly built private one-family residence in the prizes handed out by the prestigious magazine *Wallpaper Design.*

Two years ago, the architect Marcio Kogan was interviewed by this magazine and quoted as saying: "I have always admired the Modern Movement that arose in Brazil in the 1930s, which gave rise to unbelievable works built by a dozen masters of architecture like Lucio Costa, Lina Bo Bardi, Oscar Niemeyer, Rino Levi and Affonso Reidy". The Modern Movement remains current in the opinion of Gustavo Penna, an architect based in Belo Horizonte (Minas Gerais). In a 2001 interview for the magazine *Projeto Design,* he said: "Research on the Modern Movement should have continued. I would like to be building an architecture that is conceived for its location; to interpret the political, cultural and social context of Brazil and include it all in the project. It would interest me to discover what is common in this way of building architecture in Brazil, even if I had to look back and revisit the world of Aleijadinho, Lina Bo Bardi, Osvaldo Bratke and Raffaelo Berti, or reread MMM Roberto (Marcelo, Milton & Mauricio)". In the 1980s, Penna experienced the eclosion of postmodernism in Minas Gerais with architects of the likes of Éolo Maia, Jô Vasconcellos, Sylvio de Podestá, Veveco Hardy or João Diniz, among others. Notwithstanding, he kept his work at a relative distance from the formal eclecticism that characterized the works of his colleagues, and stayed well within the limits of a geometrical abstraction that gained ground in the 1990s. His key reference was Humberto Serpa, a great architect who, unfortunately, is little known outside the state of Minas Gerais.

This state has seen the rise of a very new crop of architects who, born in the second half of the 1970s and done with school at the end of the millennium, mostly got to work with the Minas Gerais postmoderns. In particular, structured around the architecture and urban planning magazine *Mínimo Denominador Comum* is a nucleus formed by Alexandre Brasil Garcia, André Luiz Prado, Bruno Santa Cecília, Carlos Alberto Maciel Danilo Matoso Macedo, Humberto Hermeto and Pedro Morais. While some of them have set up the studio Arquitetos Associados, the rest run independent practices or work for different public organisms. But all stand out and together they have reaped numerous awards in architectural competitions, among which we can mention the first prize that went to André Luiz Prado and Bruno Santa Cecília's project for an expanded Environment

Projeto Paulista, Legislative Chamber of the Federal District, Brasilia (2010)

Danilo Matoso Macedo, Army Housing Foundation, Brasilia (2010)

Museum (2010) in Rio de Janeiro's Botanical Garden. Moreover, the new crop of architects has begun to build works of greater importance, such as the Army Housing Foundation (2010) by Danilo Matoso Macedo, Elcio Gomes, Fabiano Sobreira, Newton Godoy, Daniel Lacerda and Filipe Monte Serrata.

Brazil Takes Off
The Christ the Redeemer statue in Rio de Janeiro is one of the most recognizable symbols of the city. In 2007 it was selected to vie for a place among the New Seven Wonders of the World, a public initiative of the New Open World Corporation, which, in lieu of endorsement from institutions or governments, has set up a website through which to choose from among the wonders classified by votes of over 100 million. On the cover of the November 2009 issue of *The Economist,* the title 'Brazil takes off' appeared with a photomontage depicting the statue shooting up like a rocket. Inside, an editorial followed by a coverage of fourteen pages extolled the behavior of the Brazilian economy (it also discussed the country's defects) amid the turbulences of the world crisis of 2008. Little more than six months after this report was published, Brazil's 'honeymoon' with international financial institutions and political powers turned out not to be as sweet as it had been imagined. In 2010, a 'Born in Brazil' issue of *Wallpaper* magazine declared: "We have a single objective: to offer as faithful a picture as possible of an extraordinary country at an exceptional moment of transition". The issue offered interviews with "leading Brazilian architects" of the day, among them Ruy Ohtake, Fernando de Mello Franco, Marcio Kogan, Marcelo Ferraz, Ángelo Bucci and Marcos Acayaba, all from São Paulo, as well as a "directory of Brazilian architects" that included ten young practices based in São Paulo, Minas Gerais, Curitiba, Porto Alegre and Rio de Janeiro. Naturally Brasilia and Paulo Mendes da Rocha were present as well. Considering all this, one can safely say that Brazil is on the rise. But until when?

As for works of foreign architects, on the whole they have been mediocre. Those that can be considered part of what is called architecture of spectacle, so present in past decades, are few: Álvaro Siza's Iberê Camargo Foundation in Porto Alegre; Christian de Portzamparc's City of Music in Rio de Janeiro (the construction of which is currently at a standstill); Herzog & de Meuron's Dance Theater in São Paulo; the Museum of Image and Sound in Rio de Janeiro by Diller Scofidio in conjunction with Renfro; and the competition for the Museum of Tomorrow, to which Santiago Calatrava was invited.

Some far-reaching commitments like the hosting of the Soccer World Cup of 2014 and the Olympic Games of 2016 will continue to show Brazil to the world as a country well on the rise. These are grand events involving transformations of the infrastructural kind whose good effects are predictable, although as yet none of the stadiums designed for the World Cup has especially stood out. What is so extraordinary about the transition? It is hard to tell. We can only hope that the new generations will give due honor to the past they venerate, and know to make the most of a legacy few countries have; that modernity will not be a passing fashion or mere nostalgia; that mistakes of the past will not be repeated; that our young architects will exceed the masters with the same wisdom that enabled the new moderns of the mid-20th century to help transform the country through architecture.

Gustavo Penna, Japanese Immigration Memorial, Belo Horizonte, Minas Gerais (2009)

Paulo Mendes da Rocha
Chapel of Our Lady of the Conception
Recife, Pernambuco (Brazil)

Architect
Paulo Mendes da Rocha
Collaborators
Eduardo Argenton Colonelli;
Eduardo Pereira Gurian,
Laura Guedes, Rafael Baravelli
Consultants
Sérgio Osório/Engedata (structure);
José Miranda Esteves/JME
(installations); Francisco
Dantas/Interplan (air conditioning);
Jorge Passos (stonework restoration);
Luciana Medeiros (site coordination)
Contractor
AB Corte Real
Photos
Leonardo Finotti

As if to treat the ruin like a precious relic, the new concrete roof and the glass enclosure are arranged in such a way that they do not come in contact with the hundred-year-old walls that surround the chapel.

THE STUDIO, museum and residence of Francisco Brennand sit on the remnants of an old ceramics factory, one dating back to the early 20th century, that the artist inherited from his father. The site, an estate in the historic quarter of the Brazilian city of Recife, is surrounded by an exuberant natural reserve of Atlantic shrub and the waters of the Capibaribe River. Following a long reconstruction process, the latest addition to the architectural complex is the Chapel of Our Lady of the Conception, also known as the Brennand Chapel.

The project addressed the challenge of inserting a new space and a new function into a 19th-century house in ruins. The remains of walls of tile and masonry were incorporated into the temple as the envelope of its main nave. The fragments of arches left over from the old arcade form an outer boundary around the building.

The roof, a prestressed concrete slab resting on two circular pillars positioned on the longitudinal axis of the nave, hovers over the area defined by the masterfully restored original walls. Giving the liturgical space a certain degree of privacy is a transparent crystal casing that is independent of both the roof and the walls, from which it is separated by less than a meter, creating a very unique apse aisle. These glass partitions mark a zigzagging perimeter that, by means of a play of transparencies, perspectives and reflections visible through the old doors and windows, helps amplify the small, barely 120 square meter space within.

The sacristy, reached by going down a flight of stairs, is buried in the basement level, beyond the footprint of the main body of the temple. Also carved below grade is a machine room that can be accessed directly from outside. The choir is an elongated rectangular piece with an area of 7.5 x 1.2 meters that floats 2 meters above the sanctuary floor, hanging from the column situated beside the entrance atrium. Finally, a bell tower that stands apart from the main construction, aligned with the arches, completes the program.

Placed along the outer perimeter of the building, both the atrium and the baptistry help to make the architectural complex include the landscape formed by the forest, a small pond, and the river to the south.

The chapel recuperates and incorporates the ruins of a 19th-century house located on the premises of an old ceramics factory of the Brennand family. The new prestressed concrete roof is held up by two pillars placed along the central axis of the temple's main nave, hovering over the stone walls. Set about 80 centimers from these original masonry elements is a zigzagging glass casing that gives rise to a unique apse aisle.

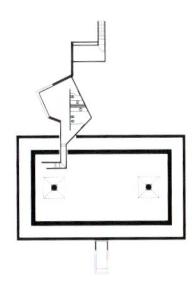

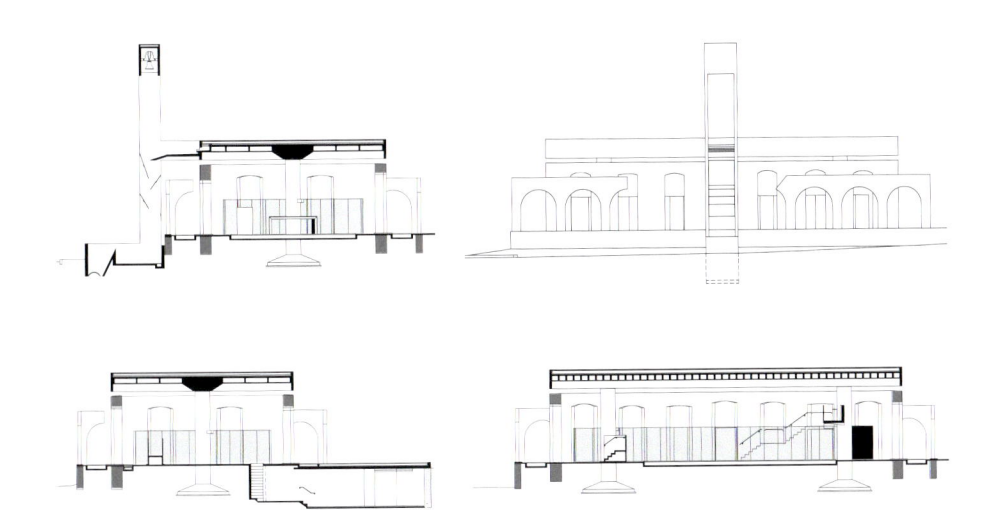

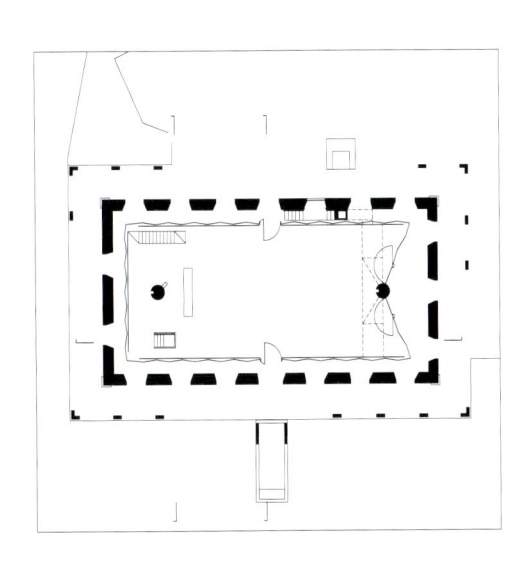

Forte, Gimenes & Marcondes Ferraz
FDE Public School
São Paulo (Brazil)

Architects
Fernando Forte, Lourenço Gimenes, Rodrigo Marcondes Ferraz
Collaborators
Renata Davi, Adriana Junqueira, Ana Paula Barbosa, Fernanda Alpiste, Paloma Delgado, Luciana Muller
Consultants
Catuta Engenharia (structure)
Contractor
Constructora Linic
Photos
Nelson Kon

The new school building has a structure that was executed using a series of prefabricated elements of reinforced concrete that together guaranteed speed of assemblage, budgetary control and quality finishes.

Resulting from a program undertaken by the São Paulo State Government, the so-called FDE Public Schools all follow a system whose industrial components have the effect of facilitating the construction of quality buildings for education. Hence the school in the municipality of Várzea Paulista has a structure whose prefabricated concrete elements guarantee speed of assembly, cost control and quality finishes.

With the intention of linking up school and community activities, a large plaza has been laid out in front of the building, for which the rough terrain had to be flattened beforehand. At the weekend, this space becomes a public square for the neighborhood. The rest of the program is distributed in two prismatic volumes. One of them has a single level for a multisport court, while the other construction rises three stories and contains the communal halls and administration areas. The building's main facade features a series of prefabricated concrete components of varying size, arranged in such a way that they form a mosaic of sorts, with irregular openings that serve to give nuance to the natural light coming into the rooms. The way they are designed frames multiple views of the landscape from within, while from outside, the facade is perceived like a gigantic panel. At night, with the lights in the classrooms on, the school takes on a lighter and more diaphanous appearance.

Behind is a double-height open gallery that is intended to be a multipurpose space. It is protected against the elements with parasols made by installing perforated aluminum sheets directly on the building's loadbearing structure of reinforced concrete. These elements, too, filter incoming sunlight while maintaining transparency and views. In this way it was not necessary to build an actual physical limit between the interior of the school and the public spaces intended for use by the community at large.

The building's envelope is rendered with prefabricated reinforced concrete pieces of varying size, arranged in such a way that they form a huge mosaic of sorts that serves to frame multiple views of the city and both gives nuance to the natural light shining in and protects the interior spaces from excess solar action. At nighttime, when all the lights in the classrooms are on, the facade of the school takes on a lighter, more diaphanous appearance.

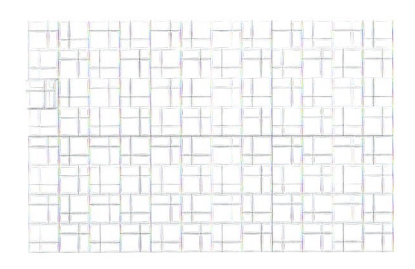

The program unfolds in two prisms: one of them contains a single level for the multisport court; the second volume rises three stories to accommodate the classrooms, administration offices and communal facilities. A large plaza gives access to the entire school complex and at weekends is a public square for the whole community. A double-height open gallery protected by 'parasols' is intended to serve as a multipurpose space.

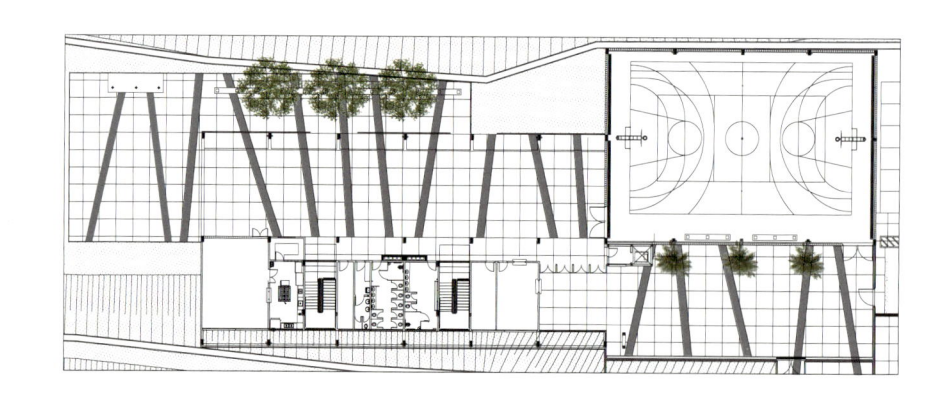

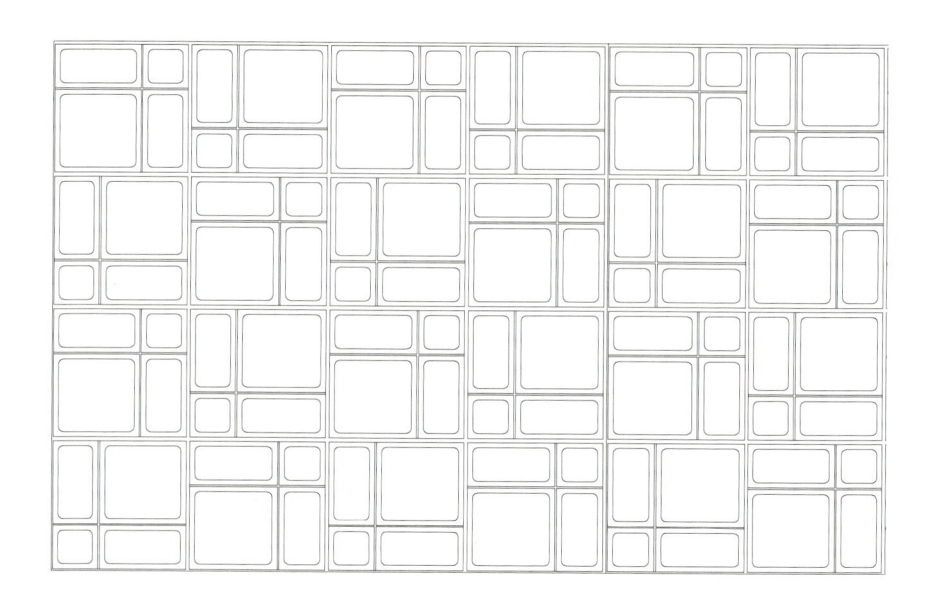

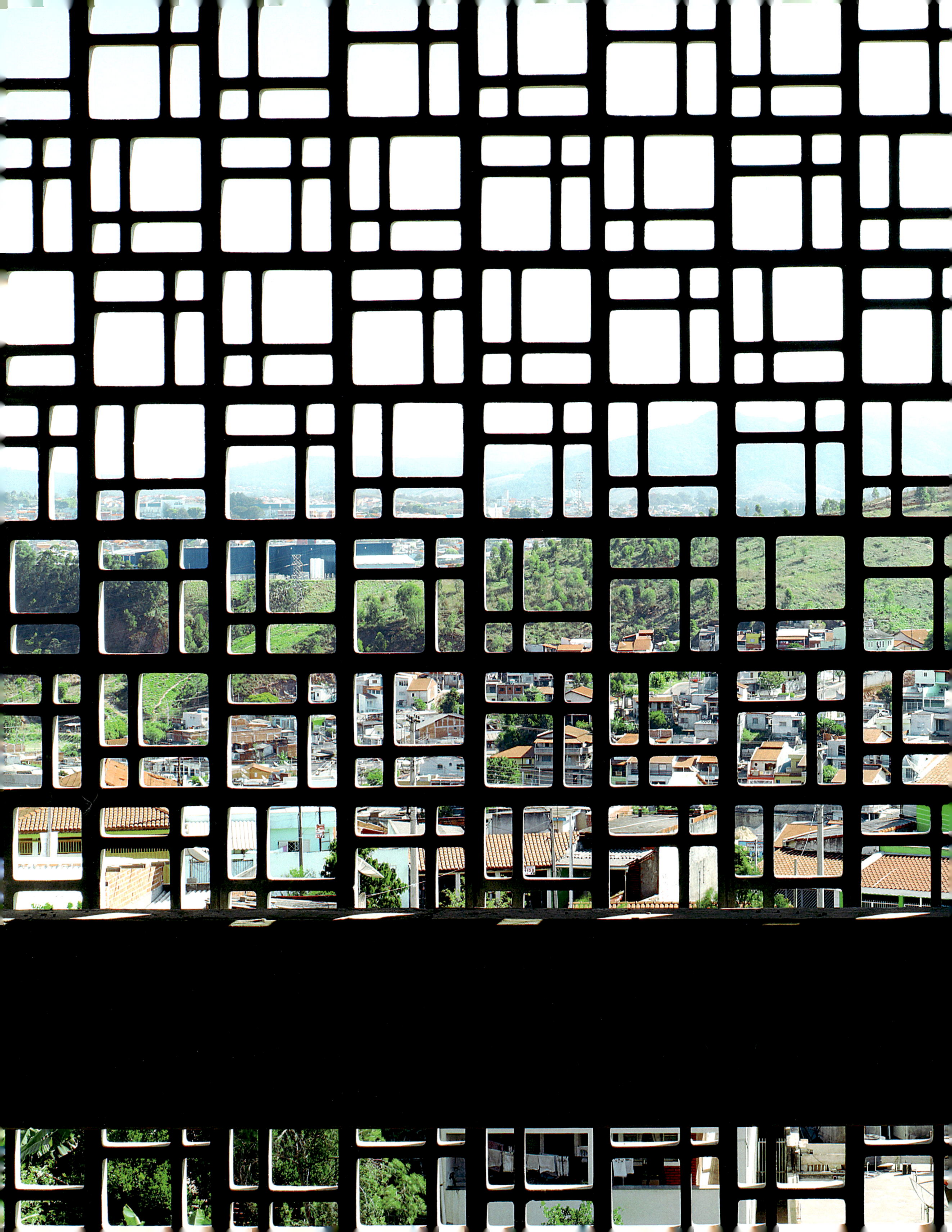

Triptyque
Office Building
São Paulo (Brazil)

THE BUILDING that houses the offices of the Brazilian advertising company Loducca is located in Jardines, one of the most exclusive neighborhoods of São Paulo. Situated in the northern part of the city, in the district of Santana, the place is characterized by the grouping of large corporate premises and recreational facilities around its main street, Luiz Dumont Villares. Meters from Paulista, an avenue of heavy traffic, rises the unique form of the advertising agency, which stands out for its complex envelope. This skin is a protection against both the strong noise pollution of the zone and the intense solar radiation of the region. Its organic appearance is a reference to the deformations that the powerful sound waves registered in the area would cause on a prismatic volume.

The main facade is conceived as a free-flowing membrane, built with a translucent skin of silk-screen printed glass protected by a panel of wooden *brises soleils,* that acts as a buffer shielding the interior spaces from external aggressions while enabling the user to establish a more controlled relationship with the urban context. Lastly, a reinforced concrete frame makes it possible to anchor the intricate enclosure system to the building's loadbearing structure.

The central staircase, also of concrete, is the main articulator of the interior. Thought out as a sculptural element, it traverses all the spaces, rising from the basement that provides for parking all the way up to the rooftop featuring a solarium. Standing out on the wooden pavement here is the concrete-topped glass box that gives access to this deck, from which one can enjoy views of the city gardens. The other floor levels accommodate the various functions of the advertising firm in such a way that the service areas are put together in a block, freeing up the rest of the space for an open-plan organization of offices and meeting rooms.

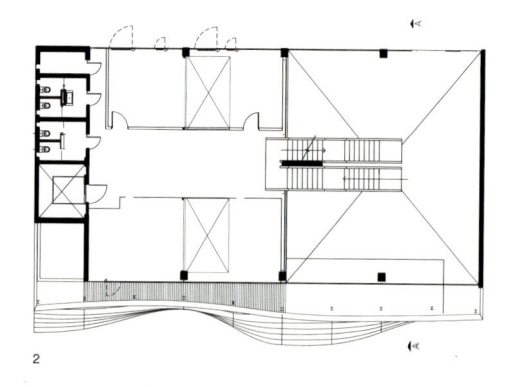

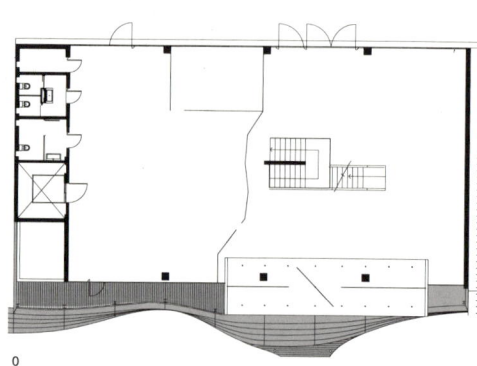

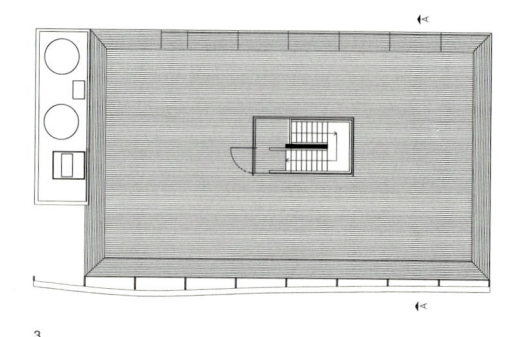

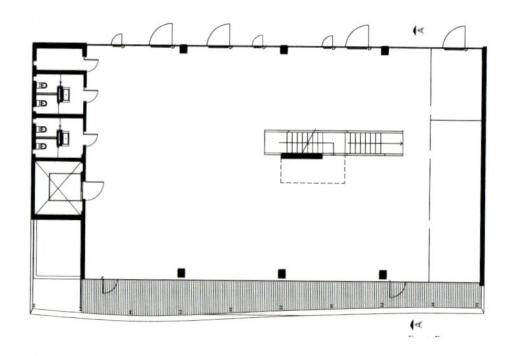

Client
Loducca
Architects
Greg Bousquet, Carolina Bueno, Guillaume Sibaud, Olivier Raffaelli, Tiago Guimarães (project leader)
Collaborators
Laura Bigliassi, Isabella Gebara, Felipe Hess, Bob Van der Brande, Flavio Miranda, Renata Pedrosa, Marc Roca Bravo, Bruno Simoes, Filipe Troncon
Contractor
Bassani+BFG
Photos
Leonardo Finotti, Fran Parente (p. 228)

A unique membrane of organic character, built with a translucent skin of silk-screen printed glass and protected by an envelope of wooden *brises soleils,* insulates the offices from the busy urban activity outside.

Conceived as a filter protecting the interior spaces from glare and noise, the free-flowing character of the facade makes reference to the deformations that the volume would suffer as a result of the powerful sound waves registered in an area where acoustic pollution is high. Inside the building, a sculptural staircase connects the management and staff offices and the meeting rooms to the solarium situated on the roof.

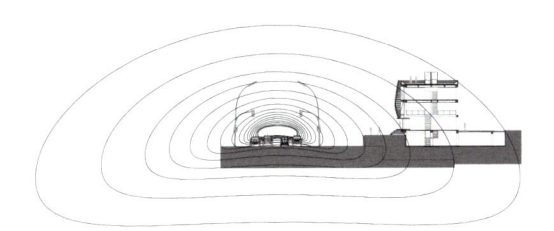

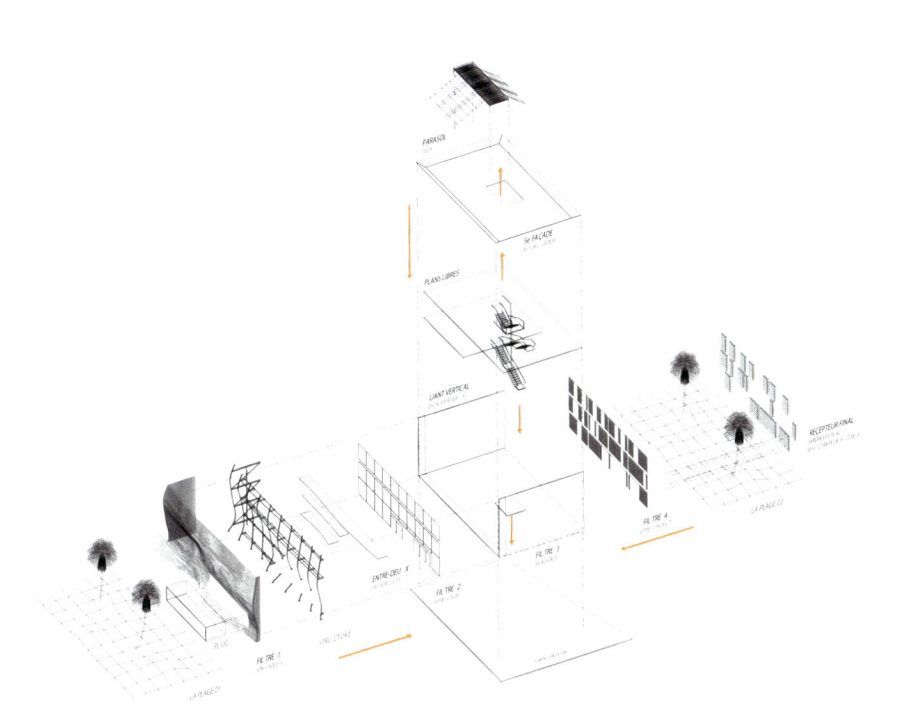

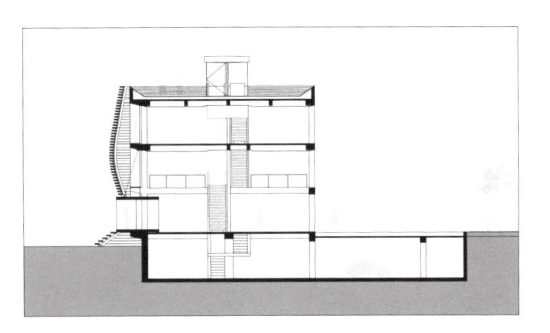

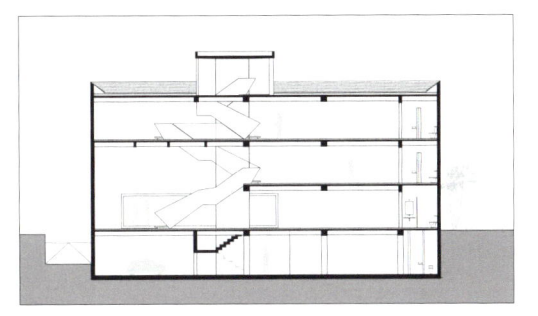

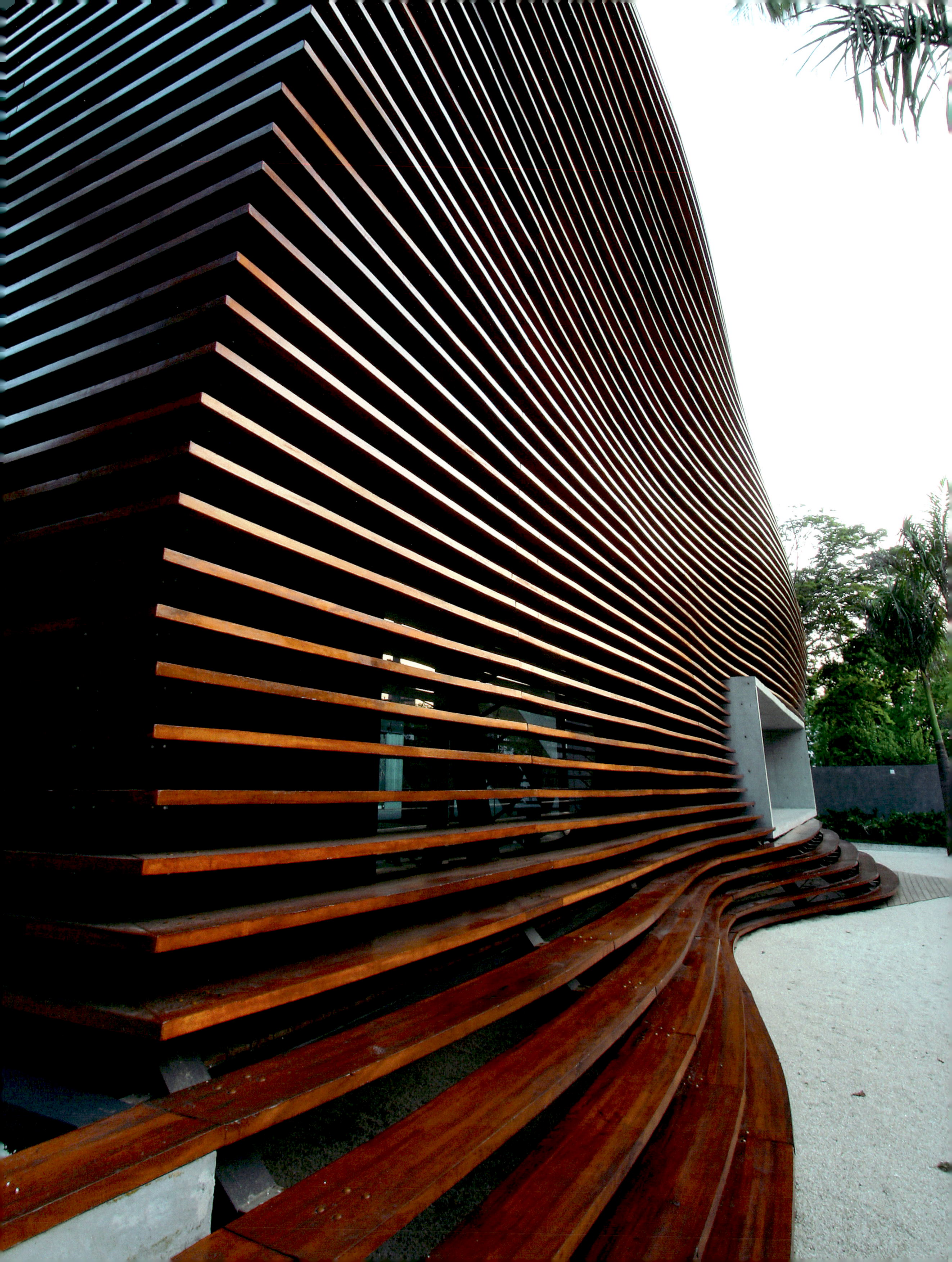

TABLE N°_50

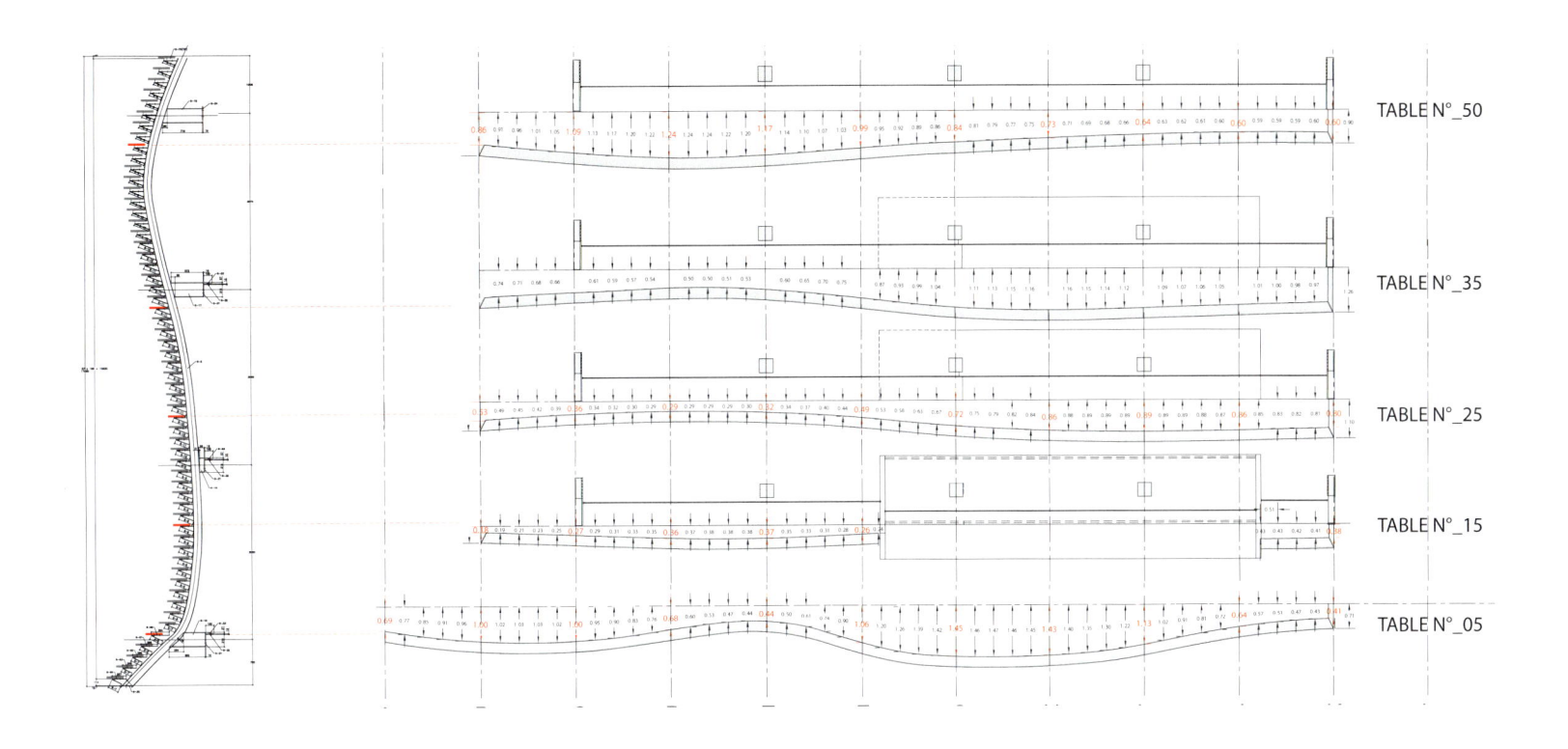

TABLE N°_35

TABLE N°_25

TABLE N°_15

TABLE N°_05

Atlas: America

Marcio Kogan
Paraty House
Paraty, Rio de Janeiro (Brazil)

Architect
Marcio Kogan
Collaborators
Suzana Glogowski, Beatriz Meyer, Eduardo Chalabi, Eduardo Glycerio, Gabriel Kogan, Lair Reis, Maria Cristina Motta, Mariana Simas, Oswaldo Pessano, Renata Furlanetto, Samanta Cafardo; Diana Radomysler, Carolina Castroviejo (interior design)
Consultants
Sf Engenharia (engineering); Gil Fialho (landscaping)
Contractor
Lock Engenharia
Photos
Nelson Kon

An overhanging slab of reinforced concrete about 8 meters long protects the main entry foyer, up from which a sculptural staircase ascends to connect the various spaces of the house to one another.

ON ONE OF THE ISLANDS of the colonial city of Paraty, halfway between São Paulo and Rio de Janeiro, sheltered in the slope of a small mountain and hidden in dense, lush forest vegetation between colossal beachside rocks, stands this unique one-family residence. Two prismatic concrete volumes take in the entire program, connected by a vertical communication core that, apart from containing the main stairs, acts as a loadbearing element on which the building's structural system rests. Through it, both constructions stretch on toward the beach with an overhang some eight meters long. In this way the house spans the irregularities of the terrain, creating ample habitable space without altering the surrounding nature.

The only path to the house starts at a dock built on the beach, a few meters from the building; residents arrive by boat. It leads directly into the main entrance hall, protected by a projecting concrete slab, after traversing a metallic bridge built over a swimming pool surrounded by a glass enclosure. This bridge brings one to the stairs leading into the lower volume, where part of the program is located: the living room, the kitchen, a service area and a lounge. With a 27 meter span, this large space benefits from huge windows facing magnificent views of the tropical landscape. On the roof of this volume is a wood-floored terrace from which to gaze out toward the bay.

The same staircase continues on to the upper floor, where the large glazed openings of the bedrooms, which are on the front part of the house, are equipped with retractable panels made of eucalyptus sticks that protect the interior spaces from the solar glare, the humidity, and the high temperatures typical of the region. Situated more inland, toward the mountainside, the other private rooms have small inner patios that are bordered by walls of reinforced concrete and lit from above. The hard texture of the concrete enclosures and the stone of the retaining walls strike a contrast with the warmth of the reed panels and the floors of fine wood. The house shelters a good collection of 20th-century furniture design, with several pieces by Latin American architects of world renown.

Two box-like bulks of reinforced concrete contain the entire program and are joined together by a vertical communation core that, aside from accommodating the main staircase, serves as a loadbearing structural system for the house. The communal areas are organized in the lower volume, the top of which is a terrace looking out to the bay, while the bedrooms and other private spaces are put in the upper prism.

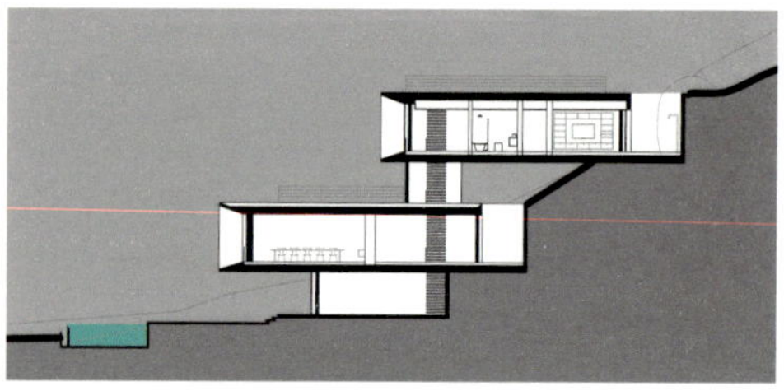

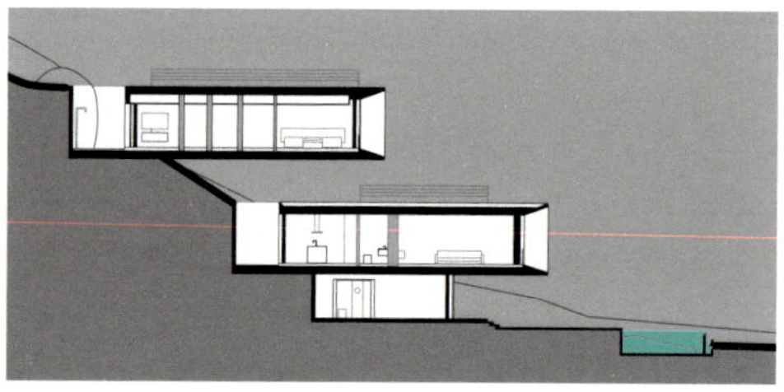

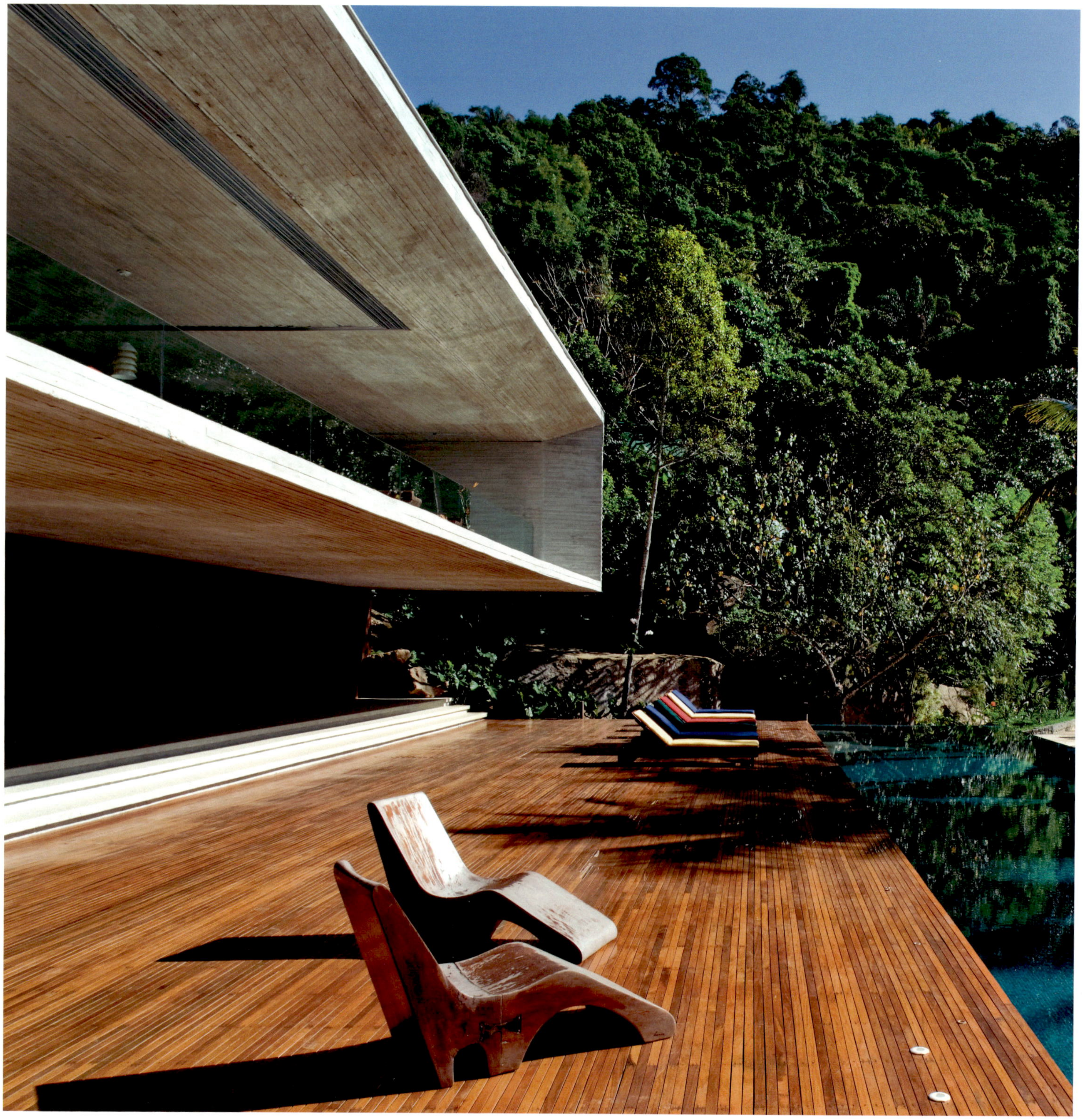

The hard texture of the building walls and retaining walls – raised with reinforced concrete and stone, respectively – strike a contrast with the warm effect of the floors of fine wood and the retractable panels made of eucalyptus sticks that have been placed on the large openings of the upper level to protect the interior spaces of the residence from solar glare, from humidity, and from the high temperatures that characterize the region.

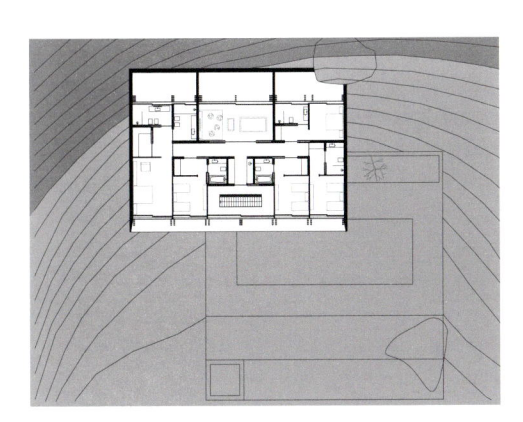

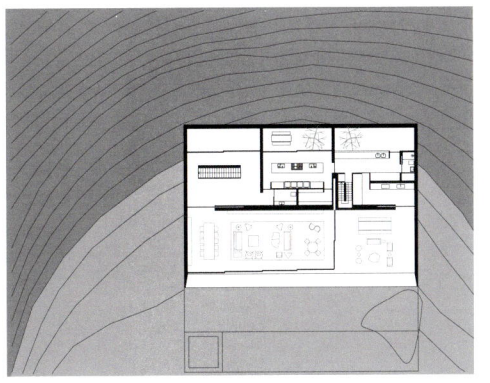

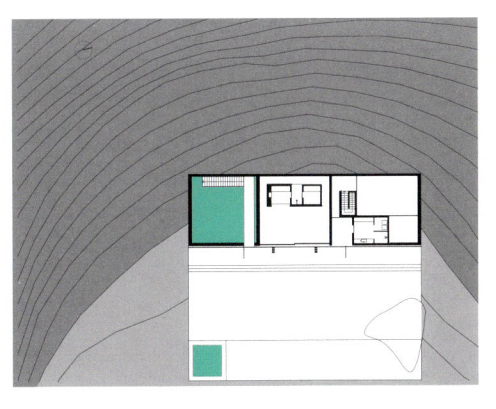

Procter & Rihl
Slice House
Porto Alegre, Rio Grande do Sul (Brazil)

Architects
Christopher Procter, Fernando Rihl
Collaborators
Dirk Anderson, James Backwell, Johannes Lobbert
Consultants
Michael Baigent MBOX, Antonio Pascuali, Vitor Pasin, Flavio Mainardi (structural engineering)
Contractor
JS Construçoes
Photos
Marcelo Nunes, Sue Barr

With a floor plan that takes the shape of a trapezoid, the house adapts to a very narrow lot by arranging the rooms in a linear sequence and by including an inner court that serves to bring in natural light.

THE CONTINUOUSLY changing nature of cities generates the appearance, through time, of odd residual sites. These present themselves as ideal laboratories for exploring new ways of living. Aware of this potential of urban residues, the client decided to buy one such lot in Porto Alegre that had gone on auction three times without obtaining a bidder on account of its difficult proportions: 38.5 x 3.7 meters.

The project is defined by slanting planes that force perspectives so that the house's different spaces appear larger than they are. The idea is not to annul the long narrow linearity of the place, but to work upon it. Entrance is through one of the far ends and into a continuous open space with a central court. A horizontal surface 7 meters long serves, in succession, as a dining table, a kitchen countertop and a garden table. The distance between walls progressively increases, giving rise to a trapezoidal floor shape that with the help of the double-height ceiling neutralizes the tunnel effect one would expect of a house squeezed into a strip of leftover urban space. Upstairs, the movement of the ceiling gives nuances to the varying degrees of privacy required. At the entrance to the bedroom, for example, it is only 2.1 meters high. On this upper-floor level is the swimming pool, whose bottom is suspended over the living space at ground level. The pool's transparent wall makes it a centerpiece, drawing the attention of those below while bathing the lower rooms with light filtered by the water.

For construction, different multimedia applications were combined with on-site work that used the traditional techniques of the region. The house presents itself as a hybrid of Brazilian elements – reinforced concrete poured into formworks made of wooden strips, open extroverted spaces, lush vegetation – and British ones – the facade's steel cladding, the pool's structural glass, the railings and gutters.

Situated in a luxurious neighborhood of the city, this one-family dwelling is fitted into a residual site measuring 3.7 x 38.5 meters, the buildability limit. City regulations called for a 4-meter setback at the edges, but because of the tight dimensions of the lot, this was respected only on the access side. The obligation to leave at least 25% of the total ground area free was complied with through a large court in the interior.

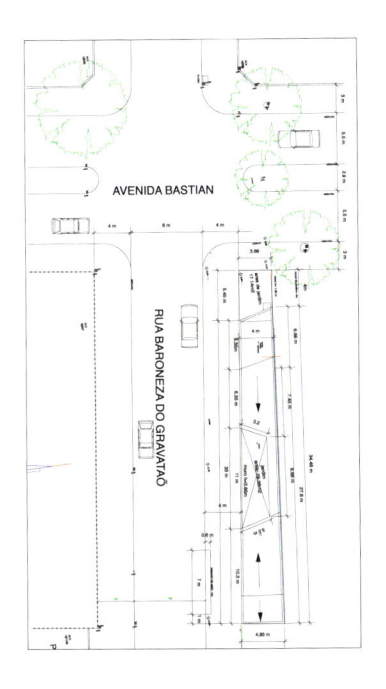

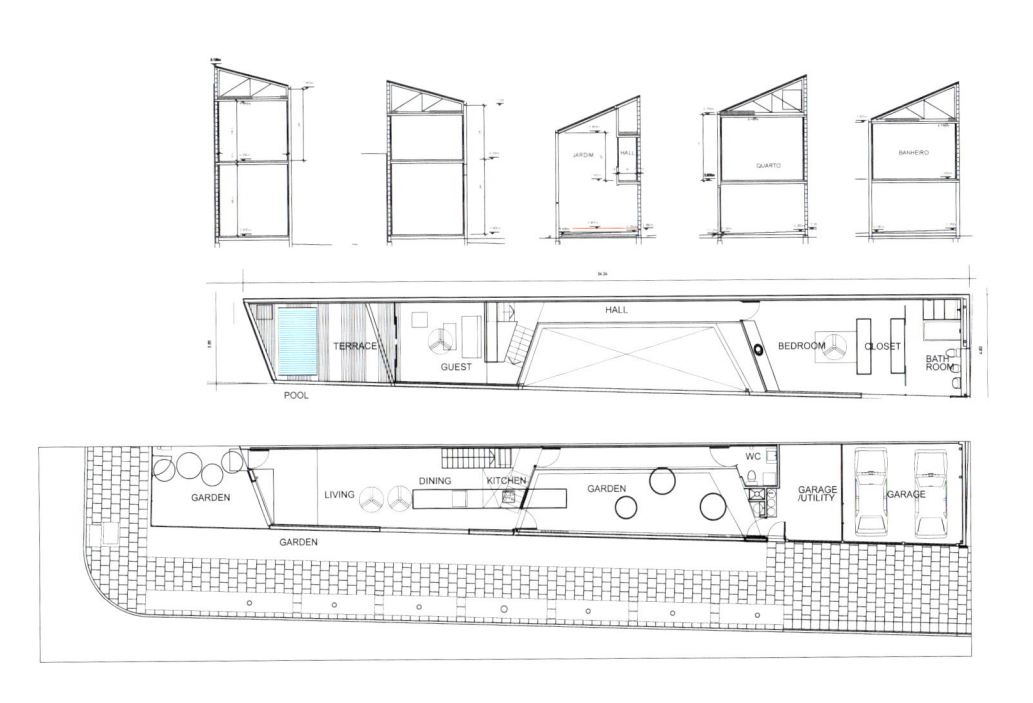

The client wanted a house that would be interesting, spatially, and executed with traditional building techniques. The walls are slanted, in a play of perspectives intended to make the dwelling's interiors seem larger than they are. The swimming pool, which hovers over the downstairs rooms and is held up by the loadbearing side walls, filters daylight through the rippling surface of the water and becomes a colored lantern at night.

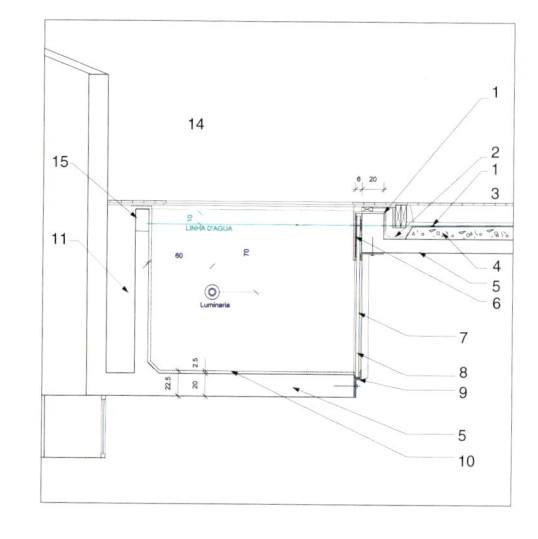

1 waterproofing
2 concrete gutter for terrace drainage
3 wooden floating pavement
4 cement mortar
5 concrete slab
6 asphaltic sheet between glass and concrete
7 laminated glass t = 3 x 10 mm
8 resin for swimming pool insulation
9 fixing of glass with steel plate
10 plaster t = 2.5 cm
11 installations void
12 concrete surface
13 45° chamfer
14 white plaster wall
15 overflow outlet

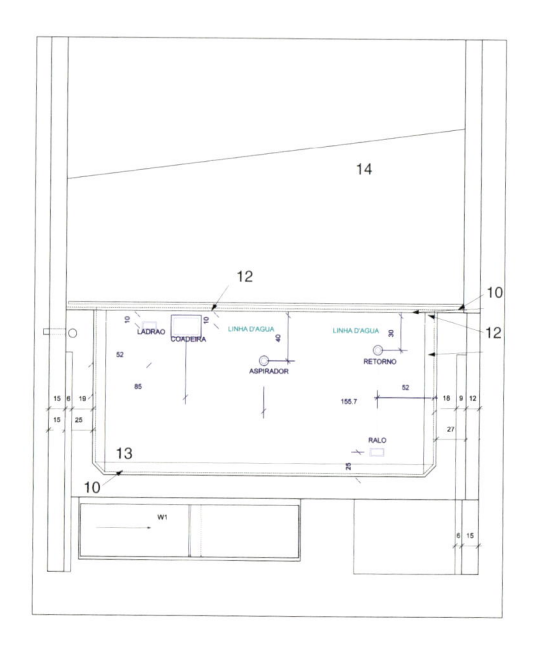

Atlas: America **237**

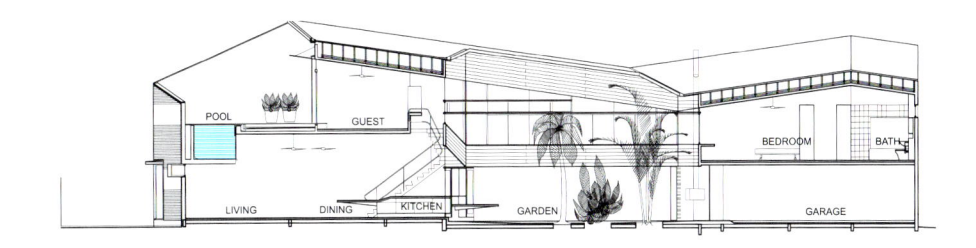

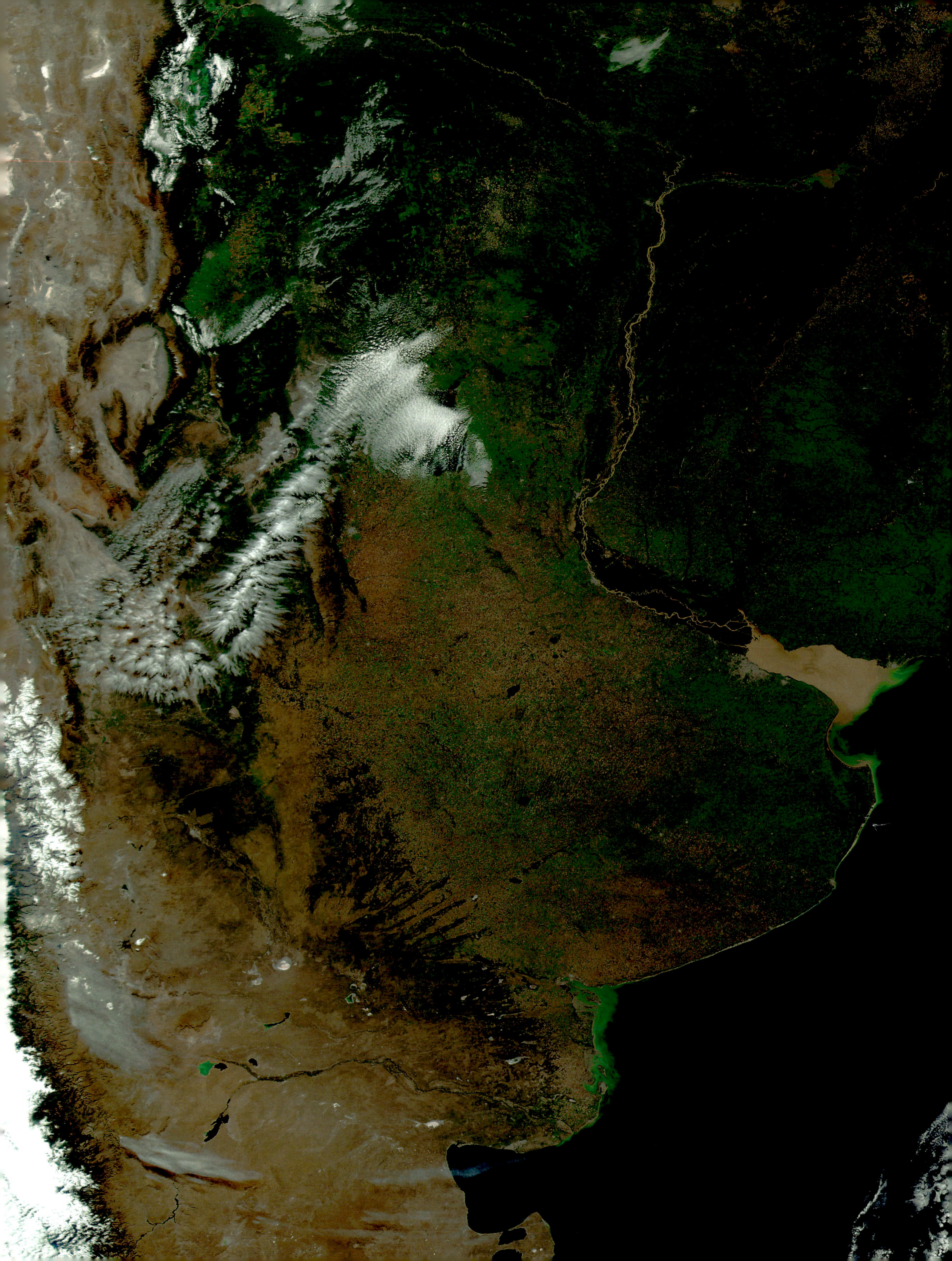

Argentina, Uruguay, Paraguay

Economic recovery from the serious crisis that devastated Argentina at the start of the century has given rise to intense activity in the architectural sector. The lack of refinement of large-scale urbanistic operations in the capital is balanced out by the quality of small interventions like the houses built by Diéguez-Fridman and other modest constructions located in provincial cities, such as the Juan and Eva Perón Mausoleum in San Vicente, by the group AFRA in collaboration with LGR and Fernández Prieto, or the two *quinchas* in Rosario by Rafael Iglesia. In Uruguay we find the sensitivity to landscape that the firm of Gualano & Gualano has demonstrated in the Shelter at the Salto del Penitente. And in Paraguay, finally, along with the Spanish Embassy by Linazasoro, the architectural scene includes the figure of Solano Benítez, with works like his Father's Tomb in Piribebuy, which synthesizes his experimental handling of materials to create an evocative place.

Jorge Francisco Liernur
Panorama after the Crisis
Argentina, Uruguay and Paraguay, Green Shoots

VSV & Asociados, Micaela Bastidas Park, Buenos Aires, Argentina (2003)

Recovery from the serious economic crisis that shook the region of the Pampas at the start of the century has given rise to intense architectural activity.

The high caliber of the modest projects that are being carried out in the provincial cities of the country strike a contrast with the poor quality of the large-scale urbanistic operations undertaken in the capital.

TEN YEARS AGO Argentina went through a crisis that was one of the worst in its history and among the most spectacular in the western hemisphere in decades. To picture its intensity, suffice it to recall that in the space of just a month, the republic saw as many as five presidents sworn in. Hard as it may be to identify its manifestations with exactitude, the effects of that convulsion, however indirectly, were bound to reach the realm of an activity like architecture, which is constituently linked to the powers that be. To attribute what has happened in recent years exclusively to that troubled start of the decade would be excessive, but there have to be profound connections between occurrences at that time and the state of things at present.

At first sight it seems evident that the architectural discipline is not living one of its richest moments; neither in terms of the creativity temperature of average production nor in terms of intensity and quality of public and private demands, and neither in the push of construction-related industry nor in the extent or depth of experimental or investigative projects. Nevertheless it would be erroneous to think that this observation of dark tones refers to a reality of stuntedness and absent constructions, works and projects alike, or to a generalized state of paralysis. On the contrary, and however paradoxical it may seem, among the most notable manifestations of architecture in Argentina in the past decade is an urban project, one which on account of its importance finds new parallels in the international scene.

The start of the 1990s saw the launching of plans to refurbish the old port zone of Buenos Aires. Covering an area of 90 hectares and against all odds, the operation has managed to survive the different political-economic misfortunes that have shaken the country and reach an advanced stage, with 2,250,000 square meters already built. The city now even has a new quarter boasting all kinds of uses, including a 350 hectare natural reserve. Pieces of architectural quality superior to the average are few, but the merits of the new urban development may lie, precisely, in its relative mediocrity. The Micaela Bastidas Park stands out here, with the architects Alfredo Garay, Néstor Magariños, Irene Joselevich, Graciela Novoa, Marcelo Vila, and Adrián Sebastián (VSV & Asociados) successfully constructing a landscape of curves, acute angles and grade differences that strike a contrast with the city's flat features and obsessively orthogonal scheme. This project is of interest, on one hand, because of the bold architecture that has generated it, with walls, ramps and a rich orchestration of spaces varying in dimensions and height, and on the other hand because of its capacity to present the public with rare situations achieved, paradoxically, through the use of local materials and native plants.

Amid a homogeneous texture of commercial constructions for dwellings and offices, some buildings sport features of value, such as the Madero Plaza Building of the studio of Aisenson, with its carefully worked classical structuring of tectonic textures and volumes that are organized around a central court, or the Forum Building of the office of McCormack. But within the imposing built mass of Puerto Madero, the only piece that is organized as a programmatic, cultural and architectural proposal with no commercial end is the Fortabat Collection Museum of Rafael Viñoly. This is a volume extruded from a circular section that defines a transparent enclosure acting as roof and facade along the dikes over which the building rises. Subjected to the rigors of the western sun, the enclosure is in turn protected by a system of mobile metal plates that act as parasols. The huge interior space is flanked by installations and a circulation system. As in other Viñoly works, the elegance of the solution is undeniable, but perhaps

240 Atlas: America

Rafael Viñoly, Fortabat Collection Museum, Buenos Aires, Argentina (2008)

Launched at the start of the 1990s, the plan to refurbish the old port zone of Buenos Aires known as Puerto Madero has suffered from political and economic misfortunes, but has given rise to a new neighborhood close to the center of the capital. Cultural and commercial buildings are going up beside a natural reserve that breaks the excessive homogeneity of the urban fabric, and with few exceptions, are of little architectural interest.

because of the complex execution process, the initial gesture of defining the section is not enough to sustain interest and maintain quality, in a balanced way, through all the aspects of the building. The example of Puerto Madero is related to the crisis because the scarcity of high-quality pieces within an operation of great institutional, economic and cultural complexity can only be explained as resulting from serious deficiencies in the professional corps.

The Influence of Globalization
The same tonality of this operation can be seen in the larger, overall scheme of Argentina's architectural production of the past years. Appearing within this general picture, nevertheless, albeit of marginal character, is a body of outstanding cases. To begin with, the proliferation of images made possible by the globalized information system has, here as well, stimulated the consumption of forms and solutions, in a dynamic resembling the workings of fashion. For some, the pleasure derived from lightness and the ephemeral shine, and the idea of being part of the most exclusive and celebrated fringes of the global world, are temptations that are difficult to resist. This does not make attainment thereof a simple task, much less when one considers that transferring this architecture to peripheral geographies involves an attempt to reproduce its forms and solutions in technological, climate and cultural circumstances that are totally different from those in which they originated.

The past decade, for example, saw a proliferation of overhanging volumes, and with it, a tendency to hide the loadbearing structure as an architectural issue, an ever more widespread use of glass of diverse characteristics, and a recourse to claddings made of artificial materials. There has also been a shift of attention from linguistic questions to processes of articulation. Composition has tended to give way to works with rhythms of patterns that seem irregular and are more or less of an open and changing nature.

The studio of Alberto Varas has a long track record behind it, with an output that has always been responsive to the swayings of the strongest international tendencies of the moment. This is how it evolved from the time it attached itself to the postulates of Team X up to the time of the postmodern protocols that triumphed in the 1980s and 1990s. In recent years, the studio has turned its attention to some of the features mentioned above: stacked volumes with overhanging pieces define the house in Pilar and patterned glass panes form the facade of the FOX building in Buenos Aires, while a solution combining both features characterizes the AFIP federal tax office in Pehuajó, Buenos Aires Province.

The architects Rosina Gramática, Juan Carlos Guerrero, Jorge Morini, José Pisani and Eduardo Urtubey (GGMPU) have likewise updated their expressive mediums in recent works, such as the restoral of the Ferreyra Palace Museum of Fine Arts or, in association with young Lucio Morini, the enlargement of the Emilio Caraffa Provincial Museum of Fine Arts, both in the province of Córdoba. In the former, besides carefully

Alberto Varas, AFIP Offices in Pehuajó, Buenos Aires Province, Argentina (2007)

Atlas: America 241

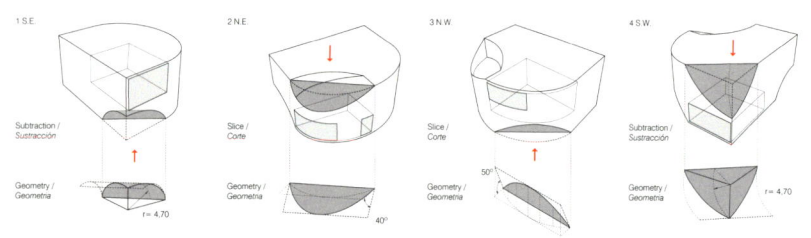

Johnston Marklee & Diego Arraigada, View House, Rosario, Argentina (2009)

Johnston Marklee & Diego Arraigada, View House, Rosario, Argentina (2009)

recuperating a marvelous early 20th-century residence, the intervention concentrates on support spaces, both in the upper plane and along the front of the building. Here we find the new vertical circulation systems and other services, in a composition that may be excessively spectacular with patterned glazings here and treatments adopting different color effects there. Within the actual museum, however, the observer perceives a more decisive use of contemporary circulation elements, such as overhanging parts. Worth mentioning, in any case, is the generous solution of the new entry, as is the response to the difficult task of connecting preexisting constructions of different characteristics.

The necessity and capacity to keep up with fashion is not a new phenomenon. It is frequent in a relatively sophisticated and cosmopolitan culture, though too far removed from the international centers that engender new ideas at best but often only bring on new silhouettes. To produce works and projects that can be placed in these series, one needs to have a strong vocation and a great amount of agility and capacity. With all the credentials to participate in them in order, Andrés Remy's Black House is a good example of this kind of ductility.

The studio of Diéguez Fridman is characterized by its eclectic inclination to diametrically opposed matrixes, but also by its remarkable suitability for resolving them in a consistent way, to the point of having begun a career of incipient international recognition. His proposals move from the relative professionalism of solutions for one-family houses or apartments – such as the Clay 2928 Building – to the digitalized contorsions of the project for the National Library of the Czech Republic or the attractive neo-form for the Gyeonggi-do Jeongok Prehistory Museum in Korea, passing through his very convincing solutions for the programs of the psychology and economics faculties of the University of Buenos Aires, which are drawn up with formal resources borrowed from international magazines.

One could safely say, also to a large extent, that the architecture of Mendoza's Parque Central, which was originally conceived by Óscar Fuentes, Daniel Becker and Claudio Ferrari and built by the latter two, is indebted to a way of going about things that is circulating in these same publications. But it is no less true that the landscaping proposal, the treatment of the terrain and the spatial qualities obtained are of a scale, quality and professionality that deserve to be highlighted.

Comprising two parallel planes of transparent glass, the Memorial to the Disappeared Detained Citizens of Uruguay, a work of Daniel Otero and Martha Kohen, resorts to a solution already used elsewhere – in the Holocaust Memorial of Boston or the Vietnam Veterans Memorial in Washington, D.C. It consists of engraving the names of the victims on a surface. But Otero & Kohen's work presents an interesting contrast with the rock of the place and, in general, a wonderful implantation charged with sensitive allusions to the particular theme being evoked.

Although rightly linked to the "keep up-to-date" made necessary by global culture, interest in the systematic resource of digital media, particularly in diagrammatic approaches, requires special attention.

Sophisticated one-family residences have gone up with exposed reinforced concrete. Sometimes these are derived from diagrammatic analyses elaborated by digital means through complex computer programs; in other cases they are the outcome of an expressive, almost artisanal treatment of this material, which is used for the roofs, for the pavements, and even to form simple furniture pieces integrated into the interior spaces.

BAK Arquitectos, XS House, Buenos Aires Province, Argentina (2007)

With the approaches, a generation of young people with graduate degrees from certain schools in the United States has begun to stand out in the international scene. Among these are Hernán Díaz Alonso, Marcelo Spina, Ciro Najle and Sebastián Khourian, and some have started to build works in Argentina. In these cases it is difficult and perhaps imprudent to rush into conclusions, although it is important to be aware of the difference between adopting formal clichés and getting involved in the development of methodological options. One could legitimately wonder about the connection between beginnings and results in the case of Marcelo Spina's House in Rosario, but in the case of Johnston MarkLee and Diego Arraigada's View House, also located in Rosario, one has to admit that the beginnings seem able to give rise to architecture of unusual characteristics.

In Search of Introspection

In general, in the space traversed by those with a personal exploratory vocation in greater tension with external stimuli, there has often been a preference for an intuitive or sensitive approach concentrated on an expressionistic, almost artisanal treatment of materials. The material most used in these quests for introspection has been exposed reinforced concrete, which has a long-running tradition in the region.

The office of BAK Arquitectos is characterized by its having initiated a search of exceptional consistency in the past years, an exploration that has taken shape in a series of summer houses situated in different forest-filled beaches in the province of Buenos Aires. Because of their locations, the dwellings are stripped to an extreme, reduced in provisions to a minimum, having only the elements necessary for use in short periods of time. Concrete is worked in the form of continuous abstract sheets of similar thickness, molded and cut like pieces of cardboard, and is used for the roofs, walls and floors and even for seats, shelves, tables and cupboards. Regulations in the region are not overly strict when it comes to cold bridges, so the material is visible on the inside and the outside, nuanced by the eloquent presentation of textures and the use of wood for both horizontal and vertical planes. In response to the sandy, unstable character of these beaches and forests, the houses appear to be held up lightly,

BAK Arquitectos, concrete house, Mar Azul, Buenos Aires Province, Argentina (2007)

The tectonic nature of materials manifests itself in the production of Solano Benítez, in Paraguay, whose works reflect an experimental research revolving around brick, as well as in the architecture that begins to sprout in the Argentinian city of Córdoba, where, using the traditional building system of wooden formworks, the qualities of reinforced concrete as a sculptural material are exploited to an extreme.

Solano Benítez, Esmeraldina House, Asunción, Paraguay (2001)

levitating on beams or supports anchoring them to the ground.

The studio has as yet only carried out a single one-family residence with brick, recalling Mies van der Rohe's Landhaus aus Backstein, which is present, moreover, in geometric compositions that are reduced to a minimum of elements, generally arranged orthogonally to one another. But contrary to the tectonic intention of the original version, here the material has been worked as if to emulate homogeneously cut sheets that are capable of sustaining themselves in the air without the help of supports, but with the texture of exposed brick.

The same attitude towards material characterizes the work of Claudio Vekstein, although his starting points are very different. The Vicente López Institute for Rehabilitation of the Disabled, designed by Marta Tello, does not make reference to any modern elementarism. On the contrary, its references are much closer to Scharoun than to Mies, and in connection to the way the material is used in Argentina, it echoes Clorindo Testa and the studio Septra's Bank of London building in Buenos Aires. The contorsions and cuts of the volume are not limited to discreet perforations of the plane, but seek to generate unexpected effects of light and sculptural drama. Moreover, Vekstein drew on the expressive potential of the numerous ramps that were needed to serve the purposes of the municipal building, which was built on a relatively narrow urban plot. The public character of the center must be taken into account when explaining the stripping of the construction: because of the reduced budget and the limited chances of proper maintenance, the sophisticated design is not applied to the finishes and the constructive details with the same degree of refinement. In a subsequent project for the security of a hospital service of the same municipality, we can discern a maturation in the architect's use of resources. Here, without ceasing to exploit his capacity to create complex spaces, he comes up with a more balanced solution of rich textures and a greater degree of dimensional and constructional pondering.

The offices of Bertolino & Barrado and Ana Etkin, both based in the land-locked province of Córdoba, use reinforced concrete more as a sculpture material with which to obtain dramatic forms, more interested as these practices are in obtaining volumetric compositions with strong contrasts. Bertolini & Barrado recently built some simple structures to accommodate the Farm Pavilion of a tourist complex in the mountainous zone of Capilla del Monte, where they exploited the allusions to wood that are implicit in the reinforced concrete which is obtained with traditional formwork systems. The building is constructed by means of frameworks of beams that blend nicely into the landscape like vine arbors, achieving a climate that is notably sensitive to the simplicity of the traditional crafts on display inside, and to a context that seems to have managed to preserve itself in the untouchable condition of an old farmhouse.

While Mónica Bertolino and Carlos Barrado try to keep up the program of their work with a serene melody in harmony with climates of 'provincial quietude', Ana Etkin puts a high degree of drama into her projects. The Don Bosco Winery and School of Viticulture in Mendoza is one of few facilities of the kind that can be said to have architectural value, among the many that the growing industry has seen spring up in the last years. Etkin shares Vekstein's interest in a Baroque approach to architecture, although unlike her colleague in Buenos Aires, she takes pleasure in experimenting with different compositional elements, from pilotis to brick walls, passing through metal claddings and reinforced concrete surfaces torn by fissures of light.

Building dramatic spaces also seems to be the focus of Marcelo Villafañe in Rosario,

X-Arquitectos, JS House, Mendiolaza, Córdoba, Argentina (2008)

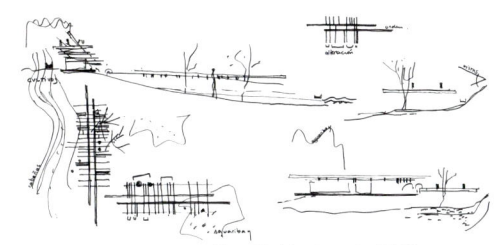

Bertolino & Barrado, Farm Pavilion, Córdoba, Argentina (2006)

as in the Raigal or the Brown House, not so much through the use of materials – reduced here to a limited and homogeneous palette – as through the tense organization of the floor plan and the interior distribution in both residences. If, excepting Clorindo Testa, the search for a marked personal expressivity has not been frequent in the architecture of modernity in Argentina, it seems to be among the features defining the works that have begun to appear in an environment that is very different and that has up to now had little repercussion in the architectural culture of the region: the Republic of Paraguay.

In this context, the work of Javier Corvalán with his Laboratorio de Arquitectura and that of Solano Benítez emerge among the most prominent manifestations. In the CPES Cultural Center in Asunción, Corvalán shows an interest in what could be identified as an architecture of 'real' materials, where what we see is what we get, not a simulacrum nor a reproduction nor a cladding. The brick, the concrete, the metal supports and the wood are in their constitution exactly what their appearance tells. And it is such honesty that determines the texture of the surfaces. Corvalán's is an architecture of bare stark truth. As a matter of fact he has continued to experiment in that direction in the enlargement of the cultural center, as well as in residences like the Getopán House, where the results come close to the limits of what is acceptable within the discipline.

Solano Benítez's path has been more homogeneous and consistent in character. His is literally a search for balances that could well tumble on the edges of stability and become dynamic if it centered on mere mechanisms instead of actual works of architecture. What subjugates Solano is the weight of the material, which can present itself through the texture of the reinforced concrete, as in the tomb in Piribebuy – made with four 7.5 meter long beams set apart from one another and supported at the far ends –, or through a thin brick surface like that used in the Esmeraldina House or the canopy in La Estancia. This is not about an expressive tension produced by formal or textural incidents; the aesthetic temperature reached by his works depends on the (a)tectonic power of his architectural ideas. In one of his recent projects, an office building, the floor slabs appear to float in the air, held up exclusively by a core of services and a transparent mesh around the perimeter.

The Use of Minimal Resources

Nevertheless, the exploration carried to intensely dramatic extremes does not define the main course of the currents that flow in the field of architectural culture in Argentina or the Río de la Plata region at large. Owing perhaps to the extraordinary disorientation that characterizes contemporary architecture, but also to the narrowness of the local spaces of creativity, the truth is that it being difficult to adopt excessive gestures or attitudes, there is a tendency to discard the roads of introspection or the search for individual expression. Along this line we can point out some examples whose effectivity comes from a large concentration of minimal elements or resources. This kind of search can be manifested in relation to building regulations, as with the Quesada Building of Óscar Fuentes. Despite it being a commercial program with low creative intensity demands, the architect comes up with rich public interior spaces and an exterior volumetry that is no less rich, thanks to a painstaking study of the limits and potentials of the technical code.

Something similar happens in the obsessive precision with which Ricardo Sargiotti (X-Arquitectos) has treated the small enlargement of a house, a light wooden-clad structure executed with the precision of a furniture piece. And in the same register we can place the house that the studio E48 built in La Plata. Corrugated

Bertolino & Barrado, Farm Pavilion, Córdoba, Argentina (2006)

A strong minimalist vocation in Argentina has generated a succession of projects that resort to a limited and homogeneous palette of materials, as in the case of the architecture that is being carried out in Rosario by Rafael Iglesia and Diego Villafañe, where the material takes on a wrinkled texture, in contrast with the sleek surfaces that characterize the works of Adamo & Faiden, a studio on the rise that concentrates its production in the capital.

Rafael Iglesia, Altamira Building, Rosario, Argentina (2008)

sheets are a tradition in the region, frequently used for sheds and for industrial, farming and fishing facilities, but also typical in homes that were built in port areas at the close of the 19th century and the beginning of the 20th. Concern for expanding the potential of the most accessible materials, particularly their tectonic capacities, is the main engine of the studies being conducted by the architect Rafael Iglesia in Rosario, whose built works without a doubt count among the most interesting and provocative in the period we are analyzing. Iglesia has been researching on the different themes and scales it has been his lot to operate in, from simple shades or *quinchas* to buildings of horizontal property.

In all of these cases, the interventions endeavor to question the performance of structural forces. He has experimented with elements as unusual as transparent plastics wrapped around used tires, tree trunks in their original state, asphaltic metallized textiles for facade claddings, and undulating stainless steel sheets for finishes. The programs are material to subvert in his hands: the communal areas of a residential building can at the same time be treated like private spaces, the housing unit can be destructured, and the public bathrooms can be made visible day and night through glazed enclosures.

Beyond the cases mentioned, thanks to a thick framework woven in the course of history, the tougher core of these lands has accommodated a culture where discreetness, restraint and rules have a lot of weight. And although this framework has been torn by the harsh realities of politics and economics, these features are what we still find in a considerable segment of contemporary production on both banks of the great river. True, sometimes discreetness and deliberate sobriety tend to be confused with lack of professionalism. But it is precisely by taking the risk of working in a very limited,

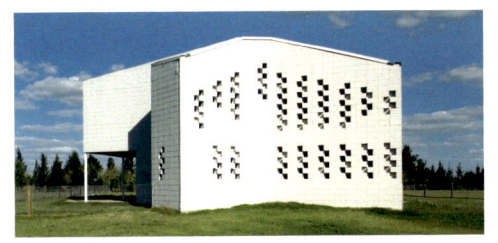

Marcelo Villafañe, Block House, Rosario, Argentina (2005)

practically vanishing space that the challenge inherent in this option is manifested.

We have already mentioned the elegance that Rafael Viñoly always pursues in his projects, especially through synthetic gestures that serve to mollify internal tensions. The airport he built in Carrasco is among the more far-reaching of interventions carried out in Uruguay in the past decade. Here, a shell or skin of sorts encloses the complex plurality of functions that a program of this kind involves. The work of Argentinian practices like AFRA, Adamo-Faiden, Mariano Clusellas or Ignacio Dahl Rocha in Argentina and Uruguay, as well as that of Uruguayan firms like MBAD and Gualano & Gualano, can be identified with these kinds of traditions.

AFRA's most important work is the Juan and Eva Perón Mausoleum in San Vicente, executed with a minimum of elements, an elementarist form, and extreme restraint. The monumental effect is achieved through a balanced handling of dimensions, proportions and distances, as well as of the interplays of dialogues and silences with which the constructions organize the park around. The reduction of expressive recourses is characteristic of the studio's work, evident in the dialogue between concrete and wood that occurs in the Summer House in Country or in recent works like the Panamericana offices or the bar Deriva in San Isidro.

Mariano Clusellas – in association with other colleagues like Cristian O'Connor, Sebastián Colle and Rodolfo Croce – has built numerous one-family houses. All of them express a conservative mindset, or at least a disdain for risks, creative adventures and stridencies. This does not mean they are of little interest, but that instead of design attention being directed at the work as a whole, the focus is on its partial aspects, its corners, thicknesses, openings and minimal compositional incidents, as we can discern in some of the architect's most balanced projects, such as the Njk, Mcmcm and Hmc Houses. In a similar register is a small house in Punta del Este by Richter & Dahl Rocha, a Swiss-based firm that recently opened an office in Buenos Aires.

The works of Adamo & Faiden are astonishing for their extreme minimalist intentions, if indeed the term can denote something more than the evocation of an architectural impossible. It is true that the small building at Arribeños 3182 could be

Adamo & Faiden, Arribeños Building, Buenos Aires, Argentina (2007)

considered a tedious application of solutions that have already been tested, and the Courtyard House a part of the series we have just mentioned. Nevertheless it must be acknowledged that in the cases of the Multi-use Space and Club House in the province of Buenos Aires, the effort of reduction reaches an intensity level that is rare in these latitudes. The former is set on the terrain like a kind of mineral formation with polished surfaces and rough edges, revealing an interior space that declaims an austerity to the point of absence; the latter floats on the mirror of water like a small shed that is at once abstract and representational.

Traversing a road with characteristics resembling the aforementioned, a group of young offices has in the past years begun to stand out in Uruguay. MBAD has built two beach houses in Punta del Este that give us a peek into a rich future output. In both houses there is a clear preference for precise definition and simple, clear-cut, forceful stereometries. And just as evident is the interest in construction, well-resolved details, and experimentation with materials: concrete, stone, wood.

It is promising to close this presentation with mention of the office of the Gualano brothers, who demonstrate a special sensitivity to location, as in the shelter at Salto del Penitente. The piece makes a splendid platform from which to contemplate the landscape it is set amid, while organically expanding, in the manner of a terrace, the floor of the entrance level. But such sensitivity is also present in his houses, treated as they are as a succession of open and closed spaces, whether with expansive plays where these appear as loose pieces, as in the dwelling in La Asunción, or tensely compacted to form part of the urban fabric, the case in El Buceo.

And special mention must go to the Multi-use Pavilion in Bolivar, an inland town of Uruguay. The stretched out, flattened volume – compressed between two concrete strips, with an exposed brick treatment following local tradition, and small skylights on top – is an excellent work. From the heart of a modest but proudly dignified reality, this pavilion illustrates for us the infinite potential of an architecture that has the capacity to be magnificent through a reasonable and discreet use of available materials, logical and comprehensive organization, and intelligent handling of measurements and proportions.

Rafael Iglesia
Quincha I and II
Rosario, Santa Fe (Argentina)

Architect
Rafael Iglesia
Collaborators
Silvio Vacca, Gustavo Farías
Consultants
Quincha II: Ingenierías
Bollero-Campodónico (structures)
Contractor
Quincha II: Artuza Construcciones
Photos
Gustavo Frittegotto

THE DEFINITION of the word *quincha* makes reference to a traditional construction system that utilizes cane, reed or other similar materials to build walls, which are subsequently covered with mud. In Argentina, moreover, the *quincha* refers specifically to the part of the house where the family gathers to prepare and enjoy the typical roast. Belonging to two single-family houses located in different residential areas of the city of Rosario, the two structures designed for this purpose have been executed with wood of a reddish brown color. The material comes from the *quebracho,* a native hardwood tree. Strongly resistant to humidity, it is habitually used to fabricate the longitudinal sleepers of railway tracks all over the country.

In Quincha I, a free-standing poolside piece in a private residence, this same wood has been used to build a structure of thick rectangular-section supports. Over the structure, sustained by a wooden trunk set at one of the corners, rests a thin slab of reinforced concrete that serves to apply compression on it. Literally jutting out of or hanging from one of the vertical planes is the furniture – a heavy table, weighing some 400 kilograms, that seems to levitate –, made with the same sleepers that have been embedded in the walls and secured with small wooden wedges. Finally, the conventional grill has been replaced here by a traditional earthenware oven.

The building of Quincha II, a small construction attached to a preexisting house, has followed the same concepts. The wooden sleepers are fastened to a concrete partition wall, wedged so as to be fixed and leveled. And sticking out from this wall are the grill, table and benches, all rendered in *quebracho* wood and protected with pieces of cowhide. The floor surfaces have been carried out with narrow rods of cane, of the kind commonly utilized in the making of fences, and are laid out on a thin layer of sand.

Annexed to single-family residences located in two different neighborhoods of the city of Rosario, both *quinchas* have been constructed around a framework of hard resistant wood taken from a native tree species.

Quincha I, a poolside construction standing free of the house, was put up with a slender slab of reinforced concrete resting directly on a structure fabricated with sleepers of colored *quebracho* wood, and on the other hand on a wooden trunk rising at one of the corners. Completing the furniture are a traditional firewood oven and a heavy, 400 kilogram table that is actually built into one of the vertical planes.

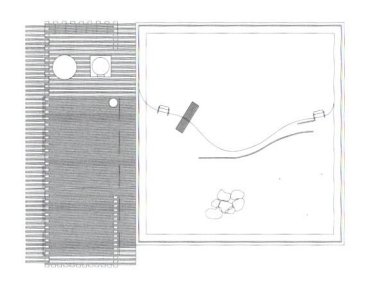

Quincha II is conceived as a small pavilion that is physically attached to the private, one-family residence. On a flooring of cane rods that are arranged over a layer of sand, a concrete wall has been erected, serving to support a wooden roof, the grill, and the table and benches all at once. The latter have been carried out with a sleeper built into the wall, from which two further wooden pieces jut out, lined with cowhide.

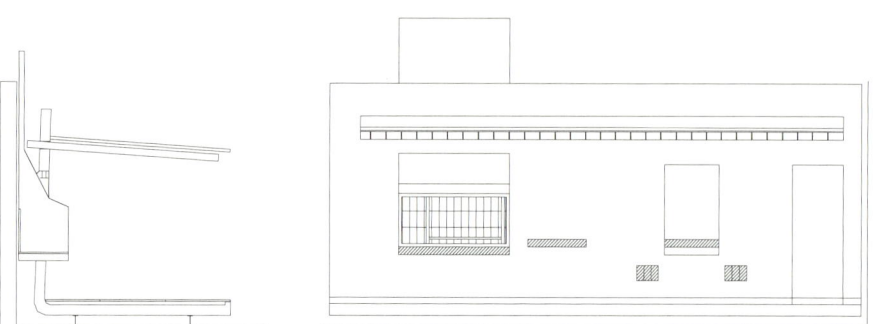

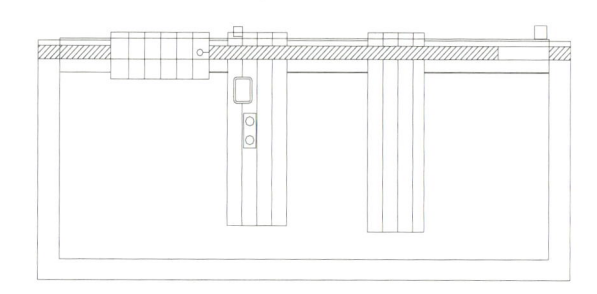

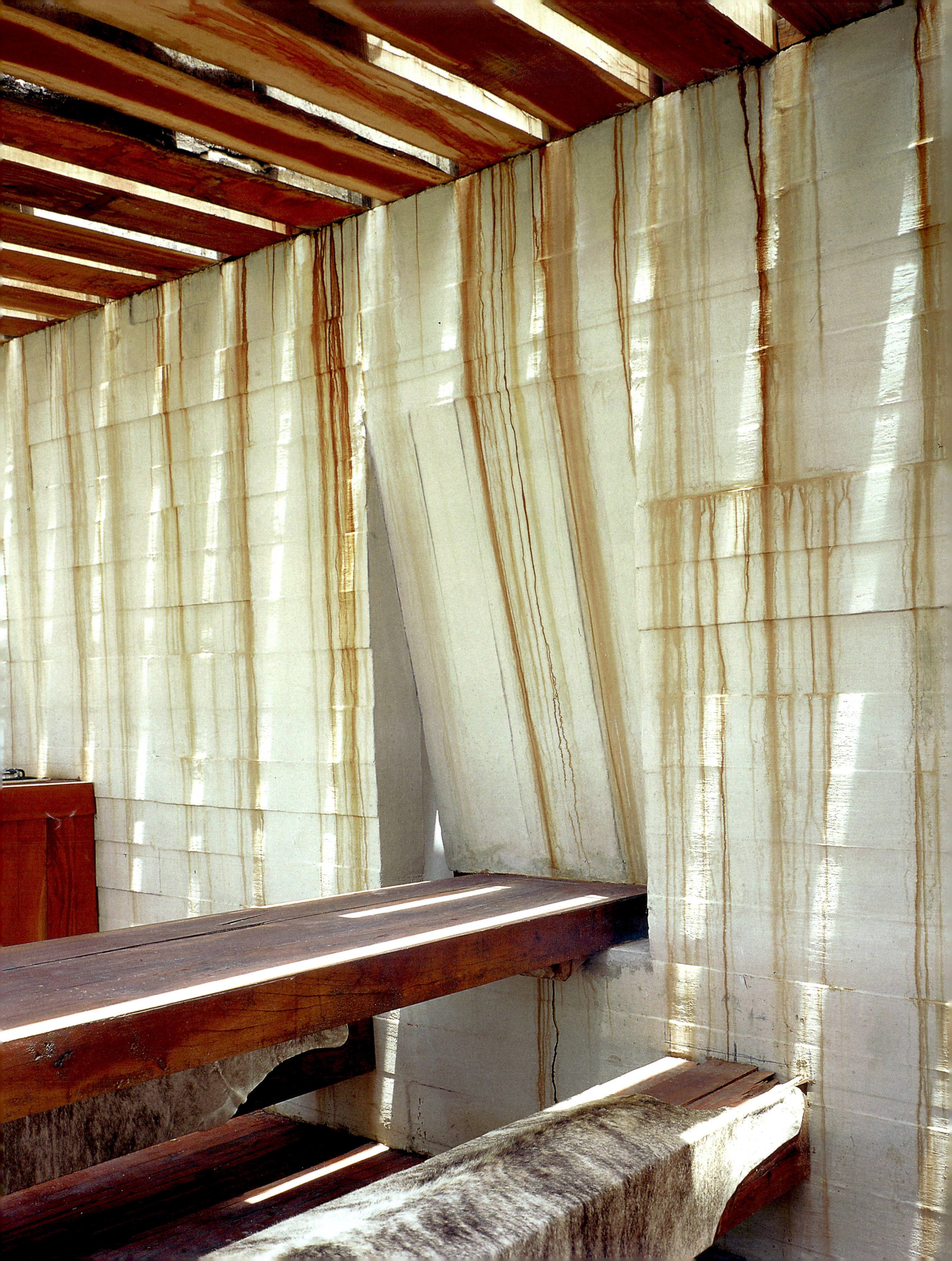

AFRA-LGR-Fernández Prieto
Juan and Eva Perón Mausoleum
San Vicente, Buenos Aires (Argentina)

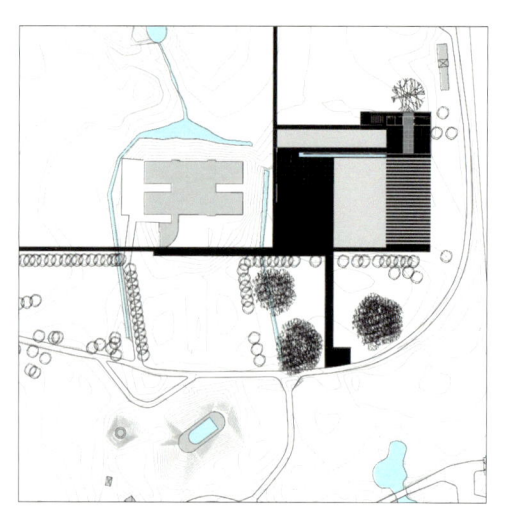

Architects
J. Fernández Castro, J. González Ruiz,
G. Lanosa, S. Armendares, P. Ferreiro;
A. Fernández Prieto (project)
Collaborators
L. Timisky, C. Spiteri, L. Bianchi,
M. Tozzini, O. Suárez, E. García,
D.Isola, S. Rodríguez, R. Dufrechou,
J. Fernández
Consultants
D. Isola (structural engineer),
GF Ingenieros (electrical engineer),
L. Luciano (wall)
Contractor
Centro construcciones
Photos
Leonardo Finotti

Located in the Argentinian city of San Vicente, the Juan and Eva Perón Mausoleum is part of a General Plan involving the restoral and revitalization of the so-called Quinta 17 de Octubre – the presidential couple's country home situated some kilometers from the center of the city of Buenos Aires – as an enclave of landscaping and architecture. The plan proposes to refurbish the facilities and old buildings besides incorporate new uses: the History Museum and the Homage Park. The first step towards building the mausoleum dates back to 2003, when the Pro Monumentos Commission announced the ideas competition that this proposal won. Taking the existing buildings into consideration, the actual pantheon is positioned at the end of a sequence of interlinked spaces reached by crossing a grove of ash and eucalyptus trees preceding the large public space of a central square. From there one proceeds to a succession of scenes: the memorial, with its podium of commemorative plaques; a path symbolizing the line of life; the Plaza del Encuentro, of concrete pigmented with the colors of local earth; and finally the pantheon, where a translucent marble tympanum facing the park stands out.

Past a grove of ash and eucalyptus trees rises the volume of the pantheon, a prism raised with a tympanum of translucent concrete facing the park and a surface of transparent glass that looks toward the wood.

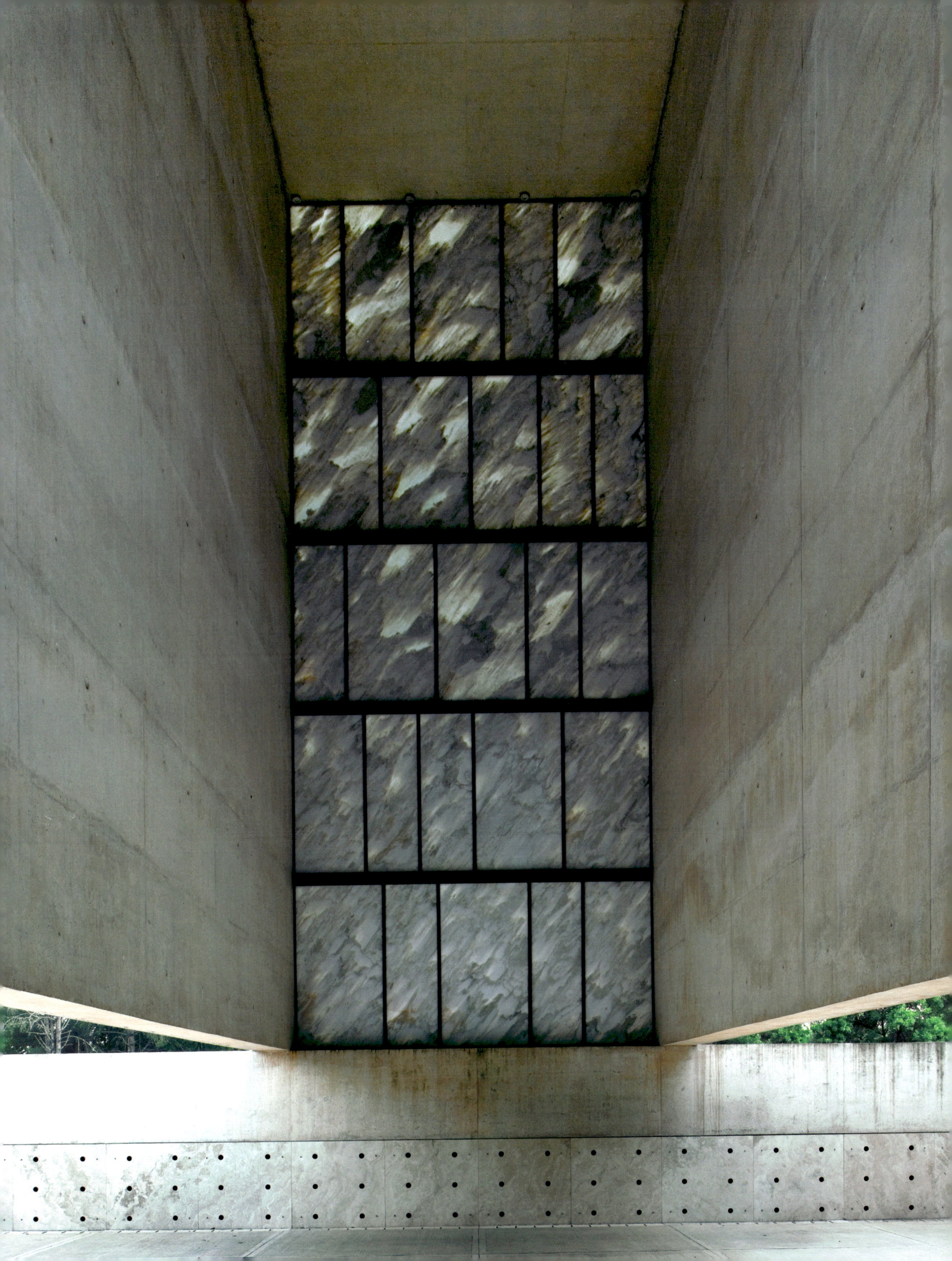

Diéguez-Fridman Arquitectos
Apartment Building
Buenos Aires (Argentina)

Architects
Tristán Diéguez, Axel Fridman, Germán Dyzenchauz (associate architect)
Collaborators
Brenda Levi, Odile L'Hardy
Consultants
Sebastián Berdichevsky (structural engineering); Pablo Pizarro (lighting); Cora Burgin (landscaping); Estudio Gigli (metal frames)
Contractor
Brunetta S.A.
Photos
Leonardo Finotti

The glass slats that protect the large terraces and the glazed partitions that divide the interior spaces together create a series of veils, which in turn generate an interplay of lights and reflections that varies as the day goes by.

LOCATED IN a residential neighborhood of Buenos Aires, the building contains eight duplex apartments which are accessed through an open-plan ground level that in turn opens on to the exterior completely and accommodates vehicular and pedestrian circulation, serving as a parking garage at nighttime and a children's playground by day. A sequence of stairs and bridges, partly covered to protect the pavement of *quebracho,* a wood which is highly resistant to humidity, then leads up to the first-floor foyers of the apartments.

From the foyer of each unit one proceeds to a double-height living room, around which the dining room and the kitchen are placed. The remaining spaces, three bedrooms and two bathrooms, are found on the second floor and receive natural light through the building's central access court.

All the first-floor living-dining areas open on to double-height terraces that are set along the main facade, sheltered intermediate spaces that act as filters between the domestic interiors and the urban environment existing beyond, with the help of a system of horizontal glass shades. A structure of steel tubes supports the aluminum profiles that in turn sustain the slats of serigraphed tempered glass. These shield the interior spaces of the apartments from excessive sunning while nuancing the views of the city outside.

The interior layout relies on translucent partitions of frosted glass facilitating the passage of natural light from room to room. The partitions also create a veil effect and a play of lights and reflections that changes as the day goes by, making it possible to protect the privacy of the rooms without giving up natural illumination.

All this is part of an attempt to surpass the limits that urban regulations impose on this part of the city, and evade the obligation to maximize profitability that is nowadays required of residential buildings.

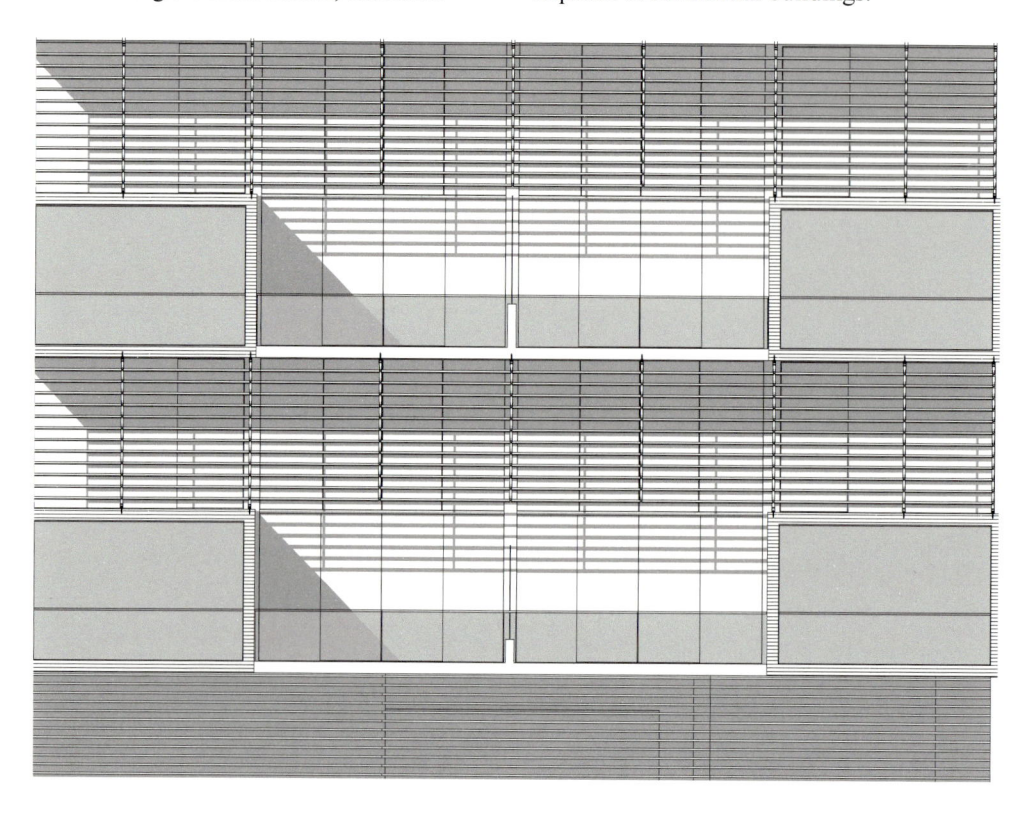

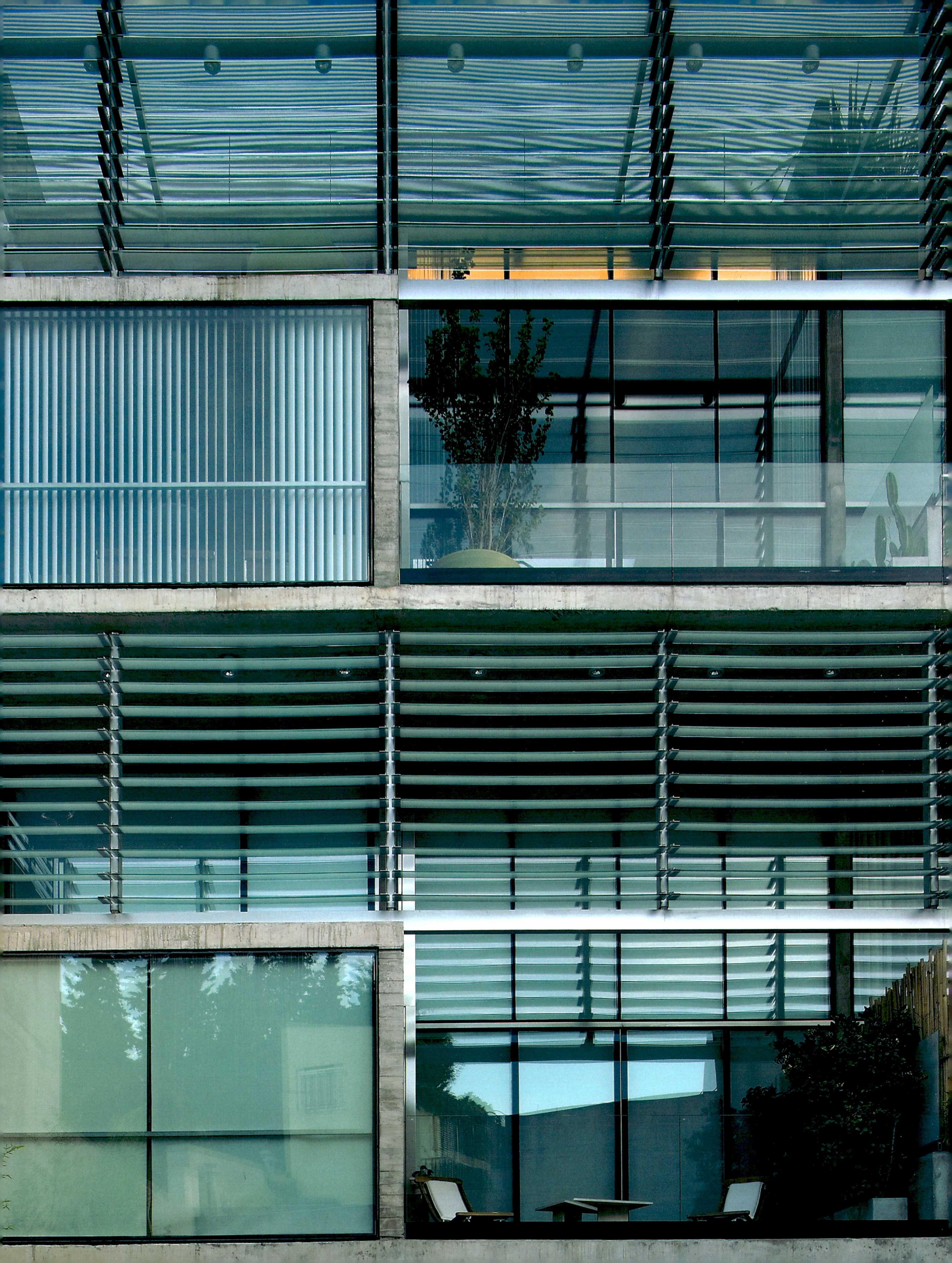

On a narrow lot located in a residential part of Buenos Aires rises a prismatic volume accommodating a total of eight duplex apartments around an open-plan ground-level communal area. Partly covered to protect the zones that are paved with *quebracho* wood, this space from which the living units are accessed serves as a playground for children during the day and as a parking garage for residents at nighttime.

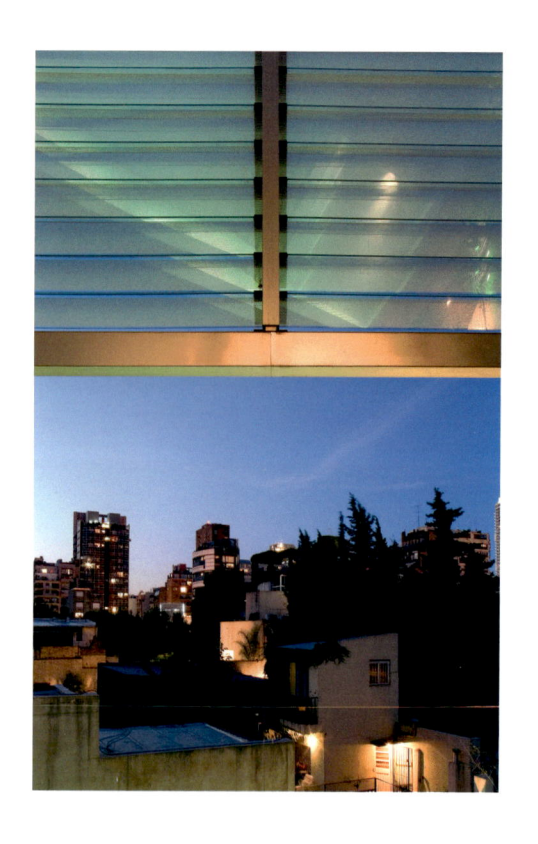

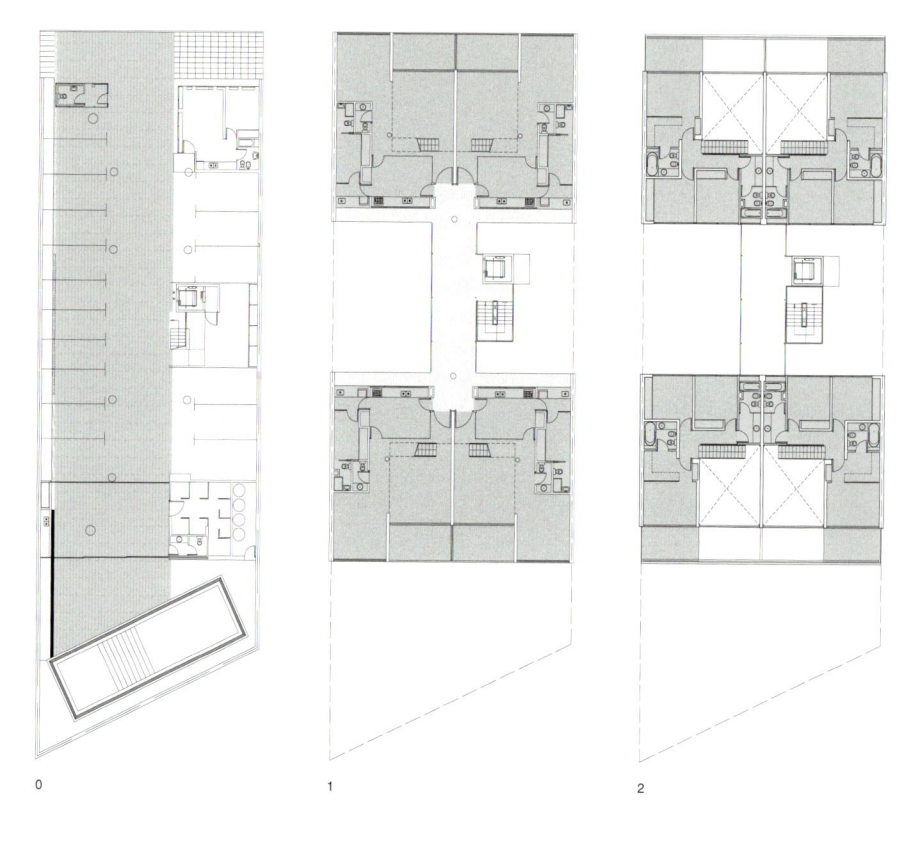

1. 10 mm thick tempered glass serigraphed with ceramic inks
2. 100x45x2 mm anodized extruded aluminum circular profile
3. 50x50x5 mm anodized extruded aluminum L-shape profile
4. structural sealing with silicon
5. 40x2 mm extruded aluminum profile
6. 50x3 mm extruded aluminum profile
7. stainless steel serrated head screw
8. 1.5 mm thick stainless steel folded sheet
9. 150x100x4.8 mm galvanized steel profile
10. steel expanding bit
11. polyamide plug divider
12. stainless steel serrated head bolt
13. anodized extruded aluminum profile
14. 50x50x5 mm steel profile

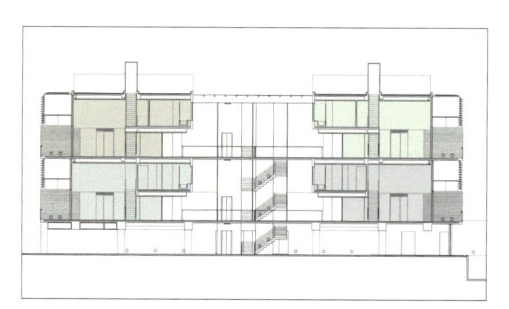

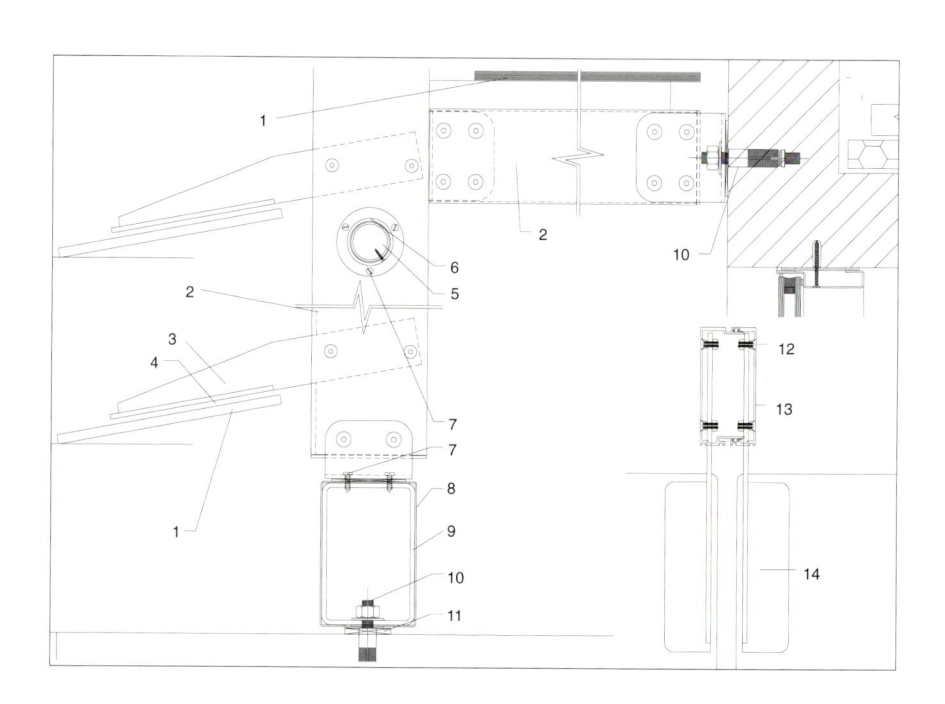

The living rooms and the main bedrooms of the apartment units look out to a double-height terrace that is protected by a system of slats. Fastened to a structure of steel supports are aluminum profiles that in turn hold up sheets of serigraphed tempered glass through which natural light is filtered and passed on to the interior spaces, shielding them from excessive sunning and framing views of the outline of the city.

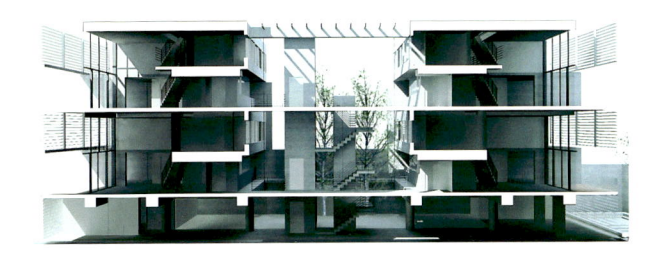

Gualano & Gualano
Shelter at the Salto del Penitente
Minas, Lavalleja (Uruguay)

Client
Ministry of Tourism
Architects
Marcelo Gualano, Martín Gualano
Collaborators
Christian Bernhardt, Lorena Díaz,
Jorge Epifanio, Ignacio de Souza
Contractor
Tresor
Photos
Ramiro Rodríguez Barilari

THE SALTO DEL PENITENTE is an over 60 meter high cliff located in a park of the mountain range of Minas, capital of the Uruguayan department of Lavalleja. To get from the entrance of the park to this shelter one has to travel approximately 16 kilometers through a prized virgin landscape characterized by steep geometries. Close to a waterfall, set deep in the rocks, rises this complex that comprises a shelter and a service area for use by small expeditions stopping for the night.

The project came about as the result of a competition that Uruguay's Tourism Ministry organized with the intention of stimulating ideas for a mountain shelter equipped with a restaurant, kitchen and toilets besides including a residence for the owner and family and providing facilities needed by people camping in the vicinity, such as changing rooms and baths. The entire program is accommodated in two distinct volumes: an elongated prism containing the services, the water deposit and a small parking area for excursionists, and the building for the actual shelter, which is reached by means of a pedestrian path and features a spatious terrace and deck from which to enjoy magnificent views of the cliff. This mirador is placed on the roof, creating a 20 meter long horizontal platform bordered by a fine steel handrail and cut over the rugged topography. From here, a staircase embedded into the building's lone wall of stone extracted from a nearby quarry brings one to the lower level of the construction, where the different spaces of the shelter are laid out: the restaurant with its broad open-air terrace and the owner's private home.

The claddings are rendered exclusively in a combination of wood and glass, and the structure is executed with exposed reinforced concrete, which makes for a neutral finish but ages well in the long run. In the face of the limited budget stipulated by the competition brief, it is also a low-cost finish requiring minimum maintenance.

Set deep in the rocks is an outdoor tourism complex that addresses its program in two distinct volumes: a prism containing services for a nearby camping site and a shelter with a rooftop viewing deck.

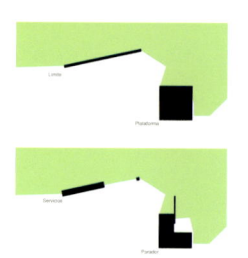

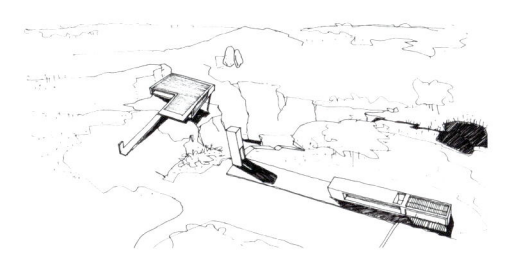

From the parking facility beside the service area – which apart from a water deposit contains the prismatic volume providing changing rooms and toilets – stretches a narrow pedestrian path leading directly to the shelter's roof. From there, a light staircase embedded into a stone wall brings one to the lower level of the building, where there is the restaurant and the terrace with views of the cliff besides the proprietor's home.

Atlas: America 259

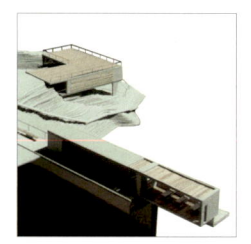

The reinforced concrete rooftop of this shelter building has been turned into a horizontal platform with sides stretching as much as 20 meters. Neatly cut over the rugged topography of the terrain and bordered by a fine handrail of stainless steel, this extensive deck treats the naturalist visitor to magnificent views of the mountainous landscape of Minas and the waterfall of Penitente Park, the principal tourist attraction of the area.

Atlas: America **261**

Solano Benítez
Father's Tomb
Piribebuy, Cordillera (Paraguay)

Architect
Solano Benítez
Collaborators
Alberto Marinoni, Silvia Ortiz, Silvio Vázquez, Oliver Ortiz, Adriana Sbetlier, Giovanna Pederzani, Gabriela Abente, Raúl Vera
Consultants
Federico Taboada (structure)
Photos
Enrico Cano

THE WORK involves a 9x9 meter square located in the midst of a very special forest landscape. Two sides are bordered by a stream of crystalline waters, while a minor course cuts through the square diagonally, giving shape to a small island. The square is formed by four concrete beams, each of which is held up by a single pillar. Because of the moisture produced by the watercourse, the spot is lush with vegetation and the beams intertwine with trees and large ferns. The place is marked from outside by the concrete structure. Leaves of *amambay*, a typical fern of the region, were inserted in the formwork of the beams' outer faces, their botanical patterns thus getting engraved on the surface of the concrete. The inner faces of the beams are covered with mirrors, in such a way that the space marked from without vanishes from within. Inside the square, avoiding the roots in the shade of the trees and filled with the sound of the stream water, is a concrete pit. This is the grave of the architect's father. The entrance, crossing the sign of the beams through the four interrupted spaces of the perimeter, densifies the air with a centripetal force, and what is present blends in, awaiting the moment when one sits beside the tomb; a moment where all presences are absorbed by the mirrors.

In a small plot of land characterized by lush forest vegetation, the place formed by four mirrors set around the grave of the architect's father effectively evokes the presence of the past in the present.

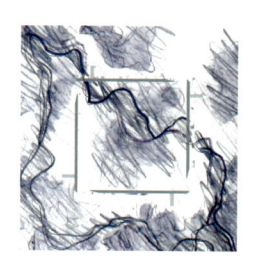

In Piribebuy, a small town situated some 84 kilometers east of the city of Asunción, in a forest spot that has come to be known as a 'branch of heaven', four beams of reinforced concrete held up by four pillars, along with four mirrors and a pit, also of concrete, define a tomb that, in the words of its author, has given him a new way of "living with loved ones who have gone because the obscenity of death took them away from us".

José Ignacio Linazasoro
Spanish Embassy
Asunción (Paraguay)

Architect
José Ignacio Linazasoro
Collaborators
Javier Puldain, Óscar Vázquez, José Ascanio, José Antonio López Cediel, Juan Carlos Corona (quantity surveyor)
Contractor
Alcallana
Photos
José Ignacio Linazasoro

With the intention of preserving most of the native trees preexisting on the site, the embassy function venues and the ambassador's residence are put together in a single compact volume on the edge of the lot.

SITUATED IN a residential area of the Paraguayan capital, the building rises near the edge of a tree-dotted plot of land, leaving ample garden ground free for holding receptions and other embassy activities. The construction's position on the highest spot of the site guarantees protection against water-related damages while giving it a dominant imposing presence when seen from the entrance, thereby asserting its representational role. The yard is fragmented by walls into spaces with varying degrees of privacy, among them the *quincho* or steak place, the 'secret garden' and the 'ambassador's patio'. The choreography of these vertical partitions creates a labyrinth of sorts on the premises.

The building's programmatic organization takes into account its simultaneous use as a one-family residence and a venue for diplomatic events. The main construction includes the private quarters of the incumbent ambassador combined with halls for official functions; a free-standing volume containing service spaces; and a lone pavilion in the swimming pool area. At ground level are the reception rooms and kitchens, while the bedrooms are distributed on the upper floors: for the ambassador's family on the first, and for the household staff on the second. This is all brought together by a central space through which light shines from above, illuminating the grand staircase that serves to connect the two main levels of the house.

The building addresses the country's tropical climate. The frequent rains call for pitched roofs and galleries, which besides providing protection against rainfall have the effect of generating a space that insulates the interior thermally. Used in combination with a structure of exposed reinforced concrete are elements coming from the vernacular architecture of Paraguay, such as the slats of *lapacho* wood of the *brises soleils* or the lattices of the main stairs, which were traditionally utilized in monastery constructions of colonial times. Similarly, in the roof, a series of modern features is complemented by the diagonal arrangement of hips, in deliberate avoidance of conventional roof systems. As for the enclosures which are rendered in brick, the material also used for the dividers in the garden, they infuse the embassy building with a language of timelessness.

At once regulating the entrance of sunlight into the interior spaces of the building and contributing to the thermal insulation of the various rooms, a series of *brises soleils* of *lapacho* wood is placed over the structure of exposed reinforced concrete. The pitched roofs and the wide galleries surrounding the ambassador's private quarters on the first upper floor are a response to the frequency of rainfall in tropical climates.

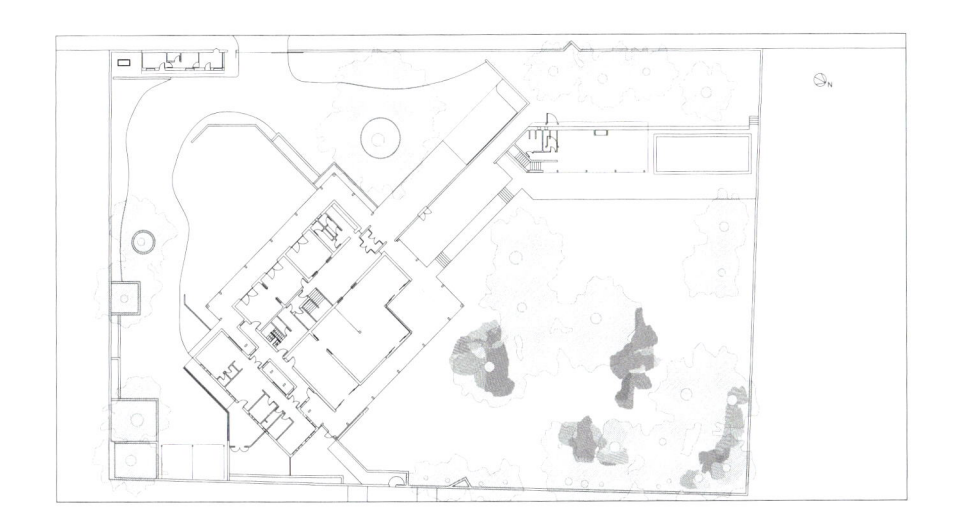

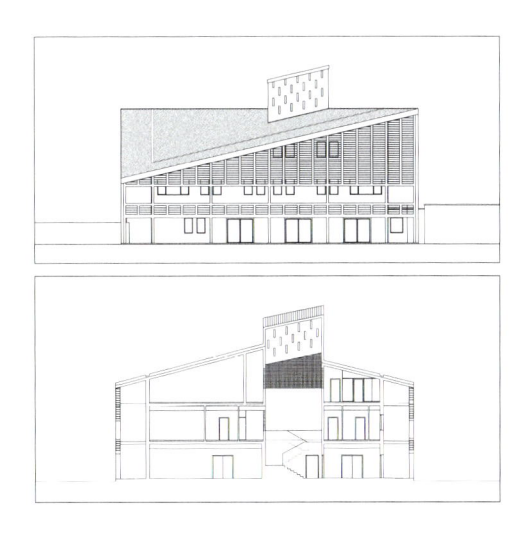

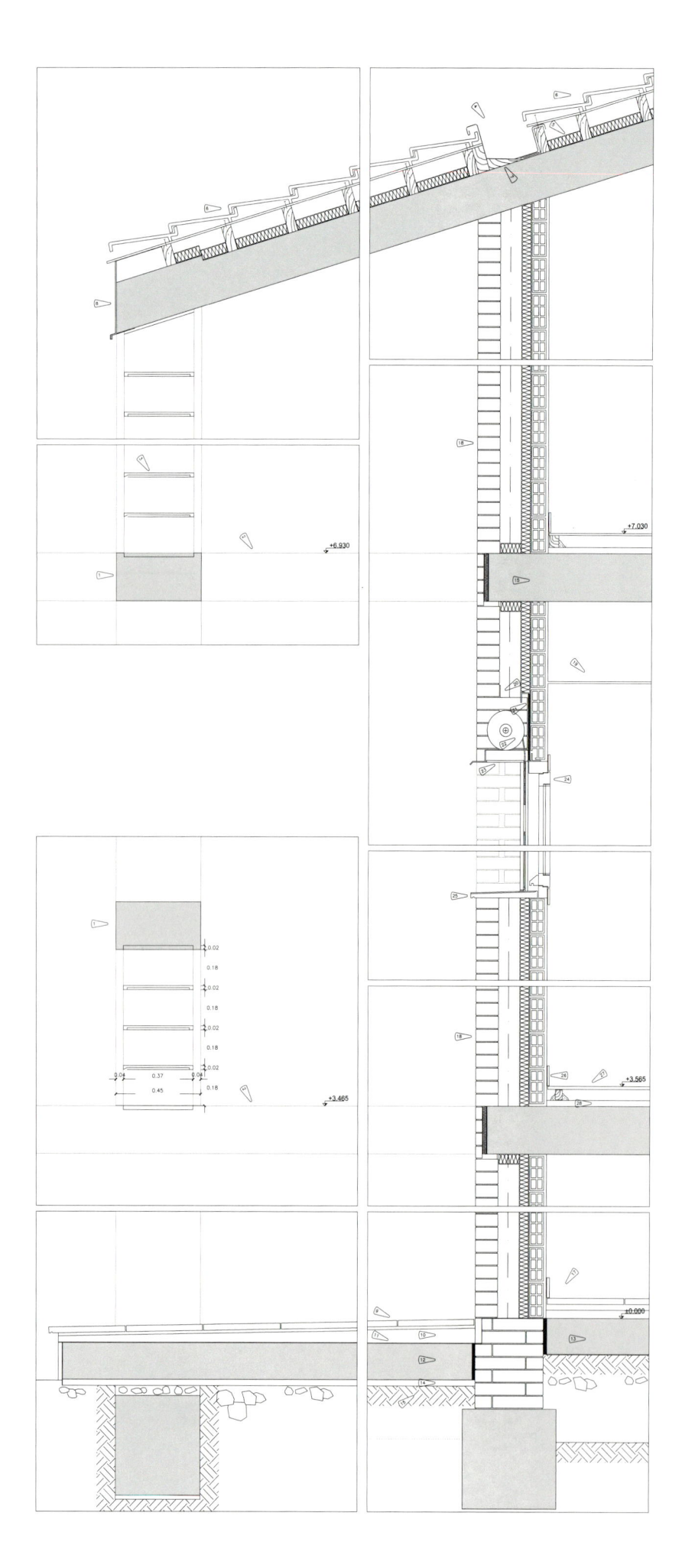

1 structure of exposed reinforced concrete	18 half-foot outer wall of exposed brick, 140 mm air chamber, thermal insulation
2 bracing beam between lattice and slab	19 plaster false ceiling
3 latticework made of 2 cm thick solid lapacho wood	20 steel L profile with antioxidant finish
4 hidden gutter of laminated zinc sheet	21 rigid thermal insulation screwed to profiles
5 rigid insulation of polyurethane foam	22 wooden blinds rollable and oscillating outward and with double articulation
6 flat ceramic tile on onduline nailed to wooden strip and screwed to slab	23 workable cover of lapacho wood, screwed to continuous border plates fastened to wall
7 wooden support for gutter	
8 solid lapacho wood finish, 6 mm laminated zinc sheet nailed to wooden finish and with run-off for rain	24 window frame of 7 cm thick solid lapacho wood, flashing joint moldings of 1.5 cm wood, mosquito net incorporated
9 exterior flooring of ceramic tiles with 40 cm sides	25 prefabricated flashing of artificial stone with run-off, embedded in brickwork
10 lightened concrete, 2% inclination	26 10x15 cm skirting board of lapacho wood
11 self-protecting leak-proof membrane	27 18 mm thick wooden platform nailed to wooden strip
12 exterior flooring, 15 cm, in reinforced concrete	28 3 cm layer of trowelled cement
13 interior flooring of reinforced concrete, self-protecting leak-proof membrane	29 3 mm thick steel profile normalized and anchored rigidly to slab
14 flowable fill	
15 building pad	30 piece of lapacho wood screwed to metal profile
16 reinforced concrete slab	
17 floor of marble tiles with 40 cm sides, 10 cm skirting board	31 1.5 cm wooden piece

266 Atlas: America

Brick walls divide the garden into smaller spaces of a more private character that are intended to serve as outdoor venues for holding a wide variety of embassy functions and events, including the area fitted out for the *quincho* or typical Paraguayan roast and the so-called 'secret garden' and ambassador's patio'. The arrangement of these vertical elements creates a labyrinth around the building that leads directly to the gallery.

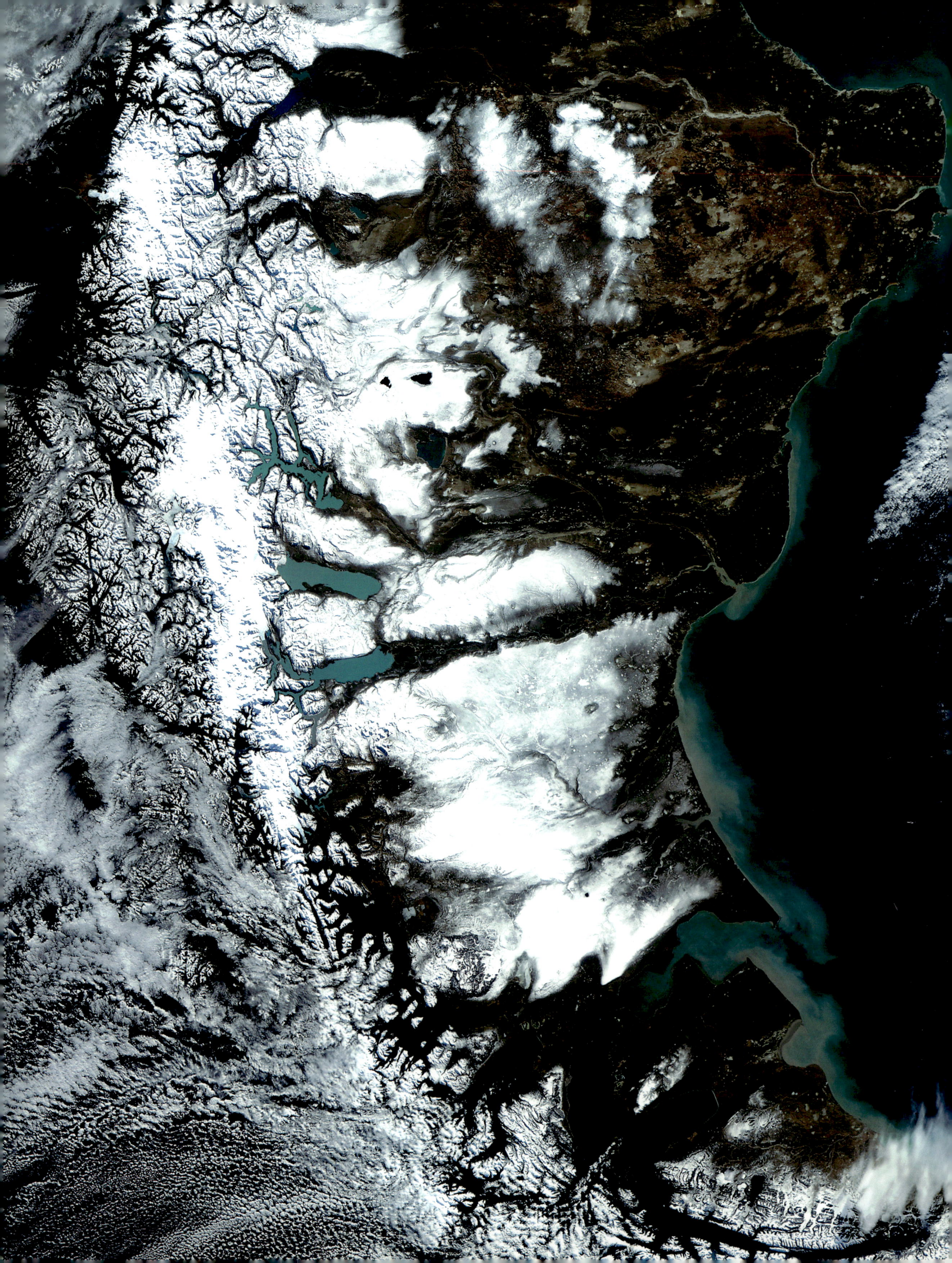

Chile

Occupying a long narrow strip of land that stretches between the southeastern coast of the Pacific Ocean and the Andes mountain range, Chile is diverse in climate and landscape. Its geography has been instrumental in the shaping of a poetic centered on interpreting the territory as a starting point of the architectural project, as reflected in the Museum of the Atacama Desert by Coz, Polidura & Volante; the graduate center in Peñalolén by Cruz Ovalle; the chapel in the Andes by Undurraga; the shelters and observation decks in Panguilemo by the Talca Group; or the Hotel Remota in Puerto Natales by Germán del Sol. Outstanding in the urban context are the refined projects carried out by Mozó for the BIP Building in Santiago and the social housing development executed by Aravena in Iquique, while attention to the constructive logic of materials has given rise to high-quality works like the one-family houses built by Radic, FAR and Pezo & Von Ellrichhausen.

Fernando Pérez Oyarzun
Excellence at the Limit
Chile, a Critical Fortune Put to the Test

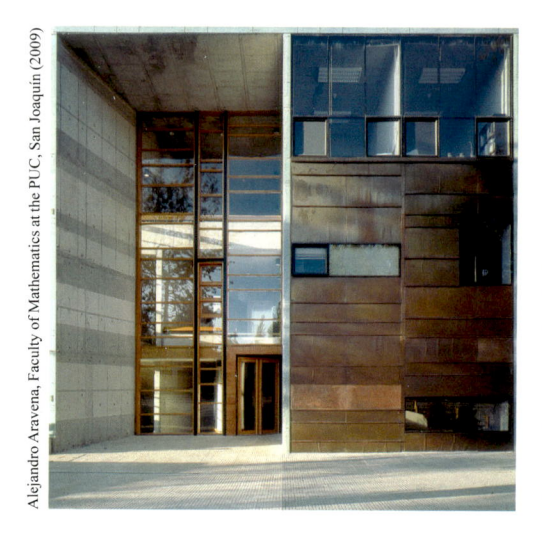

A new sensibility for working in natural landscapes and urban contexts combines with an interest in exploiting the poetics of materials.

Alejandro Aravena, Faculty of Mathematics at the PUC, San Joaquín (2009)

The elaborate projects being carried out in the cities strike a contrast with the works going up in remote areas: simple volumes inspired by vernacular traditions and marked by intimate rapport with the place.

ARCHITECTURE IN Chile has had the good fortune of enjoying a certain degree of critical acclaim in the past ten or fifteen years. Chilean architects have been basking in international attention and their works and projects have come to get included in important publications and exhibitions. This interest in the country has been accompanied by commissions coming from diverse latitudes of the globe, and professionals like Alejandro Aravena, José Cruz, Sebastián Irarrázaval and Mathias Klotz have built in China, Switzerland, Germany, the United States and Argentina. In the book *Portales del Laberinto,* the critic Jorge Francisco Liernur poses the question of whether Chile's current situation can be compared to the acclaim that was showered on Brazil in the mid-20th century.

This success is in part attributable to the surprise provoked by the unexpected appearance of a good number of quality architecture works in a place as remote as Chile. Whatever the reason, the temptation to explain current Chilean architecture in terms of an alleged 'arriving' is not satisfactory, because successes of this kind tend to be ephemeral and are not always indicative of solidity and quality. It would make more sense to talk in terms of the origins and eventual contributions of the architectural works in question, of what they have come to mean for the country, and of their connections to different social processes. This involves addressing their successes, but also their limitations, in the context of the social circumstances surrounding them. Thinking about these questions can cast some light on the meaning of recent Chilean production and lead to a more realistic and comprehensive reflection on contemporary architecture.

Any form of historic determinism proves to be insufficient as an explanation for what is happening in the field of architecture. Nevertheless, it is difficult to separate architectural results of the past years from the political and social processes that have been taking place in the country in the same period. We also have to take into account an old tradition of architectural quality that is being revisited by the young generations. In Chile, the tradition of architectural quality has profound roots dating back to the beginning of the 20th century. The country's first schools of architecture were founded during the final decade of the 19th, and were from the start attached to universities. In the mid-20th century, a good number of established architects were working in Chile and delivering works fit to address the demands of a developing country, works that came to enjoy a certain degree of international publicity.

Running parallel to this solid, qualified professional activity was a solid theoretical activity. Here, the publications of José Ricardo Morales, Juan Borchers and the School of Valparaíso were among the most prominent. They did not merely propose solutions to a variety of local problems, but also participated in a more generalized theoretical discussion. Furthermore, a significant part of this theoretical activity addressed connections to the project, giving rise to an architectural output that effectively set itself apart from the habitual forms of professional practice. The works and projects of Borchers, Suárez and Bermejo as well as the School of Valparaíso best represent this tendency, and their influence has reached today's architecture.

As in other Latin American countries, in Chile the 1970s and 1980s were strongly influenced by postmodernism, but though postmodernism had a presence in relevant publications and biennials, it did not materialize in quality works. Nevertheless, revived interest in history and increased awareness of the problems of urban form outlived the period. Towards the end of the 1980s and into the start of the 1990s, the most radical strain of postmodern historicism gave way to a keen interest in

Sebastián Irarrázaval, Hotel Indigo Patagonia, Puerto Natales (2007)

local identity and geography, vaguely inscribed within a critical regionalism that helped to liberate works and projects from the clichés of previous years.

The interest aroused by the Chilean Pavilion at the Expo of Seville in 1992 has frequently been used to mark the beginning of the international dissemination of Chilean architecture. It was built with pinewood, one of the materials promoted during the Expo as the country's export products. The materiality of pinewood was determinant not only for the pavilion's conception, but also for the evolution of the professional career of its authors, José Cruz and Germán del Sol.

The central icon of the Chilean exhibition in Seville was a large chunk of ice that was transported from the southern snowdrifts, and it was presented in such a way that Chile revealed itself as a reality removed from Latin American platitudes. The nuanced light of the interior alluded to the idea of the temperate: a reference to the climate that transcended the purely geographical.

The project was the result of an explicit theoretical position of the architects, who had tied up their years of training in Barcelona with a keen interest in the fabrications of Alberto Cruz and the School of Valparaíso. It is therefore no coincidence that the Hotel Explora in Torres del Paine (1994), which was one of their subsequent commissions, came to count among the most published works of the late 1990s. Its location in Patagonia – in the remotest area of the country's southern tip –, its use of wood and its elaborate rapport with the landscape indicate a high degree of continuity with the arguments brought into play in the Expo pavilion.

Landscape and Urban Context
That the reality of the landscape and the force of nature are, in Chile, more significant than the cultural scene is a relatively

Germán del Sol, Geometric Hot Springs at Villarica National Park, Cautín (2003)

Atlas: America **271**

Smiljan Radic, Copper House 2, Talca (2007)

Close attention to the architectural object and the material conception behind it is evident in domestic architecture, as much in the delicate and exquisite houses that Smiljan Radic or the young team of Pezo & Von Ellrichshausen build with walls of wood or metal sheeting as in the bold and concise single-family residences that Cristián Undurraga or Mathias Klotz execute with structures of reinforced concrete.

widespread conviction. And although there is a certain myth about the alleged variety of Chile's landscape, the linear arrangement of landscapes strung together like beads of a necklace, combined with the opposition of extreme conditions – from the most arid deserts to the Antarctic expanses of ice – gives it a certain peculiarity. It is not then surprising that a strong interest in the landscape has emerged among contemporary Chilean architects. They follow the footsteps of landscape architects like Oscar Prager, who stood out in the 1940s and 1950s, or Carlos Martner, whose work unfolded in the 1960s and 1970s. We should mention Juan Grimm, perhaps the most international and reputed among Chilean landscape architects, who has designed numerous parks and gardens both inside and outside of Chile. Teodoro Fernández, in turn, is equally comfortable in architecture and landscaping, and thanks to his talent we have public parks of great importance, such as Santa Inés Park (1994) in the commune of Providencia and Bicentennial Park (2007) in the commune of Vitacura, both of them in the city of Santiago.

But the landscape also tinges architecture, as in the Cemetery of the Open City of Ritoque, a work that plays with native vegetation and topography, intimately linked to the landscape. While the earlier interventions are associated with figures like Juan Baixas, Juan Enrique Mastrantonio and Bruno Barla, the more recent ones are by a group headed by Jorge Sánchez. A significant number of works undertaken in the past ten years or so are some way or another thought of as engaging in dialog with the landscape. Some cater to novel forms of tourism in remote regions, such as the buildings raised for the Explora chain, including the hotel located out in Rapa Nui (2007) by José Cruz, the Hotel Remota (2005) by Germán del Sol, and the Hotel Indigo Patagonia in Puerto Natales (2007) by Sebastián Irarrázaval. Many of these are simple but sophisticated containers resembling the elemental constructions inhabiting these places.

On very similar lines we could situate Germán del Sol's Puritama Hot Springs (2000), a delicate exercise in the insertion of a building in the landscape, while his Geometric Hot Springs in Villarica National Park (2003) – an intervention sited in a narrow canyon in the middle of the Valdiviano forest – confronts the landscape directly through a series of suspended ramps and a group of basic huts. We should also mention the delicate landscaping treatment executed by Tere Moller and José Domingo Peñafiel in the Punta Pite development (2003), on the central coast of Chile, where the principal piece is a shoreline promenade that respects the beautiful rocky seaside landscape.

In turn, for the conception of a work as seemingly removed from landscaping as José Cruz's Adolfo Ibáñez University (2002), concern for the landscape is one of the starting points. An interior is created that allows a near-tactile interaction with the Andes mountains, whisks away the obvious panoramic view of the city, and tries to separate architecture from any possible dependence on a visual spectacle. Prominent among architects of the youngest generations is the office of Polidura & Talhouk, which has built several parks, as well as DRN Arquitectos, the practice run by Nicolás del Río and Max Núñez.

The matter of taking the urban context into account took on weight and importance in the 1980s, but was marked by historicist approaches or conventional gestures of the kind that were associated with styles in vogue. But the 1990s saw a turn towards a more fecund engagement with context. Context was still considered key, but the question of how exactly to relate with it became material for reflection. This is what happens in a series of projects that in some

Mauricio Pezo & Sofía von Ellrichshausen, Rivo House, Valdivia (2005)

Cristián Undurraga, Horizon House, Zapallar (2007)

way or another rise or rest on preexisting architectural realities.

In the Sergio Larraín García-Moreno Information Center (2007), the architects Teodoro Fernández, Smiljan Radic and Cecilia Puga together constructed beside the old house of Lo Contador – the seat of the architecture school of the Catholic University of Chile – what Jesús Bermejo at some point called "a piano mobile in the basement". The complex includes a library, an archive, auditoriums and a number of classrooms, and it emphasizes the long facade of the preexisting building, creating a space that is sunken yet does not lose touch with the exterior landscape. Beside this is José Cruz's University Dining Hall (1997). A volume that delicately approaches one of the house's lateral facades, it is built in laminated wood with a folded surface where solids and voids alternate in counterpoint to the old mud walls surrounding it.

One of Alejandro Aravena's early works, the Mathematics School in the Catholic University's San Joaquín campus (1999), is a strongly contextual intervention where a new volume connects two preexisting blocks, giving rise to a compositionally rich ensemble. Similarly, the School of Medicine and Biomedical Library (2005) that he carried out for the same university, this time in its Casa Central campus, and designed with the author of this text, is embedded between existing constructions with the intention of materially and functionally connecting with a complex whose oldest pieces date back to the dawn of the 20th century.

The university neighborhood of the southern zone of the center of Santiago is an area of old private one-family residences whose inhabitants moved to the eastern part of the city in the course of the 1940s, 1950s and 1960s. Fortunately many of them have in the past years been restored as university buildings. Among the interventions carried out is Diego Portales University, where the architect Mathias Klotz has directed an operation that includes not only restorations and new buildings, but also the design of a whole network of interstitial spaces that give new meaning to the urban fabric. In this context he has carried out projects like the Faculty of Economics (2004) and the Faculty of Health Sciences (2004), and invited other architects to participate, among them Ricardo Abuauad, who built the Faculty of Architecture and Design.

One-Family Residences

If the built context has inspired a significant part of the projects that have been carried out in Chile in the past years, a complementary line of inspiration seems to be coming from the Antipodes, one involving attention to the architectural object and its material conception. Here we discern a tendency to revisit a certain poetic of construction that is opposed to another inclination, that which seeks to reestablish space as the protagonist in architecture. The architect who perhaps has most intensely adopted this approach is Smiljan Radic. In his work, appraisal of objectivity is mixed with a poetic of the material, both in representations of some of his projects – where plans of the actual installations are superposed on merely descriptive plans – and in his project descriptions for the Chica House (1996) and the San Miguel House (1997), which read like enumerations of building materials and processes. Radic has remained faithful to this idea, as we can verify for ourselves in Copper House 2 (2007), in Talca; in the services building for the Public Works Ministry (2005), in Concepción, carried out in collaboration with Eduardo Castillo and Ricardo Serpell; or in the more recently inaugurated Mestizo Restaurant (2007), where concrete beams and the monumental stone sculptures by Marcela Correa make an elemental but sophisticated shelter facing the elaborate landscape of Bicentennial Park.

Mathias Klotz, Eleven Women House, Zapallar (2004)

With the incorporation of Chile into the international markets, many an emerging company has started to look for a corporate image that is associated with its buildings, which on the whole try to reflect the process behind the elaboration of its products. Depending on typology, the firms opt for translucent materials on light steel structures, or soft technologies with traditional wooden frameworks.

This same approach seems to have been undergoing affirmation most forcefully in the studio of Izquierdo & Lehman, for which the building called The Fountainhead (1999) – executed in conjunction with Raimundo Lira and José Domingo Peñafiel – presented itself as an opportunity to aesthetically express the structural problems at hand. This is perceived in their houses and in the recent Patricia Ready Art Gallery (2008), built in collaboration with Mauricio Léniz and Mirene Elton. Finally, the role played by these technical poetics in architecture is also discernible in the notable system of self-bearing models for reinforced concrete designed by Luis Izquierdo.

Though Chilean architects like Cristián Undurraga took off from different starting points, they too have been drawn to this material poetic. The glass and quartz panels used in the Simonetti Office Building (2003) and the House-Patio (2008) – where the pulchritude of the exterior finish combines with the quality of the interior light – are proof of his efforts to conceive architecture as a problem of sensitive construction.

In turn the Retiro Chapel (2009), situated in the Sanctuary of Auco, hovers between the effectivity of the elemental design scheme that has always attracted Undurraga on one hand, and the material rotundity of a reinforced concrete structure on the other.

In its own way, the work of Mauricio Pezo and Sofía von Ellrichshausen can also be inscribed within this constructive poetic if we understand the notion in a larger sense, one that transcends the technical realm to concentrate on exploring the frontiers existing between art and architecture. The Poli House (2005), the Fosc House (2009) and the Parr House (2007) all belong to this territory, as does the Quinta Junge Building in Concepción (2009). Within the youngest set of architects, the studio WAR Arquitectos has demonstrated in the Panul Sheds (2004) how exactly the use of basic resources, when these are assembled with a high degree of constructive and conceptual rigor, can yield results of great formal sophistication and aesthetic richness.

The work of Alberto Mozó has recently received plenty of recognition, especially on account of the building he raised for the company BIP Computers (2007), rendered with glass and laminated wood. Beyond its bold design, a response to the complex conditions of the site, it is conceived as an object that can be taken apart and then recycled; that is, with a constructive rationality that addresses the most general productive and environmental questions. The building seems to put itself at the head of a new line of investigation for Mozó, a line where conception, fabrication and montage are seen as being part and parcel of one same architectural operation.

A look at the works selected in the most recent biennials of architecture suffices to realize the importance that one-family residences have had in contemporary Chile. Not only has the genre been treated with craft and quality by the likes of Izquierdo & Lehman – for whom it has been the most persistent source of commissions – or Mathias Klotz – who has even come to export his sophisticated houses to neighboring countries; there are practically no professionals of recognized prestige who

Bebin & Saxton, Aonni Mineral Water Plant, Punta Arenas (2008)

Martín Hurtado, Viña Morandé Winery, Casablanca, Valle Central (2006)

do not routinely include notable samples of the genre in their catalogs. Mathias Klotz's Eleven Women House (2004), Assadi-Pulido's 20x20 House (2005), Winkler, Saric & Fritz's W House (2008) and Rodrigo Duque's Duque House (2004) attest to the degree of sophistication that domestic architecture has attained. But the house has also provided a multitude of young professionals with opportunities to bring their talents and inspirations into play. A run-through of the catalogs of the latest biennials, or of websites like those of Barqo or Plataforma de Arquitectura, yields an interminable, almost unreconstructible list of domestic projects, many of them highly interesting. This reflects the links that exist between certain social elites and current architecture, but it also indicates that the opportunities for quality architecture remain confined to private commissions and tied to social and family connections.

Industry and Infrastructure
If there is a sure area where economic development and globalization come in contact with architecture, it is the field of industrial facilities. Chile's incorporation into international markets has helped forge the mindsets of its industrialists, who have now started to associate their buildings with the prospect of creating a corporate image, often one that makes reference to the particular production process at hand. It would not be wise to generalize, but a large number of entrepreneurs have in these past years been hiring recognized architects to design their headquarters and other premises, reviving a tradition that was very important in the mid-20th century.

And there are certain industries – wine and wood, for example – that seem to be particularly sensitive to this alliance with architecture. We can mention the works of José Cruz for Arauco, such as the wood-processing Maderas Center (2000), which show how typologies as conventional as those of industrial construction do admit rethinking. Viticultural buildings have also come to have a high level of sophistication. Numerous winegrowers have called in prestigious architects to endow their facilities with an architectural quality that is attractive to the general public. The winery for Viña Pérez Cruz (2001) by José Cruz or the one built for Almaviva (1998) by Martín Hurtado are just two prominent examples. Wood plays a leading role in both, as it does in two other works carried out by Hurtado, for the wine barrel manufacturer Nadalie (2002) and the organic fruit company Packing Greenvic (2006).

Finally we should mention other industrial sectors that have opened up space for architects. There has been plenty of recognition for projects like those carried out by Sabbagh Arquitectos for the bottling company Embotelladora Andina (1996), including the Planta Andina Norte facility, or for those of the architect Guillermo Hevia for the glass manufacturer Cristal Chile (2006) and the olive oil producer Olisur (2008). In the mineral water sector, the Aonni Mineral Water Plant (2008) by the firm Bebin & Saxton is representative of the incursion in this field by members of the youngest set of architects.

Infrastructures have been increasingly

Guillermo Hevia, Olisur Olive Oil Factory, San José de Marchigüe, La Estrella (2008)

In Santiago de Chile, amid numerous apartment buildings of poor quality that are the consequence of real estate speculation, a number of significant proposals stand out for the novel design options they present, including sophisticated enclosure materials. In turn, along the same line of experimentation, the center of the capital is the location of some new cultural and educational facilities of excellent quality.

Assadi & Pulido, Gen Building, Santiago de Chile (2010)

seen as being instrumental to urban planning and an indispensable condition for attaining higher levels of development. Chile digested this connection very thoroughly in the early 1990s, and since then the country has made considerable investments, private and public alike, in these fields: roads, port operations, metropolitan railway networks, water treatment plants, etc. All this questions the capacity of architecture to give infrastructures greater quality and cultural meaning. The cases where architects have had a part are still rare, although some examples give us an inkling of the extent to which such collaboration is possible. In roads, for example, we can mention complementary buildings like the Emergency Attention Center on the South Central Highway (2003) by the studio masarquitectos (Brahm, Bonomi, Leturia and Bartolomé), as well as the gasoline stations situated along the Costanera Norte highway and the Pronto services network for Copec (2004) by Sabbagh Arquitectos. José Domingo Peñafiel's Planta de Tratamiento de Aguas Servidas (1997), a water treatment facility in Lo Barnechea, shows up to what point infrastructures can indeed prove to be a fertile field for architecture.

Included within the overall scheme for the enlargement of Santiago de Chile's metropolitan railway network are efforts to improve the architectural quality and significance of certain stations, such as those that have been assigned to Gubbins Arquitectos. The Quinta Normal station of line 5 is prominent in this regard because it forms part of a whole new cultural area in the Matucana sector, in the vicinity of the Public Library and the Cultural Matucana 100 center, and because it explores the theme of urban signification and the hybrid character a metro station can take on.

State Commissions
The political conditions established in the country from 1990 onward were manifested in many different spheres, and state-commissioned buildings were fundamental here. The early years of democracy saw efforts to improve the urban environments of deteriorated peripheral neighborhoods through the construction of parks and public-use facilities. Juan Baixas and Enrique del Río designed the notable Mirador Interactive Museum (1999), a science and technology museum for children, a simultaneously complex and unitary space that offered a wide choice of routes with the clarity of an industrial hangar and a high degree of sophistication in the finishes and constructive details.

In another area, the reforms instituted that significantly modified penal procedures stipulated the provision, throughout the country, of judicial courts that would ensure compliance with the new legislation. The most significant courthouses were competition material when not directly commissioned to architects of renown. Outstanding among them were the courthouse for Santiago's west zone (1996), a design of Enrique Browne and Borja Huidobro, and the Justice Center of Santiago (2006), by Cristián Boza. Not all of the buildings can be said to be memorable, but all together they testify to the growing interest, on the part of public organisms, in giving architecture a sure role in the undertaking of social initiatives.

The Santiago Public Library (2005), a work of Cox & Ugarte situated on the grounds of an old government warehouse building, is surely the most significant intervention of its kind that has been carried out in Chile in the past years. This is a re-addressing of the theme of architecture and the preexisting, as well as of that of interaction between infrastructure and public space. Such interest in giving the country better infrastructural works can also be appreciated in sport stadiums, among them the Nelson Oyarzun Bicentennial Stadium in Chillán (2008) by Judson & Olivos.

Izquierdo Lehmannn, Cruz del Sur Building, Santiago de Chile (2009)

In turn the delicate location of the Palacio de la Moneda Cultural Center (2004) – in one of the most significant works of the history of Chilean architecture, the very seat of the national government –, along with its quality, surely makes it one of the major projects of recent years. Constructed on the initiative of former President Ricardo Lagos by the prominent architectural firm Undurraga Devés, it does not only provide an unprecedented exhibition space in the direct vicinity of the presidential palace, but also gives rise to an altogether new urban context: Citizenry Square.

Chile's first workers' housing law was promulgated in the year 1906. In the course of the 20th century, diverse initiatives, regulations and institutions have tried to solve a problem that is highly complex, especially considering the scarcity of resources available. The country has been a kind of research laboratory for social housing. The past twenty-five years have been considered successful in terms of returns on resources invested, of financing systems used, and of number of living units built. There has even been talk of putting an end to the housing deficit, and in fact A Roof for Chile, an organization connected to the Catholic Church, had sought to eliminate the nation's relatively few remaining informal settlements by 2010, the year of the Independence Bicentennial. But the technical problems that accompany these kinds of constructions and the social conflicts that are endemic in the vast expanses of poor settlements, consequences of the policies that have been in force to date, have made voices of alarm warn against excessive optimism.

Rising to these challenges is the purpose of initiatives like Elemental – led by Alejandro Aravena and co-founded with Pablo Allard and Andrés Iacobelli –, which has drawn special attention since it organized an international competition on the theme, or A Roof for Chile, which has transferred its experience to other Latin American countries. Such initiatives have caused a degree of social and intellectual mobilization around a theme previously quite ignored by architecture. The results are still isolated examples in comparison to the mass of social housing built by the state. But projects like the Quinta Monroy development in Iquique (2002) and the dwellings in Renca (2008), both carried out by Elemental, must be credited for offering new solutions with the tight means and resources of the state. Previous experiments with progressive housing have been reelaborated, and matters like families' attachments to their places of residence have been addressed. Not to mention the initiatives of private foundations, which have also busied themselves with improving the urban conditions of housing, but through the model of the traditional urban fabric. A case in point is the Ermita de San Antonio complex (2000) in Santiago, by Undurraga Devés. All these initiatives have tried to build a new space for an encounter between architecture and a problem of such social significance as state-protected housing.

New Alternative Forms
In the last sixty years or so, the School of Valparaíso has with continuity and in certain isolation been carrying out a unique project. The Open City of Ritoque remains in construction and reconstruction, constantly

Estudio América, Museum of Memory, Santiago de Chile (2010)

Regard for the inherent constructive logic of materials is manifested in the daring proposals that young practices have been carrying out in inhospitable places, where they use anything from pieces of recycled wood to corrugated steel sheets to form thin enclosure skins that are then fixed to structures of wooden slabs, or complex fabrics, thermal and translucent, that wrap around a core of reinforced concrete.

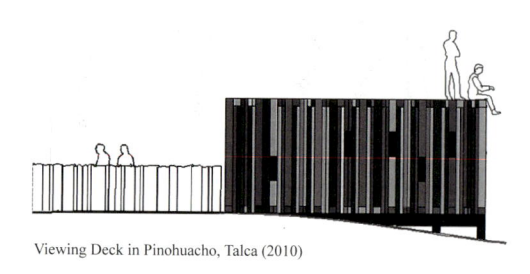

Viewing Deck in Pinohuacho, Talca (2010)

incorporating new buildings connected to academic activity. But not until the 1990s did this peculiar architectural experience become a focus of international attention, with exhibitions held at the UIA Congress in 1996, at Harvard University and at other academic and cultural centers, more recently the 'Drifts and Derivations' exhibition at Madrid's Reina Sofía Museum, which included works coming from the school and the Taller de Juan Borchers. But significant commissions aside, the pedagogical and creative activity of this school has been very constant. Its influence, not always evident, has filtered into the architectural production of Chile and can be discerned in the thinking of José Cruz, in the designs of Cristián Valdés, or in Cazú Zegers's imaginative wooden constructions in Kawelluco, in the vicinity of Pucón and Lake Villarica.

One of the latest manifestations of this kind of activity that looks for new opportunities and new parameters for the architectural practice is the School of Talca. With no direct ties to its counterpart in Valparaíso, it has continued to explore alternatives for the practice of architecture. Situated some 250 kilometers from Santiago, the small city of Talca saw the rise of a school of architecture in what originally was a campus of the University of Chile. With the architect Juan Román as director, it has imposed on its students a peculiar set of prerequisites to graduation that includes prior construction of a work, normally a small-scale one. This means finding the demand and the resources necessary to raise it. Such a pedagogical approach has managed to enthuse numerous groups of students, who see in it the prospect of bringing architecture to remote, architecture-less places, and with this, the opportunity to embark on innovative careers. Of all the members of the Talca Group, the team formed by Macarena Ávila, Cecilia Cullen, Martín del Solar, Alejandra Liebana and Rodrigo Sheward is the most representative. Using elements easily available in the different locations – such as the enormous chunks of wood used to construct the Pinohuacho viewing deck (2006) or the wine waste barrel staves that were recycled for the construction of a small public space called the National Plaza (2007) –, the group has proven its capacity to think up altogether new alternatives for the practice of architecture.

Current Challenges
There are times when a group of talented and well-directed architects are able to positively contaminate a large number of professionals, forging an implicit agreement on the type of architecture to promote. A positive contamination of this kind has come to take place in Chile, generating an output that Luis Fernández-Galiano at some point has described as 'choral', in reference to a significant body of works and architects of outstanding quality. But it is generally not in the great Chilean cities that we can appreciate the good effects of such architecture. One could say that for changes of an urban scale to be discerned, a bit more time is required, or that examples of architecture of true quality are few in any city of the world. Nevertheless, the fact is real and cause for concern.

And there are areas of the building industry where quality is not necessarily the norm, but that have an enormous impact on the urban environment. One is the sector of huge office buildings, among which it is hard to find something worth separate mention and where corporate or technical criteria prevail over quality. On the other hand, a very significant number of real estate operations tied to the construction of highrise residential buildings has appropriated the center of Santiago, most of them of poor quality not only design-wise but also in program and contribution to public space. The pending task, then,

Grupo Talca, Viewing Deck in Pinohuacho, Talca (2010)

Owar Arquitectos, Santa Clara Housing, Robinson Crusoe Island (2008)

is to forge a link between the capacity to generate quality works and operations of high urban impact. The idea is to raise the average quality of the urban fabric of Chilean cities. The recent partnering of Izquierdo & Lehman with the real estate firm Paz to build the Cruz del Sur Building (2009) is a mentionable intervention, as is the Gen Building (2010) of Asadi & Pulido. The former, with its exceptional location in the east part of Santiago de Chile, rises like an inverted pyramid that, making a show of its notable structural virtuosity, takes off from a central core to form a partly buried public commercial space. For the facade of the latter, solar panels were placed over elements of recycled metal in an attempt to plastically distinguish a conventional residential building. But these examples are exceptional cases. The same kind of affirmations can be said with regard to social housing, where the efforts of Elemental or A Roof for Chile deviate from the norm.

Only the future will allow an evaluation of the contribution of the new generations of architects, which, as in the cases of the Wall House (2008) of Frohn & Rojas or the Santa Clara Social Housing Development on Robinson Crusoe Island of Owar Arquitectos (an office run by Álvaro Benítez, Emilio de la Cerda and Tomás Folch), do not only seek new design alternatives; they are also on the lookout for new forms and new fields of action for the practice of the profession.

All this makes it possible to answer a question posed by Rafael Moneo several years ago: "How can the work of so many talented architects extend to new programs and be put at the service of social demands?" Only in the above-described conditions can architecture become a social good. Of course this will require aligning a large dose of realism with a high degree of imagination. Already many years ago now, and perhaps with similar problems in mind, José Antonio Coderch formulated a manifesto: "It's not geniuses that we need now". By saying this he was trying to propose architecture as a kind of quality craft that has the potential to bind the world of construction to everyday life. It is a good thing to remember his message nowadays, but maybe this is not the only road to take. Architecture requires imaginative individuals who are willing to take risks and able to work at the frontiers existing between different disciplines. But at the same time, it is necessary to connect their work to the real demands of society. Only in this way will architecture cease to be a luxury reserved for a few, and begin to contribute to the lives of the majority. This is a challenge involving professionals as well as schools, which have to make special efforts to make said demands present in the training of their students, but also public institutions and society at large, which need to have a clearer understanding of what architecture is able to offer.

FAR, Frohn & Rojas, Wall House, Santiago de Chile (2007)

Alejandro Aravena
Quinta Monroy Social Housing
Iquique (Chile)

Client
Regional Government of Tarapacá
Architect
Alejandro Aravena
Collaborators
Alfonso Montero, Tomás Cortese, Emilio de la Cerda
Consultants
Juan Carlos de la Llera, José Gajardo (engineering)
Contractor
Proingel
Photos
Cristóbal Palma

ELEMENTAL IS the building approach that has come to the fore with the Chilean Housing Ministry's decision to rehouse a hundred families that had for thirty years been illegally occupying a site located in the very heart of Iquique. Despite the high price of land in the city, which triples the cost of implementing social housing projects there, it was decided that the community should not be banished to cheap land on the outskirts, far from access to basic infrastructures and opportunities. The resulting project forms part of a larger government-developed program named 'Dynamic Social Housing Without Debt'. Directed at the most impoverished sectors of society, it granted every household a subsidy with which to purchase a piece of land, contribute to the necessary urbanization works, and construct a dwelling. At best, however, the limited budget only allowed for 30 square meters per unit, making future expansion inevitable.

On the other hand, if each family was assigned a lot on such a small site, it would only be possible to build thirty units. And if for a more efficient use of land the size of the individual lots was reduced to equal the perimeter of the houses, the result would be not so much efficiency as a stacking up of volumes. Highrise building was ruled out too, precluding as it did the growth of the dwellings, and the idea was that each unit should grow, with time, to at least twice its original floor area.

The building strategy proposed here allows the construction of row houses, a typology that makes it possible to achieve sufficient density to pay for the land, the central urban location of which is instrumental to the economic sustenance of the families and to the future value of the dwellings. Furthermore, because 50% of the initial square meters should stretch in the course of time, the design of the complex is porous enough to allow growth upon the structure delivered. In effect, the $10,000 subsidy is made to yield not just a basic 30 square meter housing unit, but what will eventually become an over 70 square meter home, of which only a part is given at the start. With time, the expansion will be carried out by the residents and with their own means.

Constituting a system of building row houses for the most impoverished sectors of the population, the Elemental approach guarantees solid economic and environmental conditions in new urban developments.

The houses are built upon a structure of reinforced concrete and with blocks of cement, on urban land with easy access to basic infrastructures and opportunities. For approximately $10,000, part of a 70 square meter living unit is provided, and it is up to the users to build the rest with their own means and resources. Through this system it has been possible to construct as many as 500 basic dwellings in different locations within Chile.

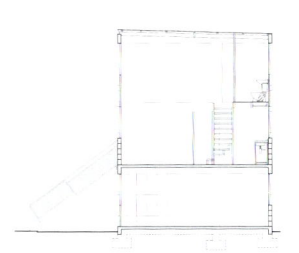

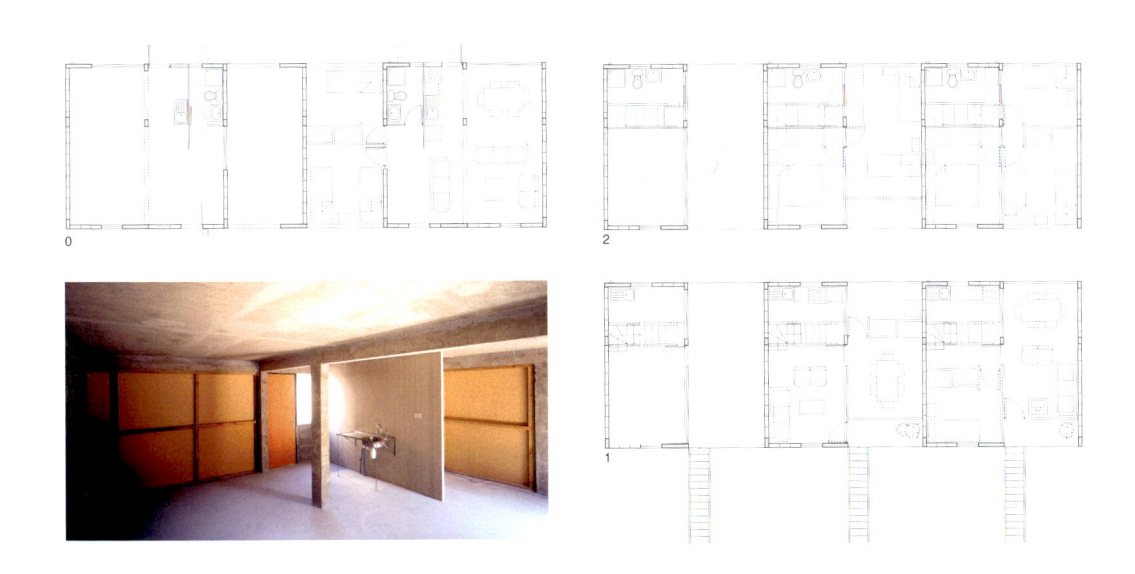

Coz, Polidura & Volante
Museum of the Atacama Desert
Antofagasta, Antofagasta (Chile)

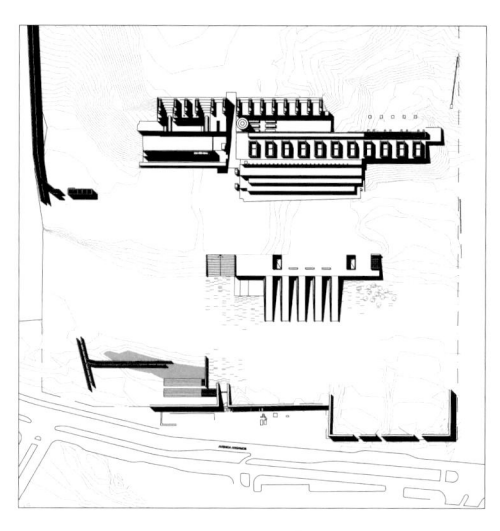

Client
Huanchaca Ruins Foundation
Architects
Ramón Coz, Marco Polidura, Iñaki Volante, Eugenia Soto
Collaborators
Carolina Agliati, Benjamín Ortiz, Diego Salinas, Carlos Valenzuela
Consultants
Santolaya Ingenieros Consultores (structural calculations);
Mónica Perez (lighting)
Contractor
Salfa Corp
Photos
Sergio Pirrone

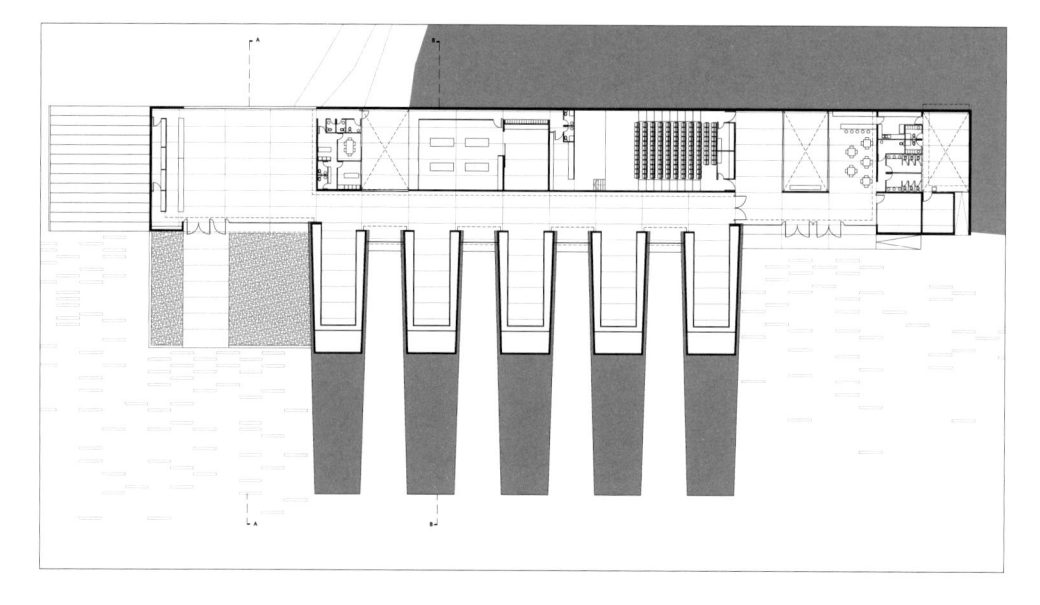

Located in Huanchaca Cultural Park, in the Atacama Desert, this museum is conceived as a mirador to the landscape and the archaeological ruins of the site, thus burying the exhibition halls under the ground.

WITH VIRTUALLY no rainfall in the course of the year, blocked from moisture by the Andes to the east and the Pacific coast range to the west, the narrow strip of land in northern Chile that is known as the Atacama Desert is said to be among the most arid places on the planet. The museum dedicated to it is situated on the southern outskirts of the city of Antofagasta, the country's mining capital, specifically beside the White Beach silver casting foundry that fell into disuse in 1902 and is known as the Huanchaca Ruins, a national monument since 1974.

Besides contributing to a large-scale urban development operation by helping to link the rapidly growing city to its no longer so distant monument, the project aimed to present the old solid masonry structures and immense walls in all their monumental splendor. So it is that the museum is mostly tucked underground, taking on a low profile in deference to the ruins, which are made to be perfectly visible not only from outside but also from within, thanks to large windows and three slightly sunken inner courtyards that simultaneously make for cross ventilation, a must in these climates.

The first courtyard engages visitors to appreciate both the museographic and the preservation activities being carried out in the institution's workshops, while the second, through operable frames, allows expanding the foyer of the auditorium and connecting it to the cafeteria, the souvenir shop and the services area located by the south entrance. The north entry has its own lobby, which serves as a temporary exhibitions hall. In this space, a long narrow fracture reveals the old ruins.

Five parallel ramps that are arranged perpendicularly to the silver foundry's rhythm of solids and voids rise from the dry terrain to the very foot of the ruins, connecting the seaward esplanade to the museum's roof terrace. The result, forming part of Huanchaca Park, is a magnificent venue for outdoor performances and events on desert evenings, stimulating the city's social, cultural and economic development. The museum's five permanent exhibition halls are housed inside these ramps and cover different fields addressing the land, life and skies of the Atacama Desert. Two of the halls tackle the geological eras that Atacama has undergone, another two are centered on mining and anthropology, and the last one is devoted to astronomy.

Atlas: America 283

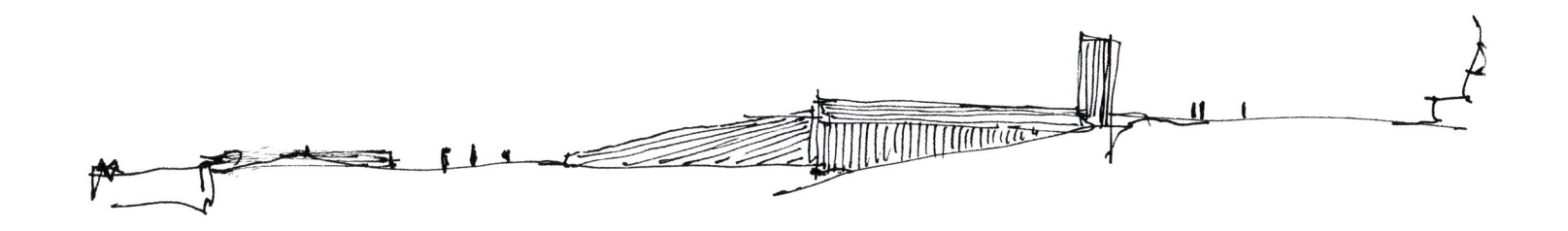

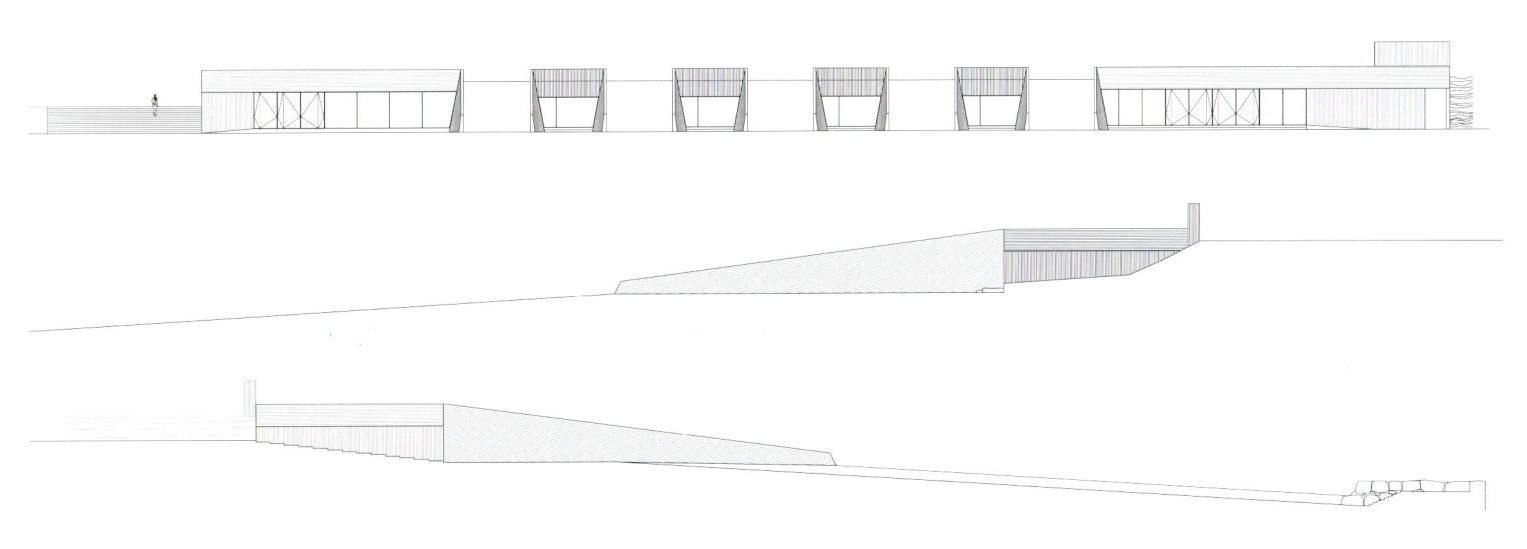

Two huge esplanades set at different levels are connected by five parallel ramps through the museum's roof, from where the visitor can contemplate the ruins of the foundry. The interior spaces are ventilated and lit through the strategic arrangement of large openings and courtyards slightly immersed in the ground, all with operable frames that make it possible to enlarge the exhibition halls and connect them to the foyer.

1. reinforced concrete wall
2. ledge of exposed reinforced concrete
3. overslab of washed reinforced concrete
4. reinforced concrete slab
5. floor of exposed reinforced concrete
6. aluminum profile frame colored dark bronze
7. fixture for fluorescent lighting
8. false ceiling structure
9. false ceiling of plasterboard to paint on
10. monolithic glass 12 mm
11. concrete pavement polished to a smooth finish
12. foundation

Atlas: America 285

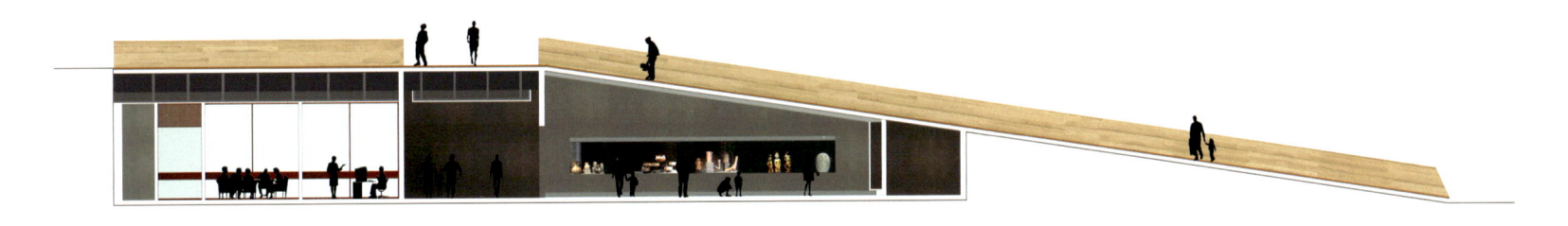

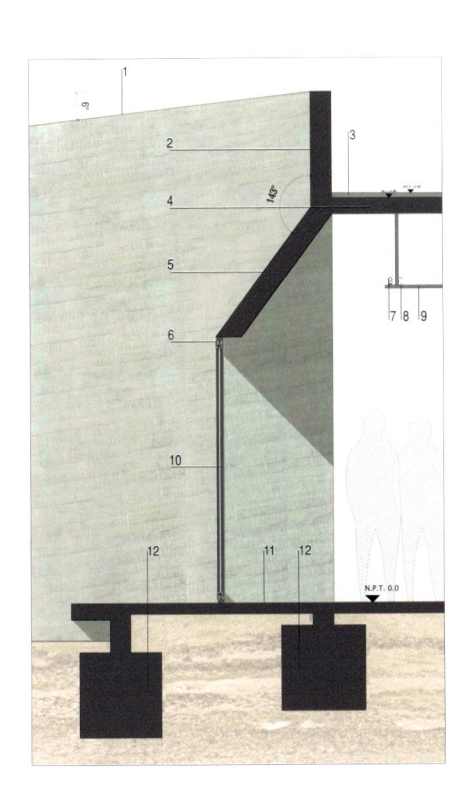

Cristián Undurraga
Retiro Chapel
Auco, Los Andes (Chile)

Architect
Cristián Undurraga
Collaborators
Cristián Larraín Bontá, Pablo López, Jean Baptiste Bruderer
Consultants
José Jiménez, Rafael Gatica Ingenieros (structural engineering); José Vicente Gajardo (altar)
Contractor
Terrano
Photos
Leonardo Finotti, Cristóbal Palma (p. 286 bottom), Sergio Pirrone (pp. 287, 289)

Located at the foot of Mount Carmelo, close to the guest house of the Sanctuary of Teresa de Los Andes and a Carmelite convent, the small chapel is conceived as a place of prayer and retreat for pilgrims.

SEVENTY KILOMETERS to the north of Santiago lies the Valley of the Andes, one of the most beautiful and agriculturally fertile areas of central Chile. There, near the city of Los Andes, are the Sanctuary of Teresa de los Andes and the Carmelite Monastery of Auco, and on the edge of the grounds, at the foot of Mount Carmelo, rises the Retiro Chapel. Standing by the guest house of the complex, the small building is conceived as a place of prayer for pilgrims who have come from afar in search of silence and retreat.

Following a strict geometry, the concrete volume rises from four hefty walls that are raised on blocks, also of concrete, then intersect to form a cruciform floor plan. Under the structure, with its gridded geometry, the ground was excavated to configure an irregularly shaped space delimited by a retaining wall of rustic stone surrounding the chapel in a random manner. It is conceived as a light well court that serves to insulate the inner space. Access into the chapel is through a snaking ramp situated on the north. Pilgrims descend it to reach the court, as in a processional path ending in the place of worship.

The interior is a box made of pieces of triangularly sectioned pieces of wood recycled from sleepers that were used in the past to build the railway lines traversing the country. The box literally hangs from the structure of reinforced concrete above it, the walls coming down to two meters above ground level to illuminate the nave from below and limit worshippers' views of the surroundings. That it seems to be in levitation contributes to the spirituality required of a temple, an atmosphere further heightened by the dark color of the wood and the lack of overhead lighting, the idea being to keep a house of prayer in penumbra. Here, contrast between rational exterior and metaphysical interior takes on a new expression of commitment to modernity.

Four blocks of concrete positioned on the terrain support a unique volume, also of concrete, that results from four beams intersecting to form a cross. Hanging from these beams is an enormous wooden box thought out to be a place for spiritual contemplation. A light well court delimited by a wall of rustic stone completely surrounds the innermost space, serving to nuance the passage of light and keep the house of prayer in penumbra.

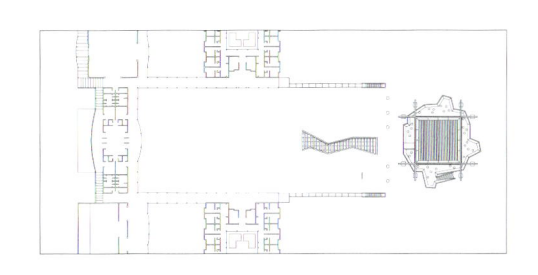

Atlas: America 287

Access to the chapel is by means of a ramp situated on the north side of the premises, along which pilgrims descend in a long processional route to the level of the court before finally entering the actual place of worship. The temple is conceived as a large levitating wooden box constructed with rectangularly sectioned pieces recycled from sleepers of the kind that were used in the past to build the railway lines traversing the country.

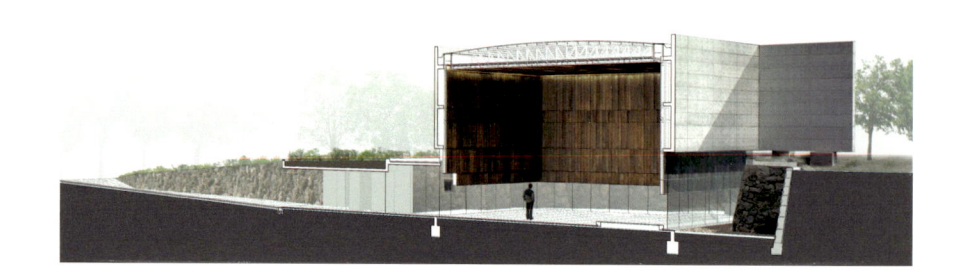

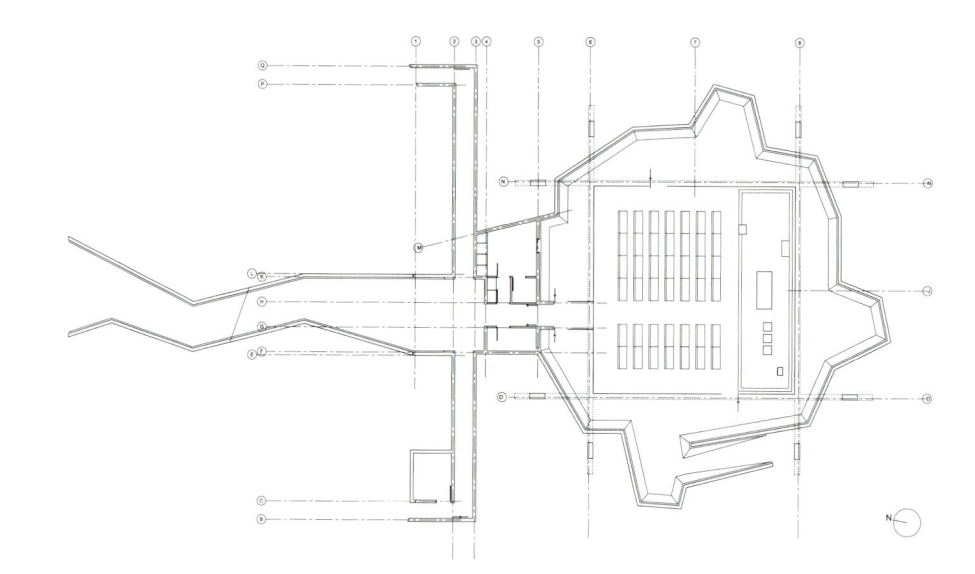

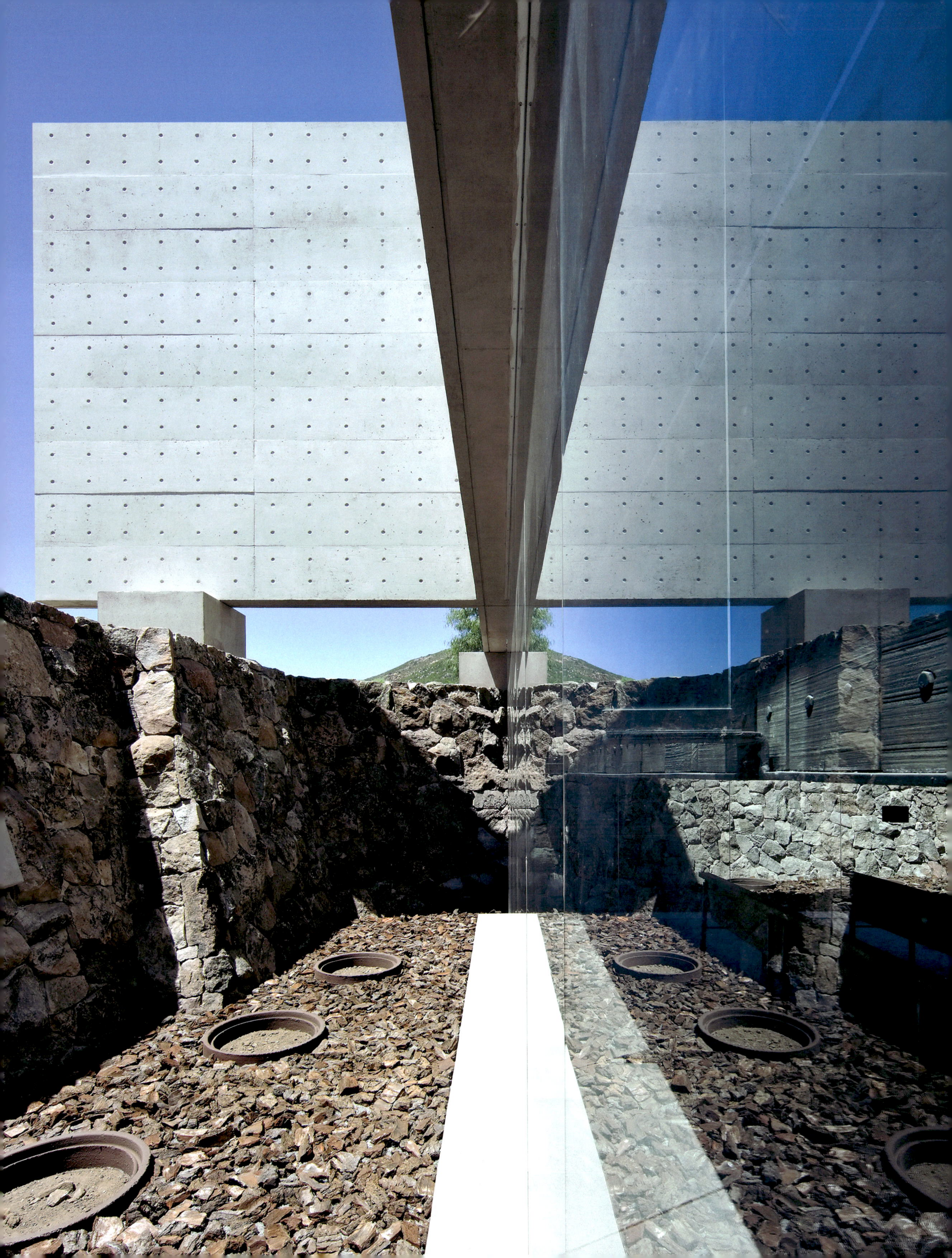

José Cruz Ovalle
Adolfo Ibáñez University Graduate Center
Peñalolén, Santiago (Chile)

Client
Fundación Adolfo Ibáñez
Architect
José Cruz Ovalle
Collaborators
Ana Turell, Hernán Cruz, Juan Purcell (associate architects); Mercedes García, Sebastián Maze
Consultants
Pedro Bartolomé / B&B Ingeniería (structure calculations); Marcelo Rodríguez / PRY (technical coordination and inspection)
Contractor
CYPCO
Photos
Roland Halbe; Juan Purcell (p. 291)

To blend in with the surrounding nature, the sinuous volumes of this academic building follow the curves of the topography, combining spaces for study and open areas for contemplation and strolling around.

THE GRADUATE CENTER is the latest addition in a large-scale operation that is currently being undertaken for a private university's newest campus in Peñalolén, on a slope in the outskirts of the Chilean capital. Besides a masterplan for the entire premises, the project involved the actual materialization of several buildings.

Those so far carried out resemble each other in material quality, color and formal language, but the most recently executed one, this graduate center, located a kilometer southeast of the rest, differs in its sinuous contours and in its volumes being set perpendicularly to the curves. In this way, instead of breaking away from nature, it seeks to merge with it. The complex addresses the slope as if it were a dimension of the place: the project unfurls northward to follow the direction of the valley, with sun-bathed patios set at multiple levels and traversed by suspended volumes that create shades. Through openings, these patios also look on to the south slope to receive the breezes blowing from that direction in the spring and summer months.

The building unfolds step by step, from tree to tree. It is not based on an abstraction of mathematical origins. Rather, its lines are traced by carefully addressing the rocks on site, skirting foliage, opening up to the beeeze or casting shadows in the patios.

The work pursues the objectives laid down at the origin: in the university, movement is intimately linked to the circular, which, with its pauses and stops, sustains the relationship between study and contemplation. In a spatiality that reveals itself at the prospect of multiple itineraries, each person chooses a particular route, so traveling from one point to another takes on the nature of a promenade. The space is continuous but never homogeneous, with twists and turns and variations of size and light, creating numerous sequences that give motion through the campus a sense of expectation: each step gives rise to new visions. The rise and fall of the terrain is repeated inside through many levels connected by ramps and stairs, transcending the usual order of 'floors'.

The center is hence an extension of the idea of architecture as simultaneously an opening or internal void and a spatial unfolding that accompanies nature to create a habitable outer perimeter. The work introduces natural light in a different way and from diverse directions to make it appear in permanent transformation. But it does so in a way that is not literal, the skylights not being simply elements that make its capture possible, but thought out to together build a sculpture of light.

The building is constructed with reinforced concrete that is painted white, thus receiving the same superficial treatment as the partitions, the stone walls and the structural elements. These contrast with the plinths of dark stone and the elements of light-colored wood that appear in the doors and the furniture. The pavements of the patios are of stone in combination with natural rocks, trees and bushes. The indoor floors are clad with bright vinyls.

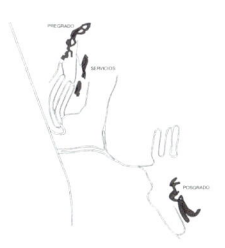

The latest campus of Adolfo Ibánez University is perched on the slopes of the hill of San Ramón, in the outskirts of the Chilean capital. About a kilometer southeast, some 600 meters further uphill, rises this new center for graduate-level studies: an ensemble of organically shaped volumes with walls of reinforced concrete painted white, plinths and pavements of dark-toned stone, and wooden frames and finishes.

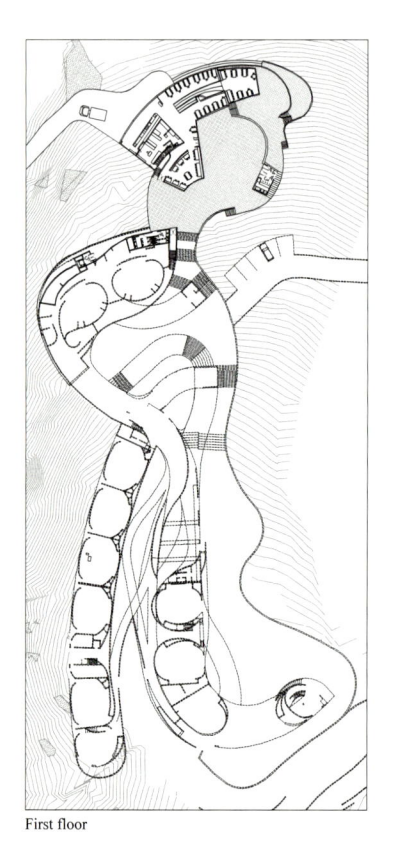

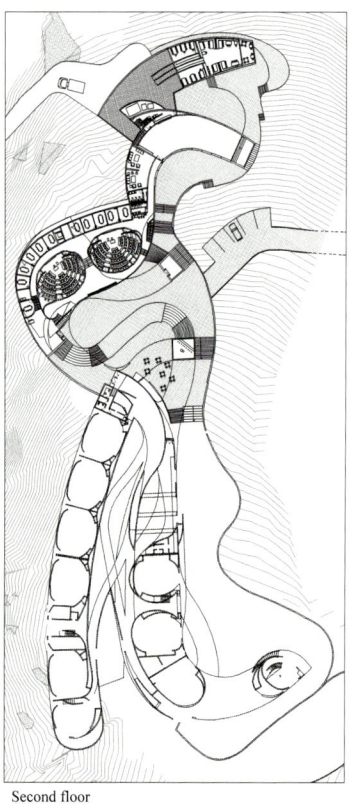

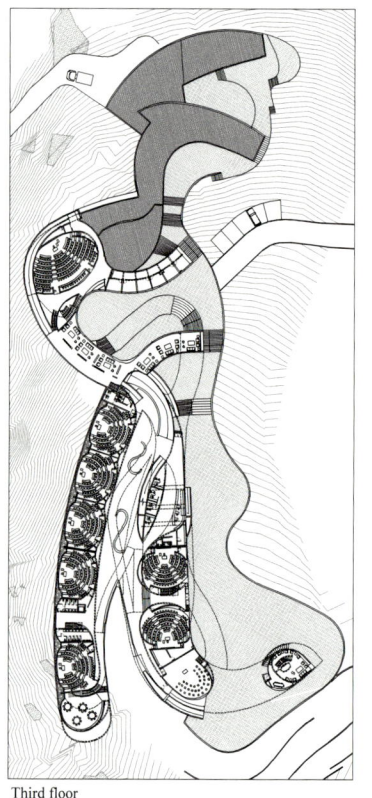

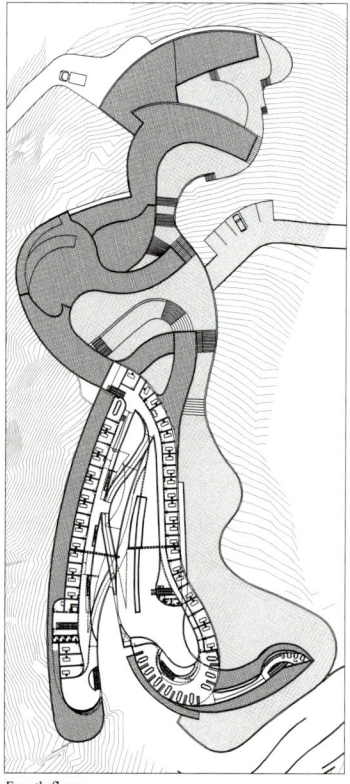

First floor   Second floor   Third floor   Fourth floor

292 Atlas: America

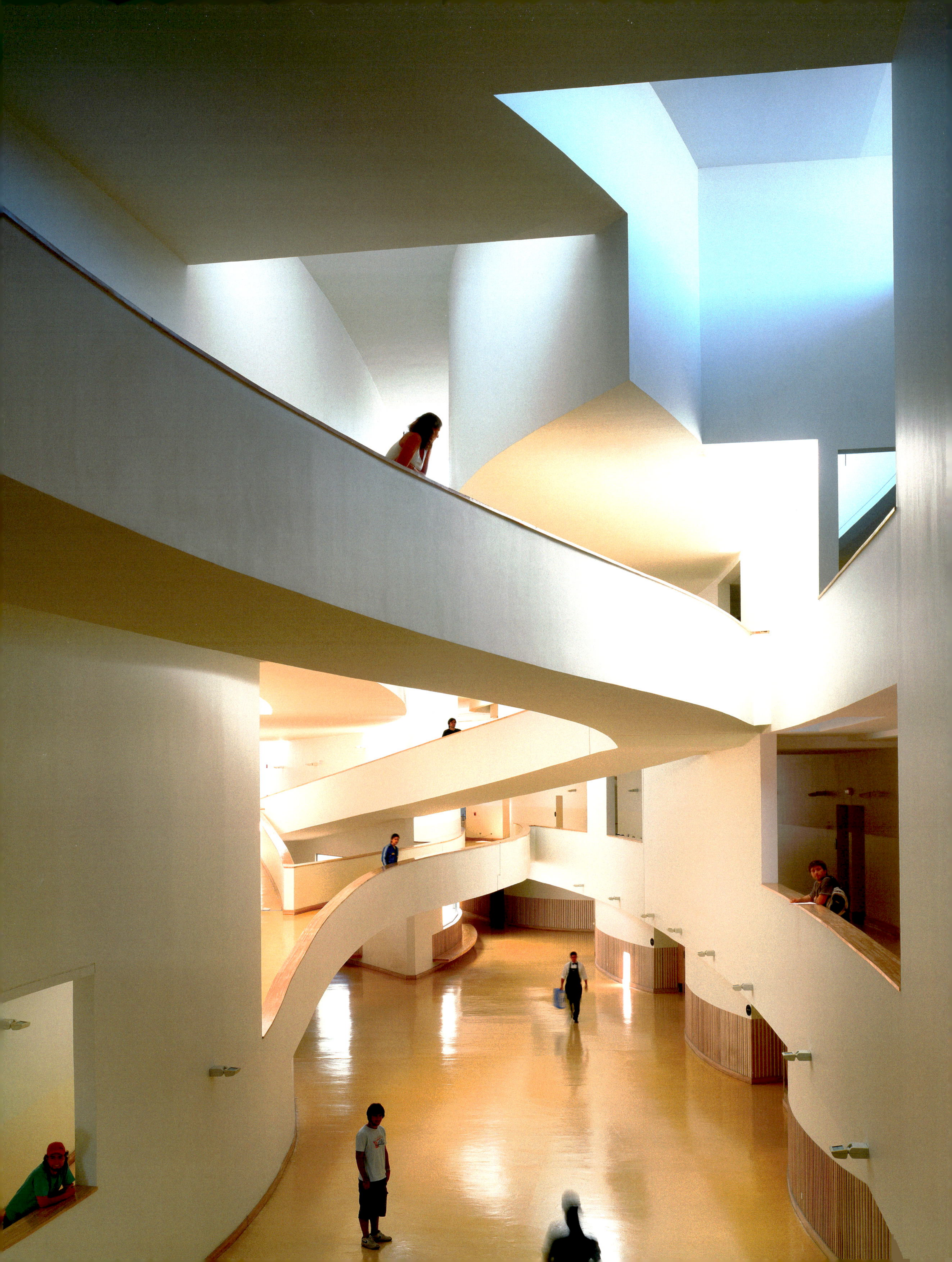

Alberto Mozó
Office Building
Providencia, Santiago (Chile)

Architect
Alberto Mozó Leverington
Collaborators
Francisca Cifuentes, Mauricio Leal
Consultants
Juan López (structural engineering); Gastón Villaroel (electricity)
Contractors
Arauco, Constructora Las Torcasas
Photos
Cristóbal Palma

The main facades of the building were carried out with laminated pieces of wood taken from renewable forests, and by means of a dry construction system that made it possible to raise them in a single day.

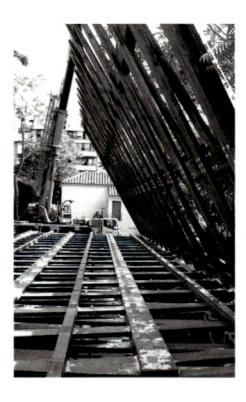

The new offices of the company BIP Computers are located in a residential enclave in the commune of Providencia, in Santiago Province. Urban planning regulations applicable to the area allow a height of up to twelve levels. The answer to this here is a volume rising only three floors and the preservation of three one-family houses that were built on the site back in 1936. In view of possible future sale of the lot, with the attendant demolition of the building, it is constructed entirely in laminated wood, making it easy to disassemble and reassemble elsewhere, recycling all the materials.

The wooden frame was put together with a single section – 9 centimeters long and 34 centimeters wide – used for the pillars, the beams, and the steps of the main staircase. The choice of Monterey Pine wood taken from renewable forests was the result of environmental considerations, which deemed that using this as building material would send fewer carbon dioxide emissions into the atmosphere.

The building's two main facades – each of them with an area of 260 square meters and weighing 12,000 kilograms – were put up in a single day. This was followed by the installation of prefabricated slabs of reinforced concrete – 30x30 centimeter squares resembling floor tiles, reinforced with metal meshes – underneath the floating wood flooring. These slabs perform better against fire and their thermal mass makes for greater energy efficiency.

Thermal and acoustic glazing consisting of double-glass windows completes the construction, with a translucent layer of polyester 15 millimeters thick giving it reflective properties. This has the effect of reducing the solar radiation penetrating it, thereby curbing both heat loss during the winter season and excessive heating in the summer months, ultimately minimizing overall energy consumption.

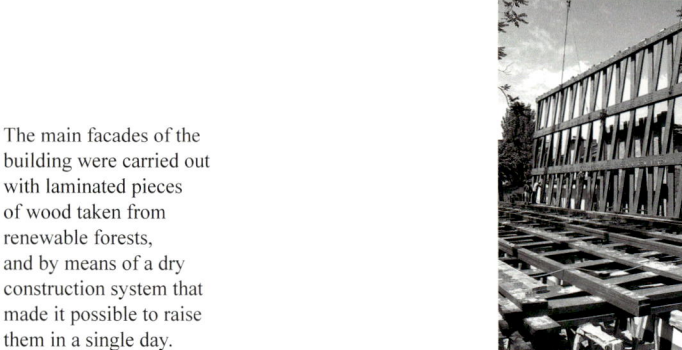

The new office building of the company BIP Computers rises on a small lot in a residential neighborhood of the commune of Providencia, in Santiago Province, between two one-family houses constructed on the site back in the 1930s. The program is organized on three open floor plans containing communal workspaces, individual offices, meeting rooms and washroom areas, all connected to one another by a spiral staircase.

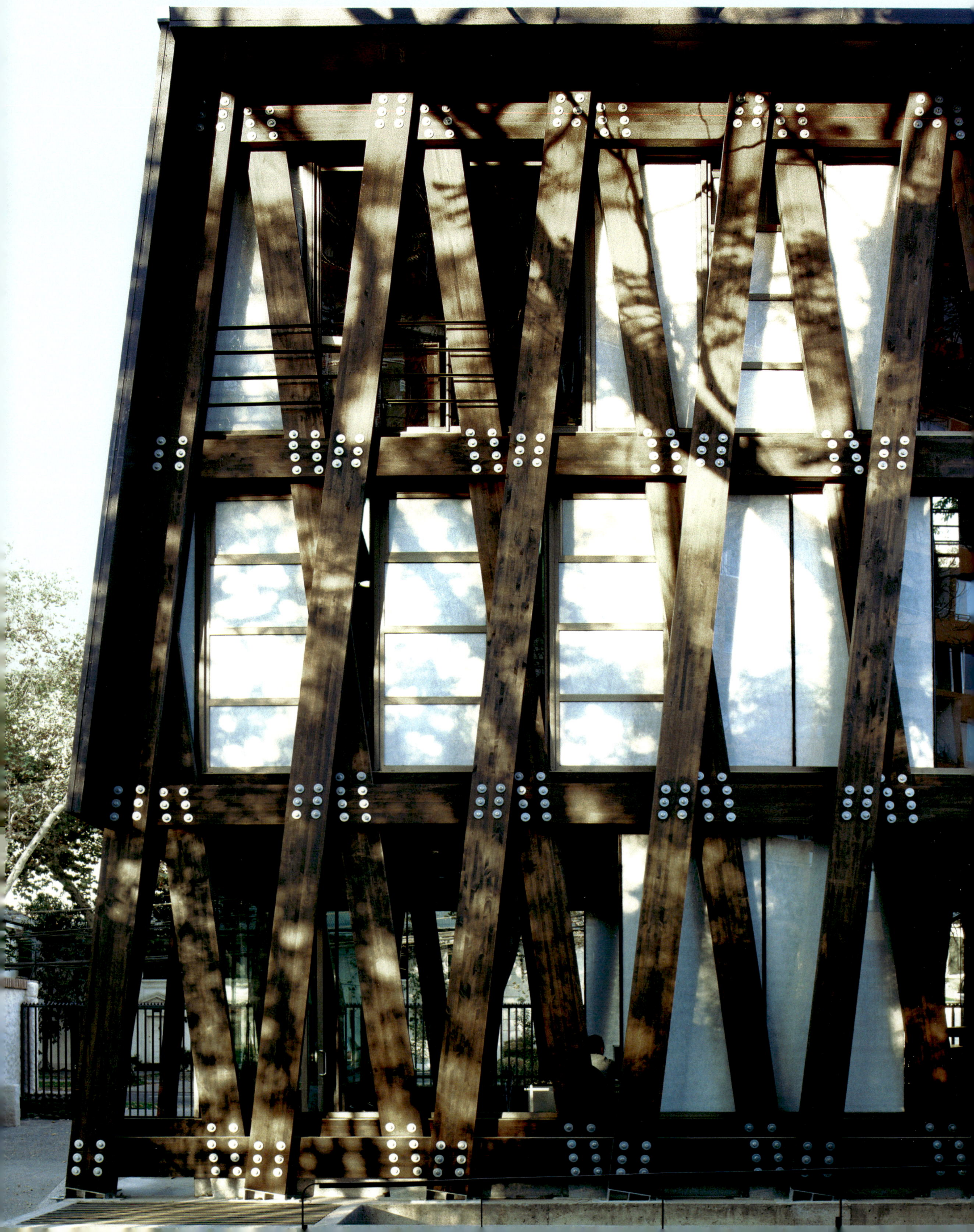

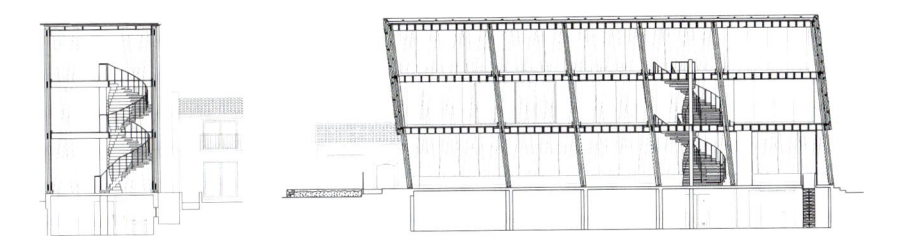

The entire structure is built with a single section of pinewood measuring 9 centimeters long and 34 centimeters wide, and it is used for the pillars, the beams and the steps of the main staircase. The facade is executed with thermal glazing formed by double-glass windows, with a layer of translucent polyester that reduces the intensity of solar radiation in the interior during the summer and prevents heat loss in the winter.

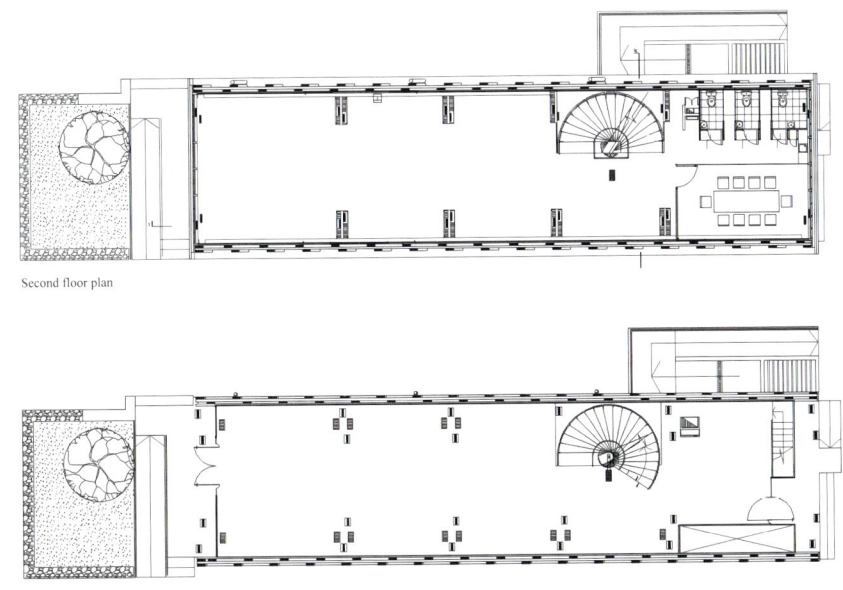

Second floor plan

First floor plan

Atlas: America 297

FAR, Frohn & Rojas
Wall House
Santiago (Chile)

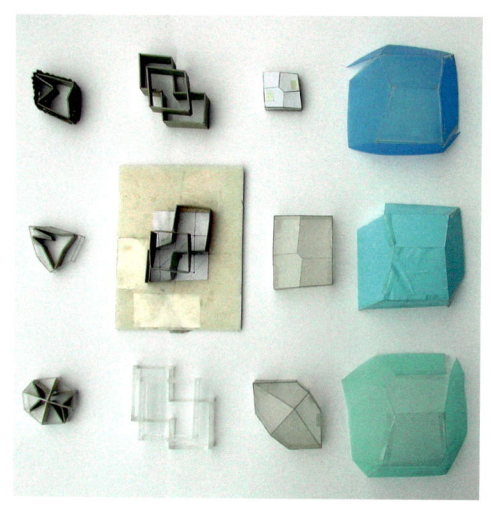

Client
Patricia Krause Senft
Architects
Marc Frohn, Mario Rojas
Collaborators
Amy Thoner, Pablo Guzmán, Isabel Zapata
Contractor
Constanzo ERIL
Consultants
Ingewag, Mario Wagner, Ernesto Villalón (structure); Nelson Quilaqueo, Central TechnoPlus/Vaillant, Christian Aguirre (bioclimate project)
Photos
Cristóbal Palma

THIS SINGLE-FAMILY house on the outskirts of Santiago escapes the noise of the Pan American Highway to embrace the slow pace of rural paths. Tall shrubs delimiting the lot it stands on, cut out against the silhouette of the Andes Mountains, enhance its isolated character. The idea of the dwelling as a set of clear-cut separations between interior and exterior is challenged, giving way to a scheme where the transition from one to the other is hazy.

The building comes about through the superposition of four envelope layers. The first is an inner core of structural reinforced concrete, clad on the inside with ceramic tile so that, working as a wet cell, it contains the house's two bathrooms. Wrapped around this nucleus is a perimeter of two large lattices built with engineered wood, formwork panels and plywood. The two lattices are stacked, one on the other, but shift position in relation to each other, so that the upper band cantilevers out by as much as 5.2 meters. The space surrounding these structures is organized to be a social zone at ground level and a workspace upstairs. The lattices are boarded up in some parts. Elsewhere they are left open to be used as shelves all along the building's envelope. A translucent skin of high-insulation polycarbonate panels unfurls around these shelves, registering shadows of trees and other outside elements and flooding the interior space with natural light while ensuring climate control. At some points, polycarbonate gives way to transparent insulating glass.

Finally a fabric of polyethylene mixed with aluminum, of the kind that is typically used in greenhouses, forms the house's outermost shell, which varies in density, depending on orientations. This veil also acts as an energy screen, filtering out as much as 70% of the harsh Chilean sunshine received by the building while serving as a protective barrier against insects.

Inspired by a camping tent, this single-family house rises on a skeleton of concrete and laminated wood, and is clad with a translucent thermal fabric that also serves to filter the views of the surrounding landscape.

Rendering the separation between interior and exterior spaces hazy, the house incorporates a complex envelope of four superposed layers. Around a core of reinforced concrete unfolds a play of lattices of laminated wood that act as structural supports and are covered with a translucent polycarbonate skin, over which is spread a fabric of polyethylene that serves, among other things, to regulate the inflow of the harsh Chilean sunshine.

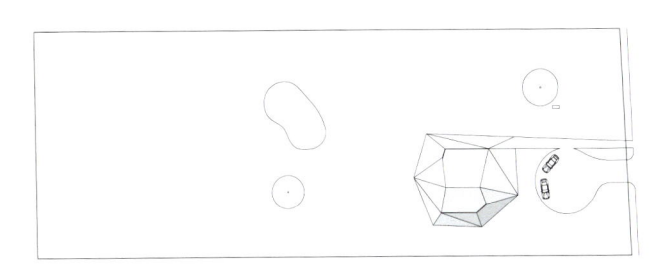

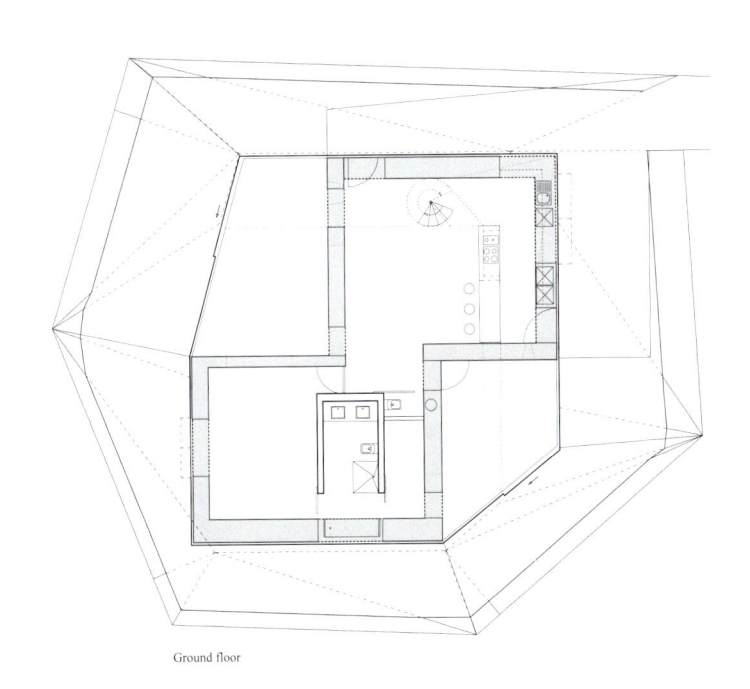

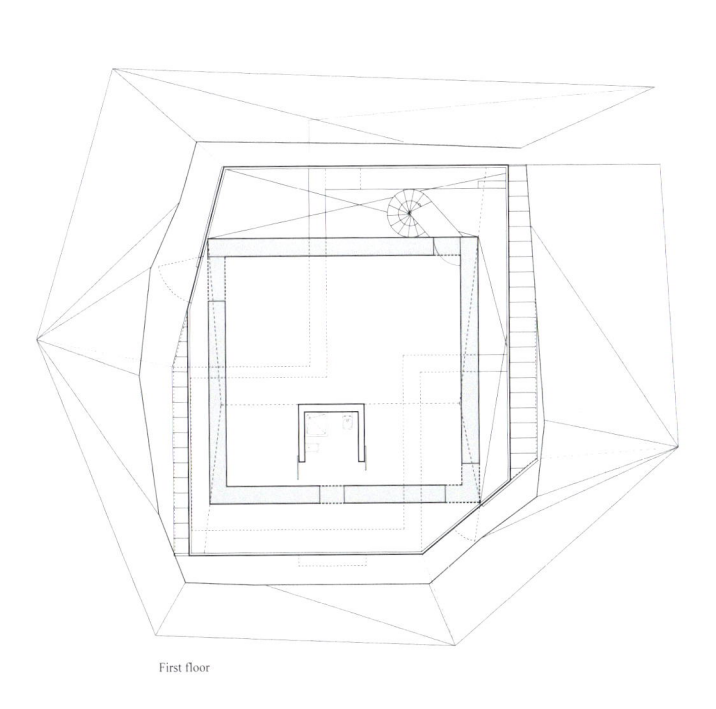

Ground floor

First floor

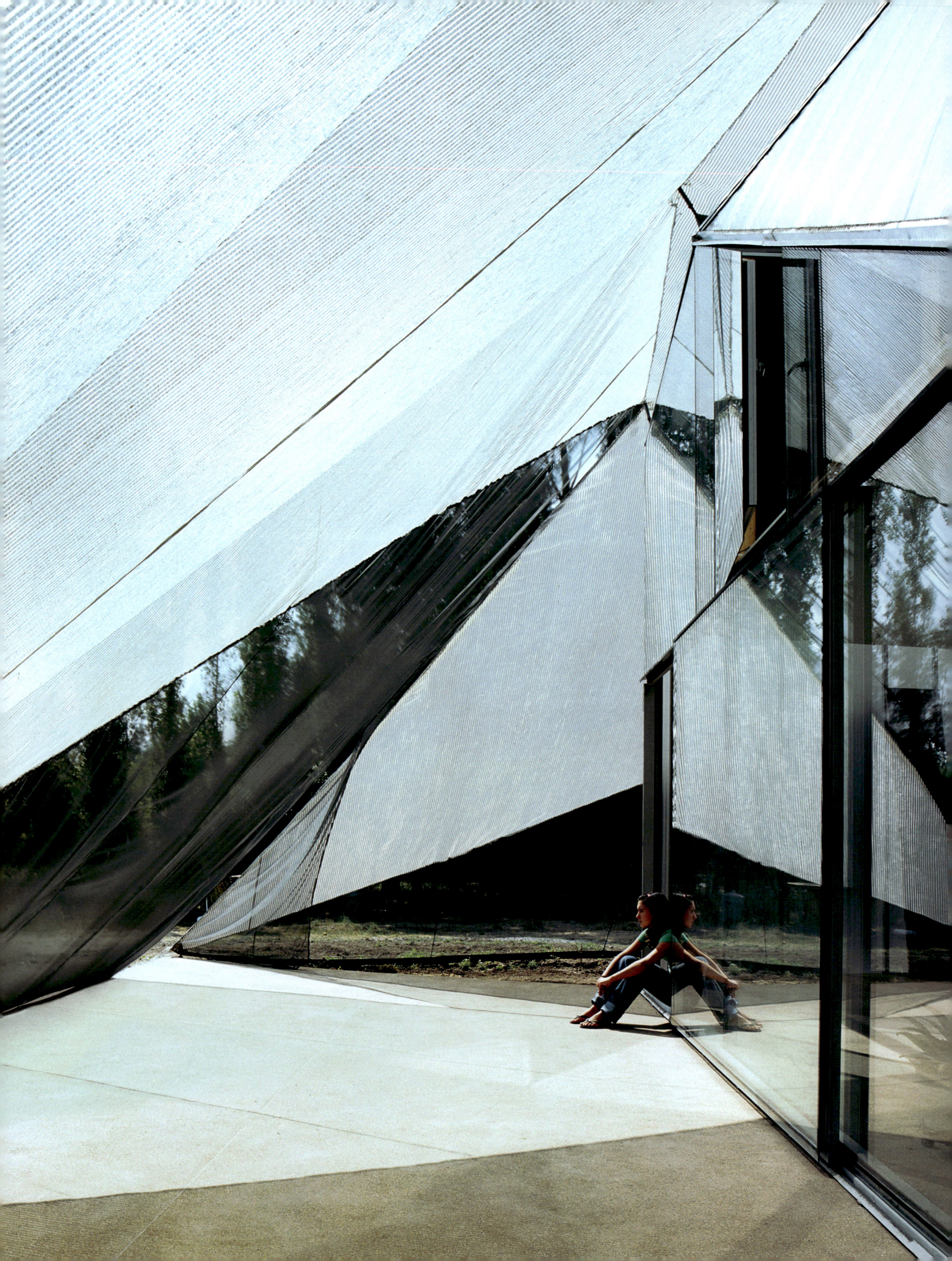

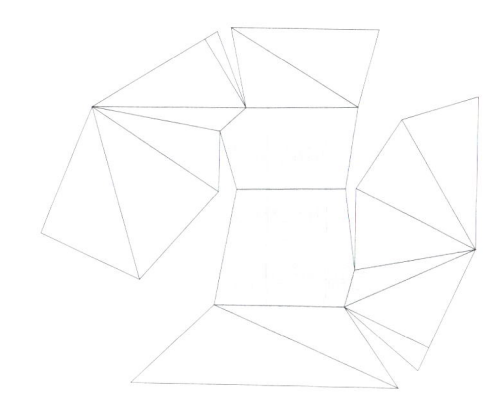

1. reflecting layer of aluminum-lined high-density polyethylene
2. polycarbonate panels 40 mm thick and thermopanels made of two transparent insulating glass sheets
3. structural plywood ledge
4. exposed aggregate concrete 10 mm
5. reinforced concrete slab 150 mm
6. polyethylene tubes for radiant heating
7. styrofoam insulation thermal panels 30mm thick
8. plywood sheets 18 mm
9. beam of yellow pine plywood 2"/8"
10. gypsum board 10 mm thick

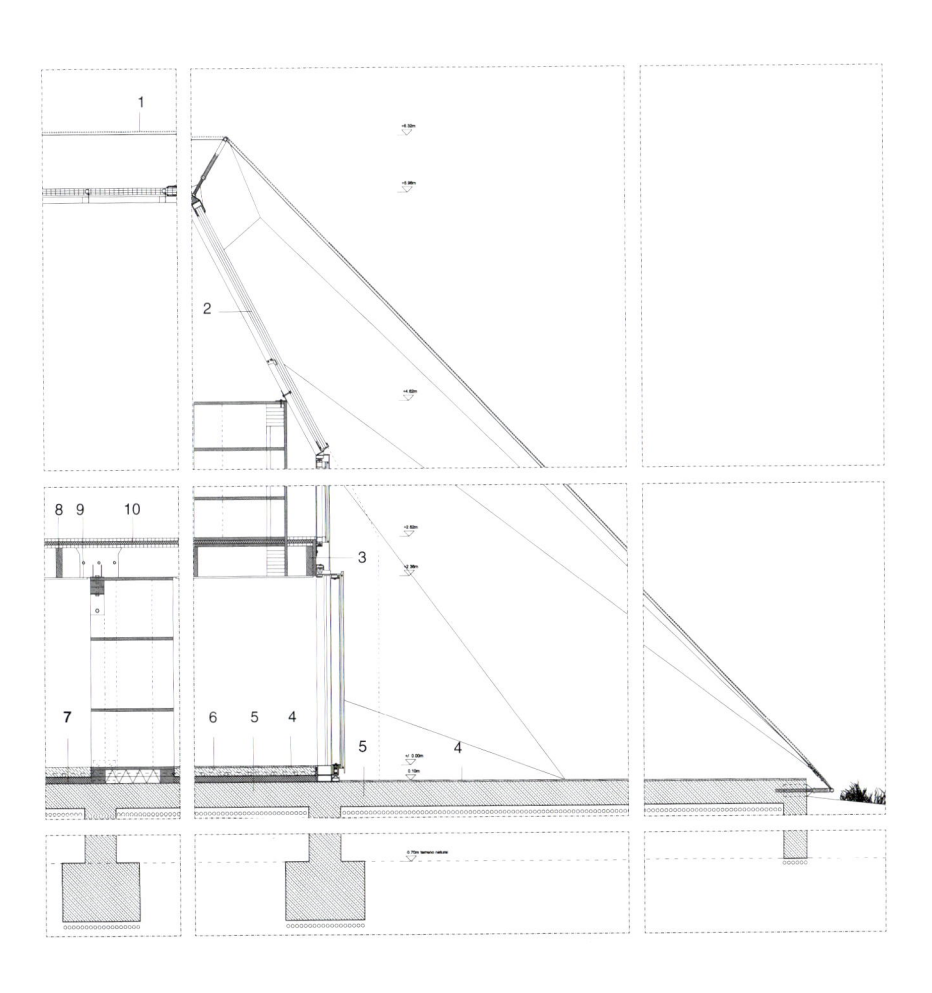

Atlas: America

Pezo & Von Ellrichshausen
Parr House
Chiguayante, Concepción (Chile)

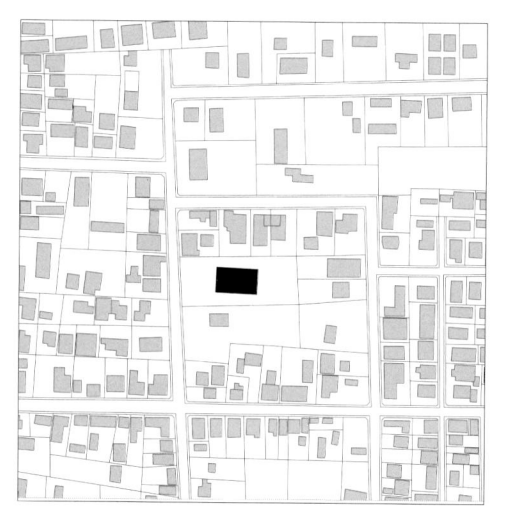

Architects
Mauricio Pezo, Sofía von Ellrichshausen
Consultants
Claudio Sepúlveda (structure); Marcelo Valenzuela, Juan Aroca, Mauricio Comas (installations); Juan Mellado, Carolina Merino, María Paz Palma (models)
Photos
Cristóbal Palma

SITUATED IN A mountainous landscape that is characteristic of the commune of Chiguayante, northwest of the city of Santiago, this unique one-family house stands on a small farm estate where the owner spent his childhood, a place lush with local vegetation including a wide variety of trees, from palm to *araucaria* and cherry to walnut. The program unfolds horizontally on the property in a single level, through separate pieces chained to one another and accommodating different uses, in accordance with the scheme of the typical Chilean country house.

Built with traditional materials evoking the old wooden farmhouse that stood on the site until not long ago, fourteen prisms are truncated to allow the zenithal lighting of the interior spaces, which are organized in an irregular and rather labyrinthine arrangement around nine open-air inner courtyards. These openings are positioned in such a way that they have the effect of alleviating the density that come from chaining together all the rooms at ground level. There are no very large rooms, but instead small spaces intended for specific uses, some of these made roomier by raising the ceiling to the equivalent of two floors.

Over a framework constructed with large pinewood trusses go the pitched roofs clad with small metal tiles. The use of this material to build traditional roofs illustrates the at once industrial and artisanal conception of the project. The exact locations of the truncations accommodating the aluminum-framed skylights are strategic, each case in close coordination with the position of the furniture and also depending on the dimensions of the room. Because the roofs are markedly steepened and made to descend toward the courtyards, there are hardly any shadows cast in these exterior spaces, which then fully perform their role as markers of a transition between the house and the surrounding landscape.

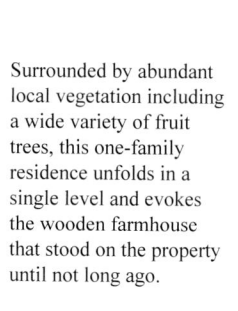

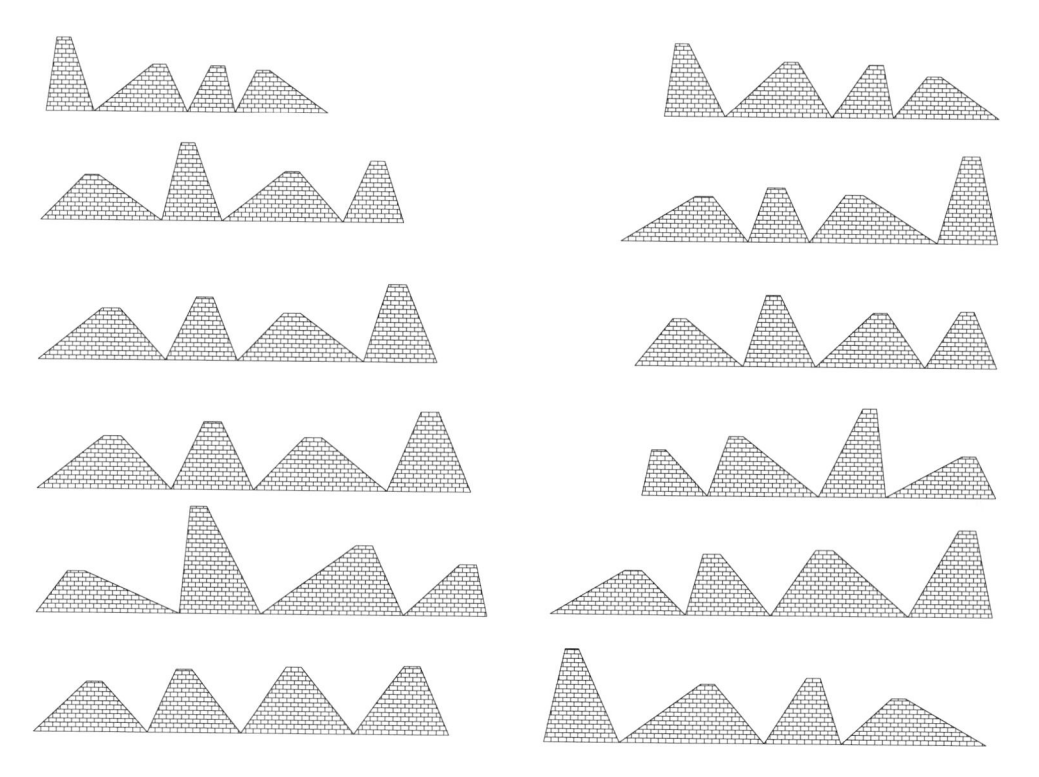

Surrounded by abundant local vegetation including a wide variety of fruit trees, this one-family residence unfolds in a single level and evokes the wooden farmhouse that stood on the property until not long ago.

Truncated prisms built with traditional materials contain the various rooms of the house, which are organized around nine courtyards that string together the volumes in an irregular, somewhat labyrinthine arrangement. The courtyards serve to mark a transition between the interiors and the surrounding garden area, while alleviating the density that results from concentrating the domestic spaces on the ground level.

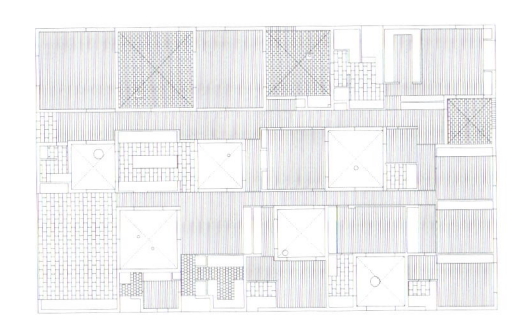

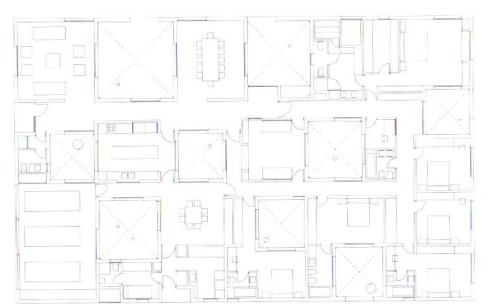

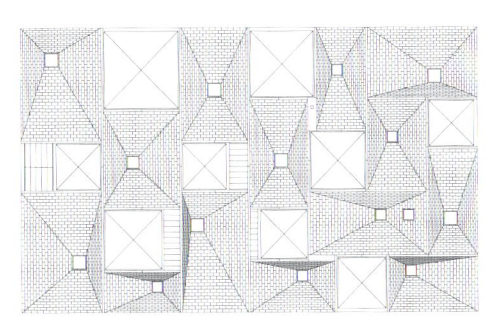

Each of the volumes has a structure built with pinewood trusses, over which rises a pitched roof clad with metal tiling that opens on top to illuminate the interior through large aluminum-framed skylights. These overhead openings are positioned strategically, in accordance with the size of the room in question and the specific use assigned to it, or depending on the arrangement of the furniture pieces inside.

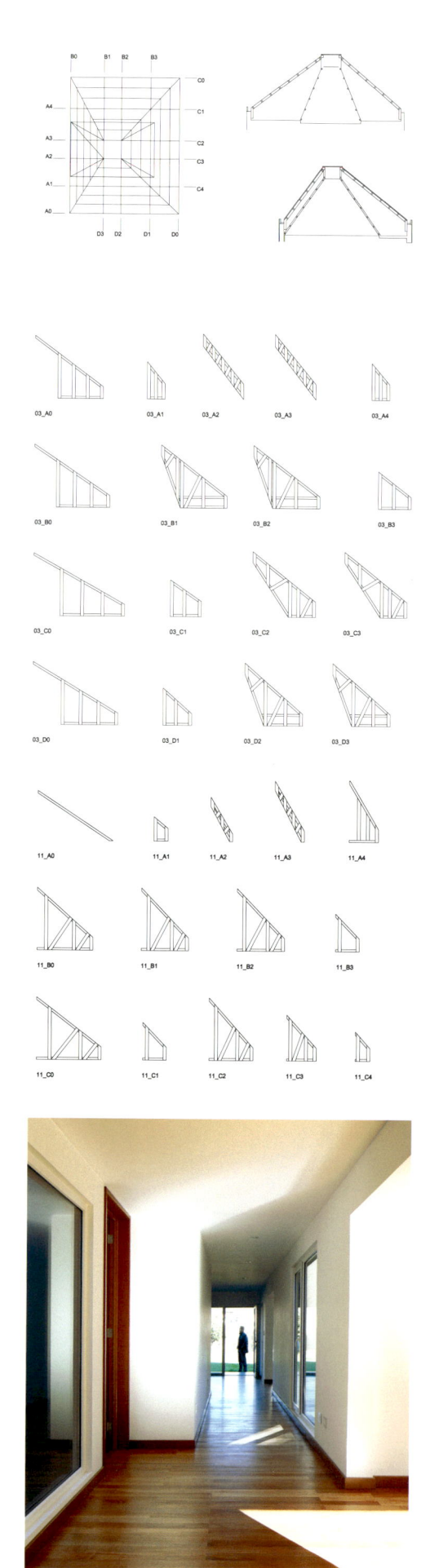

1	25x45 cm metal tile with thermal glaze	7	stucco, 25 mm plastering and painting mortar	15	wood floor board
2	vapor barrier	8	reinforced concrete	16	suspended ceiling
3	pinewood strip separated 40 cm	9	natural ground	17	pinewood cleat
4	15 mm structural slab	10	10 cm hardcore bed	18	pinewood beam
5	thermal insulation, 30 mm mineral wood	11	vapor barrier, 0.05 mm polystyrene membrane	19	thermal insulation
6	PVC frame painted in white and walnut	12	10 cm concrete layer	20	roof structure
		13	leveling mortar	21	aluminum skylight
		14	pavement cleat	22	bricklaying
				23	15x15x10 cm paving granite stone floor

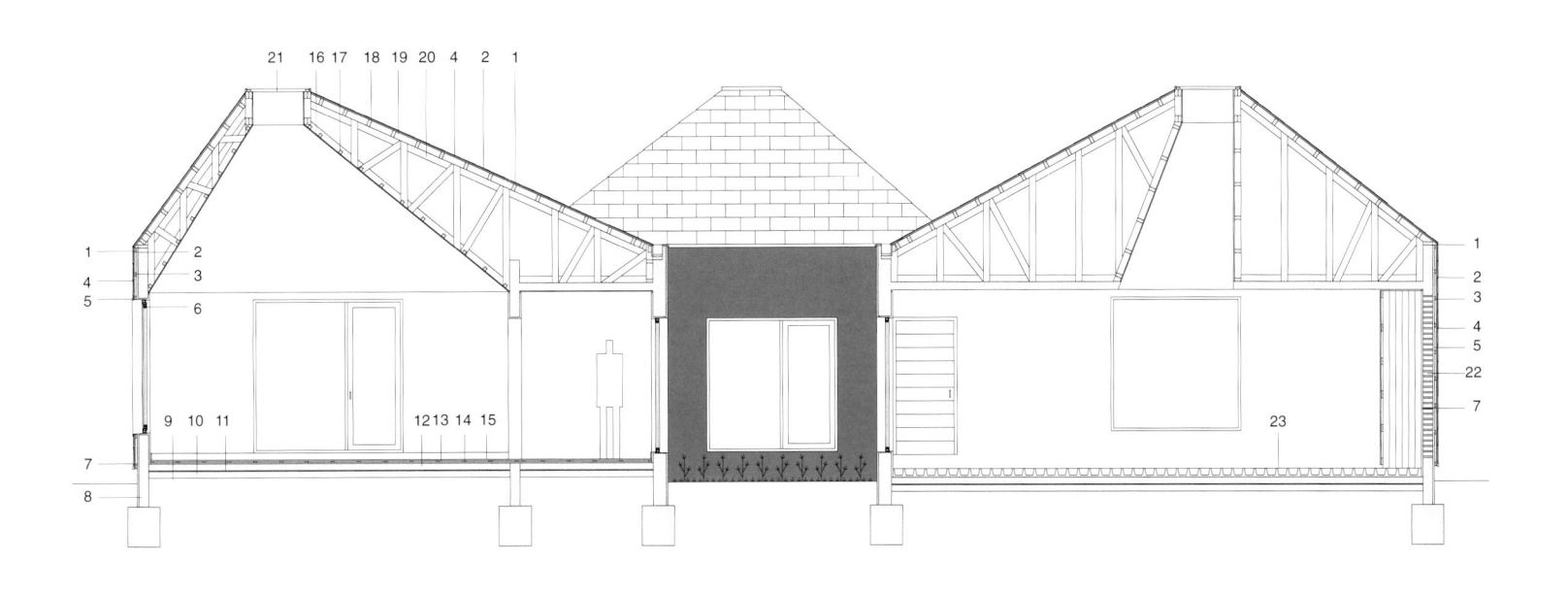

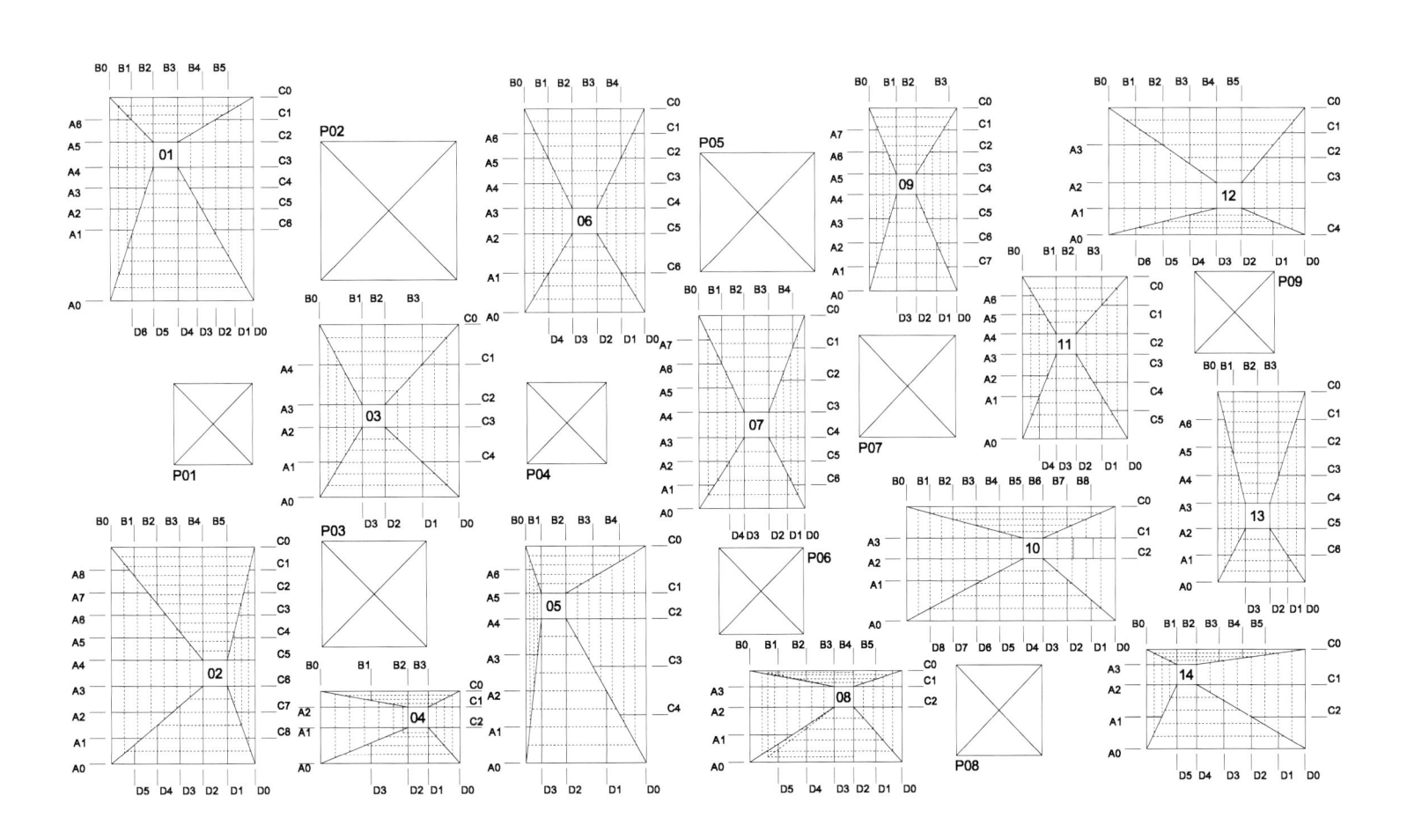

Atlas: America 305

Smiljan Radic
Copper House 2
Talca (Chile)

Client
Manuel O'Ryan, Constanza Pérez
Architect
Smiljan Radic
Collaborators
Loreto Lyon, Danilo Lazcano, Augusto Vergara, Gonzalo Torres, Hugo Lagos (model photos)
Contractor
Covasa
Photos
Cristóbal Palma

Clad with modularized lighweight copper sheets arranged over a structure of steel, this one-family residence located between mountain ranges echoes the surrounding land's thick carpet of fallen leaves.

THIS ONE-FAMILY residence is located between the precipitous mountain ranges stretching parallel to the coast to the west and the Andes, a few kilometers from the Chilean city of Talca. The copper sheet that covers the roof and the exterior walls – the architect's second experiment with this material, after the house he built in Nercón – is instrumental in defining the building's exterior image, to the point of giving it its name. In the previous house, the undulating texture of the copper seemed to take on a historic role, copying the claddings of galvanized steel that were used for the houses and churches of Chiloé until the early 20th century. In this construction, too, the texture imitates certain general features of the surroundings.

Modularized in lightweight sheets 38.5 centimeters wide, 95 centimeters tall and 0.5 millimeters thick, the alloy of eletrolytic metal makes it possible to configure a volume that echoes the abundant layers of fallen leaves carpeting the surrounding land. As for the volume itself, simple geometries give way to an outline that undergoes slight deformations here and there to vary the ceiling heights on section, in accordance with the uses of the succeeding interior spaces. The rectangular perimeter of the house is also altered to make the most of the northern light.

The floor plan is an inversion of the CR House in Santiago, which was built a year before. At the center of the single level is an inner courtyard with a wooden floor, around which the various rooms are arranged. The layout of the domestic program is such that the three bedrooms are separated from the house's shared areas. The light that comes in through the courtyard guides interior circulation in winter, and in summer the glazed surfaces open up to allow diagonal movement. In this way, the different rooms merge with the garden and landscape in a single uninterrupted space.

On land situated outside the city of Talca stands a compact construction that is perforated in the interior by a narrow courtyard with a wooden floor, around which the different spaces of the private dwelling are organized on a single level. During the winter months, the residents circulate around this void, whereas in summer, its glazed surfaces are opened to allow diagonal movement and generate spatial continuity.

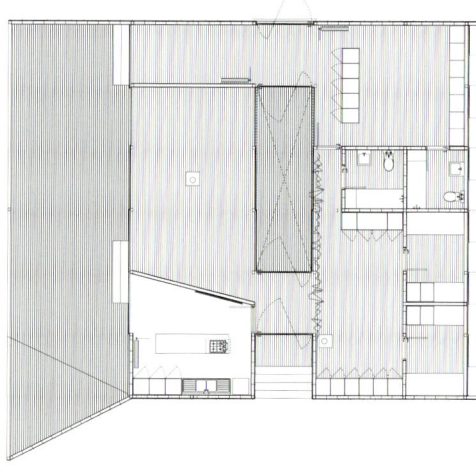

1. cladding of electrolytic copper crimped and modularized in sheets 38.5 cm wide, 95 cm tall and 0.5 cm thick
2. plasterboard panel painted white
3. cladding with board of wooden sheets
4. pavement of wooden floating floor
5. operable wooden frame
6. collapsible stainless steel frame
7. structure of stainless steel profiles
8. foundation, footings of reinforced concrete

Atlas: America 309

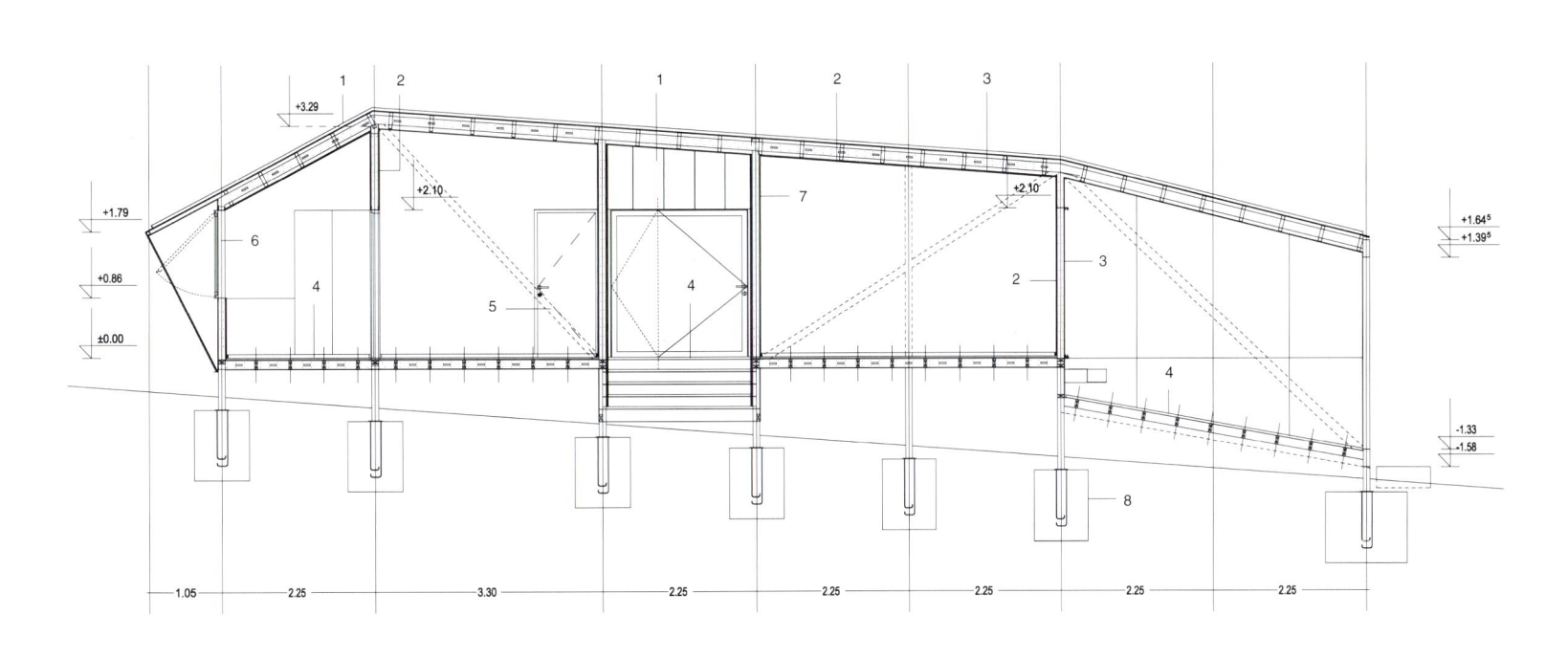

Grupo Talca
Tourist Shelter and Observation Decks
Panguilemo, Talca (Chile)

AT A DISTANCE of forty kilometers from the city of Villarica is a small community of woodcutters formed by eleven families dedicated to the exploitation of local tree species (*mañío, tepa* and *coigüe*) and the cultivation of land for their own subsistence. Aware of the need to preserve the environment, the young members of the community have developed an agrotourism project to ensure that the woods are reforested whilst offering trails for hiking and horseback riding to excursionists. The resulting alteration of the environment made it necessary to build a hut that could be a shelter for hunters in the winter and an orientation and meeting point for trekkers in the summer, as well as a vantage point from which to contemplate the landscape that stretches from the Villarica volcano to the Calafquén and Panguipulli lakes.

Furthermore, creating a new route connecting Chile's inland drylands through the coastal mountain range are seven 'modules' that act as markers along the route and serve as spots where naturalists stop to rest and view the surroundings. They are built with frameworks of pieces of pinewood obtained through the recycling of timber offcuts of the kind used by the region's wood industries to turn on their boilers.

Architects
Stockpiling hut and observation deck in Pinohuacho: Rodrigo Sheward Giordano
Miradors along inland drylands route: Ronald Hernández, Marcelo Valdez, Osvaldo Veliz
Collaborators
Stockpiling hut and observation deck in Pinohuacho: Germán Valenzuela
Miradors along inland drylands route: Kenneth Gleiser
Consultants
Miradors along inland drylands route: Maderas Bravo (wood)
Photos
Cristobal Palma,
Germán Valenzuela (p. 311 bottom),
Blanca Zuñiga (p. 312)

Built with 96 pieces of recycled *coigüe* wood taken from the woods of Pinohuacho, a small resting hut serves as a shelter for naturalist tourists in the summer and a refuge for hunters of wild boar in the winter.

Situated approximately eighty meters from the resting hut, at the highest point of the slope, a small observation deck offers a sweeping panorama of the Villarica volcano and the Calafquén and Panguipulli lakes beyond. A wooden fence marks the boundary that separates the naturalist tourism areas from the pastures for livestock, and delimits the road reserved for excursionists arriving on horseback from the nearby woods.

Atlas: America **311**

312   Atlas: America

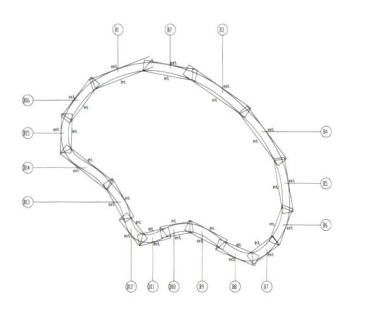

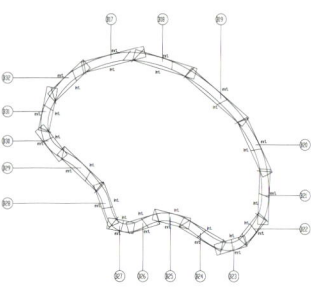

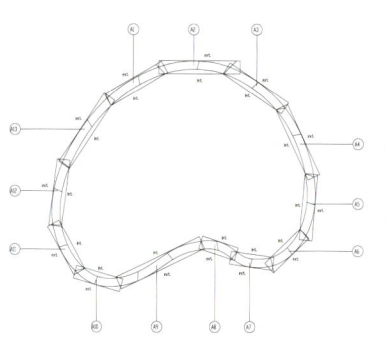

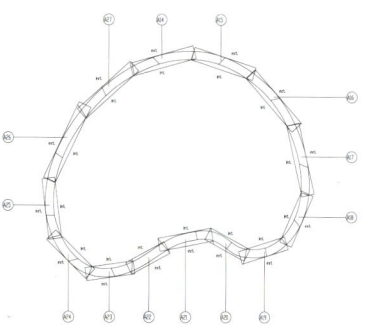

Seven unique observation decks have been erected all along a seasonal migration route stretching 138 kilometers that connected the coastal mountain range of Chile to the country's inland drylands. They are built using offcuts of pine timber salvaged from the region's wood industries, each 50 centimeters long, and grouped to create the 16-centimeter modules that serve to form the structural framework of the pieces.

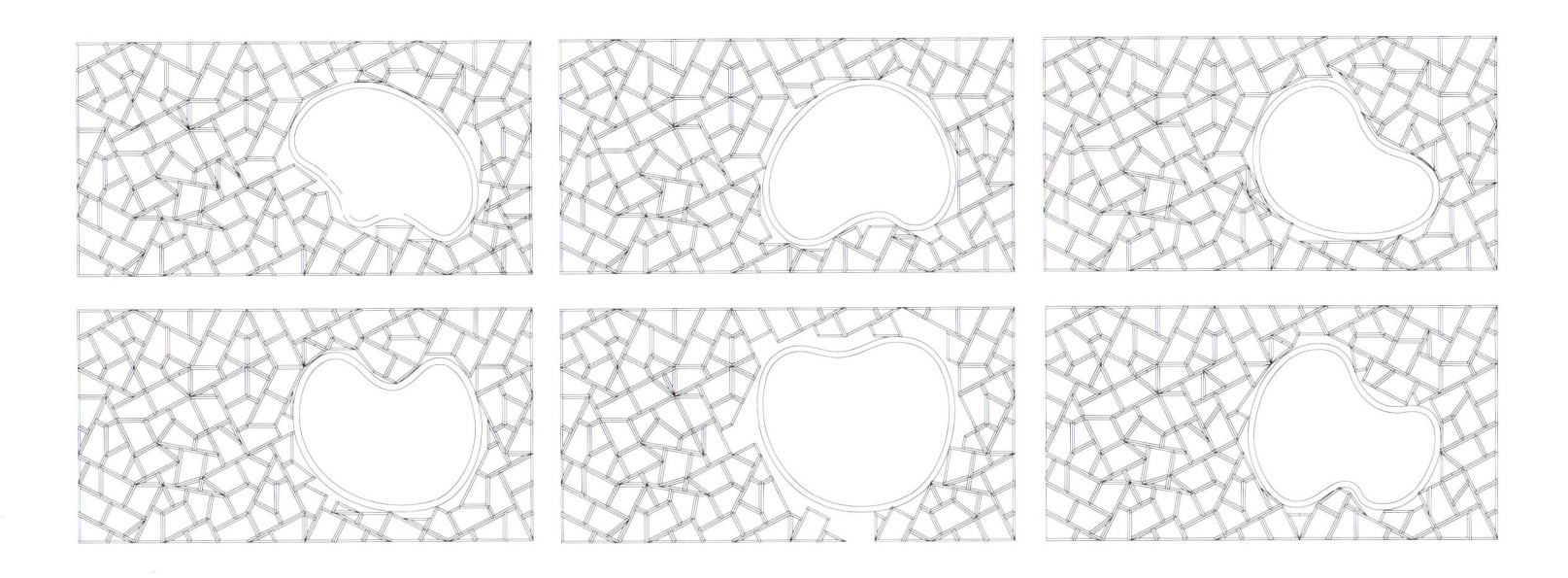

Germán del Sol
Hotel Remota
Puerto Natales, Patagonia (Chile)

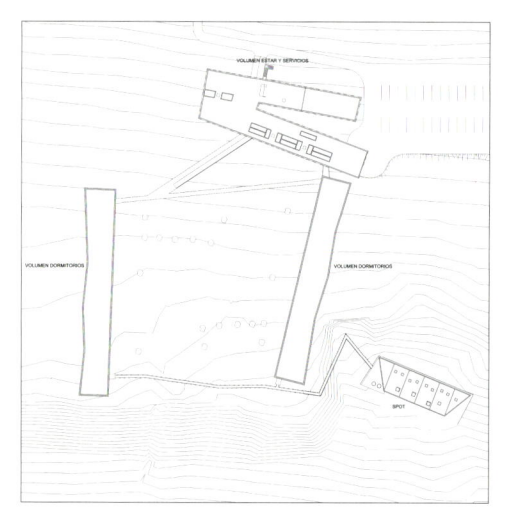

Client
Inmobiliaria Mares del Sur
Architect
Germán del Sol
Collaborators
José Luis Ibañez, Francisca Schüler, Carlos Venegas
Consultants
Pedro Bartolomé (structure); Carlos Pérez (installations); Carlos Marnell (electricity)
Contractor
Salfacorp
Photos
Cristóbal Palma

The program of the hotel complex is distributed in three buildings that are arranged to form a U, which adapts to the slope of the terrain as it stretches on and opens to impressive views of the Patagonian landscape.

IN THE SOUTHERN tip of Chile, between the Almirante Montt Gulf and the Última Esperanza Inlet, is the city of Puerto Natales, the location of this hotel complex with a floor area of some 5,000 square meters. The program is distributed in three buildings that form a U opening on to the impressive landscape. The 72 double-height bedrooms take up the two long volumes, which adapt to the sloping terrain as they stretch on, while in a third structure, a V-shaped main building, are the hotel's common facilities: dining room and sitting areas, the kitchen, administrative offices, accommodations for the staff, and two large multipurpose halls at the vertex that enjoy views of the cordillera and sea. A small construction that is slightly separated from the main building contains the swimming pool and some saunas and outdoor jacuzzis.

The field around which the main pieces are arranged brings the wilderness into the heart of the hotel. Its pasture vegetation has been preserved, and the odd boulder here and there, of the kind that abounds in this area with such a recent glacial past, reinforces the sense of emptiness of the place. This wild central plaza is traversed by long corridors, some covered and some not. Connecting the hotel spaces to one another, they allude to the paths long used to drive herds of sheep from the stockyards to the shearing barns of the region.

The landscape of southern Chilean plains colonizes the roofs, whose concrete slabs are coated with a carpet of grass grown over an asphalt membrane, which in turn is covered with black gravel for protection against ultraviolet rays. This same kind of membrane, which comes in rolls, is glued to the rainproof and windproof plywood panels enclosing the buildings' concrete structures of pillars, slabs and walls. The continuity of the facades are interrupted by PVC frames and double-glass panes that bathe the interior with the ever-changing Patagonian light.

Atlas: America 315

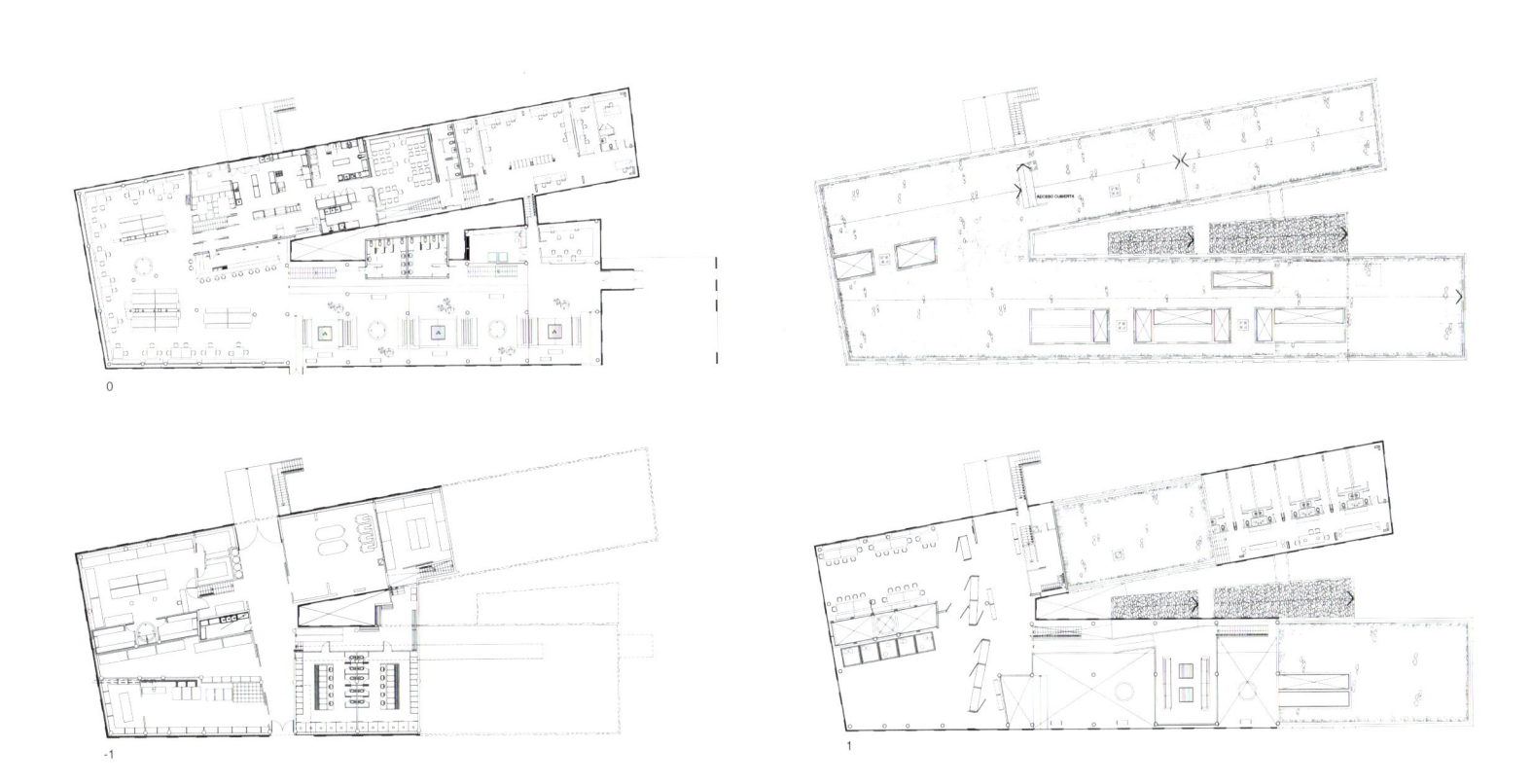

The different parts of the complex are organized around a large central open field dominated by the pasture vegetation of the place and oriented towards views of the cordillera beyond. The two longitudinal volumes accommodate the guest bedroooms, while the V-shaped volume contains the common facilities, service spaces and administration areas. All these hotel spaces interconnect by means of long corridors.

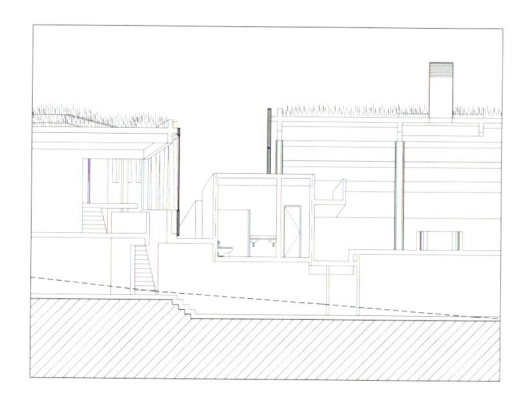

316 Atlas: America

1. lightened concrete
2. layer of expanded polyurethane
3. PVC rigid window frame
4. rain run-off of folded zinc sheet
5. Aislapol-type insulation
6. asphaltic membrane painted green
7. OSB sheet, 12 mm thick
8. smooth protective membrane
9. wooden strip, 4.5 cm wide
10. rain pipe, 115 cm thick aluminum profile
11. thermal panel for PVC window
12. U-shaped metal profile
13. volcanic sheet with plaster finish painted white
14. slate stone, 0.8 cm edge
15. PVC window frame, curtain wall
16. concrete slab, 14 cm thick
17. wooden strip, varnished and brushed
18. beam of reinforced concrete
19. concrete slab, 16 cm thick

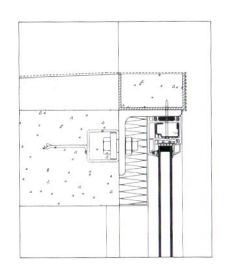

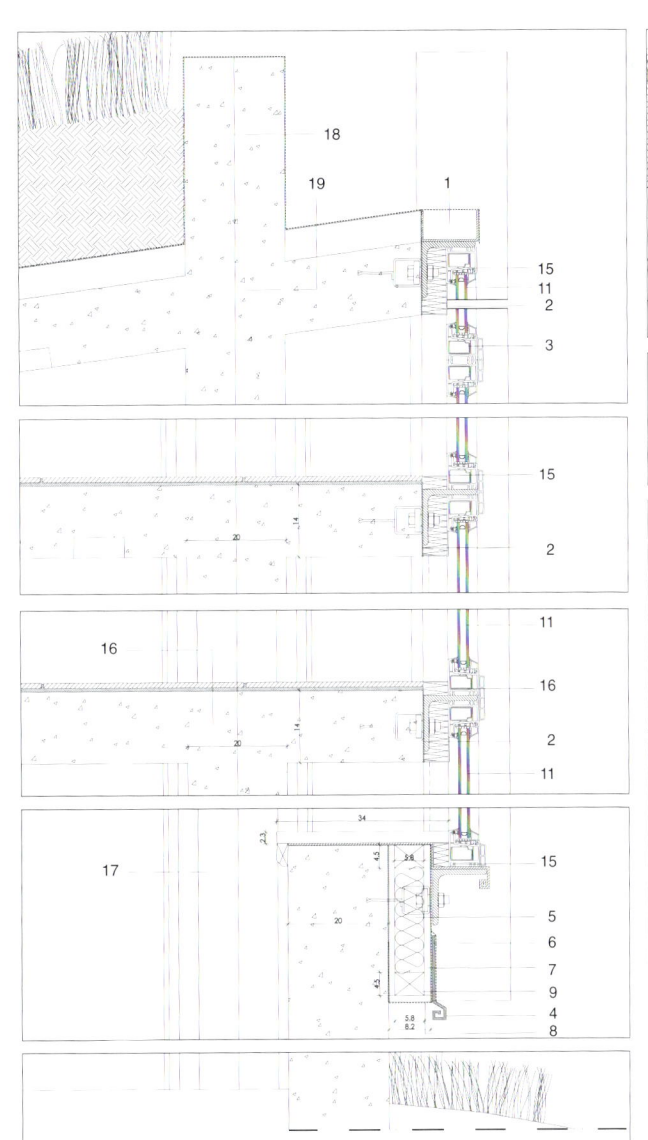

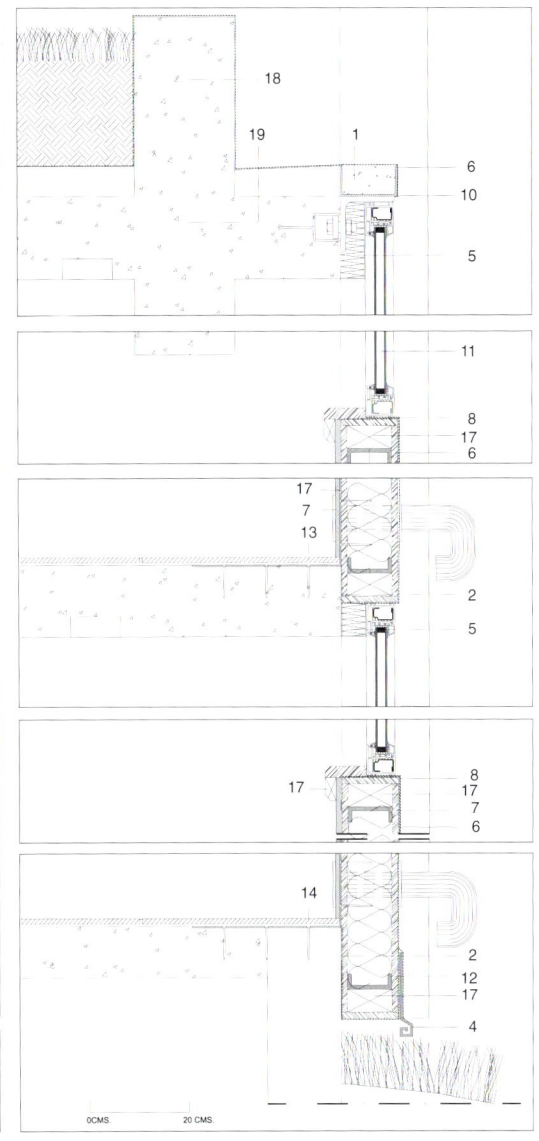

Photographic Credits

Authors of images illustrating the works published in detail appear in the data list of the respective projects. The following list serves to credit photographs found in the articles or elsewhere in the publication. The numbers refer to the corresponding pages.

Oscar Abarca: 132. Silvia Arango: 165 (bottom), 167 (bottom). Tom Arban: 19, 21 (top). Iwan Baan: 11, 22, 36, 38 (bottom), 39, 41 (bottom), 149 (bottom), 164 (bottom). Bak Arquitectos: 243. Alejandro Balaguer/Albatros Media: 133. Carlos Barrado: 245. David Barragan: 197. Marco Antonio Borsoi: 215 (bottom). Jomar Bragança: 219 (bottom). David Chipperfield Architects: 41 (top). Daniel Contreras: 200. Cordon Press: 130, 131. Sebastián Crespo: 199 (bottom). Jean Pierre Crousse: 195. Rodrigo Davila: 163 (bottom). James Dow: 20 (bottom), 21 (bottom). João Filgueiras Lima: 213 (top). LeonardoFinotti: 212 (top), 213 (bottom), 244 (top), 246, 247 (top). Tom Fox, SWAGroup: 37 (bottom). Joana França: 219. Luis Mauro Freire: 218 (bottom). Gustavo Fritegotto: 242. Paolo Gasparini: 144 (bottom), 145 (top). Juan Carlos Gaviria: 163 (top). Sergio Gómez: 169 (top). Enrique Guzmán: 166. Pedro Hiriart: 104 (bottom), 111 (top). Roberto Huarcaya: 196. Tadeuz Jalocha: 270. Yoshihiro Koitani: 105. Nelson Kon: 214 (top), 217 (bottom). NASA: 8, 9, 12, 34, 102, 128, 142, 160, 192, 210, 238, 268. Jaime Navarro: 111 (bottom). Fin O'hara: 20 (top). Jorge del Olmo: 109. Cristóbal Palma: 271 (top), 272, 273 (bottom), 275 (bottom), 277 (top), 279 (bottom). Franklin Pardon: 274. Sandra Pereznieto: 106. Maciá Pinto: 145 (bottom). Sergio Pirrone: 276. Sergio Recabarren: 279 (top). David Rego: 216. Christian Richters: 40 (bottom), 136. Paul Rivera/archphoto.com: 107. Marisol Roca: 137. Carlos Mario Rodriguez: 164 (top). Nicolás Saieh: 277 (bottom). Hugo Segawa: 215 (top). Shai Gil Photography: 15. Rodrigo Sheward: 278. Gustavo Sosa Pinilla: 241 (bottom). Ten Arquitectos: 110. Cristián Undurraga: 273 (top). Roman Viñoli: 241 (bottom). VSV Asociados: 240. Paul Warchol: 14, 16, 37 (top). Guy Wenborne: 271 (bottom).

Contributors

Silvia Arango (Bogotá, 1948) studied architecture at the University of the Andes, is a graduate in Urban Design from Oxford Polytechnic and earned her doctorate in Urbanism at the University of Paris XII. She teaches the masters degree in Architectural Theory and History and is the doctorate coordinator at the Arts School of the National University of Colombia. Visiting professor at universities in Puerto Rico, Brazil and Mexico, she has written several articles on Latin American architectural history. Her book *Las seis generaciones que construyeron América Latina. Arquitectura y ciudad,* will appear soon.

Trevor Boddy (Edmonton, 1953) is an architecture critic, consulting urban designer and curator of exhibitions like *Vancouverism: Architecture Builds the City* for the 2010 Olympic Winter Games, after previous showings in London and Paris. He has written for such magazines as *Architectural Record, Canadian Architect* and *Architectural Review,* and for newspapers like *Vancouver Sun* and *Seattle Times,* and has participated in several architecture competitions as both juror and organizer. His book *The Architecture of Douglas Cardinal* was named Alberta Book of the Year.

Frederick Cooper (Lima, 1939) graduated from the School of Architecture and Urbanism of the Engineering University of Peru. Nikolaus Pevsner was his tutor during his postgraduate studies in England, where he collaborated in *Architectural Design,* then edited by Monica Pidgeon. In Lima he created the studio Cooper, Graña, Nicolini, whose long list of works includes the prized headquarters of the Agrarian Bank in Cusco. Founder of the magazine *Arkinka* in 1996, he has written for many architectural journals, and since 2008 is dean of architecture at the Pontifical Catholic University of Peru.

Thomas Fisher (Cleveland, 1953) graduated in architecture from Cornell University and is a professor and dean of the College of Design at the University of Minnesota. He was editorial director of *Progressive Architecture* magazine in Connecticut, and has lectured or juried in several schools of architecture and professional societies. Among his published books are *In the Scheme of Things: Alternative Thinking on the Practice of Architecture, Salmela Architect, Architectural Design and Ethics: Tools for Survival,* and the recently released *Ethics for Architects.*

Jorge Francisco Liernur (Buenos Aires, 1946) is an architect, dean of the School of Architecture at the Torcuato Di Tella University, and researcher at the CONICET (National Committee of Scientific and Technical Researches) of Argentina. He has been invited professor in universities such as Harvard, the ETSAUN of Pamplona, the Central University of Venezuela and the Catholic of Chile. Author of articles published in prominent international architecture magazines, he has written books like *America Latina, gli ultimi vent'anni* and *Trazas de futuro. Modernidad y arquitectura en América Latina.*

Louise Noelle (Mexico City, 1944) graduated in History of Art from the Iberoamerican University, and obtained her masters degree from the UNAM. Editor of the magazine *Arquitectura/México* between 1976 and 1980, she is a researcher at the UNAM's Institute of Aesthetic Researches and professor of Architectural History in the same center. Member of the Academy of Arts, of the International Committee of Architectural Critics (CICA) and of DOCOMOMO International, she has written books like *Arquitectos contemporáneos de México* and *Ricardo Legorreta, tradición y modernidad.*

Fernando Pérez Oyarzun (Santiago de Chile, 1950) completed architectural studies at the Pontifical Catholic University of Chile and his doctorate at the Barcelona School of Architecture. Professor at his alma mater, he has taught and lectured at several Chilean universities and at foreign ones like Harvard and Cambridge. Both his built works and his research studies have been extensively published, especially those devoted to Le Corbusier and to 20th century architecture in Chile. His academic and research activity has been rewarded with the Sergio Larraín García-Moreno prize.

Maciá Pintó (Maracaibo, 1946) studied architecture at the University of the Andes. Professor at the School of Architecture and Urbanism of Venezuela's Central University, he has taken part in the design of academic programs and in the evaluation of academic institutions, commissioned by the University or by the Ministry of Education. He is the author, among other works, of *La casa como paradigma de la arquitectura, Carlos Raúl Villanueva* (with Paulina Villanueva), and 'Carlos Raúl Villanueva: The Synthesis with Venezuela' in *Alfredo Boulton and His Contemporaries,* published by the MoMA.

Hugo Segawa (São Paulo, 1956) completed his architectural studies and doctorate at the University of São Paulo, where he teaches at the School of Architecture. Collaborator and editor of the magazine *Projeto* between 1979 and 1995, he is regional editor of *The Journal of Architecture* and author of *Arquitectura Latinoamericana Contemporánea, Arquiteturas no Brasil 1900-1990* and *Prelúdio da Metrópole São Paulo.* He has been coordinator of DOCOMOMO Brazil and member of its international committee, and also jury member of the second Mies Award for Latin American Architecture.

Roberto Segre (Milan, 1934) studied architecture at the University of Buenos Aires and earned doctorates in Art History at that of Havana and in Regional Planning at the Federal one of Rio de Janeiro, where he teaches at the PROURB. Consulting professor at the CUJAE, he is Honorary Doctor by the FAU/ISPJAEU of Havana, member of the CICA and coordinator of DOCOMOMO in Rio. He is the author of a long list of books and essays on Latin American architecture and urbanism, and coauthor with J. Scarpaci and M. Coyula of *Havana: Two Faces of the Antillean Metropolis.*